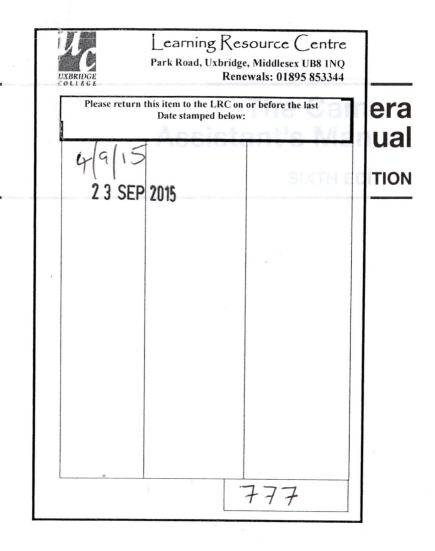

era

ual

TION

The Camera Assistant's Manual

SIXTH EDITION

David E. Elkins, S.O.C.

Focal Press
Taylor & Francis Group

NEW YORK AND LONDON

First published 1991 by Focal Press

This edition published 2013
by Focal Press
70 Blanchard Rd Suite 402, Burlington, MA 01803

Simultaneously published in the UK
by Focal Press
2 Park Square, Milton Park, Abingdon, Oxon OX14 4RN

Focal Press is an imprint of the Taylor & Francis Group, an informa business

Notices
Knowledge and best practice in this field are constantly changing. As new research and experience broaden our understanding, changes in research methods, professional practices, or medical treatment may become necessary.

Practitioners and researchers must always rely on their own experience and knowledge in evaluating and using any information, methods, compounds, or experiments described herein. In using such information or methods they should be mindful of their own safety and the safety of others, including parties for whom they have a professional responsibility.

Library of Congress Cataloging in Publication Data
Elkins, David E.
The camera assistant's manual / by David Elkins.—6th edition.
pages cm
1. Cinematography—Handbooks, manuals, etc. 2. Camera operators—Handbooks, manuals, etc. I. Title.
TR850.E37 2013
777—dc23   2013001985

ISBN: 978-0-240-81868-9 (pbk)
ISBN: 978-0-240-81869-6 (ebk)

Typeset in Melior LT Std
by MPS Limited, Chennai, India
www.adi-mps.com

Printed and bound in the United States of America by Sheridan Books, Inc. (a Sheridan Group Company).

To my wife Jan.
Your love and support gets me through each day.

Contents

5   First Assistant Cameraman (1st AC)   195

Preface

The sixth edition of this book includes much of the information from the previous five editions along with expanded sections and new information. The book was originally written for Camera Assistants working in film, and this edition is no different. I have included new information on the differences between working in the US and Britain along with information about working in digital video, but the majority of the information is still geared toward a film Assistant Cameraman.

All of this material is based on my experience and the experience of other Camera Assistants who have been trained and have worked on the West Coast of the United States. It is my understanding that there are some minor differences in carrying out certain tasks if you have worked and been trained on the East Coast. As far as what those differences are, I don't fully know. I doubt any of the differences would prevent you from obtaining work, but I wanted to make you aware of the possibility.

Chapter 3 is an entirely new chapter devoted to the Camera Trainee/Camera Production Assistant (PA). Many people break into the camera department by working as a trainee or PA on productions when they first start out. Chapters 4 and 5 contain expanded information on working in digital. Many of the sections in these two chapters have also been expanded to include new and updated information. Chapter 6, Problems and Troubleshooting, contains additional problems you may encounter and how to deal with them. Chapter 7, Film Cameras, contains a few new illustrations of cameras and magazine threading diagrams. Many of the older cameras have been removed from this chapter to make the book as up to date as possible.

Appendix A, Film Stock, contains the most current listing of film stocks that were available at the time of publication. Appendix B, Equipment, Software, and Apps, includes information on new equipment and accessories along with the names of some of the most commonly used video and digital cameras. Also included are new items in the section on Specialized Camera Accessories. All forms and checklists have been updated in Appendix C, Camera Department Checklists, Production Forms, and Labels. These forms are all available for download on the companion web site for this book

(www.cameraassistantmanual.com). Added to Appendix D, Tools, Accessories, and Expendables, is a list of special tools for the working Camera Assistant along with illustrations of some of the typical items in a Camera Assistant's toolkit. Appendix E, Tables and Formulas, contains many updated and useful tables along with new formulas you may need. The companion web site has been updated to include more of the camera and magazine illustrations along with all of the forms and checklists. For those of you who buy this new edition, you should have all the information you need to start your career as an Assistant Cameraman. For those of you who are already working in the industry, I hope that this new edition will be added to your toolkit or ditty bag to be used as a reference on the set. In a previous review of the third edition, a reviewer wrote, "I find it highly unlikely that someone who has never been on a film set would buy this book." I found that statement quite amusing because in the many years since the first edition came out, I have had many people thank me for writing the book and tell me how much it helped them when they first stepped onto a film set. Many beginners, as well as professional Assistant Cameramen, have this book in their ditty bag.

As you read this edition, you may notice that some items are repeated from one chapter to another. One of the most important aspects of the job is clear communication between crew members. Part of this communication involves repetition of orders and requests. When a Director of Photography (DP) requests a specific lens, filter, or other accessory to be placed on the camera, the Camera Assistant always repeats it back to him or her. When the DP announces the t-stop to be set on the lens for a specific shot, it is always repeated back. The repetition of the orders and requests is important to ensure smooth operation of the film set and communication among the camera crew. In light of this, I have chosen to repeat some things from one chapter to the next to stress the importance of repetition of orders. As a motion picture Assistant Cameraman, you must be constantly aware of many things happening around you during the performance of your job. There are many responsibilities and duties that a Camera Assistant should know about. You need to do your job quickly and quietly. This book is intended to be a guide for the beginner who would like to learn to become a Camera Assistant.

Because of all of the information included here, the book is also meant to be used by working professionals. When I first started in the film industry, there was no book that explained how to do the job of a Camera Assistant. Even while I was in film school, there was no course dealing with this specific area of production. All of my training came from on-the-job work experience. This book started as classroom notes that I used to teach a Camera Assistant class at Columbia

College Hollywood. It has gone through many changes and improvements through the years, and I hope that with this edition any student or beginning filmmaker who wishes to become a Camera Assistant will find it a little easier to learn the job duties and responsibilities. For those who are working as professional assistants, I hope that this new edition will be a valuable reference source that will always be close at hand. With the knowledge obtained from this book, it should be easier to obtain your first job because you will know the basics and should have no trouble applying them to actual shooting situations. While this book will provide the basic information needed to do the job, nothing beats on-the-job training. Actually being on set and doing and observing is the best way to learn.

The book starts with a description of the basics of cinematography in Chapter 1 because many readers of this book may have no previous photography or cinematography experience. This introduction will help beginners to understand much of the terminology used throughout the book. Chapter 2 contains a description of the chain of command within the camera department and how each member works with and relates to the others. As stated previously, Chapter 3 is an entirely new chapter devoted to the Camera Trainee/Camera Production Assistant. I chose to cover the job responsibilities of a Second Assistant Cameraman (2nd AC) in Chapter 4 and then move on to the First Assistant Cameraman (1st AC) in Chapter 5. My reason for this is that when most people start in the camera department, they may start as a PA, Trainee, Loader or 2nd AC. When they have worked at that position for some time, they move up to 1st AC. The length of time spent at each position depends on each person's situation or preference. Chapter 6 discusses problems that may arise and what you should do to either correct or prevent them. This is an important part of the job of a Camera Assistant. Despite careful checking of the equipment prior to production, something inevitably goes wrong at the worst possible time. If you know how to troubleshoot many of the most common problems, you will show that you are a professional and will most likely be hired on many more productions. Chapter 7 contains illustrations of most of the currently used cameras and magazines, and Chapter 8 contains some tips and guidelines on what to do before you have the job, when you are working, and after the job is over. Chapter 8 also contains information on the camera union, including how to join, examples of the fees for joining, and examples of rates of pay along with some basic information on freelance work and taxes. All of the information in these chapters is based on my experience as an Assistant Cameraman and from tips or advice that other members of the camera department have given me. The appendices cover five areas: film stock, equipment, checklists, tools and

accessories, and tables. Appendix A is a complete listing of all film stocks available from the various manufacturers at the time of publication. It lists the recommended exposure index (EI) ratings for each stock for different lighting conditions. Also included are the various roll sizes for 16 mm and 35 mm film, as well as the weights of the film cans for each full-size roll. Appendix B lists the names of the most common pieces of equipment that you will work with and should know about. It also contains information on software and applications that are available to the Camera Assistant for computers and smart phones or similar devices. Appendix C contains checklists for camera rental items, filters, and expendables that are usually needed on each production. In addition, I have included some typical production forms and labels that a Camera Assistant may need in the day-to-day performance of the job. Some of these forms and labels are modified versions of industry standard forms, and some I have specially designed based on my experience. Appendix D lists the basic tools, accessories, and expendables that a Camera Assistant needs to do the job. Appendix E contains many useful tables and formulas that you may need to refer to in the day-to-day course of your job. Following the appendices is a list of recommended books for the Camera Assistant who would like to learn more about the film industry. The Glossary lists many of the key terms used in the book and their meanings. Included in the Glossary are the items on the expendables list, camera rental items, and various filters mentioned in the book.

As you read this book, if you see anything that you believe is in error or would like to see something added, please send me an email and I will incorporate your suggestions into future editions. My email address can be found on the companion web site for this book. Best wishes for a long and successful career.

Acknowledgments

In preparing this book I have used information from many friends and colleagues. Having worked on so many productions through the years, it is difficult to remember the names of all the Directors of Photography, Camera Operators, and Camera Assistants with whom I have worked. Rather than leave out someone's name I will simply say thank you to all for your help and support in the preparation of this and all previous editions, and also thanks for all the great times on all the productions we have done together.

To the many Directors of Photography with whom I have worked, thanks for all your help and understanding. To all the Camera Operators I have had the pleasure of working alongside, thanks for your support and encouragement. To my fellow Camera Assistants who have shared many of their ideas, thanks for the many enjoyable hours of working together. To all the other crew members on the many productions on which I have worked, thanks for making each workday a little more interesting.

Cover photos of ARRI cameras courtesy of ARRI Inc. Cover photos of Panavision cameras and lenses courtesy of Panavision Inc. Thanks so much to Celia Donnoli and Franz Wieser at ARRI for the use of the ARRI camera photos. Thanks to Susan Nelson and Jim Roudebush at Panavision for the use of the Panavision camera and lens photos. And a very special thank you to Chris Ellison for the wonderful cover design for this edition. It's the best cover yet for any of the editions I have written.

I would like to extend a very special thanks to Cinematographer David W. Samuelson for his help and encouragement. Thank you so much for allowing me to reproduce many of the illustrations from your books, *Panaflex Users Manual* and *Hands-On Manual for Cinematographers*. Without your support this book would not be complete. My special thanks to Jon Fauer, author of many great books including the *Arriflex 16SR Book* and the *Arriflex 35 Book*. Thanks so much for allowing me to reproduce specific illustrations from those excellent books. Your support is greatly appreciated. To the employees at the various camera rental houses, Alan Gordon Enterprises, ARRI CSC, Birns & Sawyer, Clairmont Camera, Keslow Camera,

Otto Nemenz International Inc., Panavision Inc., Panavision Hollywood, Panavision New York, and Ultravision, thanks for all the help during the many productions and workshops we have done together. To Brian Lataille, thanks for the information about the Steadicam. Thanks to Larry Barton and Marilyn Beswick of Cinematography Electronics for allowing me to reproduce the HMI Filming Speed Cards. To Bill Russell, Guenter Noesner and Franz Wieser at ARRI Inc.; Frank Kay, Dan Hammond, Phil Radin, and Jim Roudebush at Panavision; Matt Leonetti at Leonetti Camera; Conrad Kiel and Philip Kiel at Photo-Sonics; and Grant Loucks at Alan Gordon Enterprises, thanks for letting me use the various illustrations included in the book. Thanks to Sandra Kurotobi at Fujifilm for providing copies of Fujifilm can labels. Thanks to John Mason, Mike Brown, Kerry Driscoll, and Lori Hannigan from Eastman Kodak for their support and for providing the illustrations of the Kodak film can labels. Thank you to Donald Burghardt for allowing me to reproduce pages from his book, *The Camera Log*. Thanks to Walt Rose of Foto Kem for granting permission to reproduce the FotoKem camera reports and purchase order form. Thanks to Kevin Burroughs for allowing me to reproduce his digital camera report in this edition. To David Eubank, thanks for providing the many screen shots from your excellent app, pCAM Film+Digital Calculator. Thank you to Paul Tilden for allowing me to use the pCAM screen shots containing his image. Thank you to Wayne Baker for allowing me to modify and use your Non-Prep Disclaimer form. Thank you to Simon Reeves and the staff at Chemical Wedding for granting permission to use the screen shots from the app Toland ASC Digital Assistant. Thank you very much to Chaim Kantor of International Cinematographers Guild Local 600 for providing me with information on union membership and the camera department chain of command.

Thanks to 2nd AC Leon Sanginiti, Jr. for his excellent contributions to the chapter dealing with the 2nd AC and for his input regarding some of the forms and checklists along with his help with creating the tax related forms for the chapter on Before, During and After the Job. To the late Mike Denecke, thanks for the illustration of the Timecode Slate. To Rudy at the Paramount Studios Camera Department, thanks for your help. Thanks to E. Gunnar Mortensen, Jennifer Braddock, Corey Steib and Mako Koiwai for their contributions to the updated material on working in the digital world of production.

Thank you to B. Sean Fairburn, Victor Goss, Steve Heuer, Jeff Nolde, Tony Salgado, Randy Sellars, Ryan Sheridan, David Speck, and Michael Vasovski for providing information on working in SD and HD video for previous editions. Special thanks to John Ames for

proofreading the previous material on working in video and making suggestions and contributions to that information.

Thanks to my colleague Chris Schneider for his contribution to the section on aspect ratios. Thanks to Jeremy Boon, Dane Krogman and especially Joe Lopina, for drawing some of the illustrations that I could not find anywhere else. Thanks to Matthew A. Petrosky and Steve Pedulla for their ideas and insight, and special thanks to Matt for his contributions to the forms and his knowledge of new equipment and technology. To Nicole Conn for allowing me to use the names *Demi Monde Productions* and *Claire of the Moon* in the various examples and illustrations in the book, thanks for letting me have so much fun on your film. Thanks to the late Pat Swovelin for his 2nd AC pointers. Pat, you will be missed by all who knew and worked with you. To Richard Clabaugh, who spent many hours reading the final manuscript of the first edition and offering his suggestions, thanks for your time and effort. Thanks to Jack Anderson for taking time to review the manuscript for this edition.

A very special thank you to John Le Blanc, Harper Alexander, Austin Blythe, Chase DuBose, Walker Forshee, Brittni Moore, Christopher O'Leary, Josh Quick, Drew Taylor, Eduardo Uruena, Drew Valenti, and David Robertson for their help in the shooting of the video tutorial on camera prep for this edition. Thanks to Richard Clabaugh for his help and tips on editing. And thank you to Jacob Highland for helping me to record the voiceover and for editing the finished video.

To Tim Roarke, thanks for being a great friend and colleague. To the former staff of Columbia College Hollywood, especially Allan Rossman and Dianne McDonald, thank you for your help and guidance. To Mike Hanly for giving me some insight on dealing with a camera rental house, thanks for your help. Thanks to the current and former faculty and staff at The University of North Carolina School of the Arts School of Filmmaking for their help, support, and encouragement. And thanks to all the students I have had the pleasure of teaching through the years, for their enthusiasm and spirit that reminds me every day of why I became a filmmaker.

To everyone I have worked with at Focal Press since the first edition was published, including Karen Speerstra, Sharon Falter, Marie Lee, Valerie Cimino, Tammy Harvey, Terri Jadick, Theron Shreve, Cara Anderson, Elinor Actipis, Michele Cronin, Lauren Mattos, Peter Linsley, Emma Elder and Dennis McGonagle thanks for making the writing of this edition and all previous editions a little easier because of your help and guidance. Thanks to my family and friends for being understanding and supportive of me throughout my career.

Most importantly, to my wife, Jan, thank you for your love, support, understanding and patience while I spent hours at the computer writing each edition of this book. You have filled my life with much joy and happiness, and you make each day special. With love always and forever.

Introduction

The process of motion picture photography started when George Eastman introduced the first 35mm film in 1889, and Thomas Edison, along with his assistant W. K. L. Dickson, designed the Kinetograph and Kinetoscope, also around 1889. Various reports indicate that the patent was applied for in 1891 but that it wasn't granted until 1897.

The Kinetograph was used to photograph motion pictures, and the Kinetoscope was used to view them. These early pieces of equipment were very basic in their design and use. As film cameras became more complex, a need developed for specially trained individuals to work with this new technology and equipment. Two of these individuals became known as the First Assistant Cameraman (1st AC) and the Second Assistant Cameraman (2nd AC).

One of the most well known of the early cinematographers was Billy Bitzer, who shot most of the films of Director D. W. Griffith. As a Cameraman he did all of the jobs himself: carrying the equipment, setting it up, loading film, and so on. In 1914 D. W. Griffith hired an assistant to work with the Cameraman. This assistant was called a Camera Boy, and his job was only to carry the equipment for the Cameraman. Each morning, the Camera Boy would move all of the equipment from the camera room to wherever the scenes were being shot for the day. There was a lot of equipment, and many trips back and forth were required to get everything in place. In addition, the Camera Boy was required to take notes of what was being shot. There were no Script Supervisors at that time. Around 1916, Cameraman Edwin S. Porter asked for an assistant after returning from a long location shoot. This Camera Assistant had some additional duties that the Camera Boy did not have. Because all of the early cameras were hand cranked, the Camera Assistant had to count the number of turns of the crank and keep a log of the number of frames shot. Other duties included slating the scene, keeping track of footage, loading and unloading film, carrying and setting up the equipment, and anything else that the Camera Assistant may have been asked to do. Many of these tasks are still some of the responsibilities of today's Assistant Cameramen.

As a result of these two early Cameramen having an assistant, a new position was created within the camera department. Many of

the techniques of these early Cameramen and Camera Assistants were passed on to others, and they developed into the very specific job duties that are performed today by the 1st AC and 2nd AC. Because this was such a new technology, the early Camera Assistants had no one to learn from, so they set most of the guidelines for performing their specific jobs. Each had specific responsibilities but was also capable of doing the other's job if necessary.

Today, a beginning filmmaker has a wide choice of places to get the training to work as an Assistant Cameraman. There are many colleges and universities that offer a complete curriculum dealing with motion picture production. In addition to the larger institutions, many smaller colleges and trade and technical schools offer film classes. There are also many schools and training facilities that now specialize in training filmmakers in the many crafts associated with filmmaking. In addition, there are specialized workshops that teach very specific aspects of film production. Some states have even established film training programs to train their residents for entry level production jobs so that they can get work on productions coming into their states.

There are workshops for camera operating, camera assisting, sound recording, editing, assistant directing, script supervising and much more. These workshops may be one or two days long or possibly even one or two weeks long. They are usually very intense and teach a great deal of information in a very short period of time. Instead of attending one of these schools, a beginning filmmaker may know someone in the film industry who is willing to train him or her and provide that important first break. I know many film professionals who never attended film school but obtained their training and experience by starting out working on productions. There is no right or wrong way to gain the experience. It is a matter of which way is best for you.

If you choose to attend film school or some other type of training program, the best way to gain actual production experience is to work on as many student film or low budget independent productions as possible. Even though these productions are done on a much smaller scale than most professional productions, the basics will be the same, and you can apply what you have learned in your film classes. When you start looking for that first professional job, any experience, even if it is on a student production, increases your chance of getting a job. For those who do not wish to go to film school, or perhaps cannot afford the cost, it may be a little more difficult to obtain that first job. If you have an acquaintance or relative in the film industry, it may be a little easier. For me, film school was a valuable and rewarding experience. I was hired on my first production as a Production Assistant only one month after completing film school. That led to my first job as a 2nd AC on the same film. The film crew was doing

some second-unit shooting on a weekend and needed a 2nd AC to load magazines and keep camera reports. Because I had performed similar tasks in film school, I asked to do the job and the Director of Photography (DP) gave me the chance to show that I could work for a couple of days as the 2nd AC on the second unit. The DP gave me the opportunity to prove that I could do the job, and this led to my first job on a feature film as 2nd AC with the same DP. You must be willing to work hard, not only at getting the job, but also when you have the job, to prove that you are capable of handling it. If you have been in film school recently, an excellent way to learn about available jobs is to talk to your instructors. Ask them if they know about any productions that you may be able to work on. You also should stay in contact with other film students who were in your classes. There are many web sites as well as publications that publish job opportunities on a regular basis. Two of the most popular of these publications are *The Hollywood Reporter* and *Daily Variety*. Both publications have a list of productions being done now or sometime in the future. The list often contains phone numbers or addresses to obtain more information about each production. These two publications also have web sites that contain lists of upcoming productions, and in some cases you must become a subscriber to access much of the web information. In addition to the various publications, there are many great web sites devoted entirely to the film industry, some specifically for listing jobs and crew positions that are available. Many of these are listed on the companion web site for this book.

When you first try to get a job on a film, you may be asked to work for little or no money. The production company may be just starting out and have only enough money for the basic costs of production. Or they may expect you to prove you can do the job before they offer you any pay. If you can afford to take such a job, it is an excellent way to get some experience. Three of my first jobs as a Camera Assistant were without pay, but they helped me to get paying jobs later because I had proved that I could do the job and was not afraid to work long, hard hours. Not everyone will find it necessary to work for free. I mention it only so that you know what you might encounter when you first start looking for work. The important thing to remember is not to get discouraged and give up. The film industry is a very competitive business; breaking into it may take a while. If you don't get the first few jobs you apply for, keep trying. If you want a job bad enough and are willing to work, you will eventually find one. When you do start working in the industry, always stay in contact with people with whom you have worked in the past. Call them periodically just to say hello and find out what they are doing. They may be working on a production that needs additional crew

members. Also, if you are working on a production that needs additional people, be sure to let other film professionals know about it. This process of keeping in touch with other film crew people is called *networking* and is probably one of the best ways to get jobs. Many of my jobs came from recommendations from people with whom I had worked on other productions. Also, many DPs will call me back to work with them on other productions. Another good way to break in to the business is to get a job at a camera rental company. This is a good way to learn about the wide variety of camera equipment and accessories that an Assistant Cameraman uses in the day-to-day performance of the job. Working at a rental house will enable you to meet a lot of Camera Assistants and DPs. Developing a good relationship with the Camera Assistants and DPs will most likely help you get that first job as a Camera Assistant. One problem associated with working at a rental house is the fact that you are removed from actual production work for an extended period. This may be acceptable for some people because it provides an opportunity to learn the equipment, but for others it may not work. You must decide what is the best route for you to take and then give it all you've got. No matter what route you take to break into the film industry, keep in mind that nothing beats on-the-job training. You can learn so much from just being on set and observing how things are done or actually doing the job yourself. Reading books and sitting in a classroom can give you some basics, but until you are actually on set doing the job, you will not fully understand the joy of being a filmmaker.

Good luck to all the aspiring Camera Assistants who read this book. I hope that you find the motion picture industry to be as exciting and rewarding as I have. And don't forget, work hard but have fun too.

1

Basics of Cinematography

The motion picture industry uses many terms and specialized equipment that are not used anywhere else. To perform your duties as a Camera Assistant, you need to be aware of these terms and the basics of cinematography along with the names of specific pieces of equipment. You will hear many of these terms in the day-to-day performance of your job. By introducing and explaining some of them here, I hope to make it easier for you as you read this book, as well as the first time you step onto a film set. To my knowledge all of this information is true and accurate and is based on my experience as well as research done in the compilation of this text. If you would like a more in-depth explanation about any of this information, you may consult any of the books listed in the Recommended Reading at the end of the book.

FILM FORMATS

The term *format* may be used to indicate a few different things in the motion picture industry. In most instances the term format is used to refer to the size of the film stock being used for shooting. With today's digital technology the term format may also be in reference to the type of digital camera you are using. The two primary film formats used for shooting filmed productions are 16 mm and 35 mm. Almost all professional cinematography is shot using one of these two formats. The 65 mm/70 mm format is a popular release print format but it is used very infrequently for production primarily because of cost.

All motion picture film contains perforations so that it can move through the camera. The perforations may also be referred to as perfs or sprocket holes. These are equally spaced holes that are punched along the edges of the film so that it can be transported through the camera at a constant speed. The gear mechanisms in the cameras and

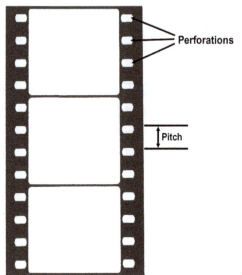
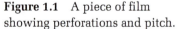

Figure 1.1   A piece of film
showing perforations and pitch.

magazines engage these perfs, moving the film smoothly through the camera. The spacing between the perforations is known as *pitch* and is defined as the distance from the top of one perforation to the top of the next perforation (see Figure 1.1).

Single Perf or Double Perf

16 mm film actually comes in two different formats. One of these has the perforations along one edge of the film, which is often referred to as single perf film. The other has the perforations along both edges of the film, which is often referred to as double perf film. Each frame of 16 mm film is two perforations high, with one perforation at the top of the frame and one at the bottom, either on one side or on both sides of the frame, depending on whether it is single or double perf. 16 mm film contains 40 frames per foot of film.

When shooting in the 16 mm format you will often hear the term Super 16. Super 16 doesn't actually refer to a different film format; it just means that you are using a larger area of the piece of 16 mm film to give you a larger image. When shooting in Super 16 you must always use single perf film in order to create the larger image size. Because there are no perforations on one side of the film, the picture area can be extended to the edge of the film for a larger image. The aspect ratio for Super 16 is 1.66:1. If you wish to shoot in the stand-ard 16 mm aspect ratio of 1.33:1, commonly referred to as *academy*

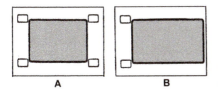

Figure 1.2 **A**, Standard 16mm frame.
B, Super 16mm frame.

aperture, you may use either single perf or double perf film. More on aspect ratios later in this chapter. See Figure 1.2 for an illustration of a standard 16 mm film frame and a Super 16 mm film frame.

35 mm film always has perforations on both sides of the film with the standard 35 mm frame being four perforations high. Standard 35 mm film contains 16 frames per foot of film. See Figure 1.3 for an illustration of a standard 35 mm film frame. The 65 mm/70 mm format is a popular release print format. Many films that are photographed on 35 mm film are enlarged to 65 mm/70 mm for release to theaters. A larger negative will result in a sharper, clearer picture when it is projected on a large theater screen. While some films have been shot using 65 mm film it is not a common practice due to the larger cost associated with rental of camera equipment, and the cost of purchasing and developing the film. See Figure 1.4 for an illustration of a standard 65 mm film frame.

Figure 1.3 35mm film frame.

Figure 1.4 65mm film frame.

VIDEOTAPE AND DIGITAL SHOOTING

Since productions began shooting on videotape, there have been many different formats used. They include ¾-inch, Beta, VHS, S-VHS, VHS-C, 8 mm, Hi8, and Digital8. Most of these formats are no longer used for shooting. Some newer videotape formats used in recent years include MiniDV (digital video), DVCPRO, and DVCAM. Whatever format you choose to use, be sure that the camera you are working with is compatible with the tapes you are using because in many cases they are not interchangeable. Check with the rental company or camera instruction manual if you are not sure.

Shooting on tape is not done that much any longer, with most non-film-type productions shooting in the digital format. The newer digital cameras have the ability to shoot on hard drives or some type of memory or media card. Some of the most common types of media cards in use today include P-2 cards, SxS Cards, and SD or SDHC. Again, be sure that you know exactly what type of recording medium your camera uses before starting production. Do some tests and be sure that you are totally familiar with your camera and all of its functions.

ASPECT RATIOS

The shape of the image frame is expressed as a ratio of its width to its height. This is referred to as the aspect ratio of the image. Since the beginning of filmmaking there have been three commonly used aspect ratios for filmed productions, which are 1.33:1, read as "one three three to one"; 1.85:1, read as "one eight five to one"; and 2.40:1, read as "two four oh to one." The 1.33:1 aspect ratio may also be referred to as academy aperture. It is 1.33 times as wide as it is high. Many of the early motion pictures were shot using this aspect ratio. Academy aperture may also be said to have an aspect ratio of 1.37:1. Older-style tube televisions had an aspect ratio which was basically the same as the academy aperture, and any films or shows shot strictly for television were usually shot using the academy aspect ratio (see Figure 1.5). The aspect ratio of the standard 4-perf high 35 mm frame of film shown in Figure 1.3 is the academy aperture of 1.33:1.

The standard aspect ratio for most theatrical motion pictures is 1.85:1. This format is usually referred to simply as "one eight five." This wider format is obtained by chopping off the top and bottom portions of the academy aperture to give an image that is exactly 1.85 times as wide as it is high (see Figure 1.5). The 2.40:1 aspect ratio is often called Cinemascope, and the image is 2.40 times as wide as it is high. In most cases, to obtain this aspect ratio, a special anamorphic

Figure 1.5   Comparison of 1.33, 1.85, and 2.40 aspect ratios. **A**, 1.33:1. **B**, 1.85:1. **C**, 2.40:1. (Courtesy of Panavision Inc.)

lens is used that squeezes the wider image onto a standard 35 mm frame of film. It is then projected through an anamorphic projection lens that un-squeezes it to produce the widescreen image. The other way to achieve Cinemascope is to shoot Super 35 mm and frame it for Cinemascope, then print anamorphic. During the printing process, the Cinemascope image is compressed or squeezed onto a square frame. During projection the image is projected through an anamorphic lens and stretched to fill the screen. Depending on whom you speak with or what reference material you use, the anamorphic or Cinemascope aspect ratio may also be listed as 2.35:1 or 2.36:1 (see Figure 1.5).

In addition to the aspect ratios previously named, two others that are commonly used are 1.66:1 and 1.78:1. As stated earlier in this chapter the 1.66:1 aspect ratio is the standard aspect ratio for the Super 16 mm film format. At one time it was also the aspect ratio for shooting most European motion pictures. The 1.78:1 aspect ratio is one of the newer ones and may also be referred to as 16 × 9 format, and is often referred to as HDTV (high-definition television). The new flat screen, high-definition televisions have a screen that has this aspect ratio, which is almost the same aspect ratio as the standard 1.85:1 theatrical movie screen (see Figure 1.6). Also see Figures 1.7, 1.8, and 1.9 for illustrations of various aspect ratios.

A

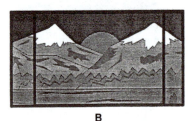

B

Figure 1.6   **A**, 1.66:1 aspect ratio.
B, 1.78:1 aspect ratio (HDTV).
(Courtesy of Panavision Inc.)

Format	Aspect Ratio	Dimensions	Description	Scale Drawing	Area
2/3" CCD	1.78:1	.3775 x .2123 in 9.59 x 5.39 mm	2/3" CCD Area		51.7 mm²
	2.40:1	.3586 x .1500 in 9.11 x 3.81 mm	2/3" CCD Area for 2.40:1 Release		34.7 mm²
16mm Film	1.37:1	.404 x .295 in 10.26 x 7.49 mm	Regular 16mm Camera Aperture		76.8 mm²
	1.66:1	.486 x .295 in 12.35 x 7.49 mm	Super 16mm Camera Aperture		92.5 mm²
Genesis	1.78:1	.930 x .523 in 23.62 x 13.28 mm	Genesis CCD Area		313.7 mm²
	1.85:1	.884 x .478 in 22.45 x 12.14 mm	Genesis CCD Area for 1.85:1 Release		272.6 mm²
	2.40:1	.884 x .370 in 22.45 x 9.40 mm	Genesis CCD Area for 2.40:1 Release		211.0 mm²

Figure 1.7   ⅔-in. CCD, 16mm, and Genesis camera aspect ratios.
(Courtesy of Panavision Inc.)

It is not uncommon when shooting to frame for two different aspect ratios at the same time. You may be shooting a feature film, but we all know that most films eventually end up on television or video. By having a combination ground glass, such as a TV/1.85 or 1.78/1.85, you can frame the shots accordingly so that they will look correct on a movie screen, as well as when formatted for television. There are many different formats for shooting, and which one to use is often the decision of the DP, Director, and sometimes even the Producer. This decision determines which ground glass is going to be ordered for the camera. See Figures 5.26 and 5.27 in Chapter 5 for examples of the ground glass found in both Arriflex and Panavision 16 mm and 35 mm cameras. For many of these the ground glasses are marked for multiple formats.

Format	Aspect Ratio	Dimensions	Description	Scale Drawing	Area
35mm 2 perf	2.40:1	.868 x .365 in 22.05 x 9.27 mm	35mm 2 perf Camera Aperture		204.4 mm²
	2.40:1	.825 x .345 in 20.96 x 8.76 mm	35mm 2 perf Extracted Area for 2.40:1 Release		183.6 mm²
	1.78:1	.614 x .345 in 15.60 x 8.76 mm	35mm 2 perf 1.78:1 Transmitted Area		136.7 mm²
35mm 3 perf	various	.980 x .546 in 24.92 x 13.87 mm	Super 35mm 3 perf Camera Aperture Some formats that can be captured 3 or 4 perf: Super 35mm 2.40 [.945 x .394 in] Super 35mm 1.85 [.945 x .511 in] Super 35mm 1.78 [.945 x .531 in]		345.6 mm²
35mm 4 perf	1.33:1	.792 x .594 in 20.12 x 15.09 mm	35mm TV Transmitted Area (SMPTE recommended practice)		303.6 mm²
	1.33:1	.832 x .624 in 21.13 x 15.85 mm	Super 35mm "Large" TV Transmitted Area		334.9 mm²
	1.85:1	.825 x .446 in 20.96 x 11.33 mm	35mm 1.85:1 Projection Aperture		237.5 mm²
	1.85:1	.945 x .511 in 24.00 x 12.98 mm	Super 35mm Extracted Area for 1.85:1 Release		311.5 mm²
	1.78:1	.945 x .531 in 24.00 x 13.50 mm	Super 35mm 1.78:1 Transmitted Area		324.0 mm²
	2.40:1	.945 x .394 in 24.00 x 10.04 mm	Super 35mm Extracted Area for 2.40:1 Release		241.0 mm²
	2.40:1	.825 x .690 in 20.96 x 17.53 mm	35mm Anamorphic Projection Aperture		367.4 mm²
	1.37:1	.980 x .735 in 24.92 x 18.67 mm	35mm Full Camera Aperture		468.3 mm²

Figure 1.8 35mm aspect ratios. (Courtesy of Panavision Inc.)

Format	Aspect Ratio	Dimensions	Description	Scale Drawing	Area
65mm 70mm	2.20:1	2.072 x .906 in 52.63 x 23.01 mm	65mm Camera Aperture		1211.0 mm²
	2.20:1	1.912 x .870 in 48.56 x 22.10 mm	70mm Projection Aperture (Panavision Super 70mm)		
	2.40:1	1.912 x .800 in 48.56 x 20.31 mm	Extracted for 2.40:1 Release		966.3 mm²

Figure 1.9 65mm/70mm aspect ratios. (Courtesy of Panavision Inc.)

With the advent of the smart phone with built-in still and video cameras, many new aspect ratios have cropped up. The most popular of these seems to be the iPhone, which has an aspect ratio of approximately 1.5:1 in the landscape mode. This is a bit narrower than the HD ratio of 1.78:1 but seems to work fine for the iPhone.

In recent years some camera manufacturers have developed 35 mm camera systems that are designed to reduce film waste. Instead of the standard four perforations per frame, these systems may use

either two or three perforations per frame of 35 mm film, resulting in a 25–50 percent saving in film use. When shooting 1.85:1 aspect ratio or 1.78:1 aspect ratio, and using 4-perf 35 mm film cameras, the top and bottom parts of the film frame are wasted. By using 2-perf or 3-perf cameras there is almost no wasted film. Check with the camera rental company for the availability of 2-perf or 3-perf pull down cameras (see Figures 1.10 and 1.11).

Figure 1.10   Example of 2.40:1 aspect ratio when shooting 35mm 2-perf. (Courtesy of Panavision Inc.)

Figure 1.11   Example of 1.85:1 aspect ratio when shooting 35mm 3-perf. (Courtesy of Panavision Inc.)

SHOTS AND COMPOSITION

A film is made up of a series of photographic images and each image in the film is commonly referred to as a frame. Each frame contains objects and shapes arranged in a composition. A sequence of frames together is commonly referred to as a shot. Visual productions, whether they are movies, television shows, music videos, commercials, video or stills, are all made up of shots. Different shots are used for different purposes and the selection of what shots to use illustrates the creative choices of the people making the production. It is critical to get the right shots which will be needed in order for the scene to play correctly and make sense to the viewer.

As a Camera Assistant you need to have a basic understanding of the various types of shots and what lens you should use to get the shot, so that you can properly perform the duties of your job. As Second Assistant you will be placing marks and slating the scene, so you need to understand focal lengths and shot names so the marks are not seen and the slate is placed properly in the frame. As the First Assistant you need to know the shot and lens to get that shot so you can calculate your depth of field and know how much room you have for error in any given shooting situation.

There are so many names and types of shots and you should have an understanding of the basic ones used on a daily basis. There is a standard set of terms used to indicate the basic shots, and you should know these. It is also important to know what the person you are working with is referring to when they ask for a specific shot. One person may ask for a choker, another may ask for a tight shot and another may say an extreme close-up, and for many these will all give you the same basic shot. Also your interpretation of a medium shot or medium close-up may not be the same as another person's interpretation so you should fully understand what they want when asking for a shot. I once worked as a Camera Operator on a small educational project and the Director/DP was constantly changing the framing of my shots. I soon figured out that his interpretation of a particular shot name was just slightly tighter than mine. Once I had it figured out I was always able to give him the shot he asked for without worrying that he would change it. Once you understand the basic terminology, the rest should come fairly easily.

For a basic sequence you will start with a wide shot of the entire scene and then move in for what is referred to as coverage for the remainder of the scene. Coverage can be defined as getting all of the various shots needed to tell the story. We have all watched television or been to the movies, so you know that as a scene progresses the camera gets closer to the actors so that you can see the emotion on their faces. You may then cut back to a wider shot or a medium wide shot and then back in to the close-up until you have everything needed for the scene. Each scene is going to be different based on the needs of the story and the artistic vision of the Director.

Rather than try to explain every possible shot here, I will mention some of the basic ones that you will use regularly. Figures 1.12 through 1.17 show illustrations of six of the most basic shots, starting wide and moving in to a very tight shot. Those shot names are listed below.

- Full Shot—A shot that shows an actor from head to toe; it may also be called a wide shot. (See Figure 1.12.)
- Cowboy or Western—A shot derived from the early westerns, the cowboy or western shot is one in which shows an actor from just above the knees to the top of the head. Its name comes from the fact that we want to see the holster hanging down from the gun belt. (See Figure 1.13.)
- Medium Shot—A shot which shows roughly half the actor's body, from just above the waist to the top of the head. (See Figure 1.14.)
- Medium Close-up—As we get closer to the actor we want to start to see more detail. This shot shows them from approximately mid chest to the top of the head. (See Figure 1.15.)

Figure 1.12   Illustration of a full shot. (Screen shot of full shot from Preview screen of Field of View section of pCam Film+Digital Calculator.) (Courtesy of David Eubank and Paul Tilden.)

Figure 1.13   Illustration of a cowboy or western shot. (Screen shot of western or cowboy shot from Preview screen of Field of View section of pCam Film+Digital Calculator.) (Courtesy of David Eubank and Paul Tilden.)

Figure 1.14   Illustration of a medium shot. (Screen shot of medium shot from Preview screen of Field of View section of pCam Film+Digital Calculator.) (Courtesy of David Eubank and Paul Tilden.)

Figure 1.15   Illustration of a medium close-up shot. (Screen shot of medium close-up shot from Preview screen of Field of View section of pCam Film+Digital Calculator.) (Courtesy of David Eubank and Paul Tilden.)

- Close-up—This is a shot that shows a person from the top of the shoulders to the top of the head. (See Figure 1.16.)

Figure 1.16   Illustration of a close-up shot. (Screen shot of close-up shot from Preview screen of Field of View section of pCam Film+Digital Calculator.) (Courtesy of David Eubank and Paul Tilden.)

- Extreme Close-up—This is a shot which shows a great amount of detail, such as the actor's eyes, nose and mouth, but can be even closer if you wish. (See Figure 1.17.)

Some other shot names that you may hear on set include the following:

- Dutch Angle—A shot where the camera is tilted laterally so that it is not level with the horizon.
- Establishing Shot—A long shot or full shot that gives the audience an initial representation of the location or setting of the scene.
- High Angle—The camera is placed above the subject or object looking down at them

Figure 1.17   Illustration of an extreme close-up shot. (Screen shot of extreme close-up shot from Preview screen of Field of View section of pCam Film+Digital Calculator.) (Courtesy of David Eubank and Paul Tilden.)

- Insert—Usually a close-up of an object used to emphasize a particular point in the scene. It may be a shot of a key in a door, a clock on the wall, a gun being pulled out of a desk drawer, etc.
- Low Angle—The opposite of the high angle in that the camera is placed below the subject or object, looking up at them.
- OTS (Over-the-shoulder)—Usually when two actors are facing each other and the camera is placed behind one actor, looking over their shoulder towards the other.

Two additional shot names that you will most often hear on a film set are the Abby Singer shot and the Martini shot. The Abby Singer is the second to the last shot of the day and the Martini is the last shot of the day.

The previous names are just a small sampling of the names of shots you will hear on a typical film set. You'll probably hear many others as you start to work. Knowing and understanding what these are will help you to do your job better.

FILM STOCK

It is important to understand how motion picture film is constructed and the terms used to refer to the three main components of a piece of motion picture film stock. If you were able to look at a cross-section of a piece of film you would see three basic components: emulsion, base, and anti-halation backing (see Figure 1.18).

Figure 1.18   Enlarged cross-section of a piece of film (not drawn to scale).

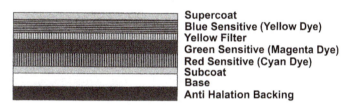

Figure 1.19   The various emulsion layers of color motion picture film.

Emulsion

Emulsion is the part of the film that is sensitive to light. It may be light brown (color film) or light gray (black-and-white film). It is comprised of silver halide crystals suspended in a gelatin substance. Exposure to light causes a chemical change in the silver halide crystals and forms what is called a latent image, meaning an image that is not yet visible. When the film is developed and processed at the laboratory, it is exposed to various chemicals, forming a visible image. The emulsion layer of a piece of color film is made up of many layers so that it can record all of the colors in the scene. These layers include filters and separate layers that are sensitive to one of the three primary colors of light. Figure 1.19 shows the many layers that make up the emulsion layer of color motion picture film stock.

Base

The base is the flexible, transparent support for the emulsion. In the early days of filmmaking, it was made up of highly flammable cellulose nitrate. Not only is nitrate highly flammable, but it can decompose over time to a flammable gas, which increases the chances of it bursting into flames. When Kodak first introduced 16 mm film in 1923, it was the first film to use the cellulose acetate base instead of nitrate. Around 1952 Eastman Kodak began manufacturing all motion

picture film with the more stable cellulose acetate base, which is still used today. Prior to that time almost all major motion pictures were shot using nitrate-based film. The cellulose acetate base is much more long lasting. It is basically a very strong piece of plastic. The base does not play a part in forming the image on the film but acts only as a support for the emulsion.

Anti-halation Backing

The anti-halation backing is the dark coating applied to the back of the film base. It is there to prevent light from passing through the film, reflecting off the internal components of the camera, and then passing through the film again, causing a flare/flash in the image or a double exposure.

TYPES OF FILM

There are two main types of film available for shooting: negative and reversal.

Negative Film

Negative film produces a negative image when it is developed, in which blacks are white, whites are black, and each color is its opposite or complementary color. A positive print must be made from the negative so that you have something that is suitable for projection and viewing. In recent years it has been very common to directly transfer the negative to videotape, and more recently to a digital format for editing purposes. During the transfer process, the colors are switched back to their positive image electronically. One of the primary advantages of using negative film is the ability to make any exposure corrections during the laboratory printing process. Negative film is also better suited to making a large number of copies, as with feature films that are being shown in many different theaters at the same time. For all professional cinematography using film, negative film is most commonly used.

Reversal Film

Reversal film produces a positive image when it is developed, and the camera original can be projected without making a print. A good

example of reversal film is Super 8 mm home movie film or slide film. It is possible to make a print from reversal, but it is not as well suited as negative film for making multiple copies. Reversal film has been commonly used in film schools when teaching beginning filmmakers how to expose and shoot film.

FILM SPEED

All motion picture film is sensitive to light in varying intensities. The term film speed is the measurement of a film stock's sensitivity to light. In other words, it is an indication of how much light is needed in order to obtain a proper exposure. The film speed is most often expressed as an EI (Exposure Index) or ISO (International Standards Organization) number. You may also hear the terms ASA (American Standards Association) or DIN (Deutsche Industrie Norm) used to indicate the film speed. Eastman Kodak and Fujifilm both designate their film speeds using the term EI, so I will use that term in all examples. Film with a lower EI number requires more light to obtain an exposure and is called slow film. Film with a higher EI number requires less light to obtain an exposure and is called fast film. For example, a film stock with an EI of 500 is more sensitive to light than a film stock with an EI of 200. Therefore, to obtain a proper exposure, you need less light with EI 500 film than with EI 200 film.

There is a standard series of EI numbers used to rate film's light sensitivity: 12, 16, 20, 25, 32, 40, 50, 64, 80, 100, 125, 160, 200, 250, 320, 400, 500, 650, 800, 1000, etc. In theory, these numbers go infinitely in both directions. If you look carefully you will notice that for the most part the values double every three numbers. There are a few variations to this rule, as when going from EI 12 to EI 25, from EI 64 to EI 125, and from EI 320 to EI 650. What this translates to is that the change in exposure from one EI value to the next is equal to one-third of an f-stop. In other words, if you double or halve your EI value, it equals one full f-stop change in exposure. In the upcoming section about f-stops, you will see that there is also a standard series of f-stop numbers. As stated in that section, each f-stop number admits half as much light through the lens as the f-stop number before it. This means that a change of one full f-stop is equivalent to either doubling the amount of light or cutting it in half. Doubling or halving the EI number is the same as halving or doubling the amount of light. As an example, the same amount of light that gives you an exposure of f/4 at EI 200 will require an f/5.6 at EI 400 or an f/2.8 at EI 100. The EI is determined by the film's manufacturer based on extensive testing of the film. This number is what the manufacturer feels will give the

best or ideal exposure of the film. Each film can label will show the recommended EI rating for the film stock for both daylight and tungsten light. You can see illustrations of film can labels from Kodak and Fujifilm in Figures 4.3 and 4.4 in Chapter 4. The ultimate decision on what speed to rate the film is up to the Director of Photography (DP) and is usually based on his or her experience in using the particular film stock.

SYNC SPEED

The term sync speed refers to the speed at which the film moves through the camera to create the illusion of normal motion. In the United States, sync speed is 24 frames per second (fps). In Britain, Europe, and Australia, sync speed is 25 fps. Anything filmed at a frame rate less than sync speed will have the illusion of fast motion when it is projected. This is often referred to as undercranking. Anything filmed at a frame rate more than sync speed will have the illusion of slow motion when it is projected. This is often referred to as overcranking. For the examples in this book, I will assume we are shooting at a sync speed of 24 fps. When shooting in the 16 mm format, at sync speed the film will travel through the camera at the rate of 36 feet per minute. When shooting in the 35 mm format, at sync speed the film will travel through the camera at the rate of 90 feet per minute. When shooting in the 3-perf, 35 mm format, at sync speed the film will travel through the camera at the rate of 67.5 feet per minute. When shooting in the 2-perf, 35 mm format, at sync speed the film will travel through the camera at the rate of 45 feet per minute. See Table E.2 in Appendix E for a list of film formats, feet per minute, and frames per foot. See Table E.3 in Appendix E for a list of film formats, meters per minute, and frames per meter.

EXPOSURE TIME

The length of time that each frame of film is exposed to light is called the exposure time or, in still photography terms, shutter speed. At sync speed, film travels through the camera at the speed of 24 frames per second. This means that each frame is traveling through the camera at a speed of $\frac{1}{24}$ of a second. Essentially, for one-half the time the film is being moved in and out of position in an area of the camera known as the gate, and for one-half the time it is being held steady in the gate so that it can be exposed to the light entering the lens. Half of

$\frac{1}{24}$ of a second is equal to $\frac{1}{48}$ of a second. For convenience this is usually rounded to $\frac{1}{50}$ of a second, and most light meters are calibrated with a setting for $\frac{1}{50}$ of a second. This is the actual amount of time that each frame of film is being exposed to the light. Therefore, at sync speed we say the standard exposure time or shutter speed for all motion picture photography is $\frac{1}{50}$ of a second. If you want to be precise, $\frac{1}{48}$ of a second is the actual exposure time when shooting with a 180-degree shutter angle on the camera, and $\frac{1}{50}$ of a second is the actual exposure time when shooting with a 172.8 degree shutter angle on the camera. Many cameras with adjustable shutter angles have a setting for 172.8 degrees. On cameras without an adjustable shutter, most DPs will still use the exposure time of $\frac{1}{50}$ of a second because the difference in the amount of light is negligible. To find your exposure time you must know the camera speed (fps) and shutter angle. See Appendix E for the formula for calculating your exposure time/shutter speed.

EXPOSURE METERS

To determine the correct exposure setting for the particular shot, we measure the intensity of the light with an exposure meter or light meter. The two basic types of light meters used for measuring the exposure of an object are incident meters and reflected meters. Any light that is falling on an object is called incident light and is measured with an incident light meter. The meter contains a white, translucent dome called a photosphere, which is mounted over a light sensor. The photosphere simulates a three-dimensional object, such as the human face, and averages the light falling on the object from all angles. The standard procedure for using an incident light meter is to stand at the position of the subject being photographed and point the photosphere toward the camera when taking the light reading (see Figure 1.20).

Any light that bounces off or is reflected by an object is called reflected light and is measured with a reflected light meter. The light that is reflected by an object is based on the color and texture of the object. A white object reflects more light than a black object. A smooth object reflects more light than a textured object of the same color. The area in which a reflected meter actually reads the light is called the angle of acceptance and the most commonly used reflected light meters are called spot meters and have a very narrow angle of acceptance, usually around 1 degree. The standard procedure for using a spot meter is to stand at the position of the camera and point the meter toward the subject being photographed (see Figure 1.21).

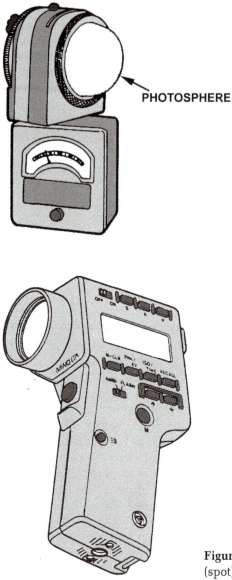

PHOTOSPHERE

Figure 1.20   Spectra incident light meter.

Figure 1.21   Minolta reflected (spot) meter.

In recent years a new type of light meter has been introduced that is becoming quite popular among cinematographers. It is a combination meter that combines an incident and reflected light meter into one compact light meter. A major advantage of the combination meter is that you no longer need to have two separate meters to measure the light (see Figure 1.22).

Figure 1.22   Sekonic combination light meter.

COLOR TEMPERATURE AND COLOR BALANCE

For professional cinematography, proper color reproduction of objects in a scene is dependent on the color temperature of the light source used to illuminate the scene. This applies when shooting film or digital formats. Each light source is a different color and therefore has what is referred to as a color temperature. The human eye cannot accurately distinguish between the different colors of light. Whether or not you are inside with tungsten lights or outside in bright sunlight, a red object looks red to your eye. But motion picture film stock is much more sensitive. When shooting in the digital format you must set specific menu items or settings on the camera so that the colors in the scene are accurately reproduced. When shooting film it is typically based on the "color sensitivity" of the film stock.

In order to determine the color temperature, scientists take an ideal substance, what they refer to as a "black body," and heat it. They then measure its temperature as it emits different colors of light. Think of this black body as a piece of steel being heated up. As this piece of steel gets hotter, it begins to glow different colors, first yellowish-orange, then red, then blue, and eventually white hot. The color of the light is then identified by the temperature at which it became that color. This temperature is called color temperature. Color temperature is measured in degrees Kelvin (K), which is a temperature scale used in physics. Reddish color light has a lower color temperature, and bluish color light has a higher color temperature.

When speaking of the colors of light we often refer to the primary and complementary colors. The three primary colors of light are

red, green, and blue (RGB). The corresponding complementary colors are cyan, magenta, and yellow (CMY). All light sources are made up of varying combinations of the three primary colors. Equal amounts of red, green, and blue light give us what is called white light. Our perception of the color of an object is based on the varying amounts of the primary colors of light that the object reflects. Our brain can process this so quickly that no matter what color temperature of light we are in, an object will always appear the same color. With film or digital we must help the process in some way. With digital we may perform what is called white balance on the camera. By white balancing the camera under the light source we are filming with, we are telling the camera what color white is for that color temperature of light. Or with many of the newer digital cameras we simply set the color temperature of the light source in the menu of the camera. When using film, we choose a film stock that is color balanced for shooting under a specific light source. The two main types of light source for professional cinematography are daylight and tungsten light. Daylight has a color temperature of approximately 5600 degrees Kelvin, written as 5600° K, and is bluish in color. Daylight is actually a combination of sunlight and skylight. Tungsten light refers to professional motion picture lighting fixtures used to create artificial light. Tungsten light has a color temperature of approximately 3200° K and has a reddish-orange color. All film stocks have a particular color balance, and when we refer to any certain film stock, we say that it is either daylight balanced or tungsten balanced. When filming in a particular light source, it is usually common to use a film stock that is color balanced for filming in that type of light. Daylight-balanced film can be shot in daylight without making any corrections or adjustments to the camera or light source to correct the color temperature. Tungsten-balanced film can be shot in tungsten light without making any corrections or adjustments to the camera or light source to correct the color temperature. You may use either film in the opposite type of light, but you must make adjustments to the light source by placing a filter on the camera or light source to correct for the difference in color temperature. Information on specific filters used on film cameras will be discussed later in this chapter.

THE CAMERA

All motion picture cameras are made up of many different components. Each camera manufacturer has its own specific design for the various parts, and these parts are usually not interchangeable from one make of camera to another. A basic motion picture camera will

usually be made up of the following components: gate, shutter, inching knob, viewing system, lens, magazine, and motor. There are many more specific components that are used on all motion picture cameras that you will learn about as you work as a Camera Assistant. For now I will discuss only these basic parts.

Gate

The gate may be described as the opening in the camera that allows light passing through the lens to strike the film. It may also be referred to as the camera aperture. We sometimes refer to the entire area within the camera where the film is exposed as the gate. As the film moves through the gate, it moves by a process known as intermittent movement.

Intermittent Movement

To the human eye, it appears that the film is constantly moving as it travels through the camera. Actually, as the film moves through the camera, each frame is held in place in the gate for a fraction of a second before it moves on and is replaced by another frame. While the film is held in the gate for this fraction of a second, it is exposed to light. The process of holding one frame of film in the gate and then moving it so the next frame is brought into position is called intermittent movement. This process of starting and stopping the film happens at the rate of 24 frames per second, which we learned earlier is called sync speed.

As the film travels through the camera, it will often pass through one or more sprocket wheels or rollers in the magazine, the camera, or both. These rollers or sprocket wheels help move the film into and out of the gate area. To relieve some of the tension on the film between its continuous movement as it passes through the rollers and the intermittent movement in the gate area, you will thread the film with a loop before it enters the gate and another loop after it exits the gate. This loop is nothing more than a slack length of film between the rollers or sprocket wheels and the gate, which acts as a buffer between the intermittent movement and the continuous movement of the film. The constant starting and stopping of the film, so that each frame may be exposed, puts a great amount of strain on the entire roll of film, which could cause the film to break. As the film starts and stops, the loops absorb the strain of the starting and stopping, instead of the entire roll of film. Each camera has specific requirements regarding the size of the loop or loops when threading (see Figure 1.23).

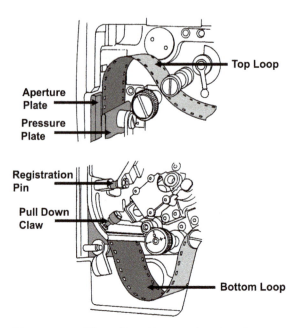

Figure 1.23 Threading diagram showing the loops and gate components in the Panavision camera. (Reprinted from the *Panaflex Users Manual* with permission of David Samuelson and Panavision Inc.)

There are four components to the gate area that work together to make this intermittent movement happen.

Pull Down Claw

To move the film, a small hook or claw engages into a perforation in the film and pulls it through the gate. This small hook or claw is called the pull down claw. Each camera contains some type of pull down claw to move the film and some of the more advanced cameras, including many 35 mm cameras and those used for special effects cinematography, contain two pull down claws, one on each side of the film frame.

Registration Pin

When the pull down claw pulls the film into the gate so that it may be exposed, it must be held perfectly still during this exposure process. A metal pin engages into the film's perforation and holds it in place

so that it may be exposed. This pin is called the registration pin. Some 16mm cameras do not have a registration pin, but because of their design, the film is held securely enough in the gate area to ensure a steady image. As with the pull down claw, some of the more advanced cameras, including many 35mm cameras and those used for special effects cinematography, contain two registration pins.

Aperture Plate

The metal plate that contains the opening or aperture through which light passes to the film is called the aperture plate. The opening may be called the gate or the camera aperture (not the same as the lens aperture or f-stop) and is usually the same size as the aspect ratio being used. The term aperture means "opening" and we often speak separately of lens apertures and camera apertures.

Pressure Plate

The area where the film is held in the gate during exposure is called the film plane or focal plane. To keep the film flat against the aperture plate during exposure, the camera contains a metal plate located behind the film that pushes it against the aperture plate and keeps it flat and steady in the gate area. This metal plate is called the pressure plate because it puts pressure against the film. I usually describe the pressure plate as being "spring-loaded," which basically means that it can move slightly forward and backward due to the different thicknesses of film. For example, black-and-white film is generally thinner than color film due to the multiple emulsion layers in the color film. Also, film from different manufacturers may be different thicknesses. And depending on the age or how the film has been stored, it could expand or contract, causing a change in thickness. By having the pressure plate "spring loaded" it enables it to put just the right amount of pressure against the film so that it lies flat against the aperture plate. If the pressure plate was firmly locked into the camera and not moveable, you may not be able to use certain films, or the film may not be held securely against the aperture plate.

When referring to the gate, most camera personnel usually are referring to the entire area in the camera that contains the pull down claw, registration pin, aperture plate, and pressure plate.

Shutter

The shutter is a spinning mechanism in the motion picture camera that controls the light striking the film. The shutter is mechanically

linked to the other parts of the intermittent movement so that its timing is synchronized with the movement of the pull down claw and registration pin. The shutter spins and alternately allows the light to either expose the film or go to the viewfinder eyepiece so that the Camera Operator may see the image. The typical shutter has a front surface mirror which directs the light to the viewfinder when the shutter is blocking the film, allowing the Camera Operator to view the shot. As the pull down claw moves the film into position, the shutter will be in the closed position so that no light strikes the film. When the frame of film is in place and being held by the registration pin, the shutter will be in the open position so that the light may strike the film and create an exposure.

Shutter Angle

The opening in the shutter that allows the light to strike the film and create an exposure is called the shutter angle. A typical shutter contains a shutter angle of 180 degrees. This is what most people consider to be the standard shutter angle for motion picture photography. On all professional motion picture cameras, you will have either a fixed 180-degree shutter or a variable shutter that can be adjusted to different shutter angles. Changing the shutter angle affects how long the film is exposed to light: Reducing the shutter angle reduces the amount of time that the film is being exposed to light, and increasing the shutter angle increases the amount of time that the film is being exposed to light. A variable shutter is sometimes used to achieve some type of exposure effect or visual effect. It sometimes helps to have a variable shutter when filming sports or any other fast action scene.

In addition, a cinematographer may want to change the exposure of a shot without affecting depth of field, and this can be achieved by changing the shutter angle. You should also be aware that there may be strobing of the lights when you close down the shutter angle. Depending on the model of the camera, the shutter may be adjusted during the shot or only while the camera is not running. Check with the rental house if you are not sure if the camera has an adjustable shutter or how the adjustable shutter operates. In most cases the shutter will be one of two types: a solid 180-degree shutter, sometimes referred to as a half-moon shutter, or a double-bladed 180-degree shutter, sometimes referred to as a butterfly shutter (see Figure 1.24).

In addition to the rotating mirror shutter, some cameras, such as those from Panavision, contain a focal plane shutter. The focal plane shutter is located at the film plane or focal plane, and it is what controls the light striking the film, while the mirror shutter is for the reflex viewing system (see Figure 1.25).

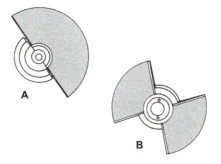

Figure 1.24 **A,** Standard or half-moon shutter. (Reprinted from the *Hands-On Manual for Cinematographers* with permission of David Samuelson.) **B,** Double-bladed or butterfly shutter. (Reprinted from the *Panaflex Users Manual* with permission of David Samuelson and Panavision Inc.)

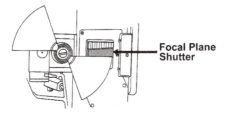

Figure 1.25   Panavision focal plane shutter. (Reprinted from the *Panaflex Users Manual* with permission of David Samuelson and Panavision Inc.)

Inching Knob

Most professional motion picture cameras contain an inching knob. This is often a small knob located either inside the camera body or on the outside of the camera. By turning this knob you can slowly advance or "inch" the film through the camera movement to check that it is moving smoothly. Whenever you thread the film into the camera, you should turn the inching knob a few turns to check that the film is traveling smoothly and not binding or catching anywhere.

Failure to turn the inching knob before turning on the camera could result in torn film and ripped perforations. Film cameras without an inching knob often have a phase button or test button which allows you to check that the pull down claw and registration pin are engaging properly in the film perforations.

Viewing System

The viewing system or viewfinder allows the Camera Operator to view the scene. Through the years of motion picture production, there have been three basic types of viewing systems used. The rack over viewing system and direct viewfinder are older viewing systems that are not used today for most professional motion picture productions and are not discussed here. The current standard viewing system for professional motion picture cameras is the mirrored-shutter reflex viewfinder system. A reflex viewfinder is one that allows you to view the image directly through the lens, even during filming. The mirrored-shutter reflex system means that the rotating shutter is actually a spinning mirror. As the shutter spins, when it is in the open position, all of the light entering the lens strikes the film and creates an exposure. When the shutter is in the closed position, all of the light is reflected off the mirror and directed to the eyepiece for the Camera Operator to view the shot (see Figure 1.26).

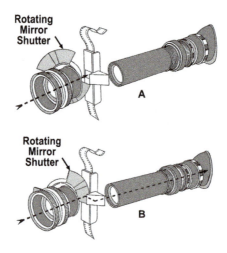

Figure 1.26   Simple mirror reflex viewfinder system. **A**, With the mirror shutter open, all light is directed to the film. **B**, With the mirror shutter closed, all light is directed to the eyepiece. (Courtesy of ARRI Inc.)

Diopter Adjustment

Because of the differences in each person's vision, the viewfinder of most cameras has an adjustable diopter. By setting the diopter according to your particular vision, the image will appear in focus when you

look through the eyepiece if the lens focus is set correctly. To adjust the diopter, it is best to remove the lens, but it can be done with the lens in place. You then point the camera at a bright light source or white surface. While looking through the eyepiece, turn the diopter adjustment ring until the crosshair or grains of the ground glass in the viewfinder are sharp and in focus. A further discussion of the viewfinder diopter adjustment is located in Chapter 5.

The Lens

A lens may be defined as a device that contains one or more pieces of optically transparent material, such as glass, which bends the rays of light passing through it, causing them to focus at a point. In a motion picture camera this point is called the film plane or focal plane, and the light creates an exposure on the film's emulsion at this point. All lenses are referred to by their focal length, and it is the focal length that determines the size of the image. The technical definition of focal length is the distance from the optical center of the lens to the film plane when the lens is focused at infinity. The optical center is a mathematical point within the lens that is determined by the lens manufacturer. The focal length of the lens is always measured in millimeters (mm).

When discussing focal length, I often say that there are three general categories: telephoto, normal, and wide angle. When filming in the 35 mm film format, it is generally accepted that a lens with a focal length of 50 mm is considered to be a normal lens because it approximates an image size that is roughly the same as that seen by the human eye. Of course, this depends on who you ask about it. There have been many opinions over the years as to what lens may be called a "normal" lens. Many of the professionals I have worked with and spoken to about this topic agree that it is a 50 mm lens, so that is the number I am using here. In the 35 mm film format, as a general rule, any lens that has a focal length less than 50 mm may be called wide angle, and any lens that has a focal length more than 50 mm may be called telephoto. To be more precise, when filming in the 35 mm format, wide angle is around 25 mm and below and telephoto is around 75 mm and above. When filming in the 16 mm film format, it is generally accepted that a lens with a focal length of 25 mm is considered to be a normal lens. In 16 mm, as a general rule any lens that has a focal length less than 25 mm (closer to 18 mm) may be called wide angle, and any lens that has a focal length more than 25 mm (closer to 35 mm) may be called telephoto.

A wide-angle lens will distort the image because it exaggerates distances and makes small rooms seem larger than they actually are. Wide-angle lenses are ideally suited for filming any handheld-type shots. A telephoto lens compresses objects together and makes them appear closer than they actually are; it is ideally suited for filming pleasing close-up shots.

Primes and Zooms

While wide angle, normal, and telephoto are categories of focal lengths, when we speak of the physical lens itself we refer to two basic types. Prime lenses have a single, fixed focal length that cannot be changed. In other words, in order to get a different shot when using prime lenses, you must either move the camera closer or farther away, or physically change the lens on the camera. Some examples of prime lenses are 18 mm, 25 mm, 32 mm, 75 mm, and so on. Zoom lenses have variable or adjustable focal lengths that can be changed during shooting. By turning a ring on the barrel of the zoom lens, you can change the focal length and therefore change the shot. Zoom lenses are most often referred to by their range of focal lengths, such as 12 mm to 120 mm (12 to 120), 25 mm to 250 mm (25 to 250), etc. These may also be referred to as 10 to 1 (10–1) zooms. You may also have a 5 to 1 zoom, 4 to 1 zoom, etc. (see Figure 1.27). A further discussion of lenses can be found in Chapter 5.

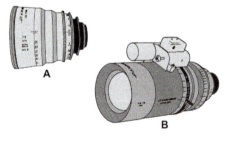

Figure 1.27 A, Prime lens. **B**, Zoom lens with motor attached. (Reprinted from the *Panaflex Users Manual* with permission of David Samuelson and Panavision Inc.)

F-stops and T-stops

All motion picture lenses contain an adjustable iris, sometimes referred to as an aperture or diaphragm, to control the amount of light that enters the lens and strikes the film. You can compare this to the iris in the human eye. A wide opening allows more light in to strike the film than a small or narrow opening. The number that refers to the size of this opening is called an f-stop. It is a mathematical calculation

equal to the focal length of the lens divided by the diameter of the aperture opening. The standard series of f-stop numbers is 1, 1.4, 2, 2.8, 4, 5.6, 8, 11, 16, 22, 32, etc. In theory, the f-stop numbers go infinitely in both directions. All lenses are marked along the barrel of the lens with these numbers. By turning the diaphragm or iris adjustment ring on the lens barrel to a specific number, you are adjusting the size of the iris diaphragm within the lens and controlling how much light gets through to the film or the digital sensor (see Figure 1.28). As I stated previously, you can think of this adjustable lens iris as being similar to the iris/pupil in your eye. In a low light or dark setting your pupil gets larger to let in more light, and in a very bright setting your pupil gets smaller to let in less light.

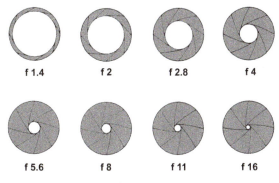

Figure 1.28   Examples of f-stop openings.

So, how does each f-stop number relate to the others? Each f-stop admits half as much light through the lens as the f-stop before it. In other words, an f-stop of 4 admits through the lens half as much light as an f-stop of 2.8. Conversely, each f-stop admits twice as much light through the lens as the f-stop after it. In other words, an f-stop of 5.6 admits through the lens twice as much light as an f-stop of 8. It is important to remember that as the f-stop numbers get larger, the opening of the iris diaphragm gets smaller.

All lenses will absorb some of the light passing through them, and as such, there is a more precise representation of the amount of light reaching the film through the lens. This is called a t-stop. While an f-stop is a mathematical calculation based on the size of the opening of the diaphragm, a t-stop is a measurement of the actual amount of light transmitted through the lens at a particular diaphragm opening. The t-stop takes into account any light that is lost due to absorption through the many optical elements of the lens. The t-stop is more

accurate and should always be used when setting the exposure on the lens. Many lenses are marked with both f-stops and t-stops, and most, if not all, professional film lenses are only marked in t-stops. F-stops and t-stops are discussed further in Chapter 5.

Magazines

A magazine may be described as a removable, lightproof container that is used to hold the film before and after exposure. Each camera uses a different type of film magazine, and some cameras don't even use magazines. In any film magazine or camera, the area that holds the fresh, unexposed raw stock is called the feed side. The area that holds the exposed film stock is called the take-up side. A further and more complete discussion of types of magazines and the procedure for loading and unloading them can be found in Chapter 4.

Motor

The three main types of camera motors that have been used throughout the years are variable, constant, and crystal. Almost all professional motion picture cameras today use a crystal motor. Today's camera motors contain a crystal that is similar to the crystal found in a quartz watch. The sound recorder also contains a similar crystal. This crystal vibrates at a precise, constant frequency, ensuring that during shooting the camera and sound recorder are running in sync so that the picture and sound will match. Most crystal motors have the ability to run at variable speeds for slow motion or high-speed filming, either by use of a built-in adjustable speed control or by using some type of optional speed control device.

Batteries

When using any professional motion picture camera, it is important to remember that they all contain DC motors and must be powered from a battery source. Depending on the camera you are using, these batteries are typically 8, 12, or 24 volts. Batteries come in different sizes and types depending on the shooting situation. The three most common types of batteries are the belt, block, and on-board. Belt batteries are often used for handheld camera work or in a situation where the block battery is not practical, such as when the camera is mounted

to a car mount or remote crane. Block batteries are the most common and are used for most studio and location work when the camera is mounted to a tripod or dolly. On-board batteries are batteries that attach directly to the camera and make a very compact package, especially for hand-holding the camera. Be sure that you obtain the proper type and voltage battery for your shooting situation. If you are unsure about the voltage needed for a particular camera, you should always check with the rental company from where you are renting the camera equipment. Chapter 5 contains illustrations of various types of batteries.

Additional Camera Components

Depending on the model and age of the camera you are using, it may have some additional components or features that are worth mentioning briefly. The footage counter may either be analog or digital, and it counts off how many feet of film pass through the camera when it is running. The analog footage counter usually contains a numbered dial that moves whenever the camera is turned on. This dial must first be set to zero when loading a fresh roll of film onto the camera. As the film travels through the camera, the numbers on the dial register the approximate amount of film footage exposed. The analog type of footage counter is not very accurate. The digital footage counter works in a similar way but is much more accurate. Whenever a new roll of film is placed on the camera, the footage counter should be reset to zero. As the film travels through the camera, the footage counter indicates precisely how much film has been used. All of the currently used professional motion picture cameras contain digital footage counters.

In addition to the footage counter, some older cameras also have a frame counter that registers the precise number of frames that have been exposed. Most professional cameras used today do not contain a frame counter.

Some older cameras have a lens turret on the front of the camera. This allows you to have two or three lenses mounted on the camera at one time. When it comes time to change lenses, you simply rotate the turret until the new lens is in line with the film plane. It is important to remember that you cannot and should not move the lens turret while the camera is running.

Many cameras also contain a buckle switch or buckle trip switch. This switch serves as a safety mechanism within the camera. If the film loop becomes too large or too small, or if the camera runs out of film during shooting, the buckle switch will turn off the camera.

SYNC AND MOS

The two types of motion picture filming are sync (synchronous) and MOS (pronounced "em-oh-es"). During filming, recording synchronous sound, such as dialog, along with the picture is referred to as sync filming. When filming without recording synchronous sound, this is referred to as MOS filming. There are a number of Hollywood legends about terminology and one of these says that the term MOS came from a German director who could not say "without sound." Instead he would say "mit out sound," which gives us the term MOS. The literal translation of the term is minus optical sound. MOS filming is used whenever there is no sound involved or the sound will be added at a later date during postproduction.

FILTERS

One of the most frequently used pieces of equipment in cinematography is the filter. It is a device that often modifies the light reaching the film to achieve a specific effect. Filters may change the overall look of the image, change or enhance the color of the image, or simply adjust for the correct color temperature. They may be placed in front of the lens, behind it, or even on the light source. For purposes of this section I will only be discussing filters used on the camera.

Most behind-the-lens filters are made of a plastic gel-type material and must be handled carefully. Some cameras contain a small filter slot in the aperture plate or directly behind the lens for the placement of behind-the-lens filters. The types of filters that can be used behind the lens are very limited. Many DPs use behind-the-lens filters if they need to place more filters in the matte box or in front of the lens, or it may simply be a matter of not wanting to see the filter when looking through the viewfinder. It is important to remember that when using behind-the-lens filters you cannot see the effect of the filter through the lens. Because of this, you should always place a reminder label on the camera whenever a behind-the-lens filter is being used. This label should indicate what type of filter it is and also that it is behind the lens. Without this label, you may forget that the filter is behind the lens. The following is an example of why this is important.

While working on a feature film as First Assistant Cameraman, I had a small problem with a behind-the-lens filter. During one day of filming, the DP asked me to place an 85 gel filter behind the lens. We were using the Panavision GII camera system, so I placed an optically correct 85 gel in one of the gel holders and inserted it in the

filter slot on the camera. I then placed a small piece of tape over the filter slot on which I wrote the number 85. At the end of the shooting day, I packed the camera away and forgot to remove the 85 gel behind the lens. The next morning the DP asked for an 85 glass filter to be placed in the matte box. I put the 85 filter in the matte box, and we proceeded to shoot. At the conclusion of shooting the first couple of shots, I suddenly remembered that the 85 gel was still in the camera. I immediately went to the DP and told him that the last scene was shot with two 85 filters on the camera, one behind the lens and one in front of the lens. He was very understanding and actually laughed about it, and told me not to worry about it because it was only $\frac{2}{3}$ of an f-stop difference, and it could be corrected in postproduction. I removed the behind-the-lens filter, and we continued to shoot. Needless to say, I was quite embarrassed and vowed to never let that happen again. That night when I packed the camera away I found my reminder tape stuck to the inside of the camera case.

For the remainder of this section I will deal only with filters that are placed on the camera in front of the lens when shooting film. Many filters require an exposure compensation based on the color and density of the filter. Keep in mind that if there is an exposure compensation, you will always open the lens aperture (f-stop/t-stop) the appropriate amount. In other words, if your exposure was an f/5.6 without the filter, and your filter requires a compensation of 1 f-stop, your exposure with the filter would be an f/4. If you are not sure about the exposure compensation of a particular filter, check with the rental company where you rented the camera equipment. A quick way to determine the exposure change for a particular filter is to take a light reading with an exposure meter in the light you are shooting under. Then hold the filter over the photosphere of the light meter and take another reading. Compare the difference and you will have determined your exposure compensation for that filter. Some of the most common filters, their effect, and any exposure compensation are covered briefly in this section. Tables E.5 and E.6 in Appendix E list the exposure compensations for some of the most commonly used filters.

Conversion Filters

The most frequently used filters are called *conversion filters*. They may also be referred to as color-correction filters. These are filters that are used to convert one color temperature to another. Because there are two different types of color balance for film (daylight or tungsten), there are two basic types of conversion filters.

85 Filter

When using tungsten-balanced film in daylight, it is standard practice to use a number 85 filter to correct the color temperature. This filter converts the daylight color temperature to the color temperature of tungsten light to match the color balance of the film stock. When using this filter, an exposure compensation of ⅔ of a stop is required. The 85 filter is orange or amber in color. Some cinematographers may use an LLD (Low Light Daylight) filter in place of the 85 when shooting tungsten film outside during the very early morning hours or very late afternoon when the sun is low in the sky. It corrects for the change in color temperature but has no exposure compensation. The LLD is a very light orange color filter.

80 A Filter

When using daylight-balanced film in tungsten light, a number 80 A filter is used to correct for the difference in color temperature. This filter converts the tungsten color temperature of the lights to the color temperature of daylight to match the color balance of the film stock. When using this filter, an exposure compensation of two stops is required. The 80 A filter is blue in color.

Neutral Density Filters

When filming outdoors in daylight, the DP may wish to reduce the amount of light entering the lens or reduce the depth of field for the shot. A neutral density filter would be used to do this. You may be shooting on a bright sunny day and the exposure meter indicates an exposure of f/22, but the lens aperture ring only goes to f/16. To obtain a properly exposed image you would place a neutral density filter on the lens. This would reduce the amount of light entering the lens and enable you to shoot at an appropriate f-stop. One reason for wanting to reduce depth of field is when filming a close-up of an actor, actress, or some object. Reducing depth of field causes the background to go out of focus, thereby drawing the viewer's attention to the subject or object being photographed. For a more complete discussion of depth of field, see Chapter 5.

Neutral density filters are usually abbreviated ND filter. The most commonly used ND filters are ND3, ND6, and ND9. These may also be referred to as ND.3, ND.6, and ND.9. When using these filters, you must remember to adjust your exposure accordingly. The ND3 (ND.3) requires an exposure compensation of one stop, the ND6

(ND.6) two stops, and the ND9 (ND.9) three stops. Neutral density filters give the Cinematographer much more control over the exposure, especially when shooting outdoors in daylight.

Polarizing Filters

A polarizing filter reduces glare or reflections from shiny, nonmetallic surfaces, such as glass and water. For example, you may wish to remove reflections from an automobile windshield. Or you may be looking into a pond or stream and wish to remove the reflections of the surroundings in the water. To remove the reflections, you would place the polarizer in front of the lens and rotate it while looking through the viewfinder until you either remove or minimize the reflections. When the correct position of the polarizer has been determined, be sure to lock it in place so that it doesn't move during the shot. Polarizing filters work best when the camera is placed at approximately a 45-degree angle to the object being photographed. Polarizers take light that is traveling in many directions and cause it to travel in only one direction. These filters are also used quite often to saturate colors when filming outdoors in daylight. It can darken a blue sky and help clouds appear whiter and puffier in the sky. When using a polarizing filter, you must typically adjust your exposure by two stops.

Combination Filters

Any filter that combines two or more filters into one filter is called a combination filter. The most common combination filters are those that combine an 85 with the series of neutral density filters to get 85ND3, 85ND6, and 85ND9. Another common combination filter is the 85 plus polarizer, which is usually called an 85Pola. When using a combination filter, add together the exposure compensation for each individual filter to obtain the correct exposure compensation. For example, when using an 85ND6, your exposure compensation would be 2 ⅔ stops, 2 stops for the ND6 plus ⅔ of a stop for the 85.

Optical Flat

A special filter that should be included in every camera package is the optical flat. It is an optically correct, clear piece of glass that has many uses. It may be placed in front of the lens to protect the lens for a shot in which something is being projected toward the camera. You may

be shooting in windy situations, where dust and dirt may be blown toward the lens, or on a beach, where water may be blown toward the lens. The optical flat will protect the front element of the lens from these items. In addition, it can be used to cut down on the noise level of the camera. Much of the noise from the camera comes out through the lens. By placing an optical flat in front of the lens, you can reduce this noise and achieve a quiet sync sound take during shooting. If the Sound Mixer asks you to place an optical flat on the camera, it usually means that he or she is hearing some camera noise through the microphone. Because the optical flat is clear, it does not reduce light and requires no exposure compensation.

The previously mentioned filters are required under certain situations, and I recommend that you always have them as part of the camera equipment package. You may need to convert color temperature, reduce light or depth of field, remove reflections, or protect the lens. Having a complete set of the previously discussed filters will enable you to handle most any situation no matter what film stock or light source you are using. When shooting film I recommend that you always have the following basic filter package:

- Set of 85 Filters—85, 85ND3, 85ND6, 85ND9
- Set of Neutral Density Filters—ND3, ND6, ND9
- Polarizer
- Optical Flat (Clear)

The following filters are some common filters that you may also use in the day-to-day shooting of your production. Their use is completely at the discretion of the Cinematographer to achieve a specific effect or look in the image.

Diffusion Filters

When speaking about diffusion filters, we may be referring to many types and styles of filters that will give a similar effect. A diffusion filter is generally used to soften the image or look of the picture. It is typically made of glass that contains a rippled surface, which prevents the light from focusing sharply. It will produce an image in which fine details are not clearly visible. It may give the appearance that the image is out of focus. One of the most common uses of diffusion filters is to minimize or soften any facial blemishes or wrinkles on an actor or actress. Some names of the most commonly used diffusion filters are Tiffen Diffusion, Harrison & Harrison Diffusion, Black Dot

Texture Screen, Black Pro-Mist, White Pro-Mist, Black Diffusion, Gold Diffusion, Soft/FX, Soft Net, Net, Supa-Frost, and Classic Soft.

One of the premier manufacturers of filters is Tiffen and some of the most popular types of diffusion filters from them are the Tiffen Black Pro-Mist, Tiffen White Pro-Mist and Tiffen Glimmerglass. The White Pro-Mist softens the image without causing it to appear out of focus. It also spreads light slightly by creating a small amount of flare from light sources, and it will slightly reduce the contrast. The Black Pro-Mist softens the image with a more subtle flare from light sources and slightly reduces contrast by lightening shadows and darkening highlights. The Glimmerglass, a new type of filter, softens fine details while adding a mild glow to the highlights.

Another major filter manufacturer is Schneider Optics and one very popular diffusion filter is the Schneider Classic Soft, which adds a glow to the image, keeping contrast under control and creating a romantic look. As with most diffusion filters, these filters require no exposure compensation.

In the early days of filmmaking, many DPs would stretch a mesh net or stocking material over the front of the lens to create the diffusion effect. Some filter manufacturers currently offer net filters that have the net sandwiched between two pieces of optically correct clear glass. Another diffusion filter is the Black Dot Texture Screen, a glass filter with a series of random black spots spread across the filter. Light that strikes this filter spreads out over a wider area, thereby diffusing or softening the image. While most diffusion filters require no exposure compensation, the Black Dot Texture Screens require an exposure compensation of one stop. Be sure to flag your lens and use a matte box whenever using diffusion, to eliminate the chance of any stray light causing exposure problems when it strikes the filter. Most diffusion filters are available in sets ranging in densities from light to heavy diffusion, usually numbers ⅛, ¼, ½, 1, 2, 3, 4, and 5. The lower the number, the less noticeable the effect of the filter.

Fog and Double Fog Filters

Fog filters may be used to simulate the effect of natural fog. The regular fog filters create a soft glow and flare in the image, with the lighter grades reducing contrast and focus. Heavier grades of the regular fog filter may create an unnatural look, and if you want a dreamlike appearance to your image you may want to use a heavy regular fog filter. The double fog filter gives you a more natural fog effect, with objects in the frame still looking sharp and in focus. With double fog filters the

overall contrast in the scene will also be reduced. Fog and double fog filters are available in sets ranging in density from very light to very heavy. No exposure compensation is needed when using these filters.

Low-Contrast Filters

To change the overall contrast of a scene, a DP may use a low-contrast filter. This causes the light from the highlight areas of the scene to bleed into the shadow areas, which produces a lower contrast. In other words, it lightens the shadows without affecting the highlight areas. Low-contrast filters do not soften the image or make it appear out of focus as diffusion filters do. As with diffusion and fog filters, they are available in varying densities. No exposure compensation is required for these filters.

Soft-Contrast Filters

A soft-contrast filter may be used to change the contrast in a slightly different manner than a low-contrast filter. It is different from the low-contrast filter because it darkens highlights without affecting the shadow areas. They are also available in varying densities. No exposure compensation is required for these filters.

Ultra-Contrast Filters

Another way to lower the overall contrast of a scene is to use an ultra-contrast filter. This filter lowers the contrast evenly throughout the scene by equally lightening the shadow areas and darkening the highlight areas. Ultra-contrast filters are available in varying densities and require no exposure compensation.

Coral Filters

To make a scene appear warmer, which gives an overall reddish-orange tint to the image, a DP may use a coral filter. The coral filter may be used when filming a sunset or a fireside scene to give the scene a warmer look. Another use of the coral filter is when filming outside in daylight. Because the color temperature of daylight changes from early morning to late afternoon, the DP may use a coral filter along with, or in place of, the 85 filter to give the scene a slightly

warmer look. Coral filters come in varying densities, and exposure compensation is required based on the density of the filter.

Enhancing Filters

To create brighter reds, oranges, and rust browns when filming outdoors, a DP may use an enhancing filter. While creating spectacular effects on the reds and oranges in the shot, it has very little effect on other colors. This filter is especially useful when filming fall foliage. It may also be used to enhance the red brick when filming a brick building or structure. Enhancing filters require an exposure compensation of one stop.

Graduated Filters

Sometimes we only want to alter a portion of the frame with a specific filter. To do this, the DP would use a graduated or grad filter. Only half of the filter contains the specific filter, while the remaining half is clear. For example, we may use a neutral density grad or a coral grad for certain effects, a blue grad to brighten a blue sky without affecting other portions of the scene, etc. Some graduated filters also come in varying densities.

Diopters

When doing extreme close-up work, we may need to use a special type of filter called a diopter on the lens. The diopter is often considered to be a type of lens, but because it is mounted in front of a standard lens, similar to a filter, it is being mentioned here. The diopter acts like a magnifying glass and allows the lens to focus closer than the lens' normal focusing range allows. Diopters come in varying strengths, as follows: $+\frac{1}{4}$, $+\frac{1}{2}$, $+1$, $+1\frac{1}{2}$, $+2$, $+3$, and so on. The higher the number, the closer the lens will focus. The glass of the diopter is curved on one side, and when placing the diopter on the lens, this curved side must face away from the lens. When using a diopter, no exposure compensation is required.

Currently more than 200 types of filters are available for the film-maker. The previously named filters are only a sampling of what is available to the Cinematographer. This small listing is intended to give you a basic understanding of the most commonly used filters. Through experimentation and use of the filters, a DP will know which

filter to use for a specific application or effect. For a list of more filters and the common filter sizes, see Appendix B and the Filters Checklist in Appendix C. To find out more information about specific filters check the companion web site for the book for links to the Tiffen and Schneider web sites.

Filter Manufacturers

There are many different manufacturers of filters, including Tiffen, Harrison & Harrison, Mitchell, Schneider Optics, Formatt Filters, Ltd, Wilson Film Services, and Fries Engineering.

CAMERA MOUNTS

Many different devices and tools are available for mounting the camera, moving it, and keeping it smooth and steady when following the action within a scene.

Tripods and Spreader

One of the most common supports for the camera is a three-legged device called a tripod. Each of the three legs of the tripod can be adjusted in height according to the shot needed. The feet of the tripod are usually placed into an adjustable brace called a spreader. The spreader holds the legs in position and keeps them from collapsing when the legs are extended or spread out (see Figure 1.29). If a spreader

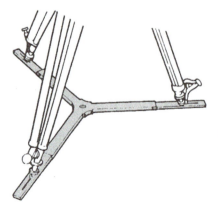

Figure 1.29 Tripod legs locked onto the spreader. (Reprinted from *Motion Picture Camera and Lighting Equipment* with permission of David Samuelson.)

is not available, many assistants use a piece of carpet measuring approximately 4 feet by 4 feet. The points of the tripod feet will grip the carpet and prevent the tripod legs from moving or spreading apart.

The two most commonly used tripods are the standard tripod and the baby tripod. Two of the most common slang terms used to refer to the tripod are sticks and legs (see Figure 1.30).

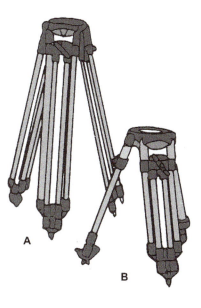

Figure 1.30 **A**, Standard tripod. **B**, Baby tripod. (Reprinted from the *Panaflex Users Manual* with permission of David Samuelson and Panavision Inc.)

Tripods will have one of two types of top castings for the head to attach to: either the Mitchell flat base or bowl shaped (see Figure 1.31).

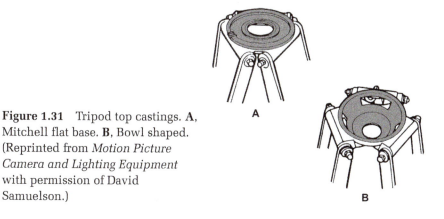

Figure 1.31 Tripod top castings. **A**, Mitchell flat base. **B**, Bowl shaped. (Reprinted from *Motion Picture Camera and Lighting Equipment* with permission of David Samuelson.)

High Hat/Low Hat

For doing extreme low-angle shots where a tripod will not work, a mounting device called a high hat or low hat is used. The high hat or low hat consists of a camera-mounting platform similar to the top casting of the tripod, mounted to a square piece of plywood. The mounting platform of the high hat or low hat may be either a Mitchell flat base or bowl shaped. By using the high hat or low hat, you can get the camera lens just a few inches above the floor (see Figure 1.32).

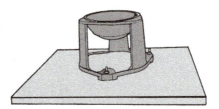

Figure 1.32   High hat with bowl-shaped top casting. (Reprinted from *Motion Picture Camera and Lighting Equipment* with permission of David Samuelson.)

Tripod Heads

To make smooth moves with the camera so that you can follow the action within a scene, the camera must be mounted onto a device called a head. This head will allow the Camera Operator to make smooth pan and tilt moves when following the action. Any horizontal movement of the camera to follow the action is called a pan or panning, and any vertical movement of the head is called a tilt or tilting. The two most common types of heads are the fluid head and gear head.

Fluid Head

Because of its ability to make smooth pan and tilt moves, the fluid head is one of the most commonly used tripod heads. The internal elements of the head contain a type of viscous fluid, which provides a slight resistance against the movements. There is often an adjustment on the outside of the head to increase or decrease the amount of resistance. Depending on the type of shot, the Camera Operator may want more or less resistance to make a smooth pan or tilt move. The pan

and tilt movements are controlled by a pan handle, which is usually mounted to the right side of the head. By moving the handle left and right or up and down, you can make smooth pan and tilt moves.

Some of the most common fluid heads are manufactured by O'Connor, Sachtler, Vinten, Cartoni, Ronford Baker, and Weaver Steadman. When you order a fluid head, be sure that it contains the same style base as the tripod top casting, either a Mitchell flat base or a ball leveling base, as shown in Figure 1.33.

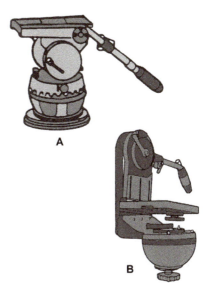

Figure 1.33 Two types of fluid heads. **A**, Sachtler head. (Reprinted from the *Panaflex Users Manual* with permission of David Samuelson and Panavision Inc.) **B**, Ronford-7 head. (Reprinted from *Motion Picture Camera and Lighting Equipment* with permission of David Samuelson.)

Gear Head

For very precise and smooth movements, you might choose to use a gear head. The pan and tilt movements are controlled by two wheels that are connected to gears or belts within the head. One of the wheels is located to the back of the head and controls the tilt; the other wheel is located on the left side and controls the pan. It takes much practice to be able to operate the gear head correctly, but when you learn it, you will most likely not want to use any other type of tripod head. On most productions, when you order equipment you should always obtain a fluid head along with the gear head because there are certain shots that just cannot be accomplished with the gear head. Some of the most common gear heads are the Arriflex Arrihead, Panavision, Panahead, Worral, and Mini Worral (see Figure 1.34).

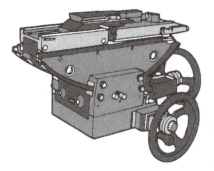

Figure 1.34 Panavision Panahead gear head. (Reprinted from the *Panaflex Users Manual* with permission of David Samuelson and Panavision Inc.)

Steadicam

A highly specialized mounting device for the camera is the Steadicam, a body-mounted harness that is worn by the Camera Operator. It consists of a vest, a special support arm, and the basic Steadicam unit onto which the camera is mounted. The arm consists of a series of springs that absorb the up-and-down movement of the camera, allowing it to give a steady image. The Steadicam allows the operator to do traveling shots where a dolly or crane is not practical, or to bring an actor from one location to another within the scene, without an edit. With the Steadicam, the operator can follow an actor while running up or down stairs or an incline, through a building, in wheelchair-mounted shots, car-mounted shots, and many other types of special shots. To be able to use the Steadicam properly, many Camera Operators attend special training classes to be certified to use the system. Since the Steadicam was first introduced to the film industry, it has gone through many changes. There have been many different models of the system, including Model I, Model II, Model III, Model III-A, EFP, Master, Pro, Ultra 2, Archer, Phantom, Clipper, Zephyr, Tango and Scout (see Figures 1.35–1.38).

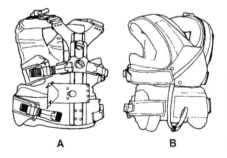

A   B

Figure 1.35 Steadicam vest. **A**, Front view. **B**, Back view. (Reprinted from the *Hands-On Manual for Cinematographers* with permission of David Samuelson.)

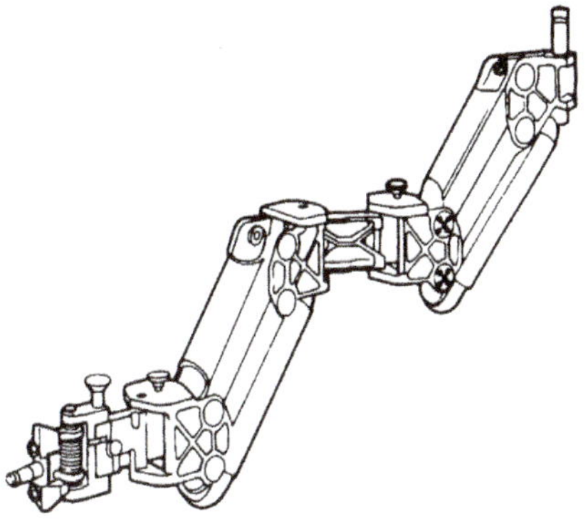

Figure 1.36   Steadicam support
arm. (Reprinted from the *Hands-On
Manual for Cinematographers* with
permission of David Samuelson.)

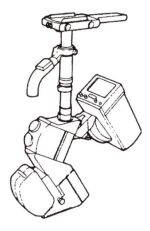

Figure 1.37   Main Steadicam unit. (Reprinted
from the *Hands-On Manual for Cinematographers*
with permission of David Samuelson.)

Dolly

A wheeled platform onto which the head and camera may be mounted
is called a dolly. The dolly often contains seats for the Camera
Operator and Camera Assistant. Not all shots in a film are stationary.
Some require the camera to move in order to follow the action within
a scene. By mounting the camera to the dolly, you can do traveling or
moving shots very smoothly. The dolly is usually placed on some type
of track so that the movement will be free of vibrations. Most dollies
contain a boom arm, which is operated hydraulically or by air pressure to raise or lower the height of the camera during a shot. When
using a dolly, the head is mounted to the dolly. The dolly contains a
mounting platform similar to the top piece of the tripod so that the

Figure 1.38 Steadicam operator using the system with an Arriflex 35BL camera (from a photo of Ted Churchill). (Reprinted from the *Arriflex 35 Book* by Jon Fauer with permission of the author and ARRI Inc.)

head may be locked firmly in place. Even when doing static shots that would normally be shot from a tripod, a dolly can be very useful in that it makes it faster to move the camera from one setup to the next. I have been on many productions in which we rarely did a dolly move, but the camera was mounted on the dolly for ease of movement around the set and location (see Figure 1.39).

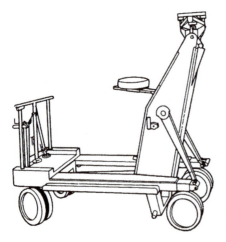

Figure 1.39 Camera dolly. (Courtesy of J.L. Fisher, Inc.)

The previously mentioned pieces of equipment are only a small sampling of the wide variety of equipment used by the camera department. As you work more frequently on different types of productions, you will learn about and use many other specialized pieces of equipment. See the lists in Appendix B and the Film Camera Equipment Checklist in Appendix C for a more complete listing of film camera equipment.

Whenever you come across a piece of equipment that you are not familiar with, ask the rental house to explain it to you so that you feel comfortable using it. Never try to use a piece of equipment that you are not familiar with.

2

The Camera Department

FILM PRODUCTIONS

The number of members in the film camera department depends on the kind of production being shot. Big-budget feature films usually have a larger crew than low-budget films, television series, TV commercials, or music videos. It also depends on whether the production is union or non-union. In the United States the typical film camera department usually consists of the following crew members:

- Director of Photography (DP)
- Camera Operator
- First Assistant Cameraman (1st AC or Focus Puller)
- Second Assistant Cameraman (2nd AC or Clapper/Loader)
- Film Loader (optional position on larger multi-camera productions)

This list is based on a union feature film and includes the basic key crew positions. All of the following lists of camera department personnel responsibilities are based on a union feature film. Each job is different, so not all of these responsibilities will be performed on every show. Some of the similarities and differences between union and non-union work are discussed in Chapter 8.

Often, when multiple cameras are being used, there will be additional Camera Operators and Assistants. The responsibilities of these additional crew members are exactly the same as the key members of the camera crew. These additional crew positions are hired on an as-needed basis and are often referred to as day players. Smaller non-union productions most likely will not have the Loader position, and often on non-union productions the DP also serves as the Camera Operator. Each member of the camera department has specific duties and responsibilities, and each position is related to the others. While the following lists include the basic responsibilities of each position, each production will be a bit different; therefore, what each

Camera Department Chain of Command

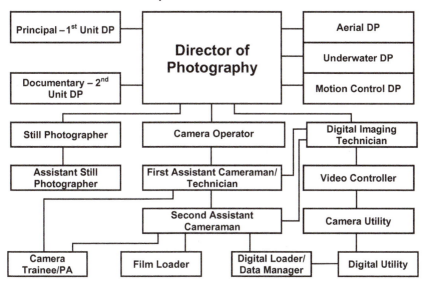

Figure 2.1 Camera department chain of command.

person does on the production may vary slightly. On some smaller productions I have actually served as both First and Second Assistant Cameraman. You must be able to make adjustments based on the type of production you are working on. The important thing to remember is to be flexible and willing to help out in any way, providing you don't step on anybody's toes or cross over into another department where your help may not be wanted or welcome. The Cinematographer or DP is the head of the camera department, and he or she is directly responsible to the Director. This chapter lists the DP and the Camera Operator responsibilities. The responsibilities of the First Assistant Cameraman (1st AC) and Second Assistant Cameraman (2nd AC) are described in detail in Chapters 4 and 5. See Figure 2.1 for an illustration of the chain of command for the camera department. This illustration also includes some of the newly established digital positions.

Director of Photography

The Director of Photography (DP) is the head of all technical departments on a film crew and is responsible for establishing how the script is translated into visual images based on the Director's vision. The DP decides which camera, lenses, filters, and film stock will be

used for the production. The DP hires or recommends the Camera Operator and often also hires or recommends the 1st AC. In some cases, mostly on non-union productions, the DP acts as Camera Operator, so there will not be an additional person serving in the position on the film crew. In hiring the 1st AC, the DP usually bases the decision on past work experience and chooses someone he or she is comfortable working with. If that person is not available, the DP may ask for a recommendation from his or her usual 1st AC or a recommendation from another DP. The position of 1st AC is very important, and the DP wants to have someone who can be trusted and is good at the job. Because the 1st AC works closest with the 2nd AC, the 1st AC usually hires or recommends the 2nd AC. Again, this is usually based on past working experiences or on the recommendation of another trusted Camera Assistant.

During shooting, all members of the camera department must work closely together as a team to get the job done. Working with the Director, the DP determines where the camera is placed for each shot and which lens is to be used. It is up to the Camera Assistants to get the camera set up each time and place all appropriate accessories on the camera for shooting. The DP determines how the lights are to be placed for each shot, and works closely with the Gaffer and the electrical department to be sure that this is carried out. When the lights are set, he or she gives the 1st AC the correct exposure (f-stop/t-stop) to be set on the lens for shooting. In addition to working closely with the Camera Assistants, the DP works closely with the Camera Operator to determine the composition for the shot. The DP, along with the Director, may also decide if there are to be any dolly moves for the shot and when they will take place.

Some DPs may have started their film careers as Camera Assistants, so they should know and understand the requirements of the job. They may have worked a few years each as 2nd AC and 1st AC. Then they may have been a Camera Operator for a few years before finally becoming a DP. The path you take and the length of time that is spent at each position is based on each person's individual circumstances. There are also many DPs who arrived at the position without ever having been a Camera Assistant. They may have been a Lighting Technician or Gaffer before becoming a DP. They also could have started their career as a documentary filmmaker or television news cameraman. If the DP has never been a Camera Assistant, he or she may not be fully aware of all the duties of the job. In any case, you must be able to work closely with the DP to get the job done. Many DPs started out working on small, low-budget films or even some student film projects. These small projects enabled them to gain valuable experience that later helped them get their first big break on a major,

big-budget production. Some DPs started out as apprentices to well-known DPs. By working with these professionals, they learned many valuable skills that helped them when it came time to start out on their own.

The following are many of the responsibilities of the DP, and are listed in no particular order within each heading:

Preproduction

- Reads the script so that he or she understands the story and has an idea of what may be involved in the shooting of the film
- Works with the Director, Production Designer, and Set Construction Supervisor to determine the look of the film and how the sets will be designed and constructed
- Assists the Director in translating the screenplay into visual images
- Attends production meetings to discuss the script and make any suggestions to help the production run smoothly
- Attends location scouts with the Director and any other production personnel to help determine the location's suitability for filming, both aesthetically and from a practical production standpoint
- Chooses camera, lenses, filters, film stock, and any other camera equipment that may be needed
- Consults with the 1st AC on any camera equipment or accessories that may be needed
- Recommends the camera rental house to use for renting equipment
- Recommends the grip and lighting equipment rental companies to use for renting equipment
- Recommends the laboratory that will process the film
- Discusses with the lab any anticipated special processing needs for the production
- Supervises any camera tests that may be necessary or arranges for them to be done
- Supervises any film tests that may be necessary or arranges for them to be done
- Supervises any lighting, costume, and makeup tests or arranges for them to be done
- Hires or recommends the members of the camera crew, the Gaffer, and the Key Grip
- Works closely with the Production Manager or Production Coordinator to determine the size of the camera, grip, and lighting crews
- Works with the grip and electric crews to determine the type and quantity of equipment needed for each department

Production

- Maintains the photographic quality and continuity of the production
- Sets the camera position, camera angle, and any camera movement for each shot based on the Director's vision
- Oversees any photographic special effects shots in collaboration with the Effects Supervisor
- Selects the lens and filter(s) required for each shot
- Determines the correct exposure (t-stop) for each shot
- Works with the Director and Camera Operator when lining up and matching action and screen direction from shot to shot
- Works with the Camera Operator to set the composition for each shot based on the Director's request
- Works with the DIT (Digital Imaging Technician) on a digital shoot to determine the overall look of each shot/scene.
- Determines whether the shot will require a dolly or crane move
- Plans and supervises the lighting of all scenes, working closely with the Gaffer and the electrical crew
- Maintains the continuity of lighting from scene to scene
- Supervises the crews for all cameras in use on the production
- Supervises each technical crew while on stage or location
- Specifies the laboratory instructions for developing and processing exposed film
- Views dailies with the Director and other production personnel
- Provides exposure meters and other necessary tools associated with performing the job

Postproduction

- Supervises the color timing of the final version of the film
- Supervises the transfer from film to videotape or digital medium

Camera Operator

The next person in line in the camera department is the Camera Operator. In the United States, the Camera Operator works closely with the DP to determine the composition for each shot as instructed by the Director. In Britain, the Director and the Camera Operator work closely together to determine the placement of the camera and the composition of the shots, while the DP, or Lighting Cameraman, as he or she is sometimes called, deals primarily with the lighting of the set.

The primary job of the Camera Operator is to make smooth pan and tilt moves to maintain the composition of the subject. The Camera Operator keeps the action within the frame lines to tell the story. Sometimes the Camera Operator may decide the placement of the camera and also may choose the lens for each shot. The 1st AC works most closely with the Camera Operator during rehearsals and the actual shooting. There may be a complicated camera move that requires zoom lens moves and many focus changes during the shot. The Camera Operator rehearses these moves with the 1st AC before shooting them to be sure they are done at the correct time during the shot. If a problem arises with any of these moves during the shot, the Camera Operator is often the only one who can detect it and must let the 1st AC know where the problem occurred so that it can be corrected for the next take. The Camera Operator rehearses any dolly moves that may have been determined by the DP and Director. The Camera Operator will often let the Dolly Grip know when it is the right time to move the dolly during the shot. The Camera Operator also works with the sound department and Boom Operator to set the placement of the boom microphone during the shot. He or she may let the Boom Operator look through the camera to see the frame size or may just tell the Boom Operator where the edge of the frame is so that the microphone is placed where it is not in the shot. The Camera Operator should tell the 2nd AC if any actors' marks are visible in the frame and if they should be made smaller for the shot. When actual shooting starts, the Camera Operator will often instruct the 2nd AC where to place the slate so that it is visible in the frame.

The following are many of the responsibilities of the Camera Operator, and are listed in no particular order within each heading:

Preproduction

- Reads the script so that he or she understands the story and has an idea of what may be involved in the shooting of the film

Production

- Ensures the proper operation of the fluid or gear head and similar equipment
- Adjusts the viewfinder diopter for his or her vision
- Adjusts the seat of the dolly for comfort and proper positioning prior to each shot
- Maintains the proper composition and framing as instructed by the Director or the DP

- Watches to make sure the proper eye lines and screen directions are maintained
- Makes smooth pan and tilt moves during each shot to maintain the proper composition
- Communicates clearly if the shot is acceptable; approves or disapproves each take after it is shot; certifies that no microphones, lights, stands, or other unwanted items were in the frame
- Works closely with the 1st AC to ensure proper focus, zoom moves, and t-stop settings for each shot
- Works closely with the 2nd AC regarding the proper size and placement of actors' marks; if the marks are seen in the shot, informs the 2nd AC to make them smaller or remove them
- Notifies the 2nd AC when the camera has reached sync speed so that he or she may slate the shot
- Works closely with the Dolly Grip during rehearsals and takes to ensure smooth dolly or crane moves
- Works closely with the sound department to ensure proper placement of microphones during each take by telling them where the edges of the frame are located
- Works closely with Assistant Directors to ensure the proper placement of background actors and extras in the scene
- During rehearsals and takes ensures that crew members and equipment are not seen in any reflective surfaces seen in the shot
- May act as DP on any second unit shooting during the production
- Views dailies with the DP, Director, and other production personnel

First and Second Assistant Cameramen

The responsibilities of the 1st AC and 2nd AC are covered in detail in Chapters 4 and 5. The following are checklists of many of the responsibilities of each of these positions, listed in no particular order within each heading:

First Assistant Cameraman (1st AC or Focus Puller)

Preproduction

- Knows and understands all professional motion picture camera equipment and accessories currently used in the industry
- Reads the script so that he or she is aware of the story and recommends any special equipment that he or she feels may be needed to carry out specific shots

- Works with the DP and/or Camera Operator to choose the camera equipment that will be used on the production
- Recommends the 2nd AC and Loader/Trainee to the DP and/or Production Manager
- Works with the 2nd AC to prepare a list of expendables, which is then given to the production office or Production Manager so that the items may be purchased
- Preps the camera package alone or along with the 2nd AC; ensures that all equipment is in proper working order

Production

- Is responsible for the overall care and maintenance of all camera equipment during production
- Mounts the camera head onto the tripod, dolly, or other support piece and ensures that it is secure and working properly
- Unpacks, assembles, and warms up the camera and all of its components at the start of each shooting day
- Does not leave the camera unattended
- Loads and unloads proper film into the camera for the shots and setups
- Resets the footage counter to zero after each reload
- Resets the buckle switch in the camera if necessary
- Keeps all parts of the camera clean and free from dirt and dust, including camera body, lenses, filters, magazines, and so on
- Oils and lubes the camera as needed
- Sets the viewfinder eyepiece for each key person who will look through the camera
- Before each shot, ensures that the camera is level and balanced
- If the camera is mounted on a tripod, ensures that it is securely positioned and leveled
- When the camera is in position for shooting, checks to be sure that no lights are kicking into the lens, causing a flare
- Places proper lens, filter, and any other accessory on the camera as instructed by the DP or Camera Operator
- Checks that lenses and filters are clean before filming
- Sets the t-stop on the lens before each take as instructed by the DP
- Measures the distances to subjects during rehearsals and marks the lens or focus marking disk
- Checks the depth of field for each shot as needed
- Follows focus and makes zoom lens moves during takes
- Adjusts the shutter angle, t-stop, or camera speed during a take as needed and as instructed by the DP

- If shooting digital knows and understands how to change/adjust settings in the camera menu, including ISO, color temperature, shutter speed, fps, etc.
- Checks that the camera is running at the correct speed during filming
- Gives the 2nd AC footage readings from the camera after each take
- After each printed take or when instructed by the DP, checks the gate for hairs or emulsion buildup and requests another take if necessary
- Supervises the transportation and moving of all camera equipment between filming locations
- Works with the 2nd AC to move the camera to each new position
- Works with the 2nd AC to be sure that all camera batteries are kept fully charged and ready for use
- If there is no 2nd AC on the production, then also performs those duties
- Orders additional or special camera equipment as needed
- Checks the call sheet daily to be sure any additional camera equipment and crew members are requested if needed
- Arranges for the return of any camera equipment no longer needed
- Arranges for the return and replacement of any damaged camera equipment
- Oversees all aspects of the camera department
- Disassembles the camera and its components at the completion of the shooting day and packs them away into the appropriate cases
- Provides all the necessary tools and accessories associated with performing the job

Postproduction

- At the completion of filming, cleans and wraps all camera equipment for returning to the rental house
- Views dailies with the DP, Director, and other production personnel

Second Assistant Cameraman (2nd AC or Clapper/Loader)

Preproduction

- On film shoots obtains a supply of empty cans, black bags, camera reports, and cores from the lab or asks the production office to arrange this
- Prepares a list of expendables with the 1st AC

- Preps the camera package along with the 1st AC
- Cleans the camera truck and/or darkroom for use during the production and ensures that each is loaded with the proper supplies and equipment
- Loads and unloads film in the magazines and places proper identification on each if there is no Loader
- Prepares media cards and labels for each when working in digital

Production

- Checks with Loader (if there is one) to be sure that all film magazines are loaded and properly labeled
- Loads and unloads film in the magazines and places proper identification on each if there is no Loader
- Checks the darkroom, if necessary, on a daily basis to be sure that it is lightproof
- Communicates with the Script Supervisor to obtain the scene and take numbers for each shot and also which takes are to be printed
- Records all information on the slate
- Records all information on the camera reports
- Checks with the Script Supervisor as to what takes are to be printed for each scene
- Helps to set up the camera at the start of each shooting day
- Marks the position of actors during the rehearsals
- Slates each scene, whether sound (sync) or silent (MOS)
- Assists in changing lenses, filters, magazines, and so on, and in moving the camera to each new position
- Sets up and moves the video monitor for each new camera setup and makes sure the cable is connected to the film camera
- Prepares exposed film for delivery to the lab and delivers it to the production company representative at the end of each shooting day
- Prepares exposed media cards for download
- When working in digital, works closely with postproduction to be sure that all footage is properly downloaded before formatting and reusing hard drives and/or media cards
- Cans and labels any film recans or short ends
- Serves as camera department contact with the production office, film laboratory, camera equipment rental house and postproduction staff of the production
- Maintains a record of all film received, film shot, short ends created, and film on hand at the end of each shooting day during the production

- Maintains an inventory of film stock and expendables on hand and requests additional film stock and supplies from the production office as needed
- Maintains an inventory of camera equipment on hand, additional equipment ordered, and any equipment that has been damaged or returned
- Distributes copies of the camera reports and film inventory forms to the appropriate departments
- Keeps a file of all paperwork relating to the camera department during the production: camera reports, daily film inventory forms, processing reports from the lab, equipment packing lists, expendable requests, etc.
- Keeps a record of all hours worked by the camera department and prepares time sheets at the end of each day
- Performs the job of 1st AC, if necessary, in the absence of the 1st AC or when additional cameras are used
- Works with the 1st AC to move the camera to each new position
- Works with the 1st AC to ensure that all camera batteries are kept fully charged and ready for use
- At the end of each shooting day, helps the 1st AC pack away all camera equipment in a safe place
- Provides all the necessary tools and accessories associated with performing the job

Postproduction

- At the completion of filming, helps the 1st AC clean and wrap all camera equipment for return to the rental house
- At the completion of filming, cleans and wraps the camera truck

Film Loader

The Film Loader is not included on all film productions but in the event you do have the luxury of having a Loader, these are some of their responsibilities:

Preproduction

- Obtains a supply of empty cans, black bags, camera reports, and cores from the lab or asks the production office to arrange this
- Prepares a list of expendables with the 2nd AC
- Cleans the darkroom for use during the production and ensures that it is loaded with the proper supplies and equipment

Production

- Maintains an inventory of all film stock initially received from the production company
- Maintains a record of all film received, film shot, short ends created, and film on hand at the end of each shooting day during the production
- Keeps a file of all paperwork relating to the camera department during the production: camera reports, daily film inventory forms, processing reports from the lab, equipment packing lists, expendable requests, etc.
- Keeps a record of all hours worked by the camera department and prepares time cards at the end of each day or week
- Checks the darkroom, if necessary, on a daily basis to be sure that it is lightproof
- Loads and unloads all film magazines during the course of filming
- Properly labels all loaded film magazines, cans of exposed film and short ends, and recans of unexposed film
- Prepares exposed film for delivery to the lab and delivers it to the production company representative at the end of each shooting day
- Distributes copies of the camera reports and film inventory forms to the appropriate departments

DIGITAL PRODUCTIONS

In addition to the preceding positions, the following positions may be found on a production that is shooting in the digital format:

- Digital Imaging Technician (DIT)
- Video Controller
- Camera Utility
- Digital Utility
- Digital Loader/Data Manager

Although all of my experience has been on film productions, I wanted to include these classifications, which are currently listed under the International Cinematographers Guild classifications. This information is by no means complete; it has been provided to me by a number of sources. If you notice any errors or omissions, please feel free to email me at the email address provided on the companion web site for this edition: www.cameraassistantmanual.com.

Digital Imaging Technician (DIT)

- Creates the equipment package for the production based on stage or location, how the show will be presented, and who will be using the equipment (film or video oriented)
- Should know each piece of equipment, how it works, and how to troubleshoot each part of the system by making recommendations regarding repair options; he or she should not be expected to repair equipment
- Preps, tests, sets up, operates, and maintains digital cameras, monitors, cables, recording devices, and other related equipment
- Should be able to make recommendations regarding options available whenever a piece of equipment goes down, but should not be expected to repair equipment
- Should know how to match the color on two or more cameras and maintain the look of the cameras if a Video Controller is not on the production
- Should understand and be able to perform shading operations that relate to gamma, gain, iris, RGB, white and black balance, detail/enhancement, matrix, and knee
- Should know and understand the internal camera menus and functions of various cameras
- Must understand and know how to read a waveform monitor and vectorscope and know how to interpret the values to the DP in "film" terminology that he or she can understand
- Verifies that audio is being recorded onto the camcorder, videotape recorder, or other recording medium
- Should know the production's entire postproduction path and how it will be finally delivered when completed
- Makes recommendations on postproduction facilities and other technical issues to keep the postproduction path as smooth and uneventful as possible
- Should establish a creative relationship with the DP so that he or she can set the color of the cameras, often before the DP asks for a specific change
- Looks out for the DP's best interest in terms of understanding what the camera package can and cannot accomplish to fulfill the DP's and the Director's vision
- Oversees the use of any down-converters (HD to other formats)

Video Controller

- Matches or shades multiple cameras to each other so that a consistent look is maintained throughout the production

- Should be knowledgeable on every master control/shading system in use for video and HD production, including video trucks, control room installations, and handheld camera control devices
- Should be knowledgeable on the NTSC system so that changes to cameras are broadcast legal
- Should be up to date on all waveform monitors and vectorscopes and be able to read and calibrate each of them
- Should attend the setup and prep session for the equipment that will be used
- Should be able to match a minimum of four cameras without the use of charts after the initial setup of the cameras, including but not limited to gamma, gain, iris, RGB white balance, RGB black balance
- Will listen to the Director or Technical Director and match or shade a camera before it is switched for live broadcast or live recording
- For sitcoms, should match all cameras during rehearsals and will make only fine changes during shooting
- Should know what the broadcasters and production companies expect in the look of their shows
- In many cases, the DIT performs the duties of the Video Controller

Camera Utility

The Camera Utility is primarily found on television shows, sitcoms, and multi-camera feature films. He or she has various responsibilities depending on the type of production. Some of those responsibilities are listed here, in no particular order:

- Assists the DIT or Video Controller in the setup of the camera
- Wrangles the many cables connecting the camera to the sound equipment, video recorders, and monitors
- Assembles each camera system and knows how to maintain proper pressure of the pneumatic camera pedestals
- Has a knowledge and understanding of multiple video formats
- On sitcoms, places marks for actors if no 2nd AC is on the production
- Switches media cards as needed if no 2nd AC is on the production
- Keeps camera reports and inventory sheets if no 2nd AC is on the production
- If shooting on a tape-based camera, records bars and tone on a few tapes before the day's shooting begins
- Assists the DIT in any manner needed, including the setup and connection of all equipment

- Should be knowledgeable on the setup of each piece of gear being used and how each piece is connected and integrates with other pieces of equipment

Digital Utility

The Digital Utility is often an additional position not found on all productions. Many of the duties are the same as those of the Camera Utility. Some of those responsibilities are listed here, in no particular order:

- Wrangles the many cables connecting the camera to the sound equipment, video recorders, and monitors
- Assembles each camera system and knows how to maintain proper pressure of the pneumatic camera pedestals
- On sitcoms, places marks for actors if no 2nd AC is on the production
- Switches media cards as needed if no 2nd AC is on the production
- Keeps camera reports and inventory sheets if no 2nd AC is on the production
- If shooting on a tape-based camera, records bars and tone on a few tapes before the day's shooting begins
- Assists the DIT in any manner needed, including the setup and connection of all equipment
- Should be knowledgeable on the setup of each piece of gear being used and how each piece is connected and integrates with other pieces of equipment

Digital Loader/Data Manager

The Digital Loader, like the Film Loader, may not be included on all digital productions. His or her responsibilities are much the same as the Film Loader but instead of loading film they are dealing with digital data. Sometimes this position is referred to as Data Manager.

- Maintains an inventory of all media cards, hard drives, and other media onto which the project is being recorded
- Maintains a record of all clips recorded and which cards, drives, or media they were recorded onto
- Works with the DIT or postproduction to be sure that all media is properly downloaded and reviewed before cards/drives are reformatted for future use

- Properly labels all media cards, hard drives, and other media
- Prepares media cards and hard drives for delivery to postproduction for downloading either during the day or at the end of the shooting day
- Provides all the necessary tools and accessories associated with performing the job

3

Camera Trainee and Camera Production Assistant (PA)

Are you just starting out in the film industry and interested in the camera department? If so, you will probably start out as a Camera Trainee or Camera Production Assistant (PA). Many film students get internships on films as a Camera Trainee or Camera PA, which gives them a foot in the door once they finish film school. The Trainee or Production Assistant working with the camera department may have little or no experience, but when starting out in one of these positions that usually doesn't matter. The important thing is to be willing to work hard and always have a smile on your face. When asked to do something, no matter what, do it happily, quickly, and safely. If you are not sure about something, always ask. The First or Second Assistant would rather you ask than do something incorrectly. Be respectful of others, learn their names, watch how other crew members conduct themselves and you will quickly learn proper on-set etiquette and procedures.

I always tell my assistants and Camera Trainees, keep your eyes and ears open at all times, especially within your department. If you hear the 1st AC and 2nd AC talking about moving the camera, get the equipment cart and video monitor ready to move along with them. If they are talking about changing a lens, you might want to bring the lens case to them to make the switch faster and easier. If you hear the First Assistant ask for a new battery, assume that the Second Assistant is going to ask you and have it standing by. No matter what is going on you will learn so much on set just by observing and listening to the other crew members.

You may not have the technical ability or knowledge right away, but by paying attention and working hard, soon the 1st AC may show

you how to change lenses or thread the camera. The 2nd AC may show you how to load a magazine with a dummy load and before long you may be doing those jobs when one of the other assistants is busy with another task. But don't ever do anything that you don't feel comfortable with and especially don't do anything unless you have been properly trained and have been given prior approval by someone higher up in the camera department.

You will undoubtedly have questions, especially if you have not been on a professional set before. It is okay to ask questions, just be sure you are not asking them at an inappropriate time. For example, don't interrupt the 2nd AC when he/she is loading a mag and ask questions about loading. Keep your questions basic at the beginning and at first they should only relate to the job responsibilities that you have been assigned. During lunch while you are all sitting around the lunch table may be a good time to ask other, more technical questions that are of interest to you. The DP and other crew members may be more willing to answer these questions during this break in the action, rather than answer them when they are in the middle of a major lighting or camera setup.

In most cases the job responsibilities of the Trainee and PA are very similar so I will be discussing both as one in this chapter. This chapter will discuss many of the job assignments and responsibilities given to the Camera Trainee and/or Camera PA as they apply to each phase of production: preproduction and production. Postproduction is not included because in most cases the Camera Trainee or Production Assistant is not involved in postproduction.

PREPRODUCTION

For the most part, the Camera Trainee or PA will not have any responsibilities during the preproduction phase of production. But depending on the size of the production or the needs of the camera crew, these crew members may be asked to help out in some way during preproduction, especially so that they can learn as much as possible about the overall process.

The First and Second Assistant may have the Camera Trainee or Production Assistant come along on the camera prep so that they can learn about all of the equipment. They may all get together to prepare the list of supplies and expendables needed for the shoot. Each production job will be a bit different, and the responsibilities of the Camera Trainee and Production Assistant during preproduction will differ accordingly.

Working with the Film Laboratory

Obtaining Laboratory Supplies

The Camera Trainee or Production Assistant has little if any contact with the laboratory during any phase of production, with the possible exception of picking up the various lab supplies needed by the camera department. If the production office hasn't already obtained the supplies for you, the Trainee or PA may be asked to go to the lab to pick up a supply of empty film cans, black bags, camera reports, spare cores, daylight spools, and boxes for the spools. All of these items are critical to the smooth operation of the camera department and will be used by the 2nd AC and/or Loader during production. During production the Trainee or PA may be assigned the task of keeping a daily inventory of the lab supplies so that they can pick up more when the supply gets low. You should never run out of film cans, black bags, cores, or daylight spools.

Choosing and Ordering Expendables

During preproduction the camera crew will prepare a list of expendables. In order to learn as much as possible I think it is a good idea to include the Trainee and PA in this discussion. They need to know what expendables are, how they are used, and why they are important to the day-to-day operation of the camera department. The list of expendables is usually given to the production office so that they may purchase these items for the camera department. There will be more on expendables in Chapter 4, Second Assistant Cameraman (AC) and Film Loader.

Preparation of Camera Equipment

In most cases the camera preparation, or prep, is usually done by the 1st AC, and on larger shows the 2nd AC and Loader may also work on the camera prep. The Camera Trainee and PA may be asked to participate so that they may learn about all of the equipment. The camera prep is important because it gives the camera crew a chance to check each piece of equipment before shooting. By doing this you know if you have everything necessary and also that everything works properly. Even if you are not scheduled to be part of the camera prep, I recommend going along so that you have a complete understanding of all the equipment being used. It also shows your professionalism

and willingness to work hard. Please see the section on camera prep in Chapter 5 for the procedures to follow. You should also look at the Film Camera Prep Checklist, Figure C.4, in Appendix C.

Preparation of Camera Truck

When using a camera truck, the camera equipment is usually loaded and organized on the truck following the camera prep. All crew members should participate in this because you will all be working with this equipment each day and should know exactly how it needs to be stored and transported. Before loading the truck, be sure that it has been cleaned out. Sweep the floor and clean off the shelves. If the truck is kept clean, there is less chance that the camera and equipment will get dirty. This is often the job of the Camera Trainee or PA.

When the truck has been cleaned, load the equipment on the shelves. The shelves should then be labeled as to what is on each of them. The labels are important to help you locate items in a hurry and are especially useful when using additional camera crew members who may not be familiar with the setup of the truck. In addition to labeling the shelves, each equipment case should be labeled with a brief description of what is inside. You can find more on loading the truck, labeling shelves and equipment cases in Chapter 4, Second Assistant Cameraman (2nd AC) and Film Loader, and Chapter 5, First Assistant Cameraman (1st AC).

PRODUCTION

When you have completed all of the preproduction procedures, it is time for filming to start. The production phase of shooting is a complex operation that requires a great deal of hard work from all crew members, especially the camera crew. As a Camera Trainee or PA you can learn so much during actual production.

Start-of-the-Day Procedures

Typically the 1st AC will build the camera and get it ready for shooting, while the 2nd AC hands them equipment. If no Loader is on the job, then the 2nd AC will get the magazines loaded and ready for the start of the day. The Camera Trainee or PA may be called upon to help the 1st AC with the setup of the camera. Since the Trainee or PA may have minimal experience, the extent of their involvement in the setup

of the camera may be as simple as carrying cases back and forth from the camera truck or equipment cart. Most First Assistants are very particular about how the equipment is handled and won't let a Trainee or PA handle any piece of equipment until the First Assistant has had time to give them the proper instruction.

But don't think that you won't learn anything by carrying cases. When you bring the cases to the First Assistant, watch how he or she does things so that in the future you may be able to help them if you know how they expect the equipment to be handled. Remember they may have been in your position just a few short years ago, and by paying attention and working hard, they moved up the ladder. You will too as long as you are willing to work hard.

Once the camera is set up, help to organize the equipment carts with the various cases that will be needed throughout the day. If you are shown how, check all filters and clean them if necessary. You may be asked to prepare a supply of camera reports for the Loader or actor marks for the 2nd AC to use during shooting. If working in digital you may be asked to label the memory cards and prepare an inventory of the cards being used on the shoot. As stated earlier, whatever job you are given, do it quickly and happily.

Camera Reports

Each roll of film shot during the production must have a camera report that shows which scenes were shot and how much film was used for each shot. Even on a digital shoot many Assistant Cameramen continue to keep camera reports. Instead of keeping track of how much film was used, these digital reports are used to keep track of how many clips were recorded on the memory card and how many gigabytes of space are used on each card.

Traditionally the 2nd AC fills out the report during production, but this task may be handled by the Trainee or PA on set. Camera reports are not that difficult to complete and a basic understanding of simple arithmetic is necessary. Learning how to properly complete a film camera report is an excellent way for the Trainee or PA to get future jobs. Just knowing how to do this important aspect of camera department paperwork is very important to camera crews looking to hire you in the future. Knowing how to fill out a film camera report will take a huge burden off of the 2nd AC and allow him/her to concentrate on assisting the 1st AC with any camera related issues. A complete discussion of the procedures for completing a film camera report is covered in Chapter 4, Second Assistant Cameraman (2nd AC) and Film Loader.

Recording Shot Information

In addition to completing camera reports it is often the responsibility of the 2nd AC to keep track of detailed information for each shot, including a basic description of the scene, lens used, t-stop, filters, focus distance, lens height, film stock, and other information. When shooting digital you will also keep track of ASA/ISO, codec, fps, total clips and total gigabytes per card. As indicated in the previous section on Camera Reports, this task may also be assigned to the Trainee or PA on the set. Appendix C contains a Camera Department Log Sheet that you may use for this record keeping (see Figures C.17 and C.18). I have also used an item called *The Camera Log*, which is a 4-inch by 6-inch spiral-bound book available at most expendables supply stores. This pocket-size book contains pages to record all of the pertinent information for each shot. It also contains pages for recording your hours worked along with basic equipment information. See Figure 4.12 in Chapter 4 for examples of pages from *The Camera Log*.

Marking Actors

During rehearsals the 2nd AC is responsible for placing marks on the floor/ground for each actor, for each position he or she takes during the scene. This is another one of those basic jobs that can be assigned to the Trainee or PA. This gives them an opportunity to be on set, watch the blocking of the scene and learn more about on-set protocol and etiquette. If you learn the simple task of how to properly give an actor a mark, you will also be able to get more entry level jobs in the future. While the "T" mark is the most common, you should learn about the other types of actor marks that are often used. Chapter 4, Second Assistant Cameraman (2nd AC) and Film Loader, includes more detail and illustrations of the various types of actor mark.

Slates and Slating

Like many of the previous sections, learning the importance of the slate and how to use the slate will take a huge burden off the 2nd AC. Most DPs and assistants are very particular about slating procedures. When viewing dailies I want slates to fill the frame whenever possible, be in focus, be legible and be used correctly. Incorrect or dark slates make it extremely difficult for the editor to know what the shot is. Learn how to slate properly and practice repeatedly until you are comfortable doing it. Always use the slate the way it is meant to be

used and don't try to perform trick slates by throwing it up in the air, spinning it around, etc. This will only show your lack of professionalism and prevent you from getting jobs in the future. Slates and slating procedures are covered in detail in Chapter 4, Second Assistant Cameraman (2nd AC) and Film Loader.

Changing Lenses, Filters, Magazines, and Accessories

When starting out it is very rare that you will be asked to help with changing lenses, filters or any other piece of equipment on the camera. When the time is right, the First Assistant will show you how to do many of these jobs, but it will take time before they may trust you to help with them. The First Assistant is responsible for the overall operation of the camera equipment and he/she is often very particular about who touches that equipment. They won't let you touch any piece of equipment until they are confident you can be trusted. Don't worry; the time will come when they will allow you to help set up the camera. The key is to be careful when handling any equipment and especially do not rush. A complete description of the procedures for changing anything on the camera can be found in Chapter 5, First Assistant Cameraman (1st AC).

Using a Video Tap and Monitor

Today most productions use a video tap incorporated into the film camera so that the Director and other key crew members can view the shot on a monitor while it is being filmed. When shooting in digital format, there is an output from the camera in order to connect the camera to a video monitor. During each shooting day, the camera is moved to many different locations and sets for the various shots. Whenever the camera is to be moved, the 1st AC will usually disconnect the video cable from the camera. If there is a Camera Trainee or PA on the production, moving the monitor may be one of the primary jobs that they are given. When moving to a new camera position the Trainee or PA should make sure that the monitor is moved along with the camera, set up, powered up, and the cable given to the First Assistant for connection to the camera for each shot.

Record Keeping and Filing of Paperwork

If you are not already aware of it, you will soon discover that the camera department requires a lot of paperwork, most of which is often filled in and prepared by the 2nd AC. This includes shot logs, camera reports

for each roll, film inventory forms, weekly time sheets, equipment records, expendables inventory, and more. When a Camera Trainee or Production Assistant is on your crew the completion and organization of much of this paperwork may be given to them, with the 2nd AC possibly checking their work periodically. It is important for the camera department to keep copies of all paperwork related to the department and I strongly recommend that you set up some type of filing system to keep all of the paperwork organized during the production. See Chapter 4, Second Assistant Cameraman (2nd AC) and Film Loader, for more information on record keeping and filing of paperwork.

Packing Equipment

At the end of each shooting day, all the camera equipment should be packed away in its proper case as quickly as possible and placed in a safe place until the next shooting day. Once the 1st and 2nd ACs feel that you can handle the responsibility, they may have you participate in this task. You probably won't be allowed to disassemble the camera alone, but will be asked to help, and they may show you how things fit together and come apart when packing up the equipment. You will assist them in this job so that you can learn all the parts of the camera package and where each item belongs in the many equipment cases. The only way you will learn about the equipment is if you are able to physically touch it and are shown how to properly use it.

Tools and Accessories

As with many other professions, you must have some basic tools and accessories so that you may do the job properly. Even as a Trainee or PA you should have some basic tools with you when working. This will show your desire to do a good job and also you won't need to rely on using others' tools on set. I recommend a basic tool bag or belt pouch with a small flashlight, multipurpose tool, 4-in-1 screwdriver, permanent markers, pens, slate marker, lens tissue and cleaner, and one of each 1-inch black and white camera tape. As you work more and see the tools that the 1st and 2nd ACs use on a daily basis, you will want to expand your tool bag/ditty bag.

Camera Trainee and PA Tips

The Camera Trainee and PA positions are entry level and you may be given what you feel are menial tasks. But the main thing that you should remember is that no matter what jobs you are given, you will

learn so much and being on a film set is such a great opportunity. Always make an attempt to learn the names of all crew members and be willing to help anybody at any time.

A positive attitude as well as your willingness to work hard will get you many job offers. And once you have more experience with equipment, all three factors will only increase the job calls.

Always arrive at least ½ hour before the call time. In my opinion, arriving before the call time is being on time and arriving right at the call time is being late. Show that you care about doing a good job by always getting there a bit early. It is important to have a great attitude on set. We all have bad days and personal things on our minds but if you let them affect your work day everyone suffers.

As a matter of professional courtesy and protocol you should let the 1st or 2nd AC know where you are at all times, even if it's to go to the restroom. Don't stray too far from the camera department. If the camera crew is working you should not be talking with other crew members in other departments, you should be helping the camera crew. Even if you are only watching them you will still learn by paying attention to how they do things. And it is very important that you should never sit down while the camera crew is working.

Always help clean and pack up at the end of the day. You will learn about equipment and how to pack it properly. Don't complain, even if everyone else is complaining. If the camera crew doesn't need you at the moment, ask if you can help the grip or lighting crew. Learning about what they do and being willing to help them will go a long way in the future when the camera crew needs help from them.

Be prepared for anything and any unusual working conditions. You should always have a bag with a change of clothing, shorts for those hot days, and jeans or other long pants for the cold all-nighters. The bag should also include underwear, sneakers, shirt, sweatshirt, cap, sunglasses, and rain gear, just to name a few key items.

Don't worry if it takes a while for the 1st and 2nd ACs to trust you to handle any of the equipment. They need to be sure that you can be trusted. At first they'll watch you to see how you handle yourself before they know whether you are an asset or a hindrance to the department. First impressions are very important so always try to put your best foot forward. Don't try to impress them by claiming to know things that you don't. It will only hurt you in the long run. At the beginning mistakes may happen and that's okay because we all make mistakes at some time or another. The important thing is to always tell someone and admit your mistake when it happens. Don't try to blame your mistakes or errors on somebody else. That's a surefire way to not get hired back in the future.

Keeping your eyes and ears open and your mouth closed is a very good way to start out when learning. Keep your eyes on the DP, 1st AC, and 2nd AC. Learn to pick their voices out of a crowd so if they ask for something you may be able to help them. You can ask questions but only at the appropriate time, and be sure that they are relevant to what is happening at the time. Show the camera crew that you can save them time by taking care of many of the little things each day and they will soon consider you an important part of the camera crew. By showing that you can stay on top of the small tasks you are given, they will eventually give you more responsibility. If you have questions I recommend writing them down, and in many cases you'll get the answers just by watching what's happening around you.

For all members of the camera crew, anticipation is a key part of the job. Try to prevent problems by taking care of things before they become problems. Keep the camera batteries charged and have a fully charged battery close by in case it is needed. Check the expendables (tape, lens cleaner, canned air, pens, markers, chalk, etc.) and if they appear to be getting low, let the 2nd AC know about it so that more may be ordered.

It is extremely important to keep all camera equipment together, and once the 1st and 2nd ACs trust you they may assign you the task of keeping all cases together in a central location when filming. You may be responsible for loading and moving the equipment carts between setups. Keeping the equipment organized and together minimizes the chance of loss or damage to the gear.

Because you are still learning, keep a small notepad and pen with you so that you can write down questions or other things throughout the day. This will help you to not forget something important that one of the assistants may have asked you to do for the department. Things get very hectic on set and it is not uncommon to forget something that is asked of you if you haven't written it down.

The previous are just a small sampling of tips for the Trainee or Production Assistant in the camera department. As you work more and more you'll develop your own set of guidelines and tips to follow. I recommend reading the Tips sections in each of the chapters for the First Assistant and Second Assistant (Chapters 4 and 5). Best of luck in the pursuit of your career in the camera department.

4

Second Assistant Cameraman (2nd AC) and Film Loader

In most cases, when you first join the camera department, you will be starting as a Second Assistant Cameraman (2nd AC) or Loader. In Britain, Europe, and Australia, the 2nd AC is most often referred to as the Clapper/Loader. The Film Loader is primarily responsible for loading and unloading film into the magazines and filling in all of the paperwork relating to the film stock shot during the production, and they rarely leave the camera truck or loading area. On some occasions, the Loader may work alongside the 2nd AC on the set to gain further experience. The current union entry-level film position is that of the Film Loader.

The job responsibilities of the Loader include some of the fundamental job responsibilities of the 2nd AC. If there is no Loader on the production, the 2nd AC does it all. If there is a Loader he or she handles the specific responsibilities of that position, which allows the 2nd AC the freedom to be on set more to assist the 1st AC. With a Loader on a shoot the 2nd AC does not have to leave set periodically to load/unload film, complete paperwork, etc. The main difference between the Loader and 2nd AC is that the 2nd AC has more responsibilities. The 2nd AC works directly with the First Assistant Cameraman (1st AC) during the production and performs many different job duties each shooting day.

Unfortunately in recent years, or on certain types of productions, producers think that there is no need for a Second Assistant Cameraman. This has become especially apparent on many small-scale digital productions. Some people compare the 2nd AC position to that of the Best Boy in the grip or electrical departments. The grip department has a Key Grip and Best Boy Grip and the electrical department has the Gaffer and Best Boy Electric. In the camera department the 1st AC is the key position, while the 2nd AC would

be the equivalent of the Best Boy in the other departments. The First Assistant must maintain the camera, configure it with specific lenses, filters and other accessories for each shot, and adjust the focus during the shot, just to name a few of the responsibilities. The Best Boy in the grip and electrical departments is responsible for organizing equipment and getting the equipment ready for upcoming shots or set-ups, which is the same thing that the 2nd AC must do for the camera department, among other things. Some producers look at the 2nd AC as just a Loader or even a Camera PA, but their job entails much more responsibility, knowledge, and special training. This person is responsible for many things within the camera department, the most important of which is the handling of the film before and after exposure, and in many cases the data management if the production is being shot digitally. The untrained and undisciplined Second Assistant Cameraman has the power to destroy hundreds of thousands of dollars of production work in an instant. They are critical to the operation of the film set and the camera department, and in many cases the 2nd AC is the hardest working person on set and often the last camera crew member to leave after wrap. The position is a key member of the camera department and not a luxury. Producers need to realize this no matter what type of production is being done. Even with more productions being shot digitally and with less being done on film, the 2nd AC is still a critical member of the team. Equipment must still be organized, actors given marks, scenes and shots properly slated, camera reports completed, and even though they are not loading or unloading film, they often handle the data management of the digital footage, backing it up onto computers and/or hard drives. Having a 2nd AC on set is always going to save the production valuable time and money in the long run.

This chapter discusses in detail each of the 2nd AC's duties and responsibilities. Because there are three different stages of production, these duties are separated into three categories: preproduction, production, and postproduction.

PREPRODUCTION

Depending on the type of production, the 2nd AC may or may not be involved in many of the preproduction activities. Preproduction is the period before the actual shooting when most of the planning and preparation for the production takes place. It has been said that the best preproduction leads to the best production. On many smaller productions, the 2nd AC will most likely not start work until filming actually begins.

But on large productions, such as television shows or feature films, the 2nd AC may play a small part in the preproduction process. The 2nd AC may have to contact the laboratory that will be processing the film to work out any details and also to obtain any of the necessary lab supplies required for the production. The 2nd AC may meet with the 1st AC to prepare the list of expendables and possibly offer ideas for the camera equipment package. And finally, the 2nd AC may work closely with the 1st AC to perform the camera prep where all of the equipment is checked to be sure it is in proper working order before shooting begins. Each production job will be a bit different, and the responsibilities of the 2nd AC during preproduction will differ accordingly.

Working with the Film Laboratory

As the 2nd AC you will often be the one person who deals with the film lab on a regular basis. You will serve as the liaison between the Director of Photography (DP) and the lab personnel. In most cases your production will be assigned one individual at the lab who will be working on your film. This will be the person you speak to each day to discuss the previous day's footage. Depending on the DP you are working with, he or she may want to speak with the lab each day to discuss the previous day's footage. Be sure to work this out ahead of time so that there is no confusion or duplication of work. It is very important to work out any specific details and procedures with the lab before production begins.

The DP may have very specific guidelines as to how the film should be handled during processing. Often during preproduction, film tests will be shot so that the DP and lab can establish these guidelines and requirements as quickly as possible. The lab may have specific requirements as to how the film should be packaged and labeled, as well as what information is required on the camera reports. Much of this information is covered in detail in the section on camera reports later in this chapter. Working this out during preproduction saves time and, it is hoped, will help to eliminate most problems during production.

The lab should know whom to contact if it finds any problems with the film. In many cases the lab contacts the production office if there are any problems, and the production office will notify the camera department, usually the 2nd AC. It is important to be made aware of any problems as soon as possible so that any reshoots can be scheduled if necessary. If the problem is camera or magazine related, you may need to obtain a different camera or magazine. You don't want

to use a particular magazine if it is repeatedly scratching the film. If the problem is film related, it may be necessary to contact the company that supplied the film to work out any of these problems. If the production company purchased short ends from one of the many companies that sell short ends, you may need to contact them about the film problem. I know of a situation in which the 2nd AC loaded film stock that was thought to be EI 500 film but that was actually EI 250 film because of an error in labeling by the film supplier. I was on a feature film production in which we had a problem with the film stock. We were using fresh factory-sealed cans of film. There was a problem with the developed image, which was eventually traced back to a manufacturing error. Working with the camera rental company, the lab, and the film manufacturer, the problem was figured out very quickly, and we were provided with new film stock so that we could reshoot. Although we did fall behind schedule briefly, it didn't affect the overall production. Please note that due to the very high quality control standards at the film manufacturers, this type of situation happens very infrequently.

Obtaining Laboratory Supplies

Part of establishing the relationship with the lab includes obtaining all of the lab supplies you will need to keep your production running smoothly. As the 2nd AC you should either go to the lab and pick up a supply of empty film cans, black bags, camera reports, spare cores, daylight spools and boxes for the spools, or ask the production company to arrange to have these items picked up. Remember to obtain the appropriate size cans and bags. These items are necessary so that you can do the job properly, and you must have them available to you during production.

The black bag is a small plastic, lightproof bag which is approximately the same size as the roll of film. It is used to protect the roll of film from light and also from scratches when it is placed in the film can. You should never place a roll of film into a film can without first placing it in a black bag. Many assistants may also refer to the changing bag as a black bag. The changing bag is not the same as the black bags used for wrapping exposed and unexposed film in a film can, so be sure you know exactly what is being referred to when someone uses the term.

The cans and bags are used to can out, which means to wrap and store any short ends and any exposed film during the production. A short end may be described as any roll of film left over from a full-size roll that is still large enough for shooting purposes. For example, you may load 1000 ft of 35 mm film into the camera and only shoot 275 ft

of it. The remaining 725 ft would be referred to as a short end because it is less than a standard full-size roll. Short ends are explained in more detail later in this chapter in the section on camera reports. The spare cores or daylight spools are needed to wind the film on the take-up side of the magazines if the magazines do not have collapsible cores. Collapsible cores will be explained later in this chapter. The camera reports will be filled out during shooting. Many times the production company will have already picked up these supplies for you, but it is a good idea to have a supply of your own in case of emergency. Keep a constant inventory of these items because you should not run out of any of them during shooting. As shooting progresses you may ask the production office to have someone pick up additional supplies as needed. Never wait until you have run out before ordering additional lab supplies. It is better to have extra supplies on hand than to run out at a critical time during shooting. I always have a supply of cans, bags, and cores at home because you never know when you will be called for a last-minute job and will need these supplies. When you start the job, your personal supply can be replenished as necessary.

In many cases the empty cans you receive from the lab will still have tape and labels from other productions on them. As soon as possible after receiving these supplies, I recommend removing all old tape and labels and placing a black bag and plastic core inside each can. During production, whenever you grab a can it will have everything in it you may need for unloading a magazine of film. If the core is not needed, you can always save it until it may be needed on your current production or on a future production. The more time you can save during shooting, the better for all concerned, especially you.

It is also important to keep the black bags and film cans clean. These will be used for any short ends or leftover film from the production, and you don't want to scratch the film by placing it in a can and bag that are dirty. When creating short ends during the production, be sure to remind the DP and 1st AC to try to use the short ends whenever short insert or pickup shots are done. The fewer short ends you have at the end of the production, the happier the production company will be.

Remember: Never run out of film cans, black bags, cores, or daylight spools.

Choosing and Ordering Expendables

During preproduction the First and Second Assistants should prepare a list of expendables. This list is then given to the production office

so that they may purchase these items for the camera department. Expendables are items that will be needed daily in the performance of your job, such as camera tape, permanent felt-tip markers, ballpoint pens, compressed air, lens tissue, lens cleaning solution, and so on. They are referred to as expendables because they are items that are used up or expended during the course of the production. In Britain expendables may be referred to as "stores" or "consumables." It is usually a good idea for the assistants and the loader to prepare the list because each may need specialty items that should be included with the basic supplies. You should also check with the DP and Camera Operator to see if there are any special items that they may need. The initial order should give you enough supplies to start filming, and as the shooting progresses, check the expendables supply regularly to see if anything is getting low and if you need to order more. When you see that additional items are needed, prepare a list and present it to the production office so that they may purchase the items for you. As a matter of professional protocol, you should only order specific amounts that you think you will need for the production. Do not over order just so you can add to your own personal supply of expendables. This is highly unprofessional and may cause you to not get hired on future productions. As you gain more experience, it will be easier for you to judge exactly how many of each item will be needed for the particular production you are working on. On most productions it is common to allow the assistants to split up any leftover expendables and keep them for their own supply. You may want to check with the Unit Production Manager (UPM) or Production Coordinator before doing this. As with lab supplies, do not wait until you run out to order expendables. It can be quite embarrassing for the 2nd AC to unload the exposed film, place it in a black bag and film can, and then discover that there is no tape to seal the can. For a complete list of the standard items on an Expendables Inventory and Checklist, see Figure C.3 in Appendix C.

Remember: Never run out of expendables that you may need to do the job.

Preparation of Camera Equipment

Camera preparation, or prep, is usually done by the 1st AC, but many times on larger productions the 2nd AC will also help with the camera prep. The camera prep is important because it gives the Camera Assistants a chance to check each piece of equipment before shooting. By doing this you know if you have everything necessary and also that

everything works properly. Even if you are not scheduled to be part of the camera prep, I recommend going to the rental house on the day of the prep so that you have a complete understanding of all the equipment being used. It also shows your professionalism and willingness to work hard. Please see the section on camera prep in Chapter 5 for the procedures to follow. You should also look at the Film Camera Prep Checklist, Figure C.4, in Appendix C.

Preparation of Camera Truck

When the camera prep has been completed, and if you are using a camera truck, the equipment should be loaded onto the truck. Before loading the truck, be sure that it has been cleaned out. Sweep the floor and clean off the shelves. If the truck is kept clean, there is less chance that the camera and equipment will get dirty. Once the truck has been cleaned, load the equipment on the shelves. The shelves should then be labeled as to what is on each of them. The labels are important to help you locate items in a hurry and are especially useful when using additional camera crew members who may not be familiar with the setup of the truck. In addition to labeling the shelves, each equipment case should be labeled with a brief description of what is inside.

When loading the camera truck, common sense is the key. Do not place camera, lenses, or filters on high shelves because they may fall while the truck is moving. These items should be kept on middle or lower shelves for ease of accessibility and safety. Most camera trucks have a workbench where you will perform the daily camera setup and maintenance. The workbench may also be a good area to work on the paperwork associated with the camera department. The camera case and accessory (AKS) case are often kept under the workbench so that they may be accessed easily each shooting day.

Most shelves in the camera truck have a lip along the front edge to help prevent the cases from sliding off during transport. In addition, all shelves should have a provision for attaching some type of tie-down strap or bungee cord across them to prevent cases from sliding off during transport. By using a logical system and order as to how the truck is loaded, you will be able to quickly set up at the start of each day and locate any item in a hurry.

When working with film one of the key items that is often included in the camera truck is a nitrogen tank with a regulator, hose, and nozzle. This tank is used for blowing dirt and dust off the camera equipment and especially for cleaning out the film magazines before loading and after unloading film. If you will be using a nitrogen tank

in the truck, be sure that it is secured in such a way that it will not tip over during transport. You should also be sure that you have the proper size and type of nozzle for the tank. An incorrect fitting will cause serious problems. Make sure the gauge you are using is made for nitrogen tanks and not some other type of gas. If not, you will get incorrect readings on the gauge. Many assistants use some type of small compressed air can on the set, but the nitrogen tank is the best thing to have when working out of a camera truck. If the truck is equipped with a darkroom, it should be cleaned and stocked with all necessary supplies. Make sure you have tape for sealing cans along with empty cans, black bags, cores, camera reports, inventory forms, permanent markers, pens, and everything you need in the darkroom so that you may do your job quickly and efficiently. See the next section on setting up your darkroom. Figure 4.1 shows a typical camera truck setup.

Figure 4.1   Typical camera truck setup. (Reprinted from the *Arriflex 35 Book* by Jon Fauer with permission of the author and ARRI Inc.)

Preparation of Darkroom

When using a darkroom, whether it is on a stage or on a camera truck, you should first ensure that it is lightproof. The best way to do this is to go into the darkroom, close the door, turn off the light, and stay in for at least five minutes to allow your eyes to adjust to the dark. After approximately five minutes, hold your hand 12 in. from your face with your fingers spread apart. If you are able to see the outline of your hand, then light is leaking in. Find the leaks and plug them or cover them with tape. Check along the floor, walls, and ceiling, and along the door frame where the door closes. Never use a darkroom until you are sure that it is completely lightproof. Also, be sure that

the door has a lock on the inside to prevent anyone from opening it while you are loading or unloading film. The controls for the darkroom light should also be located inside the darkroom so that there is no chance of someone turning on the light while you are loading or unloading film. The darkroom should be checked regularly to ensure that no light is leaking in. It should especially be checked daily if it is located on a camera truck that has been driven from location to location. The shifting and swaying of the truck during driving can cause the seams of the walls, floor, and door of the darkroom to separate.

When you are sure that the darkroom is lightproof, you should clean and stock it with all necessary supplies and equipment. Only the items that are needed for the loading and unloading process should be kept in the darkroom. Any additional items may be stored on other shelves in the camera truck so they do not clutter the darkroom. Set up the darkroom in a neat and orderly manner, with each item having an assigned location. This will help you do the job much faster so you do not have to search for something each time you load or unload. It is very important to keep the darkroom clean. Dirt and dust from a dirty darkroom can get inside the magazines and cause scratches on the film. Take the few extra minutes each day to be sure that your darkroom is clean and orderly and ready for use.

Camera tape, pens, permanent felt-tip markers, compressed air cans, empty cans, cores, camera reports, and inventory forms should all be kept within easy reach. Before using the darkroom, be sure that you have everything you need to load or unload the film. You don't want to discover after you have opened the film magazine that all the film cans are in a box outside the darkroom. Always be sure to separate the raw stock and short ends from the exposed film. Raw stock is any fresh, unexposed film, and short ends are short, unexposed rolls of film left over from a full roll. Figure 4.2 shows a typical film darkroom setup.

If working in digital you will obviously not need a film darkroom, but if using a truck with a darkroom you may want to use it as a secure area to download and transfer all the footage from the hard drives/memory cards. Having a secure area that you could even lock from the outside will ensure that the footage, along with your computers, hard drives, battery backups and other equipment, is safe and secure when you are away from the truck or darkroom.

PRODUCTION

Now that you have completed all of the preproduction procedures, it is time for filming to start. Putting a large production together is a complex and time-consuming operation that requires collaboration,

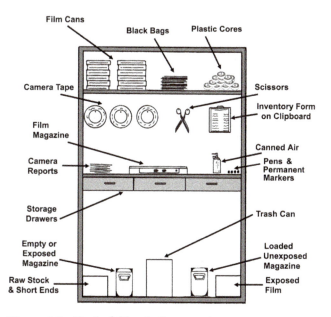

Figure 4.2   Typical film darkroom setup.

dedication and endurance from everyone involved. The production phase of shooting is a complex operation that requires a great deal of hard work and attention to detail on the part of all involved, especially the 2nd AC and Loader.

Proper performance of the duties and responsibilities of the 2nd AC and Loader is vital to the smooth operation of the production. You must keep track of how much film is shot, how many rolls are used, which scenes and how many takes of each are shot, along with many other aspects of the job. You must be very organized and able to jump in at a moment's notice with any piece of information or equipment needed during shooting. An average feature film may shoot over 100,000 ft of film, using over 100 rolls of film. Each day will require many shots and setups to get the day's work completed. All of this information must be accurately kept track of by the 2nd AC and/or Loader.

Start-of-the-Day Procedures

As the Loader, the first thing you should do each day is check with the 1st AC or DP to see what film stock is needed for the day and load up all of the magazines if they are not already loaded. If you were able

to get all of the magazines loaded the night before, then you should double check all of your paperwork and inventory forms from the previous day and get the forms ready for today's shooting. If you haven't already done so, prepare a supply of camera reports for the day's shooting. If you are also keeping track of camera crew hours, double check the time sheets and call sheets to be sure that you have all of the correct information recorded. Do an inventory of your lab supplies and expendables to be sure that you will have enough. I recommend having enough for at least three to five days unless you know that the end of production is coming soon. It won't hurt if you have cans, bags, cores, and other lab supplies left after the production. You can always take them with you for use on the next job. If it has not been done by the Trainee or PA, check the inventory of expendables to be sure you have enough of everything, especially 1-in. cloth tape for wrapping exposed cans and short ends. Check with the First and Second Assistants to see if they need any expendables and prepare an order for the production office. As with lab supplies, if it is coming up to the end of the production, you should not order expendables that you won't need. Although it is common practice for the assistants to split up the expendables at the end of the show, you don't want to place a large order two days before shooting ends simply to pad your own personal supply of expendables. Once all that is done you can then help the 2nd AC get the gear together and ready for the 1st AC to set up the camera.

As the Second Assistant you should help the First Assistant with the setup of the camera. Have all of the necessary cases open and hand things to the 1st AC as they are needed. When the camera is set up you should prepare all of the equipment carts. Check that all filters and lenses are clean. Also prepare marks for the actors. If you establish a daily routine, the job will go much more smoothly, and you should have fewer problems on set.

Setting Up the Camera

At the start of each shooting day, the camera must be set up and made ready to shoot as quickly as possible. But before that takes place, the DP should be able to start setting up for the first shot with the Director. Quite often they will use a Director's viewfinder, which is a device that allows them to see the shot as it would look through the lens. You can set the viewfinder for the aspect ratio of the production and dial in the specific focal length of the lens. While looking through the viewfinder you will have a very good approximation of how the shot will look through the camera from the position at which you are

standing. Many Cinematographers and Directors use a Director's view-finder that allows the actual camera lenses to be attached to it. It is up to one of the assistants, usually the 1st AC, to get this set up as soon as possible. But if the 1st AC is busy building the camera, then either the 2nd AC or Loader should make sure this is taken care of.

The actual setting up of the camera is usually handled by the 1st AC. The 2nd AC stands nearby and hands them pieces of equipment as they are asked for. It is important for the 2nd AC to know and understand the proper setup of the camera system in case he or she must step in and serve as 1st AC in an emergency or when additional cameras are used. The procedure for setting up the camera is discussed in detail in the section Setting up the Camera in Chapter 5.

Organizing Equipment

While the First Assistant is setting up the camera and getting it ready for the first shot, the Second Assistant usually ensures that all needed camera equipment is nearby. They may recruit the Trainee or Camera PA to assist in this task. Keep any camera equipment that will be needed throughout the shooting day as close to the camera as possible, without being in the way of other people or equipment. Camera equipment includes lenses, filters, magazines, and accessories.

As part of their kit, most assistants have a handcart or dolly to keep camera equipment cases on. These carts enable the assistant to keep all of the cases neat and organized yet quickly movable when there is a new camera setup. For many years the most common types of carts or dollies used for moving camera equipment cases were the Magliner brand folding cart or the Rubbermaid cart. The Magliner Gemini Jr. and Gemini Sr. or a similar type of cart sold by Filmtools in California, called the Liberator cart, were the typical carts used by assistants. They both collapse for shipping and storage and can be set up quickly when needed. These carts are still used quite frequently by First and Second Assistant Cameramen, but a newer cart made by Backstage Equipment, called the TR-04 Cart, is one of the favorites among today's Assistant Cameramen. Each of these carts can be very expensive depending on the options you choose, but you will soon discover that they are worth the price. With all of the cases on set, you will discover very quickly how time saving it is to wheel the equipment from one setup to the next rather than carry each case individually. See Figures D.1, D.2, D.3, and D.4 in Appendix D, for illustrations of the Backstage TR-04, Magliner and Rubbermaid carts.

Most assistants also keep their tools and accessories near the camera during shooting. The Camera Assistant's ditty bag, containing

basic tools and accessories, should also be kept on the cart during filming. It is also common to keep the DP's meter case on one of the camera
equipment carts. The carts should be set up so that things on set run
as efficiently as possible. It is common to have one cart designated as
the lens cart, with all lens cases, lens accessory cases, and filter cases
kept on this cart. Another cart would be set up with magazines, extra
camera batteries, and other accessories such as high hat, tripods and
matte box, and anything else that may be needed. I often take all of the
accessories like hard mattes, follow-focus whips, hand grips, etc., and
remove them from the hard side equipment case and place them in a
large canvas bag which can be hung on the handles of the cart. The LL
Bean Boat and Tote Bag or the Harrison Ditty Bag is perfect for this. I
also mount two large hooks on the Magliner nose plate which are used
for the standard and baby tripod. I remove the tripods from their cases,
place them upside down on these hooks, and secure them to the cart
with bungee cords. The more compact you can make your carts, the
easier your job will be each day. The assistant's set bag and DP's meter
case would usually be placed on the second cart.

In addition, if you are using more than one camera, it is advanta-
geous to have a separate cart designated for each camera's accessories.
Many assistants also set up their carts with drawers that can be used
to store some of the most commonly used expendables, such as AA,
AAA, and nine-volt batteries, along with markers, pens, Velcro, lens
tissue and fluid, and more. It is not uncommon to have two, three, or
even more camera equipment carts on a large-scale production.

Just like the assistant's ditty bag, every camera cart is going to be
set up differently and customized by the individual as to what works
best for them. When bringing equipment to the set, keep in mind that
you may not need everything from the camera truck. Bring only what
will be needed for the basic shots. Use your best judgment based on
the previous day's needs along with the location and types of scenes
that will be shot. Look at the call sheet for the day's work so that you
know what scenes will be shot. For example, if you will be shooting
mostly interiors in a very small room, you probably won't need the
150–600 zoom lens, or if shooting night exteriors, you probably won't
need the set of 85 or ND filters. Use your best judgment as to what
equipment should be on set at any given time, but if you are unsure,
bring it all so that if you do need something, the production is not
held up while you go to the camera truck to retrieve the item. It is
important for the camera equipment to be as close as possible to the
shooting location so that any delays can be avoided. I remember one
production that I was on where the Location Manager had the grip/
lighting truck parked directly in front of the location and the camera
truck parked two blocks down the street. After about two hours of the

2nd AC needing to be shuttled back and forth to the camera truck, the Location Manager made arrangements for the truck to be moved closer to the location.

Another important thing to keep in mind when bringing equipment to the set is where you will put it. When filming on practical locations, such as private homes or businesses, you should scout the location upon arrival to find a room or area close to the shooting area where you can set up a home base for the camera department. This is important so that you have everything needed in close proximity to the camera and so you don't have to continually run back and forth to the camera truck or to another area of the location to get a piece of equipment. Be sure to check with the Location Manager or AD to be sure that the room or area can be used to stage equipment. Keep in mind that the grip and electric departments will also be looking for an area to stage their equipment, and you all must work together. Don't block their equipment with camera carts and cases, and hopefully they will be equally courteous when they stage their equipment.

Film Stocks

As the camera crew member responsible for loading and unloading the film, the Second Assistant and Loader should be aware of the currently available film stocks. For many years the two companies that manufactured film stock for professional motion picture productions were Eastman Kodak and Fujifilm. Although Fujifilm no longer manufactures motion picture film for production, many of the examples in this book include references to Fujifilm products, just in case you have the opportunity to work with it.

When I started out in the early 1980s there was also another company called Agfa. Because the most widely used film in the motion picture industry is manufactured by Eastman Kodak, most of the examples in this book will use Eastman Kodak Color Negative Film. I am not saying that Eastman Kodak is better, but most of the productions that I have worked on have used Eastman Kodak motion picture film. See Figures 4.3 and 4.4 for illustrations of Eastman Kodak and Fujifilm film can labels.

Both Kodak and Fuji have used series of numbers to designate the specific film stock. To distinguish between 16 mm and 35 mm film stock, Eastman Kodak designates the film stocks that use the prefix 72 as 16 mm and any film stocks that use the prefix 52 as 35 mm. For example, 7218-365-2502 would be Eastman Kodak Color Negative 16 mm film stock and 5217-121-2302 would be Eastman Kodak Color Negative 35 mm film stock. The numbers 7218 and 5217 refer to what

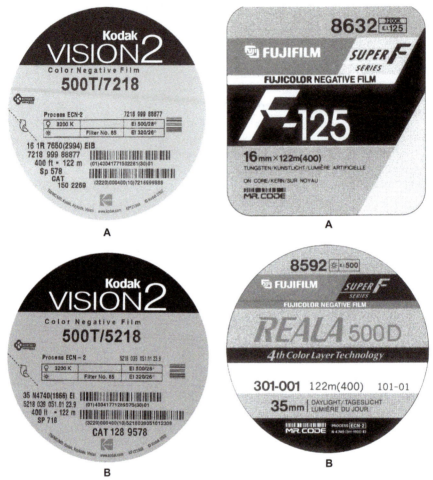

Figure 4.3 **A**, Eastman Kodak 16 mm film can label. **B**, Eastman Kodak 35 mm film can label. (Courtesy of Eastman Kodak Company.)

Figure 4.4 **A**, Fujifilm 16 mm film can label. **B**, Fujifilm 35 mm film can label. (Courtesy of Fuji Photo Film U.S.A. Inc.)

we commonly call the film type, 365 and 121 are the emulsion numbers, and 2502 and 2302 are the roll numbers of that particular emulsion. It is customary to include both the emulsion number and roll number when asking for the film's emulsion number and when writing it on magazine labels and camera reports. Fujifilm designated its film stocks using the prefix 86 for 16 mm film stock and 85 for 35 mm film stock. For example, Fujifilm Color Negative 8673-701-012 is 16 mm film where 8673 is the film type, 701 is the emulsion number,

and 012 is the roll number for the emulsion. Fujifilm Color Negative 8583-301-001 is 35 mm film where 8583 is the film type, 301 is the emulsion number, and 001 is the roll number for that emulsion. See Table A.1 in Appendix A for a complete listing of all current motion picture film stocks available at the time of publication of this edition.

Film Stock Packaging Sizes

In addition to knowing which film stock to use, you must know what size rolls are available from each manufacturer. The size of the roll that you use will be based on the camera and magazines you are using. Certain cameras only accept specific size rolls. 16 mm film is available on rolls ranging in length from 100 to 800 ft, and 35 mm film is available on rolls ranging from 100 to 1000 ft. See Table A.2 in Appendix A for a complete listing of all currently available motion picture film stock packaging sizes.

Film stock may be packaged on a daylight spool or on a plastic core. Daylight spools, sometimes called camera spools, allow you to load or unload the film in daylight or subdued light, while film wound onto a plastic core must be loaded and unloaded in complete darkness. See Figure 4.5 for an illustration of 16 mm and 35 mm daylight spools, and Figure 4.6 for an illustration of 16 mm and 35 mm plastic cores.

Figure 4.5   **A**, 16 mm daylight spool. **B**, 35 mm daylight spool.

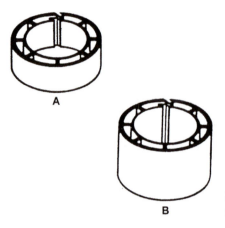

Figure 4.6 **A**, 16 mm 2-in. plastic core. **B**, 35 mm 2-in. plastic core.

Camera Reports

Camera reports are one of the most important, if not the most important, documents completed by the camera department. For film productions they are used to track how much film is used for each camera roll, and they identify the film stock for the camera crew, the lab personnel, production staff, and the editor and assistant editor. Each of these people uses information on the camera report, so it is imperative to fill it out neatly and correctly. One of the biggest mistakes the Second Assistant can make is to neglect the camera report.

Every magazine loaded with film and each roll of film shot during the production must have a camera report that shows which scenes were shot and how much film was used for each shot. Each lab has its own style of camera report, and each one contains very similar basic information. It is common practice to use the report from the lab that will be processing the film, but if this is not possible, then any camera report will suffice. I have designed a generic film camera report that can be used when you don't have specific lab reports available (see Figure C.10 in Appendix C). The generic report is also available for download on the companion web site for this book. The Second Assistant or Loader should prepare a supply of camera reports by filling out the top section of several reports during camera prep (or prior to the first day of shooting).

When the magazine is placed on the camera, the camera report for that roll of film is often attached to the back of the slate or to a clipboard so that you have a hard writing surface for entering the information. The 2nd AC fills out the information for each take, recording the footage information from the camera either by looking at the camera footage counter or by asking the first AC.

Much of the following information is for working on features, television movies, or episodic television shows. When working in commercials or music videos, many assistants do not keep as detailed camera reports as they do on other types of productions. Some assistants even develop a shorthand for the camera reports when working on commercials and music videos because things are moving so quickly on the set. Often just general notes are taken about the individual roll instead of take-by-take notes and footage numbers. Be sure to work it out ahead of time regarding how you should complete camera reports for commercial and music video productions.

No matter what style of camera report you use, most of the basic information on it is the same. I separate all camera reports into two basic sections, the heading section and the shooting section. The heading of the report should contain most of the following information: production company, production title, production number, Director, DP, magazine number, roll number, camera number, footage, film type, emulsion number, date, and developing instructions. The basic heading information, such as the production company, production title, Director, and DP, should be self-explanatory. The production number is a number assigned to that particular production by the company that is filming it. The company may have many different productions going on at the same time, and one way to keep track of them is to assign a different number to each one. When filming a television series, it is customary to assign a new production number to each new episode being filmed. Check with the production office to see if the production you are working on has been assigned a specific production number.

The magazine number is typically the serial number of the magazine in which the film is loaded. Many assistants prefer to assign numbers to the magazine, such as 1, 2, 3, and so on. If you choose to number the magazines in this manner, you must keep a written record showing which magazine serial number corresponds to your numbering system. The magazine number is useful if there is a problem with a particular roll of film. If there is a problem with a magazine (or *mag*), you can check the camera report to see which magazine was used and have it repaired or replaced if necessary. Rather than assign a separate number to the mags, I prefer to use the serial number of the mag so that there is less confusion. I recommend placing a small piece of tape on the outside of the magazine with the magazine serial number written on it so that I don't have to search for it when things get rushed. Often the serial number is engraved inside the magazine, and it may not be possible to view it when film is loaded in the magazine.

The roll number space is left blank until the magazine for that camera report is placed on the camera. Once the magazine is on the camera and the film threaded, then the subsequent roll number can be assigned

and written on the mag label and on the camera report. The common practice is to number the rolls sequentially starting with roll number one (1) on the first day of film and progressing from there. The second roll placed on the camera would be roll two (2), the next roll three (3), and so on. Each time a new roll is placed on the camera, it is assigned a new number, whether it is a full roll of film or a short end. When you start a new shooting day, the starting roll number will usually be the next higher number from the one you ended with on the previous day. For example, on day number 10 of shooting, you ended with roll number 57. When you start day number 11, the first roll placed on the camera will be roll number 58. The only exception to this practice is if you do not remove the last roll of film from the camera on the previous day and continue with it on the next day; or, if you remove a roll from the camera without breaking it, with the intention of using it again later in the day, when you later place this roll back on the camera, it will retain its original roll number. It is not common to continue a roll from one day to the next because on most professional productions all footage shot on a particular day should be sent to the lab for processing.

If more than one camera is being used, it is standard practice to assign a letter to each camera, and the roll number would then be a combination of the camera letter and the roll number, such as A-1, A-2, B-1, B-2, and so on. It is a good idea to check with the Editor or the production company to see how they would like the roll numbers labeled each day. If you only use one camera, it is common to not designate a letter for that camera. I was on one production in which we started with roll number 1 each day. I found this to be a bit confusing, but it is what the production company or Editor wanted, so I did not question it.

The footage space would be filled in with the size of the roll of film that is loaded into the magazine (400 ft, 1000 ft, 250 ft, etc.). Remember that the footage amount may be less than the actual size of the magazine. Often a short end will be loaded into a magazine instead of a full roll of film. The film type refers to what film stock you are using, for example Kodak 7205, 7212, 5218, 5229; Fujifilm 8622, 8653, 8563, 8592; and so on. The emulsion number is the emulsion number and roll number listed on the film can label. For example, if you are using Eastman Kodak 16 mm Color Negative 7218-032-1902, the film type is 7218 and the emulsion number is 032-1902. For Eastman Kodak 35 mm Color Negative 5218-197-1102, the film type is 5218 and the emulsion number is 197-1102. If you are using Fujifilm 16 mm Color Negative 8632-271-5846, the film type is 8632 and the emulsion number 271-5846.

When film is manufactured, it is made in very large rolls, approximately 54 in. wide. These rolls are then sliced into 16 mm or 35 mm wide rolls. From these large 16 mm or 35 mm rolls, smaller rolls are cut, which is what you receive when you order a 400 ft, 1000 ft, or other size roll from the manufacturer. For example, using

the film number 5218-197-1102, 5218 is the film type, 197 is the emulsion number, and 1102 the roll number cut from the larger roll. When filling in the camera report, you should always include all of the numbers following the film type in the space labeled emulsion number. Figures 4.3 and 4.4, shown previously, are examples of Eastman Kodak and Fujifilm 16 mm and 35 mm film can labels.

The date on the camera report corresponds to the date that the roll of film is exposed. The developing instructions are usually given to you by the DP. Some examples of developing instructions include develop normal, one-light work print, prep for video transfer, time to gray card or grayscale, print all, and print circle takes only.

Because much of the heading information, such as production company, production title, Director, and DP, will remain the same during the production, it may be filled in prior to production to save time. I recommend filling out a batch of camera reports beforehand so that when you are in the midst of shooting and get rushed, at least you will have some reports ready to use. Many times, the film type, emulsion number, and footage amount may also be filled in before production if you are using only one or two film stocks and one or two roll sizes for the entire production. Prepare a stack of camera reports for each film stock and roll size so that you will be prepared when things start to get a bit crazy on the set. Anything you can do to save time will help you in the long run.

During shooting you will fill in the shooting portion of the camera report with the following information: scene number, take number, dial reading, footage, remarks, G (Good), NG (No Good), W (Waste), T (Total), and SE (Short End). Figures 4.7 through 4.9 illustrate examples of the different styles of camera reports. Each one of these different styles is discussed separately later in this section.

In most cases you will receive the scene number and take number from the Script Supervisor. Write these numbers in the appropriate spaces on the report. At the end of each take, check the footage counter on the camera to obtain the dial reading. If you cannot see the footage counter, ask the 1st AC to give you the information. It is common for the 1st AC to call out the reading to you at the end of each take, or they may give you a hand signal to indicate the number on the camera footage counter. (See Chapter 5 for more information on hand signals.)

Most professional motion picture cameras have a digital footage counter. When a new roll is placed on the camera, the footage counter should be reset to zero. Each time the camera is turned on, the numbers on the footage counter get progressively higher. To make the addition and subtraction on the camera report easier, we traditionally round all camera footage amounts to the nearest 10 and then enter that amount in the DIAL space of the camera report. As most of us learned in elementary arithmetic, if the number ends in 0, 1, 2, 3, or 4, round it down, and if it ends in 5, 6, 7, 8, or 9, round it up. For example, if

the camera footage counter shows a reading of 247, round it to 250. On the camera report, next to the appropriate scene and take number, write the number 250 in the dial column. Because of the small size of the spaces on the camera report, many camera assistants will drop the zero and write the number 25 in the dial column for this example. Use whatever method is best for you.

To determine the footage amount for each take, subtract the previous dial reading from the one just recorded. For example, if the previous dial reading on the camera report is 210 and the present dial reading is 250, the footage for the present take is 40 (250–210). Table 4.1 shows an example of camera footage counter amounts and the corresponding dial reading and footage amounts for each. The information in Table 4.1 is used in each of the three different styles of camera

Table 4.1 Camera Footage Counter Amounts and Corresponding Camera Report Dial and Footage Amounts

Camera Footage Counter	Camera Report Dial	Camera Report Feet
66	70	70
121	120	50
162	160	40
205	210	50
247	250	40
279	280	30
364	360	80
433	430	70
498	500	70
550	550	50
607	610	60
649	650	40
703	700	50
754	750	50
802	800	50
836	840	40
885	890	50
942	940	50
968	970	30

reports so that you can compare the differences between each report. The first camera report style is shown in Figure 4.7.

The SD column is not common but on this report it may be used to indicate whether the scene was shot sync or MOS. If the shot was done with sync sound, write S in the column for sync, and if it was done without sound, write M in the column for MOS. Most assistants, including myself, do not use this column but prefer to write the sound information in the Remarks column of the report.

In the Remarks column of the report, you may record a variety of information, including filters used, f-stop/t-stop, focal length of the lens, camera to subject distance, lens height, MOS (if the shot was done without sound), tail slate or second slate, or any other information that the DP or 1st AC wants written on the report. You also may note whether the shot was interior (int), exterior (ext), day (day), or night (nite). There is no set rule as to what information should go in the Remarks column. Check with the DP and 1st AC to see if they want anything written in this space. Each production is different.

CAMERA REPORT

Co. Submitted By: **Demi Monde Productions** P.O.#:

Bill To: **Demi Monde Productions**   Date Exposed: Phone Contact

Picture Title: **Claire of the Moon**   Loader:

Director: **N. Conn**   D.P.: **R. Sellars**   Sheet of

ROLL # **5**   ☐ BLACK & WHITE   ☑ COLOR
EMUL.# **5218**   — **237 4862**   MAG # **10146**
DEVELOP   FOOTAGE **1,000**
☑ NORMAL ☐ PUSH____STOP(S)   ☐PULL____STOP(S)
FILM WORKPRINT ☐ PRINT ALL ☑ PRINT CIRCLED TAKES
VIDEO PREP & TRANSFER ☐ TRANSFER ALL ☑ TRANSFER CIRCLED TAKES
   TRANSFER AT____ fps ☐ EDGE # PUNCH

FOTOKEM
FILM AND VIDEO
FOTO-KEM INDUSTRIES, INC.
2801 W. Alameda Ave. • Burbank CA 91505
8 1 8   8 4 6   3 1 0 1   V o i c e   M a i l
Production Services Fax 818 841 7532
Customer Services Fax 818 841 0630

SCENE NO.	TAKE	DIAL	FEET	SD.	REMARKS	SCENE NO.	TAKE	DIAL	FEET	SD.	REMARKS
54	1	70	70			82 A	(2)	700	(50)		
	(2)	120	(50)				(3)	750	(50)		
	3	160	40			82 B	(1)	800	(50)		
	(4)	210	(50)				2	840	40		
54 A	(1)	250	(40)			36	(1)	890	(50)		
	2	280	30				(2)	940	(50)		
82	(1)	360	(80)				3	970	30		
	2	430	70								
	(3)	500	(70)			Out At 970'				G	600
	4	550	50			Develop Normal				NG	370
	(5)	610	(60)			Prep for Video Transfer				W	30
82 A	1	650	40							T	1,000

2050-60 (9/00)   THIS CAMERA REPORT SUBJECT TO PROVISIONS ON THE REVERSE SIDE
OPEN 24 HOURS A DAY, 7 DAYS A WEEK

Figure 4.7   Example of one camera report style. (Courtesy of FotoKem Industries, Inc.)

color by deluxe **deluxe laboratories**
1377 North Serrano Ave., Hollywood, CA 90027   (213) 462-6171

CAMERA REPORT
SOUND REPORT   No. 179450

DATE _____ CUSTOMER ORDER NUMBER _____
COMPANY **Demi Monde Productions**
DIRECTOR **N. Conn**   CAMERAMAN/RECORDIST **R. Sellars**
PRODUCTION NUMBER OR TITLE **Claire of the Moon**
MAGAZINE NUMBER **10146** _____ ROLL NUMBER **5**
TYPE OF FILM / EMULSION **5218 237 4862**
PRINT CIRCLED TAKES ONLY: ☑ ONE LITE   ☐ TIMED

SCENE NO.	TAKE	DIAL	PRINT	REMARKS
54	1	70		
	②	120	50	
	3	160		
	④	210	50	
54 A	①	250	40	
	2	280		
82	①	360	80	
	2	430		
	③	500	70	
	4	550		
	⑤	610	60	
82 A	1	650		
	②	700	50	
	③	750	50	
82 B	①	800	50	
	2	840		
36	①	890	50	
	②	940	50	
	3	970		
			G	600
	Out At 970'		NG	370
	Develop Normal		W	30
TOTAL	Prep for Video Transfer		T	1000

All contracts with this company are accepted with the understanding that all film delivered to it is covered by the owner against loss. This company takes every necessary precaution for the safekeeping of the film, but assumes no responsibility for its loss.
DEL-82 (10/90)

Figure 4.8   Example of a second camera report style. (Courtesy of Deluxe Laboratories.)

For the type of camera report shown in Figure 4.8, write the scene and take numbers as you did in the previous style of report. Round the dial reading and write the amount in the Dial or Counter column, depending on which type of report you are using. Some reports use the term Dial and some use the term Counter, but the information that you place in this space is the same. In the Print column, you only write the footage for the takes that are to be printed. The information in the Remarks column is the same as in the previous example. As you can tell from looking at the third type of camera report shown in Figure 4.9, the only sections that are the same in the shooting portion of the report are the Scene Number and Remarks columns. Instead of writing the dial readings in one column and the footage amounts in another column, only the footage amounts are written in the space for

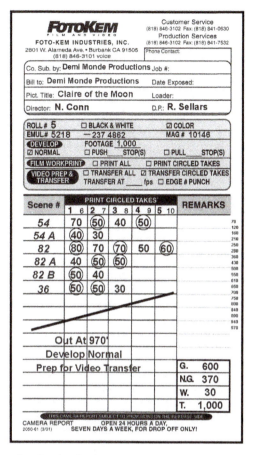

Figure 4.9   Example of a third camera report style. (Courtesy of FotoKem Industries, Inc.)

the particular take number. Column 1_6 is for take 1 and take 6, column 2_7 is for take 2 and take 7, and so on. Because there is no space for the dial readings, many assistants usually make their own column along either the left or the right edge of the report as shown in Figure 4.9. As shown in this figure, the dial readings are written along the right edge of the Remarks column. So, for this camera report style, scene 54, take 1, was 70 ft; take 2 was 50 ft; take 3 was 40 ft; and so on.

Notice that on each of these styles of camera reports, certain take numbers and footage amounts have been circled. After each setup, the Script Supervisor will tell you which takes are to be circled. These are the takes that the Director likes and wants to consider for use in the editing of the film, and they are called the good or printed takes. Circling lets the lab know which takes are to be printed or transferred

during processing. If the film is being transferred to videotape or some digital format, the circled takes are the takes that will be transferred. Although it is no longer common, before the advent of digital editing, a work print would be made of the film for editing purposes. When making a work print, most labs would not print circled takes in 16 mm because it is cheaper to print the entire roll, but for a video or digital transfer, circled takes are used in 16 mm. When circling particular takes, it is common practice to also circle the corresponding footage amounts and I recommend this in order to make it easier to add up the footage.

No matter what format you are shooting, 16 mm, 35 mm, or digital, I recommend always circling the good takes and if shooting film then you should circle the corresponding footage amounts for each take. The camera report serves as a record for the Editor and Director to know which takes were the best and are to be considered for use in the finished film. During editing, they can refer to the report and know immediately which takes the Director liked during shooting. The circled takes are called good (G) takes. The takes on the film camera report that have not been circled are called no good (NG). If for some reason you circled a take and then the Director decided not to print it, draw slashes through the edges of the circle and write "Do Not Print" in the Remarks column. An example of a circled take that is not to be printed is shown in Figure 4.10.

SCENE NO.	TAKE	DIAL	FEET	REMARKS
54	1	70	70	
	2	120	50	
	3	160	40	
	⊘4⊘	210	⊘50⊘	DO NOT PRINT
54 A	1	250	40	
	2	280	30	

Figure 4.10 Marking a circled take to indicate that it is not to be printed.

At the bottom right in the shooting portion of most camera reports, there are usually spaces labeled G (Good), NG (No Good), W (Waste), SE (Short End), and T (Total). If the camera report does not have any of these labels, write them in yourself. "G" stands for GOOD and will be the total amount of footage for all circled takes. Write the total footage for all circled takes on the report in the section marked G. "NG" stands for NO GOOD and is the total amount of footage for all takes not circled. Mark the total footage for all non-circled takes in the section marked NG. "W" stands for WASTE and may be the amount of film left over after the good and no good totals are added together,

depending on the length. "SE" stands for SHORT END and may be the amount of film left over after all the good, no good, and waste totals are added together. "T" stands for TOTAL and is the total amount of film loaded into the magazine for the particular roll of film. You should add up the totals for G and NG, and subtract this amount from the total amount of film loaded into the camera. This remaining amount of film, if any, may either be called Waste or a Short End depending on the length. If it is waste, write it in the section marked W (Waste). If it is a short end, mark it in the section marked SE (Short End).

A short end is a roll of film that is large enough to use for shooting and is remaining from a full-size roll. In other words, let's assume you loaded a 1000 ft roll of film into the camera and only shot 370 ft. The 370 ft of exposed film would be sent to the lab for developing with all other film shot during the day's shooting. The remaining 630 ft (1000−370) is left over and is called a short end. As a general rule, for 35 mm format, the traditional short end amount is anything that is more than 100 ft, and anything that is less than 100 ft is called waste. When I worked at one of the major Hollywood studios, the studio camera department had a policy that anything less than 200 ft was waste, and anything more than 200 ft was a short end for 35 mm. As a general rule, for 16 mm format, anything more than 40 ft is a short end, and anything less than 40 ft is waste. The waste footage is traditionally kept by the assistants to use during camera prep when scratch testing the magazines. They may also be used when practicing loading film on a new camera or magazine that you have never used. These waste rolls of film are usually called dummy loads. In Britain a dummy load may be referred to as gash stock. Unless told otherwise by the production company or studio, use the figures shown in Table 4.2 for short end and waste values.

Table 4.2   Typical Waste and Short End Amounts for 16 mm and 35 mm

Film Format	Waste	Short End
16 mm	Under 40 ft	Over 40 ft
35 mm	Under 100 ft	Over 100 ft

The combined total of G, NG, W, and SE should equal the total amount of footage loaded in the magazine. If it doesn't you should check your arithmetic. This total amount is written in the section marked T (Total). Before removing the magazine from the camera, the 1st AC will often cover the lens by placing their hand in front of it and run the camera for approximately 10 ft so that there will be a dark area of film at the end of the roll for safety reasons. If you remove the magazine immediately after the last take, you may fog the last few frames of the shot. This

10 ft of film can be included in the good or no good totals, or you may consider it to be waste. That decision is up to you. As long as the numbers add up correctly nobody will really care if you call it no good or waste. The important thing to remember is that the total of G, NG, W, and SE must equal the amount of film loaded in the magazine for that roll. At the bottom of the report, after the last take, write the amount of footage that the roll ended at. For example, if the last dial reading on the camera report is 970 ft, you would write "OUT AT 970." If the roll of film rolled out during the last take, write the amount of footage that the roll ended at or write "ROLLOUT." Whenever possible, it is better to reload the camera than to risk having a rollout, because when the film rolls out, you will often lose the end of the last take and if the performance was good, it cannot be used. If you are in doubt as to whether you should reload or risk rolling out, check with the DP or Director and let one of them make the decision. For example, I have been in the situation where after shooting a take that was 90 ft long and according to the footage counter on the camera I had 100 ft of film left in the magazine, the Director said he wanted to shoot another take of the scene. I have learned not to fully trust the footage counter or the film manufacturer when it comes to the size of the film roll. Rather than make the decision myself to take the chance and shoot with the remaining 100 ft of film, I usually check with the DP or Director. If either one chooses to take the risk and shoot another take, and the film rolls out, it is his or her responsibility. Whenever the film does roll out, write at the bottom of the report "SAVE TAILS" as an indication to the lab to process the roll to the very end. In addition, it is common to write any developing instructions at the bottom of the report. The instructions may include the following: develop normal, one-light print, time to grayscale, time to color chart, push one stop, print circle takes only, prep for video transfer, transfer circle takes only, and so on. Figures 4.7, 4.8, and 4.9 show the G, NG, W, SE, and T at the bottom of each camera report, as well as the developing instructions.

Often the magazine may be loaded with a short end of film. When quickly looking at the camera report, you might assume that it contains a full roll of film unless there is some indication otherwise. The camera report should be marked in some way to indicate that it is a short end. This eliminates confusion so that you don't risk running out of film in the middle of a shot because you forgot that it was a short end. The standard procedure for marking a camera report for a short end is to draw a diagonal line across the shooting part of the report from the lower left to the upper right. This should be done before filling in the information on the report so that each time you look at the report this diagonal line will remind you that it is a short end. You should also write the footage in the lower left corner and circle the amount. A typical camera report for a short end is shown in Figure 4.11.

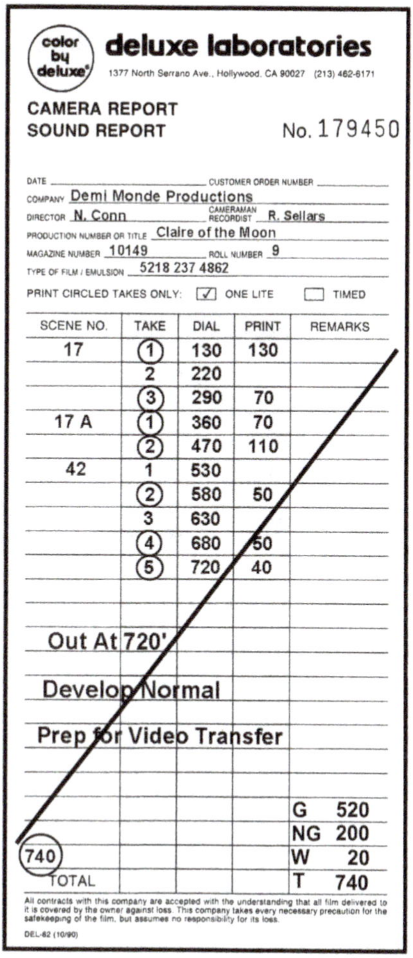

color by deluxe® **deluxe laboratories**
1377 North Serrano Ave., Hollywood, CA 90027 (213) 462-6171

CAMERA REPORT
SOUND REPORT

No. 179450

DATE ______ CUSTOMER ORDER NUMBER ______
COMPANY Demi Monde Productions
DIRECTOR N. Conn CAMERAMAN RECORDIST R. Sellars
PRODUCTION NUMBER OR TITLE Claire of the Moon
MAGAZINE NUMBER 10149 ROLL NUMBER 9
TYPE OF FILM / EMULSION 5218 237 4862

PRINT CIRCLED TAKES ONLY: [✓] ONE LITE [ ] TIMED

SCENE NO.	TAKE	DIAL	PRINT	REMARKS
17	(1)	130	130	
	2	220		
	(3)	290	70	
17 A	(1)	360	70	
	(2)	470	110	
42	1	530		
	(2)	580	50	
	3	630		
	(4)	680	50	
	(5)	720	40	

Out At 720'

Develop Normal

Prep for Video Transfer

G	520
NG	200
W	20
T	740

(740) TOTAL

All contracts with this company are accepted with the understanding that all film delivered to it is covered by the owner against loss. This company takes every necessary precaution for the safekeeping of the film, but assumes no responsibility for its loss.

DEL-62 (10/90)

Figure 4.11 Example of a completed film camera report for a short end.

Each time you load a magazine with a fresh roll of film, a camera report should be attached to it. As stated earlier in this chapter, to save time, many 2nd ACs prepare a supply of camera reports with most of the heading information filled in ahead of time. Fill out as much information as possible in the heading so that the report is ready for shooting. This includes the production company, production title, Director, and DP. When you load the magazine, any additional heading information, such as film type, emulsion number, and magazine number, can be filled in on the report before attaching it to the magazine. Some labs will preprint the heading information on the report for you. This saves time during the loading process. If you have some of the heading information filled in ahead of time, each time a magazine is loaded only a

small amount of information needs to be added to the report. This is discussed further in the section on loading magazines.

Sometimes it may be necessary to remove a partially shot roll of film from the camera, knowing that it will be used again later the same day. When doing this, remember not to break or cut the film when removing the magazine. You should also mark the frame in the gate with an "X" before removing it from the camera, so that when you place the magazine back on the camera you can line up the film exactly as it was before removing it. Attach the camera report to the magazine and place the magazine back in its case for later use. When the partially shot roll is placed back on the camera, the roll number remains the same, as mentioned earlier. Be sure to inform the Script Supervisor that you are using a roll from previously in the day and that it is not a different roll number but rather the same roll number as before.

Each time a new magazine is placed on the camera, the 2nd AC should take the camera report from the magazine and place it on the back of the slate, on a clipboard, or some other type of hard surface. This gives a smooth writing surface to write out the report during shooting. Some assistants prefer to use a clipboard for the report; some use the back of the slate. You may use whichever system is more convenient for you. Be sure to write clearly and legibly on the camera report so that the people at the lab, the Editor, and any other people who need it will be able to read the report without any difficulty. Camera reports used when shooting digital are a bit different than film camera reports and will be discussed later in this chapter.

Recording Shot Information

Throughout the course of filming, it is often the responsibility of the 2nd AC to keep track of specific, detailed information for each shot, including a description of the scene, lens used, t-stop, filters, focus distance, lens height, film stock, angle of the camera tilt, and other information. Appendix C contains a Camera Department Log Sheet (Figures C.17 and C.18) that you may use for this record keeping. I have also used an item called *The Camera Log*, which is a 4×6-in. spiral-bound book available at most expendables supply stores. This pocket-size book contains pages to record all of the pertinent information for each shot. It also contains pages for recording your hours worked along with basic equipment information. See Figure 4.12 for examples of pages from *The Camera Log*. In addition, the application called Toland ASC Digital Assistant for the iPhone, iPad, and iPod Touch contains a feature that allows you to record specific information about a shot. Figure 4.13 shows a screen shot image of the Log feature of Toland ASC Digital Assistant.

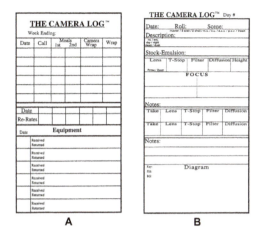

Figure 4.12   A, *The Camera Log* page for recording hours worked and equipment information. **B**, *The Camera Log* page for recording shot information. (Courtesy of Donald Burghardt.)

Figure 4.13   Log screen shot from Toland ASC Digital Assistant. (Courtesy of Chemical Wedding.)

Magazines

A magazine may be described as a removable lightproof chamber that is used to hold the film before and after exposure. There are two basic types of magazines in use today: coaxial and displacement. When we speak about the areas within the magazine, and if the camera accepts internal loads, we refer to the area holding the fresh unexposed raw stock as the feed side, while the take-up side holds the exposed film after it has run through the camera.

The coaxial magazine has two distinct compartments, one for the feed side and one for the take-up side. The feed and take-up rolls are parallel to each other, with a common dividing wall between them. The magazine is called *coaxial* because the feed and take-up rolls share the same axis of rotation. Because there are two separate compartments, it is much easier to do the loading and unloading of the magazine. During the loading process, only the feed side needs to be loaded in the dark; the take-up side can be loaded in the light. During the unloading process, the take-up side must be unloaded in the dark, and the feed side may be unloaded in the light, unless there is a short end. If there is any short end left in the magazine, then the feed side also must be unloaded in the dark. The coaxial magazine typically mounts to the rear of the camera.

A displacement magazine is so named because as the film travels from the feed side to the take-up side, it is displaced from one side to the other. There are typically two different types of displacement magazines: the single-chamber displacement magazine and the double-chamber displacement magazine. On most displacement magazines the feed side is toward the front of the camera, and the take-up side is toward the back of the camera as the magazine sits on the top of the camera. During shooting, the film moves from the feed side to the take-up side, or the film moves from the front of the camera to the back. This typically causes a shift in weight on the camera, so the camera must be periodically rebalanced, usually after each take.

The single-chamber displacement magazine contains both the feed and the take-up rolls in the same compartment. Because of this, the entire loading and unloading process must be done in the dark. Single-chamber displacement magazines are smaller than a corresponding double-chamber displacement magazine. This is because the single-chamber magazine is not able to hold a full roll of film on both the feed side and the take-up side at the same time. As the feed roll gets smaller, the take-up roll gets larger during shooting, so the film is displaced from the feed side of the magazine to the take-up side.

The double-chamber displacement magazine has two distinct compartments that share a common dividing wall between them. One compartment holds the feed roll of film and one holds the take-up roll. The double-chamber displacement magazine may be handled the same as

the coaxial magazine during the loading and unloading process. In other words, the feed side must be loaded in the dark and the take-up side may be loaded in the light during loading, and the take-up side must be unloaded in the dark during unloading. Unlike the single-chamber displacement magazine, the double-chamber displacement magazine has the ability to hold a full roll in each of the feed and take-up compartments.

Some newer cameras use a variation of the displacement magazine called active displacement. During operation of the camera, the feed and take-up rolls actually shift position within the magazine during filming to compensate for the transfer of the film from the feed roll to the take-up roll. This allows the magazine, and therefore the overall camera, to be smaller in size and much more compact.

It is a good idea to be familiar with the loading and unloading procedures for as many different magazines as possible. Figure 4.14 shows two sides of a coaxial magazine. Figures 4.15 and 4.16 show the single-chamber and double-chamber displacement magazines. Figure 4.17 shows the Aaton 35 active displacement magazine.

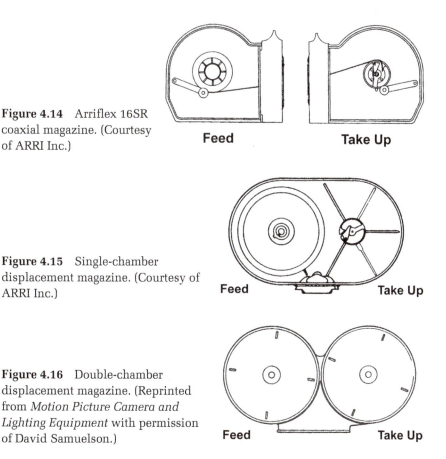

Figure 4.14   Arriflex 16SR coaxial magazine. (Courtesy of ARRI Inc.)

Feed   Take Up

Figure 4.15   Single-chamber displacement magazine. (Courtesy of ARRI Inc.)

Feed   Take Up

Figure 4.16   Double-chamber displacement magazine. (Reprinted from *Motion Picture Camera and Lighting Equipment* with permission of David Samuelson.)

Feed   Take Up

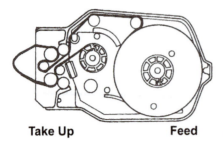

Take Up   **Feed**

Figure 4.17 Active displacement magazine. (Courtesy of Aaton Inc.)

Loading Magazines

Loading film into the magazines is primarily the Loader's responsibility, but if the production does not have a Loader, then it falls to the 2nd AC to handle this. Before loading any magazine, clean it thoroughly to remove any dirt, dust, or film chips. Blow out the magazine using some type of compressed air or nitrogen tank. Also check the magazine to see if it contains any electrical contacts where it attaches to the camera. It is important to keep these contacts clean; otherwise the film will not travel properly through the magazine. Be sure that the darkroom, changing bag, or changing tent is clean and that you have all the necessary items before you start to load any magazines.

You should have camera tape, permanent felt-tip markers, camera reports, extra cores, film cans, and so on. Most important, be sure that you have the correct film stock to load into the magazine. When opening a fresh can of film be very careful when removing the sealing tape from the can. If you remove it too quickly or too hard you will create sparks or static electricity that could streak your film. This will happen especially when working in a very dry climate. Remove the tape very slowly to prevent this from happening. If possible, put a wet cloth in the darkroom or even in the changing tent to prevent static electricity. When a fresh roll of raw stock is removed from the film can and black bag, it will have a small piece of tape on the end to hold the roll together. Be sure to remove all of the tape from the end of the roll and place it inside the bottom of the film can. Many camera or magazine jams have occurred because of a small amount of tape left on the roll. As with the sealing tape on the can, you should also remove this piece of tape slowly so you do not create sparks or static electricity. See Figure 4.18 for an example of the tape used to hold the end of the film to the roll. Once you have removed the film from the black bag, and placed it on the core adapter in the feed side of the magazine, place the black bag back in the film can and put the lid on the can to reduce the chance of the piece of tape or the black bag getting stuck in the magazine during the remainder of the loading process.

Figure 4.18 **A**, Example of sealing tape from 16 mm roll of Kodak film. **B**, Example of sealing tape from 35 mm roll of Kodak film.

Some magazines require a plastic core on the take-up spindle or core adapter onto which the exposed film will be wound. You should have extra cores available in this case. The best way to secure the film to the plastic core is to fold approximately one inch of the film against itself, keeping the edges of the film straight against each other. This gives you a double thickness of film, which should grab the slot in the core more securely. Position the core so that the slot is facing in such a way that, as it rotates, the film is pulled tight against the core. You want to be sure that, as the core rotates, the film does not pull loose from the slot in the core. By positioning the slot correctly, the film will be pulled tight as the core rotates, eliminating any chance of the film coming off the core (see Figure 4.19).

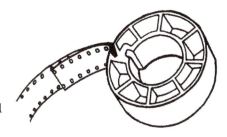

Figure 4.19 Securing the end of the film to a plastic core.

Certain magazines have what is referred to as a collapsible core on the take-up side. The collapsible core is so named because when you first place the film onto the core and lock it, the core expands slightly. Upon unlocking the core in order to remove the exposed film,

the core will collapse slightly, making it easier to remove the exposed roll of film. When the film is first placed on the collapsible core, it is inserted into a slot and locked in place. When locking the film onto the core, place it so that the end of the film is approximately halfway into the slot. Do not place it in the slot in such a way that the end of the film touches the edge of the core. During shooting, while the core is turning, the film may rub against the inside edge of the core and cause unnecessary noise in the camera. When you are ready to remove the exposed film from the take-up side, release the lock; the core will collapse and you can then remove the roll of film from the magazine. Figure 4.20 shows a collapsible core.

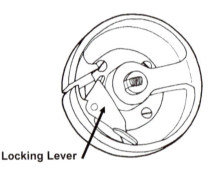

Locking Lever

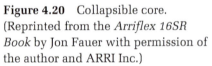

Figure 4.20 Collapsible core. (Reprinted from the *Arriflex 16SR Book* by Jon Fauer with permission of the author and ARRI Inc.)

Some cameras have the ability to accept internal loads, commonly referred to as daylight spools or camera spools. When using daylight spools you don't need a magazine. This mostly applies to some older 16 mm cameras but there are a few 35 mm cameras that also accept daylight spools. In this case, you should have extra daylight spools available onto which the exposed film may be taken up. See Figures 4.5 and 4.6 for illustrations of daylight spools and plastic cores. Some magazines will accept a daylight spool, but I do not recommend doing this because as the spool rotates, the flanges of the spool may rub against the interior of the magazine, causing unnecessary noise during shooting.

For ease of loading and threading the film, the end of the film should have a straight edge, and it should be cut so that the cut bisects the perforations. This enables the end of the film to engage in the sprockets of the rollers located in the magazines and cameras. Before loading a roll of film into a magazine, you may need to cut the film so that you bisect a perforation. This makes it easier to thread the film into a magazine that contains geared teeth or sprocket wheels. Remember, you will need to do this in the dark so that you do not

expose the film stock. Be very careful if you need to cut the film in a darkroom, and especially if you are using a changing bag or changing tent, so that you do not cut the bag or tent. Cutting the end of the film straight is usually only necessary on short ends. Most fresh raw stock is cut in such a way to make it easier to thread the film in the dark (see Figure 4.21).

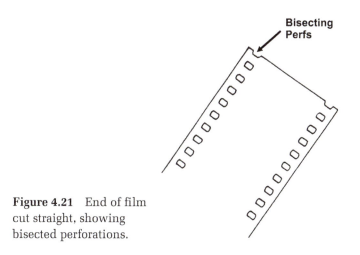

Figure 4.21 End of film cut straight, showing bisected perforations.

Now that you have loaded the magazine with film, an identification label must be placed on the magazine lid to identify what type of film is loaded along with other information specific to that roll of film and to the production. On a coaxial magazine, the identification label should be placed on the take-up side of the magazine. On the displacement magazine the label is placed somewhere in the center of the lid. The identification label should contain the following information: production company, production title, date loaded, footage loaded, film type, emulsion number, roll number, and magazine number. If more than one person is loading magazines on the production, the Loader's initials also should be written on this piece of tape. For the roll number you should write "ROLL #," leaving a blank space following so that you can enter the actual number once the magazine is placed on the camera.

It is common to make the magazine identification label from a piece of 1-in. wide white camera tape and a black permanent felt-tip marker. But many assistants may use a color-coding system for labeling the magazines, especially if they are using more than one type of film stock. For example, use white tape for slow-speed film, yellow tape for medium-speed film, blue tape for daylight film, and red tape

for high-speed film. This is especially useful when you are in a hurry because you don't have to take time to read the label to know what type of film is loaded in the magazine. The color of the tape indicates the type of film being loaded. Table 4.3 is a suggestion of what color tape to use based on some of the currently available Eastman Kodak Color Negative films. Keep in mind that not all film stocks are listed in the table; the system shown is based on the color-coding system I have used successfully for many years. You may adjust this to suit your particular shooting needs, depending on how many different film stocks you are using on your production.

Table 4.3 Camera Tape Color-Coding System When Using Various Films

Kodak	EI	Tape Color	Ink Color
$7201/5201$ $7203/5203$	50 D	White	Blue
$7207/7207$	250 D	Blue	Black
$7213/5213$	200 T	Yellow	Red
$7219/5219$ $7230/5230$	500 T	Red	Black

D = Daylight, T = Tungsten

If you are unable to use a tape color-coding system because of budget constraints or other reasons, you may still color code the film by using 1-in. wide white camera tape with a different color marking pen for each film stock. This may not work as well as using different color tape because you may not be able to distinguish the ink color from a distance, but if you don't have the various colors of tape, using white tape and various colored markers may be your only option. The important thing to remember is that if you develop a system, you should stick with it; don't change it from production to production.

The magazine label is usually 6- to 8-in. long and may look like the ones shown in Figures 4.22 and 4.23. Some film expendables supply stores offer a special 2-in. wide tape that is imprinted with spaces to write in certain information for the mag label. An example of this type of tape label is shown in Figure 4.24. When using this tape label, the exposed footage amount would be entered once you unload the magazine.

Date	Production Company Production Title	Roll # Mag #
		Loader
Footage	Film Type Emulsion Number	Initials

A

Figure 4.22 **A**, Information to be included on a magazine ID label. **B**, Completed magazine ID label.

10/29/91	Demi Monde Productions "Claire of the Moon"	Roll #7 Mag # 10143
1000'	5218 - 237 - 4862	DEE

B

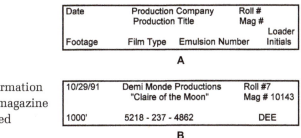

Figure 4.23 Magazine identification label in place on the magazine. (Magazine reprinted from the *Panaflex Users Manual* with permission of David Samuelson and Panavision Inc.)

Figure 4.24 Example of preprinted 2-in. tape magazine label.

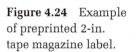

PROD:					DATE:
STOCK#	MAG#	LOADED FOOTAGE	EXPOSED FOOTAGE	ROLL#	
LOADER:					

In humid conditions, 1-in. cloth camera tape usually does not stick very well to magazines, equipment cases, film cans, etc. I have been told that when working in very humid conditions an excellent substitute for the cloth camera tape is vinyl electrical tape. It comes in ¾-in. width and is available in white, black, red, yellow, green, orange, violet, and blue. It can be used to wrap film cans, label cans, and equipment. You can write on it with most permanent felt-tip markers. Although I have never used it, I do plan on trying it out the next time I am working in humid weather.

When the magazine has been loaded, place a piece of tape over the magazine lid lock as a safety measure. On many magazines it is recommended that you wrap tape around the edges where the lid attaches to the magazine to prevent light leaks and as an additional safety measure to keep the lid from coming off. This is especially important when filming outside in bright sunlight because the

intensity of direct, bright sunlight for an extended period on a magazine may cause fogging of the film even from a very small light leak. If you are using the color-coding system for the magazine identification labels, the tape used for sealing the lid should be the same color as that used for the identification label. Figure 4.23 shows a magazine that has been taped around the edges of the lid. When the magazine has been loaded and an identification label has been attached, you should also attach a camera report to it. The key heading information of the report should already be completed, so now you only have to fill in the footage loaded, film type, emulsion number, magazine number, and so on. Tape the camera report to the magazine so that it is ready for use when the magazine is removed from its case and placed on the camera. When the magazine is then removed from its case for use, the camera report is already attached, and you do not have to search to find a report. The report should be removed from the magazine and placed on the back of the slate or clipboard for use during filming. Before handing a new magazine to the 1st AC, be sure to write in the proper roll number on the identification label. When you have finished using a particular magazine and roll of film, the camera report should be reattached to it, and the magazine placed back in the case. When you or the Loader takes the magazine to the darkroom to unload and reload, the report is there so you can complete the unloading process without having to locate the report for that roll of film.

If the magazine is loaded with a short end, the footage amount on the identification label should be circled in a contrasting color so that it stands out. In addition, you should make an additional, smaller identification label with only the footage marked on it, which is placed alongside the larger identification label. This smaller label is generally about 1 or 1½ in. long. When the magazine is loaded onto the camera, place this smaller piece of tape near the footage counter of the camera. Each time you or the 1st AC looks at the footage counter to obtain the dial readings, you will be reminded that there is a short end in the magazine. The short end identification label and smaller reminder label are shown in Figure 4.25.

When using short ends for filming, be aware that the labels on the cans may not always be completely accurate. This is often true for short ends that are purchased from an outside supplier, but may also be the case with short ends that you or somebody else has created during the course of production. You may be using short ends that the production company had left from a previous production. If you are careful when loading and unloading, and if you keep accurate records, the footage amounts for short ends that you create should be fairly accurate. However, when using short ends from another source, you may load a magazine with what you think is a 370 ft short end only to

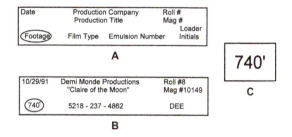

Figure 4.25   **A**, Information to be included on a short end ID label. **B**, Completed short end ID label. **C**, Example of the small short end reminder label.

discover that the film rolled out after 325 ft. Whenever this happens you should keep a record listing the amounts indicated on the can labels versus the actual amount that ran through the camera. In some cases the production company may be able to obtain additional film stock at no charge to make up for this discrepancy. I recommend keeping a record of short ends using the Short End Inventory Form that I have created, which can be found in Appendix C (Figure C.15).

After the magazines have been loaded, you should place them in their case and attach another identification tape to the lid of the case for each magazine inside. This is just a small piece of tape with the footage amount written on it. Many assistants may also place a small identification tape on the sides and/or front of the case. If you are using the color-coding system, use the same color tape used on the magazine identification label. Using the color-coding system saves time because you do not have to pick up the magazine or open the case to know what type of film is loaded. An illustration of a properly labeled magazine case is shown in Figure 4.26.

During the day's shooting, there will be many times when you will be required to unload and load magazines. When is the right time to go to the darkroom and reload any used magazines? It depends on the individual circumstances of the particular production that you are working on. If there is a 2nd AC and a Loader on the production this is not an issue. The Loader is most often not involved in any on-set activities so there will always be enough time for him/her to load and unload magazines. With a Loader on your shoot you should never have to wait for a magazine to be unloaded and reloaded with film.

If there is no Loader and the 2nd AC is also responsible for the loading/unloading of film, they must wait until there is an opportunity for them to leave the set without affecting the overall operation of the camera department. In most cases, when there is a new lighting

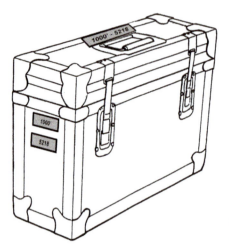

Figure 4.26 Magazine case showing identification tape on top and side.

setup being done, the 2nd AC will usually have enough time to complete the reloading process. As the 2nd AC you must always check with the 1st AC to see if it is acceptable to leave the set and do this job. The 1st AC usually has a lot on his or her mind and may not realize that you have two or three magazines that need to be reloaded. Let the 1st AC know the situation, and if it is convenient, you will be allowed to reload. If you are shooting a lot of film, you may have to leave the set during shooting; just be sure to work it out with the 1st AC so your on-set duties can be covered for the brief time you will be away from the set. You should never wait until all of the magazines have been shot before reloading. This could result in the production having to stop shooting until you have time to load more film. If you keep ahead of this throughout the day, the filmmaking process will go much more smoothly, and there should be no delays because a magazine is not ready. Always try to find out ahead of time from the DP what film stock you will be using the next day and load the magazines before you go home for the night.

During the loading process, mistakes can happen, and there may be an instance when you accidentally expose a fresh roll of film to the light, or worse, expose an exposed roll. In a rush you may open the magazine or the film can in the light, or possibly the lid of the magazine was not locked properly and unexpectedly opened in the light. You should immediately place this exposed roll of film in a black bag and put it back into the film can. Wrap the can with 1-in. white camera tape and place a warning label on the can that reads, "FILM EXPOSED TO LIGHT—DO NOT USE." This warning should be written on the top of the can and also along the edge on the sealing

tape. Place this can in a safe place away from all fresh raw stock, short ends, and exposed film that has been shot. You do not want to risk loading this film by accident and trying to shoot with it.

Finally, if film is accidentally exposed, do not try to hide it. Notify the 1st AC immediately so that it can be brought to the attention of the DP and then to the Production Manager. By telling the appropriate people about this as soon as possible, you will show that you are a professional, and they should understand that it was probably only an accident and you did not do it intentionally. By trying to hide it you will only cause problems for yourself, including losing your job and possibly not getting future jobs.

Fortunately, in the course of my time working as a 2nd AC I never flashed a roll of film that had already been shot, but I do remember the first time that I accidentally flashed a fresh, unexposed roll of film. I was in the darkroom at a rental house, and the DP knocked on the door to ask me a question. I became distracted and accidentally opened the feed side of the coaxial magazine that I had just finished loading. I immediately informed the DP, and fortunately he was extremely understanding about it. He actually laughed about it. We got another roll of film, and the good thing was that I didn't lose the job and continued to work with the DP for many productions following that incident.

Unloading Magazines

As with loading magazines, unloading magazines also falls to the Loader if there is one on the production. Otherwise it will be the 2nd AC that handles the unloading of all film from the magazines. Before unloading or downloading magazines, check that you have everything needed to can out the film. You should have empty cans, black bags, black and white camera tape, and so on. Always remove the exposed film and place it in a black bag and can before removing any short end or waste. When unloading a roll of film that is on a plastic core, place the thumb of one hand on the inside edge of the core, and, using your other hand on the outside edge of the roll, gently lift the roll of film with the core off the take-up spindle. As the roll starts to come up and off the spindle, slide your hand under the roll to keep the film from spooling off. When using a collapsible core, release the lock on the core, place your thumbs inside the core, and gently pull the roll of film up so that your thumbs are inside the center of the roll to prevent the film from coming out from the center. Keep your fingers tight against the outer edge to prevent the film from spooling off the end of the roll. Once off the core you should gently place the roll in the black bag and into the film can. It is usually not necessary to place a plastic

core into the center of the roll unless the lab requests it. If you are not sure check with the lab to see how they would like you to deal with it. Most labs that I worked with as a Second Assistant didn't require a core in the center. When placing an exposed roll in the black bag you should never tape the end of the film to the roll. Seal the can with 1-in. black cloth camera tape to indicate it is an exposed roll of film. The standard industry procedure for wrapping a can of exposed film is to use 1-in. black cloth camera tape. Some assistants use special red tape that is imprinted with the words "EXPOSED FILM—OPEN IN DARKROOM ONLY." A roll of this preprinted tape actually costs more and is smaller in size than a roll of 1-in. black cloth camera tape so I always use the black camera tape. After you have sealed the can, place the identification label from the magazine on the film can along with the top copy of the camera report. If the exposed film can contains less than the total amount of film loaded into the magazine you should cross out the amount indicated on the label and write in the amount that was exposed. This will avoid any confusion when the film gets to the lab for processing.

Be sure that the camera report is completely filled out with all the proper takes circled; that the footage amounts are totaled for Good, No Good, Waste, Short End, and Total; and that the lab instructions are written on it. You should always have the Script Supervisor double check the report and initial it so that you are sure that the correct takes are circled. When the can of exposed film is ready, keep it in a safe place away from any raw stock so that it does not get reloaded by mistake. See the section Preparing Exposed Film for Delivery to the Lab later in this chapter for a more detailed discussion of paperwork and preparing exposed film for delivery to the lab. If there is any film left in the feed side of the magazine, remove it now. If it is a short end, it must be unloaded in the dark. You will know if it is a short end or waste based on the totals on the camera report. Use the amounts discussed earlier in this chapter to determine if it is a short end or waste. If it is a short end, place it in a black bag and in a film can, and wrap it with tape. A general rule is to wrap all short end cans of unexposed film in 1-in. white camera tape. However, as I have mentioned before, if you have been using a color-coding system, wrap the film can in the appropriate color tape. Place a label on the can containing the short end so that you know how much and what type of film is in the can. Using the appropriate color tape, place an identification label on the can with the following information: date, footage, film type, emulsion number, and the words "SHORT END." Put your initials on this label so that if there are any questions about the roll the production company should know who to ask. The label for a short end roll of film is shown in Figure 4.27. See Appendix C for a custom short end label that you may use for labeling short end film cans (Figure C.26). This custom label

may be downloaded from the companion web site of this book for your personal use. Whenever placing short ends in a film can it is very important that all old tape and labels be removed from the can so that there is no question as to the type of film and size of the roll inside the can. In addition to placing a label on the lid of the sealed can, you should write the footage amount of the size of the short end on the tape sealing the edge of the can. Examples of properly labeled cans containing a short end are shown in Figures 4.28 and 4.29.

Date	**SHORT END**		
Footage	Film Type	Emulsion Number	Loader Initials

A

10/29/03	**SHORT END**	
740'	5218 - 237 - 4862	DEE

B

Figure 4.27 **A**, Information to be included on a short end label. **B**, Completed label for a short end roll of film.

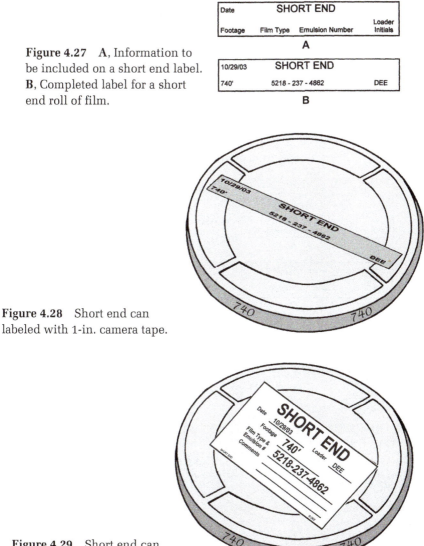

Figure 4.28 Short end can labeled with 1-in. camera tape.

Figure 4.29 Short end can labeled with custom label.

There may be times when you have to can up a roll of raw stock that was loaded but not used. It may be the end of production and filming is completed. When this happens, place the film in a black bag and into a film can. If possible, use the original film can. Seal the can with the appropriate color tape, and place an identification label on the can. This label should contain the following information: date, footage, film type, emulsion number, and the word "RECAN." The initials of the assistant who unloaded the film should also be placed on this label. Write the footage on the piece of sealing tape on the edge of the can. The label for a recan roll of film is shown in Figure 4.30. See Appendix C for a custom recan label that you may use for labeling recan film cans (Figure C.27). This label may be downloaded from the companion web site of this book for your personal use. Examples of properly labeled cans containing a recan roll are shown in Figures 4.31 and 4.32.

As when loading a magazine, accidents can also happen when unloading. If you accidentally expose to light a roll that has been shot, you should tell the 1st AC and DP immediately. This situation is much more serious than exposing a fresh roll of film. By exposing a roll that has already been shot, you are now requiring the production company

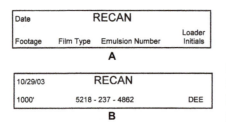

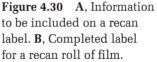

Figure 4.30   A, Information to be included on a recan label. **B**, Completed label for a recan roll of film.

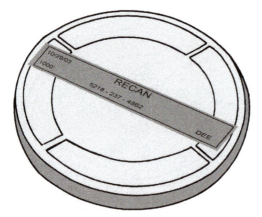

Figure 4.31   Recan roll of film labeled with 1-in. camera tape.

Figure 4.32   Recan roll of film labeled with custom label.

to reshoot everything that was on that particular roll. Hopefully the footage on the roll can be easily reshot that day or on another day. This will most likely cost the production company a lot of unexpected money and may result in you losing your job, even if it was only an accident. Don't try to hide it because it will be found out eventually when they are looking for the footage during postproduction. This will seriously damage your reputation and most definitely result in you losing the job and most likely not being hired for future jobs.

The important thing to remember when loading and especially when unloading film is not to be rushed and to take your time. Rushing can only cause costly mistakes, not only to the production company, but also to you if you lose the job. Don't let anybody rush you during the loading or unloading of any film magazine.

Using a Changing Bag or Changing Tent

If a darkroom is not available, you should have a changing bag or changing tent available for loading and unloading magazines. As a professional 2nd AC you must have your own changing bag or changing tent. It should be a standard part of your kit or ditty bag. If you don't have one of your own, they are available for rental at most camera rental houses, but I strongly urge you to invest in one. If necessary, ask the production company to rent one along with the camera equipment. An assistant will often rent a changing bag or tent just to have an extra in case of emergencies. The changing bag is actually two bags, one within another. They are sewn together along the edges and along the sides of the two sleeves, which have elastic cuffs. At the top

of each bag is a zipper so that you have access to the inside of the bag. With the zippers closed and your arms in the sleeves, you have a completely lightproof compartment for loading and unloading magazines. The changing tent is an item that has become available in recent years and is much easier to use than a changing bag. I wish that the changing tent was available when I first started out as an assistant because it is a great item to have in your ditty bag or kit. It is similar in size and shape to a changing bag, but instead of lying flat, it forms a lightproof tent in which you load and unload magazines. Creating a tent over the working surface makes it so much easier for the assistant to load and unload film in comfort. You don't have the bag resting on top of your arms, on top of the film, or on top of the magazines while trying to load or unload film. This helps to eliminate the possibility of the tent becoming caught in the magazine when closing and attaching the lid. Most assistants today have a changing tent instead of a changing bag. Figure 4.33 shows a changing bag and a changing tent.

It is important to remember when using a changing bag or tent to not panic if something goes wrong. The area inside the tent or bag is very small and confined, and you should take your time when

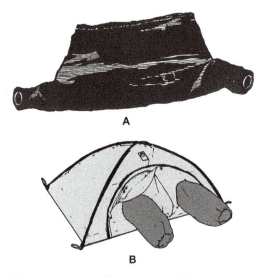

A

B

Figure 4.33 **A**, Changing bag. (Reprinted from the *Arriflex 16SR Book* by Jon Fauer with permission of the author and ARRI Inc.) **B**, Changing tent. (Reprinted from the *Arriflex 35 Book* by Jon Fauer with permission of the author and ARRI Inc.)

working in the tent/bag. One of the most common problems encountered when unloading film is that the core will come out of the center and the film will start to spool off the roll from the center. When working in a small changing bag with a 35 mm film magazine, this can be especially frustrating because of the lack of space to work in the bag. If this happens with the exposed roll of film, do not try to force the core back into the center of the roll. Carefully place the film back into the center of the roll without the core, and continue the unloading process normally. Most labs that I have worked with have told me that it is not necessary for a core to be placed in the center of the roll to develop and process the film. As with an exposed roll of film, if the core comes out of a roll of unexposed raw stock or a short end, do not try to force the core back into the center of the roll. Place this roll into a black bag and can, and start over with a new roll of film. If something does go wrong while you are working in a changing bag or tent, remember, never open the bag/tent or remove your arms until all film, whether exposed or unexposed, is in a black bag and in a film can.

Before using the bag or tent, always turn it inside out and shake it to remove any loose film chips or material that may have become stuck in the bag from previous use. To check the bag for light leaks, place it over your head; when your eyes have adjusted to the darkness, see if any light is leaking in. It is best to do this outside in bright sunlight or inside in a well-lighted room so that you can better see any light leaking in. This may sound pretty silly and you will look foolish doing this, so I recommend doing it when nobody else is around. If any holes are found, they may be covered with black camera tape or gaffer tape if they are not too large. When loading a magazine, place it in the inner bag with the can of unexposed raw stock. If necessary, be sure to place an empty core on the take-up side of the magazine before placing it in the bag or tent. Close both zippers of the bag or tent and then insert your arms into the elastic sleeves so that the elastic is past your elbows. When the magazine lid is removed, some assistants place it under the magazine to conserve space in the bag. Load the film in the usual manner and then place the lid back on the magazine, being careful not to catch the changing bag or tent between the magazine and the lid. Be sure that the lid is securely locked on the magazine before removing your arms from the bag and opening the zippers. Place the proper label on the magazine and tape the lid around the edges. Place the film black bag back in the can, replace the lid on the can, and put the can aside so that it is ready when it is time to unload the magazine.

The unloading process is the reverse of the loading process, as described earlier. Be sure that the bag is clean and free from dirt, dust, and film chips. Place the magazine in the inner bag along with

the appropriate number of cans and bags to can out any exposed film, short ends or recans. Again, remember to not remove your arms or open the bag until all film is placed in black bags and film cans.

When you are finished using the changing bag or changing tent, always shake it out to remove any film chips or other foreign matter. Follow these instructions for folding the changing bag:

1. Lay bag flat and close both zippers.
2. Fold arms in toward center of bag.
3. Fold bag one-third up from the bottom.
4. Fold bag one-third down from the top.
5. Fold bag once more from either top or bottom.
6. Fold bag one-third from the right to the left.
7. Fold bag once more from the left.

Keep the bag in a secure place so that it remains clean and cannot become ripped or torn.

The changing tent is folded in a similar manner. Follow these instructions for folding the changing tent.

1. Remove support rods, lay tent flat, and close both zippers.
2. Fold arms in toward center of bag.
3. Fold bag in half from the bottom.
4. Fold support rods and lay them on the tent.
5. Carefully roll tent up tightly and place it in its carry bag so that it remains clean and cannot become ripped or torn.

Whenever using a changing bag or changing tent while working as a 2nd AC or Loader, I recommend never wearing any type of clothing, such as loose sweaters, that have fibers or threads that could get into the magazines. These small fibers or threads could scratch the film and create additional shooting time if scenes need to be reshot. The process of placing your arms in the bag or tent could cause fibers or threads to become loose and fall into the magazine. In addition, if you wear a watch that has an illuminated dial, it should be removed before going into the darkroom or placing your hands in the changing bag or changing tent. The light from the dial could cause a slight fogging on the edges of the film depending on the exposure index of the film. It is always better to take that extra step and be safe.

Marking Actors and Camera Positions

While on set, one of the most important jobs of the 2nd AC is to place the marks for the actors. Marks are usually small strips of tape or some other object placed on the floor/ground as an indication of where the

actor is supposed to stand or stop during the shot. Marks are typically placed during the blocking rehearsal for the scene. Any time an actor stops and does something or speaks a line, a mark must be placed for him or her. These marks are sometimes referred to as action points. For example, if an actor walks in the door and stops, then walks over to a table and stops, and then goes to the window for the remainder of the scene, there will be one mark at the door, one at the table, and a final mark at the window. Actors use these marks so that they know where to stand, the 1st AC uses them for focus measurements, and the DP uses them for lighting purposes. The marks are usually made with the ½-in. or 1-in. colored paper tape that you ordered with the expendables order. Some assistants may disagree with me on this but I recommend using only paper tape for actors' marks when working inside. The adhesive on the paper tape is not as strong as the adhesive on the cloth camera tape, so there is less chance of damage when removing the paper tape from the floor or carpet of a private home or business or other interior location.

When placing marks, you should always make a small tab on the end of the tape. This is sometimes referred to as tabbing your tape. By making a small tab on the end of the piece of tape, it is easier to remove later on. If the floor or ground is seen in the shot, place marks for the rehearsal and then remove them or make them very small for the actual shot. You may be able to use a color of tape that is close to the color of the floor surface. If the mark is small enough, the camera may not pick it up in the shot, but the actor should still be able to see it if necessary. If you are working outside or on a surface where you cannot place tape marks, use anything that is handy, such as leaves, sticks, twigs, rocks, etc. Ideally, when working outside, and if the ground is seen in the shot, you would use something that would blend in with the surroundings and not look like an actor's mark. When working on pavement or concrete, many assistants use chalk to make the marks for the actor. Just remember to remove any marks before shooting so that they are not visible on film. I once worked on a television series, and in one episode a scene required two characters to meet up with each other on the street. The 2nd AC placed a large chalk mark on the pavement for each actor. Unfortunately, when it came time to film the shot, nobody said anything about the marks; they were not removed before shooting and were clearly visible in the finished show.

If more than one actor is in the scene, each actor's marks should be a different color if possible. This makes it easier and less confusing for each actor. When ordering the expendables you should order different colors of paper tape for this purpose. The most common type of mark used is the T-mark, shaped like the letter "T" and measuring

3- to 5-in. wide by 3- to 5-in. high. A T-mark is placed with the horizontal portion of the T just in front of the actor's toes and the vertical portion extending between the actor's feet (see Figure 4.34). Often when the actor has to stop at a very precise spot, a sandbag will be placed on the ground at the spot so that when the actor touches the sandbag he or she knows that they are in the correct place. In Britain a mark may also be placed along the side of the actor's foot and this is commonly referred to as a "sidey."

Figure 4.34   Example of a T-mark.

Another type of mark is the toe mark. These are usually 3- or 4-in. long strips of tape placed at the end of each actor's foot (see Figure 4.35).

Figure 4.35   Example of toe marks.

A variation of the toe mark is the V-mark. It consists of two strips of tape placed at each actor's foot in the shape of the letter V (see Figure 4.36).

Figure 4.36   Example of a V-mark.

One final and more precise form of mark is a box created with tape that is placed completely around the actor's feet (see Figure 4.37).

Figure 4.37   Example of a box mark.

Although it is rare, there may be a situation when two different actors must stop on the same mark. Rather than use one color of tape and expect one of the actors to remember, it is common to use the two marks, using the specific colors designated for each actor, and place them very close together, slightly overlapping them so each actor can see their color. An example of this is shown in Figure 4.38.

As stated previously, it is common to purchase different colors of tape for the actor's marks so that each actor will have a different color mark. In the rare case that you cannot do this, how do you distinguish actors' marks when using the same color tape for each actor? It's actually quite simple. Using a permanent marker, you can add stripes or some other pattern to each separate mark in order to distinguish one actor's mark from another. Be sure to use the same pattern

Figure 4.38   Example of the same mark for two actors.

for a specific actor so that there is no confusion. An example of this is shown in Figure 4.39.

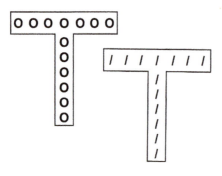

Figure 4.39   Marks for two actors with the same color tape.

An actor's mark and the actor's ability to "hit" the mark are critical to the 1st AC and Camera Operator being able to do their jobs properly. When an actor misses his or her mark it affects the composition and the focus of the shot. Some actors are great at hitting their marks, others not so much. The First Assistant will often ask for a few other marks to be placed on the floor as reference points in case the actor does miss the mark. Be prepared to work with your 1st AC and place these additional marks if asked.

Rather than keep five or six large rolls of tape with them, which can get bulky if attached to your belt, some assistants make up a marking board which they keep nearby during the blocking rehearsal. Some even attach it to the back of the slate so that it is always handy. During preproduction, or downtime on set, make a bunch of marks in each color and attach them to this marking board. Then when you need to mark an actor you already have some marks pre-made and can quickly remove a mark from the board and place in on the floor for the

actor. As your marking board gets low on marks, make up some new ones or have the PA or Trainee do it so that you never run out.

When working outside, marking actors can be difficult when it comes to using tape. When working outside there are a number of different types of marks that you may use. You could purchase small shot bag style T-marks or similar marks which work great when outside and you cannot use tape. There are also shot bag style marks called "sausage" marks which are simply a small shot bag about 1 in. wide and 5- or 6-in. long. The shot bag T-marks and "sausage" marks come in a variety of colors and some assistants have these in their ditty bags or toolkits. Some assistants purchase rubber matting or even t-shaped metal brackets from home improvement stores. They will cut small T-marks from the rubber mat and then cover these or the metal brackets with various colors of tape to use outside. I have also heard of an assistant who uses colored golf tees as marks when working outside on grass. The tees are easy for the actor to see but barely, if at all, visible to the camera. Use whatever is best and easiest for you.

In addition to marking actors, the 2nd AC often works with the DP and Director while they are discussing the upcoming shots. Often the DP and Director will walk around the set, with the Director's viewfinder, trying to determine camera placement and lens choice for upcoming shots. During this process the 2nd AC will place tape marks on the floor and mark them to indicate the direction that the camera should be pointing and the focal length of the lens. When it comes time to place the camera for the shot, the DP and Director have a general reference point.

Slates

The slate is used to identify the pertinent information for each scene shot during the production and should be a standard item in the assistant's ditty bag. The information on the slate includes the basics, such as production title, Director's name and Cinematographer's name, and it also includes specifics about the particular shot, such as scene number, take number, and roll number. The slate may also be marked to indicate which camera is photographing the shot, if more than one camera is being used on the production. There are two basic types of slates: sync and insert. The sync slate is used any time you are recording sound. The top part of the slate contains two pieces of wood that are usually painted with diagonal black and white lines. The two pieces are hinged together, with the bottom portion attached to the slate. These pieces of wood, along with the slate, are sometimes referred to as the clapper. Some assistants use a sync slate that has the

clapper or wooden part that is painted with colored stripes that correspond to the colors of a typical color chart. The type of slate and clapper is up to the individual Camera Assistant. An example of a sync slate is shown in Figure 4.40.

Figure 4.40   Sync slate.

Another type of sync slate is the time code or electronic slate. These types of slates have become more common because everything that we film these days is being edited on computers. When using the time code slate there is a very precise electronic clock installed in the sound recorder and often in the camera, although it is not necessary in the camera. These clocks produce a signal that is recorded on the sound track and also along the edge of the film. The slate contains a digital readout display showing hours, minutes, seconds, and frames. When the sticks of the slate are clapped together, the display freezes momentarily and the image is recorded on film. This precise time information is recorded on the soundtrack, and in the editing process it is a simple matter of matching up the sound with the picture that has the same time code information. These time code slates were first used quite extensively on music videos over the years, but they have become more and more prevalent on features, television shows, and commercials as well (see Figure 4.41).

The insert slate is usually a much smaller version of the sync slate, and it usually does not contain the wooden clappers. The typical insert slate is approximately 4 in.×6 in. in size. It is often used when shooting MOS shots or, as the name implies, when shooting inserts. The sync slate may be used for inserts or MOS shots without clapping the sticks together. There are a few different styles of insert slate, and one example is shown in Figure 4.42.

Figure 4.41 Timecode slate.
(Courtesy of Denecke Inc.)

DATE	UNIT	CAMERA
SCENE	TAKE	ROLL
CAMERAMAN		PROD. NO.

Figure 4.42 Insert slate.

The information written on the sync and insert slate is usually as follows: production title, Director, Cameraman (DP), roll number, scene number, take number, int/ext, day/nite, and the date. Often when using more than one camera, a separate slate is designated for each camera. In this case, the slate would also have the camera letter written on it so that the Editor can easily distinguish which camera photographed the particular shot. When using the insert slate, the unit number and the production number may also be written on the slate.

The production title is the working title of the film during shooting. The Director is the name of the person who is directing the film. It is standard to write the first initial and last name of the Director and the Cinematographer in the appropriate spaces on the slate. The roll number refers to the camera roll number that is being shot at the time. The scene number, which corresponds to the scene in the script that is being filmed, should be obtained from the Script Supervisor. "INT" means that you are filming on an interior set, and "EXT" refers to an

exterior set. "DAY/NITE" refers to the time of day that the scene takes place. The date is the month, day, and year that you are filming. Much of this basic information may be placed on the slate using stick-on vinyl lettering or a label made with a laminated label maker that can be purchased from any office supply store. If you don't have the stick-on letters or label maker, you may simply write this information on a piece of 1-in. wide white camera tape and place it on the slate. The information that is continually changing, such as the roll, scene, and take numbers, would usually be written on the slate by using some type of erasable marker. The most commonly used slates are made of a material that allows you to use a dry-erase marker to record the information. Only use a dry-erase marker to write on the dry-erase type of slates. Never use any type of permanent marker because you will not be able to remove the writing once it has dried.

Before each shot, check with the Script Supervisor for the scene number and take number. Always write the numbers clearly on the slate to make it easier for the Editor to read. Often when only shooting a portion of a scene, the scene numbers are written with a letter added, such as 15A or 37B, etc. When doing this, the number is in reference to the scene number and the letter indicates that it is a portion of the scene or a new camera angle, etc. It is standard to start with the letter "A" and continue through the alphabet as you shoot different portions of the scene. The Script Supervisor will tell you when to add a letter, which letters to use, and when to change scene numbers or letters.

In some cases the 2nd AC must call out the scene and take number when slating. Instead of calling out the letter, they will usually use a specific word that begins with that letter. Each assistant has their own system and words that they may use when slating and for the most part that is left entirely up to the assistant. If you want a standardized listing I recommend using the standard words that have been adopted by the military, as shown in Table 4.4.

If you wish to use your own words please keep in mind some basic rules for protocol and etiquette. Don't use words that could be offensive to some. Keep them short and simple, one or two syllables at most. Some letters that are not usually used for slating are I, O, Q, S, Y and Z, which can resemble numbers when written hurriedly. The letter I can resemble the number 1, O and Q can resemble the number 0, S can resemble the number 5, Y can resemble the number 4, and Z can resemble the number 2. Check with the Script Supervisor to find out which letters not to use when slating scenes. I have included all letters in the above table just in case you need to use them when slating.

In Britain the system of slating is bit different. Instead of using scene and take numbers as is done in the United States, they use slates and take numbers. The first shot on the first day of shooting

Table 4.4   Military Alphabet that may be Used When Slating

Letter	Common Word
A	Alpha
B	Bravo
C	Charlie
D	Delta
E	Echo
F	Foxtrot
G	Golf
H	Hotel
I	India
J	Juliet
K	Kilo
L	Lima
M	Mike
N	November
O	Oscar
P	Papa
Q	Quebec
R	Romeo
S	Sierra
T	Tango
U	Uniform
V	Victor
W	Whiskey
X	X-ray
Y	Yankee
Z	Zulu

would be indicated as Slate 1, Take 1. The next is Slate 2, then Slate 3, and so on. The scene often has a separate place on the slate and many assistants will leave that space blank because a record of the scene number is kept by the Script Supervisor. I have been told that the

process of slating using slate instead of scene has become less prevalent in recent years and on many types of productions in Britain they use scene numbers as is done in the United States.

When using more than one camera, the roll number would be a combination of the camera letter and the number of the roll of film, for example roll number A-1, A-2, A-3, B-1, B-2, and so on. If only one camera is used, the assistant may still use the A prefix for all roll numbers to avoid any confusion by the Editors. If more than one camera is used, it is recommended that you have a separate slate for each camera, and mark the lettering on each slate in a different color to distinguish one slate and camera from the other. For example, when using two cameras, the A camera slate may be labeled in red letters and the B camera slate in blue letters.

Slating Procedures

During shooting, the 2nd AC is responsible for slating each shot, whether it is sound (sync) or silent (MOS). Remember to obtain the correct scene and take number from the Script Supervisor. The Sound Mixer also needs to know the scene and take number as well. At the start of production you should always work it out with the Sound Mixer how shots are going to be slated. Often the mixer will have a small microphone at his/her cart and will pre-slate the shot. What this means is that once they get the upcoming scene and take number from the Script Supervisor, they will turn on the mixer and record the scene and take number onto the recording device. Then when it is time to roll camera and sound, the 2nd AC only needs to call out, "Marker," before clapping the sticks together. This results in a cost saving for the Producer because you are not wasting film running through the camera while you call out the scene and take number. When it is time to roll the shot, the recorder is ready to go. If the Sound Mixer cannot pre-slate or chooses not to pre-slate, you can slate the scene without wasting film. During the process of getting ready to roll for the shot, after the Assistant Director calls, "Roll sound," and the Sound Mixer calls, "Speed," the 2nd AC will call out the scene and take numbers before rolling camera. Once the scene and take number have been recorded, the camera is then started by either the 1st AC or Camera Operator, and the 2nd AC will then clap the slate. As long as the scene and take number are recorded on the sound recorder and the camera photographs the slate, it doesn't matter what procedure you use. It is very important that you hold the slate still when slating and then hold it for a half second before exiting the frame. The slate must be kept still so that the Editor can read it properly.

Based on my experience on the many productions that I have worked on, the standard procedure for rolling the shot and slating a sound take is as follows, assuming that the Sound Mixer has pre-slated the shot.

1. The First Assistant Director (1st AD) calls for quiet on the set.
2. 1st AD calls for sound to roll.
3. The sound recorder is turned on and the Sound Mixer calls out, "Speed."
4. Upon hearing the Sound Mixer, the Camera Operator or 1st AC turns on the camera.
5. When the camera reaches the proper speed, the Operator or assistant calls out, "Rolling," or some other command to indicate that the camera is running.
6. The 2nd AC, who has been waiting patiently in front of the camera, usually calls out, "Marker," and claps the sticks of the slate together, holding them still for a half second before exiting the frame.

While waiting for the camera to be turned on and to reach speed, the 2nd AC should be holding the slate in the frame with the clapper sticks held open at approximately a 45-degree angle to each other. Do not hold the clapper sticks closed, open and then clap them when slating. This will only confuse the Editor. The sticks should always be held open before slating a sync sound shot.

With the time code slate, holding the sticks open allows the time code to run freely. When the sticks are clapped together, the time code freezes on the display for a brief moment. It is important to hold the slate still for a half to one second after slating so that the numbers on the display can be read clearly. After the time code numbers appear, the date appears before the slate goes blank. This additional information on the slate also helps to keep the shots better organized in postproduction.

It is quite common for the Sound Mixer to wait about five seconds after rolling with time code before calling out, "Speed." This is called pre-rolling and is important for syncing the dailies in postproduction because it often takes around five seconds for the time code equipment, both sound recorder and time code cameras, to lock when they are rolling. Without allowing the pre-roll, the Editor may be unable to sync the footage because the camera and sound device were not running in sync.

While it is the job of the Camera Operator to frame the slate properly, the 2nd AC must know exactly where to place it so that it fills the frame and the Camera Operator does not have to move the camera to photograph the slate. Position the slate in such a way that it

is not too big or too small in the frame. A general rule for positioning the slate in front of the camera so that it can clearly be seen is as follows: For 35 mm film, hold the slate 1 ft from the camera for every 10 mm in focal length. For example, with a 50 mm lens the slate should be held 5 ft away; for 25 mm, 2½ ft; for 100 mm, 10 ft; and so on. For 16 mm film, hold the slate 2 ft from the camera for every 10 mm in focal length. For example, with a 50 mm lens the slate should be held 10 ft away. It is not necessary to measure this distance, only to approximate it so the slate fills up the frame. The slate should also be well lit so that the information on it can be read clearly. When filming in a dark set, be sure to have a good, powerful flashlight to illuminate the slate, or you may even have an electrician set up a small light that is turned on for the slate and then turned off before the action of the scene begins. In order to avoid any glare from lights hitting the slate you should tilt it slightly forward and/or to the side so that it can be seen and photographed clearly. The 1st AC should adjust the focus to the slate so that it is easy to read and not blurry and out of focus, and may also briefly open the f-stop if necessary to photograph the slate properly. When the slate has been photographed, the focus and f-stop will be shifted back to the correct position for the scene. It is quite common for the Operator and 1st AC to call out, "Set" after slating to indicate that they are ready for the Director to call, "Action." Again I must stress the importance of holding the slate still when clapping the sticks and for a half to one second after slating so that it can be read clearly. One thing that upsets me greatly when watching dailies (other than out of focus shots) is slates that are not clear and easy to read. Many assistants who are new to slating will move the slate in a downward motion when clapping the sticks. This causes a blurred image, making it difficult for the Editor to read the slate.

It is also important that you do not cross the frame after slating whenever possible. If you slate from the right, then exit to the right; if you slate from the left, then exit to the left. This is a courtesy to the actors as well as the Camera Operator. Sometimes it may not be possible to do this because of lights, C-stands, set walls, furnishings, or actors preparing to enter the shot. Be sure to watch where you go after a shot. A shot can be ruined because the 2nd AC does not watch where he or she moves after slating the shot and ends up standing in front of a light, causing a shadow on the actor, or moves in the way of the dolly. In any event, know your escape route after slating and be sure that others are aware as well. If there is simply no other place for you to go, then crouch down below the camera until the shot is complete. I have had to do this on more than one occasion. Just be sure it's not in front of the dolly when there is a dolly move planned or else everyone will be surprised.

It's usually fairly easy to get the slate in the frame when working with wide-angle lenses but with longer telephoto lenses it is more difficult. You don't want to waste time by having the Camera Operator or 1st AC try to tell you to raise or lower the slate or move it camera left or right. One of the easiest ways to almost guarantee the slate will be in frame on longer lenses is to hold it over the actor's mark and at the approximate height of the lens. The more practice you get with this the better you will become. The objective is for the 2nd AC to always put the slate in frame so that the Camera Operator doesn't have to reframe the shot after the slate has been clapped.

When slating a close-up shot of the actor, it is often necessary to hold the slate very close to the actor's face. When doing this it is important to not clap the sticks so loudly that you startle the actor and ruin his or her concentration. The sound microphones are very sensitive, and for a close-up shot they will be very close to the actor, so a light clap is sufficient. Sometimes when clapping the slate for a close-up shot the 2nd AC will call out, "Soft sticks" just before clapping the slate. Check with the Sound Mixer to see if this is necessary.

Often the slate will not be framed properly, or it may be missed completely by the Camera Operator, and the Camera Operator will call for second sticks or a second marker. Be prepared so that if this happens you can insert the slate quickly into the shot, and when the Camera Operator tells you that it is framed properly, call out, "Second sticks" or "Second marker," before clapping the sticks together. Whenever you do second sticks, be sure to note it in the Remarks column of the camera report and to notify the Script Supervisor. There are also situations in which it is not possible or practical to clap the slate at the beginning of the scene. When this happens, you do what is called a tail slate. For a sync shot, the tail slate is clapped the same way as a head slate, the only difference being that the slate is held upside down in the frame and is photographed at the end of the scene (see Figure 4.43). In some instances, for example when you are working with inexperienced actors, child actors who may be scared by the loud clap, or animals, it may be advisable to tail slate the shot so that you don't distract or upset the actor, who may be trying to get into character or remember his or her lines. If you know before the shot that you will be doing a tail slate, you should photograph the slate at the beginning with the clapper sticks closed just as a record of the scene information. This is commonly referred to as getting an ID and can usually be done before actually rolling for the shot. Hold the slate in front of the camera, focus on it, and roll for a few seconds to record the basic information. Be sure that all of the proper information for the shot is on the slate, such as the roll, scene, and take numbers. This will allow the Editor to see the information for the

Figure 4.43 A tail slate is always held upside down at the end of the shot.

shot at the beginning of the take. Tell the Sound Mixer whenever you are doing a tail slate. When the Director calls, "Cut," the sound and camera should continue to roll, at which point the 2nd AC calls out, "Tail slate," and inserts the slate into the frame, upside down, before clapping the sticks together. Always make note of a tail slate in the Remarks column of the camera report and notify the Script Supervisor. In Britain a tail slate is commonly referred to as an end board (EB). When slating at the end, the 2nd AC would call out, "Slate 14, Take 2, on the end." In addition, it is common practice in Britain to write E/B on the slate after the take number, for example SC 15, Tk 2 E/B.

If you use two cameras on a production and they will be rolling together, there are a couple of different ways that you may slate the scene, separate slates or a common slate. When doing separate slates, each camera is slated individually, using a separate slate for each camera. When sound and cameras are rolling, the cameras are slated in order. Each slate is held in front of its respective camera. The 2nd AC slates the A camera first, then the B camera, then the C camera, and so on. When doing separate slates, the 2nd AC calls out the camera letter before clapping the sticks. For example, when using two cameras labeled A and B, the 2nd AC calls, "A camera marker," before slating the A camera, and then, "B camera marker," before slating the B camera. With multiple cameras you may need the help of another crew person to do the slates. When doing a common slate, you should photograph an identification slate before the shot, showing the correct roll, scene, and take numbers for each camera. When sound and cameras are rolling, you would then use only one slate, held so that the back of the slate is facing both cameras. The 2nd AC calls out, "A and B cameras, common marker," before clapping the sticks together. Instead of using a slate held with its back to the cameras, many 2nd ACs have a large set of clapper sticks that are used when doing

common slates (see Figure 4.44). These larger sticks are easier to see, and tell the Editor that it is a common slate for more than one camera.

Figure 4.44   Large clapper sticks.

There are a number of ways that you may slate an MOS shot with a sync slate. Because there is no sound for an MOS shot, you want to be sure that the Editor knows that the sticks have not been and will not be clapped. The most obvious way to do this is to hold the slate with the sticks closed and your hand over them. Many assistants hold the sticks in an open position with their hand in between the two sticks to indicate that they have not been or cannot be clapped together. In any case, when slating an MOS shot, be sure to indicate it clearly on the slate and also on the camera report. When slating MOS shots, be sure to do it the same each time so that you don't confuse the Editor or Assistant Editor. If they ask you to slate an MOS shot a particular way, you should always honor their wishes. It is important to maintain peace and harmony among your fellow crew members.

Properly slating a shot is important, and many beginners don't realize the importance of doing it correctly or even doing it at all. During postproduction the Assistant Editor is responsible for syncing up the film dailies, and he or she must be able to read the slate so that it can be placed within the film in the proper place. If the information on the slates, including the scene and take information, cannot be read, the Assistant Editor's job becomes much more difficult and time consuming.

Changing Lenses, Filters, and Magazines

Please note that much of the following information will be repeated in this section in Chapter 5. Repetition is important in the day-to-day performance of your job and so that you fully understand many of the aspects of the job.

Whenever you are asked to place a new lens, filter, or any other accessory on the camera, it should be done as quickly as possible so that the DP or Camera Operator can line up the shot. But don't rush

the process because you don't want to drop one of the most expensive pieces of film equipment, thereby causing delays in production, not to mention the strong possibility of one or more of the Camera Assistants losing their job. You must develop a protocol for this procedure and make sure that each assistant knows precisely what their job is during the change of the item, and everything should go smoothly.

The standard procedure for changing lenses, filters, or accessories on the camera is as follows. As soon as the DP calls for a change in lens or filter, the First Assistant repeats the request so that the DP and the 2nd AC hear. This lets the DP know that the request was heard and that it was heard correctly, and it lets the 2nd AC know to retrieve the item from the equipment case/cart. The 2nd AC should repeat the request so that the 1st AC knows that it was heard correctly. While the 2nd AC is getting the new item the 1st AC removes the old item from the camera and prepares the camera to accept the new item, whether it is a lens, filter or other accessory. If changing lenses, the 2nd AC should remove the lens caps and leave them in the lens case, set the focus to infinity, f-stop/t-stop to its most wide open setting and, if a zoom, set the focal length to the most wide-angle setting as he/she brings the new lens to the camera. The 2nd AC should also check the front and rear lens elements for dirt, dust or smudges. Don't clean it yet though. I'll explain the procedure for cleaning lenses later on in Chapter 5, First Assistant Cameraman (1st AC). Once at the camera the 2nd AC will exchange the new lens for the old lens. When changing prime lenses I recommend placing the old lens in the 2nd AC's palm, with the front element face down. This allows them to get a secure grip on the lens without dropping it. This is the procedure that I was taught when I first started and it has worked perfectly for me throughout the years. You should develop a system for exchanging lenses that works best for you and stick with it. I am only making recommendations based on my professional experience. Remember, when exchanging items both assistants should give some type of indication that they have a firm grip on the item so that the other person knows that it is all right to release it. I usually say, "Got it," when exchanging items with my assistant and this is what I recommend for you. This lets him or her know that I have a firm grip on it and they can let go. The 2nd AC should also say, "Got it," when they have a firm grip on the piece of equipment. No matter how big or small the equipment is, when exchanging items always indicate that you have a firm grip so that there is no chance of anything getting dropped. While the 1st AC places the new item on the camera, the 2nd AC places the old one back in the equipment case. If changing lenses, once the lens has been approved by the DP you can then remove it for cleaning if necessary. In most cases the DP does not want to wait for you to clean

the lens before looking through it. What if it turns out to not be the right focal length? You have now wasted valuable time cleaning a lens that won't be used for the shot. This is usually the standard protocol when changing lenses or filters but I always check with the DP at the beginning of a show as to the protocol he/she prefers when changing anything on the camera. I especially do this if it is a DP that I have not worked with in the past. If changing filters the same basic protocol is followed. While the First Assistant removes the old filter, the Second Assistant gets the new filter from the case, checks it for dirt or smudges, but doesn't clean it right away. Any filter change should be made quickly so that the DP and Operator can see it and approve it first. Once it is approved, then you can take a moment to clean it if necessary. When changing or adding any other accessories to the camera, the 1st AC makes the camera ready for the item, while the 2nd AC retrieves it from the proper equipment case.

When changing from a prime lens to a zoom lens or from a zoom lens to a prime lens, to save time you should bring both lens cases to the camera to make the change quicker and easier. When the change has been completed, you may then return both cases to the cart or storage area. Also, when changing lenses you may have to change the lens support rods and support brackets because of the physical size or weight of the lens. When bringing the lens from the case, the 2nd AC should remember to bring the appropriate lens support rods, support brackets and accessories when required.

When changing anything on the camera it is very important never to leave an equipment case open when you are away from it. If a case is in use you should lock at least one of the latches. This makes it easier to open when you have to go back into the case. Any case that is not in use should have both latches secured. There have been a few times when I have picked up a case that my assistant or the camera intern forgot to latch. Fortunately, in most cases I realized it in time before any of the contents spilled out. During filming, there are many different camera setups, and the equipment must be moved many times during the day. If a case is not latched and someone else picks it up to move it, there could be disastrous results. Lenses, filters or accessories could come tumbling out of the case and become damaged. If someone outside of the camera department did pick up an unlatched case and spill its contents, it would not be the fault of the person picking up the case but rather the fault of the camera crew member who failed to secure one of the latches. You never know when a Grip or Electrician may suddenly decide to place a C-stand or light exactly where your cases are. If you close and secure at least one of the latches of the cases, you can be confident that even if somebody else moves the case, the contents will be safe.

When changing magazines and before handing the new magazine to the 1st AC, you should write the new roll number on the identification label, remove the camera report from the magazine, and place the report on the back of the slate or on the clipboard. If the magazine contains a short end, remind the 1st AC of this and tell him or her to place the small reminder tape next to the footage counter. A good 2nd AC will never hand a new magazine to the 1st AC without first writing the new roll number on the identification label.

Using a Video Tap and Monitor

Today most productions use a video tap incorporated into the film camera so that the Director can view the shot on a monitor while it is being filmed. During the camera prep, all of the needed accessories and cables should have been obtained for the video system. During each shooting day, the camera is moved to many different locations and sets for the various shots. Whenever the camera is to be moved, the 1st AC will typically disconnect the video cable from the camera. If there is no Camera Trainee or PA, it is usually the responsibility of the 2nd AC to be sure that the monitor is moved along with the camera, set up, powered and connected for each shot. Just be sure that whenever the camera moves, the monitor moves along with it as quickly as possible and is connected to the camera for the Director and other production personnel to view the shot.

Preparing Exposed Film for Delivery to the Lab

At the end of each shooting day, it is customary to send all film that has been shot to the lab for processing. As I mentioned in the section on unloading magazines, all exposed cans of film should have the proper identification label on them, along with the top copy of the camera report. This assists the lab so that it knows which shots to print and what, if any, special instructions need to be followed during the developing process. Check with the Script Supervisor regarding the circled or printed takes. The best time to check with the Script Supervisor is at the time you place a new magazine on the camera. When you take the old magazine off the camera, give the camera report for that roll to the Script Supervisor, who will check to ensure that the correct takes are circled, and then return it to you. Total up the amounts and write the Good, No Good, Waste, Short End, and Total footage amounts on the camera report. You should also place an additional piece of tape on the can, with the developing instructions

to the lab printed on it. Some examples of specific developing instructions include: develop normal—prep for video transfer, develop normal—one-light print, push one stop, develop only–no work print. There are many other types of developing instructions that may be used (see Figures 4.45 and 4.46). Check with the DP before sending any film to the lab to be sure that you have included all the developing and processing instructions.

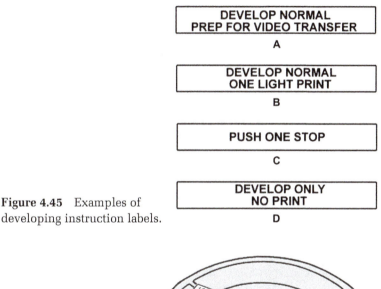

Figure 4.45 Examples of developing instruction labels.

Figure 4.46 Magazine identification label and developing instructions label on exposed film can.

In place of, or in addition to, the magazine identification and developing instructions piece of tape, some assistants may use a pre-printed label that is filled in with the appropriate information and placed on the exposed film can. This label may look like the one shown in Figure 4.47. See Appendix C for a custom film can label that

```
Laboratory          _____

Date        _____    Prod #      _____

Prod. Co.           _____

Prod. Title         _____


Exposed Footage     _____

Film Type           _____


Camera      _____    Mag #    _____    Roll #    _____


☐ Process Normal        ☐ One Light Print        ☐ Best Light Print

☐ Prep for Transfer     ☐ Time to Gray Scale     ☐ Timed Work Print

☐ Time to These Lights      —  _____    —  _____

☐ Other             _____
```

Figure 4.47   Example of a blank film can label.

you may use for labeling exposed cans of film (Figure C.25). This label may be downloaded from the companion web site of this book for your personal use. When sending the film to the lab, it is common for the 2nd AC to prepare a purchase order form that details the specific developing instructions for that day's filming. Some production companies use their own purchase order form, and some laboratories have their own form that they require you to use. An example of a standard laboratory purchase order can be seen in Figure 4.48. In addition to other forms, I have created a general Film Developing Purchase Order form that can be seen in Appendix C (Figure C.11) and is also available for downloading on the companion web site to this book.

The information on the purchase order (PO) should include complete contact information for the production company. This includes name, address, telephone number, and contact person. The title of the production and production number should be clearly indicated on the PO. The PO should list the total number of cans being sent to the lab, total footage, roll numbers and the film type, format (16 mm or 35 mm), and whether it is color or black-and-white film. The type of processing (normal, prep for video transfer, one-light work print, etc.) and any special instructions should be listed on the PO as well. Many assistants will prepare a separate PO for any special or unusual developing instructions such as pushing, pulling, skip bleach, or forced processing of a roll or rolls of film. One copy of the PO is sent to the lab with the film. Each film can must have a copy of the camera report for that

FotoKem
F I L M   A N D   V I D E O
FOTO-KEM INDUSTRIES, INC.

2801 W. ALAMEDA AVE., BURBANK, CA 91505
(818) 846-3101

Laboratory Purchase Order
FILM DAILIES ONLY

(LAB USE ONLY)
TOTAL FILM ROLLS
TOTAL SOUND REELS
NOTES:
RECEIVED BY
TIME RECEIVED

Date: Customer P.O. #   Customer Code:

Company: Open Acc.   COD   MOA

Address: City: State: Zip:

Phone Number: Contact For Negative Report:

IF THIS ORDER IS TO BE SHIPPED PLEASE FILL IN THE SHIPPING INFORMATION AT BOTTOM OF THE PAGE

TITLE: _____

PROCESSING	FILM WORKPRINT/FILM DAILY	VIDEO TRANSFER
☐ Color Size: ☐ 16 mm	NOTE: THIS SECTION IS FOR FILM PRINTING ONLY!	VIDEO DAILIES
☐ B + W ☐ 35 mm ☐ Super 16	INSTRUCTIONS	Please Contact Video Scheduling to arrange for video tape Dailies
☐ Process Normal Roll # _____		VIDEO PREP.
		☐ Normal Video Prep for Telecine
☐ Special Processing Roll # _____		☐ Special Video Prep for Edge No. Encoding
PICTURE ORIGINAL		☐ Film Transfer At FotoKem
VAULT RETURN		☐ Outside Transfer

Note: Unless circled takes are requested, all dailies print orders will be "print all." No circled takes available in 16mm.

NOTES:

Work Authorized By: _____   Order Written By: _____
* FOTOKEM'S TERMS CONTROL
ALL WORK IS ACCEPTED SUBJECT TO FOTOKEM'S TERMS, SEE SELECTED TERMS ON THE REVERSE SIDE.

SHIPPING & DELIVERY INSTRUCTIONS

Deliver to:

Address: City: State: Zip:

Phone Number: Attention:

VIA: ☐ COD   ☐ Prepaid

PLEASE FILL OUT THIS ORDER AS COMPLETELY AS POSSIBLE. IT WILL HELP US DO A BETTER JOB FOR YOU.

THERE IS A MINIMUM CHARGE OF $45.00 PER ITEM (UNLESS OTHERWISE INDICATED)

Figure 4.48   Example of a film laboratory purchase order. (Courtesy of FotoKem Industries, Inc.)

roll attached to the can. A copy of the PO should be given to the production office, and the camera department should always keep a copy.

Send the exposed film to the lab as soon as possible. Each lab usually has a specific cutoff time each day for when the film must be

delivered for it to be ready the following day. The 2nd AC or Loader should know the cutoff times for the lab being used. Until the exposed film is ready to be sent, keep it in a cool, dry place away from direct sunlight and away from any raw stock so that it does not get loaded by mistake. See the Storage and Care of Motion Picture Film section later in this chapter for information on the proper care and storage of film stock. When you are ready to send the film, it is common to stack the cans four or five high and tape them together. You should invert the top can so that you do not tape over the attached camera report. If the film is to be shipped, place it in a sturdy corrugated-cardboard shipping box, and fill any unused space with crumpled newspaper or other packing material to prevent the cans from moving around during shipping. If the film is to be shipped, label the box on all sides "EXPOSED FILM—KEEP FROM RADIATION" or "EXPOSED FILM—DO NOT X-RAY." See Appendix C for a custom X-Ray Warning Label that you may use for labeling shipping cartons of exposed cans of film (Figure C.28). This label may be downloaded from the companion web site of this book for your personal use.

Shipping Film (Exposed and Unexposed)

If you will be filming on a distant location that requires you to ship film to the laboratory, it is best to make prior arrangements with one of the professional shippers such as DHL, Federal Express, or UPS. This is usually handled by the Production Manager or Production Coordinator of the show. Most of these companies use their own planes for shipping and usually do not use any type of X-ray equipment to scan packages being shipped within the United States. If you are planning to ship your film with any commercial shipping company, you should have the production office check with them before shipping to ensure that your film will not be X-rayed and will be transported safely. Be aware that if you package your film for shipping and ship it as freight on a passenger airline, it will be subject to the same high intensity X-ray machines that checked baggage goes through. In any event, any time you ship motion picture film, you should always label all sides of the shipping carton with the following warning: "DO NOT X-RAY, MOTION PICTURE FILM."

Film, X-Rays, and Carrying Film on Planes

Be especially careful when transporting film on a commercial plane. Although some of the X-ray equipment used to check baggage emits

a very low level dose of radiation, it can still cause a fogging on the film. Film can tolerate some X-ray exposure but excessive amounts may result in noticeable fog and grain. This is especially true for very high-speed films. Many airports are currently using a new type of X-ray equipment to examine luggage that is checked in at the ticket counter. This equipment uses a more intense X-ray beam, and no matter what they tell you at the airport, it will cause fog damage to any exposed or unexposed film stock. It is also not recommended to hand-carry film when traveling by plane, but if you must do so, you or the Producer or Production Manager should request that it be inspected by hand. You should have your changing bag or changing tent available because the security officer will want to open some of the cans to ensure that it is indeed film inside of them. Unfortunately, this is very time consuming and inconvenient, but it is still worth the time to avoid having fogged film. If you do plan to hand-carry any film on a plane, the Producer, Production Manager or somebody from the production office should contact the security people at the airport well in advance and ask how they would like to handle the situation. They should ask if they would be willing to conduct a manual inspection of the packages that contain the film. If not, the only alternative may be to ship the film using one of the standard commercial shipping companies mentioned previously.

If you are traveling with film in foreign countries you must be especially careful when transporting film. You not only have to worry about X-rays but also the security and customs agents wanting to open film cans to inspect them, potentially ruining all of the production's hard work. The best thing to do before any of this happens is to contact the airport personnel and explain details of your travel and the special needs regarding film stocks. Ask them for the recommended steps you can take to insure the safe and expeditious transportation of your film stock. As with travel in the USA, you may want to simply make arrangements with one of the professional shipping companies that deal with international shipments, and simply ship the film back to your home base without hand-carrying it on the plane. If you arrange in advance with a shipper, you shouldn't need to worry about the cans of film being opened or exposed to X-ray radiation.

Ordering Additional Film Stock

When you have completed filling out the daily film inventory forms at the end of each shooting day, be sure you have enough film on hand to continue filming. As the film inventory gets low, notify the production office that you need additional film stock. A good rule to follow

is to have at least enough film on hand for three to five days of filming. Of course, if it is the last couple of days of filming, you may not need to order any additional film stock. Be especially aware of holidays and weekends during the shooting schedule because you will not be able to order film on these days. Also be aware of where the film is being sent from. If you are filming on the East Coast of the United States and the film is being shipped from the West Coast, be sure to allow enough time for the film to arrive. Whenever you receive any additional film stock, remember to record the amounts on the daily film inventory form. If possible, obtain a copy of the packing list that came with the film so that you have proof of how much was sent. On larger shows, the production office often keeps a reserve supply of film at the office and only sends what is needed on set for a few days at a time. Be sure that you are aware of how much and what type of film the production office has in reserve supply. You should keep an inventory, starting with the amount at the start of production, and as the office sends you film from this reserve, you should subtract that amount from your current inventory balance. This inventory should be separate from your daily inventory form that is filled out each day after filming. If the office orders more film from the manufacturer for their reserve supply, this additional amount should be communicated to the 2nd AC and/or Loader so that the inventory totals can be adjusted accordingly. Keeping a separate record of film inventory from the production office often allows you to double check amounts if there is a question later on. The more detailed and accurate your records, the fewer problems you should have at the conclusion of the production. When ordering additional film stock, be sure to double check with the DP regarding the type of film he or she wants. If you have been using the same film stock throughout the production, it may not be necessary to check. But if you have been using many different film stocks, checking with the DP will most often ensure that you have the correct film on hand. You should look at any advance shooting schedules so that you know what scenes are coming up and plan accordingly. If there are any scenes that are quite long, you will want to have plenty of 1000-ft loads on hand. If the DP indicates there will be handheld or Steadicam shots, you will want to have plenty of 400-ft loads. If upcoming scenes require multiple cameras, you must have plenty of film on hand for each camera. By keeping a constant check on the film inventory and looking at upcoming schedules or shot lists, you will eliminate a lot of problems later on. Nothing is worse than running out of film at a critical time during production because the assistant or Loader didn't look ahead and plan properly. Appendix C contains a Raw Stock Inventory Form (Figure C.16) and a Film Stock Request Form (Figure C. 19) that can be used when

requesting additional film stock from the production office. Like other forms, these can also be found on the companion web site for this book.

When a new shipment of film arrives I recommend making magazine identification labels for each can of film. As discussed previously in the section on marking actors, you may want to create a mag ID label board with many pre-made marks on it. You can make these marks during off time on set or have the PA or Trainee make them. Then when a new supply of film arrives and you are loading magazines, the labels are already created with the basic information. Once placed on the mag you only have to add a few bits of info like mag number and roll number. This saves time later when you are rushing to load magazines. Or you may make labels with the basic information on them and place these labels on each film can. Each time a magazine is loaded, remove the label from the can or label board and place it on the magazine, and fill in the remainder of the information. When the magazine is then placed on the camera, be sure to write in the roll number before handing it to the 1st AC.

Using Short Ends and Recans

You should be very careful if you are considering using short ends or recans on your film projects. This is especially true if you don't know the origin of the short ends or recans. As discussed previously, a short end is any film left over from a full roll of film. These may be saved by the production company to be used on future productions, or they may be sold to a business that specializes in selling short ends and/ or recans. If the production company purchases short ends from one of these companies it is recommended that you send a small sample of the film to the lab for testing to be sure that there is nothing wrong with the film. You never know if it had been subjected to exposure to radiation, heat or chemicals, or the age of the film, which could affect the film's ability to accurately reproduce colors or to be exposed properly. Be sure to check with the DP or somebody in production before doing this. It's not your decision and should be made by somebody with more authority. With recans you need to be aware of some of the same things as with short ends. If you don't know where the recans came from, you may also want to test one or two of them before shooting. Again, you may not know how it was stored, its age or if it was exposed to X-rays. And finally, even if you purchase film in its original, sealed cans, unless you are purchasing it directly from Kodak you still should be concerned about shipping and storage conditions of the film before you purchased it. You should only trust film stock

purchased directly from Kodak. Anything else should be tested before use.

Storage and Care of Motion Picture Film

Unexposed Film

All motion picture films are manufactured to very high quality standards, and the proper storage and handling of these films are important. Motion picture films are sensitive to heat, moisture, chemicals, and radiation. The following information is based on the recommendations of Eastman Kodak, the manufacturer of all currently used motion picture film.

For short-term storage of less than six months, original cans of unopened raw stock should be kept at a temperature of 55°F or lower and at a humidity level below 60 percent. For long-term storage of more than six months, film should be kept at a temperature of between 0°F and −10°F and at a humidity level below 60 percent. It is very important to remember that when removing any film stock from cold storage, it must be allowed to properly warm up before the can is opened. Failure to allow the film to reach the proper temperature before opening the can will cause condensation to form on the film, resulting in spots in your photographic image. Never open a film can immediately after removing it from cold storage. Film should be allowed to warm up slowly, and you should never try to rush the warming-up process. I once had a film student place a couple of cans of film under a 2000-watt light in an attempt to warm up the film faster. This is not recommended, and I would never do it under any circumstances. Table 4.5 lists the recommended warm-up times for motion picture films as recommended by Eastman Kodak. In addition, film should be kept away from any chemicals or fumes that could cause contamination of the emulsion layers. It should not be stored near any exhaust or heating pipes or in direct sunlight. All film stock should also be kept away from any exposure to radiation.

Table 4.5   Recommended Warm-Up Times for Sealed Cans of Motion Picture Film

Film Format	Warm Up Time
16 mm	1–1½ hours
35 mm	3–5 hours

Exposed Film

After exposure, film should be unloaded from the magazines as soon as possible, placed in a black bag and film can, and properly sealed with camera tape in preparation for delivery to the lab. All cans of exposed film should be sent to the lab as soon as possible. If there is any reason that exposed film cannot be sent to the lab within a reasonable amount of time, it should be kept at a temperature of 70°F or lower and at a humidity level below 50 percent. As with unprocessed film, you should also keep processed film away from any chemicals or fumes that could cause contamination of the emulsion layers. It should not be stored near any exhaust or heating pipes or in direct sunlight and should also be kept away from any exposure to radiation.

Film Inventory and Record of Film Shot

Throughout the production you will shoot a large amount of film as well as receive shipments of film stock. You should have a supply of daily film inventory forms so that you may keep an inventory of all film stock received and shot. In most cases, the production company needs an inventory of each different film stock, as well as a grand total for all film stocks combined. For example, if you are using Eastman Kodak 35 mm Color Negative 5218 and 5274 on your production, you may have three separate totals for the film inventory, one for 5218, one for 5274, and one for the combined total of both. When keeping the inventory, you may use a standard inventory form or make up one of your own. A large part of the production's budget is spent on film stock, and it is important to keep accurate records in case there are any questions during the production. I was once hired on a show and was told that the previous assistants had been caught stealing film stock, so it was important to keep proper records that could be periodically reviewed for accuracy. Examples of two different types of daily film inventory forms can be found in Figures 4.49 and 4.50.

These are only two examples of styles of inventory forms I have used during my career. There are many other styles out there, and you may design your own based on what works best for you. These two forms can also be found in Appendix C (Figures C.13 and C.14) and are also available for downloading on the companion web site to this book.

At the end of each shooting day, after the equipment has been packed up and the film sent to the lab, the 2nd AC prepares a daily film inventory form that contains the following information: film received; each roll number shot; a breakdown of Good, No Good,

DAILY FILM INVENTORY						Page #		of	

Prod. Co.:					Day #:		Date:	
Prod. Title:							Prod. #:	
Laboratory:								

Film Type:

LOADED	ROLL #	GOOD	NG	WASTE	TOTAL	SE	FILM ON HAND	
							Previous	
							Today (+)	
							Today (-)	
							Total	
							400' Rolls	
							1000' Rolls	
							Short Ends	
							Other	
TOTALS	**GOOD**	**NG**	**WASTE**	**TOTAL**	**Comments:**			
Today								
Previous (+)								
Total to Date								

Film Type:

LOADED	ROLL #	GOOD	NG	WASTE	TOTAL	SE	FILM ON HAND	
							Previous	
							Today (+)	
							Today (-)	
							Total	
							400' Rolls	
							1000' Rolls	
							Short Ends	
							Other	
TOTALS	**GOOD**	**NG**	**WASTE**	**TOTAL**	**Comments:**			
Today								
Previous (+)								
Total to Date								

TOTAL FILM USE	GOOD	NG	WASTE	TOTAL	TOTAL FILM ON HAND	
Today					Previous	
Previous (+)					Today (+)	
Total to Date					Today (-)	
					Total	

DFI-1   © DEE

Figure 4.49 Daily film inventory form #1.

Waste, Short End, and Total footage for each roll; film on hand at the end of the day; totals for each day; and a running total for the entire production. Be careful when totaling up these numbers because it is important to the production office to account for every foot of film used on the production. It is easy at the end of a long shooting day to make a mistake in calculations, so be sure to use a calculator. If you have time I recommend checking your figures from the previous

| DAILY FILM INVENTORY | | | | | | Page # | | of | |

Prod. Co.:   Day #:   Date:
Prod. Title: Prod. #:
Laboratory:

FILM TYPE	ROLL #	LOADED	GOOD	NO GOOD	WASTE	TOTAL	SE
TOTALS		LOADED	GOOD	NO GOOD	WASTE	TOTAL	SE
	Today						
	Previous (+)						
	Total to Date						

Film on Hand	Film Type					**TOTALS**
Previous Balance						
(+) Received Today						
(−) Used Today						
Total To Date						

DFI-2   © DEE

Figure 4.50   Daily film inventory form #2.

day's shoot each morning. You will be more awake and refreshed after a good night's sleep and better able to catch any small errors in arithmetic.

When these reports have been filled out, give a copy to the production office along with copies of the camera reports for each roll. You should also keep a copy of any reports for the camera department in case there are any questions later. I recommend taking all of the camera reports for a particular day and stapling them to the inventory form for that day. This way if there is ever any question later on, you will have everything for that day all together and will not have to search for it. When using more than one camera, keep separate totals for each camera, as well as combined totals for all cameras.

Completing Film Inventory Forms

The following example shows how to fill out the daily film inventory forms and how each day's totals relate to the next day's daily film inventory form.

Example   You have been hired as the 2nd AC on a feature film. The film is called *Claire of the Moon* and is being produced by Demi Monde Productions. The Director is Nicole Conn, and the Director of Photography is Randy Sellars. The DP has decided to use two film stocks for this shoot, Eastman Kodak 5218 and 5274. He will be doing some handheld shots, so he will need 400-ft rolls in addition to 1000-ft rolls.

On the first day of production, the following film stock is received:

- 5,200 ft of Eastman Kodak 5274-148-0739
  Four 1000-ft rolls
  Three 400-ft rolls
- 5,400 ft of Eastman Kodak 5218-237-4862
  Three 1000-ft rolls
  Six 400-ft rolls

On the second day of production, the following film stock is received:

- 7,000 ft of Eastman Kodak 5274-148-0739
  Five 1000-ft rolls
  Five 400-ft rolls
- 5,000 ft of Eastman Kodak 5218-237-4862
  Three 1000-ft rolls
  Five 400-ft rolls

Figures 4.51 through 4.67 show the completed camera reports and completed daily film inventory forms for day 1 and day 2. So that you may become familiar with the different styles of camera reports and inventory forms, I have chosen to use examples of each style of camera report for each day. On a typical production you would only use one type of camera report form.

On an actual production you would only use one camera report style from a single lab and one daily film inventory form and not mix them. I have included the various styles to help you better understand how to complete the different styles of reports and forms.

Using the information from the preceding camera reports and inventory forms, the following section breaks down the information and shows where it comes from for each style of daily film inventory form. In examples where information is to be transferred from one day's inventory form to the next day's form, I have included the section from each form for each day.

Co. Submitted By: Demi Monde Productions	P.O. #
Bill To: Demi Monde Productions	Date Exposed:
Picture Title: "Claire of the Moon"	Loader:
Director: N. Conn D.P.: R. Sellars	

ROLL # 1 ☐ BLACK & WHITE   ☒ COLOR

EMUL. # 5274 — 148 0739   MAG #   10161

DEVELOP FOOTAGE __400__
☒ NORMAL   ☐ PUSH ____ STOP(S)   ☐ PULL ____ STOP(S)

FILM WORKPRINT ☐ PRINT ALL   ☒ PRINT CIRCLED TAKES

VIDEO PREP & ☐ TRANSFER ALL ☐ TRANSFER CIRCLED TAKES
TRANSFER   TRANSFER AT ____ fps   ☐ EDGE # PUNCH

SCENE NO.	TAKE	DIAL	FEET	SD	REMARKS	SCENE NO.	TAKE	DIAL	FEET	SD	REMARKS
32	1	80	80								
	②	120	㊵								
	③	160	㊵								
32 A	1	210	50								
	②	270	㊿								
32 B	①	300	㉚								
32 C	1	320	20								
	②	360	㊵								
						DEVELOP NORMAL				G	210
						1 - LITE PRINT				NG	150
										W	40
	OUT AT 360									T	400

Figure 4.51 Completed camera report for roll #1.

DATE		CUSTOMER ORDER NUMBER		
COMPANY	Demi Monde Productions			
DIRECTOR	N. Conn	CAMERAMAN	R. Sellars	
PRODUCTION NO. OR TITLE	"Claire of the Moon"			
MAGAZINE NUMBER	10109	ROLL NUMBER	**2**	
TYPE OF FILM / EMULSION	5274-148-0739		400'	
PRINT CIRCLED TAKES ONLY:	☒ ONE LITE	☐ TIMED		

SCENE NO.	TAKE	DIAL	PRINT	REMARKS
32 C	①	40	40	
	②	80	40	
32 D	①	150	70	
36	1	170		
	②	190	20	
	3	200		
36 A	1	220		
	②	240	20	
	3	260		
	④	280	20	
36 B	①	350	70	
	2	390		
		OUT AT 390'		
		DEVELOP NORMAL		
		ONE LITE PRINT		
			G	280
			NG	110
			W	10
			T	400

Figure 4.52 Completed camera report for roll #2.

Co. Sub. by: Demi Monde Productions	Job #:
Bill to: Demi Monde Productions	Date Exposed:
Pict. Title: "Claire of the Moon"	Loader:
Director: N. Conn	D.P.: R. Sellars

ROLL # 3   ☐ BLACK & WHITE   ☒ COLOR

EMUL. # 5218 — 237 4862   **MAG #**   10146

DEVELOP FOOTAGE _1000_
☒ NORMAL   ☐ PUSH ____ STOP(S)   ☐ PULL ____ STOP(S)

FILM WORKPRINT ☐ PRINT ALL   ☒ PRINT CIRCLED TAKES

VIDEO PREP &   ☐ TRANSFER ALL ☐ TRANSFER CIRCLED TAKES
TRANSFER   TRANSFER AT ____ fps   ☐ EDGE # PUNCH

SCENE #	1	6	2	7	3	8	4	9	5	10	REMARKS
79	30		(40)		(40)		30				30 / 70
79 A	(20)										110 / 140
79 B	0		(30)								160 / 160
79 C	20		(20)								190 / 210
79 D	30		(30)								230 / 260
79 E	(10)		(10)								290 / 300
79 F	(20)										310 / 330
94	(20)		20		(40)						360 / 370
99	60		(80)		50		(70)				410 / 470
											550 / 600 / 670
			OUT AT 670								
			DEVELOP NORMAL								
			1 - LITE PRINT								
							G.		430		
							N.G.		240		
							W.		0		
							T.		670		
							SE		330		

Figure 4.53   Completed camera report for roll #3.

| DAILY FILM INVENTORY | | | | | | Page # | 1 | of | 1 |

Prod. Co.:	Demi Monde Productions		Day #: 1	Date:
Prod. Title:	Claire of the Moon			Prod. #:
Laboratory:				

Film Type:	5218						
LOADED	**ROLL #**	**GOOD**	**NG**	**WASTE**	**TOTAL**	**SE**	**FILM ON HAND**	
1,000	3	430	240	0	670	330	Previous	0
							Today (+)	5,400
							Today (-)	670
							Total	4,730
							400' Rolls	2,400
							1000' Rolls	2,000
							Short Ends	330
							Other	0
	TOTALS	**GOOD**	**NG**	**WASTE**	**TOTAL**	**Comments:**		
	Today	430	240	0	670			
	Previous (+)	0	0	0	0			
	Total to Date	430	240	0	670			

Film Type:	5274						
LOADED	**ROLL #**	**GOOD**	**NG**	**WASTE**	**TOTAL**	**SE**	**FILM ON HAND**	
400	1	210	150	40	400	0	Previous	0
400	2	280	110	10	400	0	Today (+)	5,200
							Today (-)	800
							Total	4,400
							400' Rolls	400
							1000' Rolls	4,000
							Short Ends	0
							Other	0
	TOTALS	**GOOD**	**NG**	**WASTE**	**TOTAL**	**Comments:**		
	Today	490	260	50	800			
	Previous (+)	0	0	0	0			
	Total to Date	490	260	50	800			

TOTAL FILM USE	**GOOD**	**NG**	**WASTE**	**TOTAL**	**TOTAL FILM ON HAND**	
Today	920	500	50	1,470	Previous	0
Previous (+)	0	0	0	0	Today (+)	10,600
Total to Date	920	500	50	1,470	Today (-)	1,470
					Total	9,130

DFI-1   © DEE

Figure 4.54   Completed daily film inventory form #1 for day 1.

DAILY FILM INVENTORY						Page #	1	of	1

Prod. Co.:	Demi Monde Productions				Day #:	1	Date:		
Prod. Title:	Claire of the Moon						Prod. #:		
Laboratory:									

FILM TYPE	ROLL #	LOADED	GOOD	NO GOOD	WASTE	TOTAL	SE
5274	1	400	210	150	40	400	0
5274	2	400	280	110	10	400	0
5218	3	1,000	430	240	0	670	330
TOTALS		LOADED	GOOD	NO GOOD	WASTE	TOTAL	SE
Today		1,800	920	500	50	1,470	330
Previous (+)		0	0	0	0	0	0
Total to Date		1,800	920	500	50	1,470	330

Film on Hand	Film Type	5218	5274				TOTALS
Previous Balance		0	0				0
(+) Received Today		5,400	5,200				10,600
(−) Used Today		670	800				1,470
Total To Date		4,730	4,400				9,130

DFI-2   © DEE

Figure 4.55 Completed daily film inventory form #2 for day 1.

Co. Submitted By: Demi Monde Productions		P.O. #
Bill To: Demi Monde Productions		Date Exposed:
Picture Title: "Claire of the Moon"		Loader:
Director: N. Conn	D.P.: R. Sellars	

ROLL # **4** ☐ BLACK & WHITE ☒ COLOR

EMUL. # 5274 — 148 0739   MAG #   10149

DEVELOP FOOTAGE __1000__
☒ NORMAL   ☐ PUSH ___ STOP(S)   ☐ PULL ___ STOP(S)

FILM WORKPRINT ☐ PRINT ALL   ☒ PRINT CIRCLED TAKES

VIDEO PREP &   ☐ TRANSFER ALL ☐ TRANSFER CIRCLED TAKES
TRANSFER   TRANSFER AT ___ fps   ☐ EDGE # PUNCH

SCENE NO.	TAKE	DIAL	FEET	SD	REMARKS	SCENE NO.	TAKE	DIAL	FEET	SD	REMARKS
24	1	70	70				3	670	40		
	②	160	⑨⓪			97	①	690	②⓪		
	3	200	40				2	720	30		
	④	240	④⓪			135	①	780	⑥⓪		
24 A	①	290	⑤⓪				②	830	⑤⓪		
	2	340	50				3	870	40		
	③	400	⑥⓪			146	1	910	40		
10	1	430	30				②	940	③⓪		
	2	450	20								
	3	470	20				OUT AT 940	G	490		
	④	500	③⓪					NG	450		
	5	530	30					W	60		
	⑥	560	③⓪			DEVELOP NORMAL		T	1000		
10 A	1	600	40			ONE LITE PRINT					
	②	630	③⓪								

Figure 4.56 Completed camera report for roll #4.

Co. Sub. by: Demi Monde Productions	Job #:
Bill to: Demi Monde Productions	Date Exposed:
Pict. Title: "Claire of the Moon"	Loader:
Director: N. Conn	D.P.: R. Sellars

ROLL # 5   ☐ BLACK & WHITE   ☒ COLOR

EMUL. # 5274 — 148 0739   MAG #   10161

DEVELOP FOOTAGE __400__
☒ NORMAL   ☐ PUSH ___ STOP(S)   ☐ PULL ___ STOP(S)

FILM WORKPRINT ☐ PRINT ALL   ☒ PRINT CIRCLED TAKES

VIDEO PREP &   ☐ TRANSFER ALL   ☐ TRANSFER CIRCLED TAKES
TRANSFER   TRANSFER AT ___ fps   ☐ EDGE # PUNCH

SCENE #	PRINT CIRCLED TAKES					REMARKS
	1 6	2 7	3 8	4 9	5 10	
7	⑥⓪	20	⑦⓪	40		60 / 80
7 A	40	③⓪	③⓪	10	20	150 / 190
7 B	③⓪	②⓪	20			230 / 260
						290 / 300
						320 / 350
		OUT AT 390				370 / 390
		DEVELOP NORMAL				
		1 - LITE PRINT				
					G.	240
					N.G.	150
					W.	10
					T.	400

Figure 4.57 Completed camera report for roll #5.

Co. Submitted By: Demi Monde Productions	P.O. #
Bill To: Demi Monde Productions	Date Exposed:
Picture Title: "Claire of the Moon"	Loader:
Director: N. Conn	D.P.: R. Sellars

ROLL # **6**   ☐BLACK & WHITE   ☒ COLOR

EMUL. # 5218 — 237 4862   MAG #   10014

DEVELOP FOOTAGE ___1000___
☒ NORMAL   ☐ PUSH ___ STOP(S)   ☐ PULL ___ STOP(S)

FILM WORKPRINT ☐ PRINT ALL   ☒ PRINT CIRCLED TAKES

VIDEO PREP &   ☐ TRANSFER ALL ☐ TRANSFER CIRCLED TAKES
TRANSFER   TRANSFER AT ___ fps   ☐ EDGE # PUNCH

SCENE NO.	TAKE	DIAL	FEET	SD	REMARKS	SCENE NO.	TAKE	DIAL	FEET	SD	REMARKS
5	1	20	20			57	②	810	㊵		
	2	40	20				3	850	40		
	③	130	㊿				④	920	㊆		
	④	200	㊆								
	⑤	280	㊵								
5 A	1	300	20					OUT AT 920'			
	②	400	⑩⓪								
5 B	①	440	㊵								
	2	520	80								
	③	550	㉚								
12	1	590	40			DEVELOP NORMAL					
	②	660	㊆			1 - LITE PRINT				G	680
	③	730	㊆							NG	240
	4	750	20							W	80
57	①	770	⑳							T	1000

Figure 4.58   Completed camera report for roll #6.

DATE		CUSTOMER ORDER NUMBER		
COMPANY	Demi Monde Productions			
DIRECTOR	N. Conn	CAMERAMAN	R. Sellars	
PRODUCTION NO. OR TITLE	"Claire of the Moon"			
MAGAZINE NUMBER	10250	ROLL NUMBER	7	
TYPE OF FILM / EMULSION	5218-237-4862			
PRINT CIRCLED TAKES ONLY:	☒ ONE LITE		☐ TIMED	

SCENE NO.	TAKE	DIAL	PRINT	REMARKS
33	1	30		
	2	50		
	③	70	20	
	④	100	30	
33 A	1	130		
	②	170	40	
33 B	①	200	30	
	2	220		
	3	240		
	④	270	30	
	5	290		
	⑥	320	30	
33 C	1	360		
	②	420	60	
107	①	490	70	
	2	520		
	③	580	60	
		OUT AT 970'		
			G	370
	DEVELOP NORMAL		NG	210
	ONE LITE PRINT		W	0
			T	580
			SE	420

Figure 4.59 Completed camera report for roll #7.

DAILY FILM INVENTORY							Page #	1	of	1

Prod. Co.:	Demi Monde Productions		Day #:	2	Date:	
Prod. Title:	Claire of the Moon				Prod. #:	
Laboratory:						

Film Type: 5218

LOADED	ROLL #	GOOD	NG	WASTE	TOTAL	SE	FILM ON HAND	
1,000	6	680	240	80	1,000	0	Previous	4,730
1,000	7	370	210	0	580	420	Today (+)	5,000
							Today (-)	1,580
							Total	8,150
							400' Rolls	4,400
							1000' Rolls	3,000
							Short Ends	750
							Other	0
	TOTALS	GOOD	NG	WASTE	TOTAL	Comments:		
	Today	1,050	450	80	1,580			
	Previous (+)	430	240	0	670			
	Total to Date	1,480	690	80	2,250			

Film Type: 5274

LOADED	ROLL #	GOOD	NG	WASTE	TOTAL	SE	FILM ON HAND	
1,000	4	490	450	60	1,000	0	Previous	4,400
400	5	240	150	10	400	0	Today (+)	7,000
							Today (-)	1,400
							Total	10,000
							400' Rolls	2,000
							1000' Rolls	8,000
							Short Ends	0
							Other	0
	TOTALS	GOOD	NG	WASTE	TOTAL	Comments:		
	Today	730	600	70	1,400			
	Previous (+)	490	260	50	800			
	Total to Date	1,220	860	120	2,200			

TOTAL FILM USE	GOOD	NG	WASTE	TOTAL	TOTAL FILM ON HAND	
Today	1,780	1,050	150	2,980	Previous	9,130
Previous (+)	920	500	50	1,470	Today (+)	12,000
Total to Date	2,700	1,550	200	4,450	Today (-)	2,980
					Total	18,150

DFI-1   © DEE

Figure 4.60 Completed daily film inventory form #1 for day 2.

DAILY FILM INVENTORY						Page #	1	of		1

Prod. Co.:	Demi Monde Productions				Day #:	2	Date:			
Prod. Title:	Claire of the Moon						Prod. #:			
Laboratory:										

FILM TYPE	ROLL #	LOADED	GOOD	NO GOOD	WASTE	TOTAL	SE
5274	4	1,000	490	450	60	1,000	0
5274	5	400	240	150	10	400	0
5218	6	1,000	680	240	80	1,000	0
5218	7	1,000	370	210	0	850	420

	TOTALS	LOADED	GOOD	NO GOOD	WASTE	TOTAL	SE
	Today	3,400	1,780	1,050	150	2,980	420
	Previous (+)	1800	920	500	50	1470	330
	Total to Date	5,200	2,700	1,550	200	4,450	750

Film on Hand	Film Type	5218	5274				TOTALS
	Previous Balance	4,730	4,400				9,130
	(+) Received Today	5,000	7,000				12,000
	(−) Used Today	1,580	1,400				2,980
	Total To Date	8,150	10,000				18,150

DFI-2   © DEE

Figure 4.61 Completed daily film inventory form #2 for day 2.

The following section refers to Daily Film Inventory Form #1 in Figure 4.62.

- FILM TYPE: The type of film you are using: Eastman Kodak 7213, 7219, 5245, 5296; Fujifilm 8632, 8552; etc. In this example you are using Eastman Kodak 35 mm Color Negative 5218.
- LOADED: The size of the roll of film loaded into the magazine. In this example it is a 1000-ft roll.

- ROLL #: The camera roll number from the camera report. In this example you have roll number 3.
- GOOD (G): The total of good or printed takes from the camera report for each roll.
- NG (NO GOOD): The total of no good takes from the camera report for each roll.
- WASTE (W): The amount of footage left over that cannot be called a short end. Less than 40 ft in 16 mm and less than 100 ft in 35 mm is considered to be waste.
- TOTAL: The total of GOOD plus NO GOOD plus WASTE.
- GOOD + NO GOOD + WASTE = TOTAL.
- SE: The amount of footage left over that is too large to be called waste. More than 40 ft in 16 mm and more than 100 ft in 35 mm is considered to be a short end.

Film Type:	5218					
LOADED	ROLL #	GOOD	NG	WASTE	TOTAL	SE
1,000	3	430	240	0	670	330

Figure 4.62   Breakdown of information for daily film inventory form #1.

The following section refers to daily film inventory form #1 in Figure 4.63.

- TOTALS: The total amount of all roll numbers combined for each category: GOOD (G), NO GOOD (NG), WASTE (W), and TOTAL.
- TODAY: The totals for all roll numbers shot today for each category: GOOD (G), NO GOOD (NG), WASTE (W), and TOTAL. In this example, for day 1, the total good for roll numbers 1 and 2 combined is 490, total no good is 260, total waste is 50, and total is 800.
- PREVIOUS (+): The totals for all roll numbers shot previous to today, obtained from the previous day's report, from the section labeled Totals—To Date. In this example, for day 1, there are no previous amounts because it is the first day of filming.
- TOTAL TO DATE: The combined total for all roll numbers shot today plus the totals for all roll numbers shot previous to today. These amounts are then written on the next day's daily inventory report in the section labeled Totals—Previous (+).

Film on Hand:

- PREVIOUS: The total amount of footage on hand at the start of the day for each film stock, obtained from the previous day's report, from the section labeled Film on Hand—Total. In this example, for day 1, you had no film on hand at the start of the day because it is the first day of filming, and on day 2 you had 4400 ft on hand at the start of the day. This was the amount on hand at the end of day 1.
- TODAY (+): The total amount of footage received today for each film stock.
- TODAY (−): The total amount of footage shot today for each film stock.
- TOTAL: The combined total of previous, plus footage received today, less footage shot today, for each film stock.
- PREVIOUS + TODAY (+) −TODAY (−) = TOTAL: This is the total amount of footage on hand at the end of the shooting day. This amount is then written on the daily inventory report for the next day in the section labeled Film on Hand—Previous.

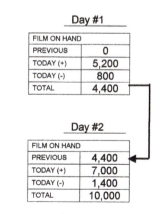

Day #1

TOTALS	GOOD	NG	WASTE	TOTAL
TODAY	490	260	50	800
PREVIOUS (+)	0	0	0	0
TOTAL TO DATE	490	260	50	800

Day #2

TOTALS	GOOD	NG	WASTE	TOTAL
TODAY	730	600	70	1,400
PREVIOUS (+)	490	260	50	800
TOTAL TO DATE	1,220	860	120	2,200

Day #1

FILM ON HAND	
PREVIOUS	0
TODAY (+)	5,200
TODAY (-)	800
TOTAL	4,400

Day #2

FILM ON HAND	
PREVIOUS	4,400
TODAY (+)	7,000
TODAY (-)	1,400
TOTAL	10,000

Figure 4.63 Breakdown of information for daily film inventory form #1.

The following section refers to daily film inventory form #1 in Figure 4.64.

Total Film Use—All Film Stocks

- TOTALS: The total amount of all roll numbers, for all film stocks combined for each category: GOOD (G), NO GOOD (NG), WASTE (W), and TOTAL.
- TODAY: The combined total for today only, for all film stocks for each category: GOOD (G), NO GOOD (NG), WASTE (W), and TOTAL.
- PREVIOUS (+): The combined total for all film types shot previous to today for each category: GOOD (G), NO GOOD (NG), WASTE (W), and TOTAL. This amount is obtained from the previous day's daily report form from the section labeled Total to Date.
- TOTAL TO DATE: The combined total of all film stocks shot today plus the total of all film stocks shot previous to today. These amounts are then written on the next day's daily inventory report in the section labeled Totals—Previous (+).

Total Film on Hand:

- PREVIOUS: The combined total amount of footage on hand at the start of today for all film stocks, obtained from the previous day's report, from the section labeled Total.
- TODAY (+): The combined total amount of footage received today for all film stocks.
- TODAY (−): The combined total amount of footage shot today for all film stocks.
- TOTAL: The combined total of previous footage, plus footage received today, less footage shot today for all film stocks.
- PREVIOUS + TODAY (+) − TODAY (−) = TOTAL: This is the total amount of footage on hand at the end of the shooting day. This amount is then written on the daily inventory report for the next day in the section labeled Total Film on Hand—Previous. Remember, these figures are combined totals for all film stocks on hand during the production.

Day #1

TOTALS	GOOD	NG	WASTE	TOTAL	TOTAL FILM ON HAND	
TODAY	920	500	50	1,470	PREVIOUS	0
PREVIOUS (+)	0	0	0	0	TODAY (+)	10,600
TOTAL TO DATE	920	500	50	1,470	TODAY (-)	1,470
					TOTAL	9,130

Day #2

TOTALS	GOOD	NG	WASTE	TOTAL	TOTAL FILM ON HAND	
TODAY	1,780	1,050	150	2,980	PREVIOUS	9,130
PREVIOUS (+)	920	500	50	1,470	TODAY (+)	12,000
TOTAL TO DATE	2,700	1,550	200	4,450	TODAY (-)	2,980
					TOTAL	18,150

Figure 4.64   Breakdown of information for daily film inventory form #1.

The following section refers to Daily Film Inventory Form #2 in Figure 4.65.

- FILM TYPE: The type of film you are using: Eastman Kodak 7213, 7219, 5245, 5277; Fujifilm 8632, 8552; etc. In this example you are using Eastman Kodak Color Negative 5218 and 5274.
- ROLL #: The camera roll number from the camera report. In this example you have roll numbers 1, 2, and 3.
- LOADED: The total amount of footage loaded in the magazine for that roll number. In this example roll number 1 is a 400-ft roll, roll number 2 is a 400-ft roll, and roll number 3 is a 1000-ft roll. GOOD + NO GOOD + WASTE + SE = LOADED.
- GOOD (G): The total of good or printed takes from the camera report for each roll.
- NO GOOD (NG): The total of no good takes from the camera report for each roll.
- WASTE (W): The amount of footage left over that cannot be called a short end. Less than 40 ft in 16 mm and less than 100 ft in 35 mm is considered to be waste.
- TOTAL (T): The total of GOOD plus NO GOOD plus WASTE. GOOD + NO GOOD + WASTE = TOTAL.
- SE: The amount of footage left over that is too large to be called waste. More than 40 ft in 16 mm and more than 100 ft in 35 mm is considered to be a short end.

FILM TYPE	ROLL #	LOADED	GOOD	NO GOOD	WASTE	TOTAL	SE
5274	1	400	210	150	40	400	0
5274	2	400	280	110	10	400	0
5218	3	1,000	430	240	0	670	330

Figure 4.65   Breakdown of information for daily film inventory form #2.

The following section refers to daily film inventory form #2 in Figure 4.66.

- TOTALS: The total amount of all roll numbers, for all film stocks combined for each category: LOADED, GOOD (G), NO GOOD (NG), WASTE (W), TOTAL, and SE.
- TODAY: The combined total for today only, for all film stocks, for each category: LOADED, GOOD (G), NO GOOD (NG), WASTE (W), TOTAL, and SE.
- PREVIOUS (+): The combined total for all film types shot previous to today for each category: LOADED, GOOD (G), NO GOOD (NG), WASTE (W), TOTAL, and SE. This amount is obtained from the previous day's daily report form from the section labeled Total to Date.
- TOTAL TO DATE: The combined total of all film stocks shot today plus the total of all film stocks shot previous to today. These amounts are then written on the next day's daily inventory report in the section labeled Totals—Previous (+).

DAY # _____1_____

TOTALS	LOADED	GOOD	NO GOOD	WASTE	TOTAL	SE
Today	1,800	920	500	50	1,470	330
Previous (+)	0	0	0	0	0	0
Total to Date	1,800	920	500	50	1,470	330

DAY # _____2_____

TOTALS	LOADED	GOOD	NO GOOD	WASTE	TOTAL	SE
Today	3,400	1,780	1,050	150	2,980	420
Previous (+)	1,800	920	500	50	1,470	330
Total to Date	5,200	2,700	1,550	200	4,450	750

Figure 4.66   Breakdown of information for daily film inventory form #2.

The following section refers to daily film inventory form #2 in Figure 4.67.

- FILM ON HAND/FILM TYPE: These columns are left blank for you to fill in with the film stock you are using. In this example you are using Eastman Kodak Color Negative 5218 and 5274.
- TOTALS: The combined totals of previous film on hand, film received today, film shot today, and film on hand at the end of today for all film stocks.
- PREVIOUS BALANCE: The total amount of film on hand at the start of today for each film stock. In this example, for day 1, you had no film on hand at the start of the day because it is the first day of filming. This information is obtained from the previous day's inventory report form from the section labeled Total to Date.
- (+) RECEIVED TODAY: The total amount of footage received today for each film stock. In this example, for day 1, you received 5400 ft of film stock 5218 and 5200 ft of film stock 5274.
- (−) USED TODAY: The total amount of footage shot today for each film stock.
- TOTAL TO DATE: The total of footage on hand at the end of today, which is the combined total of the previous amount of footage on hand plus the amount of footage received today less the amount of footage shot today: PREVIOUS BALANCE + RECEIVED TODAY − USED TODAY = TOTAL TO DATE. This amount is then written on the daily inventory report for the next day in the section labeled Previous Balance.

DAY # ____1____

FILM ON HAND	FILM TYPE	5218	5274				TOTALS
Previous Balance		0	0				0
(+) Received Today		5,400	5,200				10,600
(−) Used Today		670	800				1,470
Total to Date		4,730	4,400				9,130

DAY # ____2____

FILM ON HAND	FILM TYPE	5218	5274				TOTALS
Previous Balance		4,730	4,400				9,130
(+) Received Today		5,000	7,000				12,000
(−) Used Today		1,580	1,400				2,980
Total to Date		8,150	10,000				18,150

Figure 4.67 Breakdown of information for daily film inventory form #2.

Distribution of Reports

When all the paperwork is completed, you should distribute copies to the appropriate departments. The production office should receive a copy of the daily film inventory form with copies of the day's camera reports attached. The 2nd AC or the Loader should keep copies of all daily film inventory forms and camera reports for the camera department. Most lab camera reports consist of four copies. The top copy is always attached to the film can that is sent to the lab with the exposed film. One copy goes to the Editor, one copy to the production office, and the camera department keeps one copy. You should staple the camera reports to the daily film inventory form for each day so that it will be easier to answer any questions later. In most cases, the production office copy is given to the 2nd Assistant Director (AD) so that he or she may fill out the daily production report.

Record Keeping and Filing of Paperwork

As you have discovered from previous sections of this chapter, the camera department requires a lot of paperwork, most of which is filled in and prepared by the 2nd AC or Loader. This includes shot logs, camera reports for each roll, film inventory forms, weekly time sheets, equipment records, expendables inventory, and more.

I strongly recommend that you set up some type of filing system to keep all of the paperwork organized during the production. You may choose to use a plastic or cardboard file box with various sections for each type of form or paperwork. Set up your file box with separate, labeled file folders for each type of form, paperwork, invoice, or packing slip. An accordion-type file, which is available at most office supply stores, is also great for separating and keeping all of the various paperwork encountered during production. You may choose to use three-ring binders to organize the paperwork. Whatever system you use, just be sure that it is organized in such a way that anybody can find a particular piece of information when necessary. Customize your filing system depending on the needs of the particular production. In addition to the previously mentioned paperwork, other sections in your filing system include equipment received, equipment returned, film ordered and received, expendables ordered and received, short end inventory, raw stock inventory, individual and departmental time sheets, and so on. You should have copies of all packing lists for anything received by the camera department, as well as anything returned by the camera department. Each time you receive or return a piece of equipment, enter the date and description of the equipment on the

appropriate form. This way, if there are any questions later, you can check your records. Equipment received and equipment returned are discussed in a following section.

On many productions the 2nd AC or Loader may be responsible for keeping time sheets for each member of the camera department. In some regions of Britain most crew members fill in their own time cards. Appendix C contains a Camera Department Weekly Time Sheet (Figure C.20) on which you can keep track of the hours worked for each member of the department. The time sheet contains spaces to record the start or call time, start and end time of the first and second meal break, wrap time, total regular hours, total overtime hours, and overall total hours worked for each day and week. The time sheet is based on a typical time card that is used by many of the payroll companies in the motion picture industry. See Figure 8.3 in Chapter 8 for an illustration of a standard film industry crew time card. When filling out the time sheets, it is common to record the time using military time. Military time is based on a 24-hr clock instead of the 12-hr a.m. and 12-hr p.m. clock. Hours are typically broken down into tenths of an hour. Each six-minute time period equals $\frac{1}{10}$ of an hour. For example, a call time of 8:30 a.m. would be written as 8.5, and a wrap time of 8:30 p.m. is written as 20.5. Using military time along with tenths of an hour makes the calculation of total hours each day much easier. Table 8.1 in Chapter 8 shows tenths of an hour conversion. Each day you should mark down the hours worked by each member of the camera department, and at the end of the week fill out the time cards for each.

The important thing to remember is to be as complete and organized as possible so that the production will go smoothly and problems will be minimized. Expendables and film stock must be replenished often during a large production. You should keep accurate inventory records of both of these. I have included many different forms in Appendix C that make it easier for you to keep track of these. You may use the Expendables Inventory and Checklist (Figure C.3) not only to order your expendable supplies but also to keep track of the inventory of those items. It is important not to run out of expendables during production, especially black and white camera tape. You would be in a serious predicament if you were unloading rolls of exposed film and had no black camera tape to wrap the film cans. Appendix C contains two versions of a Daily Film Inventory Form (Figures C.13 and C.14), a Short End Inventory Form (Figure C.15), and a Raw Stock Inventory Form (Figure C.16). By using all of these forms, you should be able to keep a very accurate record of all film stock and be able to answer any questions during and after the shoot.

Throughout a production you may receive additional equipment and send equipment back to the camera rental company. A piece

of equipment may become damaged and need to be sent back for replacement. You may have some special shots that require certain special pieces of equipment. There may be scenes scheduled for shooting that require additional cameras. It is important to keep track of all of this equipment. Appendix C contains an Equipment Received Log (Figure C.6) and a Returned Equipment Log (Figure C.7) that you can use to keep track of all of this information. Whatever paperwork is required for the camera department, the 2nd AC or Loader should have complete and accurate records that should be easy to locate quickly if needed. It is also important to hold on to this paperwork for a brief period after production has been completed. You never know when you may have to refer back to an invoice, time sheet, or camera report. Many years ago I remember receiving a telephone call from an Editor a few months after a production had wrapped. He was working on a particular scene and could not find the copy of the camera report with the scene and take number on it. By going back through my files I was able to locate my copy of the camera report, which I immediately faxed to him.

Performing the Duties of First Assistant Cameraman

From time to time the 2nd AC may be called on to act as 1st AC on some shots. There may be an additional camera, or the 1st AC may have to leave for some reason. As the 2nd AC you should have a basic knowledge and understanding of the job requirements of a 1st AC in case this happens. If someday you plan on moving up from 2nd AC to 1st AC, the more knowledge you have about the job, the better your chances are of moving up. I once worked as a 2nd AC on a feature film that used multiple cameras for a series of shots. Instead of hiring an additional 1st AC, I was asked to move up to 1st AC on the second camera. This was not the first time I received a bump up on a show, and because I knew and understood the job of a 1st AC, the DP was comfortable with my pulling focus on the second camera. It didn't hurt that the camera had a wide-angle lens with a lot of depth of field, so there was little chance I could mess up the shot. After doing this on a few more productions and when I felt more comfortable performing the job of the 1st AC and especially pulling focus, I made the official move to 1st AC and no longer accepted 2nd AC jobs. Chapter 5 discusses in detail all the responsibilities of the job of a 1st AC.

Packing Equipment

At the end of each shooting day, all the camera equipment should be packed away in its proper case as quickly as possible and put in

a safe place until the next shooting day. Remember, the sooner you pack everything away, the sooner you go home for the day. Check all areas of the location to be sure that you have all the camera equipment and nothing is left behind. Place all equipment in the camera truck, or if you are shooting on a stage, place it in a safe area on the stage. Many stages have a designated room for the camera department for the storage of equipment. This room also may contain a darkroom for loading and unloading the film. Any camera equipment should be placed in its case and not left out where it could become damaged. This equipment is very valuable and should be handled carefully. It will be much easier to locate something if it is put away each time instead of left lying around. I don't recommend leaving the camera set up from one day to the next. You never know what will happen overnight. This is usually referred to as a "Walkaway." See the section in Chapter 5 entitled End-of-the Day Procedures for more information on the Walkaway.

Tools and Accessories

As with many professions, you must have some basic tools and accessories so that you may do the job properly. When first starting out, you should have a very basic toolkit or ditty bag, and as you gain more experience and work more frequently, you can add things as you feel they are needed. Some are common tools, while others are specialized pieces of equipment that are unique to the film industry.

In addition to the basic tools, an assistant should also have a small inventory of expendables, film cans, cores, camera reports, etc. There may be many times when you are called for a job at the last minute, and you may have no time to acquire some of these items. By having a small amount on hand, you will always be prepared for most job calls that you get. See Appendix D for a list of the common tools and equipment that should be included in an Assistant cameraman's ditty bag, toolkit, or AKS case.

Many people today carry some type of smart phone or other electronic device like an iPhone, iPad, iPod Touch, or laptop computer, and the Assistant Cameraman will often have one or more of these on the set. Having one of these devices along with many of the cinematography related applications (apps) installed will save both the 1st and 2nd AC much time in the performance of their jobs. It also helps to have a basic understanding of word processing and spreadsheet software. Many camera manuals are currently available in PDF format, which can be saved onto a laptop computer or one of the handheld devices and referenced quickly on set if needed.

In addition, all of the forms, checklists, and labels in Appendix C are available for download on the companion web site for this book. They are available as Word document templates and PDF forms. By downloading them to your laptop computer, you will have every form needed to make your job go smoothly. If possible, you should ask the UPM about a rental fee for the use of your laptop computer when negotiating your deal memo for the production. Just be aware that if anything goes wrong or your computer is lost or damaged while on production, it may not be covered by the production insurance. You should work this out ahead of time with the production office.

I have also found it important to have on set a personal bag that contains a change of clothes, extra work shoes or sneakers, along with foul weather or rain gear. You never know when you must change clothes or have additional clothing in case of extreme weather conditions. Having an extra sweatshirt, thermal underwear, and cold-weather boots can make the difference between being warm and comfortable on a shoot or freezing. I bring this bag with me on any long-term jobs and keep it on one of the top shelves in the camera truck. In addition to clothing items, I also keep a small first aid kit, basic toiletry kit, and extra towels in the bag. You never know when you will find yourself away from home and in need of many of these items. See Appendix D for a complete listing of the suggested items in this bag.

2nd AC/Loader Tips

Many of these tips apply only to the 2nd AC and Loader, and some of them also apply to the 1st AC. As you read this book you will notice that some of them are repeated in Chapter 5, First Assistant Cameraman (1st AC). In the course of the day-to-day performance of your job, you will often repeat orders back to someone to indicate that you heard them. I believe that repetition is important in the proper execution of your job, and that is why some of these tips are repeated in Chapter 5. It can only help to reinforce the importance of them.

Always arrive to work at least half an hour before the call time. If your call time is 7:00 a.m., then plan on arriving at 6:30 a.m. Check the call sheet and maps the night before so you know your route for the next day. This shows your willingness to work and also your professionalism. If you get in this habit from the very beginning, it will stick with you throughout your career. It also allows for any unexpected delays you may encounter on the way to the job. No matter what, you should always be on set before the 1st AC, ready to begin the workday.

Your attitude is a big part of the reason why you get hired for a job and why you keep the job. One of the first questions that may be asked about you when you are being considered for a job is "How does he get along with others?" or "Does she have a good attitude?" If you are constantly complaining or whining, nobody is going to want to work with you. Have a positive attitude every day on the set. Leave your personal problems at home. If you do, everybody will want to work with you.

Find out which lab is processing the film and establish a relationship with the lab as soon as you are hired. Work it out with the DP and the production office regarding who will be speaking with the lab each day regarding the previous day's footage. Be sure to have all the supplies needed for loading and unloading film. Know the name and telephone number of your lab contact, and be sure to give that person your contact information. Check the darkroom regularly to be sure that it is lightproof. This is especially important when working out of a darkroom on a camera truck. As the truck is driven from location to location, it may be traveling over varied road surfaces. This may cause the walls, ceiling, and door of the darkroom to shift, creating cracks for light to leak in. I recommend checking the camera truck darkroom at the beginning of each shooting day.

Prepare a supply of camera reports beforehand with all of the basic heading information. You may also be able to include film stock information if only using one or two stocks. This saves time during production when you are in a hurry and need a new camera report. It's also a good idea to prepare magazine identification labels beforehand. You can complete all of the basic information, place a label on the side of each film can, and then when the film is loaded, write the magazine number on the label and place the label on the magazine. When preparing a label for a short end of film, be sure to circle the footage amount in a contrasting color to indicate that a short end is loaded into the magazine. If possible, color code magazine labels according to the type of film you are using. By glancing at a magazine or magazine case, you will know what type of film is loaded without having to read the label. You may do this by using different color cloth camera tape for each film stock or by using a different color marker and white tape. When loading fresh film, be very careful when removing the sealing tape on the can and on the roll so that you don't create static electricity. If you remove the tape too quickly, the sparks created could streak the film. Also be very careful when removing the small piece of tape from the actual roll of film. Pulling it off too quickly will also create static electricity and sparks that could streak your film.

Keep your eyes and ears open at all times during rehearsals. Nothing is more irritating to a DP or 1st AC than calling for something from the 2nd AC and hearing nothing but silence. Always respond so that they know that you heard them. Watch rehearsals and be prepared to place marks for actors and camera positions. These marks may change and you should always be prepared to move them if necessary. Directors and DPs don't want to wait for the 2nd AC to make a mark and place it for an actor. Prepare actor marks ahead of time and place them on an unused slate or some other surface. This saves a great deal of time when rehearsing a scene because you only have to quickly remove a mark from the board and place it on the floor for the actor. Color code actor marks so that each actor has his or her own specific color. You may even ask the actor which color he or she would like. Keeping the actors happy makes you look good.

The 1st AC must stay close by the camera and the DP to assist them in any way necessary. The 2nd AC is there to assist the 1st AC by getting equipment when needed, moving equipment for each new setup, and anything else that may be required by the 1st AC, Camera Operator, or DP. This even includes getting drinks or a snack for the 1st AC, Camera Operator, and DP if necessary. This added bit of attention can go a long way to those above you and insure that you will get called for that next job. The camera must never be left unattended, and if the 1st AC must step away, the 2nd AC stands by until he or she returns. Unless the entire cast and crew are on a break, the camera should never be left unattended. When breaking for lunch or any other all-crew break, and the camera will be left unattended, the lens should be removed, the head should be locked, power turned off, battery disconnected and the camera should always be covered. If working outside during the day, the camera can be covered with a space blanket with the silver side facing out. This helps to reflect the sunlight off the camera and keep it cooler.

When charging batteries, you should charge only those that have been used. This should prevent them from building up a memory. Always rotate batteries so that each one gets used equally. After charging, cover the cable port with a piece of white 1-in. camera tape to indicate the battery is charged. Any battery that is not working should be marked with 1-in. red camera tape. Change the battery at lunchtime so that you start the second half of the day with a fresh battery. If filming on location or on a stage be sure that it has been prearranged with the location or stage owners that you may charge the batteries. I know of a situation where an assistant plugged in batteries to charge at the location, and because of a charger malfunction, the location burned down. You should work it out ahead of time where the batteries will be charged. If you can make arrangements for the batteries

to be charged on location or some other location, you should not take batteries home with you to charge because of the previous incident regarding a short and fire. On most of the productions that I worked on I took the batteries home with me to charge and thankfully never had a problem. If there is a problem, in most cases it will not be covered by the production insurance. The production company should make the arrangements as to where batteries will be charged when they are not in use. If charging batteries on location, be sure that the power to the outlets is not turned off in the evening, otherwise you will arrive to work the next day and have no charged batteries. If necessary, you should obtain extra batteries so that there is always adequate power for the equipment.

As the Loader, whenever you are not loading/unloading film or doing paperwork, you should try to be on set as much as possible to assist the 1st and 2nd AC in their duties. But always check with the 1st and 2nd to be sure that this is acceptable to them. Being on set also lets the DP know that you want to learn as much as possible from the other assistants so that some day you may make the move up to their position. Don't be afraid to ask questions. How else will you learn and be able to move up when the time comes?

Even though things must get done as quickly as possible, never run on the set. There are too many cables, equipment, and people on the set. Someone running needlessly and then tripping and getting hurt can cause many more problems. Nothing is that important. You can get things done quickly without running.

When working around the camera, keep your talking to a minimum. If it's necessary to talk, then speak in a low voice or take the conversation off set. The DP may be discussing the shot with the Director or the Gaffer, or the Director may be talking with the actors. Keep quiet and listen to what is going on. If it's necessary to speak with someone, either wait until the time is right or ask him or her to go to another area of the set where it may be quieter. Above all, there is no yelling on any film set. This is a sign of a true nonprofessional. And absolutely NO SMOKING anywhere near the camera or camera equipment.

The entire camera department is a team and must work together. Things that happen within the camera department should remain within the camera department. This is especially important for the 1st AC, 2nd AC, and Loader. If you, as the 2nd AC, must leave the set for any reason, you should inform the 1st AC. If the 1st AC needs you for something and doesn't know where you are, he or she may have to leave the camera unattended to take care of a particular matter like changing lenses or filters. The 1st AC should also inform you whenever he or she leaves the set. This is standard professional courtesy

within any of the departments on a film set. Each department must always be represented on set, at all times.

If you are having personality conflicts with someone in your department or in another department on the crew, try to speak with the person directly, away from the set. Work it out between yourselves so that you can at least have a good working relationship. You may not like the person, but you should at least be able to work together without any conflict.

Whenever any piece of equipment is called for, you should repeat it back to confirm that you heard the request and that you heard it correctly. If your name is called out, you should also respond so that whoever called will know that you heard him or her. As stated previously, repetition is an important element in the proper performance of your job.

When getting a piece of equipment from a case, be sure to close and lock one latch when leaving it. Even if you will be coming right back to the case, at least one latch should be locked. While you are away from the case, somebody may need to move it, and if none of the latches are locked and someone picks up the case, spilling its contents, it will be blamed on the last person who used the case, not the person who picked it up. Camera assistants and trainees have been fired from productions for failure to secure at least one latch of an equipment case.

When changing magazines be sure to enter the new roll number on the ID tape before handing the magazine to the 1st AC. Never give the 1st AC a magazine that does not have an identification label on it, and be sure that this label is completely filled in.

When preparing to shoot any scenes, be sure to obtain the proper scene and take numbers from the Script Supervisor. Place this information on the slate so that it is ready when the camera rolls. As soon as the camera cuts, change the take number to the next highest number so you are ready in case the Director decides to film the shot again. Be prepared to change the scene and take numbers on the slate quickly if the shot changes. Write any information on the slate legibly so that it can be read by all concerned, especially the Editor.

As stated earlier, keep your eyes and ears open at all times so that you are constantly aware of what is happening on the set. As you become familiar with a particular working style of the 1st AC and DP, you should be able to anticipate their requests and be ready when they do make a certain request. The DP may always use a particular lens or filter for the close-up and another for the wide shot. By paying attention and listening you will know when a new scene is being shot and will have the lens or filter ready when it is called for. Watch the DP and Director when they are blocking out the scene. If possible,

listen to what they are saying. They may be discussing using a particular lens for the next shot, and you can have the lens ready when it is called for. Knowing where the next scene or setup is located will give you an idea of where the camera is to be placed, and it will also be an indication of where you can move the equipment so that it is close by.

Unless you are told or asked by the 1st AC, never go into his or her toolkit, front box, or ditty bag without permission. If something is needed from these, the 1st AC will either get it personally or give you permission to get it. You wouldn't like someone using your tools without permission, so treat the 1st AC with the same consideration. It's like going into someone's home without permission. It's all about professional courtesy and common sense.

Know where all the camera equipment is at all times. Keep all equipment organized and in its proper place. If it is kept in the same place all of the time, it can easily be located when you are in a hurry. This applies to both the camera truck and equipment carts. When on stage or location, you should have some type of four-wheeled cart, such as the Magliner equipment cart or Rubbermaid utility cart, for moving the equipment from place to place. You will have many equipment cases to deal with each day, and it is much easier and quicker if they can be wheeled from place to place instead of individually carried. Whenever the camera is moved to a new location, the cart or carts should also be moved as quickly as possible.

Most important, if you make a mistake, tell someone immediately, usually the 1st AC, and if you are the Loader, tell the 2nd AC. This information should be communicated quietly so as not to alarm anybody else. It may not be as bad as you think, and keeping it between the 1st AC, 2nd AC, and Loader usually allows you to take care of it without anybody finding out. If you must tell the DP or any other production personnel, do it quickly and quietly.

Filmmaking involves a lot of what many people refer to as "hurry up and wait." There is often a lot of downtime on the set for the assistants while a new lighting setup is being done, etc. While it may be tempting to take the opportunity to sit down and relax for a few minutes, as soon as you do somebody from production will walk by and think you are goofing off. When it is necessary for you to take a break and sit, it is most important you should be as close to the set as possible so that if you are needed you will hear your name called and nobody needs to search for you. Try to find a job or task that you can do while sitting, so even if somebody walks by, you are still busy working. Perhaps you can prepare some camera reports and inventory forms for future filming days. Or you can make film can or magazine labels for upcoming rolls of film. You could clean equipment cases, inventory equipment, organize the camera carts, and much more.

There is a lot that can still be done while you are sitting down. You get off your feet for a little while but are still active, and everyone will be impressed with your work ethic and attitude.

As a 2nd AC, you must be able to work very closely with the DP, the Camera Operator, and the 1st AC. Keep in mind that everybody does things differently. Be flexible, and when working with a new crew, try to do things the way they want. After a while you will develop a system of doing things that works best for you. But don't forget that you will always have to adjust your way of doing things when working with others who have their own system. Remember, the DP or 1st AC are probably the ones who hired you for the job, so if they want things done a certain way, you should do it their way. Showing your willingness to adjust to their way of doing things will only encourage them to hire you for future projects. As you become more comfortable working with certain crew members, you may suggest an alternative way of carrying out a task if it works better for you. Each job will be slightly different, and as you work more and more it will be much easier for you to judge when and if you can suggest alternatives to doing a particular task.

When filling out the time sheets/time cards for the camera crew, be sure that you have all of the times, rates, addresses, phone numbers, etc., correct so that there are no errors in somebody else's paycheck. Don't be afraid to check and double check with each crew member before turning in the paperwork to production.

It's a good idea to have some basic tools and expendables in your pouch, or nearby on the camera cart in case of emergency. Keep some extra strips of Velcro in your pouch, assorted video connectors, including BNC barrels, t-connectors and RCA to BNC adapters, small rolls of tape, etc. When working with any Arriflex cameras you might want to keep a 1.3 mm, 1.5 mm, and 3 mm allen wrench with you in case of any needed adjustment on the camera. Each job will be different from the previous job, so adjust things accordingly. If you have some basic items on you or nearby, it will save time and only make you look better because you will always be prepared. Believe me, people will notice this and remember when it comes to hire a Loader or 2nd AC for future projects.

Always maintain a positive and professional attitude, and if you are ever unsure of something, do not be afraid to ask. Always do your job to the best of your ability, and if you make a mistake, admit it so that it can be corrected. Remember that someday you may be in the position of the 1st AC, DP, or Operator and will deal with the same situations and problems, and you would want the persons working for you to act professionally.

Resources

During your career as an Assistant Cameraman, you will rely on a variety of professional resources to enable you to do your job completely. This includes camera manufacturers and rental companies, expendables companies, film laboratories, sellers of film raw stock, professional organizations, and many more. You should have all contact information for these companies readily available in case you need something at the last minute or in case of emergency. Most of us have some type of smart phone or other electronic device like an iPod or iPad. Using the Contact App in both of these, you should set up files with the addresses and contact information for all of the companies that you deal with on a daily basis in the performance of your job.

Rather than list here all of the possible names, addresses, telephone numbers, and email addresses for the various companies, I have created a Links page on the companion web site for this book. Because companies move and change addresses, telephone numbers, and email addresses quite frequently, it's not practical to list them in the book. The Links page of the web site will be updated on a regular basis so that you should be able to have the most current information for any of the companies that are listed. In addition to the various companies and suppliers that you will be dealing with, the web site also includes many links to industry-related web sites for listing your résumé and searching for jobs, as well as sites for related departments, such as grip and lighting. In addition to the Links page, I have created a page on the web site with recommended cinematography apps for the iPhone, iPad, and iPod Touch. If you have web sites or know of any web sites or apps that you would like to see included, please feel free to contact me by email.

POSTPRODUCTION

Postproduction is the time after the shooting of the film is done. This is the time when the editing is completed and all promotional and distribution details of the production are worked out and finalized. The 2nd AC may work only one or two days during postproduction, depending on the size of the project. On very small projects there may be no postproduction time for the 2nd AC. The entire wrap-up may be completed at the end of the last day of filming or may be done solely by the 1st AC. Postproduction for the camera department means that all equipment must be cleaned, checked, and packed away so that it can be returned to the rental company. A final inventory of film

stock and expendables is usually done and turned in to the production office. If a camera truck was used, it should be cleaned out for the next production's use. Finally, the 2nd AC packs up all his or her gear and gets ready for the next job call, where the entire process starts all over again.

Wrapping Equipment

Either on the final day or immediately following the final day of production, the camera equipment, camera truck, and anything else related to the camera department must be wrapped. This means that everything should be cleaned and packed away. All equipment must be inventoried, cleaned, packed, and sent back to the camera rental house. The wrap can take anywhere from a few hours to an entire day, depending on the size of the camera package. Rarely does it take more than one day to wrap out the camera department unless it is an unusually large production with multiple cameras and equipment. Usually the 1st AC wraps out the camera equipment, while the 2nd AC wraps out the truck, darkroom, and film stock. Many times, if it is a small production, only the 1st AC wraps the camera equipment. All equipment should be cleaned and any tape or other markings removed from equipment and cases. All equipment should be placed in the proper equipment case. If you look at the Expendables Inventory and Checklist in Appendix C (Figure C.3), you will notice that I have listed cleaning supplies. I believe that it is important to send equipment back to the rental company in the same or better condition than when you received it. This means cleaning each piece of equipment before placing it in the equipment case. If you show the rental company that you take care of their equipment, they will be more inclined to help you in the future. You should have a copy of the original packing slip listing all of the equipment so that you may use it to double check that you are sending back everything that you received. Any discrepancies should be reported to the production office immediately. The truck and darkroom should be left clean for the next job. A final inventory of the film stock should be done, and all remaining film raw stock should be packed in boxes for the production office.

WORKING IN DIGITAL VIDEO

With so many productions being shot in the digital format these days, I thought it would be a good idea to include some basic information about the job responsibilities of the Camera Assistants when working

in that format. Most of my production experience has been working on film productions, so I have obtained this information from colleagues who have more experience in this area. To my knowledge, it is as complete and accurate as possible. Special thanks go out to all who contributed to the information in this section.

Unfortunately, many producers believe that you don't need a full crew when shooting a digital production. In fact, you should have the same number of crew positions in the camera department as when shooting film. Depending on the type of production, but especially if you are doing a film-style shoot, there should always be a separate Camera Operator so that the DP can be near the monitor when shooting to ensure that the image looks correct. You need a 1st AC and a 2nd AC because of the additional equipment needed along with the variety of cables that may be connected to the camera. The shots still must be kept in focus, marks placed for actors, slates recorded, reports filled out, and much more. Although there is no loading of film involved when working in digital, a 2nd AC should still be hired. Many DPs feel that a 2nd AC is needed now more than ever because of all of the cables and equipment to move every time you move the camera to a new setup. On many digital shoots, there may be both a 2nd AC and a Digital Utility person, or there may be only one of these positions. Whatever name or title you give to this person, the person hired will perform many of the tasks listed later. To keep with the standard film titles that I am most familiar with, I will use the term 2nd AC when referring to this job classification even though the Digital Utility person may do many of these tasks.

Preproduction

As stated earlier in this chapter, the 2nd AC works with the 1st AC to prepare the list of supplies and expendables needed for the production. Many of the expendable items are the same as for a film shoot, but you probably won't need as much 1-in. cloth camera tape since you won't be loading and unloading film. The tape may still be used for labeling equipment and other uses as with a film production. Some items unique to digital productions are SD cards as well as a sensor cleaning kit. Some cameras have the ability to update the firmware in the camera. The SD card is used to download the updates and install them in the camera. In addition to the SD cards you should also have a card reader for downloading the updates. The SD cards should be at least 4GB in size. Both of these may be ordered with the expendables, but it is recommended that the 2nd AC have some of their own in their ditty bag. The sensor cleaning kit is used to

periodically clean dirt or dust from the recording sensor of the digital camera.

Although most productions now use some type of memory card or hard drive, you may be working on a production using a tape-based camera. If using a tape-based camera you should obtain a supply of tapes and prepare the labels for these tapes with the basic production information. Anything you prepare beforehand will save you time in the long run. When shooting digital and using memory cards or hard drives you should number these just as you would number the film magazines. In the digital format we continue to use the term "Magazine" and "Mag Number" on camera reports but instead of referring to a film magazine you are referring to a particular memory card or hard drive. The "mag number" remains the same throughout the production, but each time you use it, a different roll number is assigned. Because there is no need for a darkroom for loading and unloading film, a camera truck equipped with a darkroom is still important because the 2nd AC will often use the darkroom as their area where they import the footage into the hard drives and/or computers before sending it to postproduction. You need a secure area to do this so that you are not disturbed and don't make a mistake. And with any production, the truck will still be necessary for the transportation of equipment, although it may be set up differently from a standard film camera truck. The 2nd AC may work with the 1st AC and/or Digital Utility person to clean and load the truck with all of the equipment.

Production

As with a film production, when all preproduction procedures have ended it is time for filming to start. Putting any production together, whether film or digital, can be a complex and time-consuming operation that requires both dedication and endurance from everyone involved. The production phase of a digital shoot can be as complex as a film shoot or it may be a very simple production. In any event, a great deal of hard work and attention to detail is required on the part of all involved, especially the 2nd AC. Proper performance of the duties and responsibilities of the 2nd AC is vital to the smooth operation of the production. You must keep track of memory cards or hard drives, which scenes are shot and how many takes of each are shot, check the settings of the digital camera, monitor, or other equipment; and many other aspects of the job. You should be very organized and able to jump in at a moment's notice with any piece of information or equipment needed during shooting. Each day will require many shots

and setups to get the day's work completed. The 2nd AC must accurately keep track of all of this information.

Setting Up the Camera

The 2nd AC often helps the 1st AC set up the camera at the beginning of the shoot day. The 2nd AC helps set up and connect the monitor to the camera and helps the Digital Imaging Technician connect the camera to any external recorder and other devices, if necessary. Because there may be more cables involved with a digital production, the 2nd AC should be familiar with all of the cables and their proper connection. If there are multiple lenses and accessories, the 2nd AC will retrieve those items very much like what is done on a film set. Be sure to have spare batteries, memory cards, lenses, filters, and the focus chart near the camera at all times. You may also want to have your laptop computer nearby for ease of downloading the footage after it has been shot. Depending on what camera system you are using, you may need additional hard drives for recording or downloading the footage. These are often rented along with the camera equipment.

Camera Reports

Camera reports are still used when shooting digital but are a bit different than film style camera reports. With digital camera reports you should keep track of scene and take numbers and may also need to record clip numbers, project fps, ASA/ISO, codec, color temperature and other information from the camera or recorder. When starting productions you typically set some base settings into the camera. Many of these settings are written on the camera reports for reference. One of these settings is referred to as codec, which is a derived from the words compression and decompression or coder and decoder. The codec is the digital sampling rate, which is the ratio used to digitize the luminance and color components of an image. Some common codecs are ProRes 422 LT, ProRes 422 HQ, and ProRes 444. The ASA/ISO is the exposure index setting and has a direct impact on the overall image related to the color temperature that you set on the camera. The color temperature is based on the light source you are filming under. Most digital cameras have a base or native color temperature of the sensor. This is the ideal color temperature in which the lowest overall gain is applied to the red, green, and blue pixels, which also results in the lowest video noise in the image. The project fps is the number of frames per second that the time code is counting and is the frame rate used for playback of QuickTime clips. On some cameras you set your project fps to the usual 24 or 30 fps, and if you wish to

shoot a shot either in high speed or slow motion, you would adjust the fps of the sensor.

Some assistants who I have known say that it is not necessary to record much of this information, but that will vary depending on the production, the camera being used and, most importantly, the requirements of the Director of Photography. Many DPs working in digital have very specific requirements as to how the camera is set up and what information is kept track of. I recommend keeping detailed notes so that if there is any question you have a record for all the shots. The Script Supervisor often has extensive notes regarding the specifics of the shot, actor movements, etc., but in most cases the 2nd AC will also keep extensive notes regarding camera settings so that there is no chance for error. When working with many of the newer digital format cameras such as the Arriflex Alexa or Red One, Epic or Scarlet it is common to keep track of clip numbers and the amount of data space used for each clip along with other information that is specific to shooting on digital. These cameras record onto a hard drive or a memory card, so you will want to keep a record of how many gigabytes the shot required so you know when to download the footage and start with a clean card or fresh hard drive.

Check with the 1st AC or DP on the production to find out what information they want you to keep track of on the camera report. You may also need to keep track of any other information about how the camera is set up, shutter angle, white balance, filters used either in front of the lens or set into the camera menus, and any unique adjustments to the settings in the menus. This information should be recorded onto a camera report, and if there is not enough space on the camera report for all this information, I recommend keeping a separate log book. Examples of digital camera reports can be found in Figures 4.68 and 4.69.

Using many different versions of digital camera reports I have designed a general camera report specifically for digital that can be found in Appendix C. This Digital Camera Report (Figure C.12) is also available for download on the companion web site for this book.

Magazines

When shooting digital you don't use film magazines as when shooting film but the term is still used in reference to the media cards or hard drives. On large productions you may have 25–30 media cards. Each of these is assigned a number just like when using film magazines. If you are recording to a hard drive, then the drive is given a "mag" number. If the card or hard drive has a serial number, then I recommend using that number as your mag number. Each time the footage is

ARRI ALEXA
ARRI DIGITAL CAMERA REPORT

CAMERA #	REEL #

PRODUCTION	DIRECTOR
DATE	DIRECTOR OF PHOTOGRAPHY
1ST AC	2ND AC

MAG #	SHEET #

SCENE	TAKE	CLIP	FPS	REMARKS	SCENE	TAKE	CLIP	FPS	REMARKS

LOADER	SIGNATURE

Designed By: Kevin J Burroughs

Figure 4.68 Example of a digital camera report. (Courtesy of Kevin J. Burroughs.)

transferred and the card or drive formatted to continue shooting, you would assign a new "roll" number but the mag number would stay the same, just as when shooting film. Be aware that you should not confuse the recording drives with the backup drives. Backup drives are used to download and store footage that has been shot. They must be labeled differently and kept separate and away from all recording drives so that there is no confusion.

Marking Actors

Just as in film production, actors still must be given marks for lighting and focusing purposes. The 2nd AC will place tape on the floor for each actor's position during a shot or scene. It's a good idea to have marks prepared ahead of time so that you are not holding up the production. Look at the section on marking actors earlier in this chapter.

Slates and Slating Procedures

Again, just like in film, you should use a slate to identify the roll, card or hard drive numbers, scene or clip, and take numbers for each shot according to the needs of the production. You never know when or if the camera, recorder, or editing system may malfunction.

FOTOKEM
Digital Camera Report

Date
/ /

Camera Roll #
☐ Mono
☐ Stereo

Mag#

Production Co:

Title: Episode:

Director: DP:

D.I.T. / Data: Contact #:

Format: ☐ ARRIRAW (.ari) ☐ Canon (.mov) ☐ EPIC (.r3d) ☐ ProRes (.mov) ☐ RED MX(.r3d) ☐ Other

Record Media: ☐ Compact Flash ☐ Recorder Mag ☐ SSD Mag ☐ SxS ☐ Other:

Project Frame Rate: ☐ 23.98 ☐ 25 ☐ 29.97   **FPS / Varispeed:**

Shutter Speed: **Shutter Angle:**   **ISO/EI:**

Kelvin / WB: ☐ 3200 ☐ 5400 ☐ other: **Int. Audio:** ☐ 2ch ☐ 4ch ☐ TOD T.C.

Scene	Take	Clip/File	Comment

www.fotokem.com/digitalcamreport   2801 W Alameda Ave. Burbank, CA 91505 (818) 846-3101

Figure 4.69 Example of a digital camera report. (Courtesy of FotoKem Industries, Inc.)

Many productions today don't use a slate, but I strongly recommend that you use one whenever possible to properly identify the shots. Episodic or long-format television and features quite often use a slate. As stated previously when discussing shooting film, a tail slate is one that is photographed at the end of the take. There has been some discussion as to whether a "tail slate" is necessary when shooting digital, since each shot is separated from the previous shot by the fact that it is a digital file. You may want to check with the Script Supervisor, or even the Editor if possible, whether they would like you to do a traditional tail slate when shooting digital.

Moving the Camera and Setting Up the Video Monitor

Whenever the camera needs to be moved to a new setup or camera position, the 1st AC will disconnect all cables from the camera and pass them to the 2nd AC, who assists in moving the camera to its new location. When the camera position is established, the cables can be reconnected. At the start of the day, the 2nd AC most often will set up a monitor for the DP and Director and connect it to the camera or video recorder. Any additional monitors for other people to see may also be initially set up by the 2nd AC, but during the course of the shooting day, the primary responsibility is to move and set up the monitor for the DP and Director. Any other monitors being used may require another crew member, such as a Camera Trainee or Production Assistant, to move and connect them for any camera moves because the 2nd AC has other responsibilities to attend to.

Preparing Media Cards and Hard Drives

Although you will not download film and prepare it for delivery to the lab, you still must prepare media cards, hard drives, camera reports, and other paperwork for delivery to the Editor, production office, or postproduction facility. Be sure that all media cards and hard drives are labeled correctly with all of the pertinent production information. Each should be numbered and may have a separate camera report with it showing all of the scene numbers, take numbers, and clip numbers. When removing a media card from the camera, the 1st AC should mark it in such a way to indicate that it has been used or is "HOT" and must not be used until the footage has been downloaded and checked by postproduction. Typically the 1st AC would mark the card with Red tape to indicate that it is "HOT" and ready to be downloaded. The 1st AC should write the roll number on the red tape so that there is no confusion, and then give the hot card to the 2nd AC. The 2nd AC should physically give the card to the Loader or DIT for

downloading. Once downloaded, the card should be marked in green tape to indicate that is ready to be reformatted. The card with green tape is then physically delivered back to the 2nd AC, who then gives it to the 1st AC for formatting in the camera. It is best to format the cards in the camera that is using them so that there are no issues with the firmware.

Ordering Additional Media Cards

Just as you must keep a careful watch on your film inventory for a film production, you must also be sure that you have enough media cards when working in digital video. You should never run out of cards. It is common practice to start a production with an appropriate number of media cards so running out would not be a problem. But if you get into a situation where you need to get more cards, notify the DP and UPM immediately. You should never rush to recycle and format a used memory card without being completely sure that it has been downloaded and backed up in at least two places. Be sure to request the proper format and size cards. Be aware of the differences between regular media cards and Pro or other media cards. In many cases, they may not be interchangeable. For example, when working with the Arriflex Alexa you must use Sony SxS Pro Cards. The Sony SxS-1 Cards or other third party SxS Cards are not supported by the Alexa.

Storage and Care of Media Cards

It is critical to have a system where you keep used or HOT memory cards separate from blank, formatted cards that are ready to use. Many assistants keep them separated in small plastic storage boxes, with one box marked in red tape to indicate a HOT card that needs to be downloaded and one box marked in green tape to indicate that the cards are good to GO, have been formatted and can be used. The important thing is to never reuse a card until the footage has been downloaded, backed up, and checked. Always keep cards away from magnetic fields and electronic motors.

Videotapes, X-Rays, and Magnetic Fields

Unlike when traveling with film, airport X-rays do not affect or damage digital media cards. There have been extensive tests conducted. But if you are still uncomfortable transporting media cards and having them pass through the X-ray machines, you could still request that they be hand inspected.

Tools and Accessories

Many of the same tools and accessories required for film are required when working in digital production. Although you may not use them all, I am a firm believer in the saying "It's better to have it and not need it than to need it and not have it." Have the appropriate tools and materials available for cleaning the sensor. You should never use any commercially available compressed air for cleaning the sensor. The chemicals in the product can and will damage the sensor, causing a major repair bill before the camera can be used. You should have a supply of various video connectors and video cables in your ditty bag as well. You never know when you may need a specific connector or when a cable may break, and having the right replacement could save a production time and money. When working with the Alexa or other HD cameras you should have one or two SD memory cards, up to 4GB in size, along with an SD card reader. These are used to download/ upload any software updates for the camera as well as LUT files and frame grabs. There are also some specialized tools from Arri that may be used on both film and digital cameras.

Postproduction

As with film productions, postproduction is the time when the editing is completed and all promotional and distribution details of the production are worked out and finalized. Just as when working in film, the 2nd AC may or may not be involved in the postproduction for the camera department, which is primarily checking and cleaning all camera equipment so that it may be returned to the rental company. The 2nd AC may do a final inventory of media cards and expendables for the production office. If a camera truck is used, it should be cleaned out for the next production's use. And finally, the 2nd AC packs up all his or her gear and gets ready for the next job call, when the entire process starts all over again.

Wrapping Equipment

When wrapping equipment and packing it away at the end of the day or at the end of the shoot, you should follow the same procedures as outlined in the Wrapping Equipment section for film shoots. If you will continue to shoot on another day and the camera is being shipped to a new location, it is a very good idea to write down all of your camera settings so that if settings change during transportation you can reset the camera to its original settings for shooting. Once you arrive

at the new location you should check the camera settings to be sure that nothing has changed. Some cameras have the ability to lock the settings so that they do not change. If your camera has this feature, be sure to lock everything before transporting or moving the camera.

REVIEW CHECKLIST FOR SECOND ASSISTANT CAMERAMAN (2ND AC OR CLAPPER/LOADER)

Preproduction

- On film shoots obtains a supply of empty cans, black bags, camera reports, and cores from the lab or asks the production office to arrange this
- Prepares a list of expendables with the 1st AC
- Preps the camera package along with the 1st AC
- Cleans the camera truck and/or darkroom for use during the production and ensures that each is loaded with the proper supplies and equipment
- Labels all media cards and hard drives with "mag" numbers so that they are ready to be used for recording

Production

- Checks with Loader (if there is one) to be sure that all film magazines are loaded and properly labeled
- Loads and unloads film in the magazines and places proper identification on each if there is no Loader
- Checks darkroom, if necessary, on a daily basis to be sure that it is lightproof
- Communicates with the Script Supervisor to obtain the scene and take numbers for each shot and also which takes are to be printed
- Records all information on the slate
- Records all information on the camera reports
- Checks with the Script Supervisor as to what takes are to be printed for each scene
- Helps to set up the camera at the start of each shooting day
- Marks the position of actors during the rehearsals
- Slates each scene, whether sound (sync) or silent (MOS)
- Assists in changing lenses, filters, magazines, and so on, and in moving the camera to each new position
- Sets up and moves the video monitor for each new camera setup and makes sure the cable is connected to the film camera

- Prepares exposed film for delivery to the lab and delivers it to the production company representative at the end of each shooting day
- Prepares exposed media cards for download
- Cans and labels any film recans or short ends
- Serves as camera department contact with the production office, film laboratory, and camera equipment rental house
- Maintains a record of all film received, film shot, short ends created, and film on hand at the end of each shooting day during the production
- Maintains an inventory of film stock and expendables on hand and requests additional film stock and supplies from the production office as needed
- Maintains an inventory of media cards used, total number of clips on each roll, and total gigabytes on each roll
- Ensures that "Hot" cards are delivered to Loader/DIT for downloading and checking before cards are reformatted for use
- Maintains an inventory of camera equipment on hand, additional equipment ordered, and any equipment that has been damaged or returned
- Distributes copies of the camera reports and film inventory forms to the appropriate departments
- Keeps a file of all paperwork relating to the camera department during the production: camera reports, daily film inventory forms, processing reports from the lab, equipment packing lists, expendable requests, etc.
- Keeps a record of all hours worked by the camera department and prepares time sheets at the end of each day
- Performs the job of 1st AC, if necessary, in the absence of the 1st AC or when additional cameras are used
- Works with the 1st AC to move the camera to each new position
- Works with the 1st AC to ensure that all camera batteries are kept fully charged and ready for use
- At the end of each shooting day, helps the 1st AC pack away all camera equipment in a safe place
- Provides all the necessary tools and accessories associated with performing the job

Postproduction

- At the completion of filming, helps the 1st AC wrap and clean all camera equipment for return to the rental house
- At the completion of filming, cleans and wraps the camera truck

REVIEW CHECKLIST FOR FILM LOADER (LOADER)

The Film Loader is not included on all film productions, but in the event you do have the luxury of having a Loader, these are some of their responsibilities.

Preproduction

- May obtain a supply of empty cans, black bags, camera reports, and cores from the lab or asks the production office to arrange this
- Prepares a list of expendables with the 2nd AC
- Cleans the darkroom for use during the production and ensures that it is loaded with the proper supplies and equipment

Production

- Maintains an inventory of all film stock initially received from the production company
- Maintains a record of all film received, film shot, short ends created, and film on hand at the end of each shooting day during the production
- Keeps a file of all paperwork relating to the camera department during the production: camera reports, daily film inventory forms, processing reports from the lab, equipment packing lists, expendable requests, etc.
- Keeps a record of all hours worked by the camera department and prepares time cards at the end of each day or week
- Checks darkroom, if necessary, on a daily basis to be sure that it is lightproof
- Loads and unloads all film magazines during the course of filming
- Properly labels all loaded film magazines, cans of exposed film and short ends, and recans of unexposed film
- Prepares exposed film for delivery to the lab and delivers it to the production company representative at the end of each shooting day
- Distributes copies of the camera reports and film inventory forms to the appropriate departments
- Provides all the necessary tools and accessories associated with performing the job

5

First Assistant Cameraman (1st AC)

After two or three years, you probably will move up from Second Assistant Cameraman (2nd AC) to First Assistant Cameraman (1st AC). In Britain, Europe, and Australia, the 1st AC is usually referred to as the Focus Puller. During production the 1st AC works directly with the 2nd AC, the Camera Operator, and especially the Director of Photography (DP).

The position of 1st AC requires great attention to detail. The 1st AC should stay as close as possible to the DP during shooting and be prepared for any number of requests. Keeping your eyes and ears open at all times and never being too far from the DP or the camera is a sign of a good 1st AC. A good 1st AC must be able to anticipate what the DP wants and respond to it immediately. You should know as much as possible about a wide variety of camera equipment and accessories.

The more you know, the more jobs you will get. One of the primary responsibilities during shooting is to maintain sharp focus throughout each shot. The 1st AC is also responsible for the smooth running of the camera department and maintenance of all camera equipment, as well as many other duties. This chapter discusses in detail each of the 1st AC's duties and responsibilities. These duties are separated into three categories: preproduction, production, and postproduction.

PREPRODUCTION

On most productions, the 1st AC will usually be involved in many of the preproduction events. This involvement usually requires meetings with the DP to discuss the camera equipment and film stock that will be used for the shoot. There may also be preproduction meetings with

many of the key crew members to discuss the production. The 1st AC will often discuss the expendables order with the 2nd AC before it is submitted to the production office. In addition, the 1st AC must perform the camera prep, which is when all of the camera equipment is checked and tested to be sure that it is in proper working order before production. The camera prep is perhaps the most important job of the 1st AC during the preproduction stage. Each job may be a bit different, but the camera prep is as important to a one-day commercial shoot as it is to a six-week feature or nine-month television series. The 1st AC wants to feel confident that when he or she walks onto the set, he or she has all of the equipment needed and that everything works properly.

Choosing Camera Equipment

During preproduction, the DP will often prepare a list of camera equipment that will be needed on the production. Many times this list is prepared with the 1st AC, and sometimes the DP prepares the list and then sends it to the 1st AC for additional items to be added. Because the 1st AC works with the equipment daily, he or she usually knows which accessories are needed to make the shooting go as smoothly as possible. The DP will choose the camera, lenses, and filters, and the 1st AC usually determines which accessories are needed to complete the camera package. You should have a working knowledge of all camera systems, as well as the accessories for each, and have copies of rental catalogs from various rental houses to help in choosing the proper equipment. Camera rental houses will give you a copy of their current rental catalog at no charge, and most are available online. Appendix C contains a Film Camera Equipment Checklist (Figure C.1) that can be used to prepare the initial camera package order. This form is also available for download from the companion web site of this book. The web site also contains a Links page to many of the camera rental companies in the film industry.

Choosing and Ordering Expendables

During preproduction you should make a list of the expendables (consumables in Britain) needed for the camera department. As discussed in Chapter 4, this list is prepared by both the 1st AC and the 2nd AC. Each may need specialty items to do his or her job, which should be included along with the standard items. The standard expendables are items that will be needed in the daily performance of your job, such as camera tape, permanent felt-tip markers, ballpoint pens, compressed

air, lens tissue, lens cleaning solution, and so on. They are referred to as expendables because they are items that are used up or expended during the course of the production. The size and type of production determines which items and how many of each is needed. After the initial order, the 2nd AC, Loader or Camera PA/Trainee is responsible for checking the supply on a regular basis to make sure that you do not run out of anything. For a complete list of the standard items on a camera department expendables list, see the Expendables Inventory and Checklist in Appendix C (Figure C.3).

Preparation of Camera Equipment

Before you shoot one frame of film, the camera and all related accessories must be checked to be sure that everything is in working order. When you know when the production will begin filming and the equipment has been ordered, contact the rental house and arrange a time when you can do the camera prep, or the Production Manager may have already made the arrangements and will let you know when to prep the camera. A camera prep can take anywhere from a couple of hours to a few days or even a week depending on the size of the production and the amount of equipment. Early in my career I was given a full week to prep the camera package for a low-budget feature film. Even though I didn't need a full week, I was able to do a thorough prep to be sure that I had everything and that it worked properly.

Be sure to allow enough time to complete the prep so that you are not rushed and are able to check each piece of equipment thoroughly. Also be sure that you are adequately compensated for the prep. It should be part of your original deal. Many productions try to pay a half-day rate for your prep. I don't agree with this because no matter how long the prep takes, you are being taken out of the workforce for an entire day. You should get paid your full-day rate for the prep. I'll leave that decision up to you when the time comes and will say that there have been many jobs that I did that only paid a half-day rate for prep. My feeling is a half-day rate is better than nothing, but each person's situation is going to be different. When you go to the rental house, take along your tools and accessories. Have some dummy loads of film to use for scratch testing the magazines. A dummy load is a small spool of film left over from previous shoots and is listed as waste on the camera report. Instead of throwing out the dummy load, many assistants save these short lengths of film for use during the camera prep.

The primary purpose of doing the camera prep is to ensure that you have all the necessary camera equipment and accessories and that

they are in working order and work together. Each item, no matter how small, must be checked and tested. Starting with the spreader, tripod, and head, you should assemble the entire camera package. Each accessory is attached to the camera and tested. Lenses are checked for sharpness and accurate focus; magazines are tested for noise and to be sure that they don't scratch the film, etc. Power cables are checked to be sure that they work properly. If you find any piece of equipment that does not perform satisfactorily during the prep, send it back immediately and request a replacement. Keep in mind that the one thing you don't check during the camera prep is probably the one thing that will not work at some point during the production, and even if you check everything, something will inevitably go wrong during the production. It's just a fact of life on a film set: Sometimes things don't go smoothly no matter how much preparation you do. The Film Camera Prep Checklist includes the many items found in a typical camera rental package and describes what you should check for during the camera prep. Remember, all items on the list may not be needed on every production. Because of the many different types of productions and the differences between DPs and what equipment they use, it would be impossible to come up with one checklist to cover all possible shooting situations. I have listed the most basic items that will be found on many productions. You can modify this checklist to suit your particular production needs. All camera packages may not have every item listed. Appendix C contains a Film Camera Prep Checklist for your use (Figure C.4). When you arrive at the rental house, the first thing you should do is a preliminary inventory check to see if you have most of the items on your camera equipment list. Compare the rental house listing with any list prepared by you, the DP, and/or the production company. I recommend lining up the cases, opening them, and giving them a quick visual check to see if you have all of the basic items. As you spend time checking each item, you will most likely discover some items that you didn't originally catch when doing the preliminary inventory check. As stated earlier, compare your equipment list with the list that the rental house has prepared for your production.

Sometimes the production company may tell you that there isn't enough money in the budget for a prep. This may happen because the production company doesn't see the need and wants to spend the money elsewhere. If they don't want to pay for a prep then there isn't much you can do. However, what you can do is tell them what equipment you need, hope it's there and if it isn't there on the first day of production, be sure to be clear with them that you won't be held accountable for any equipment not ordered or not in working condition. If the camera gear is coming from one of the better rental

houses, you can probably rest assured that everything you need will be there. The best thing to do is to keep a positive attitude and do the best job you can under the circumstances. It doesn't pay to stress out over something beyond your control.

Because of the tendency now more than ever for production companies to not schedule a prep, I have created a form called the Non-prep Disclaimer which basically states that the Camera Assistant won't be held responsible for any missing equipment or any equipment that doesn't work at the start of production. The form should be sent to the production company with instructions for them to sign it and send it back so that there is no question or problem later on. The Non-prep Disclaimer that I created is a modification of a similar form used by Los Angeles-based Camera Assistant Wayne Baker. Wayne has granted permission for me to modify his form and use it in the book. An example of this form can be found in Appendix C (Figure C.5) and on the companion web site for the book.

The Rental House

Before going to the camera rental house to prep, you should contact the staff to be sure that everything is ready for you. They will tell you what time they have scheduled for the prep for your particular production. When you arrive, all or most of your equipment should be set aside in an area where you can work. At the rental house you should first check their list against the list that you made with the DP to be sure that you have everything. If any item is missing, request it immediately. A technician or prep tech from the rental house will be assigned to you, and this is the person you will communicate with about any problems or questions regarding your equipment.

As a Camera Assistant, please be aware that the rental house prep tech's job is not simply to pull the items requested off a shelf. Before you arrived at the rental house, the tech has done the same prep, if not a more in-depth prep, as the one you will be doing. Each piece of equipment has been thoroughly checked to be sure that it works. And because you are the person who is responsible for the equipment on the production, it is to your advantage to check each item before production begins.

The camera and equipment you have requested will most often be prepared for you and be ready at the time scheduled for the prep. However, remember that you are not the only production that the rental house is dealing with at that time; therefore, all of your equipment may not be ready. The prep tech may be working with more than one production company, so you should have a little patience when asking for something if you do not get it right away. The prep

is usually scheduled a few days prior to production, and you should be prepared to work around the rental house's schedule. The rental house will do its best to accommodate your schedule, but sometimes you may have to prep a little earlier or later than planned. If you need to add any items to your list, be sure that you have the approval from your production company and the rental house because a deal may have been previously negotiated. Additional equipment may not be part of the original agreement, and the production company needs to know what add-ons you have requested so they can authorize it and make additional arrangements with the rental company. If it is an item that is absolutely necessary, the rental house will most often work out an arrangement that is agreeable to all concerned. As a Camera Assistant, it is important to have a good working relationship with the camera rental house. If you have treated the staff and their equipment properly in the past, they will be more inclined to help you out when a production company does not have a large budget but you need a few additional items. I was working for a small production and prepping the camera package at one of the major camera rental houses in Hollywood. They had worked out a special price deal for the equipment with the rental house. I asked for a few items that were not included in the original camera package. Because of the excellent relationship that I had with the rental house, the few additional items that I requested were included in the camera package at no additional charge because the rental house knew me, trusted me, and, most important, knew that I would take care of their equipment.

A negative attitude will not be tolerated at the rental house. A rental house tech told me of one show that he had prepped where the production company only had a specific amount of money that they could spend for the equipment. The AC attempted to get more equipment than the production company was prepared to pay for and was told that he could not have the items. The AC then began to throw a fit, claiming these were items that were needed to do the show properly and they must be included. Needless to say, he did not get the items and was not very welcome in the rental house after that. A good attitude can go a long way in this business, and a bad attitude will stop you in your tracks. You'll get a bad reputation very fast, and very few people will want to work with you.

The rental house prep tech is there to service the needs of the AC and production company regarding the equipment needed for production, but the prep techs are not your personal servants and do not jump when called. The prep tech is there to help, and if you are unfamiliar with a piece of equipment, please ask about it. The prep tech would rather spend the time answering the question and showing you how something works than fixing it after it was broken through error.

But remember, you must be patient as to how quickly your questions are answered because there are other rentals going out at the same time.

Although I have worked in the industry for quite some time and have worked with many of the currently used camera systems, I sometimes forget things. I have heard it said many times, "If you don't use it, you lose it." I was doing a prep and came across a piece of equipment that I had not used for a long time. I asked the prep tech to answer some questions about the equipment. He was busy at the time but said he would come back when he could. I continued with the prep, and when the prep tech finished what he was doing, he returned to me to answer the questions. If you have forgotten how something works, don't be afraid to ask. It's better to admit that you don't know or don't remember how something works than to try to figure it out and risk damaging an expensive piece of equipment. In addition, there will be times when you are prepping a piece of equipment that you have never used before. You should always ask the rental house prep tech for help on any unfamiliar piece of equipment.

The prep will usually go faster if you have a system that you follow. Sticking to your system helps to facilitate efficiency and make the prep go quickly and smoothly. However, for various reasons a rental house may not have an item ready, may need to make an exchange, or may even have to get the item from another rental house. You must be flexible and willing to adjust your prep routine if necessary. Remember, you don't have to rush through a prep if you have a scheduled prep time. The rental house will not close on you if they are the ones who cause a delay with a piece of equipment.

I remember one prep I did for a very large-scale music video for a major music star. The initial prep involved three complete 35 mm camera packages. I arrived at the rental house around 9:00a.m. and proceeded to prep the cameras. At approximately 5:00p.m. I received a telephone call from the Production Manager telling me that they were adding another complete camera package. After working out my additional fees for the prep, I handed the telephone to the rental house technician. I knew that they were scheduled to close at 6:00p.m. After hanging up the phone, I asked the rental house technician what we were going to do. He said that he would stay with me until all the cameras were prepped and ready for shipping. At approximately 10:15p.m. I finished and left the rental house. I had done many preps at the rental company, the production was a very large show for them, and they were willing to work with the Production Manager and me so that the prep could be completed.

The following checklist contains most of the basic items that you will find on a film camera shoot and what you should check on each.

As stated earlier, each camera package will be different and as such each prep will be different.

Camera Prep Checklist

1. Spreader
   - Runners slide smoothly and lock in all positions.
   - Tripod points fit and lock into receptacles.

2. Tripods
   - Be sure to obtain standard tripod and baby tripod.
   - Legs slide smoothly and lock in all positions.
   - Legs lock securely onto spreader.
   - Wooden legs are free from cracks and splinters.
   - Top casting accommodates the head base (flat or bowl).

3. High hat or low hat
   - Is mounted on smooth, flat piece of wood.
   - Top casting accommodates the head base (flat or bowl).
   - Top casting should be the same as the tripod top casting.

4. Fluid head
   - Base fits tripod top casting and locks securely (bowl shaped or Mitchell flat base).
   - Head includes a quick-release plate allowing for fast removal of the camera from the head.
   - Camera lockdown screw of quick-release plate fits into camera body, adapter plate, riser plate, or sliding base plate.
   - Pan and tilt movement is smooth at all tension settings.
   - Tension adjustments for pan or tilt engage and do not slip.
   - Head balances properly with complete camera, lens, and magazine setup attached.
   - Pan and tilt locks securely in all positions.
   - Eyepiece leveler attaches to head securely.
   - Head contains a mounting bracket for the Camera Assistant's front box.

5. Dutch head
   - Base fits into quick-release opening of fluid head.
   - Tilt movement is smooth at all tension settings.
   - Tension adjustments for tilt engage and do not slip.
   - Tilt locks securely in all positions.

6. Gear head
   - Base fits tripod top casting and locks securely. (All gear heads have a Mitchell flat base.)
   - Head includes a quick-release plate that allows the fast removal of the camera from the head.

- Camera lockdown screw of quick-release plate fits into camera body, adapter plate, riser plate, or sliding base plate.
- Pan and tilt movement is smooth at all speed settings.
- Gears shift smoothly.
- If head contains a tilt plate, it operates smoothly and locks securely in all positions.
- Pan and tilt locks securely in all positions.
- Eyepiece leveler attaches to head securely.
- Head has a mounting bracket for the Camera Assistant's front box.

7. Sliding base plate
   - Sliding base plate mounts securely on quick-release plate of head, and adapter plate mounts securely on camera body.
   - Camera adapter plate slides smoothly and locks in all positions (see Figure 5.1).

8. Camera body
   - Camera body fits securely on head, adapter plate, or quick-release plate.
   - Interior is clean and free from emulsion buildup or film chips.
   - All rollers are clean, free from any burrs, and move smoothly.

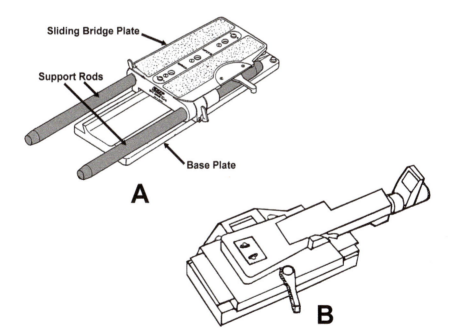

Figure 5.1   **A**, Arriflex sliding base plate. (Courtesy of ARRI Inc.), **B**, Panavision sliding base plate. (Reprinted from the *Panaflex Users Manual* with permission of David Samuelson and Panavision Inc.)

- Aperture plate, pressure plate, and gate are clean and free from any burrs.
- Inching knob works properly.
- Pull down claw and registration pin operate smoothly and are not bent.
- Aperture plate is the proper aspect ratio for the production you are shooting.
- Lens port opening is clean.
- Mirror is clean and free from scratches. (Do not clean the mirror yourself. If it is scratched or dirty, tell someone at the rental house immediately.)
- Behind-the-lens filter slot is easily accessible. (Not all cameras accept behind-the-lens filters.)
- Magazine port opening is clean.
- Flange focal depth is set correctly.
- Electrical contacts in magazine port openings are clean.
- Footage counter and tachometer function properly.
- On/off switch functions properly.
- The movement of the shutter, pull down claw, and registration pin is synchronized.
- Variable-speed switch functions properly.
- Camera maintains speed at different speed settings.
- Pitch adjustment operates properly.
- Buckle trip switch operates properly. (Not all cameras have a buckle trip switch.)
- Power ports and accessory ports all function properly.
- Camera heater functions properly. (Not all cameras have an internal heater.)
- Ground glass or viewing screen is clean and is marked for the correct aspect ratio.
- Variable shutter operates smoothly through its entire range of openings.
- Long and short eyepieces mount properly and focus easily to the eye.
- Eyepiece heater functions properly.
- Eyepiece magnifier functions properly.
- Contrast viewing filter on eyepiece functions properly.
- Eyepiece leveler attaches to eyepiece securely.
- Illuminated ground glass markings function properly and are adjustable in intensity.
- Obtain rain covers for all cameras if you will be shooting in any situations where the camera may become wet (rain, snow, in or near any water—beach, pool, etc.).

9. Magazines
   - Magazines fit securely on camera body.

- You have high speed magazines for high speed cameras and regular magazines for regular cameras. (On most cameras these are not interchangeable.)
- Doors fit properly and lock securely.
- Interior is clean and free from dirt, dust, and film chips.
- Footage counter functions properly.
- Film moves smoothly through all film channels and rollers.
- Different size magazines obtained for various shooting situations: 200 ft, 400 ft, 1000 ft, etc.
- Electrical contacts on magazine are clean and free from dirt.

10. Scratch test magazines
- Check all magazines on all cameras to be sure that they do not scratch film.
- Load a dummy load of film into each magazine and thread it through the camera. Be sure that the dummy load is fresh film stock that has not been previously run through a camera.
- Run approximately 10–20 ft of film through the camera.
- Remove the film from the magazine take-up side and examine it for scratches or oil spots on the base and on the emulsion side. (Turn the film from side to side while looking at it under a bright light. If there are any scratches on either side, they will be noticeable.)
- If you find any scratches, request a replacement magazine.
- On variable speed cameras, run film at various speed settings.

11. Barneys
- A barney is a padded cover used to reduce or eliminate noise from the camera or magazine.
- Obtain the proper size barney for each size magazine.
- If necessary, obtain a separate barney for the camera.
- With heated barneys check that the heater functions properly.

12. Lenses
- Check that lenses have the same type of mount as that on the camera and that each lens mounts securely to the camera body.
- Front and back glass elements are clean and free from scratches and imperfections.
- If any imperfections or scratches are found on the lenses, be sure to notify the rental house personnel immediately.
- Iris diaphragm operates smoothly.
- Focus gears of follow focus attach securely to lens.
- Focus ring operates smoothly.
- Remote focus and zoom controls fit securely and operate smoothly.
- Focus distance marks are accurate.

- When checking focus distance marks, be sure that the lens is marked on both sides of the barrel. If not, wrap a thin piece of tape, such as artist's chart tape, around the lens and transfer the focus marks to the opposite side.
- On zoom lenses the zoom motor operates smoothly.
- Zoom lens tracks properly (see step 13).
- Zoom lens holds focus throughout the zoom range.
- Lens shade mounts securely to each lens.
- Matte box bellows fits securely around all lenses. If not, obtain various sized rubber donuts to make a tight seal between lenses and matte box.

13. Zoom lens tracking
    - Check that the shifting of the image is minimal when zooming in or out.
    - While looking through zoom lens, line up the crosshairs of the ground glass on the focus chart or on a point in the prep area where you are working.
    - Lock the pan and tilt so the crosshairs remain centered on the point.
    - While looking through the camera, zoom the lens in very slowly and then out very slowly, and watch to see if the crosshairs remain centered on the point throughout the length of the zoom. They may shift a small amount, and this is usually acceptable.
    - If the crosshairs do not remain centered on the point or shift more than just a little, have the rental house check the lens.

14. Power zoom control and zoom motor
    - Mounts securely to the lens and operates smoothly, both zooming in and zooming out.
    - Variable speed adjustment is accurate.
    - Camera on/off switch functions properly (if available; see Figure 5.2).

15. Focus eyepiece
    - With the lens removed, point the camera at a bright light source or white surface.
    - While looking through the eyepiece, turn the diopter adjustment ring until the crosshairs or grains of the ground glass are sharp and in focus.
    - Lock the adjustment ring and mark it so that it can be set to the proper position each time you look through the camera.
    - Wrap a piece of tape around the barrel of the diopter adjustment ring and mark it so that it can be set to the proper mark for each person who looks through the camera.

16. Check focus of each lens
    - Mount a lens on the camera.
    - Set the aperture to its widest opening (lowest t-stop number).

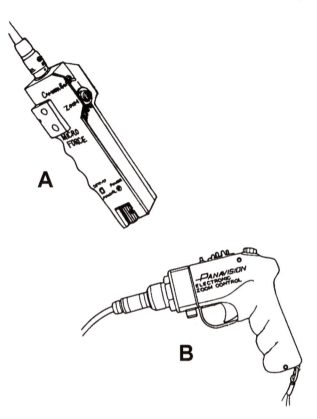

Figure 5.2   A, Microforce zoom control. (Reprinted from the *Arriflex 35 Book* by Jon Fauer with permission of the author and ARRI Inc.) **B**, Panavision zoom control. (Reprinted from the *Panaflex Users Manual* with permission of David Samuelson and Panavision Inc.)

- Using your tape measure, place a focus chart at specific distances from the camera. Base the distances on how the lens is marked. If the lens has focus marks at 5, 6, 7, 8, 10, 12, and 15 ft, place the focus chart at these distances and check the lens at each distance (see Figures 5.3 and 5.4).
- If the lens does not have enough focus markings, you may need to make your own. Using the focus marks from the previous step, you may want to determine precise marks for 9, 11, 13, and 14 ft. Wrap a thin piece of tape, like artist's chart tape, around the barrel of the lens and, using a focus chart and your tape measure, determine the other marks that you may need. In many cases this will save you a great deal of time in the long run because you won't have to do it on set.

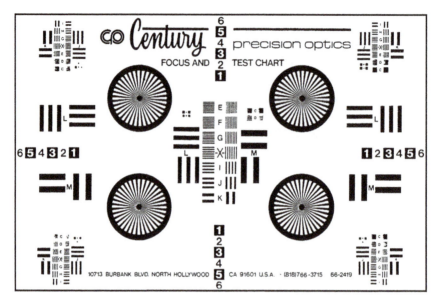

Figure 5.3 Century Precision Optics focus test chart. (Courtesy of Century Precision Optics.)

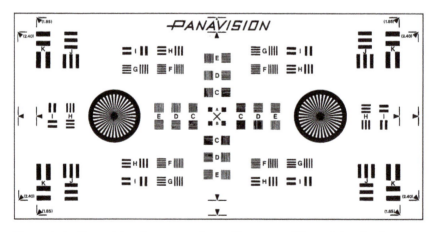

Figure 5.4 Panavision focus test chart. (Courtesy of Panavision Inc.)

- At each distance look through the viewfinder eyepiece and focus the chart by eye.
- Compare the eye focus to the distance measured and see if they match.
- If the eye focus does not match the measured focus, have the lens checked by the rental house lens technician.

- Check each lens at various distances, including the closest focusing distance and infinity (∞). Some lenses are not marked for their closest focusing distance. You may need to wrap a thin piece of tape around the barrel of the lens and mark it for its closest focusing distance.
- Check it at 1 ft intervals or, as stated previously, at markings on the lens.
- With zoom lenses, check the focus with the lens zoomed in all the way (its longest or tightest focal length).
- Telephoto lenses must be checked at more distances than wide-angle lenses because telephoto lenses have less depth of field.

17. Follow-focus mechanism
    - Mount follow-focus mechanism securely on the camera or support rods, and be sure it operates smoothly with each lens. Check that gear fits properly to lens gear.
    - If necessary, obtain different focusing gears for prime lenses and zoom lenses.
    - Check to be sure that you have all accessories and that they mount and operate properly (focus whip, speed crank, right-hand extension, focus-marking disks, etc.; see Figures 5.5 and 5.6).
    - In Britain the speed crank may also be referred to as a jimmy bar or tommy bar.

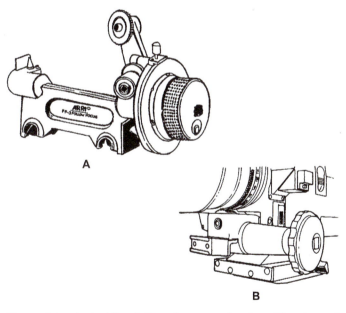

Figure 5.5   A, Arriflex follow-focus mechanism. (Courtesy of ARRI Inc.) **B,** Panavision follow-focus mechanism. (Reprinted from the *Panaflex Users Manual* with permission of David Samuelson and Panavision Inc.)

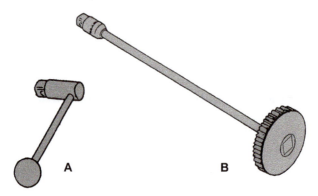

Figure 5.6   A, Speed crank. **B**, Focus whip.
(Reprinted from the *Arriflex 535 Instruction Manual*
with permission of ARRI Inc.)

18. Matte box
    - Matte box mounts securely on the camera.
    - Matte box operates properly with each lens; does not vignette with wide-angle lenses.
    - Matte box has proper adapter rings and rubber donut or bellows for each lens.
    - Filter trays are the correct size for the filters being used.
    - Be sure to have the correct number of filter trays. Matte boxes are available with two, three, four, or more filter trays depending on the needs of the production.
    - Filter trays slide in and out smoothly and lock securely in position.
    - Rotating filter trays or rings operate smoothly and lock securely in position.
    - Eyebrow mounts securely and can be adjusted easily.
    - Hard mattes mount securely and are the correct size for each lens (see Figure 5.7).

19. Filters
    - Each filter is clean and free from scratches.
    - Filters are the proper size for filter trays or retainer rings.
    - Filters cover the entire front element of the lenses being used.
    - Sliding filter trays for graduated filters operate smoothly and lock securely into position.
    - Rotating polarizer operates smoothly.
    - Always obtain an optical flat or clear filter with any filter set.
    - Obtain complete sets of filters for all cameras when using more than one camera.
    - Are graduated filters hard edge or soft edge?

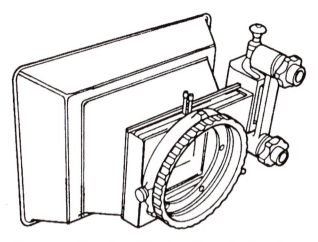

Figure 5.7 Matte box. (Reprinted from the *Panaflex Users Manual* with permission of David Samuelson and Panavision Inc.)

20. Obie light (eye light)
    • Obie light mounts securely and operates correctly at each setting.
    • Be sure that you have extra bulbs for the light.

21. Lens light (assistant's light)
    • Lens light mounts securely and operates properly.
    • Lens light is supplied with spare bulbs.

22. Precision speed control
    • Check that it operates correctly for both high speed and slow motion by running film through the camera at various speeds.
    • When set to a specific speed, it holds that speed without varying.
    • If using an external speed control, be sure to have extra cables.

23. HMI speed control
    • When using HMI lights be sure that the camera has an HMI speed control so that you may adjust the speed to the correct number when filming. (HMI lights can cause the image to flicker if the camera is not run at certain speeds or shutter angles.) See Figures 5.8 and 5.9 for HMI filming speeds and shutter angles.

24. Sync box
    • When shooting TV screens, computer monitors, and projectors, use a sync box to eliminate the roll bar. If possible, the camera should have a variable shutter so that you can sync the camera to the monitor or screen.

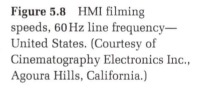

CINEMATOGRAPHY
electronics

60 Hz

HMI FLICKERFREE FILMING SPEEDS

Speed (fps) At Any Shutter Angle		With Specific Shutter Angles		
		fps	Shutter Angle	
120.000	6.666	66.667	200°	
60.000	6.315	65.000	195°	
40.000	6.000	63.333	190°	
30.000	5.714	57.600	172.8°	
24.000	5.454	56.667	170°	
20.000	5.217	55.000	165°	
17.143	5.000	53.333	160°	
15.000	4.800	50.000	150°	
13.333	4.000	48.000	144°	
12.000	3.750	46.667	140°	
10.909	3.000	45.000	135°	
10.000	2.500	43.333	130°	
9.231	2.000	36.667	110°	
8.571	1.875	35.000	105°	210°
8.000	1.500	33.333	100°	200°
7.500	1.000	26.667	80°	160°
7.058		25.000	75°	150°

© 2000 Cinematography Electronics Inc.

ALWAYS USE FILM TESTS TO VERIFY RESULTS

5321 Derry Ave., Suite G, Agoura Hills, CA 91301 USA
Phone (818) 706-3334   Fax (818) 706-3335
E-mail: info@CinemaElec.com
Website: www.CinematographyElectronics.com

Figure 5.8   HMI filming speeds, 60 Hz line frequency— United States. (Courtesy of Cinematography Electronics Inc., Agoura Hills, California.)

- When shooting at 30 frames per second (fps) or, more precisely, 29.97 fps, the shutter angle should be set to 180 degrees.
- When shooting at 24 fps or, more precisely, 23.976 fps, the shutter angle should be set to 144 degrees.

25. Video tap and monitor
   - Video tap camera mounts securely and properly to the film camera.
   - Focus and gain controls operate properly.
   - Iris control operates properly.
   - Video tap can be adjusted so that the image is centered on the monitor and is clear and easy to view.
   - Check that you have all cables and connectors necessary for the video tap and that they work properly. You should have various lengths of video cables and power cables for various shooting situations (10 ft, 25 ft, 50 ft). In addition, be sure to have a supply of video connectors for connecting the cables to a television monitor,

50 Hz

CINEMATOGRAPHY electronics

HMI FLICKERFREE FILMING SPEEDS

Speed (fps) At Any Shutter Angle		With Specific Shutter Angles		
		fps	Shutter Angle	
100.000	5.555	55.556	200°	
50.000	5.263	54.167	195°	
33.333	5.000	52.778	190°	
25.000	4.761	48.000	172.8°	
20.000	4.545	47.222	170°	
16.666	4.347	45.833	165°	
14.285	4.166	44.444	160°	
12.500	4.000	41.667	150°	
11.111	3.333	40.000	144°	
10.000	3.125	38.889	140°	
9.090	2.500	37.500	135°	
8.333	2.000	36.111	130°	
7.692	1.250	30.556	110°	
7.142	1.000	29.167	105°	
6.666		27.778	100°	200°
6.250		24.000	86.4°	172.8°
5.882		22.222	80°	160°

© 2000 Cinematography Electronics Inc.

ALWAYS USE FILM TESTS TO VERIFY RESULTS

5321 Derry Ave., Suite G, Agoura Hills, CA 91301 USA
Phone (818) 706-3334   Fax (818) 706-3335
E-mail: info@CinemaElec.com
Website: www.CinematographyElectronics.com

Figure 5.9 HMI filming speeds, 50 Hz line frequency—Europe. (Courtesy of Cinematography Electronics Inc., Agoura Hills, California.)

video recorder, or other device. Connect video monitor to camera and adjust video camera to obtain the best picture.

26. Handheld accessories
    - If the production involves any handheld shots, be sure you have the necessary accessories, which should attach securely and operate properly (left and right hand grips, shoulder pad, handheld follow focus, clamp-on matte box or lens shade, 400-ft or 500-ft magazines, on-board batteries, etc.).
    - Connect the hand grip with an on/off switch and be sure that it operates properly (see Figure 5.10).

27. Remote start switch
    - Connect remote start switch to camera and ensure that it operates properly.
    - Be sure to have extra cables and the proper length cables for different shooting situations (dangerous shots, car shots, stunts, etc.).

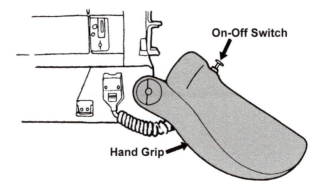

Figure 5.10   Right hand grip with on/off switch on Arriflex 16 SR camera. (Reprinted from the *Arriflex 16SR Book* by Jon Fauer with permission of the author and ARRI Inc.)

28. Batteries and cables
    - Be sure that all batteries are the correct voltage for the camera system being used.
    - All cables should be in good condition and have no frayed or loose wires.
    - There should be no loose pins in the plugs.
    - Battery cables should be of various lengths for different shooting situations.
    - Cables should be compatible with batteries, 3-pin or 4-pin.
    - At least two battery cables should be obtained for each camera being used.
    - At least two batteries should be obtained for each camera being used.
    - Extra batteries should be available for each camera in case you will be shooting high speed.
    - If you will be shooting any handheld shots, you should have at least two battery belts or on-board batteries.
    - Each battery should have a charger, either built in or separate (see Figures 5.11, 5.12, and 5.13).

29. Camera tests
    - At the end of the camera prep, the DP may ask you to perform some specific tests. These tests will be shot on film, so be sure to have access to some lights and have a light meter with you. You usually need only one 400-ft roll of film for these tests, depending on how involved the tests are. If you don't have your own light meter, then borrow one from the DP. Be sure to properly slate each shot of these tests with all information included on the slate. Keep a detailed

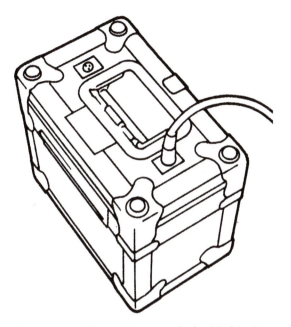

Figure 5.11   Panavision 24-volt double block battery. (Reprinted from the *Panaflex Users Manual* with permission of David Samuelson and Panavision Inc.)

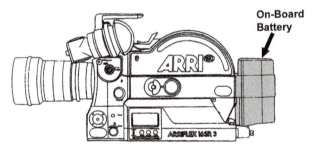

Figure 5.12   Arriflex 16 SR3 camera with onboard battery. (Courtesy of ARRI Inc.)

camera report for the test as well. The slate and camera report should include the name of the production, type of test, lens focal length, focus distance, t-stop, filter name and strength, and any other pertinent information. This will be very helpful when viewing the

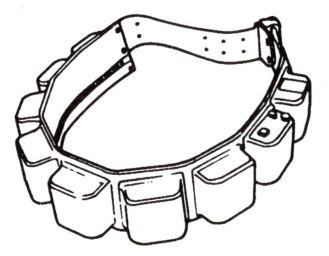

Figure 5.13 Belt battery. (Reprinted from *Motion Picture Camera and Lighting Equipment* with permission of David Samuelson.)

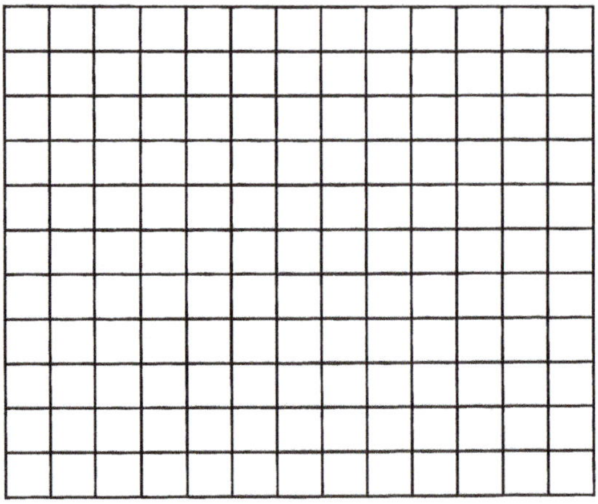

Figure 5.14 Registration test chart.

test and will better enable the DP to make final decisions about the equipment.

A. Film registration test
- Check that the registration of the camera is accurate by filming a registration test chart (see Figure 5.14).
- I recommend shooting the registration test first on the roll. This test requires that you shoot a double exposure,

which means that you shoot one exposure, rewind the film, and shoot another exposure. It is much easier to do at the beginning of the roll than somewhere in the middle.

• Thread the film in the camera and mark the exact frame where you start, using a permanent felt-tip marker (see Figure 5.15).

Figure 5.15 Mark the starting frame for the registration test.

• Line up the registration test chart through the eyepiece so that the crosshairs of the ground glass are centered on the lines of the chart (see Figure 5.16).

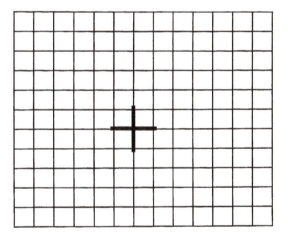

Figure 5.16 Positioning of crosshair on registration chart for shooting the first exposure.

• Lock the pan and tilt on the head.
• Shoot approximately 30 ft of the chart at one stop underexposed.
• Carefully remove the magazine, do not break the film, and go into the darkroom or use a changing bag or changing tent.
• You will need to wind the film back to the very beginning of the roll to find the start frame. This should be done by

hand and not run back through the camera if the camera has a reverse mode. (As stated earlier, I recommend shooting the registration test first on the roll because it is easier to wind the film back to the beginning of a roll than to a place in the middle.)

- Place the magazine back on the camera, and thread the film so that the original mark is again lined up in the gate.
- Release the pan and tilt of the head, and reposition the camera to line up the registration chart through the eyepiece so that the crosshairs of the ground glass are centered within one of the boxes of the chart (see Figure 5.17).

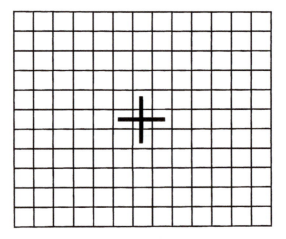

Figure 5.17   Positioning of crosshair on registration chart for shooting the second exposure.

- Lock the pan and tilt on the head.
- Shoot approximately 50 ft of the chart again at one stop underexposed.
- When the film is projected, there will be two sets of chart lines on the screen. If the registration of the camera is correct, there should be no movement of the lines. There are some important things to remember when shooting the registration test. You should never rewind the film in the camera. Some cameras have the ability to run in reverse, and you may be tempted to use this feature to quickly rewind your film back to the beginning for the second exposure. Instead, remove the magazine from the camera and, in a darkroom or changing

bag or tent, rewind the film by hand back to the beginning of the roll. I have been told by some laboratories that when you rewind the film in the camera, there is too much stress on the film and the perforations, possibly even stretching the film. This will have an adverse effect on how the registration test looks and could give you false results. Although it takes a bit longer, it is better in the long run to always rewind the film by hand when doing the registration test.

B. Lens focus calibration test
   • Place each lens on the camera, and frame the focus chart so that the entire chart is framed by the lens.
   • Photograph the focus test chart at various distances to be sure that the lens maintains sharp focus.
   • Make sure the image is sharp in the center, as well as on the left and right sides of the frame and the top and bottom of the frame.
   • Shoot the focus test with the lens open to its widest aperture whenever possible.

C. Lens color balance test
   • Place each lens on the camera and photograph a color chart to check that there is consistent color balance between lenses.
   • Check to see that each lens reproduces all colors the same way.
   • If you do not have a color chart, cut a variety of color photographs out of magazines and paste them on a sheet of poster board, and shoot this for the color balance test.

D. Filter test
   • Place various filters on the camera and photograph a live subject to see the effect of each filter.

30. Pack and label all equipment
   • Label each case on the top and sides with camera tape (just a brief description of what is in each case so that you can find things quickly: CAMERA, 1000-ft MAGS, FILTERS, PRIMES, ZOOM, HEAD, AKS, etc.; see Figure 5.18).
   • If you will be using more than one camera on the production, label each camera case and its corresponding accessories with the same color tape. (For example, all A camera and accessory cases would be labeled in red tape, and all B camera and accessory cases would be labeled in blue tape.)
   • If you will be working out of a camera truck, label the shelves for each piece of equipment the same as the cases.

Figure 5.18   Proper labeling of equipment cases.

For a definition of each item on the camera prep checklist, see the Glossary.

Keep in mind that each prep you do will be a bit different. The rental house you are dealing with, the type of production, what equipment you are checking, along with many other factors, will affect your prep. The preceding checklist is a basic guide for you to use; it is by no means a complete list. It would be impractical to try to list every possible piece of equipment you may have on your production. I have only listed the basic items that you will encounter on most camera preps that you do.

When doing the camera prep, be as thorough as possible, and check every little item in each equipment case. This is important not only for when you are shooting but also when you do the camera wrap at the end of shooting. If you have checked everything completely and it is listed on the original order, there should be no questions when the equipment is returned to the rental house.

Once the prep is completed you usually contact the production company and they will send a teamster with the camera truck to pick up the equipment, or if it is a small production they may simply send a Production Assistant with a van to pick up the gear. On rare occasions you may be asked to transport the equipment in your personal

vehicle. I don't like to do this too often because keep in mind that you will have a camera package worth thousands of dollars in your personal vehicle, making you personally responsible for it. I once had a complete Panavision Gold 35 mm camera package in my vehicle. The package was valued at $350,000 and, needless to say, I was very careful on the drive home that evening.

There are some important things to remember when packing the equipment in your vehicle or in any vehicle for transport. If using an industry standard camera truck there will be shelves and tie-down straps for the equipment cases. Chapter 4, Second Assistant Cameraman (2nd AC) and Film Loader, contains a section entitled Preparation of Camera Truck that discusses the procedure for loading cases into the camera truck. When transporting the camera equipment in your personal vehicle you would use many of the same common-sense tips as when using a camera truck.

Ideally you would have a vehicle that is completely contained, but if using a pickup truck with an open bed, be sure to have a tarp or tarps to cover the cases. Place all cases flat on their widest base to prevent them from tipping during transport. If you will not be transporting any passengers, place camera, lenses and other expensive gear in the passenger seat. Lens cases are usually smaller so they can go on the floor of the passenger side, while the camera case can be placed on the seat. Don't stack any other cases on top of these so that they don't fly off in the event of a sudden stop or accident. Whenever possible try to avoid stacking cases on top of each other. But if you must stack equipment cases, keep the larger, heavier cases on the bottom and small cases placed on top of them, against the back of your seat or a wall of the vehicle. This helps to prevent them from moving around during transport. Any time you stack cases, be sure to secure them with bungee cords and/or tie-down ratchet straps. You should have bungee cords and ratchet straps as part of your AC kit that are used for securing the camera to different camera mounts, so you can use these to secure the cases in your vehicle. If you don't have any of these, standard sash cord or rope will work as well. Whenever using any type of tie-down straps, bungee cords or rope, it is a good idea to loop the strap or cord through the handles of the cases rather than simply place it over the case. This provides a little bit of added security in the event something tries to move during transport. The more you pack equipment in various vehicles the better and faster you will become at it. A little extra time and effort spent in securing the gear will save you a mountain of headaches later on.

The camera prep is not always a guarantee that nothing will go wrong with the equipment. An experience I had during one of my preps illustrates this. I was hired to work on a commercial that was to

shoot for two days in and around Los Angeles. The camera prep took about half a day the day before we were scheduled to start shooting. The DP stopped by the rental house during the prep to see if everything checked out okay. The next day's call time was 5:00a.m., and the location was about a one hour drive away. When I arrived at the location, I proceeded to set up the camera. I connected the battery and turned on the camera. Nothing happened. The camera would not run. After checking all of the batteries and power cables, I telephoned the rental house at their 24-hr number. When I explained to the camera technician what was happening, he instructed me to change one of the internal fuses in the camera. After changing the fuse, the camera still would not run, so it was decided that the production company would return to Los Angeles, get another camera, and shoot the scenes in the studio that were scheduled for the next day. After exchanging the camera, everything went smoothly. I later found out that there was an additional fuse in the camera that could only be accessed and changed by a camera technician, and it was this fuse that had blown out, causing the camera not to run. This is an excellent example of why you should do a camera prep.

It also shows that a camera prep is not always a guarantee that something won't go wrong. Without doing the camera prep, I would have had no way of knowing if the camera had been in working order when it was picked up. At least I knew the camera had been working and the problem was no fault of mine. And since the DP had also stopped by the rental house during the prep, he knew that the camera had been working. He was able to explain this to the client on the first morning while I was attempting to get things working.

PRODUCTION

The prep is done, the film and expendables have been ordered, the camera truck is loaded and set up for production, and it's now time for filming to start. As stated in Chapter 4, the production phase of shooting is a complex operation that requires a great deal of dedication, hard work, and attention to detail on the part of all involved.

This is especially important to the 1st AC. The proper performance and execution of the duties and responsibilities of the 1st AC are vital to the smooth operation of the production. You must set up the camera each day, keep it clean, change lenses and filters, load film into the camera, and, most important, keep the shot in focus during filming. You must pay close attention to detail and be ready to make quick decisions. You are one of the key people the DP relies on during filming. If you let the DP down, you let down the entire crew.

Start-of-the-Day Procedures

The first thing you should do each day is set up the camera. Place the camera on the head, which is mounted to either the tripod or the dolly. If the camera and head are being placed on a tripod, many assistants often use a piece of carpet in place of the spreader under the tripod. The points on the tripod legs dig into the carpet, creating a firm support for the tripod and camera. This also sometimes makes it easier when moving or repositioning the camera. This piece of carpet usually measures 4 ft×4 ft. Remember that there are times when you must use the spreader, so you should always have one available. If working in Britain be prepared to have one or more grips working with you in the setup of the camera. They are responsible for all camera support, including tripods, heads, dollies, etc., and work more closely with the camera department in that regard than grips in the United States.

If necessary, oil the camera movement and clean the gate and aperture plate to remove any dirt, dust, or emulsion buildup. Check to be sure that the interior of the camera is clean and free from any film chips or dust. Set up the camera with all the basic components except for a magazine and a lens. Attach the various accessories to it, including the follow focus, matte box, eyebrow, eyepiece leveler, lens light, and so on. While the 1st AC sets up the camera, the 2nd AC is often nearby, handing pieces of equipment to him or her. When you have the basic camera built, some assistants like to run the camera to warm it up. Before doing this you should check with the rental house to see if this is okay. With many film cameras it's not a good idea to run them without film. But if you can run the camera without film to warm it up, the general rule is to run the camera for approximately the length of the first roll of film that you will be placing on the camera. For example, if the first roll being placed on the camera is 400 ft, reset the footage counter to zero, and then warm up the camera until the footage counter shows "400." After the camera has warmed up, you can then place the magazine and lens on it.

You should never place a lens on the camera or remove a lens from the camera while it is running. The shutter spins while the camera is running during the warm-up, and it may hit the back of the lens if the lens is not placed on the camera properly. If the camera has an internal heater you should connect the heater to a battery to warm up the camera. In any event be sure to check with the rental house so that you follow the proper warm-up procedures.

Unless the DP requests a specific lens, I recommend placing a wide-angle lens on the camera. This allows the DP or Camera Operator to see as much of the scene as possible when he or she first looks through the camera. It's a good idea to establish a procedure at

the beginning of the production regarding what lens to place on the camera at the beginning of each day. The DP may request a specific lens, such as the 25–250 zoom or the widest prime lens you have, or he or she may even tell you not to place a lens on the camera until the first shot has been decided upon. Open up the aperture to its widest opening and set the focus to the approximate distance so that the scene can be viewed clearly. When the camera is warmed up, place the first magazine on it and finish making it ready for the first shot. Be sure to let the DP and Camera Operator know as soon as the camera is ready for use. This setup procedure should take approximately 15–20 minutes from start to finish. It is important to get the camera set up as quickly as possible at the start of each day, but never trade safety for speed. In other words, set it up quickly, but don't go so quickly that you could make mistakes. On most union productions the call time for the assistants is approximately twenty minutes before the DP and Camera Operator. By the time the DP and Camera Operator arrive on set, the camera should be set up and ready to look through for the first setup of the day. Check that the viewfinder is clean and set to the proper position for the Camera Operator or DP to look through it. Nothing is more annoying to an Operator or DP than looking through a viewfinder that is not set for his or her eye and looking at an out-of-focus or soft image.

When the camera is set up and the first camera position and angle are established, you should ensure that all needed camera equipment is nearby. The 2nd AC may have already done this while you were preparing the camera, but it doesn't hurt to double check. Keep any camera equipment that will be needed throughout the shooting day as close to the camera as possible, without being in the way of other people or equipment. Camera equipment includes lenses, filters, magazines, and accessories.

As part of their kit, many assistants have some type of handcart or dolly to keep camera equipment cases on. These carts enable the assistant to keep all of the cases neat and organized yet quickly movable when there is a new camera setup. The two most common types of carts or dollies that have been used for moving camera equipment cases are the Magliner Gemini Jr. and Gemini Sr. They both collapse for shipping and storage and can be set up quickly when needed. Many Camera Assistants also use a cart made by Rubbermaid. The Magliner carts can be very expensive depending on the options you choose, but you will soon discover that they are worth the price. Many assistants today use a much larger cart manufactured by Backstage Equipment. It can be outfitted with camera mounts, tripod hooks and a wide variety of accessories to make your job easier. It's up to you to decide which cart is best for you. With all of the cases on

set, you will discover very quickly how time saving it is to wheel the equipment from one setup to the next rather than carry each case individually. See Figures D.1, D.2, D.3, and D.4 in Appendix D for illustrations of the Backstage, Magliner, and Rubbermaid carts. Chapter 4, Second Assistant Cameraman (2nd AC) and Film Loader, contains a detailed section on the organization of equipment on set.

Loading and Unloading Film in the Camera

Whenever a new magazine is placed on the camera, notify the DP and Camera Operator so they know that the camera will not be available to them while you complete the reload. Reloading the camera with film should take only a minute or two depending on the camera and your level of experience. Before a new magazine is placed on the camera, clean the interior of the camera body with compressed air. Check and clean the gate and aperture plate to remove any emulsion buildup. If possible, remove the gate and aperture plate for cleaning. When cleaning the gate, never use any type of sharp tool that could scratch it and cause scratches on the film emulsion. To clean emulsion buildup, use one of the orangewood sticks that you obtained with the expendables. Clean the gate and aperture plate with compressed air.

When the new magazine is placed on the camera, reset the footage counter to zero so that the dial readings and footage amounts on the camera report will be accurate. Remember to write the roll number on the identification label of the magazine if this has not already been done by the 2nd AC. If the magazine contains a short end, place the small identification label next to the footage counter as a reminder that the magazine does not contain a full roll of film. In addition, when placing a magazine on the camera, the size and weight of the roll could affect the balance of the camera. Check and rebalance the camera if necessary so that the Camera Operator will not have difficulty in operating the shot because of an unbalanced camera. Also, remember that when using a camera with displacement magazines, as the film travels through the camera it is displaced from the front of the camera to the back. This will cause the camera to become unbalanced after every shot, so you should periodically check the balance during shooting and adjust it as required. If necessary, place a sound barney on the magazine after it has been placed on the camera. When you have completed loading the magazine and film on the camera, notify the 1st Assistant Director (AD), DP, and Camera Operator that the camera is now ready for use.

If you remove a partially shot magazine and plan to finish shooting it later in the day, always mark an "X" on the frame of film in the

gate. This allows you to line up the film properly when you place the magazine back on the camera later in the day. Please see the detailed explanation of this in Chapter 4.

Keeping the Camera Clean

One of the most important things to remember during filming is to keep the camera clean. Dirt or dust on the camera not only looks unprofessional, but can also cause big problems if it gets into the camera body, the magazines, on lenses or filters, in the gate, or on the mirror shutter. The smallest speck of dirt can cause emulsion scratches on the film and ruin a whole day's shooting. Clean the camera each day when it is set up. Clean the inside with compressed air. Keep the outside of the camera body clean by using an inexpensive 2-in. wide brush to remove the dust and dirt. If the exterior of the camera body becomes exceptionally dirty, wipe it off with a damp cloth. Never use the damp cloth to clean lenses or filters. As stated earlier, clean the gate using an orangewood stick and compressed air. When oiling the camera movement, remove any excess oil by using a cotton swab or foam-tip swab. Each time a new lens or filter is placed on the camera, check it for dirt, dust, or smudges. If the lens or filter needs to be cleaned, don't make everybody wait while you clean it. First place it on the camera so that the DP can look at the shot and determine if it is the correct lens or filter. When it has been approved for the shot, you should then have enough time to remove it and clean it before shooting. There will usually be a lighting change of some type that gives you enough time to do the cleaning. If not, you must inform the DP or Camera Operator that the lens or filter must be cleaned before anything can be shot with it. The proper way to clean lenses and filters will be explained further in the Lenses section in this chapter.

Oiling and Lubricating the Camera

The movement in many motion picture cameras must be oiled at regular intervals. If you are not sure whether you should oil the movement or how often to oil it, always check with the rental house when you do the camera prep. The rental house also should give you a small container of oil.

In addition to oiling the movement, it is sometimes necessary to lubricate the pull down pins with a small drop of silicone liquid to prevent squeaking. Panavision cameras require a drop of the supplied silicone liquid on the felt pads at the base of the aperture plate. As the

pull down claws finish their downward movement, they rub across these pads, picking up just enough silicone to prevent any squeaking as they enter the film perforations at the top of their movement.

Some cameras need to be oiled every day; others only require oiling on a weekly or monthly basis. Check with the rental house because you can do just as much damage by oiling too much as by not oiling enough. Panavision says that, as a general rule, their cameras should be oiled on a daily basis depending on how much film is being shot each day. The exception to this rule is when using the new Panavision Panaflex Millennium camera. According to the operation manual for the Millennium, the movement should be lubricated every two weeks or after 100,000 ft of film has run through the camera. Panavision high-speed cameras must be oiled after every 1000 ft of film has been shot whenever you film at speeds greater than 60 fps. Panavision film cameras have anywhere from seven to thirteen oiling points in the movement, depending on which model you are using. They usually have an oiling diagram on the inside of the door to the camera body, and a small container of Panavision oil is included in the camera accessory case.

Arriflex cameras use a different type of movement and do not need to be oiled nearly as often. Some Arriflex cameras require oiling only every few months or after a specified amount of film has been run through them. The oiling of Arriflex cameras is most often handled by the rental house technicians and rarely by the Camera Assistant in the field.

If using Panavision cameras, when you do oil the movement, it is necessary to place only one drop of oil on each oiling point. Be very careful not to get any oil in the gate or on the mirror. If the oil does get onto the film, it will show up as spots on the exposed negative. If you should get any excess oil in the movement, remove it by using a cotton swab or foam-tip swab from your expendables supply. Be very careful when using the cotton swabs so that you do not leave any of the lint from the cotton tip in the movement. If lint gets into the gate, it can cause hairs on the emulsion. If you do find it necessary to place a drop of silicone liquid on the pull down claw, or sometimes on the aperture plate, be extra careful not to get any of the silicone in the movement because it could damage the movement.

Another thing to remember when oiling the camera is to only use the oil supplied by the rental house or recommended for that particular camera. Never use Panavision oil on Arriflex cameras or Arriflex oil on Panavision cameras. It is a good idea to have a supply of the different oils in your kit with your tools and accessories. This way, if you do not get any oil from the rental house, you will be prepared and be able to oil the camera movement when necessary. Figures 5.19–5.25

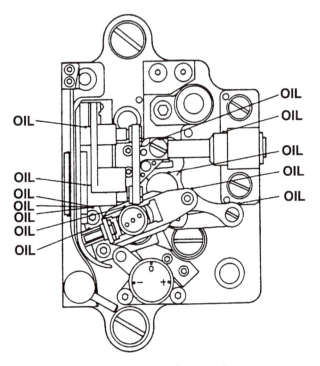

Figure 5.19   Panavision Panaflex 16 oiling
points. (Reprinted from the *Hands-On Manual
for Cinematographers* with permission of David
Samuelson.)

show the oiling points for some of the Panavision cameras that require
oiling most often.

*Remember: Never over oil the camera movement. Use only the sup-
plied or recommended oil for a particular camera. When in doubt,
check with the rental house.*

Setting the Viewfinder Eyepiece

The viewfinder eyepiece must be set for each key person who looks
through the camera. On most productions the key people are the
Director, DP, Producer, Camera Operator, and 1st AC. On commercials
it may also be set for the client or agency people. Because each person's vision is different, you will need different settings on the eyepiece so that the image will appear sharp and in focus to each person
who looks through it.

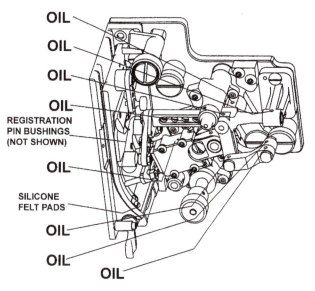

OIL
OIL
OIL
OIL
REGISTRATION
PIN BUSHINGS
(NOT SHOWN)
OIL
SILICONE
FELT PADS
OIL
OIL
OIL

Figure 5.20 Panavision Panaflex Millennium oiling points, side view. (Courtesy of Panavision Inc.)

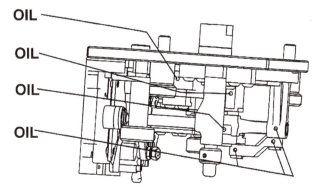

OIL
OIL
OIL
OIL

Figure 5.21 Panavision Panaflex Millennium oiling points, top view. (Courtesy of Panavision Inc.)

To focus the eyepiece, it is best to first remove the lens if possible. Aim the camera at a bright light source or white surface. While looking through the eyepiece, turn the diopter adjustment ring on the eyepiece until the crosshairs or the grains of the ground glass appear sharp and in focus.

Professional motion picture cameras are available with a variety of ground glass formats for shooting depending on a number of

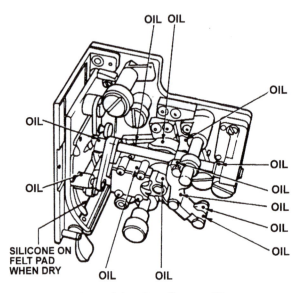

Figure 5.22 Panavision Panaflex 35 oiling points. (Reprinted from the *Hands-On Manual for Cinematographers* with permission of David Samuelson.)

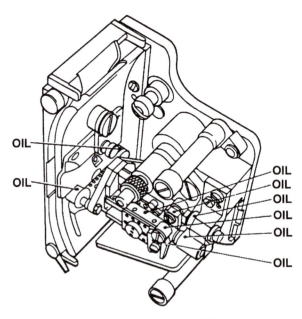

Figure 5.23 Panavision Panastar oiling points. (Reprinted from the *Hands-On Manual for Cinematographers* with permission of David Samuelson.)

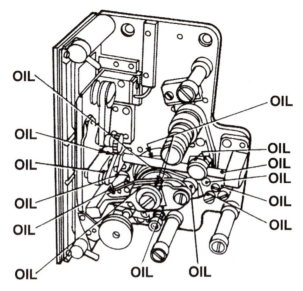

Figure 5.24 Panavision Super PSR oiling points. (Reprinted from the *Hands-On Manual for Cinematographers* with permission of David Samuelson.)

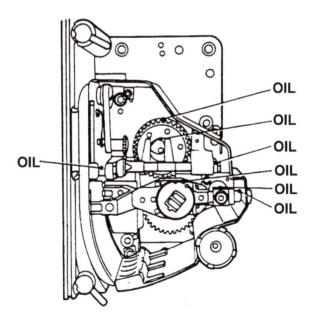

Figure 5.25 Panavision 65 mm camera oiling points. (Reprinted from the *Hands-On Manual for Cinematographers* with permission of David Samuelson.)

factors. The DP should discuss the needs with the Director and production company, as well as discuss the options with the rental company prior to renting the camera equipment. Figures 5.26 and 5.27 show examples of ground glass formats. These illustrations are only a very small sampling of what is available to the filmmaker.

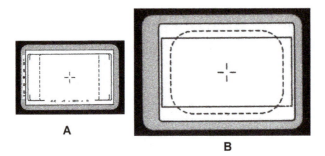

Figure 5.26   A, Arriflex Super 16 mm ground glass. B, Arriflex 35 mm ground glass. (Courtesy of ARRI Inc.)

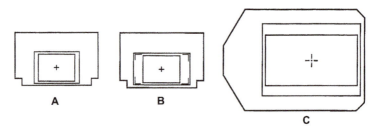

Figure 5.27   A, Panavision Regular 16 mm ground glass. B, Panavision Super 16 mm ground glass. C, Panavision 35 mm ground glass. (Courtesy of Panavision Inc.)

Some eyepieces have a diopter ring with a number scale so that you may set the viewfinder for an individual by turning the ring to the number that corresponds to his or her vision. In most cases I recommend that you wrap a thin piece of white paper tape or artist's chart tape around the diopter ring so that it can be marked for each person's setting. Have the Camera Operator, DP, and Director set the eyepiece for their vision, and mark the tape accordingly. You should also set the viewfinder for your vision. Then whenever one of these key people looks through the camera, you can set the eyepiece to their setting. Figure 5.28 shows the viewfinder marked for the key people who may look through the camera.

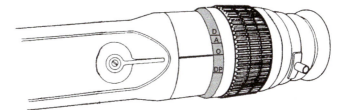

Figure 5.28   Eyepiece showing marks for each person's setting: D = Director, A = 1st AC, O = Camera Operator, DP = Director of Photography.

Note: Always remember to set the viewfinder back to the Camera Operator's mark before shooting.

To focus the eyepiece while the lens is still on the camera, first be sure that the aperture is set to its widest opening. Look through the lens and adjust the focus until everything is out of focus. If using a zoom lens, zoom in to its most telephoto focal length. Aim the camera at a bright light source or white surface. Turn the diopter adjustment ring on the eyepiece until the crosshairs or grains of the ground glass appear sharp and in focus. If you wear eyeglasses, remove your glasses before setting the viewfinder eyepiece for your vision.

Just as important as keeping the camera clean is keeping the eyepiece clean. Many eye infections have been passed on from too many people looking through the eyepiece. Be sure to clean the glass and rubber eyecup of the eyepiece regularly throughout the shooting day. Also keep some type of eyepiece cover in place during shooting. Many expendables stores sell a chamois cover made for specific camera eyepieces. I have also used terry cloth wrist bands that you can purchase at most sporting goods stores. They are very durable, absorb perspiration, and can be washed and reused.

Lenses

The basic definition of a lens is that it is an instrument that bends light waves in such a way as to produce an image of the object from which the light was reflected. The lens directs the reflected light from an object onto the film emulsion, producing a photographic image of the object. When referring to a lens, the DP will call for it by its focal length. Focal length is defined as the distance from the optical center of the lens to the film plane when the lens is focused to infinity. The focal length of the lens is an indication of how much of the scene the

lens will see from a given camera position. Focal length is always expressed in millimeters (mm). A lens with a short focal length, such as 12 mm, 18 mm, 24 mm, etc., will see a bigger area of the scene than a lens with a long focal length, such as 85 mm, 100 mm, 150 mm, etc.

Some DPs use a slightly different terminology when referring to specific lenses. This terminology is not used frequently, but it is worth mentioning in case you work with someone who does refer to a lens in this manner. A 25 mm lens may be referred to as a 1-in. lens, 50 mm as 2-in., 75 mm as 3-in., and 100 mm as 4-in. This is based on the fact that 25 mm is approximately equal to 1 in., and so forth.

Keep in mind that it is practically impossible to manufacture a perfect lens. All lenses will have some type of imperfection. Some anamorphic lenses give better results when filming a curved surface than when filming a flat surface. On some lenses the focus may shift when opened to their widest aperture. See the information in the Focusing Tips section about the yellow and blue witness marks on some Panavision lenses. Some zoom lenses give the appearance of zooming when shifting focus. This phenomenon is called breathing. Some zoom lenses do not track accurately throughout the range of the zoom, which often requires a slight movement (panning or tilting) of the camera to maintain proper composition.

Prime Lenses and Zoom Lenses

The two main types of lenses are prime and zoom. Prime lenses have a single fixed focal length, such as 25 mm, 35 mm, 50 mm, 65 mm, and so on. Zoom lenses have variable focal lengths, which means that you can change the focal length by turning a ring on the barrel of the lens. Zoom lenses are available in many different ranges, including 10–100, 20–100, 12–120, 25–250, 150–600, and so on. The 10–100, 25–250, and 12–120 ranges may be referred to as ten-to-one (10–1) zooms. The 20–100 range is called a five-to-one (5–1) zoom, and the 150–600 is called a four-to-one (4–1) zoom, and so on. These abbreviated names for the lenses are equal to the ratio of the tightest focal length of the lens to its widest focal length. The zoom lens sizes mentioned are only a small sampling of the different zoom lenses available today. Check with the rental house to see what size zooms they have. The Film Camera Equipment Checklist in Appendix C (Figure C.1) contains a more extensive listing of the prime and zoom lenses that are currently available.

While prime and zoom may be specific types of lenses, the general categories of lenses may be classified as wide angle, normal, or telephoto. This is in reference to the area of the scene that they see. A wide-angle lens sees more of the scene than a telephoto lens. A

normal lens is called that because it approximates the angle of view or field of view as seen through the human eye when standing at the same position as that of the camera. Telephoto lenses are lenses that have a very large focal length, such as 200 mm, 300 mm, 400 mm, 600 mm, and even 1000 mm. They allow you to photograph a close-up of an object or a subject from a great distance. Telephoto lenses may also be referred to as *long* lenses, and wide-angle lenses may be referred to as *short* lenses.

When working with lenses you should be familiar with some of the terminology used. One term, lens perspective, is an indication of the area that the lens sees. It may also be referred to as the lens field of view. It is an indication of how much of the scene will be visible when looking through the lens. Wide-angle lenses have a larger field of view than telephoto lenses. Another commonly used term regarding lenses is lens speed. The lens speed is an indication of the widest f-stop or t-stop setting of a particular lens. Fast lenses will have a smaller lens speed and are often used for nighttime photography. For example, a lens speed of 1.9 means that the widest aperture setting of the lens is a t/1.9.

You must also be aware of the type of lens mount on the camera you will be using. Unfortunately (or fortunately) lenses are not interchangeable from one camera system to another. Currently, the two most common lens mounts are the Panavision Mount (PV), which is standard on all Panavision cameras, and the Arriflex PL Mount, which is standard on all newer Arriflex cameras. Some of the older Arriflex 16 mm cameras use the Arriflex Standard Mount or Arriflex Bayonet Mount. There are adapters available so that you may use these lenses on a camera with a PL Mount. The PL in the name means Positive Lock. Be sure that the lenses you are using have the same type of mount as that of the camera you will be using; if they do not, then you must have some type of adapter or you cannot use them.

A situation that you may encounter with lenses is the possibility of using 35 mm lenses on a 16 mm camera. Although this rarely happens, it is important enough to mention here briefly. There is basically no difference in your image if using 35 mm format lenses on a 16 mm camera. For example, an 18 mm lens is an 18 mm lens whether it is placed on a 35 mm camera or on a 16 mm camera. It will give you the same image on both. The field of view or angle of view will be the same as if you were shooting in 35 mm format. When checking your depth of field, be sure to use 35 mm tables and circles of confusion. Focus witness marks are the same, but you should always check them just to be sure. Through the years there has been much discussion on this topic. If you are in doubt, I recommend shooting extensive tests to be completely sure.

Although I don't recommend it, some people have used 16 mm lenses on a 35 mm camera. You must be very careful when doing this because with some wide-angle lenses the spinning shutter of the camera may hit the rear element of the lens. Also, because the lenses are made for 16 mm cameras and the smaller 16 mm film frame, the area covered by these lenses may not cover the entire 35 mm film frame. Be sure to carefully check if you plan on doing this.

Most lenses you will use are called spherical lenses. They are the standard types of lenses used for many filmed productions. When you are shooting for extreme widescreen presentation, you will often shoot using anamorphic lenses. An anamorphic lens is one that squeezes or compresses the image horizontally so that a widescreen image can fit onto an almost square 35 mm film frame. During projection, the image is projected through a similar anamorphic lens that unsqueezes the image, creating a widescreen image on the screen. As stated in Chapter 1, the aspect ratio for anamorphic is usually referred to as 2.40:1, but it may also be called 2.35:1 or 2.36:1.

Whenever a lens is not being used, it should be capped on both the front and rear elements and placed in a padded case. The padding will help to cushion the lens and protect it from shocks and vibration. The internal elements of the lens can become loosened very easily if the lens is not protected or handled properly. When you are filming in dusty conditions or any situation in which something may strike the front of the lens, it is a good idea to use a clear filter called an optical flat. As stated in Chapter 1, an optical flat is simply a clear piece of optically correct glass placed in front of the lens as a means to protect it. Optical flats are available in the same standard sizes as filters. It is much less expensive to replace a filter that has become scratched than to replace the front element of the lens. This brings up a story that a DP colleague of mine once told me. He was shooting a scene of a plane taking off as the actors leaped into it. As the plane fired up, it spun around and a lot of sand and gravel were kicked up directly into the front element of the lens. The front element of the lens was severely scratched, and the production company ended up paying for a new lens. If they had only placed an optical flat in front of the lens, the production could have saved a great deal of money.

All professional lenses have a coating on the front element and should be cleaned only when absolutely necessary. I was taught that you should first use compressed air or a blower bulb syringe to blow off any dirt or dust. Many assistants don't like to use the compressed air on a lens but I believe if you are careful and only spray in very short bursts you should be fine. If you are not sure or are not comfortable using compressed air, then I recommend only using the blower bulb syringe. If there are no smudges or fingerprints, then there is

nothing more that you need to do to clean the lens. If the lens has any fingerprints or smudges, clean it with lens cleaner and lens tissue. After the dirt and dust have been blown away, moisten a piece of lens tissue with lens cleaning fluid. Wipe the surface of the lens carefully, using a circular motion. While the lens is still damp from the lens solution, use another piece of tissue to remove the remaining lens cleaning fluid from the lens. I have seen some assistants apply the lens cleaning fluid directly to the lens element, but I don't recommend doing this because of the curvature of the front element of the lens. The fluid can travel along the element of the lens and sometimes get between the lens housing and the glass curved element, ending up behind the glass. As a result, you have no way to remove the fluid from the back of the lens glass. The important thing to remember is that you should never use a dry piece of lens tissue on a dry lens surface. Small particles of dirt and dust may still be on the coating and will cause scratches. Also, never use any type of silicone-coated lens tissue or cloth to clean lenses.

Use the same method for cleaning lenses when cleaning filters. First clean the filter with compressed air, and then use lens cleaner and lens tissue. Another good way to clean the filter is by breathing on it and wiping off the moisture with a piece of lens tissue or a special filter cloth. You should never use this method when cleaning lenses.

Remember   Clean lenses only when absolutely necessary. Never use a dry piece of lens tissue on a dry lens. Never use silicone-coated lens tissue or cloth to clean a lens.

Checking for Lens Flares

Each time the camera or lights are moved to a new position, you should check that no lights are kicking or shining directly into the lens, which will cause a flare in the photographic image. A flare could cause an overall washing out of the image or create a streak of light in the image, so objects in the scene don't have sharp detail. If you have a French flag or eyebrow on the camera, you may be able to adjust it to eliminate the flare. The eyebrow may also be called a sunshade, or in Britain a top chopper (see Figures 5.29 and 5.30).

You also may be able to eliminate the flare by placing a hard matte on the matte box. The hard matte is snapped in place onto the front of the matte box, and it contains a cutout based on the focal length of the lens being used. The hard matte allows light to enter only the small cutout in the matte, while the rest of the matte blocks the light, thus preventing a flare in the image. See Figure 5.31 for an illustration of hard mattes and a matte box with a hard matte in place.

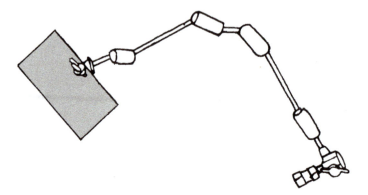

Figure 5.29   French flag attached to articulating arm.

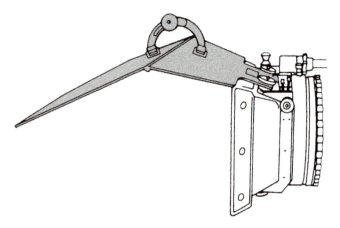

Figure 5.30   Eyebrow (sunshade) in place on matte box to eliminate lens flare. (Reprinted from the *Panaflex Users Manual* with permission of David Samuelson and Panavision Inc.)

If the flare cannot be removed at the camera, request that a flag be set by one of the Grips to keep the light from kicking into the lens. There are a few different ways to check for lens flares. One is to place your face directly next to the lens, looking in the direction that the lens is pointed in. Look around the set to see if any lights are shining directly at you, which means they are shining directly into the lens. Another way to check for flares is to stand in front of the camera, face the lens, and move your hand around the lens or matte box. If you see a shadow from your hand falling across the lens, there is probably a light flaring the lens from the angle of the shadow.

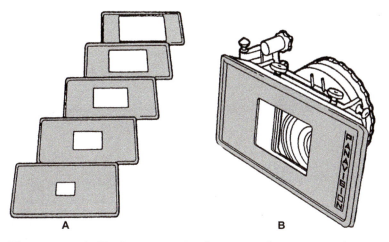

Figure 5.31   A, Hard mattes. **B**, Hard matte in place on matte box.
(Reprinted from the *Panaflex Users Manual* with permission of
David Samuelson and Panavision Inc.)

A third way to check for flares is to place a convex mirror directly in front of the lens, with the mirror side facing the set. Any lights that may be causing a flare can be seen in the mirror. Be sure to stand in a position so that you are not blocking the mirror, and also blocking any lights that could be causing the flare. If you find a flare, it must be removed from the front element of the lens by the hard matte, French flag, eyebrow, or grip flag.

Remove lens flares from the matte box and filter as well as the lens. Any light striking the matte box or filter can still reflect into the lens, causing a flare in the image. Checking the lens for flares takes a certain amount of experience and cannot be fully explained or understood unless you are in an actual shooting situation. Whenever you are not sure if there is a lens flare, ask one of the Grips to help or to double check for you. Also remember that if you are using a telephoto lens, a flag will work best when placed at a distance from the lens. In other words, the more telephoto the lens, the farther away the flag needs to be to remove any flare.

Depth of Field

Depth of field may be defined as the range of distance within which all objects will be in acceptable sharp focus, including an area in front of and behind the principal point of focus. There will always be more

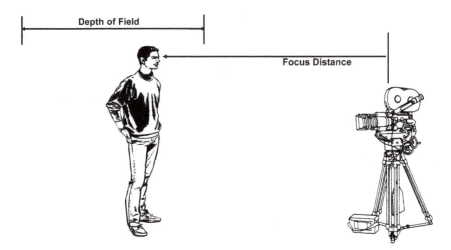

Figure 5.32   Basic principle of depth of field. (Camera illustration reprinted from the *Panaflex Users Manual* with permission of David Samuelson and Panavision Inc.)

depth of field behind the principal point of focus than in front of it. This is generally referred to as the one-third-two-thirds rule ($\frac{1}{3}$–$\frac{2}{3}$), which says that there is approximately $\frac{1}{3}$ of the depth of field in front of the point of focus and $\frac{2}{3}$ behind the point of focus (see Figure 5.32). There are a number of factors that directly affect the depth of field for any given situation. These factors include the focal length of the lens, f-stop, distance to the subject, and the format you are shooting. The smaller your shooting format, the more depth of field you have, so generally 16 mm has more depth of field for a given situation than 35 mm. To calculate your depth of field you must know the following:

1. Focal length of the lens
2. Size of the aperture (f-stop)
3. Distance from subject to the camera film plane

To find the depth of field for a particular situation, you may use the depth-of-field tables available in many film reference books or one of the commercially available depth-of-field calculators. The problem with most of the depth-of-field tables in many books is that they list only a limited number of focal length lenses. An example of a depth-of-field table is shown in Figure 5.33 .

For the depth-of-field table our focal length is 50 mm. Let's use an aperture of 2.8 and a distance of 15 ft to determine our depth of field. Knowing these three factors enables you to read that the depth of field is from 13 ft, 4 in. to 17 ft, 3 in. What happens if you are using a

Lens Focal Length = 50mm								Circle of Confusion = .001"
f 1.4	**f 2**	**f 2.8**	**f 4**	**f 5.6**	**f 8**	**f 11**	**f 16**	**f 22**
LENS FOCUS DISTANCE NEAR FAR	NEAR FAR	NEAR FAR	NEAR FAR	NEAR FAR	NEAR FAR	NEAR FAR	NEAR FAR	NEAR FAR
3' 3' 3' 1"	2' 11" 3' 1"	2' 11" 3' 1"	2' 11" 3' 1"	2' 10" 3' 2"	2' 10" 3' 3"	2' 9" 3' 4"	2' 8" 3' 6"	2' 6" 3' 9"
4' 3' 11" 4' 1"	3' 11" 4' 1"	3' 11" 4' 2"	3' 10" 4' 3"	3' 10" 4' 4"	3' 8" 4' 5"	3' 7" 4' 8"	3' 5" 5'	3' 2" 5' 6"
5' 4' 11" 5' 1"	4' 10" 5' 2"	4' 10" 5' 3"	4' 9" 5' 4"	4' 8" 5' 6"	4' 6" 5' 9"	4' 4" 6'	4' 1" 6' 8"	3' 9" 7' 7"
6' 5' 10" 6' 2"	5' 10" 6' 3"	5' 9" 6' 4"	5' 7" 6' 6"	5' 6" 6' 8"	5' 3" 7' 1"	5' 7' 7"	4' 8" 8' 7"	4' 3" 10' 2"
7' 6' 10" 7' 3"	6' 9" 7'4"	6' 7" 7' 5"	6' 6" 7' 8"	6' 3" 8'	6' 8' 6"	5' 9" 9' 2"	5' 3" 10' 9"	4' 10" 13' 6"
8' 7' 9" 8' 4"	7' 8" 8' 5"	7' 6" 8' 7"	7' 4" 8' 11"	7' 1" 9' 4"	6' 9" 10'	6' 4" 11'	5' 9" 13' 4"	5' 2" 17' 8"
9' 8' 8" 9' 4"	8' 7" 9' 6"	8' 4" 9' 9"	8' 2" 10' 2"	7' 10" 10' 8"	7' 5" 11' 7"	6' 11" 13'	6' 4" 16' 4"	5' 8" 23' 8"
10' 9' 7" 10' 5"	9' 5" 10' 8"	9' 3" 10' 11"	8' 11" 11' 5"	8' 7" 12' 1"	8' 1" 13' 4"	7' 6" 15' 3"	6' 9" 20'	5' 11" 32'
12' 11' 5" 12' 8"	11' 2" 13'	10' 11" 13' 5"	10' 6" 14' 1"	10' 15' 2"	9' 4" 17' 1"	8' 7" 20' 5"	7' 8" 30'	6' 9" 67'
15' 14' 1" 16' 1"	13' 9" 16' 6"	13' 4" 17' 3"	12' 8" 18' 5"	12' 20' 4"	11' 23' 11"	10' 30' 10"	8' 9" 59'	7' 7" INF
20' 18' 5" 21' 11"	17' 10" 22' 10"	17' 1" 24' 2"	16' 1" 26' 7"	14' 11" 30' 8"	13' 6" 39' 10"	12' 63'	10' 2" INF	8' 7" INF
25' 22' 7" 28' 1"	21' 8" 29' 7"	20' 7" 31'11"	19' 1" 36'	17' 5" 44'	15' 5" 66'	14' 168'	11' INF	9' INF
50' 41' 1" 64'	38' 72'	35' 88'	31' 131'	27' 376'	22' INF	19' INF	14' INF	11' INF

Figure 5.33 Depth-of-field table: focal length of lens = 50 mm, film format = 35 mm.

focal length lens that is not listed in the book? How do you find your depth of field? Most assistants, myself included, usually use one of the commercially available depth-of-field calculators. Some of these devices allow you to dial in the focal length, f-stop or t-stop, and subject distance and then read the depth of field. When I first started working as a First Assistant, two of the most commonly used depth-of-field calculators were the Guild Kelly Calculator for both 16 mm and 35 mm, and the Samuelson Mark II Calculator (see Figures 5.34 and 5.35).

Assistant Cameraman David Eubank has developed an application that is available for the iPhone, iPad, or iPod Touch. The app is called pCAM Film+Digital Calculator and can be found on the iTunes web site and can be downloaded directly to your device. You can find out more information on pCAM Film+Digital Calculator at

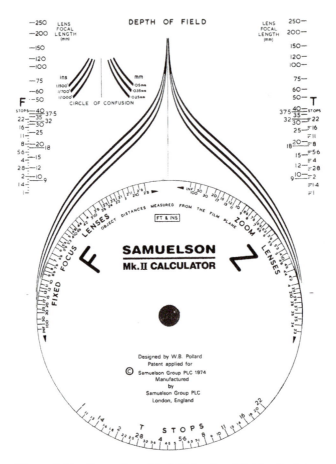

Figure 5.34   Samuelson Mark II depth-of-field calculator.

David Eubank's web site at www.davideubank.com. The application is a great tool for calculating depth of field quickly. You first choose the format you are shooting. Then you enter the f-stop, focus distance, and the focal length of the lens, and the near and far limits of your depth of field are shown on the screen (see Figure 5.36).

There are many other excellent applications for the iPhone, iPad, and iPod Touch. One of these is Toland ASC Digital Assistant, developed by Chemical Wedding. This app has some of the same features as pCAM Film+Digital Calculator, including depth of field. Toland ASC Digital Assistant also has a feature for keeping camera logs as discussed previously in Chapter 4. Figure 5.37 shows a screen shot of the depth-of-field screen from Toland ASC Digital Assistant. Further discussion of some of the other features of pCAM Film+Digital

Figure 5.35 Guild Kelly depth-of-field calculator.

Calculator and Toland ASC Digital Assistant can be found later in this chapter in the Using Computers and Technology section. While there are many other apps that calculate depth of field it would take up too much space in this book to list and show them all. I have chosen to show only two of them here but many others are listed on the companion web site for the book.

When expressing your depth of field, it should always be stated as a range from the closest point to the farthest point and not as a single number. By always stating your depth of field as a range of distance, it will help you to remember your limits or the actor's limits for a particular scene or shot. When using depth-of-field tables, remember that the depth of field is different depending on whether you are working with 16 mm, 35 mm, or digital. The circle of confusion chosen for the particular format you are shooting will have a bearing on your depth of field. The circle of confusion for 16 mm is generally accepted to be 0.0006 in., while the circle of confusion for 35 mm is generally accepted to be 0.001 in. The definition of circle of

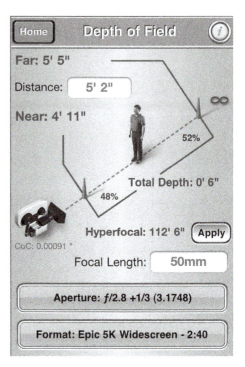

Figure 5.36 Depth of field screen shot from pCAM Film+Digital Calculator. (Courtesy of David Eubank.)

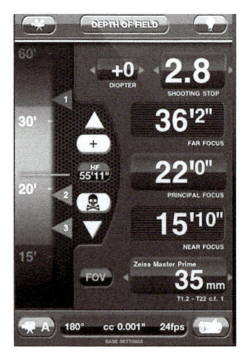

Figure 5.37 Depth of field screen shot from Toland ASC Digital Assistant. (Courtesy of Chemical Wedding.)

confusion can be quite confusing itself and depends on whom you are speaking with about the subject. Rather than try to explain it here I recommend looking at some of the cinematography books listed in the Recommended Reading section at the end of the book. Please bear in mind that depth of field is not an exact science and is based on different lens characteristics and designs. Depth-of-field limits should be used only as a guide, and for most shooting situations the limits for near and far distances will be acceptable.

The following examples illustrate how each of the three factors affects the depth of field:

1. Size of the aperture or f-stop: You have more depth of field with larger f-stop numbers (smaller aperture openings) than with smaller f-stop numbers (larger aperture openings) as long as the focal length and subject distance remain the same. *Example:* A large aperture, such as f/2.8, has less depth of field at a specific distance than does a small aperture, such as f/8, at the same focal length and the same distance (see Figure 5.38).
2. Focal length of the lens: You have more depth of field with wide-angle lenses than with telephoto lenses as long as the f-stop and subject distance remain the same. *Example:* A wide-angle lens, such as 25 mm, will have more depth of field at a specific distance and f-stop than a telephoto lens, such as 100 mm, at the same distance and f-stop (see Figure 5.39).
3. Subject distance from the camera: You have more depth of field with a distant subject than with a close subject as long as the f-stop and focal length remain the same. *Example:* An object 20 ft from the camera at a specific f-stop and focal length has more depth of field than an object 8 ft from the camera at the same f-stop and focal length (see Figure 5.40).

You will often be in a situation where there are two actors in the scene at different distances from the camera, and the Director would like to have both of them in focus for the shot. Common sense would say that if you were to focus ½ the distance between the two, they should both be in focus. But due to the principles of depth of field, this is not the case. When holding focus on two different objects in the same scene, one closer to the camera than the other, you do not set the focus at a point halfway between the two. You would actually focus on a point that is ⅓ the distance between the two objects to have both of them in focus. This is related to the principle discussed earlier that says ⅓ of your depth of field is in front of the point of focus and ⅔ of the depth of field is behind it. This principle or theory is often referred to as the ⅓ rule. Remember that this is a theory that does not work in every situation. You must check the depth-of-field

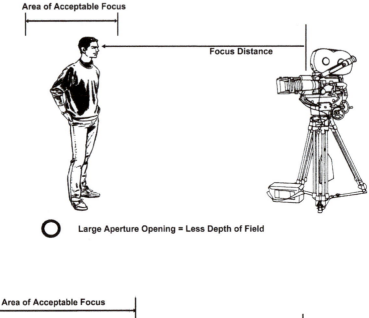

Large Aperture Opening = Less Depth of Field

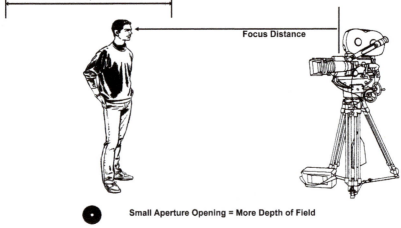

Small Aperture Opening = More Depth of Field

Figure 5.38 Diagram illustrating how the size of aperture (f-stop) affects distance. (Camera illustration reprinted from the *Panaflex Users Manual* with permission of David Samuelson and Panavision Inc.)

tables or use the depth-of-field calculators to be sure. It will depend on the depth of field for the ⅓ point (the point of focus). Check to see if the distance to each object falls within this range of your depth of field. If it does, then the ⅓ rule works. If not, you may need to change one of the variables. You may need to move the objects or subjects closer together, change the focal length of the lens, change the

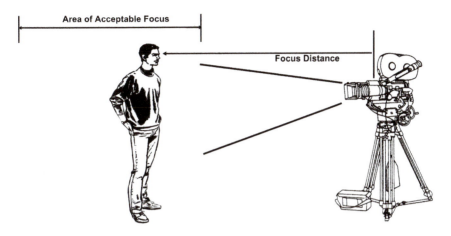

20mm Wide Angle = More Depth of Field

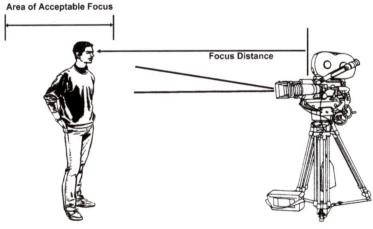

75mm Telephoto = Less Depth of Field

Figure 5.39   Diagram illustrating how the focal length of the lens affects depth of field. (Camera illustration reprinted from the *Panaflex Users Manual* with permission of David Samuelson and Panavision Inc.)

lighting, or keep only one of the actors in focus at a time. You should always check with the DP about whether you should split the focus or whether you should favor one actor over another in the scene. Splitting the focus between two subjects can be dangerous, though. Each subject may be just on the edges of the depth of field, and when you split the focus between them, they both end up looking a bit soft and slightly out of focus. Many DPs with whom I have spoken prefer

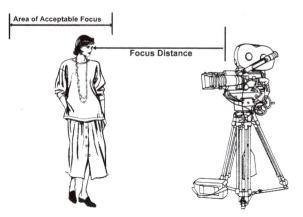

Close Subject = Less Depth of Field

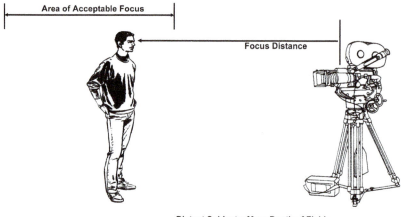

Distant Subject = More Depth of Field

Figure 5.40   Diagram illustrating how the subject distance affects depth of field. (Camera illustration reprinted from the *Panaflex Users Manual* with permission of David Samuelson and Panavision Inc.)

to have the 1st AC keep the focus on the person who is speaking and then shift the focus when the other subject is speaking. This is the method that I prefer, and I feel that it looks more natural. By shifting the focus, it brings the viewer's attention to the person who is important at that particular point in the scene. I know of an assistant who claimed that you should always focus on the actor getting the higher salary. Hopefully he was joking at the time.

The following example illustrates the ⅓ rule. *Example:* The first object is 8 ft from the camera, and the second object is 14 ft from the camera. Using the ⅓ rule, set the focus at 10 ft to have both objects in focus. The distance between the two is 6 ft (14 − 8 = 6). One-third of this distance is 2 ft (6 ÷ 3 = 2). Set the focus at 10 ft (8 + 2 = 10). Using the depth-of-field table from Figure 5.33, we see that this example will work only for f-stop numbers of f/11 or higher (see Figure 5.41).

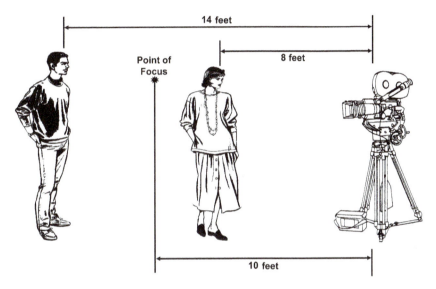

Figure 5.41 Diagram illustrating the ⅓ principle for splitting focus between two objects. (Camera illustration reprinted from the *Panaflex Users Manual* with permission of David Samuelson and Panavision Inc.)

Another special situation when working with depth of field is called the hyperfocal distance. The hyperfocal distance may be defined as the closest focus distance to the lens that will also be in focus when the lens is focused at infinity (∞). Another way to describe hyperfocal distance is to say that it is the closest point of acceptable focus when the lens is focused at infinity. You must check the depth-of-field tables to find out your hyperfocal distance for a given focal length and f-stop. If you are using the pCAM Film+Digital Calculator or Toland ASC Digital Assistant apps, the hyperfocal distance will be indicated on the depth-of-field screen for your particular situation. If you refer back to Figure 5.36, you will see that for that particular example the hyperfocal distance is 112 ft, 6 in. If you refer back to Figure 5.37, you will see that for that particular example the hyperfocal distance is 55 ft, 11 in. If you set the focus of the

lens to the hyperfocal distance, your depth of field will be from ½ the hyperfocal distance to infinity. In other words, setting the focus to the hyperfocal distance gives you the maximum depth of field. For the above example, if you set the focus to 112 ft, 6 in, your depth of field will be from 56 ft, 3 in to infinity. Appendix E contains tables listing hyperfocal distances for both 16 mm and 35 mm film formats (Tables E.9 and E.10).

When calculating the depth of field, you should always use f-stops. Depth-of-field tables and calculators base all depth-of-field calculations on f-stop numbers and not t-stop settings. Use the t-stop only when setting the aperture on the lens. It's important that you remember to not take the depth-of-field calculations too literally. The focus does not fall off abruptly at the near and far range of depth of field. It is more of a gradual decrease to where a point that is sharp and in focus becomes a blurred circle that is out of focus.

F-stops and T-stops

In professional cinematography, many lenses may be calibrated in both f-stops and t-stops. An f-stop is a mathematical calculation based on the size of the diaphragm opening, and the t-stop is a measurement of the actual amount of light transmitted through the lens at each diaphragm or aperture opening of the lens. The f-stop is determined by dividing the focal length of the lens by the diaphragm opening. This gives us an indication of how much light should get through the lens in a perfect world. The f-stop doesn't accurately represent the amount of light coming through the lens because it doesn't take into account the amount of light loss caused as the light passes through the many glass elements within the lens. But remember that all exposure meter readings are given in f-stops, and all depth-of-field tables and charts are calculated using f-stops. The t-stop is a measurement of exactly how much light is transmitted through the lens. Because it takes into account the light loss as it passes through the many glass elements of the lens, it is much more accurate. Because the t-stop is an actual measurement and is more accurate, it should always be used when setting the exposure on the lens. Many times a lens will be calibrated for both f-stops and t-stops. In referring to the exposure readings and aperture settings, most camera personnel will use the terms f-stop and t-stop interchangeably.

When the DP gives you the exposure reading for a particular shot, repeat it back to him or her. This reminds the DP of what he or she told you and also enables the DP to change the exposure if necessary. Most DPs try to maintain a constant exposure, especially on

interior locations, so if they forget to give you an exposure reading, you probably will be safe if you set the aperture to the setting of the previous shot. Always check with the DP for each new setup to be sure that you set the correct exposure.

If for some reason you forget to set the exposure, or you set the wrong exposure, notify the DP immediately. He or she will then request another take of the shot with the exposure set correctly. As a professional you should admit the mistake at the time it is made rather than to try to cover it up. We're only human and mistakes do happen. If you do not let the DP know about the error, it will be discovered when the dailies are viewed and the shot comes up on the screen either underexposed or overexposed. As a result, you may lose the job.

When setting the stop on the lens, you should open the lens to its widest opening and then close down to the correct stop. This will compensate for any sticking that may occur in the leaves of the diaphragm if you just changed from one stop to another. *Example:* You are using a lens that has a widest opening of 1.4. The lens is currently set at 5.6. The DP instructs you to change the stop to a 4. Open up the lens all the way to 1.4 and then stop down to the new setting of 4.

As mentioned in Chapter 1, the standard series of f-stop or t-stop numbers is 1, 1.4, 2, 2.8, 4, 5.6, 8, 11, 16, 22, 32, 45. Each number represents one full f-stop, and each full stop admits ½ as much light as the one before it. For example, f/4 admits half as much light through the lens as f/2.8. See Figure 1.28 in Chapter 1 for examples of f-stop/t-stop numbers and the corresponding diaphragm openings. In the preceding example, I used the terms *open up* and *stop down* when referring to the changing of the f-stop opening. When we say stopping down or closing down the lens, it means that the diaphragm opening gets smaller, and the numbers get larger. Opening up the lens means that the diaphragm opening gets larger, and the numbers get smaller. Increasing the stop is the same as opening up the lens, and decreasing the stop is the same as stopping down the lens. When you change from one f-stop or t-stop number to a larger number (smaller opening), you are closing down or stopping down the lens. When you change from one f-stop number to a smaller number (larger opening), you are opening up the lens. Opening up the lens by one stop will double the amount of light striking the film, and closing down by one stop will halve the amount of light. *Example:* The current aperture setting is t/5.6. Stopping down or decreasing it by one stop makes the aperture become t/8. Opening up or increasing it by one stop makes the aperture become t/4. The numbering system for the t-stops and f-stops is the same as mentioned previously.

Because of the physical limitations in the design and manufacture of lenses, it is not possible to make a lens of uniform

photographic quality. This means that the image at the edges of the lens may not be as sharp as the image closer to the center of the lens. Many lens manufacturers recommend that you not use the edges of the lens by stopping down approximately two stops from the widest f-stop or t-stop setting. This is called your *critical aperture*, and in theory it will give you the sharpest image.

When the DP tells you the f-stop or t-stop to be set on the lens, he or she may say it in a number of different ways, for example "halfway between 2.8 and 4," or "the stop is 3⅓," or "it is a 3.4," and so on. I recommend discussing with the DP how he or she will give you the stops so that you understand exactly what the DP means. One person's interpretation of "4½" may not be the same as another person's interpretation. There are actual numbers for the intermediate f-stops/t-stops listed previously. See Table E.4 in Appendix E for the intermediate f-stop/t-stop settings for ¼, ⅓, ½, ⅔, and ¾ of the way between full stops.

Whenever you film at a frame rate other than 24 fps, you must change the stop to compensate for the new frame rate. If you film at speeds faster than 24 fps, less light strikes each frame of film, so you must increase your exposure. If you film at speeds slower than 24 fps, more light strikes each frame of film, so you must decrease your exposure. Table E.7 in Appendix E shows the f-stop/t-stop compensation for various changes in frames per second.

It also may be necessary to adjust your exposure when you are using certain filters on the camera. Some filters decrease the amount of light passing through the lens, while others have no effect on the amount of light. Any exposure change will always be an increase, requiring you to open up the aperture. Tables E.5 and E.6 in Appendix E lists some of the most commonly used filters and the amount of f-stop or t-stop compensation, if any, for each. There are many other filters in use that require some type of exposure compensation. Check with the camera rental house about the filters you are using. It will also be necessary to adjust your exposure when you are filming with a different shutter angle set on the camera. The standard shutter angle on a motion picture camera is 180 degrees. The maximum shutter angle you can achieve with some film cameras is 200 degrees. In most cases, changing your shutter angle involves making it smaller than normal to achieve a desired effect on the film. When reducing the shutter angle, you are causing less light to strike your film as the shutter spins, so you must open your lens aperture accordingly. Table E.8 in Appendix E shows the f-stop or t-stop compensation for changes in shutter angle.

In some shooting situations you may use a lens extender for a particular shot. A lens extender allows you to increase the focal

length of the lens. It gives you an inexpensive way to obtain a longer focal length lens without actually renting additional lenses. Two of the most common lens extenders are the 1.4x and the 2x extenders. For example, a 150 mm lens becomes a 300 mm lens when using a 2x extender. When using one of these, you should keep in mind that the aperture will effectively be less than the aperture without the extender. The amount of aperture change is based on the value of the extender. For example, a 10–100 T4 lens becomes a 20–200 T8 lens when using the 2x extender. You should also keep in mind that the image quality when using an extender will not be as good as without the extender. However, as stated earlier, they are an inexpensive way to get a tighter shot without renting additional lenses.

Changing Lenses, Filters, and Accessories

Whenever you are asked to place a new lens, filter, or any other accessory on the camera, it should be done as quickly as possible so that the DP or Camera Operator can line up the shot. But don't rush the process because you don't want to drop one of the most expensive pieces of film equipment, thereby causing delays in production, not to mention the strong possibility of one or more of the Camera Assistants losing their job. You must develop a protocol for this procedure and make sure that each assistant knows precisely what their job is during the change of the item, and everything should go smoothly.

The standard procedure for changing lenses, filters, or accessories on the camera is as follows. As soon as the DP calls for a change in lens or filter, the First Assistant repeats the request so that the DP and the 2nd AC hear. This lets the DP know that the request was heard and that it was heard correctly, and it lets the 2nd AC know to retrieve the item from the equipment case/cart. The 2nd AC should repeat the request so that the 1st AC knows that it was heard correctly. While the 2nd AC is getting the new item the 1st AC removes the old item from the camera and prepares the camera to accept the new item, whether it is a lens, filter or accessory. If changing lenses the 2nd AC should remove the lens caps and leave them in the lens case, set the focus to infinity, f-stop/t-stop to its most wide open setting and, if a zoom, set the focal length to the most wide-angle setting as he/she brings the new lens to the camera. The 2nd AC should also check the front and rear lens elements for dirt, dust or smudges. Don't clean it yet though. Once at the camera the 2nd AC will exchange the new lens for the old lens. When changing lenses I recommend placing the old lens in the 2nd AC's palm, with the front element face down. This allows them to get a secure grip on the lens without dropping it.

Remember, when exchanging items both assistants should give some type of indication that they have a firm grip on the item so that the other person knows that it is all right to release it. I usually say, "Got it," when exchanging items with my assistant and this is what I recommend for you. This lets him or her know that I have a firm grip on it and they can let go. The 2nd AC should also say, "Got it," when they have a firm grip on the piece of equipment. No matter how big or small the equipment is, when exchanging items always indicate that you have a firm grip so that there is no chance of anything getting dropped. While the 1st AC places the new item on the camera, the 2nd AC places the old one back in the equipment case. Once the lens has been approved by the DP you can then remove it for cleaning if necessary. In most cases the DP does not want to wait for you to clean the lens before looking at it. What if it turns out to not be the right focal length? You have now wasted valuable time cleaning a lens that won't be used for the shot. This is usually the standard protocol when changing lenses or filters but I always check with the DP at the beginning of a show as to the protocol he/she prefers when changing anything on the camera. I especially do this if it is a DP that I have not worked with in the past. When changing filters the same basic protocol is followed. While the First Assistant removes the old filter, the Second Assistant gets the new filter from the case, checks it for dirt or smudges, but doesn't clean it right away. Any filter change should be made quickly so that the DP and Operator can see it and approve it first. Once it is approved, then you can take a moment to clean it if necessary. When changing or adding other accessories to the camera, the 1st AC makes the camera ready for the item while the 2nd AC retrieves them from the proper equipment case.

As stated in Chapter 4, don't leave an equipment case without closing the case and securing at least one of the latches on the case. I recommend always securing both latches on any case before you walk away from it, but if you are in a rush, at least one latch will be sufficient until you can get back to the case. There have been a few times when I have picked up a case that my assistant or the Camera Trainee forgot to latch. Fortunately, in most cases I realized it in time before any of the contents spilled out. During filming, there are many different camera setups, and the equipment must be moved many times during the day. If a case is not latched and someone else picks it up to move it, there could be disastrous results. Lenses, filters or accessories could come tumbling out of the case and become damaged. If someone outside of the camera department did pick up an unlatched case and spill its contents, it would not be the fault of the person picking up the case but rather the fault of the camera crew member who failed to secure one of the latches.

When placing a new lens on the camera remember to engage the follow-focus gear and adjust the position of the matte box if necessary. If using a zoom motor, check that it is engaged on the gears of the lens, the power cable is connected, and it works properly. Look through the eyepiece after changing a lens to be sure that it is focused properly; that there is no vignetting; that the matte box, hard matte, or lens shade is not cutting into the shot; and that the shutter is cleared for the Camera Operator to view the scene. If you are not able to look through the eyepiece, ask the Camera Operator to check for you. Also, when changing lenses, you may have to change the lens support rods because of the physical size of the lens. When bringing the lens from the case, the 2nd AC should remember to bring the appropriate lens support rods and any support brackets that may be required. When changing lenses it may also often be necessary to rebalance the camera, such as when you change from a prime lens to a zoom lens or vice versa. Remember to check the balance whenever any new piece of equipment has been added to or taken away from the camera. The camera must be balanced properly for the Camera Operator to do his or her job correctly. If you are using any filters, a small identification label should be placed on the side of the matte box or camera stating which filter is in use. Without this reminder tag, the DP, Camera Operator, or 1st AC may forget which filter is in place and then forget to compensate the exposure. Many assistants, myself included, have a set of small engraved filter tags that are used whenever a filter is placed in the matte box. These tags have Velcro on the back, and during the prep I usually place a small piece of Velcro on the matte box. When using a particular filter, I attach one of these engraved tags to the Velcro strip that I placed on the side of the matte box. Placing a tag on the matte box or camera reminds the 1st AC and the DP that there is a filter in front of the lens (see Figure 5.42).

Focus Measurements and Following Focus

During most scenes the actors will be moving to various spots on the set, and during the rehearsals the 2nd AC will place tape or some other type of mark on the floor or ground for each actor's position for the scene. It is the First Assistant's job to keep the actors in focus for every position they are in during the scene. During the rehearsal the 1st AC will measure the distance from the camera film plane to the actor for each position and each camera position of the shot. There are times when actors don't stop on their marks, so at least by knowing the distances to these marks you should be able to estimate their distance from the camera. Actors' marks were discussed in detail

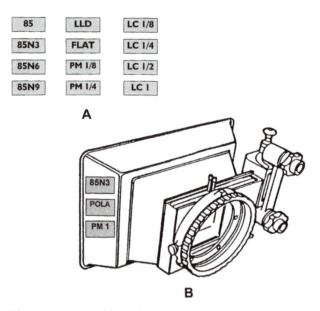

A

B

Figure 5.42   A, Filter identification tags. **B,** Filter
identification tags in place on matte box. (Reprinted
from the *Panaflex Users Manual* with permission of
David Samuelson and Panavision Inc.)

in Chapter 4. Focus may also be obtained by eye through the viewfinder and this will be discussed later in this section. For beginners,
it is important to remember that the focus measurement is taken from
the film plane of the camera to the actor or subject. The film plane is
the point in the camera where the film sits in the gate and where the
image comes into focus on the film; it is from this point that all focus
measurements are taken. On most professional motion picture cameras, there is a pin or hook attached to the body of the camera that is
precisely in line with the film plane. The 1st AC will connect the tape
measure to this pin or hook to measure the focus distance. There is
often a special symbol engraved or painted on the side of the camera
to indicate the positioning of the film plane (see Figure 5.43).

If it is not possible or convenient to measure to the actor during rehearsals, obtain focus marks by measuring to the positions of
the stand-ins or use your 2nd AC or Camera Trainee as a stand-in.
The stand-ins will stand at the marks for each actor so that you can
measure the distance. Just before you get ready to shoot the scene,
you may need to double check these focus measurements when the
actual actors step in. This is especially important on scenes that

Figure 5.43   Mark indicating the film plane on a motion picture camera.

involve critical focus marks where you have very little depth of field. After a shot has been completed, if you have any doubts about the focus, ask for a moment to check the focus of the actor on his or her mark to determine if the focus was good, or you may ask the Camera Operator if he or she noticed any focus problems with the shot. If you are unsure, the Camera Operator is the best person to tell if the focus was sharp or not. The Camera Operator is the only person who sees the image through the viewfinder, and he or she will be able to see any shifts or problems with the focus of the image. Because many older video taps were not very accurate, I did not rely on the video tap image to judge the focus unless I had checked its accuracy beforehand. Many of the newer video taps and small monitors are actually very good for judging focus. The important thing is to check the accuracy of the video tap and monitor before relying on it for judging focus. This will often be done during the camera prep.

When obtaining the focus measurements, you should do it as quickly and unobtrusively as possible without interfering with the Director, actors, or other crew members. A good Camera Assistant is one who is efficient, quick, invisible, and quiet. There are so many people on the set that any idle chatter or unnecessary noise tends to be distracting to crew members who are trying to work and also to the actors who are trying to rehearse their lines. It is important to remember to never let anyone rush you when obtaining your focus marks or distances. The most beautiful lighting, set design, costumes, makeup, and performance are not worth anything if the shot is out of focus.

When obtaining your focus mark or measuring the distance to subjects, you must be aware of a special situation that often arises. When you are filming the reflection of a subject, such as in a mirror, you must first measure the distance from the camera to the mirror and then to the subject. For example, if the distance from the camera to the surface of the mirror is 10 ft, and the distance from the mirror to the

subject is 5 ft, then you would set the focus of the lens to 15 ft (10 + 5 = 15) to have the reflection of the subject sharp and in focus.

In most cases you will be in one of the following four situations regarding focus for a shot:

1. Stationary camera and stationary actor
2. Stationary camera and moving actor
3. Moving camera and stationary actor
4. Moving camera and moving actor

If an actor and camera are stationary, focusing is actually pretty simple. Measure the distance to the actor and set this distance on the focus barrel of the lens. When an actor or camera or both are moving, focusing during the shot becomes more challenging and sometimes, for me, more fun. When the camera is stationary and the actor is moving in the scene, such as walking toward or away from the camera, the 1st AC will often place tape marks or chalk marks on the ground as reference points for focusing. Depending on the complexity of the shot, the lens being used and the f-stop/t-stop setting, there may only be a beginning mark and an end mark, or there may be these two marks plus many in-between marks. The focus marks are usually placed about 1 ft apart, but the easiest and best way is to place them according to the markings on the lens.

When I am placing focus marks, I usually base my marks on how the lens is marked. For example, if the lens has focus markings at 5, 6, 7, 8, 10, 12, 15, and 20 ft, I place focus reference marks according to these distances. When following focus, it is much easier for me to hit an exact mark on the lens rather than having to guess. As an actor passes these marks, the 1st AC adjusts the focus to correspond to the distance measured to each point. If the ground or floor is seen in the shot, the 1st AC would measure to various places on the set, such as pieces of furniture, paintings on the wall, light switches, etc. If filming outdoors you could use trees, shrubs, rocks, fences, sign posts, etc., as reference points.

If the actor is stationary and the camera is moving during the scene, either toward or away from the actor, the assistant usually places marks in line with one of the dolly wheels at 1-ft intervals or, as stated above, according to the marks on the lens. As the dolly wheel moves past these marks, the assistant adjusts focus to correspond with each mark. When placing these marks, I have found that it is easier to line them up with the center of the dolly wheel (axle). Finally, if both the actor and camera are moving, focusing can become much more difficult, challenging, and even fun, depending on how you look at it. Each shot is going to be different and it's not possible or practical for me to try to explain every possible scenario when doing

a shot with moving camera and dolly. The only real way to get good at pulling focus is to practice and actually do it.

I have done many shots where the camera on the dolly is moving backward while the actor is walking toward the lens. Whenever possible it helps if the actor can maintain the same walking speed and distance from the camera throughout the shot. However, for some shots this is not possible. Unfortunately, many actors don't do the same thing twice. During the rehearsal they play the scene one way, and then for each subsequent take, something is different. You must learn to adapt quickly because the focus of the shot is your responsibility.

The Dolly Grip is an important part of this in that he or she must maintain the proper dolly speed as well. One of the tools that I use to help with the focus of this type of shot is a laser pointer. I position the pointer so that the point of light hits the floor at a specific distance from the camera, for example 8 ft. I also check that the point is out of the frame of the shot. As the actor and camera are moving together, if the actor gets too close or too far away from this point, I can usually accurately judge the distance and adjust the focus accordingly. If it is a tight enough shot, you may be able to place focus marks on the floor, but too many marks can often confuse rather than help you. The laser pointer method can also be used if the actor is moving away from the camera that is following him or her. But when you have the camera moving on one plane and the actor on another, things can get very interesting to say the least. Because each situation is different and no two shots are alike, you need to work out the best and easiest way to focus a complicated moving shot. As you work more and more, you will develop your own system for focusing and marking.

Because of the principles of depth of field, focus marks are not as critical when using a wide-angle lens, and you may not need to measure to as many points as you would if you were shooting with a long focal length or telephoto lens. For each distance measured, the 1st AC will mark the lens or focus-marking disk accordingly so that he or she may rack focus or follow focus during the scene. The focus-marking disk is a circular white piece of plastic that is attached to the follow-focus mechanism. Using a grease pencil or erasable marker, the 1st AC marks the disk according to the distances measured for the shot. Some assistants will wrap a thin piece of tape around the barrel of the lens and place the focus marks on it for the shot. I personally don't like to use the focus-marking disks on the follow-focus mechanisms and usually leave them in the equipment case when setting up the camera. I prefer to mark the lens directly either by wrapping a thin piece of chart tape around the barrel or marking the lens directly with some type of erasable marking pencil (see Figures 5.44 and 5.45).

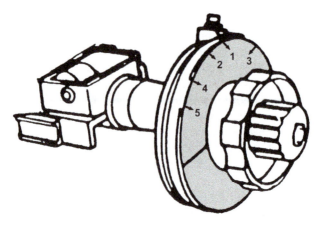

Figure 5.44   Focus-marking disk on follow-focus mechanism marked for following focus. (Reprinted from the *Panaflex Users Manual* with permission of David Samuelson and Panavision Inc.)

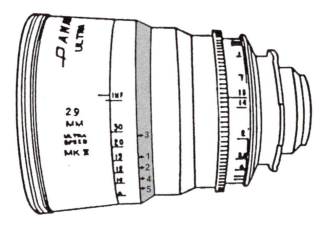

Figure 5.45   Lens marked for following focus. (Reprinted from the *Panaflex Users Manual* with permission of David Samuelson and Panavision Inc.)

In addition, the assistant may place a reminder tape near the lens with the distances listed on it for the particular shot. It is a good idea for the 1st AC to keep a small notepad to record the focus distances and lens sizes for each scene. This information may be written in *The Camera Log* book that was discussed in Chapter 4. Many times you may do a shot of one actor for a scene, and then later in the day you need to do a reverse-angle shot of another actor or actors for the same scene. The

shots should be made with the same focal length lens and at the same distance as the first shot so they will match when edited together. If you have the numbers written down for the previous shot, it will be no problem to match the focal length and distance for the matching shots.

When you are filming on a sound stage, permanent sets, or practical locations, you often can measure the length and width of each set and record these distances on a sheet of paper or in your notepad for future use. This way if you are in a rush situation and are unable to obtain all of your focus measurements, you can estimate the distance based on where the camera is placed on the set. After a while you should become experienced at guessing the distances with some degree of accuracy. If you have a complicated focus move to do, request at least one rehearsal before shooting the scene.

You may also obtain the focus marks by looking through the eyepiece and focusing on the subject by eye. You then make a mark on the lens to indicate the focus. Always open the aperture on the lens to its widest opening when obtaining focus marks by eye. On a zoom lens, you should zoom in to the tightest focal length to obtain an eye focus. When you have the focus mark, return the zoom to its correct focal length for shooting. On all lenses, remember to set the correct t-stop setting after obtaining eye focus marks.

Following focus or pulling focus is a very precise and exact job, and it can be learned only by actually doing it. It takes much practice and experience to be able to do it well and cannot be explained fully in any book. One important thing to remember when pulling focus is to keep a very light touch on the follow-focus mechanism. The Camera Operator must follow the action within a scene, and he or she does not want anything to prevent smooth pans or tilts with the camera because the 1st AC had a tight grip on the focus knob.

Getting Your Marks

For the First Assistant Cameraman, obtaining your focus marks is just as important as keeping the shot in focus. The actor's focus is determined by their distance from the camera film plane. This distance is determined by measuring using some type of tape measure or other measuring tool. Today you have many different tools at your disposal to help you in getting accurate focus marks. You should always have two different types of tape measures, the cloth or "soft" tape measure and the metal "hard" tape measure. The soft tape measure is commonly available in 50 ft lengths and the hard tape is often 20 or 25 ft in length. In recent years more and more assistants also use some type of laser measuring devices. A very popular one of these is the Hilti PD-40 laser measuring device.

The cloth or soft tape measure is the most commonly and most often used tape measure. It is usually made of fiberglass, 50 ft long and wound onto a spool for ease of use. It is one of the best tools for getting precise focus measurements. The 1st AC hooks the end of the tape onto the pin or hook located at the film plane of the film camera and then walks out from the camera to the actor or subject to get a precise measurement. You should always use this type of tape measure when you know you will have little depth of field and when you need to get multiple focus marks very quickly. I usually place a piece of 1-in. camera tape on the back of the case so that I can write down multiple measurements, which I then transfer to the lens (or focus disk) when I go back to the camera. Keep in mind that with repeated use the soft tape may stretch over time so you should periodically check it with the metal or hard tape to be sure that it is accurate.

The "hard" tape is a standard steel tape measure that you have seen most carpenters use. As with any of the tools you will use in the day-to-day performance of your job, I recommend purchasing a good quality "hard" tape that will last a long time. One that has at least a ¾-in. or 1-in. wide blade is best because you can extend it out at least 10 ft or more before it won't stand out and begins to bend. Stanley makes one of the best and it is called a FatMax tape. The hard or metal tape allows the 1st AC to stand at the camera and extend the tape out toward the actor to obtain a quick measurement. Often times the experienced actor will grab the end of the tape and hold it near their eye for you. You must be very careful when using the metal tape so that you don't hit anybody with it. Pay close attention to where the end of the tape is at all times. Also be sure that you are holding it at the film plane so that your measurements are accurate.

Laser tape measures are very accurate and are best used when you have a lot of depth of field and need to have an accurate measurement to the actor or subject. Be very careful when using one so that you are not shining it in the actor's or anybody's eyes. It's best to point these at their chest and you can compensate the small distance between their eyes and chest. Laser tape measures are best used when you have to focus on an object or subject that is a great distance from the camera and you cannot use the soft or hard tape, and cannot get an accurate eye focus. They are especially useful when doing shots with long telephoto lenses.

When measuring your focus you always start at the film plane of the camera. Hook your tape measure onto the camera and measure to each subject in the scene. Make sure you know which part of the subject you want in focus. For an actor it is most often their eyes, but in some cases it may be another part of their body. Be sure you know this before the camera rolls on the shot. You should also get focus

marks for some reference points in the scene such as pieces of furniture, paintings on a wall, light switches, etc. Once you have all of your marks, place them on the lens or follow-focus marking disk.

When pulling focus with the camera mounted to a dolly I usually use the center of the dolly wheel as my reference point. Since the camera is mounted toward the front of the dolly I usually use the front wheel that is on the side of the dolly that I am working from. I always place a mark at the beginning of the dolly move and another at the end. As stated previously, other marks will often be based on the way the lens is marked. Since you'll have less depth of field as the camera gets closer to the subject, you should have more marks close to the subject. This works best for simple dolly moves, such as moving in on a subject or pulling back from the subject. If moving in you will have more marks closer to the end of the move, and when pulling back you'll have more marks at the beginning of the move.

Focusing Tips

First Assistant Cameraman Mako Koiwai gives a great piece of advice when it comes to focusing: "The only focus reference that is worth anything is one that doesn't move." This is great when doing product shots for commercials or tabletop cinematography, but unfortunately that rarely happens when working with actors. Hopefully the following tips will help you not only when you first start out but also as you continue to work more and more as a First Assistant Cameraman/Focus Puller.

To become a better Focus Puller, there are some key things that you should be aware of and remember. If the lens doesn't have enough distance marks on it, make your own. Wrap a thin piece of artist's chart tape around the barrel of the lens, and, using a focus test chart, determine the distances you need and mark them on the tape. This should be done during the camera prep so that you are prepared for any shot during production.

Most important, you must be close to the camera, be able to see the lens, and be able to see the actor and your focus marks to follow focus accurately. Try not to position yourself perpendicular to the camera, which will require you to constantly turn your head from the lens to the actor to see what is happening. By the time you turn your head back to the lens, the actor is in a new position, and you have missed the focus. It is best to position yourself slightly toward the back of the camera near the Camera Operator so that your line of sight is along the barrel of the lens and to the actor. Now, instead of having to turn your head constantly, you only have to move your eyes slightly from the lens to the action, and you should have no problem keeping

the shot in focus. The type of shot, the position of the camera, the position of the actor, etc., often determine which side of the camera you must be on. Be prepared to work on the right side of the camera, which many Camera Assistants refer to as the "dumb side" because there are usually no focus marks on the lens or controls for the camera on that side. If you are working with Arriflex cameras with a PL lens mount, you will be able to reposition the lens so that you can see the focus marks from the dumb side, but with Panavision cameras and some older lenses, you may have to make your own focus marks so that you can follow focus properly. In recent years I have seen more and more Panavision lenses with focus marks on both sides, so it is usually not an issue. During the camera prep you should wrap a piece of tape around the barrel of the lens and transfer the distance marks to the opposite side so that you will be prepared in case you are in this situation.

Some Panavision lenses have two witness marks for aperture and focus: one blue mark and one yellow mark. The t-stop numbers on the lens are also in blue and yellow. The blue numbers are usually the first two aperture numbers on the lens; the rest are yellow. When using the blue t-stop numbers, set the aperture according to the blue witness mark. You also set your focus according to the blue witness mark for focus. When using the yellow t-stop numbers, set your aperture and your focus using the appropriate yellow witness marks. In the event your aperture setting is between one of the yellow and blue numbers, set your aperture and focus the same distance between the yellow and blue witness marks on the lens.

Determine the distance between the outstretched fingers of one hand and the outstretched fingers of the other hand when your arms are extended straight out to your side. This measurement is most often equal to your height. Also know one-half this distance. This will come in handy when you need to get a quick focus estimate. When guessing or estimating the focus, keep in mind that the distance is from the film plane and not from the front of the lens or front of the matte box. Know the distance from the film plane to the front of the matte box or front of the lens.

When not working, watch people and how they naturally move. When two people are talking to each other they may lean closer or move closer to each other. When someone gets up from a seated position they often lean forward as they get up. Each of these will have an effect on the focus of your shot. Don't just measure to the person standing or sitting still. Ask them to get up out of the chair so you can see how far they lean forward. Get a couple of additional measurements for each of these scenarios so that you are prepared for the unexpected during the shot.

If the operator tells you that the focus is soft on a close-up shot, you are probably focused too close. Whenever this happens you should carefully shift the focus back slightly. When working in one location or set for an extended period, always try to measure the length, width, and diagonal distances of the room and jot these down in a notepad. Then if you are in a rush situation, you can usually estimate the focus based on the position of the camera and subject within the room.

Close-ups on an actor are one of the most difficult shots to pull focus on. People don't generally stand perfectly still when seated or standing so you will need to get a minimum of three marks for most close-up shots. This is especially important because you will have little depth of field on these shots. The three basic marks that you will need are for their natural seated or standing position for the scene, where they may lean in to make a point or listen to somebody else in the scene, and where they may lean back during some point in the scene. When people are standing they often have a tendency to rock back and forth so getting the lean-in mark and lean-back mark are important. Actors usually understand what your job is and they obviously want to look good so they are willing to work with you to get your focus marks. Just be sure to be respectful and polite when asking them to show you their lean-in position and lean-back position for a shot. They will respect you for your professionalism.

There may be times when the 1st AC just cannot pull focus, most often on an extremely long lens, such as 1000 mm. I was in this situation on a feature film, and because the actors were so far away from the camera, I could not judge where they were in relation to focus reference points or landmarks in the shot. In this situation, the Camera Operator did his own focus. Don't be afraid to pass off the focus to the Camera Operator if you feel you just can't do it. When working with long telephoto lenses, pulling focus can be very tricky, as indicated in the previous example. But don't let that intimidate you. One very effective way to get focus marks when doing a long lens shot is to get a number of eye focus marks along the path of the actor's movements. You will need to ask the Camera Operator if you can have a few minutes to look through the lens while your Second Assistant walks the shot. Have the 2nd AC start at the farthest part of the shot and place a mark. Call this mark number one. While you are looking through the viewfinder, with the f-stop/t-stop wide open, get an eye focus setting and make a mark on the lens. Then set the stop to the working stop for the shot and ask your assistant to walk toward the camera and stop them at the point where they go unacceptably soft. Have them place another mark for this spot and label this as mark number two. Continue this process until the 2nd AC reaches the end of the shot, placing subsequent marks at each spot where you tell them. As the

shot progresses, your assistant will call out the marks to you, either standing near you and whispering in your ear so as not to disrupt the sound recording, or using a walkie-talkie and calling them out as the actor moves past each mark. Instead of watching the action and trying to turn the focus at the same time, you should only look at the lens barrel and rely on your assistant to accurately call out the marks. Following these steps should make it easier for you to pull focus on a long lens shot.

For most shots there will be no question as to which actor should be in focus. It will usually be whoever is facing the camera while speaking. With two or more actors in the scene, you may be in a situation where you may choose to split the focus. This means you will set the focus at a point in between the actors so that both will be in focus for the shot. Remember that you must check your depth of field for all actors' positions, along with the point of focus, to be sure that they fall within the acceptable depth of field. If one or more actors in the shot do not fall within the acceptable depth of field for your focus point, then you will most likely adjust the focus during the shot to favor whoever is talking and/or looking toward the camera. Or, you may split the focus between the two, which means setting the focus to a point in between them so that both are in focus. Splitting focus can be a dangerous thing, especially if the actors are on the edges of the depth of field. You may get to the dailies screening and discover that they are both soft. In most cases it is usually best to focus on the actor who is speaking or the lead actor in the scene. In any situation, if you are not sure who to keep in focus, you should always check with the DP. If the DP does not know the answer, he or she will then check with the Director. Whenever in doubt, it is best to check rather than find out in dailies that you focused on the wrong person. When checking your depth of field, be aware of the final presentation format of the production. A production done exclusively for video may be more forgiving with regard to focus than a big-budget feature film that will be projected on a large theater screen. Focus that looks acceptable in video may be out of focus and unacceptable on the big screen.

Get in the habit of guessing distances. Before measuring the distance for a shot, guess the distance and see how good you are at estimating. When I first started, I used to get together with another assistant friend and we used to practice guessing distances. We would set up a 35 mm SLR still camera at one of our homes. Each of us would point out an object in the room, and the other person would have to guess the focus and set it on the lens. Then we would look through the lens and focus by eye and compare our guess to the actual focus. It helped us to be better prepared when we started working steadily as 1st ACs. When marking the lens or follow-focus marking

disks, don't put so many marks on them that you get confused during the shot. The same thing applies to placing tape marks on the ground for focus reference. Too many marks will only confuse you.

When doing a critical focus move with the camera and actor moving together, you may want to use a laser pointer to project a point on the floor that is a specific distance from the camera. As the camera and dolly move together, you will be able to use this point as a reference if the actor and dolly get too close together or too far apart. I discussed this early in the section on focus measurements and following focus. Because the cloth or fiberglass tape measure may stretch over time, you should periodically check it against your metal tape measure for accuracy. If it has stretched, throw it out and get a new one.

Many assistants have a Mini Maglite flashlight in their toolkit or ditty bag. This is an excellent tool to use when getting critical eye focus. Remove the head of the flashlight (the part containing the lens) and hold the light next to the object you are getting the eye focus for. The bright light will "pop" into focus, thereby enabling you to get very accurate critical eye focus marks for any situation.

Each shot will be different with regard to how fast or slowly you turn the follow-focus device. Because the markings on the lens follow a logarithmic progression, with the closer focus marks being farther apart on the lens and the farther distances being closer together, pulling focus on a moving shot requires you to adjust your speed as the camera and subject get closer together or farther apart. You cannot simply turn the lens at the same speed for the entire shot, even if the actor is moving at the same speed. For example, for a shot where the subject is getting farther away from the camera, you must turn the focus knob faster when shifting focus for a move from 6 to 8 ft and more slowly when shifting focus for a move from 10 to 20 ft. In other words, you start out turning the focus knob faster and slow down as the actor gets away from the lens. The marks on the lens for 6 and 8 ft are farther apart than the marks for 10 and 20 ft. It is the reverse for a shot where the subject is getting closer to the camera: you start out turning the focus knob slower and then speed up as the actor gets closer to the lens. One of the biggest mistakes when first starting out as a First Assistant is pulling focus at the wrong speed.

On a dolly move, be sure to place your own marks on the ground for the dolly wheel closest to you. You should also work out a system with the Dolly Grip on signals to be used in the event the Dolly Grip misses his or her mark. Remember, if the Dolly Grip misses his or her mark and you hit your mark, the shot will most likely be soft and out of focus.

Have fun with pulling or following focus, but always remember that you are only human and not perfect. If you feel the need,

double check your marks before rolling on the shot. Also don't make too many marks on the ground/floor or on the lens. Always watch the rehearsals so you know where the actors are for each part of the scene. It is often necessary for the First Assistant to look at the script so that they know the precise line the actor will say before getting up from the chair, moving to the door, or any other movement. By knowing when this happens you won't be too early or too late with the focus change. Don't be afraid to ask for another take if you feel that you missed the focus. Check with the Camera Operator if you are unsure about the focus of a shot. It's better to do it again and get it right than to watch a soft shot in dailies. By speaking up at the time, you will be respected for your professionalism.

Zoom Lens Moves

In addition to pulling focus, the 1st AC may also be required to do a zoom lens move, which means changing the focal length of the zoom lens during the shot. The focal length of the lens may change from wide to tight or from tight to wide or anywhere in between. The important thing to remember when doing a zoom lens move is to start and end the zoom move very smoothly. Any sudden starts and stops are distracting when viewed on the screen. I compare the principle for starting or stopping a zoom move with the way you take off or stop your car at a traffic light. The proper way is to start out slowly and work up to the proper speed. Start the zoom move slowly and work up to the proper speed so that it does not look like a jerky, quick start. As you start to reach the end of the zoom move, you should slow down the speed until you stop completely.

Many zoom lens changes are done along with some type of camera move, either panning, tilting, dollying, or booming. When doing any type of zoom lens change along with a camera move, the zoom lens change should start a fraction of a second after the camera move starts and end a fraction of a second before the camera move ends. This helps to hide any sudden starts or stops in the zoom lens move and makes the zoom less noticeable to the viewer. Most zoom controls and zoom motors have a switch or dial that allows you to adjust the speed of the zoom. During the rehearsal, work out the correct zoom speed with the DP or Camera Operator. If you have a complicated zoom move to do, request at least one rehearsal before attempting to shoot the scene.

There may be some instances when you have to do a zoom lens move for a shot on a lens that does not have a zoom motor. This is called a manual zoom move. You should keep a light touch on the

lens, and, if possible, use some type of zoom stick so that your hand is not on the actual lens, which could restrict the Camera Operator's movement. A few years ago I was working with another assistant who had a device that he was using to do a manual zoom move on a lens that did not have a zoom motor. It was actually a jar opener that is available in many specialty kitchen stores. This jar opener has a plastic handle with a rotating knob on one end and a metal strap on the other end. By turning the knob you can lengthen or shorten the metal strap so that it fits around the barrel of the lens. You can then position it accordingly to allow you to follow focus or zoom without having your hand actually on the lens barrel. I have used mine on a few low-budget jobs where we did not have a zoom lens motor. See Figure D.13 in Appendix D for an illustration of the jar opener that can be used for zooming or following focus. Just like following focus, zoom lens moves require much practice and experience to be able to do them well and cannot be explained fully in any book. Practice, practice, practice, and before long you will be an expert at both zoom moves and following focus.

Shooting the Shot

When getting ready to shoot the shot there should be a series of last minute checks that you go through before rolling the camera. These can be done very quickly without disrupting production or causing any delays. These are listed in no particular order.

1. Focus—Double check that you have all the marks needed and know exactly who or what you are supposed to be focusing on for each part of the scene.
2. F-stop/T-stop—Confirm with the DP that you have set the proper shooting stop on the lens for the scene. You may have changed lenses or opened up the stop to check an eye focus, so always double check the stop. I usually get the DP's attention and simply say, "Our stop is a 5.6 (or whatever the stop is), right?" In most cases he/she will confirm that you are correct or change the stop just before you roll. Better to check than to get to dailies and have a shot either over- or underexposed.
3. Film—Does the magazine have enough film for the shot? If not, be sure to reload as quickly as possible, or let the DP know that you may rollout. The DP will then check with the Director and tell you whether or not you should reload. You should also check to be sure that you are shooting with the proper film speed (EI/ISO). Failure to have the correct film speed loaded in the

magazine and camera can produce disastrous results when you view the dailies.

4. Camera Speed—Are you shooting at sync speed or at a different frame rate? If you are shooting at a different frame rate than 24 fps be sure that the f-stop/t-stop has been adjusted accordingly.

5. Battery—Is the battery fully charged? This relates to the previous item because if you are shooting at a higher frame rate than 24 fps you want to be sure that you have enough power for the shot.

6. Shutter Angle—Is the shutter angle setting of the camera correct? It usually stays the same but if you are doing any type of special effects shot or the DP is trying to achieve a specific "look" to the image you may want to double check this.

If any of the above items need to be corrected, be sure to do it before rolling the camera. If you stay on top of things during the day, there should be no problem. It's the Camera Assistant who slacks off and forgets even one of these items that doesn't get hired for that next job. The true professional almost never forgets any of these important items. Some assistants simply use the term "FAST" as a reminder to check everything before rolling. F = Focus, A = Aperture (t-stop), S = Shutter Angle, T = Tachometer (fps). Use whatever system works best so that you hopefully never have a problem.

Footage Readings

After each take, the 1st AC will often call out the dial readings from the camera footage counter to the 2nd AC. These amounts are entered in the correct space on the camera report for the particular shot. To make the mathematics easier when totaling up the figures on the camera report, it is customary to round all dial readings to the nearest 10. As most of us learned in elementary school, if the number ends in four or less you round down, and if it ends in five or more you round up.

Example: The camera footage counter shows a reading of 274. Because this number ends in a 4, we round down, and it becomes 270. For this dial reading the 1st AC will drop the zero at the end and call out "27." The 2nd AC will then record either "27" or "270" in the "DIAL" column on the camera report for that particular shot.

Most often after a take the set becomes very noisy. The Director may be talking to the actors, the DP may be discussing the next lighting setup with the Gaffer or giving instructions to other crew members, and so on. It is a good idea to always remain as quiet as possible when working on a film set. In some cases it may not be practical

to call out the camera footage counter dial readings as stated above. When that is the case, there is a standard set of hand signals used to give dial readings. They can be used by the 1st AC when he or she is too far away from the 2nd AC. Figure 5.46 shows the standard hand signals used for footage counter dial readings.

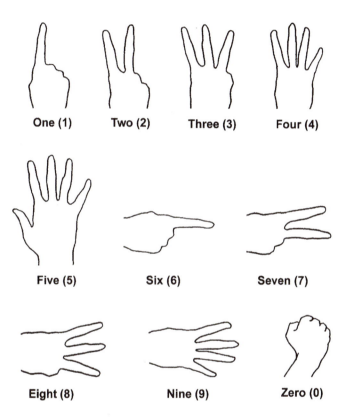

One (1)   **Two (2)**   **Three (3)**   **Four (4)**

Five (5)   **Six (6)**   **Seven (7)**

Eight (8)   **Nine (9)**   **Zero (0)**

Figure 5.46   Hand signals for camera footage counter dial readings.

Checking the Gate

After each printed take, it is standard procedure for the 1st AC to check the gate for hairs, which are very fine pieces of emulsion or dust that may have gotten in the gate and will show up on the screen as a large rope in the frame. As was discussed in Chapter 1, the gate is the opening in the aperture plate that the light passes through from the lens to the film. Most often if a hair is found, you should remove

the hair and do another take to ensure that you have a clean shot. The DP will usually look at the gate to double check it because he or she has the final say on whether you should do another take. In some cases the DP will trust the assistant's judgment and not even look at the gate. Be sure to work this out on the first day of production, especially if you are working with a new DP. Many times another take is not necessary even if there is a hair. The hair may be so small that it does not reach into the frame. There are generally three accepted ways to check the gate for hairs: remove the gate, remove the lens, and look through the lens.

- Remove the gate—This can obviously be done only on cameras that have a removable gate and aperture plate. Turn the inching knob so that the registration pin and pull down claw are away from the film and the gate. Remove the film from the gate and then remove the gate. When you hold the gate up to the light, you should be able to see any hair along the edges. This is not always an accurate way to check for hairs because when you remove the film from the gate, the hair may stick to the film and be pulled out with it. When you look at the gate, you will not see any hair and assume that the gate is clean. You cannot remove the gate on many cameras, so this method may not be used on all cameras. Be sure to check with the rental house if you are not sure whether the camera you are using has a removable gate.
- Remove the lens—Remove the lens from its mount. Then turn the inching knob to advance the shutter until you can see the emulsion in the gate while looking through the lens port opening. Using a small flashlight or magnifier with a built-in light, examine the emulsion along the top, bottom, and sides to see if there is any hair, which would be visible against the bright background of the film emulsion. I prefer to use this method whenever possible. If removing the lens is too difficult or time consuming, I use one of the other methods.
- Look through the lens—Open the aperture on the lens to its widest opening. Turn the inching knob until the emulsion is visible in the gate as you look through the lens. Place a small flashlight alongside your face and look right down the barrel of the lens. The lens will act as a magnifier for the gate, allowing you to see any hair along the top, bottom, or sides of the gate. This method works best with lenses that are 40 mm or longer in focal length. When using this method with a zoom lens, be sure to zoom the lens in to its longest focal length. Unfortunately, I have never been able to master this technique, but I know quite a few Camera Assistants who use this method successfully. If a hair is

found, clean the gate and aperture plate with compressed air and an orangewood stick. When cleaning any emulsion from the gate, use only an orangewood stick or special nonmetallic tool. When you have cleaned the gate, double check it before shooting any additional shots.

Moving the Camera

The camera must be moved frequently throughout the day. If the camera is mounted to a dolly, the Dolly Grip will usually move it to each new setup. One of the Camera Assistants, usually the 1st AC, should walk alongside the dolly, with one hand on the camera to steady it while the dolly is moving. The dolly may have to travel over rough terrain or over lighting cables. If the terrain is too rough, it may be a good idea to remove the camera and carry it or place it on one of the camera carts to move it to the next setup. The bouncing of the dolly can shake loose the elements of the lens or possibly even damage the camera. If you feel it would be safer, remove the lens before transporting the camera to a new position.

When the camera is mounted on a tripod, it is the sole responsibility of the Camera Assistants to move the camera to each new position. Many Camera Assistants pick up the entire tripod with the head and camera attached and carry it to the new position. One of the best ways to do this is as follows: Aim the lens so that it is in line with one of the legs of the tripod. Lock the pan and tilt locks on the head. Lengthen the front leg of the tripod (the one that the lens is in line with). Crouch down and place the shoulder pad of the tripod between your shoulder and the head, with the extended tripod leg in front of you. Lean into the tripod legs, and with your left and right hands grab the shorter left and right legs of the tripod and slowly push them in toward the lengthened front leg. The two shorter legs will fold up, forcing all of the weight onto the one extended leg. The camera will lean into your shoulder, making it easy to pick up. Stand up, and the camera, head, and tripod should be balanced on your shoulder. To place the entire system back on the ground, first crouch down and set the long tripod leg on the ground. Grab the left and right legs, and bring them back to their normal position to form a triangle with the extended leg. Loosen the extended leg and return it to its original length. The camera is now ready for shooting at the new setup.

The previous method usually works best when the tripod is placed on a carpet or outside on the ground without a spreader attached. When using a spreader, the tripod legs often will not fold up with the spreader attached, so you may have to remove the spreader

before moving the camera using this method. Another way to move the camera on a tripod is for the 1st AC to remove the camera from the head and carry it or place it on the camera cart while the 2nd AC carries the tripod and head. Always remember to level and balance the head whenever you move the camera to a new setup. Use whichever method is easier and safer for you. Never try to carry something if you do not feel it is safe or you don't think that you can handle it. I often set up the high hat and additional head on one of the camera carts. Or if you have one of those completely tricked out camera carts, you will most likely have a mount for the head built into the cart. When moving the camera I usually remove it from the tripod or dolly head and place it on the head on the camera cart. It makes it much easier to move and minimizes the chance of damage to the camera or lens.

Once you have completed moving the camera be sure that the head and camera are level, whether they are mounted on a dolly or on a tripod. If working with a fluid head be sure that the pan handle is in the proper position for the Camera Operator. You may have repositioned it to move the camera. Also place the viewfinder in the proper position for the Operator. Check that the shutter is clear, the focus is set to the approximate focus for the shot (or infinity), and the f-stop/t-stop is wide open so that the Camera Operator and DP can set up for the shot. Each time the camera is moved, bring along all other needed equipment and accessories, including lenses, filters, magazines, and so on. When the DP requests a piece of equipment, he or she will not want to wait because you left some of the cases back at the last camera position. If the cases are on a dolly or handcart, all you need to do is wheel it to the new position. Otherwise the cases must be hand-carried to the next setup. It is the Camera Assistant's responsibility to make sure that the camera equipment is moved quickly and safely and is near the camera throughout the day. If you require any help moving or carrying the equipment, do not hesitate to ask one of the Production Assistants on the set. And if you have a Camera PA or Trainee, they can help move equipment. It is much better to ask for help than to try to do it all yourself and risk getting hurt or dropping and damaging the equipment. No matter what, don't be rushed when moving the camera and related equipment. Do it quickly, but do it safely.

Performing the Duties of Second Assistant Cameraman

There will be times when you are working on a production that does not have a 2nd AC. It may be a small production, such as a music video or commercial, or perhaps the production just doesn't have a

big enough budget to afford an additional assistant. If this is the case, the 1st AC also carries out the duties of 2nd AC. Because you are now doing two separate jobs, it is important to remember not to be rushed while working. The Director and DP should understand that it sometimes takes a little longer to get certain things done. If for any reason you need help, do not hesitate to ask other crew members. I have done many commercials and music videos where I was the only Camera Assistant on the job.

End-of-the-Day Procedures

Packing Equipment

At the end of each shooting day you usually pack all camera equipment away in its appropriate case and store everything in a safe place until the next shooting day. If you are working out of a camera truck, place and secure all of the cases on their appropriate shelves. If you are working on a sound stage, you will often have a room or special area where all of the equipment is stored at the end of each shooting day.

The Walkaway

There is the rare occasion when you will be walking away from the location and leaving the gear set up to continue using it the next day. I don't like to do this but if the DP gives the approval, then there are some procedures you should follow to guarantee the safety of the equipment. First make sure that the camera is as low as possible on its mount. If it is on a tripod, lower the legs to their lowest point and lock them securely. It couldn't hurt to place a sandbag on the tripod or spreader to secure it as well. If on a dolly, lower the boom arm of the dolly to its lowest point. Placing the camera as low as possible will prevent it from tipping over. Next you should always disconnect the battery and remove the lens from the camera. Be sure that the camera head is securely locked and that you cover the camera with a space blanket or some other type of camera cover. Finally, make sure all other camera gear is in its appropriate case, on the equipment carts, and in a secure location before leaving for the day.

As I stated earlier, walking away and leaving the camera set up is rare, but use common sense and you will have no problem. In most cases though you will disassemble the camera at the end of each day and place everything in the appropriate equipment case, on the carts or in the camera truck before leaving for the day.

Tools and Accessories

As mentioned in Chapter 4, with many professions you must have the basic tools and accessories so that you may do the job properly. When first starting out, you should have a very basic toolkit or ditty bag, and as you gain more experience and work more frequently, you can add things as you feel they are needed. In Britain this is often referred to as a standby bag. Some of the tools are common everyday tools, while others are specialized tools or pieces of equipment that are unique to the film industry. In addition to the basic tools, you should also have a small inventory of expendables and film cans, cores, camera reports, etc. There will be many times when you are called for a job at the last minute, and you may have no time to acquire some of these items. By having a small amount on hand, you will always be prepared for most job calls that you get.

Many 1st ACs often wear some type of belt pouch or fanny pack to keep the most commonly used tools or accessories with them at all times. Quite often these pouches are specifically made for Camera Assistants or they may be as simple as a basic fanny pack. Choose whatever will work best for you. Wearing a belt pouch can be good for some and not so good for others. Wearing a pouch is good in that you have the basic essentials and most often used tools close and easily accessible. But some don't like to wear a pouch because they can be uncomfortable and cumbersome, they make it difficult to move around when working in tight quarters, items can fall out if working too quickly, and they can be too full of stuff, making their use counterproductive. It's up to the individual to decide for themselves what works best.

Instead of wearing a pouch, which can become very cumbersome when packed full of tools and accessories, some 1st ACs have an item called a front box, which contains all of the basic items needed each day for shooting. The front box is most often constructed of wood and has a metal bracket on the back that allows you to mount it directly on the front of the head under the camera. It contains items such as a depth-of-field calculator, cloth and metal tape measures, permanent markers, mini flashlight, slate markers, lens tissue, and lens cleaner. The front box may also be used to hold the DP's light meters. By mounting this on the head, the 1st AC has the basic supplies needed for shooting and does not have to be encumbered by wearing a large pouch filled with these tools and supplies. An illustration of a front box is shown in Figure D.25 in Appendix D. If you do choose to wear some type of belt pouch, the same items previously listed should be in the pouch. See Appendix D for a list of the common tools and equipment that should be included in an Assistant Cameraman's ditty bag or toolkit.

As discussed in Chapter 4, it is important to have a personal bag on the camera truck or on set. This bag should contain a change of clothes, extra sneakers, or work shoes along with foul weather or rain gear. You never know when you will be in a situation where you must change clothes or have additional clothing in case of extreme weather conditions. Having an extra sweatshirt, thermal underwear, and cold-weather boots can make the difference between being warm and comfortable on a shoot or freezing. I bring this bag with me on any long-term job and keep it on one of the top shelves in the camera truck. In addition to clothing items, I also keep a small first aid kit, basic toiletry kit, and extra towels in the bag. You never know when you will find yourself away from home and in need of many of these items.

Using Computers and Technology

As mentioned in Chapter 4, today's Camera Assistant often has a smart phone and/or other electronic device like an iPod, iPad, or laptop computer. Each of these devices can save both the 1st and 2nd AC much time in the performance of the job. A laptop computer or iPad can be used for much of the camera department record keeping as well as other applications.

The pCAM Film+Digital Calculator and Toland ASC Digital Assistant apps for your iPhone, iPad, or iPod Touch were briefly discussed in the section on depth of field. Each of these have many additional useful features for the cinematographer. Some additional features of the pCAM Film+Digital Calculator app are the ability to see your field of view for a particular shot, see a preview of your image, how to calculate any exposure change when using filters, changing film speed, changing camera speed or changing shutter angle, matching focal lengths when shooting with different cameras, calculating your running time to film length, focus splits, shooting time to screen time, HMI flicker free speed calculation, color correction, diopter settings, macro settings, time lapse settings, underwater distances, scene illumination calculation, light coverage, mired shift and standard conversions. The application also includes a Siemens star and an insert slate. See Figures 5.47 through 5.51 for screen shots of some of these various features of pCAM.

The Toland ASC Digital Assistant application has many additional features for the cinematographer, including a camera setup screen where you can set the specific settings for the camera you are using, including system format, camera type, camera format, aspect ratio, film stock, and lens type. You can also set your base settings for

Figure 5.47 Field of view screen shot from pCAM Film+Digital Calculator. (Courtesy of David Eubank.)

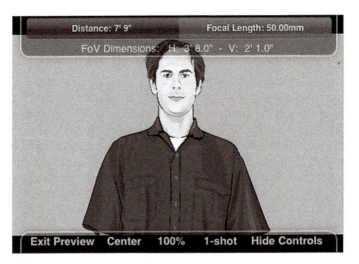

Figure 5.48 Image preview screen shot from pCAM Film+Digital Calculator. (Courtesy of David Eubank and Paul Tilden.)

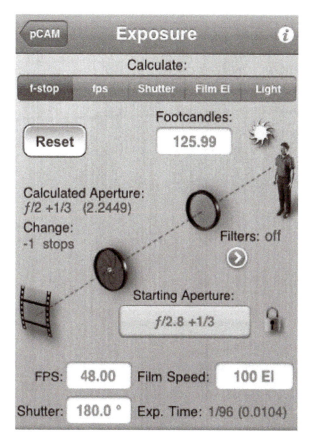

Figure 5.49 Exposure change screen shot from pCAM Film+Digital Calculator. (Courtesy of David Eubank.)

the project you are shooting, including circle of confusion, fps, shutter angle, power line frequency, and f-stop fractions. A sub-page of the camera screen allows you to change the fps and shutter angle to see the effect it will have on screen time and exposure, and also whether or not you will have a flicker problem when using HMI lights. The application also has a field of view function which allows you to see a preview of your image dependent on the focal length and distance from the camera. There is also a diopter screen allowing you to enter diopter information to see how you can shoot extreme close-ups. And the app also contains a camera log which allows you to keep track of specific information relating to the shot, like scene and take number, roll number, mag number, lens height, lens tilt, and more. See Figures

Figure 5.50   Focal length match screen shot
from pCAM Film+Digital Calculator. (Courtesy of
David Eubank.)

5.52 through 5.55 for screen shots of some of the features of Toland
ASC Digital Assistant.

1st AC/Focus Puller Tips

Previously in this chapter I made the following statement, "A good
Camera Assistant is one who is efficient, quick, invisible, and quiet."
Related to this is a comment that I once read from another Camera
Assistant that said, "Nobody notices what I do, until I don't do it."
The job of an Assistant Cameraman is critical to the smooth opera-
tion of the production, but in many cases a lot of what we do goes

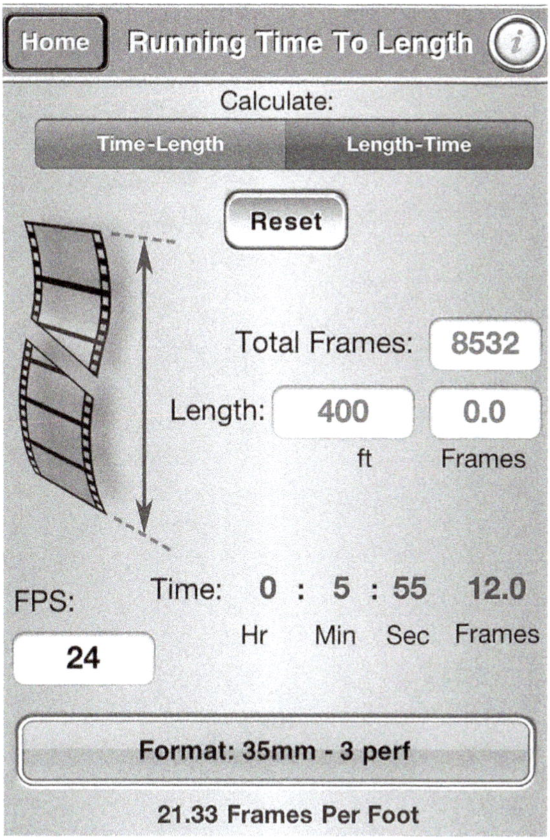

Figure 5.51 Running time to film length screen shot from pCAM Film+Digital Calculator. (Courtesy of David Eubank.)

unnoticed until we make a mistake. The important thing is to work hard, be professional, and minimize the mistakes that can happen. After all, we are only human and nobody is perfect. The following tips are designed to help you do your job better and get hired on as many productions as possible.

Always arrive to work at least ½ hour before the call time. If your call time is 7:00a.m., then plan on arriving at 6:30a.m. This shows your willingness to work and also your professionalism. If you get in this habit from the very beginning, it will stick with you throughout your career. It also allows for any unexpected delays you may encounter on the way to the job. In my opinion, arriving on time is being late and arriving early is being on time. No matter what, you should always be on set before the DP.

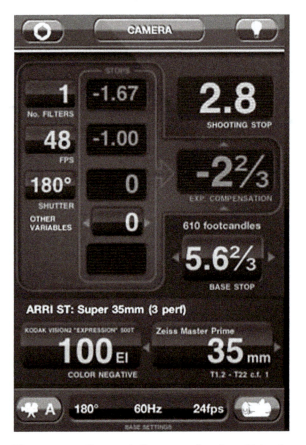

Figure 5.52 Camera info screen shot from Toland ASC Digital Assistant. (Courtesy of Chemical Wedding.)

Your attitude is a big part of the reason why you get hired for a job and why you keep the job. The first questions that are often asked about you when you are being considered for a job are, "How does he or she get along with others?" and "Does he or she have a good attitude?" If you are constantly complaining or whining, nobody is going to want to work with you. Have a positive attitude every day on the set. Leave your personal problems at home. If you do this, everybody will want to work with you, and you will get so many job calls that you will have to start turning down jobs.

You may not realize it, but as an Assistant Cameraman it is important for you to dress appropriately. This may not seem that important, but you will be working long hours, sometimes in

Figure 5.53 Shutter and fps screen shot from Toland ASC Digital Assistant. (Courtesy of Chemical Wedding.)

uncomfortable situations and locations. Long gone are the old days of Hollywood when most of the crew dressed in suits and ties. Today comfort is most important. Be prepared to get dirty in the day-to-day performance of your job. You will be asked to get into a variety of positions and must be able to move freely. Don't wear tight pants or shirts that can restrict your movement and make it difficult for you to do your job. You will be working near the camera so I recommend wearing dark colors so that you don't risk your clothing reflecting any light and causing problems for the actors. I also discuss this in Chapter 8, Before, During, and After the Job, but don't wear any shirts with slogans or sayings on them that could be offensive to others. There will be many times that you are filming outside on hot sunny days, so you

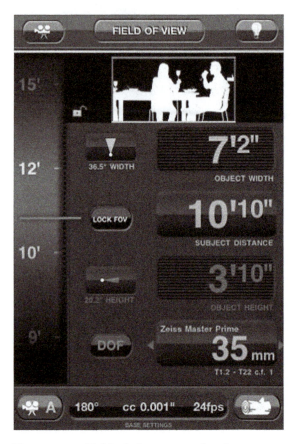

Figure 5.54 Field of view screen shot from Toland ASC Digital Assistant. (Courtesy of Chemical Wedding.)

should always have a hat with you to protect yourself, shade your eyes, and prevent sunburn on your scalp. One of the most important things to remember is to always wear comfortable shoes. You are going to be on your feet for long hours and need to be comfortable. If your feet hurt, it will cause you to not concentrate fully on your job and you could make mistakes, especially when pulling focus. And finally, always have an extra set of clothing with you just in case of emergency.

The following applies to all members of the camera department but is especially important for the First Assistant and Camera Operator. Learn the actors' names as quickly as possible. If trying to get their attention to stand on a mark or show you their movement, it can be quite embarrassing if you don't know their name. Take the

Figure 5.55 Log screen shot from Toland ASC
Digital Assistant. (Courtesy of Chemical Wedding.)

daily call sheet and cut out the section that has the actors' names. Tape it to the side or back of the camera so the 1st AC and Camera Operator can reference it if needed. And if new actors are working on any given day, be sure to replace the sheet on the camera with the updated list of names. Knowing the actors' names when speaking to them will gain their respect and show that you are a true professional. Actors usually take time to learn the names of the crew that they are working with and you should show them the same respect.

The entire camera department is a team and must work together. This is especially important for the 1st AC and 2nd AC. If you must leave the set for any reason, you should inform the DP, Camera Operator, or 2nd AC. Never leave the camera unattended. You may also notify the Dolly Grip if you can't find any other member of the

camera department. Unless the entire cast and crew are on a break, the camera should never be left unattended. When working around the camera, keep your talking to a minimum. If you must talk, then talk in a low voice or take it off set. The DP may be discussing the shot with the Director or the Gaffer, or the Director may be talking with the actors. If it's necessary to speak with someone, either wait until the time is right or ask him or her to go to another area of the set or off set where it may be quieter. Above all, do not yell on any film set. This is a sign of a true nonprofessional.

Whenever the DP calls for a piece of equipment, you should repeat it back to confirm that you heard the request and that you heard it correctly. If your name is called out, you should also respond so that whoever called will know that you heard him or her.

Get your focus marks as soon as you know what is happening in the shot. Use the stand-ins to check your focus so that you are prepared when it's time for the shot. If stand-ins are not available, then have your 2nd AC or camera PA/Trainee stand on the marks. If necessary, request a rehearsal so that you can confirm your marks. A good assistant is always prepared and doesn't have to be reminded to do his or her job. If you are having personality conflicts with someone in your department or in another department on the crew, try to speak with him or her about it. Work it out between yourselves so that you can at least have a good working relationship. You may not like the person, but you should at least be able to work together without any conflict.

Keep your eyes and ears open at all times so that you are constantly aware of what is happening on the set. As you become familiar with a particular working style of the DP, you should be able to anticipate requests and be ready when he or she does make a certain request. The DP may always use a particular lens for the close-up and another for the wide shot. By paying attention, you will know when a new scene is being shot and will have the lens ready when it is called for. Also, pay close attention to what filters are used for certain shots and have them ready before they are requested. Watch the DP and Director when they are blocking out the scene. Listen to what they are saying. They may be talking about using a particular lens for the next shot. Get the lens case and any accessories close by so you can change the lens quickly. Watching where they are discussing or blocking the shot will give you an idea where the camera is to be placed, and it will also be an indication of where you can move the equipment so that it is close by. Keep all equipment organized and in its proper place. If it is kept organized and on the camera carts at all times, it can easily be located when you are in a hurry. This applies to both the camera truck and equipment carts. When on stage or location, you should have some type of four wheel carts such as the Magliner, Liberator, Backstage, or Rubbermaid

carts for moving the equipment from place to place. You will have many equipment cases to deal with each day, and it is much easier and quicker if they can be wheeled from place to place instead of individually carried. Whenever the camera is moved to a new location, the cart should also be moved.

Most important, if you make a mistake, tell the DP immediately. This information should be communicated to the DP quietly so as not to alarm anybody else. The mistake may not be as bad as you think, and you may be able to take care of it without anybody finding out. As a 1st AC you must be able to work very closely with the DP, Camera Operator, and 2nd AC. Keep in mind that everybody does things differently.

Be flexible, and when working with a new crew, try to do things the way they want. After a while you will develop a system of doing things that works best for you. But don't forget that you will always have to adjust your way of doing things when working with others who have their own systems. When you are in charge, then you can request that things be done your way.

Don't be afraid to constantly check with your 2nd AC to be sure that all magazines are loaded, enough film is on hand, memory cards or hard drives have been backed up, expendables are fully stocked, and more. As the 1st AC, you are in charge of the overall running of the camera department, and by checking and double checking you will be sure that everything is running smoothly. Remind your assistant that it is in the best interests of both of you that the department looks good. Your constant checking is not an indication that you don't trust the 2nd AC, only that you want to be sure that there are no problems. If the department is run efficiently, you both have a better chance of being hired back by the DP for future jobs.

If you must shoot a locked-off shot or a shot where the camera may be mounted on a car mount, crane, or other device, it's important to ensure that the focus and t-stop of the lens are locked off. You may not be able to be alongside the camera during the shot, so you should secure these various components of the lens with a small piece of camera tape. The movement of the car or crane could cause the f-stop or focus to shift during the shot, which would adversely affect your image. By taping them in position, you will not have to worry about problems when viewing the dailies. If using a zoom lens, you should also tape off the focal length so that it doesn't change during the shot. It's better to take the extra time and be safe than to have to shoot the shot over on another day.

When cleaning lenses, always put the lens fluid on the tissue before wiping the lens. Never apply lens fluid directly on the lens element because it could work its way behind the glass and then you

would have no way to clean it. And only clean lenses with fluid and tissue when absolutely necessary.

When threading film into the camera, be sure to check your threading with the inching knob before running the camera at speed. This will ensure that the film is traveling smoothly and will not break when you start the camera. Always use extra support when using long telephoto or zoom lenses. Failure to properly support the lens will affect the lens mount and could also affect the flange focal depth.

There will be instances when you may need to keep track of specific information for matching a shot. You may do a close-up of an actor in the morning but won't be doing the matching close-up of the other actor until later in the day. It may be a matter of lighting or shooting all shots looking in one direction on the set before you turn the camera around so the matching shot may be done hours later. In this situation there are certain bits of information that you should record in your log book or someplace else so you can refer to them later on. Measure the height of the lens from the floor. It's up to you whether you measure to the bottom of the lens, middle of the lens, or top of the lens as long as you are consistent. Next measure the distance to the first actor so you can match that later on. It may be necessary to know the angle of the camera, so you may want to have a tool called an Inclinometer which measures the degree of tilt of the fluid or gear head. There are a couple of iPhone apps that allow you to do this if you don't have an Inclinometer. And if shooting in the digital format you may want to also keep a record of all of the specific camera settings for the matching shot. And also be sure to write down the focal length and f-stop/t-stop setting of the lens. A situation that you may also be in that is similar to the above is when you need to match the same shot. You should keep track of all of the above information plus you should place a mark on the floor/ground so that you can place the camera back in the exact same spot if it does become necessary to match the shot.

When using diopters on the lens, use the lowest strength and combine it with a longer focal length lens for best results. When filming in dusty, sandy, or windy conditions, always cover the camera and protect the lens with an optical flat. Dust and sand can work their way into the small crevices on the camera body and could cause a major problem with the motor, movement, and film. If you don't have any type of camera barney, use a sound blanket or even a large plastic trash bag to protect the camera. Anything that protects the camera is better than nothing. This is especially important when working with blood special effects. Hollywood movie blood is very sticky and can be difficult to remove if allowed to dry. Always cover the camera and lens when working around any type of blood special effect, even if the effects person assures you that it won't hit the camera. I would rather

take the extra precaution than have to spend an hour or more trying to clean the blood off the equipment.

If attaching nets to the back of lenses, do not use rubber cement, superglue, or nail polish. Always use ½-in. transfer tape (also known as snot tape). Any of the other glues or adhesives could damage the coating on the lens element.

Establish a good relationship with the Dolly Grip. Your focus marks are only accurate if the Dolly Grip hits the marks as well. Work out a system of how the Dolly Grip will communicate to you during a shot if he or she misses intended marks.

Remove the lens and unplug the battery when breaking for lunch. Unless you are coming back to the same setup after lunch, move the camera to a safe and secure location. Lower the camera on the tripod or ask the Dolly Grip to lower the boom arm of the dolly so that the camera is as low as possible to avoid the possibility of it tipping over while you are away from it. And always cover the camera when leaving it for lunch or some other purpose. I usually cover the camera with a space blanket secured with a couple of grip clamps.

As I mentioned in Chapter 4, in the 2nd AC/Loader Tips section, filmmaking involves a lot of what many people refer to as "hurry up and wait." There is often a lot of downtime on the set for the assistants while a new lighting setup is being done, set walls are being moved, etc. You may be tempted to take the opportunity to sit down and relax for a few minutes, and as soon as you do, the Producer or Director will walk by and think you are goofing off. When it is necessary for you to take a break and sit, it is most important you should be as close to the set as possible so that if you are needed you will hear your name called and nobody needs to search for you. I worked on a few television series where I was the "B" camera First Assistant and in some cases the Director only wanted the "A" camera for a particular shot or shots. This gave me a chance to sit and take a break but I always stayed near the set so that I could be ready if called for. When taking a break, try to find a job or task that you can do while sitting, so even if somebody walks by, you are still busy working. Help the 2nd AC inventory the equipment or clean and organize the cases on the camera carts. Maybe you have been filming for many weeks and the labels on the cases need to be replaced. Check the lenses and filters for dirt, dust, and scratches and clean them if necessary. There is a lot that can be done while you are sitting down. You get some rest and are off your feet for a little while but are still active, and everyone will be impressed with your work ethic and attitude.

Always stay calm and maintain a professional attitude, and if you are ever unsure of something, do not be afraid to ask. Don't watch the clock. People will notice and you will be looked upon as someone

who really doesn't want to be there. If asked to stay a bit longer to complete a shot, don't moan and complain about it. Be positive and enthusiastic and willing to work harder. Of course, if you are expected to work an unreasonable number of hours, then it is appropriate to speak up. Just do it in the right manner so that you are not looked upon as someone who is always complaining and is not there for the good of the production. Producers and Directors should know better than to mistreat their crews and expect them to work excessive hours without the proper rest periods.

If you treat people with respect, they will treat you the same. Always do your job to the best of your ability, and if you make a mistake, admit it so that it can be corrected. Remember that someday you may be in the position of Camera Operator or DP, dealing with the same situations and problems.

Resources

During your career as an Assistant Cameraman, you will rely on a variety of professional resources to enable you to do your job properly and completely. This includes camera manufacturers and rental companies, expendables companies, film laboratories, sellers of film raw stock, professional organizations, and many more. You should have all contact information for these companies readily available in case you need something at the last minute or in case of emergency. Rather than list here all of the possible names, addresses, telephone numbers, and email addresses for the various companies, I have created a Links page on the companion web site for this book. Because companies move and change addresses, telephone numbers, and email addresses quite frequently, it's not practical to list them in the book. The Links page of the web site will be updated on a regular basis so that you should be able to have the most current information for any of the companies that are listed. In addition to the various companies and suppliers that you will be dealing with, the web site also includes many links to industry-related web sites for listing your résumé and searching for jobs, as well as sites for related departments, such as grip and lighting. If you have web sites or know of any web sites of interest that you would like to see included, please feel free to contact me by email.

POSTPRODUCTION

As stated in Chapter 4, postproduction for the camera department means that all equipment must be cleaned, checked, and packed away

so that it can be returned to the rental company. A final inventory of film stock and expendables is usually done and turned in to the production office. Invoices and all other paperwork must be turned in to the production office. If a camera truck was used, it will probably be cleaned out for the next production's use. Finally, the 1st AC packs up all of his or her gear and gets ready for that next job call, where the entire process starts all over again.

Wrapping Equipment

At the completion of filming, the camera equipment, camera truck, and anything else relating to the camera department must be wrapped. This means that everything should be cleaned and packed away. All equipment must be cleaned, packed, and sent back to the camera rental house. Usually the 1st AC wraps out the camera equipment, while the 2nd AC wraps out the truck, darkroom, and film stock. If it is a small production, only the 1st AC does the wrap. This process usually takes a few hours, or possibly a whole day, and is often done the same day shooting ends or the day after the last day of shooting. Clean all camera equipment and place it in the proper cases. Remove any identification labels that were placed on the equipment during the camera prep before putting the equipment in the case. The cleaning of all cases and equipment may seem like a lot of wasted work, but it lets the rental house know that you are a professional and care about the equipment you work with. I always order some type of cleaning supplies with my expendables order so that I can keep the cases clean during a production and also so that I can thoroughly clean everything before returning it to the rental house. The rental house will also feel that the next time they send out equipment for you they do not have to worry about it. You should have copies of all packing lists for all equipment received since the beginning of the production. If you find anything missing, notify the production office immediately so that they are not surprised when the rental house calls them.

WORKING IN DIGITAL VIDEO

With so many productions being shot in the digital format these days, I thought it would be a good idea to include some basic information about the job responsibilities of the Camera Assistants when working in that format. Most of my production experience has been working on film productions, so I have obtained this information from colleagues who have more experience in this area. To my knowledge, it is

as complete and accurate as possible. Special thanks go out to all who contributed to the information in this section.

Often a Camera Operator may come from a background of shooting television. When shooting with some older, pedestal-mounted cameras, the focus is controlled by the Camera Operator. Unfortunately, in the earlier days of digital some Producers seemed to think that if the Camera Operator can focus with these types of camera, they can focus any camera and therefore a 1st AC is not needed. This may work with these older pedestal-mounted systems with a focus device on the handle, but it doesn't work when shooting with a standard fluid head or gear head. In most cases, both hands are being used to operate the head and, as such, there is no way for the Camera Operator to also pull focus. Pulling focus on an HD digital camera is just as critical as when shooting 35 mm film. The size of the sensor on most HD digital cameras is equivalent to a frame of 35 mm film. Because of the perception that there is a greater depth of field in HD, shots are often done with the aperture set wide open, giving the least depth of field. In this situation, critical focus is very important, and a separate Focus Puller is essential to quality images. Keep in mind that pedestal-mounted cameras are almost exclusively used for studio news and studio multi-camera shoots, such as sitcoms. Pedestal-mounted cameras are not used in the field, and therefore it would be quite difficult for the Operator to pull focus if he or she were using a gear head or even a fluid head, as stated previously.

A 1st AC with an electronic news gathering (ENG) background may be very helpful when working in digital, but it is not necessary. Many 1st ACs come directly from film backgrounds and must learn all of this information for the first time on the first digital shoot that they do. As more and more productions have moved to shooting digital, there are more qualified Camera Assistants to work on these types of productions.

Some of the duties of a 1st AC on digital productions are described in the following sections.

Preproduction

As stated in the section on film productions, the 1st AC will usually be involved in many of the preproduction events on a digital shoot as well. This involvement usually requires meetings with the DP to discuss the camera equipment that will be used for the shoot. There may also be preproduction meetings with many of the key crew members to discuss the production. The 1st AC will often discuss the expendables order with the 2nd AC before it is submitted to the production

office. In addition, the 1st AC will be involved in the camera prep with the Digital Imaging Technician (DIT) to be sure that all camera equipment is in proper working order before production.

Choosing and Ordering Expendables

Many of the expendable items needed on a film production will also be needed on a digital production. The 1st AC will prepare this list, usually along with the 2nd AC. In addition to the standard expendables, you may want extra video connectors and memory cards on hand in case of emergency. Because there are so many cables involved in video, having a proper connector or adapter can make the difference between shooting and waiting around to get the connector so you can shoot. SD cards are often used for updating the firmware on cameras, so you should get one or two of these with the expendables order.

The Rental House and Preparation of Camera Equipment

The 1st AC should contact the rental company to arrange the day and time that you will prep the camera equipment. If the production is a film-style shoot, the 1st AC will usually work with the DIT at the prep to be sure that the system works properly and also to allow him or her to become familiar with what equipment will be used. If it is a prep for a multi-camera video-style shoot, the 1st AC may not even be involved in the prep of the equipment. Many digital cameras use up much more power than film cameras, so be sure you have extra batteries and chargers available for shooting.

You never know what mode you will be shooting in so be sure that you have all accessories and equipment needed for studio, hand-held, crane, and Steadicam shooting situations. You should have enough media cards for each camera being used. A minimum of four cards per camera is recommended, but if there will be any high-speed shooting you may want to have extras. Test each lens to be sure that it covers the sensor of the camera, record some images and play them back to be sure that everything records properly.

Production

It's now time for filming to start. As stated previously in this chapter, the production phase of shooting is a complex operation that requires a great deal of dedication, hard work, and attention to detail on the part of all involved. This is especially important to the 1st AC. The proper performance of the duties and responsibilities of the 1st AC is

vital to the smooth operation of any production. You must pay close attention to detail and be ready to make quick decisions. You are one of the key people who the DP relies on during filming. If you let the DP down, you let down the entire crew.

Setting Up the Camera

On film-style shoots, the 1st AC sets up the camera, often working with the 2nd AC. At the start of each day, you should set up the camera, check the back focus, white balance/black balance, and all camera settings so that the camera is ready for the first shot. User-defined switches must be properly set according to the DP's request; all setup menus must be checked to be sure that the settings are correct. Some cameras have slots for memory cards, where the DP may have programmed specific looks for certain shots. The 1st AC should know how to read the card and set the settings according to the DP's request. Specific "looks" for different shooting situations are saved as scene files so that they can be accessed at a later time. This is most often done by the DIT, but the 1st AC should know where the files are saved and how to retrieve them.

There may be back-focus adjustments that need to be set. Back-focus problems are not necessarily due to problems with the lens but are often due to the lens mount of the camera. On some cameras, the metal used in the design of the camera may be susceptible to expansion or contraction, which will affect the back focus. Check with the rental house when checking out the camera.

Most of the newer digital cameras use lenses that are very similar to the film-style lenses. With some older-style digital video cameras, zoom lenses would have the zoom motor built in, with a rocker-style lever used to control the zooming in and out of the lens. Today that it not the case. Most zoom lenses used today are exactly like those used on film cameras, with a separate zoom motor and control that must be attached to the iris rods of the camera and engaged on the gears of the lens. You should know how to set up and calibrate these zoom controls as well as the controls for focus and iris motors that may be used on the lens.

Be sure that all batteries are fully charged or being charged so that they are available throughout the day. The 1st AC must be familiar with the many menus in the digital cameras so that he or she has access to basic functions like EI/ASA/ISO settings, shutter speed, gain settings, codec, fps, and color temperature settings. Many of these things are left to the Digital Imaging Technician, but the 1st AC should know them as well because in many cases there is no DIT on the production or the DIT is assigned other responsibilities such

as cataloguing and downloading the footage. In addition to the many menu settings on the camera, the 1st AC must also know and understand all of the external controls, switches, and connections on the camera.

There are many cables for the external video, on-board monitor, electronic viewfinder, and more that must be connected to the camera. The 1st AC should know where all of these cables are to be connected because there are typically more cables and connections than when using a film camera.

You will be working with a variety of accessories such as Preston lens control, cmotion, Cine Tape, etc. It is very important to know how to set up these items so that you can do your job properly. Make sure that you have all the cables and connections for all the above accessories along with all other accessories that you will be using. Because you will have a number of cables connected to the camera, you should develop a system of color coding and managing the cables in a streamlined process. Proper cable management will prevent any problems and delays when moving the camera.

Because all HD production monitors are different, you should know how to make sure that the color matches from one monitor to the next and that they each work in both AC and DC modes. You should know how to navigate through the menus of each monitor so that you can make fine adjustments as necessary. Some shoots use paint boxes or external camera control units. On smaller shoots without a Digital Imaging Technician, the 1st AC should know how to double check settings and control the camera using one of these units. If possible, it is a good idea for the 1st AC to spend a full day with the camera and the instruction manual so that he or she can become familiar with their many functions and controls. At the very least you should know how to change the ISO, color temperature, shutter speed, and frames per second.

Loading and Unloading Media Cards into the Digital Camera

The 1st AC will be responsible for changing media cards in the camera, being sure to format the cards before using them. Before formatting make sure that the previously recorded material has been copied, backed up, reviewed, and approved. Formatting a media card before confirming that the previous material has been saved is as bad as flashing a shot roll of film. You don't want to do it. As stated previously, be sure to have plenty of media cards available for the shooting you are doing. When formatting cards it is recommended that you format them in the camera that will be using them so that the firmware is the same, especially when using multiple cameras.

Swapping Hard Drives

As with media cards, be sure that any material recorded on an external hard drive has been copied, backed up, reviewed, and approved before formatting. Be sure to have enough hard drives with the appropriate amount of storage space for the type of shooting you are doing.

Lenses (Primes and Zooms)

When changing lenses, check the front and back elements to be sure that they are clean and free from scratches or imperfections that could affect your image. As with the discussion on film lenses, unless there are major smudges or marks on the lens element, it should be cleaned with lens fluid or tissue only when absolutely necessary. When changing lenses, you should always check the back focus to be sure that it is set properly before shooting.

Checking for Lens Flares

Whenever the camera is in position and the lights are set for the shot, you should check for any lens flares using the same methods as when working with film cameras.

Focusing and Depth of Field

With the newer-style digital cameras, back focus should not be as much of an issue as it was with earlier tape-based video-style HD cameras. On many of the older cameras, back focus could go out at any time without warning, so you needed to check it often. On newer digital cameras, it is not quite as critical, but you should know how to check it. It's one of those things that can't be explained, but back focus will go out at the worst possible time, and the 1st AC will get blamed for it. A few years ago I was Camera Operator on an HD digital production, and we had to check back focus after almost every take. We were using one of the earlier HD tape-based cameras. On today's newer cameras, back focus usually does not go out as often, as previously indicated.

As with shooting film, measuring the distance is the best way to get your focus marks. If the back focus is set correctly, then your measurements will give you sharp focus, but if the back focus of the camera is off, your focus measurements will be useless.

Just what is back focus? Back focus is related to another term that you may be familiar with, flange focal depth. Back focus is the distance between the rear element of the lens and the film plane or

sensor. Flange focal depth is the distance between the lens mount flange and the film plane or sensor. Both of these are critical and must be correct for the specific camera you are using. When both of these are correct, your focus marks on the lens will be accurate. Back focus can usually be adjusted in the field by the Camera Assistant, while flange focal depth most often needs to be checked and set by a rental house lens technician using a device called a collimator. Be sure that your lens mount on the camera as well as the lens mount flanges on the lens are clean. Even a small piece of dust on either of these could throw off your focus.

With the newer cameras there is no universal way of checking back focus so I strongly urge you to have a copy of the manual available. Manuals for most of the current cameras can be found on the companion web site for the book. Use your prep time to become completely familiar with how to adjust the back focus, so that when you need to do it on set, you won't feel pressured or rushed because you know how to do it. For the simple way to check back focus you should follow these steps:

1. Place a focus chart or Siemens star chart on a wall or mount it to a C-stand (see Figure 5.56).

Figure 5.56   Siemens star as seen on most focus test charts. (Courtesy of Century Precision Optics.)

2. Set the camera at the height of the chart and 8–10 ft from the chart. Make sure that the distance matches a distance mark on the lens.
3. Use a zoom lens or prime lens of at least 50 mm focal length. If using a zoom lens, zoom in all the way so that the chart fills the frame.
4. Open the f-stop/t-stop to its widest opening. Depth of field must be minimum so you can accurately judge the focus of the chart.
5. Focus by eye using the camera viewfinder or monitor. Do not use a small on-board monitor but the largest monitor that you have available.
6. Check that the eye focus matches the focus marking on the lens for the distance that the camera is from the chart.
7. If the focus is not correct, the way to adjust it may be different depending on the camera and lenses you are using. In many cases you can follow the steps that follow.
8. Use a zoom lens, zoom out to the widest-angle focal length of the lens, loosen and adjust the back-focus knob until the chart is in focus.
9. Zoom back in to the tightest focal length and watch the monitor to see that the chart remains in focus.
10. Repeat these steps until the chart is sharp at the widest-angle focal length, the most telephoto focal length, and all focal lengths in between.

Depth of field for HD is going to be slightly different than the depth of field for 16 mm film and 35 mm film. If you don't have an iPhone, iPad, or iPod Touch there is a simple to use HD depth-of-field calculator which is manufactured by the Guild of British Camera Technicians and is available from many expendable companies. It is very easy to use and allows you to determine your depth of field for a given shot. The previous apps for the iPhone, iPad, and iPod Touch, pCAM Film+Digital Calculator and Toland ASC Digital Assistant, each have settings in the depth-of-field settings of the app for various digital formats.

Focus markings on some lenses are often not very accurate and sometimes they are nonexistent. This is usually only the case if you are using ENG-style lenses. They are usually not as precise as motion picture camera lenses as far as image quality and focusing capabilities, and for the most part are not used in today's production world. Many of the cine-style HD lenses, such as Digi primes, and the Arriflex Alura Zooms, are very accurate with their witness marks. All the standard HD digital cameras can be fitted with a follow-focus and matte box system; even the Prosumer grade Panasonic HVX 200 can be fitted with a follow focus on its built-in lens.

If you don't have accurate focus markings on the lens, focus marks are often obtained by eye, sometimes relying on the monitor image to judge if it is sharp. Many times the operator or 1st AC will zoom all the way in wide open, get a mark, and the 1st AC will mark it on the lens with a grease pencil or mark it on a piece of tape wrapped around the barrel of the lens, and then reset the lens to its original frame and stop.

Some cameras have a mark on the camera to indicate the film or sensor plane. If not, you should determine where the film plane is during the camera prep and mark it on the side of the camera. This will help during production if you are measuring your focus distances.

A DP friend of mine told me about a time he was shooting with an HD camera using SD lenses. The camera had a witness mark on the body to indicate the focus plane (film plane for you film camera people). For two days the assistant was measuring focus from this mark on the camera body. Unfortunately, they discovered that the SD lenses had a mark on the front of them, which you were supposed to measure from. So for two days the focus marks were all off by over 1 ft, and the shots were out of focus. This situation was most likely due to the fact that they were using ENG-style lenses. When using these lenses, SD or HD, the assistant must measure from the front of the lens and not the film plane. Again, this pertains to ENG-style lenses, not cinestyle lenses. If you are unsure which you are shooting with, check the markings on the side of the lens with the measured distance. It should be obvious. When in doubt, always check critical focus on the larger monitor that you will always have on set. If using a video-style lens, make sure it is for HD. The previously described problem occurred in the early stages of HD and is very rare today. It is much more difficult today to get an SD lens for an HD camera. As with film cameras, today's digital cameras have a witness mark or post onto which you can attach your soft tape measure for measuring the focus to the actors. This witness mark or post is usually in line with the location of the sensor on the digital camera.

During an HD production I operated on a few years ago, all focus was obtained by eye. Because my assistants couldn't see the large monitor, they would adjust the focus while the DIT or DP watched on the monitor and let them know when it was sharp. This was very time consuming and frustrating for the 1st AC who was pulling focus. Everything worked out fine, but it took much longer than getting your focus marks in film. This happened with one of the earlier cameras, and I don't think it would be as much of an issue using any of today's digital video cameras.

It is not unusual on a digital show to shoot the rehearsals. This can be very frustrating for a Camera Assistant or Operator, and many

times you will not get a chance to get marks. Of course, this is no excuse for it being out of focus, so if marks are needed, say something before shooting. It's always best to have a large-screen monitor (at least 19 in.) to be able to clearly see the focus. These are great for going into the field. In a studio situation, a larger (25 in.) monitor would be ideal.

Moving the Camera

Moving the camera between setups can be much more time consuming than when shooting with a film camera. Even with a film camera, you will have a battery cable that connects the battery and often a video cable connected to the camera's video tap. But when shooting video, you may have more cables to contend with. Color coding your cables can make it easier to reconnect them after a camera move.

White Balancing

With many of the newer digital cameras you don't perform a traditional white balance at the beginning of the day or at the beginning of each lighting change. It is determined by the lighting color temperature and the ISO/EI setting that you set in the menu of the camera. However, if you are using an older camera that requires the traditional white balance, you should perform this at the beginning of each day and whenever you change your lighting color temperature. Many of the newer cameras have an automatic white balance setting or it is determined by the menu settings in the camera. Depending on the lighting source you are using, tungsten or daylight, once you set the color temperature setting in the camera's menu, it is the same as using a specific color balanced film stock in that lighting source. In this case there would be no need to white balance because it would be taken care of by the menu settings.

Tools and Accessories

You will need your same complement of tools and accessories when working on digital productions. Although you may not use them all, I am a firm believer in the saying, "It's better to have it and not need it than to need it and not have it." Depending on the production, you may want to have your own backup hard drives and extra media cards along with a laptop computer for downloading the footage. Many assistants also have a battery backup system in case of a power failure. You don't want to lose that valuable footage. As stated earlier, you should have an assortment of video connectors and cables.

Postproduction

As stated in Chapter 4, postproduction for the camera department means that all equipment must be cleaned, checked, and packed away so that it can be returned to the rental company. A final inventory of expendables is usually done and turned in to the production office. Invoices and all other paperwork must be turned in to the production office. If a camera truck was used, it will probably be cleaned out for the next production's use. Finally, the 1st AC packs up all of his or her gear and gets ready for that next job call, where the entire process starts all over again.

Wrapping Equipment

When wrapping equipment and packing it away at the end of the day or at the end of the shoot, you should follow the same procedures as outlined in the Wrapping Equipment section for film shoots. If you will continue to shoot on another day and the camera will be shipped to a new location, I recommend writing down all of your camera settings on a piece of paper, so that in the event the settings change during transportation, you can reset the camera to its original settings for shooting. If the camera menu has the ability to lock the settings, you should do this before moving the camera. If the buttons get pressed during the move, the menu settings won't change if it is locked.

REVIEW CHECKLIST FOR FIRST ASSISTANT CAMERAMAN (1ST AC OR FOCUS PULLER)

Preproduction

- Knows and understands all professional motion picture camera equipment and accessories currently used in the industry
- Reads the script so that he or she is aware of the story and recommends any special equipment that he or she feels may be needed to carry out specific shots
- Works with the DP and/or Camera Operator to choose the camera equipment that will be used on the production
- Recommends the 2nd AC and Loader/Trainee to the DP and/or Production Manager
- Works with the 2nd AC to prepare a list of expendables, which is then given to the production office or Production Manager so that the items may be purchased

- Preps the camera package alone or along with the 2nd AC; ensures that all equipment is in proper working order
- During prep makes sure that there are enough media cards for each camera

Production

- Is responsible for the overall operation of the camera department during production
- Is responsible for the overall care and maintenance of all camera equipment during production
- Unpacks, assembles, and warms up the camera and all of its components at the start of each shooting day
- Mounts the camera head onto the tripod, dolly, or other support piece and ensures that it is secure and working properly
- Does not leave the camera unattended
- Loads and unloads the proper film or media cards into the camera for the shots and setups
- On film cameras, resets the footage counter to zero after each reload
- On film cameras, resets the buckle switch in the camera if necessary
- On digital productions, sets all menu settings as instructed by the DP
- Keeps all parts of the camera clean and free from dirt and dust, including camera body, lenses, filters, magazines, and so on
- Oils and lubes the camera as needed
- Sets the viewfinder eyepiece for each key person who will look through the camera
- Before each shot, ensures that the camera is level and balanced
- If the camera is mounted on a tripod, ensures that it is securely positioned and leveled
- When the camera is in position for shooting, checks to be sure that no lights are kicking into the lens, causing a flare
- Places proper lens, filter, and any other accessory on the camera as instructed by the DP or Camera Operator
- Checks that lenses and filters are clean before filming
- Sets the t-stop on the lens before each take as instructed by the DP
- Measures the distances to subjects during rehearsals and marks the lens or focus-marking disk
- Checks the depth of field for each shot as needed
- Follows focus and makes zoom lens moves during takes
- Adjusts the shutter angle, t-stop, or camera speed during a take as needed and as instructed by the DP

- Checks that the camera is running at the correct speed during filming
- Gives the 2nd AC footage readings from the camera after each take
- After each printed take or when instructed by the DP, checks the gate for hairs or emulsion buildup and requests another take if necessary
- Supervises the transportation and moving of all camera equipment between filming locations
- Works with the 2nd AC to move the camera to each new position
- Works with the 2nd AC to be sure that all camera batteries are kept fully charged and ready for use
- If there is no 2nd AC on the production, then also performs those duties
- Orders additional or special camera equipment as needed
- Checks the call sheet daily to be sure any additional camera equipment and crew members are requested if needed
- Arranges for the return of any camera equipment no longer needed
- Arranges for the return and replacement of any damaged camera equipment
- Oversees all aspects of the camera department
- Disassembles the camera and its components at the completion of the shooting day and packs them away into the appropriate cases
- Provides all the necessary tools and accessories associated with performing the job

Postproduction

- At the completion of filming, wraps and cleans all camera equipment for returning to the rental house
- Views dailies with the DP, Director, and other production personnel

6

Problems and Troubleshooting

This chapter deals with problems and troubleshooting methods to use when you have equipment-related problems. Other types of problems that you may encounter in the day-to-day performance of your job, such as location issues or personality conflicts with other crew members, are covered in other chapters.

Troubleshooting may be described as a careful system of finding the cause of a problem and correcting it. When something goes wrong, find out why, and then correct or eliminate the problem. You need common sense and logic, as well as knowledge of the equipment you are working with. If you are familiar with the equipment, it is only a matter of using a step-by-step procedure to find and correct almost any problem that you encounter. I recommend always having the instruction manual for the particular camera you are working with close at hand. Most manuals are now available in PDF format so if you have a laptop computer, iPad or other device it's now even easier to have the manual with you without the need to carry a paper copy.

Being familiar with the equipment involves not only the ability to put the pieces together but also feeling comfortable with the equipment. Treat the camera and its accessories gently. Do not force any pieces of equipment that will not fit together. When placing the camera on the head or base plate, slide it on gently and do not just slam it in place. Don't slam the Arriflex SR magazines onto the camera. Place them on firmly but gently. The better you take care of the equipment, the fewer problems you should have. When you do encounter a problem, the first and most important thing is not to panic. Stop for a moment and think about what the problem is and then try to determine the most logical cause of the problem. Try to fix it, and if it doesn't work, continue trying to correct the problem by process of elimination. Try the obvious first, eliminate what is not causing the problem, and eventually narrow down the possible choices and hopefully you will find out the cause.

It is very important that you check only one thing at a time. For example, if the camera won't run and you change the battery, the power cable, and the fuse at the same time, how will you know which of these was the cause of the problem? Finding the cause of most problems should usually take only a few minutes, but there will be some instances when you cannot find the cause yourself and then must telephone the rental house and ask for help. Most reputable camera rental houses have a 24-hour number to contact in case of an emergency. Never be afraid to contact the rental house regarding any questions you may have about the equipment. They would rather have you ask about something than to try to do it incorrectly. When a problem occurs, it is often best to try to keep it within the camera department whenever possible. Sometimes you don't even need to tell the Director of Photography (DP) about it. He or she has enough to think about and doesn't need to be worried about small camera problems. Many times you will be able to fix or correct the problem without anybody ever knowing that there even was a problem. For example, if a magazine keeps jamming, have the 2nd Assistant Cameraman (AC) contact the rental house and arrange to swap the magazine out for a new one. Let the Unit Production Manager or Production Coordinator know that a magazine needs to be exchanged. This can be done in a short period of time without the DP ever knowing about it. The DP doesn't need to be bothered with something as minor as a magazine problem. Just deal with it, and he or she never has to know there was a problem. It's all part of being a professional.

When something does go wrong, remain calm and don't freak out. There is no use causing panic on the set, especially among the Director, DP, Assistant Director, or other crew members. A few years ago I was working on a 16mm shoot with an Arriflex SR2 that was owned by the DP. The matte box didn't quite fit tightly on the support rods no matter what I did. While moving to a new setup I picked up the camera, and the matte box fell off. One of the filter trays that held an enhancer filter fell to the floor, causing the filter to shatter into many pieces. Unfortunately, everybody was looking directly at me, and instead of panicking I simply apologized to the DP and told him that I would have a new filter on set within the hour. I made a call to an expendables supply company that was just down the street from our location and arranged for a Production Assistant to pick up the new filter, which, by the way, I charged to my personal account. By the time the DP had the new setup lit and ready to shoot, the replacement filter had arrived. I didn't panic and get upset but rather took responsibility and handled the situation in a calm and professional manner. Things will go wrong, and they may or may not be your fault. If you act like a professional and handle the problem quickly, you may

still be in trouble, but everybody should respect you for the professional manner in which you handled the situation.

Because it is not possible to foresee every problem, I have mentioned some of the typical ones that can and will happen in the course of a film production. Many of these things have actually happened to me or one of my colleagues on various shoots. Sometimes I was able to correct the problem quickly, but other times I had to call the rental house and ask for their advice or have a technician come to the location to fix or replace the camera or accessory. I have also tried to group these in categories so that they are easy to locate. Some of the film-related problems may relate to both cameras and magazines but the issue is only covered in one of the sections. Be sure to check both sections if you cannot find a specific problem listed in one of the headings.

CAMERA PROBLEMS

Camera Will Not Run

When the camera will not run, first check to see if the battery is connected to the camera. This is the most logical and most common reason why the camera won't run. Also check to see if the battery contains a full charge and if it is the correct voltage for the camera being used. Be sure that you have the proper voltage battery for the camera system you are using. The battery may be dual voltage, and the switch on the battery may be in the wrong position. If the camera has one, check the buckle trip switch inside the camera to see if it is in the proper position. The buckle trip switch shuts off the camera when there is a rollout or when film becomes jammed in the camera. Reset the switch if necessary, which should correct the problem. If the battery is connected and the buckle trip switch is in its proper position, try a new battery cable. If this doesn't work, try a new battery.

Often you may have to give the battery cable a closer inspection to locate a problem. It may even be necessary to take the plug apart to check that all the internal wires of the cable are properly connected to the connections on the end of the plug. This won't be apparent without taking the plug apart. You should have a soldering iron in your ditty bag in case you need to repair and re-solder a broken cable. Many assistants have battery- or propane-powered soldering irons in their kits, which can be used anywhere. These are especially good when working in remote locations and you don't have access to electricity. If you do need to make any minor repairs to cables, it is best to take them off set and do the repair on the camera truck or out of view

of the cast and crew. Producers and Directors can get a little nervous if they see one of the Camera Assistants taking equipment apart and attempting to repair it.

Some cameras have a safety feature built into them that will not allow the camera to run if the camera body door is not closed completely. Make sure the door is closed and latched before turning on the camera. If the camera still will not run, and you are able to access any fuses, check and change the fuse or fuses if necessary. You can change the electronic circuit boards in some cameras, including those from Panavision. I believe that it is a good idea to first check any fuses before resorting to changing the electronic circuit boards. If all of these actions still do not correct the problem, call the rental house for help. As I stated earlier, it is important to remember when this or any problem occurs to check only one thing at a time. Before changing fuses or circuit boards, always disconnect power to the camera. When trying to determine why the camera will not run, disconnect all electrical accessories from the camera and try to run it. This helps to determine if any accessories are causing the problem. Check all electrical accessories one at a time to see which one, if any, may be causing the problem. Sometimes simply disconnecting everything, including the camera from the battery, waiting a few minutes, and then reconnecting everything will solve the problem.

Most of the newer cameras have a computer processor that controls the camera functions. These can malfunction, especially when there are temperature changes in the shooting environment. Simply disconnecting power for a few minutes and then reconnecting may be enough to fix this problem. Some cameras have a thermal fuse, and if this fuse trips, you need to power off the camera and leave it off for a few minutes before powering it back up again. Also, many newer cameras have a master power switch that must be turned on before you can run the camera. If the master power switch is not turned on, pushing the Run button of the camera will have no effect.

When mounting the camera to the head or sliding base plate, you will most often screw a ⅜–16 bolt or screw into the bottom of the camera. This is the standard size bolt/screw used to mount most professional motion picture cameras. Some cameras have circuit boards in their base. Using a mounting bolt or screw that is too long may cause it to come in contact with the circuit boards, shorting them out and causing the camera to not run. Be sure to check that you are not using a bolt or screw that is too long before mounting the camera.

Some cameras require a minimum and maximum voltage amount for them to run. This is not controlled by the Camera Assistant but is something that is preset in the camera at the factory. In other words, if for some reason the battery voltage falls below a certain level or

rises above a certain level, the camera will automatically shut off and not run. Check your camera manual and battery voltage whenever this happens. Be sure that the battery is functioning properly so that these amounts are within the guidelines for the camera system you are using. Finally, if the camera does not run, be sure to check that the Run switch is in the "on" position.

If the camera won't run, check the speed setting. You may have the camera speed set to a speed outside the range of the camera. Be sure you know the speed range of the camera you are using to ensure the proper running speed. If you are filming in extreme cold weather conditions, be sure that the camera is properly winterized for shooting in the cold. If not, it may run slowly or not at all.

Camera Does Not Stop When Switched to "Off"

The camera may not stop when switched to the "off" position, especially when you are using a hand grip with an on/off switch or a zoom control with an on/off switch. If there are any accessories plugged into the camera that contain an on/off switch, check to see that this switch is in the "off" position. If it is in the "on" position, the camera will continue to run when you turn the main camera Run switch off.

As stated in the Camera Will Not Run section, when mounting the camera to the head or sliding base plate, you must screw a ⅜–16 bolt or screw into the bottom of the camera. Some cameras have circuit boards in their base. Using a mounting bolt that is too long may cause the bolt to come in contact with the circuit boards, shorting them out, which may cause the camera to continue running. Be sure to check that you are not using a bolt that is too long before mounting the camera.

Camera Starts and Stops Intermittently

If the camera starts and stops intermittently, the battery might not be fully charged. Changing batteries should correct the problem. If the battery cable is loose, reinsert it into either the camera or the battery. A loose wire in the power cable can also be one of the causes that you might not be able to see by just looking at the cable. If you suspect this, try wiggling the cable at the point where it is connected to the camera and also where it is connected to the battery to see if this causes any change. If the camera starts and stops, it is a good indication that there is a short in it. You should have a voltmeter in your

tool bag and you should use it to check the contacts on the cable to see if there is current flowing through the cable. Try a new cable, and have the other one checked as soon as possible. If you have a soldering iron and solder available, you may be able to repair a damaged power cable without sending it back to the rental house.

On Panavision cameras you may find it necessary to change the circuit boards to correct this problem. Each Panavision camera comes supplied with an extra set of circuit boards as part of the camera package. The important thing to remember when changing circuit boards is to always change all of the circuit boards at the same time. Never replace just one or two of the boards. Send the old boards back to the rental house and request a replacement set to have on hand.

Faulty accessories or a variable-speed control may be the problem as well. If you have any accessories or a variable-speed control attached to the camera, try removing these items and running the camera without them attached. A faulty video sync box or external speed control may also cause the camera to start and stop intermittently. If you suspect any of these external devices, have them checked as soon as possible.

As stated earlier, if the camera won't run or stops running, check the speed setting. A speed setting outside of the speed range of the camera motor may cause the camera not to run properly, to suddenly stop running, or to not run at all. Be sure you know the speed range of the camera you are using to ensure the proper running speed.

Camera Stops While Filming

The most common reason that the camera stops while filming is that the film jams in either the camera or the magazine. Check that the loops are the proper size, and adjust them if necessary. Again, if the loop is set in the magazine, it must be removed from the camera and rethreaded, or a new magazine must be placed on the camera. When the film jams it can become ripped or torn, leaving a piece of film stuck in the magazine throat or in the gate of the camera. The important thing to remember when clearing any film jam is not to force any part of the camera or magazine. Gently slide the film from side to side or up and down until it will come out cleanly. If you try to force it out, you can damage the camera movement or the gears of the magazine. After clearing any film jam, clean the camera with compressed air to remove any film chips or emulsion that may have become trapped in the gears of the movement.

Another common cause of the camera stopping is that the film has rolled out. Many cameras have a safety feature built into them

that shuts off power to the camera when it runs out of film. Be aware of the footage counter when filming so this does not happen. Also, when threading the new magazine on the camera, be sure to reset the buckle switch, if the camera has one, so that the film travels smoothly through the camera.

Camera Is Noisy

The most common reason for a noisy camera is that the film is not threaded properly in the camera. The top or bottom loop may be too large or too small, causing the movement to work harder to move the film through the camera, which results in the movement being a little noisier than usual. Rethread the camera, and set the loops to the proper length.

On many cameras the loop may be set when threading the magazine, so you may need to rethread the magazine or change magazines. Check that all rollers are closed and that the film perforations are engaged on the sprockets correctly. If the camera has an adjustable pitch control, adjust it so that the camera is running as quietly as possible when it is threaded correctly. Sometimes none of these solutions makes the camera any quieter, so the only thing to do is to cover the camera with a sound barney to cut down on the noise. If the Sound Mixer is picking up any camera noise, you may also need to place an optical flat in front of the lens to minimize the noise being picked up by the sound microphones.

I have also found that some film stocks cause the camera to run more noisily than others. Because of differences in the manufacturing of the different film stocks and emulsions, some film may be slightly thicker or thinner than other film. This is also true when shooting black-and-white versus color film. Black-and-white film is generally slightly thinner than color film and may cause the camera to be noisier as the film is running through it.

I was once working on a low-budget, independent production, and the camera ran more noisily than usual. The Director asked me if there was anything that could be done, and I explained that it was because of the film stock we were using. The film was from a different manufacturer than the film stock we had used previously. The Director was not satisfied with my explanation, so he telephoned the person from whom he had rented the camera and asked that he come to the location to check the camera. When he arrived, he asked me what film stock we were using. When I told him what it was, he told the Director that I was correct and that it was the film stock that was causing the noise problem and that there was nothing he could do

about it. He left and we continued to shoot with a sound blanket over the camera to muffle the noise.

Shutter Does Not Spin (No Flicker Seen through the Viewfinder)

While a shutter rarely fails to spin, I have heard of an instance when the Camera Operator could not see any flicker through the viewfinder when shooting. This is a good indication that the shutter is not spinning. The camera was running and film was traveling through the camera and magazine, but the shutter was not spinning. Unfortunately, there is really nothing you can do in the field, and if this occurs, you should contact the rental house immediately and return the camera. The one time that I know of this happening there was a drive belt that had broken. This was the belt that turned the mirror shutter when the camera was running or when you turned the inching knob. This belt could only be replaced by a camera technician at the camera rental company.

Unable to Thread Film into the Gate Area

If you are unable to thread film into the gate area, be sure that you have turned the inching knob to advance the pull down claw so that it is withdrawn from the aperture plate. Also, check to see if the registration pin is withdrawn from the gate area. These are the two most common reasons why you cannot thread the film. If after checking these two items you still encounter the problem, check to see that there are no film chips stuck in the gate area, preventing the film from threading properly. If the camera has a removable aperture plate, be sure that it is inserted correctly. Also check that the pressure plate is in the proper position.

Camera Door Does Not Close

On some cameras the door does not close when the keeper arms on the sprocket roller are not closed or when the registration pin is pulled away from the gate for threading. Be sure that both of these are in the correct position for filming and the door should close properly. Also check the edges around the door where it meets the camera to be sure that there are no obstructions, such as a piece of film. Clean out anything that may be blocking the door, and it should close properly.

Film Jams in Camera

If the film jams in the camera, the film loop could be the wrong size. Rethread the camera or the magazine and adjust the loops to the proper size. If the magazine is not threaded properly, it can cause the camera motor to work harder to move the film through the camera, which results in the film becoming jammed. Be sure that all sprocket keepers are closed and the film is moving smoothly through the gate. Before running the camera, you should always check the threading with the inching knob after placing a new magazine on the camera.

Film Rips or Has Torn Perforations

Film may rip or have torn perforations for the same reasons that cause the film to jam. Improper loop sizes can result in the film becoming ripped or torn as it goes through the camera or magazine. Check the loop size in the camera, and adjust it if necessary. Rethread the magazine, and adjust any magazine loops accordingly. Panavision cameras have a small pin located inside the camera body that is used as a guide when setting your loop size. If the top loop is too long, it may catch on this pin and tear the perforations. Be sure to check your threading and loop size by turning the inching knob before running the camera. Also, be sure to clean out the magazine and/or camera if you find torn film chips.

Film Loses Loop

If the film loses the loop, check the pull down claw and registration pin to be sure that they are not bent in any way. Incorrectly threading the camera or magazine can cause loss of the loop. When threading, be sure that you set the correct loop size in the camera or magazine. Also check to be sure that the film is properly engaged on the sprocket rollers and that the sprocket roller guides are engaged correctly. If the camera has one, you may also need to adjust the pitch control to quiet the camera and ensure that the proper loop size is maintained.

Camera Does Not Run at Sync Speed

One reason that the camera does not run at sync speed may be a problem with the battery. A weak battery could affect the speed of the camera. Replace the battery with one that is fully charged, and the camera should run at sync speed. Another common cause is that the motor

switch on the camera is set to the variable position instead of the sync position. Reset the switch to the sync position. On Panavision cameras, a malfunctioning circuit board could also cause this to happen. If you can, change the circuit boards to see if this corrects the problem. Also, if the magazine or the camera is threaded incorrectly, it may have an effect on the motor, causing it to lose speed. Check the threading of both and adjust as necessary.

As I stated, when discussing the problem of the camera starting and stopping intermittently, check any accessories that may be attached to the camera. Disconnect the accessories and run the camera to see if this corrects the problem.

Viewing System Is Blacked Out

When you cannot see anything through the eyepiece, there is something blocking the viewing system. This could be due to one of a number of problems. The most obvious is that the lens cap is on the front of the lens. The shutter may be closed, which makes the eyepiece dark. Turn the camera on and off quickly, or turn the inching knob to clear the shutter. The eyepiece may be set to the closed position, which allows no light to enter the eyepiece. Check the eyepiece control lever, and set it to the open position for viewing. Or if the eyepiece has a magnification lever for critical eye focus, check that it is not partially open or closed, which would make it difficult to see through the eyepiece. When the lens is stopped down to its smallest aperture, it may be difficult to see anything when looking through the eyepiece. Also, if there are any neutral density filters in front of the lens, they darken the image when viewed, making it appear totally dark. Another reason may be simply that there is someone or something blocking the lens. Many cameras also have a switch or lever that is used to switch the viewing system when filming with anamorphic lenses. Check to see if this switch or lever has been bumped and is blocking the viewing system or is not in the proper position for the lenses being used.

When doing certain special effects shots and using some older cameras, you may be using a camera that contains a rack over viewing system. If the viewfinder is not in the correct position, you will not be able to see when looking through it. Be sure to place it in the correct position for viewing.

A Fuse Blows When Connecting Electrical Accessories

Blowing a fuse when connecting electrical accessories is a common problem that can be easily corrected. The important thing to

remember when connecting any electrical accessories is always to disconnect the power to the camera before attaching the accessories. If the camera has a master power switch, be sure to turn it off before connecting or disconnecting any electrical accessory and before disconnecting the battery from the camera. If the camera is connected to a power source, the connection of any electrical accessory may cause a power surge to the motor, which will then cause a fuse to blow. It is best to turn off the power and disconnect the battery before connecting any external electronic accessory to the camera.

When Shooting a Television Monitor or Computer Screen, a Roll Bar Moves through the Screen

The frame rate for video is different than the frame rate for film. As such, when filming a television monitor with a film camera you will usually see a horizontal bar moving through the frame. When shooting TV screens and computer monitors you need to match the frame rate so that you can eliminate or minimize the roll bar. This is best accomplished by using a sync box attached to the camera. Ideally, the camera should also have a variable shutter so that you can sync the camera to the monitor or screen. When shooting at 30 frames per second (fps) or, more precisely, 29.97 fps, the shutter angle should be set to 180 degrees. When shooting at 24 fps or, more precisely, 23.976 fps, the shutter angle should be set to 144 degrees. If shooting dialog scenes in which the screen is visible, it is best to shoot at 24 fps to maintain the sync of the dialog. Be sure that your camera has an adjustable shutter so that you may do this. If you need to shoot at 30 fps with the 180-degree shutter, dialog may need to be dubbed in postproduction.

MAGAZINE PROBLEMS

Film Cones When Removing from Magazine

When unloading the film from the magazine the film may begin to "cone," which means that the film comes out from the center of the roll. This especially could happen when unloading the exposed film from a magazine with a collapsible core. But it can also happen if the take-up is wound onto a plastic core. If this happens the most important thing is to not panic. If not too much film has come out from the center of the roll you should be able to carefully feed it back into the center of the roll. If not, then you may need to break the film

and create more than one roll to send to the lab. You may lose a portion of a shot when the film is developed but this is better than losing an entire roll of film. Because this could affect the shot or shots, I strongly recommend that you always inform the 1st AC and the DP whenever this happens.

Film Does Not Take Up

Many camera magazines have electrical contacts built into them so that when they are connected to the camera, the torque motor of the magazine receives power. If these contacts are dirty, the film will not take up properly. Check the contacts and clean them if necessary. Some cameras also have the ability to run either forward or in reverse. If the switch is in one position on the camera and the opposite position on the magazine, the film will not take up properly. Make sure that the switches on the camera and magazine are in the same position. Check the take-up side of the magazine to see if the film end has come off of the take-up core. Rethread the camera, and this should correct the problem.

Check to be sure that you are using the proper magazine on the camera. You may have a newer model of camera and be trying to use an older model of magazine. Also, with some manufacturers, there are separate magazines for high-speed and regular-speed cameras. These magazines are usually not interchangeable between cameras.

Incorrect magazine tension or a damaged magazine clutch may also be the cause of film not taking up in the magazine. If you suspect either of these things, it is best to swap out the magazine for a new one and let the rental company deal with it. Many assistants don't have the proper tools or qualifications to adjust the magazine tension. Plus, most rental companies would prefer that an assistant not try to repair their equipment.

If you are using film on a daylight spool and the take-up reel is also a daylight spool, be sure to check that the flanges of the spool are not bent, preventing the film from winding properly on the spool.

If the film does not take up and you are using an older camera that uses a rubber or leather belt to drive the take-up side, check that you have the right size belt and that it is connected properly to the magazine. It is very rare in today's world that you may be using one of these older cameras, but in case you do, you should always have a spare drive belt with the camera equipment. On magazines that use the drive belt, the belt must be placed on the correct side of the magazine for it to take up properly. It should be connected either to the feed side or the take-up side, depending on whether the film is

going forward or in reverse. Check the belt and adjust it as necessary. Check with the rental house so that you are sure how to connect the belt properly. Have extra belts available in case one breaks while filming.

Magazine Is Noisy

The film spooling off the core and rubbing against the side of the magazine may cause magazine noise. Hold the magazine flat in your hands, and give the cover of the magazine a firm slap so that the film settles back onto the spool or core. When the magazine is already placed on the camera, give both sides of the magazine a firm slap to force the film back onto the spool. Be very careful when doing this so that you slap both sides of the magazine at the same time. You don't want to run the risk of knocking the magazine off the camera and possibly damaging the camera or magazine.

If the film loop is set when threading the magazine, an incorrect-sized loop may also cause the magazine to be noisy. To correct this, rethread the magazine so that the loops are the proper size. There are some newer magazines that have a timing adjustment. Check with the rental house if you are not sure how to adjust the timing on the magazines that have this feature. A film jam inside the magazine may also make it noisier than usual. If the noise gets progressively louder, you should probably stop using the magazine, remove it, and rethread the camera with a new magazine. Have the 2nd AC check the noisy magazine, and if necessary, swap it out at the rental company for a new magazine.

There Are Scratches on the Film

Whenever the film gets scratched, scratch test the entire system as you did during the camera prep (see Chapter 5). The cause of the scratches could be from a problem inside the magazine throat or in the gears or rollers of the magazine. It could also be coming from inside the camera at any number of places. There may be dirt or emulsion buildup in the gate that should be cleaned out before you continue to shoot. Dirt or dust in the magazine can also cause scratches on the film. The best way to determine where the scratch is occurring is to place the magazine on the camera and thread the camera normally. Run some film through the camera. Using a permanent ink marker, place an "X" on the film at the following places: where it exits the magazine, enters the gate, exits the gate,

and reenters the magazine. Check the film at these marks to determine where the scratches occurred. An incorrect loop size may also cause scratches on the film. If necessary, you may have to send some of the magazines, or even the camera, back to the rental house for replacement or repair. In extreme cases, scratches on the film may be caused by damaged or faulty film stock or even by improper handling at the processing laboratory.

LENS-RELATED PROBLEMS

Lens Will Not Focus

One reason the lens may not focus is that the lens is not seated properly in the lens mount. This means that the lens is not correctly mounted on the camera. Remove the lens and check the lens mount of the camera to see if there are any obstructions. Thoroughly check and clean the lens mount, and then reinsert the lens. Also, check the back of the lens to see if there is anything preventing the lens from mounting properly. If the lens and the lens mount seem all right, reinsert the lens and check the focus again.

Another reason that the lens might not focus is that the ground glass of the camera is inserted incorrectly. Check the ground glass, and reinsert it if necessary. The ground glass should be inserted into the camera with the matte or dull side facing toward the mirror of the shutter.

Another cause of lens focus problems is that the lens is damaged. Check this by using a focus chart and checking the lens as you did during the camera prep. Place the chart at various distances from the camera, and then check the eye focus mark on the lens to see if they match. If a problem is detected when comparing the eye focus to the measured focus, the lens should be returned to the rental house for repair, and a replacement lens should be obtained.

A few years ago I was 1st AC on a feature film. One of the shots we did was a very long master dolly move that led two characters through a large building. After the first take, the Camera Operator said the shot was soft and out of focus, so we did it again. We did two more takes, but each time the Camera Operator said it was soft when we cut the camera. The DP, Camera Operator, and I each checked the lens focus by eye and arrived at approximately 30–40 ft. The measured distance was approximately 7 ft, which is exactly where I had it focused for each take. I removed the lens and gave it a light shake, and it sounded like a baby rattle. The elements inside the lens had all come loose. After some investigation we discovered that some of

the crew had a contest during the lunch break to see who could make the boom arm of the dolly go up and down the fastest. Unfortunately, they did this with the camera and lens on the dolly. This caused the lens elements to come loose, which caused our focus problem. So now when I break for lunch, I always remove the lens from the camera as a safety precaution.

One of the most common reasons that the lens appears out of focus when looking through the eyepiece is that the diopter adjustment of the eyepiece was changed when you were away from the camera. Each time someone looks through the eyepiece, check that the diopter adjustment ring is set to the appropriate mark. Because each person's vision is different, the image may look sharp and in focus to one person but blurry and out of focus to another. If you are looking through at somebody else's setting, you may not be able to get a proper focus. See Chapter 5 for the procedure on setting the eyepiece diopter for your vision.

A heavy fog or diffusion filter in front of the lens may prevent you from obtaining a sharp image through the viewfinder. Check the lens with the filters removed to see if you can obtain proper focus. In addition, a behind-the-lens filter may also create focus problems, which will only be apparent when viewing dailies because the filter is not visible through the viewfinder. If you are planning on using any behind-the-lens filters, it is a good idea to shoot some tests beforehand to be sure that there will be no focus problems.

Many lenses have focus markings in feet and also in meters. The marks are often on opposite sides of the lens, so you must be careful when placing the lens on the camera that the proper markings are facing you. I know of an instance of a 1st AC placing the lens on the camera with the meter markings facing him. He measured the distance in feet and inches but set the focus according to the meter scale, thinking it was feet and inches. Needless to say, all of the shots were out of focus until he realized what he had done.

Some lenses have a setting for macro photography. Unless it is a macro shot, you will not be able to focus a shot with the lens in the macro setting. Place the lens in its normal setting, and it should focus properly.

Finally, check to be sure that both the front and rear elements of the lens are clean. Dirty or smudged lens elements make it quite difficult to obtain proper focus of the image.

If you are working with video cameras, the back-focus adjustment of the lens may be off, which will cause the lens to not focus properly. Check and adjust the back focus; this should correct the problem. See Chapter 5, First Assistant Cameraman (1st AC) for the procedure for adjusting the back focus.

Image Is Fogged When Looking through Viewfinder

You need to be aware of the storage conditions of the lenses. The lenses may have been stored in a cold truck overnight. When you bring those lenses into a warm building first thing in the morning, condensation will build up on the lenses, causing them to fog and making it impossible to see through the lens and obtain proper focus. When the lenses have been in a cold environment and you will be shooting in a warm environment, I recommend bringing them into the warm environment as soon as possible, opening the lens cases and removing all lens caps so that the lenses can become accustomed to the warm air as quickly as possible. When they have been in the warmer environment for a short period, the condensation should be gone, and you will be able to obtain an accurate focus. Make sure that all condensation is gone before attempting to use the lenses. Carefully inspect them to be sure that there is no condensation inside the lenses. If necessary, you may use a hair dryer to warm up the lenses and remove condensation.

Zoom Lens Motor Runs Erratically

If the zoom lens motor runs erratically, there may be a short in the zoom control or in the power cable from the motor to the control. Replace the zoom motor power cable; if this does not correct the problem, replace the zoom control. Check the motor gear where it attaches to the lens. There may be some chips in the motor gear teeth or lens gear teeth that could cause the motor to slip. Replace the motor gear or lens gear as necessary. The zoom motor may also run without your having to touch the zoom control. Some zoom controls have an adjustment inside the control that must be set to prevent the motor from running without being engaged. Be sure to check with the rental house before attempting to take apart any piece of equipment.

Zoom Lens Does Not Zoom throughout Its Entire Range of Focal Lengths

Some zoom lenses, especially those for 16mm cameras, have a macro setting so that you can do extreme close-up shots. To set the lens in macro, you usually press a button on the side of the lens and move the zoom control ring into the macro range marked on the lens. This limits the range of the zoom, and when you

look through the lens and zoom, it appears that you are focusing. Because the lens is now in the macro setting, you are actually focusing when you turn the zoom ring of the lens. This allows you to get an extreme close-up of an object. So, if you are shooting 16mm and attempting to zoom and the lens does not move throughout its entire range, it may be in the macro setting. Simply press the macro button on the side of the lens and move the zoom barrel until it is back in normal mode.

Lens Flares Are Seen When Looking through the Viewfinder

Lens flares are usually an indication that there is a light or lights shining directly into the camera lens. Placing a hard matte on the matte box or adjusting the matte box eyebrow will most often eliminate these flares. A French flag attached to the camera will also help to eliminate any lens flare. Sometimes you may have to request that a Grip set a flag between the camera and the light so that the flare is eliminated. Keep in mind that often you will not see a lens flare through the lens. You must stand in front of the camera and look at the lens from various angles to see most lens flares. Some assistants will use a convex shaped mirror placed in front of the lens to look for lens flares. If you see any lights in the mirror there is a good chance that they are causing a flare in the lens.

Unable to Adjust F-stop/T-stop

With most lenses, when you adjust the f-stop/t-stop ring on the lens, you will see the exposure change through the eyepiece. While working on one of the many television series that I have done in my career, I placed a 200mm lens on the camera for a shot. The cinematographer gave me the stop for the exposure and while attempting to adjust the stop, the t-stop ring on the side of the lens would not move. I looked through the eyepiece and could not see anything happening. I then removed the lens and while holding it up to the light and looking through the lens, I could see that many of the leaves of the iris adjustment had come loose and were floating freely inside the lens. To my knowledge the lens had not been dropped or mishandled in any way so I am not sure as to why this happened. There was obviously nothing I could do on set, so we sent the lens back to the rental house and proceeded to change the shot so we could get it with one of the other lenses in our camera package.

BATTERY PROBLEMS

Battery Loses Power

Loss of battery power is one of the most common problems you will encounter. The battery may not be fully charged. Try to completely discharge the battery and then place it on charge overnight. If this does not solve the problem, then have the battery checked and replaced if necessary. You should never go out on a shoot with only one battery, just in case this does happen. By having an additional battery, you will not have to stop filming until another one can be obtained. At the very minimum, you should have at least two batteries, but I recommend always having three.

Battery Will Not Hold Charge

Another common battery problem that you may encounter is that the battery will simply not hold a charge. This is most common with older batteries that have been repeatedly charged and discharged during their lifetime. If the battery will not hold a charge, the power will drop very quickly once you connect it to a piece of equipment. As with the previous problem, you should try to completely discharge the battery and then place it on charge overnight. If this does not solve the problem, then have the battery checked and repaired or replaced if necessary. It may be a simple case of needing to replace the cells of the battery. As I also stated previously, at the very minimum you should have at least two batteries for every camera you will be shooting with, but I recommend always having three.

VIDEO ASSIST PROBLEMS

Image on Video Monitor Is Out of Focus or Is Tilted to the Side

On most camera video taps there are adjustments for both the focus and the position of the image on the outside of the video tap. If the image on the monitor is out of focus or tilted, turn these adjustment knobs until the image comes into focus or the image is in the correct position. If this still does not correct the problem, remove the cover of the video tap, if you can, and turn the adjustment knobs that are located inside. Sometimes, if the video tap is not firmly mounted to the film camera, the image appears tilted or out of focus. Check to be sure that it is mounted securely and correctly to the camera.

There Is No Image on Video Monitor

In addition to the adjustments for focus and image position, most video taps have an iris adjustment for filming under different lighting situations. If you have an image through the lens and you know that the video tap is connected and working properly, check to be sure that the iris of the video tap is properly adjusted for viewing the image. Either open or close the iris until you obtain an acceptable image on the video monitor.

TRIPOD AND HEAD PROBLEMS

Tripod Head Does Not Pan or Tilt

The most obvious reason that the tripod head will not pan or tilt is that the pan and tilt locks are engaged. Check the locks for each, and release them if necessary. Check the head to be sure that there are no obstructions that could prevent the head from panning or tilting. Remove any obstruction, and the problem should be corrected. Never force the head in either direction. You may worsen the problem, making it impossible for you to correct in the field. The head must then be sent to the rental house for repair, and a replacement head needs to be sent to you. On gear heads, check that the gear adjustment lever is not in the neutral position. When it is in neutral, turning either the pan or tilt wheel has no effect on the head. Place the pan and tilt gear adjustment lever in one of the gear positions, which should allow you to pan and tilt with ease. On most gear heads there are usually two sets of locks for the pan and tilt. One is for the pan and tilt wheel controls to lock them in position, and the other is for the actual pan and tilt movements to physically lock them in position, even when the gears are in the neutral position. Be sure that all locks are released before trying to pan or tilt the gear head.

Tripod Legs Do Not Slide Up or Down

Quite often, when you are in a hurry you may forget to release the locks for the legs before attempting to adjust the height of them. By releasing the tripod leg locks, they should slide up and down smoothly. Tripod legs get dirty after much use and usually begin to stick when you try to adjust them. Clean the legs regularly, and if you are using aluminum or metal tripods, spray them with a light coat of silicone spray. This should keep them in working order and help them last longer.

WEATHER AND ENVIRONMENTAL-RELATED PROBLEMS

Shooting in Extreme Cold Weather

If you will be working in extreme cold weather situations for an extended period, leave the camera equipment in the camera truck at night so that it remains at a consistent cold temperature throughout the production. If it is necessary to bring the camera equipment inside after being in a cold camera truck overnight, warm it up as quickly as possible so that condensation does not form. Open all lens, filter, magazine, and accessory cases so they can reach room temperature. Remove all lens caps to help the lenses warm up and to eliminate condensation.

Whenever possible, obtain the appropriate size barney for the camera and magazines so that you can protect them as much as possible from the cold. Also, be sure to let the rental house know if you will be doing any extended filming in cold weather. They may need to add a special heater element or change the lubricant in the camera to one that is better suited to the cold.

You should also keep in mind that the film stock can become very brittle in cold temperatures and should be used as soon as possible after you have removed it from the manufacturer's sealed can. You may want to keep loaded magazines in a warm, dry location until ready for filming, but sometimes it is actually better to keep loaded magazines in the same environment and temperature that you will be shooting in. I worked on a music video that was shot in Boulder, Colorado, in late November. We were filming outside using an Arriflex 16 SR2 camera. At the DP's request I loaded all of the magazines, placed them in their case, and kept them outside with us during shooting. There were no problems with film breaking during shooting because it wasn't going from one temperature to another, which could actually cause more problems than keeping the film in the temperature at which you are filming. In any case, use your best judgment and always consult with the DP if you are unsure.

Shooting in Extreme Heat

Film stock may deteriorate very quickly if it is subjected to very high heat for even short periods of time. When working in extreme heat, you should have coolers or some other type of insulated container to keep the film in. Film should be kept in the cooler or insulated container in a cool, dry location whenever possible. You should never place ice in the cooler because any melting ice could seep into the

film and damage it. In addition, you should process any film as soon as possible after it has been exposed. See the section in Chapter 4 on proper storage of motion picture film before and after exposure.

Filming in or Around Salt Water and Camera and Magazine Fall into the Water

Before taking any equipment from the rental house, and you know that you will be filming around salt water, ask them what you should do if any of the equipment falls into the water. The following procedure is the accepted method, but you should check with the rental house beforehand just to be safe. First, rinse the camera and equipment completely in fresh water as soon as possible. Don't worry about getting the camera wet. It's already wet from the salt water. Salt water is highly corrosive and can damage the working parts of the camera very quickly. The faster it is removed, the fewer problems you may have. Don't allow a fully loaded magazine of film to dry. Rinse off the magazine completely, with the film still inside, and if possible ship the entire magazine, packed in fresh water, to the lab for processing. I was once told a story about a 1000-ft magazine containing a full roll of exposed film that had fallen into salt water. The assistant immediately removed the magazine from the salt water, immersed it in a cooler of fresh water, and sent it to the lab packed in the fresh water. The lab was able to process the film, and there was very little, if any, damage to the image.

COLOR BALANCE/FILTER PROBLEMS

Filters Don't Fit in Matte Box

When performing the camera prep you should have obtained proper size filters for the matte box and filter retainer rings that you will be using. On very rare occasions you need to use a different size filter in the matte box. If the filter is smaller than the matte box, you should be able to make an adapter from a piece of foam core which will hold the filter securely and also fit into the matte box filter slot. Cut the foam core to the size of the matte box filter tray. Then make a cutout in the center of this piece to hold the filter. Try to make the filter opening just a bit smaller than the dimensions of the filter. You can then wedge the filter into the cutout and the foam core will hold it in place. A couple of pieces of tape along the edges will ensure that the filter doesn't fall out. If it is a filter that is smaller than the standard

filters you have been using, always check to be sure that the filter is not seen when looking through the viewfinder.

Shooting Outside Using Tungsten-Balanced Film Without an 85 Filter

If you are using negative film, the lab can usually correct the color during processing. If necessary, you may use an orange color gel, which is the same color as the number 85 glass filter, in front of the lens. Eastman Kodak manufactures a gel that is called an 85 Wratten Gel. It gives the same effect as an 85 glass filter placed in front of the lens and is optically correct so there are no imperfections which could affect the image.

While the Kodak Wratten Gel looks very similar to a CTO lighting gel, the Wratten Gel is optically superior to the lighting gel. I recommend ordering some of these Wratten Gels when ordering the expendables so that you have them available in case of emergencies. Many assistants carry these gels in their ditty bags just in case they encounter this situation. Be sure to properly adjust the exposure setting when using an 85 Wratten Gel or glass filter. The 85 gel filter may also be used in cameras that accept behind-the-lens filters, such as most of the cameras from Panavision. If you don't have the filter, you may instruct the lab to make corrections during the transfer. The corrections may also be made during the postproduction process, depending on the editing system and software you are using.

Shooting Inside with Tungsten Light Using Daylight-Balanced Film Without an 80A Filter

This problem is similar to the previous one. You may use a number 80A Kodak Wratten Gel in front of the lens to correct the exposure. A few years ago a production company that I was working for mistakenly purchased daylight-balanced film for a shoot that was being done entirely on stage using tungsten lights. I sent a Production Assistant to a local camera shop to purchase a Kodak 80A Wratten Gel filter. I taped the filter to the optical flat in the matte box, and the DP made the necessary lighting and exposure changes. We shot the commercial, and it turned out just fine. As with the 85 filter, be sure to adjust your exposure accordingly when using the 80A Wratten Gel or glass filter. As stated in the previous example, if you don't have the filter, you may instruct the lab to make corrections during the transfer. The

corrections may also be made during the postproduction process, depending on the editing system and software you are using.

DEVELOPED IMAGE PROBLEMS

Projected Image Is Shaky or Unsteady

A shaky or unsteady projected image will only be noticed after the film has been exposed, developed, and projected. The most common cause of this problem is improper registration of the camera movement. What this means is that the film is not positioned properly in the gate area, and as a result it is not moving through the mechanism smoothly. If you suspect a problem with the camera movement, you should shoot some tests before sending the camera back for repair or replacement. If you don't have time to shoot tests, I recommend sending the camera back to the rental house and obtaining a new camera. Let the rental house determine what the problem is.

On some cameras, there may not be a problem with the camera, but rather the magazine was not placed on the camera properly or the film was simply not placed securely in the gate area during threading. You should eliminate any of these causes before sending the camera back to the rental house. During the camera prep, the 1st AC should shoot a registration test to check the registration of the camera. Unless the camera has been mishandled, dropped, or otherwise shaken or jarred in some way, the registration should not suddenly be off if you correctly checked it during prep. In addition to problems with the camera registration, shaky images may also be caused by film stock with irregularly punched perforations, an error in printing the film, or possibly unsteady projection. If you can shoot some tests using a different batch of film stock, this will help to determine if the error is in the film's perforations. Checking with the lab and seeing if there is any problem with their machines that print the film will confirm or eliminate that cause, and double checking the projector threading should confirm or eliminate any projector problems.

Projected Image Is Out of Focus

Many of the causes discussed with regard to the lens not focusing also apply to a projected image that is out of focus. A few additional causes of out-of-focus images that would most often only be noticed after the film has been shot and processed are discussed next.

If the film was not set in the gate area securely, the film may have moved slightly as it moved through the camera. This can be a registration problem that requires the camera to be serviced, and a new camera must be obtained to continue shooting. The flange focal depth of the camera may be off, which would cause the image to be out of focus. You may still be able to focus the image through the viewfinder, but the image on film will not be in focus. If you have one available, you should check the depth with a flange focal depth gauge to be sure it is set properly according to the camera manufacturer. If you do not own a flange focal depth gauge, it may be best to contact the rental company to obtain a new camera and have them check the old camera.

The lens markings may be off, and unless you checked the lenses completely during the camera prep, you may not notice this. If you suspect this problem, you should thoroughly check each lens using a focus test chart.

The 1st AC may have based the focus setting on incorrect depth-of-field calculations. This should be noticed when looking through the viewfinder, but depending on the shooting conditions, it may be difficult to judge until you see the projected image.

Another reason the image may be out of focus is that the 1st AC or Camera Operator may have focused the image by eye with the viewfinder diopter set to an incorrect setting. It is still possible to focus an image by eye and with the diopter incorrectly set, but the image will not be in focus when it is photographed on film.

Projected Image Contains Spots or Lines

When viewing the developed film, you may notice spots or lines in the image. The lines may appear randomly, or they may appear in a regular pattern. A scratch on the negative may be white or light green in appearance. In many cases it can be repaired by the lab. You should run some test film through the camera and magazines to see if you can determine where a scratch occurred. If it is a camera or magazine problem, you should obtain replacement equipment from the camera rental house before continuing to film.

Spots on the image may be caused by condensation on the film stock. If the film has been refrigerated prior to shooting, it is very important to warm it up for the proper amount of time before attempting to open the can and load the film. If the film can is opened too soon before the film is warmed up, condensation will form on the film, causing spots in the image. See Table 4.5 in Chapter 4 for the

proper warm-up times for 16mm and 35mm motion picture film. Black dots in the image may also indicate dust on the print.

Image Is Not Aligned During the Video Transfer

If you will be removing a partially shot magazine and plan to finish shooting it later in the day, always mark an "X" on the frame of film in the gate. This allows you to line up the film properly when you place the magazine back on the camera later in the day.

I know of a situation in which a DP had a magazine removed from the camera, and the assistant neglected to mark the frame of film. The magazine was later placed back on the camera, and they finished shooting with that roll. The DP took the developed film to a transfer house to have it transferred to video. During the transfer process, when it came to the point in the film where the magazine had been removed, the shots were off by two perforations. The color timer had to rethread the film to continue the transfer. I had never heard of this happening before, but based on this DP's description, I will now always mark the film when removing a partially shot magazine. It's a small thing, but it can save some confusion and headaches later on.

SHOOTING IN FOREIGN COUNTRIES

Shooting in Countries Using a Different Electrical System

When planning to film in another country, especially one that uses a different electrical system than that used in the United States, be sure that you have the proper electrical adapters or converters with you. This is especially important if you are taking equipment from the United States to another country. You will need to charge batteries, power a laptop computer, and use other electrical devices. Having the proper adapters or converters can mean the difference between a smoothly running shoot and a disaster. If you don't have the proper converters or adapters, it may be necessary to rent certain equipment from a rental company in the country in which you are filming.

TROUBLESHOOTING TIPS

I have often found that the simplest solution is often the best when it comes to troubleshooting. Sometimes when you encounter a problem,

it is best just to disconnect or disassemble everything and then connect or assemble it again. Surprisingly, this sometimes works to correct whatever the problem was. There may have been a loose connection somewhere that is corrected simply by removing and then reattaching the item. I actually had a Camera Assistant telephone me from across the country to ask how to get the Microforce zoom motor to work on an Arriflex 35BL camera. He explained everything he had done, and the motor just would not operate properly. I suggested that he disconnect all accessories and the battery from the camera and then reconnect them. After doing this, he reported that everything worked fine. While he was not able to determine why there was a problem, at least he didn't have the problem any longer, and shooting could continue. In any case, be sure to have the item in question checked as soon as possible.

Try the obvious solution first, and then continue in a step-by-step manner until you find out what the cause of the problem is. Remember to only check one thing at a time. You will most likely encounter some different problems from those listed here, but if you are familiar with the equipment, you should have no trouble finding and correcting almost any problem that you come across. If you are not sure of how to fix a particular problem, call the rental house for help. Most rental houses will send a technician to your location if you cannot fix the problem in the field. Don't try to fix something yourself if you are not sure what to do. And as I stated earlier, remain calm; don't panic. Quite often you can solve many problems without anybody else on the crew even knowing that the problem occurred.

If you come across any problems and solutions that are not mentioned here, please email me at the address on this book's companion web site. I may use it in future editions. Good luck and happy shooting.

7

Film Cameras

As an Assistant Cameraman you will be working with many different film camera systems throughout your career. You should be familiar with as many different cameras as possible. This chapter contains basic information, such as format, magazine sizes, and simple line drawings of the threading diagrams of cameras and magazines, for most of the film cameras that are currently used in the film industry. I have also included the type of lens mount and the speed range for most of these cameras. For the lens mount listings, PL refers to the standard "Positive Lock" Arriflex lens mount, and PV refers to the standard Panavision lens mount. Please note that the speed range listed is only when running cameras in the forward running mode. It is not the speed range when running the cameras in reverse. While some cameras may have the ability to run in reverse, I have chosen not to list those speeds here to avoid any confusion. For illustrations of cameras and magazines that are not included here, please check the companion web site for this book at www.cameraassistantmanual.com. The threading diagrams included here are not meant to teach you how to load magazines or thread cameras. They are intended only as a reference in case you have forgotten about a specific camera system. If you want to learn how to load magazines or thread cameras, you should contact a camera rental house that has the particular camera you are interested in. I strongly recommend that you obtain instruction manuals and reference books for all professional cameras that you will be working with. Many companies have electronic versions of the manuals posted on their web sites. You can access many of these sites from the companion web site for this book. I have also included links to specific camera manuals on the companion web site. You never know when you will be working with a certain camera, and it may be many months between jobs with a particular camera. Having the instruction manuals or books for all cameras will allow you to refresh your memory for any cameras and equipment that you may have

forgotten. To learn more about any of these cameras, speak with a representative at any professional motion picture camera rental house.

Remember   These illustrations are to be used only as a reference.

AATON A-MINIMA

Format: 16 mm
Magazine size: 200′ Coaxial
Lens mount: PL
Forward speeds: 1–32 fps, 1–50 fps with external 12-volt battery

For camera and magazine illustrations and threading diagrams, see Figures 7.1 and 7.2.

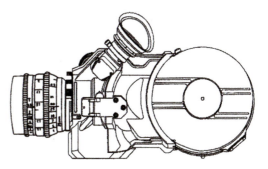

Figure 7.1   Aaton A-Minima
16 mm camera. (Courtesy of
Aaton.)

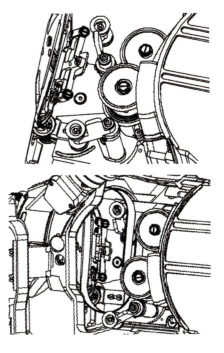

Figure 7.2   Aaton A-Minima camera
threading. (Courtesy of Aaton.)

AATON XTERÀ AND XTR-PROD

Format: 16 mm
Magazine sizes: 400' and 800' Coaxial
Lens mount: PL
Forward speeds: 3–75 fps

For camera and magazine illustrations and threading diagrams, see
Figures 7.3 through 7.5.

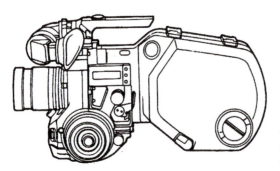

Figure 7.3   Aaton Xterà
and XTR-Prod 16 mm
camera. (Courtesy of Aaton.)

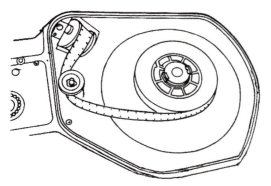

Figure 7.4   Aaton Xterà and
XTR-Prod magazine, feed
side. (Courtesy of Aaton.)

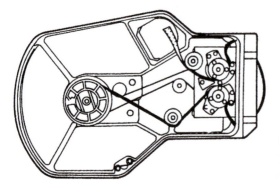

Figure 7.5   Aaton Xterà and
XTR-Prod magazine, take-up
side. (Courtesy of Aaton.)

AATON 35-III

Format: 35 mm
Magazine size: 400′ Active Displacement
Lens mount: PL
Forward speeds: 2–40 fps

For camera and magazine illustrations and threading diagrams, see Figures 7.6 and 7.7.

Figure 7.6   Aaton 35-III camera. (Courtesy of Aaton.)

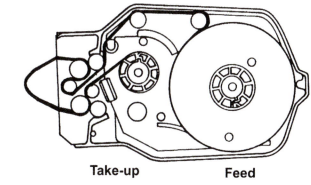

Figure 7.7   Aaton
35-III magazine.
(Courtesy of Aaton.)

Take-up   **Feed**

AATON PENELOPE

Format: 35 mm
Magazine size: 400′ Displacement
Lens mount: PL
Forward speeds: 3–40 fps

For camera and magazine illustrations and threading diagrams, see Figures 7.8 and 7.9.

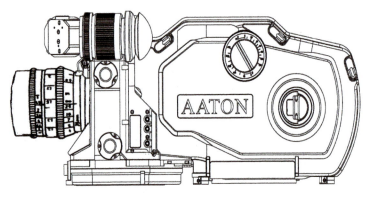

Figure 7.8 Penelope camera. (Courtesy of Aaton.)

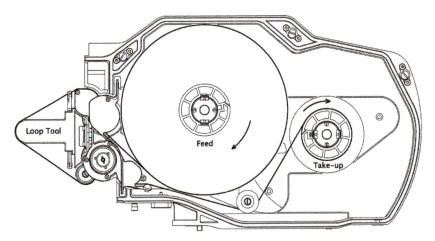

Figure 7.9 Penelope magazine. (Courtesy of Aaton.)

ARRIFLEX 16 SR1, 16 SR2, AND 16 SR3

Format: 16 mm (high-speed model also available)
Magazine sizes: 400′ and 800′ Coaxial
SR1 and SR2 lens mount: Arri Bayonet; SR3 lens mount: PL
SR1 and SR2 forward speeds: Regular, 5–75 fps; High speed, 10–150 fps
SR3 forward speeds: Regular, 5–75 fps; High speed, 5–150 fps

For camera and magazine illustrations and threading diagrams, see
Figures 7.10 through 7.13.

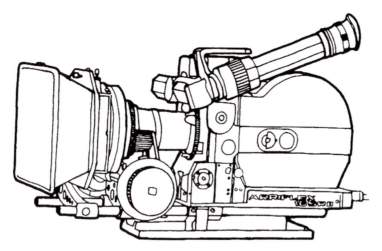

Figure 7.10   Arriflex 16 SR1 and 16 SR2 camera. (Reprinted
from the *Arriflex 16SR Book* by Jon Fauer with permission of the
author and ARRI Inc.)

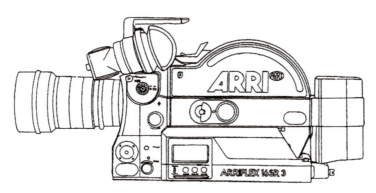

Figure 7.11   Arriflex 16 SR3 camera. (Courtesy of ARRI Inc.)

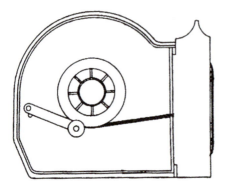

Figure 7.12   Arriflex 16 SR 400′ magazine, feed side. (Courtesy of ARRI Inc.)

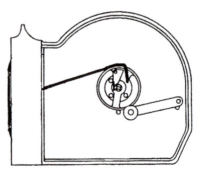

Figure 7.13   Arriflex 16 SR 400′ magazine, take-up side. (Courtesy of ARRI Inc.)

ARRIFLEX 416

Format: Super 16 mm
Magazine size: 400′ Coaxial
Lens mount: PL
Forward speeds: 416 and 416 Plus, 1–75 fps; 416 Plus HS (High Speed), 1–150 fps

For camera and magazine illustrations and threading diagrams, see Figures 7.14 through 7.16.

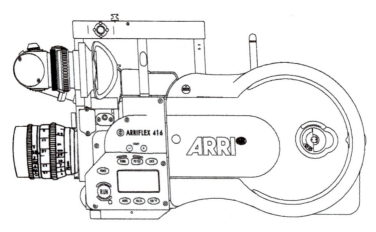

Figure 7.14   Arriflex 416 camera. (Courtesy of ARRI Inc.)

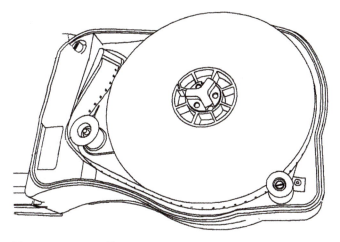

Figure 7.15 Arriflex 416 magazine, feed side. (Courtesy of ARRI Inc.)

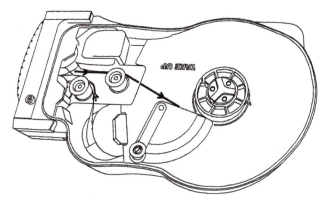

Figure 7.16 Arriflex 416 magazine, take-up side. (Courtesy of ARRI Inc.)

ARRIFLEX ARRICAM LITE (LT)

Format: 35 mm
Magazine sizes: 400′ and 1000′ Displacement Studio, 400′ Active Displacement Lite Shoulder, 400′ Active Displacement Lite Steadicam
Lens mount: PL
Forward speeds: 1–40 fps

For camera and magazine illustrations and threading diagrams, see Figures 7.17 through 7.20.

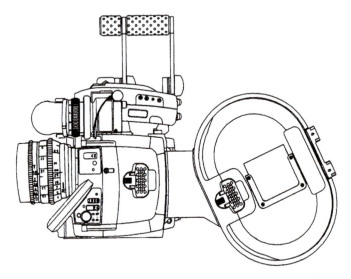

Figure 7.17 Arriflex Arricam Lite camera. (Courtesy of ARRI Inc.)

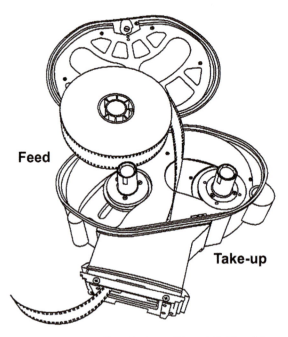

Figure 7.18 Arriflex Arricam Lite 400′ Shoulder magazine. (Courtesy of ARRI Inc.)

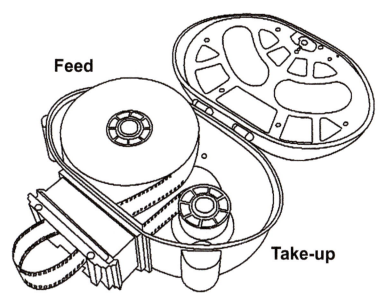

Feed

Take-up

Figure 7.19   Arriflex Arricam Lite 400′ Steadicam magazine. (Courtesy of ARRI Inc.)

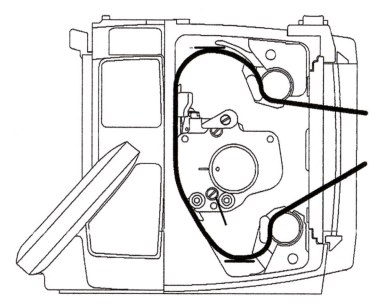

Figure 7.20   Arriflex Arricam Lite camera threading. (Courtesy of ARRI Inc.)

ARRIFLEX ARRICAM STUDIO (ST)

Format: 35 mm
Magazine sizes: 400′ and 1000′ Displacement Studio
Lens mount: PL
Forward speeds: 1–60 fps

For camera and magazine illustrations and threading diagrams, see Figures 7.21 through 7.23.

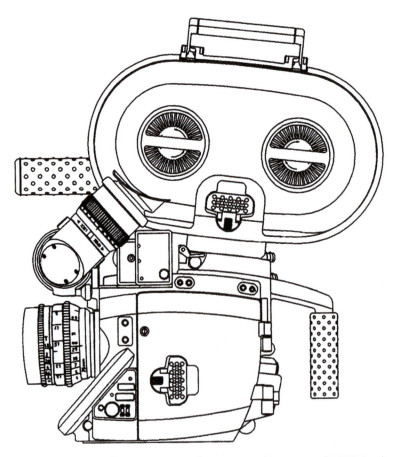

Figure 7.21   Arriflex Arricam Studio camera. (Courtesy of ARRI Inc.)

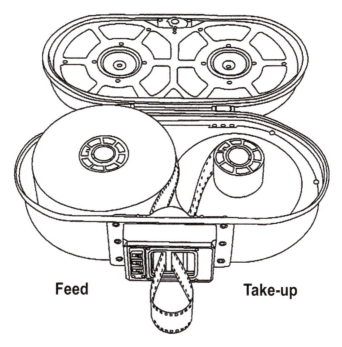

Feed

Take-up

Figure 7.22 Arriflex Arricam Studio 400′ magazine. (Courtesy of ARRI Inc.)

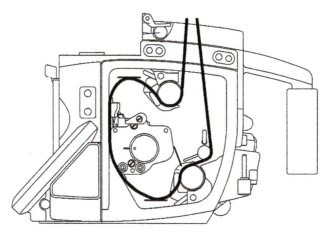

Figure 7.23 Arriflex Arricam Studio camera threading. (Courtesy of ARRI Inc.)

ARRIFLEX 235

Format: 35 mm
Magazine sizes: 200′ and 400′ Displacement Shoulder, 400′ Steadicam
Note: Camera will also accept Arriflex 435 400′ magazines and
Arriflex 35-3 200′ and 400′ magazines.
Lens mount: PL
Forward speeds: 1–60 fps

For camera and magazine illustrations and threading diagrams, see
Figures 7.24 and 7.25.

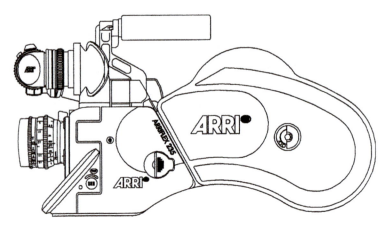

Figure 7.24   Arriflex 235 camera. (Courtesy of ARRI Inc.)

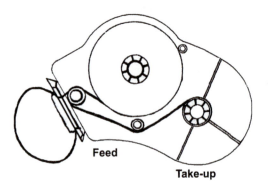

Figure 7.25   Arriflex 235 400′ magazine.
(Courtesy of ARRI Inc.)

ARRIFLEX 535A AND 535B

Format: 35 mm
Magazine sizes: 400′ and 1000′ Coaxial
Lens mount: PL
Forward speeds: 4–50 fps

For camera and magazine illustrations and threading diagrams, see Figures 7.26 through 7.29.

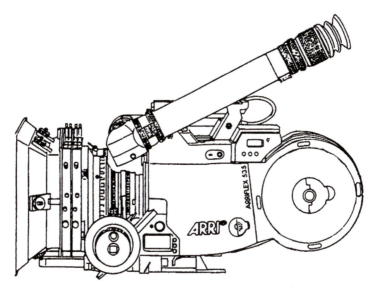

Figure 7.26   Arriflex 535 camera. (Courtesy of ARRI Inc.)

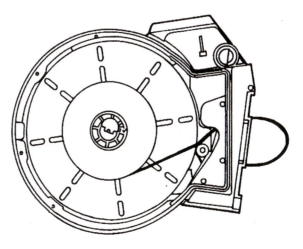

Figure 7.27   Arriflex 535 magazine, feed side. (Courtesy of ARRI Inc.)

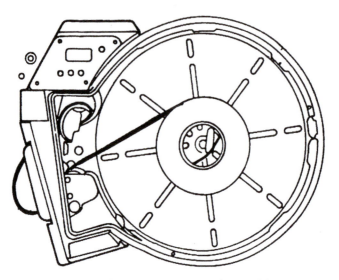

Figure 7.28   Arriflex 535 magazine, take-up side. (Courtesy of ARRI Inc.)

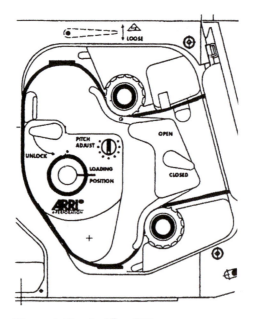

Figure 7.29   Arriflex 535 camera threading. (Courtesy of ARRI Inc.)

ARRIFLEX 435

Format: 35 mm
Magazine sizes: 400′ and 1000′ Displacement, 400′ Displacement
Steadicam
Lens mount: PL
Forward speeds: 1–150 fps

For camera and magazine illustrations and threading diagrams, see
Figures 7.30 through 7.32.

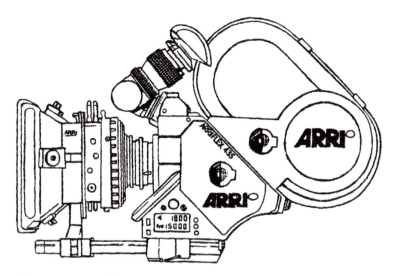

Figure 7.30   Arriflex 435 camera. (Courtesy of ARRI Inc.)

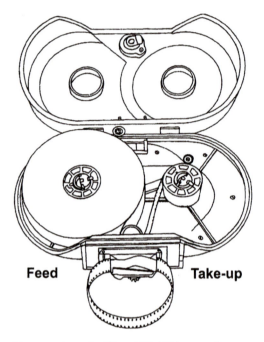

Feed   **Take-up**

Figure 7.31   Arriflex 435 400′ magazine. (Courtesy of ARRI Inc.)

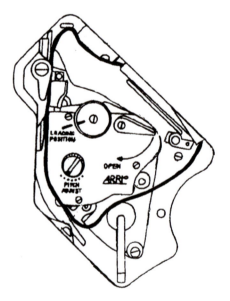

Figure 7.32   Arriflex 435 camera threading. (Courtesy of ARRI Inc.)

ARRIFLEX 35BL3 AND 35BL4

Format: 35 mm
Magazine sizes: 400′ and 1000′ Coaxial
Lens mount: PL
Forward speeds: 6–40 fps

For camera and magazine illustrations and threading diagrams, see Figures 7.33 through 7.36.

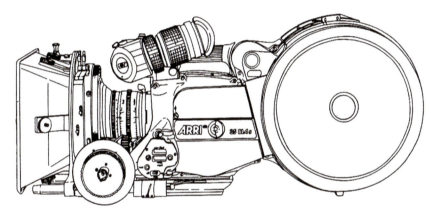

Figure 7.33 Arriflex 35BL camera. (Reprinted from the *Arriflex 35 Book* by Jon Fauer with permission of the author and ARRI Inc.)

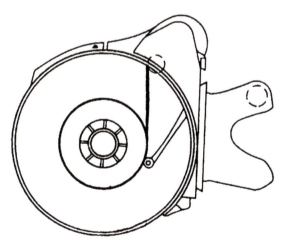

Figure 7.34 Arriflex 35BL magazine, feed side. (Courtesy of ARRI Inc.)

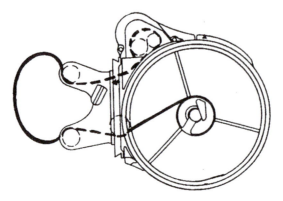

Figure 7.35   Arriflex 35BL magazine, take-up
side. (Courtesy of ARRI Inc.)

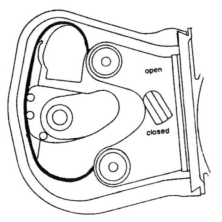

Figure 7.36   Arriflex 35BL camera
threading. (Courtesy of ARRI Inc.)

ARRIFLEX 35-3

Format: 35 mm
Magazine sizes: 200′, 400′, 1000′ Displacement, 400′ Coaxial hand-
held shoulder, 400′ Displacement Steadicam
Lens mount: PL
Forward speeds: 5–50 fps, 5–130 fps with external control

For camera and magazine illustrations and threading diagrams, see
Figures 7.37 through 7.43.

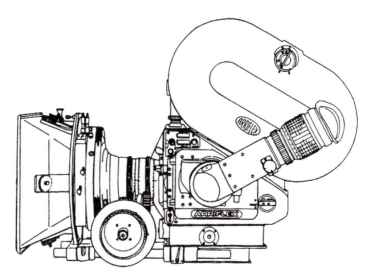

Figure 7.37 Arriflex 35-3 camera. (Reprinted from the *Arriflex 35 Book* by Jon Fauer with permission of the author and ARRI Inc.)

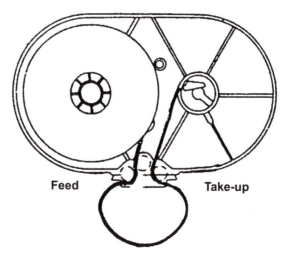

Feed   Take-up

Figure 7.38 Arriflex 35-3 400′ magazine. (Courtesy of ARRI Inc.)

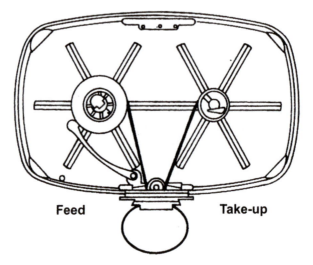

Feed   **Take-up**

Figure 7.39   Arriflex 35-3 1000′ magazine. (Courtesy of ARRI Inc.)

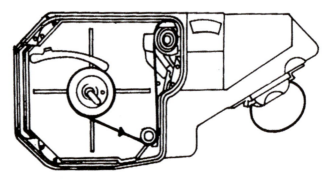

Figure 7.40   Arriflex 35-3 shoulder magazine, feed side. (Courtesy of ARRI Inc.)

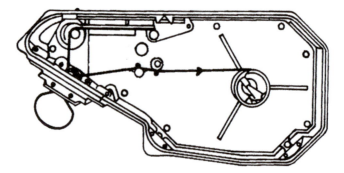

Figure 7.41   Arriflex 35-3 shoulder magazine, take-up side. (Courtesy of ARRI Inc.)

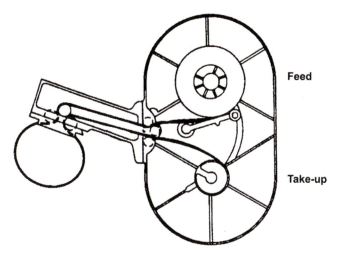

Figure 7.42   Arriflex 35-3 Steadicam magazine. (Courtesy of ARRI Inc.)

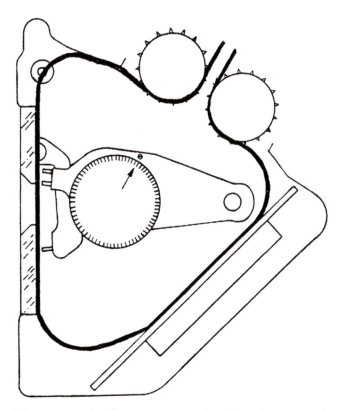

Figure 7.43   Arriflex 35-3 camera threading. (Courtesy of ARRI Inc.)

ARRIFLEX 765

Format: 65 mm
Magazine sizes: 500′ and 1000′ Displacement
Lens mount: PL
Forward speeds: 2–100 fps

For camera and magazine illustrations and threading diagrams, see Figures 7.44 through 7.46.

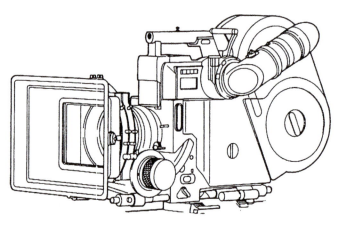

Figure 7.44   Arriflex 765 camera. (Courtesy of ARRI Inc.)

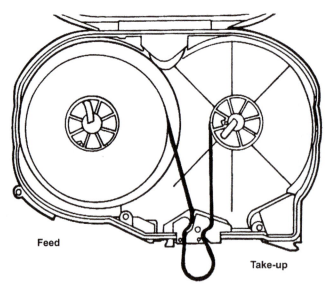

Feed

Take-up

Figure 7.45   Arriflex 765 magazine. (Courtesy of ARRI Inc.)

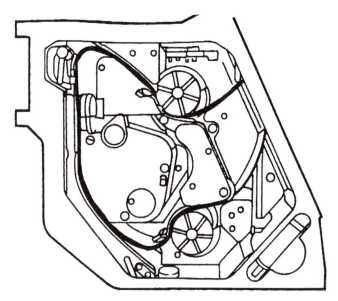

Figure 7.46   Arriflex 765 camera threading. (Courtesy of ARRI Inc.)

MOVIECAM COMPACT AND MOVIECAM SUPER AMERICA

Format: 35 mm
Magazine sizes: 500′ and 1000′ Displacement
Lens mount: PL
Forward speeds: 2–50 fps

For camera and magazine illustrations and threading diagrams, see Figures 7.47 through 7.52.

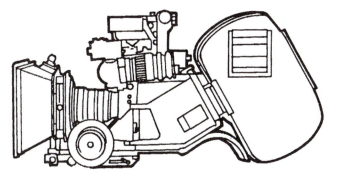

Figure 7.47   Moviecam Compact camera. (Reprinted from the *Hands-On Manual for Cinematographers* with permission of David Samuelson.)

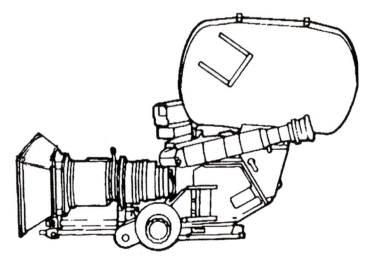

Figure 7.48   Moviecam Super America camera. (Reprinted from the *Hands-On Manual for Cinematographers* with permission of David Samuelson.)

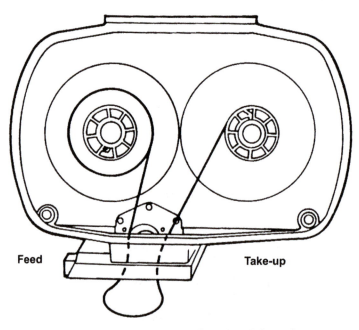

Feed

Take-up

Figure 7.49   Moviecam magazine. (Reprinted from the *Hands-On Manual for Cinematographers* with permission of David Samuelson.)

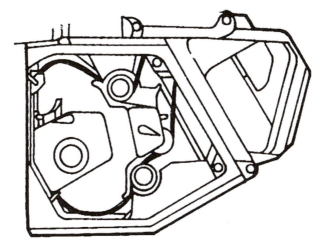

Figure 7.50 Moviecam Compact camera threading, top load. (Reprinted from the *Hands-On Manual for Cinematographers* with permission of David Samuelson.)

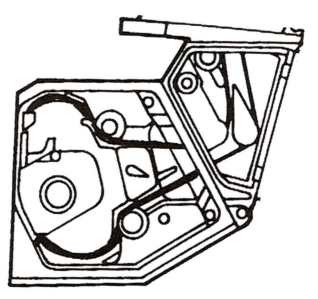

Figure 7.51 Moviecam Super America camera threading, top load. (Reprinted from the *Hands-On Manual for Cinematographers* with permission of David Samuelson.)

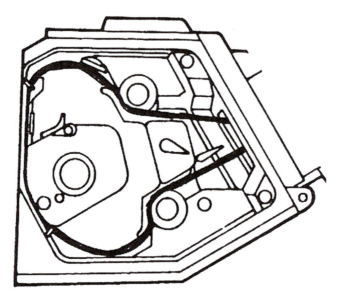

Figure 7.52   Moviecam camera threading, slant load. (Reprinted from the *Hands-On Manual for Cinematographers* with permission of David Samuelson.)

MOVIECAM SL

Format: 35 mm
Magazine sizes: 500′ and 1000′ Active Displacement
Lens mount: PL
Forward speeds: 2–40 fps

For camera and magazine illustrations and threading diagrams, see Figures 7.53 through 7.55.

Figure 7.53 Moviecam SL camera. (Reprinted from the *Hands-On Manual for Cinematographers* with permission of David Samuelson.)

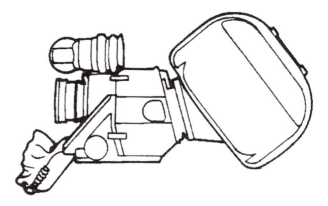

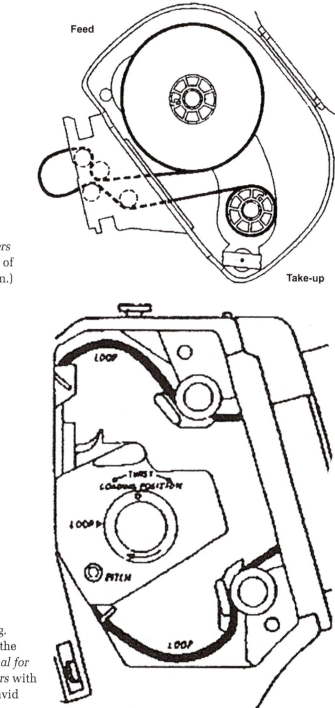

Figure 7.54
Moviecam
SL magazine.
(Reprinted from
the *Hands-On
Manual for
Cinematographers*
with permission of
David Samuelson.)

Feed

Take-up

Figure 7.55
Moviecam SL
camera threading.
(Reprinted from the
*Hands-On Manual for
Cinematographers* with
permission of David
Samuelson.)

PANAVISION PANAFLEX 16

Format: 16 mm
Magazine sizes: 500′ and 1200′ Displacement
Lens mount: PV
Forward speeds: 4–50 fps

For camera and magazine illustrations and threading diagrams, see Figures 7.56 through 7.58.

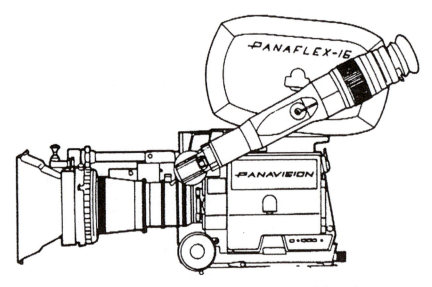

Figure 7.56   Panavision Panaflex 16 camera. (Reprinted from the *Hands-On Manual for Cinematographers* with permission of David Samuelson.)

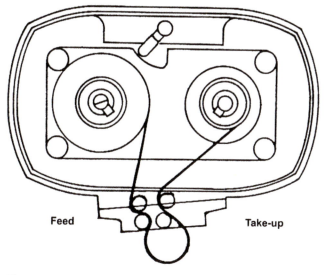

Figure 7.57 Panavision Panaflex 16 magazine. (Reprinted from the *Hands-On Manual for Cinematographers* with permission of David Samuelson.)

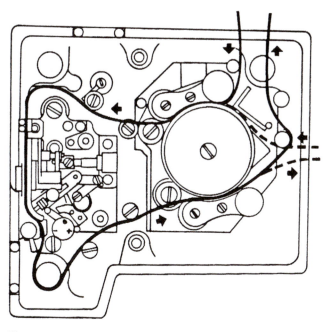

Figure 7.58 Panavision Panaflex 16 camera threading. (Reprinted from the *Hands-On Manual for Cinematographers* with permission of David Samuelson.)

PANAVISION PANAFLEX GOLD AND GII

Format: 35 mm
Magazine sizes: 250', 500', and 1000' Displacement
Lens mount: PV
Forward speeds: Gold, 4–34 fps; GII, 4–40 fps

For camera and magazine illustrations and threading diagrams, see Figures 7.59 through 7.61.

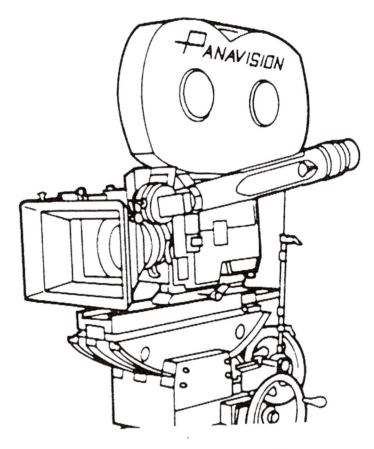

Figure 7.59 Panavision Panaflex Golden and GII camera. (Reprinted from the *Hands-On Manual for Cinematographers* with permission of David Samuelson.)

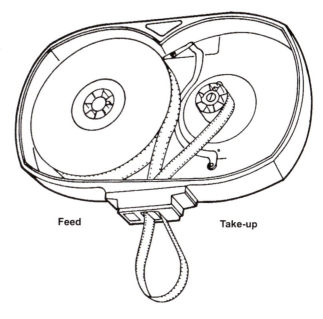

Figure 7.60
Panavision Panaflex
Standard 35 mm
magazine—Golden,
GII, Millennium,
Platinum, Panaflex
X, and Panastar.
(Reprinted from
the *Hands-On
Manual for
Cinematographers*
with permission of
David Samuelson.)

Feed   Take-up

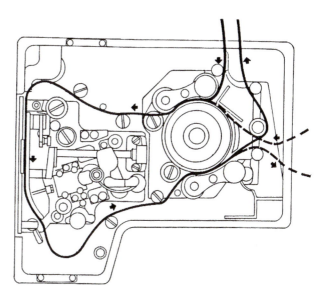

Figure 7.61
Panavision Panaflex
Golden and GII
camera threading.
(Reprinted from
the *Hands-On
Manual for
Cinematographers*
with permission of
David Samuelson.)

PANAVISION PANAFLEX MILLENNIUM AND MILLENNIUM XL

Format: 35 mm
Magazine sizes: 400' and 1000' Displacement
Lens mount: PV
Forward speeds: Millennium, 3–50 fps; Millennium XL, 3–50 fps

For camera and magazine illustrations and threading diagrams, see
Figures 7.62 through 7.64. See Figure 7.60 for standard magazine
threading diagram.

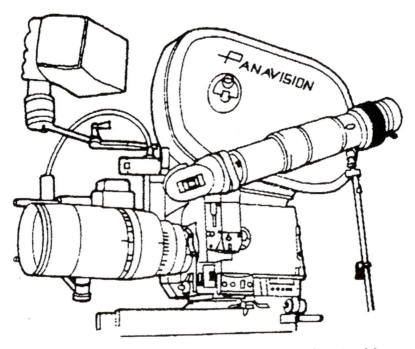

Figure 7.62   Panavision Panaflex Millennium camera. (Reprinted from
the *Hands-On Manual for Cinematographers* with permission of David
Samuelson.)

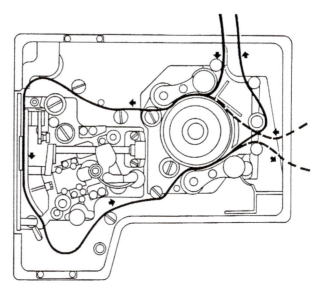

Figure 7.63
Panavision Panaflex
Millennium
camera threading.
(Reprinted from
the *Hands-On
Manual for
Cinematographers*
with permission of
David Samuelson.)

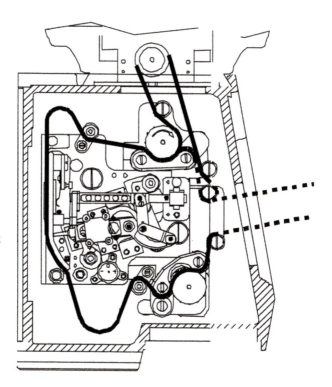

Figure 7.64
Panavision Panaflex
Millennium XL
camera threading.
(Reprinted from
the *Hands-On
Manual for
Cinematographers*
with permission of
David Samuelson.)

PANAVISION PANAFLEX PLATINUM

Format: 35 mm
Magazine sizes: 250′, 500′, and 1000′ Displacement; 1000′ reversing
Displacement
Lens mount: PV
Forward speeds: 4–36 fps

For camera and magazine illustrations and threading diagrams, see
Figures 7.65 through 7.68. See Figure 7.60 for standard magazine
threading diagram.

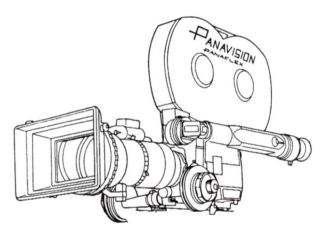

Figure 7.65
Panavision Panaflex
Platinum camera.
(Reprinted from
the *Hands-On
Manual for
Cinematographers*
with permission of
David Samuelson.)

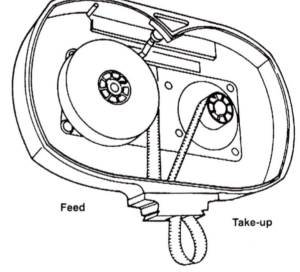

Figure 7.66
Panavision Panaflex
reversing magazine,
forward-running mode:
Platinum and Panastar.
(Reprinted from the
*Hands-On Manual
for Cinematographers*
with permission of
David Samuelson.)

Feed

Take-up

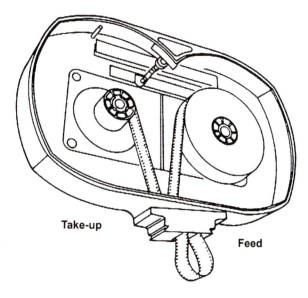

Figure 7.67
Panavision Panaflex
reversing magazine,
reverse-running mode:
Platinum and Panastar.
(Reprinted from the
*Hands-On Manual for
Cinematographers* with
permission of David
Samuelson.)

Take-up

Feed

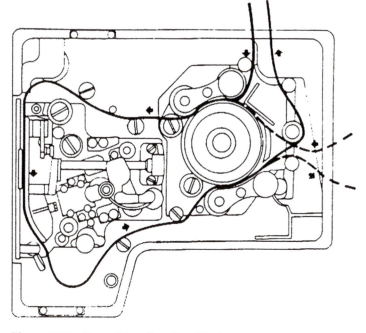

Figure 7.68   Panavision Panaflex Platinum camera threading.
(Reprinted from the *Hands-On Manual for Cinematographers*
with permission of David Samuelson.)

PANAVISION PANASTAR II

Format: 35 mm High Speed
Magazine sizes: 500′ and 1000′ Displacement; Panastar II only: 1000′ reversing Displacement
Lens mount: PV
Forward speeds: 6–120 fps

For camera and magazine illustrations and threading diagrams, see Figures 7.69 and 7.70. See Figure 7.60 for standard magazine threading diagram. See Figures 7.66 and 7.67 for reversing magazine threading diagrams.

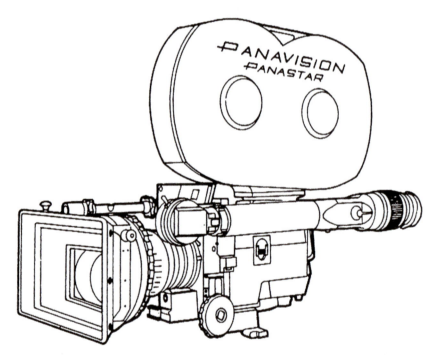

Figure 7.69 Panavision Panastar camera. (Reprinted from the *Hands-On Manual for Cinematographers* with permission of David Samuelson.)

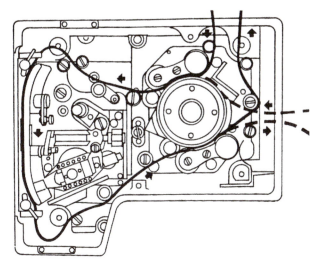

Figure 7.70
Panavision Panastar
camera threading.
(Reprinted from
the *Hands-On
Manual for
Cinematographers*
with permission of
David Samuelson.)

PANAVISION PANAFLEX 65

Format: 65 mm
Magazine sizes: 500′ and 1000′ Displacement
Lens mount: PV
Forward speeds: 4–32 fps

For camera and magazine illustrations and threading diagrams, see
Figures 7.71 through 7.73.

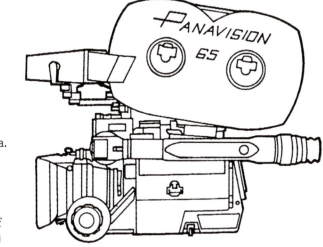

Figure 7.71
Panavision
Panaflex 65 camera.
(Reprinted from
the *Hands-On
Manual for
Cinematographers*
with permission of
David Samuelson.)

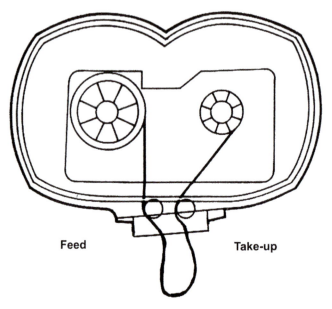

Figure 7.72 Panavision Panaflex 65 magazine. (Reprinted from the *Hands-On Manual for Cinematographers* with permission of David Samuelson.)

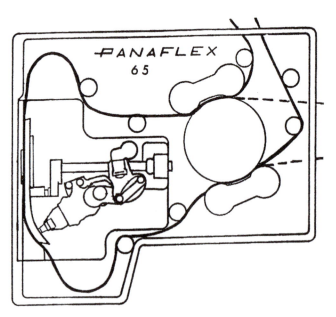

Figure 7.73 Panavision Panaflex 65 camera threading. (Courtesy of Panavision Inc.)

PANAVISION 65 MM HIGH SPEED

Format: 65 mm
Magazine sizes: 500′ and 1000′ Displacement
Lens mount: PV
Forward speeds: 4–72 fps

For camera and magazine illustrations and threading diagrams, see Figures 7.74 through 7.76.

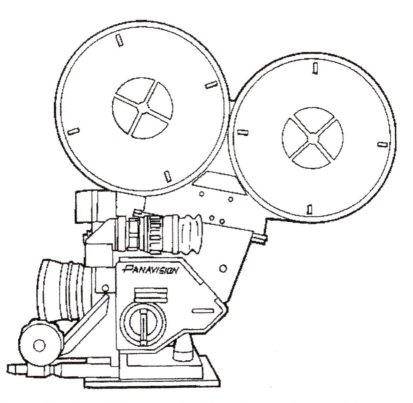

Figure 7.74   Panavision 65 mm High Speed camera. (Reprinted from the *Hands-On Manual for Cinematographers* with permission of David Samuelson.)

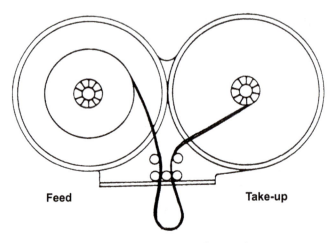

Figure 7.75 Panavision 65 mm High Speed magazine. (Reprinted from the *Hands-On Manual for Cinematographers* with permission of David Samuelson.)

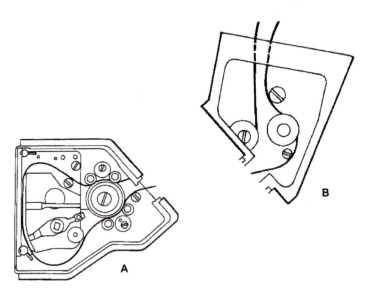

Figure 7.76 Panavision 65 mm High Speed camera threading. **A**, Camera threading. **B**, Top-mount adapter. (Reprinted from the *Hands-On Manual for Cinematographers* with permission of David Samuelson.)

PANAVISION 65 MM HANDHELD

Format: 65 mm
Magazine sizes: 250', 500', and 1000' Displacement
Lens mount: PV
Forward speeds: 4–72 fps

For camera and magazine illustrations and threading diagrams, see Figures 7.77 through 7.79.

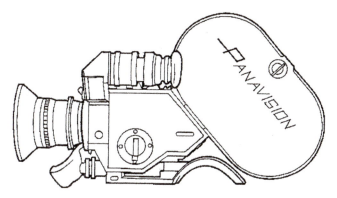

Figure 7.77   Panavision 65 mm Handheld camera. (Reprinted from the *Hands-On Manual for Cinematographers* with permission of David Samuelson.)

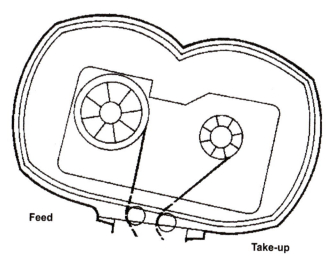

Figure 7.78   Panavision 65 mm Handheld magazine. (Reprinted from the *Hands-On Manual for Cinematographers* with permission of David Samuelson.)

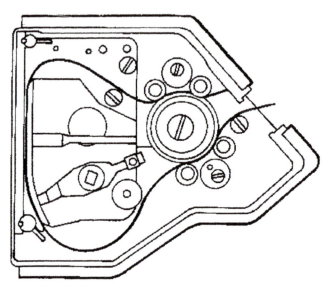

Figure 7.79 Panavision 65 mm Handheld camera threading. (Reprinted from the *Hands-On Manual for Cinematographers* with permission of David Samuelson.)

PHOTO-SONICS ACTIONMASTER 500

Format: 16 mm and Super 16 mm High Speed
Magazine sizes: 400′ Coaxial Daylight Spool Loading
Forward speeds: Standard 16 mm, 10–500 fps; Super 16 mm, 10–360 fps

For camera and magazine illustrations and threading diagrams, see Figures 7.80 and 7.81.

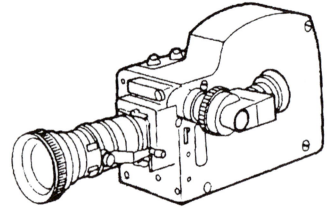

Figure 7.80
Photo-Sonics
Actionmaster
500 camera with
400′ magazine.
(Courtesy of
Photo-Sonics Inc.)

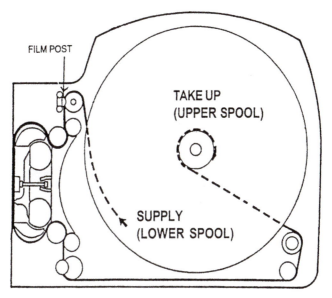

Figure 7.81   Photo-Sonics Actionmaster magazine, film path outline. (Courtesy of Photo-Sonics Inc.)

PHOTO-SONICS 1VN

Format: 16 mm and Super 16 mm High Speed
Magazine sizes: 100′ Daylight Spool Load, 100′ and 200′ Core Load
Forward speeds: 24–200 fps

For camera and magazine illustrations and threading diagrams, see Figures 7.82 and 7.83.

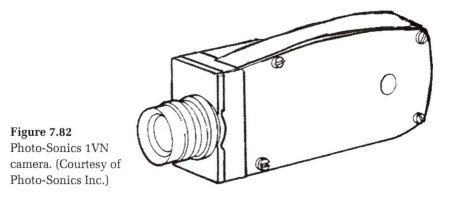

Figure 7.82
Photo-Sonics 1VN camera. (Courtesy of Photo-Sonics Inc.)

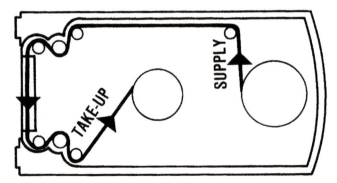

Figure 7.83 Photo-Sonics 1VN camera threading. (Courtesy of Photo-Sonics Inc.)

PHOTO-SONICS 35-4B/4C

Format: 35 mm High Speed
Magazine size: 1000′ Displacement
Forward speeds: 85–3250 fps

For camera and magazine illustrations and threading diagrams, see Figures 7.84 through 7.87.

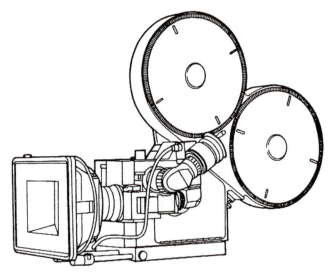

Figure 7.84 Photo-Sonics 35-4B/4C camera. (Courtesy of Photo-Sonics Inc.)

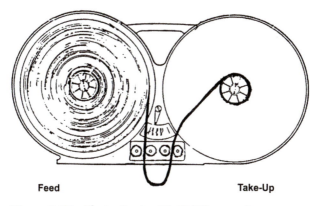

Figure 7.85 Photo-Sonics 35-4B/4C magazine. (Courtesy of Photo-Sonics Inc.)

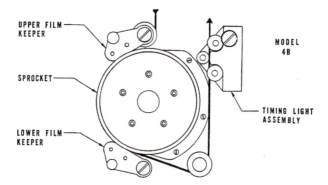

Figure 7.86 Photo-Sonics 35-4B camera threading. (Courtesy of Photo-Sonics Inc.)

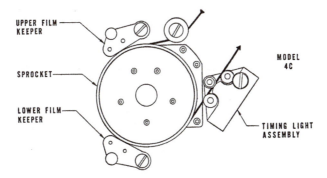

Figure 7.87 Photo-Sonics 35-4C camera threading. (Courtesy of Photo-Sonics Inc.)

PHOTO-SONICS 35-4E/ER

Format: 35 mm High Speed
Magazine size: 1000′ Displacement
Forward speeds: 6–360 fps

For camera and magazine illustrations and threading diagrams, see
Figures 7.88 through 7.90.

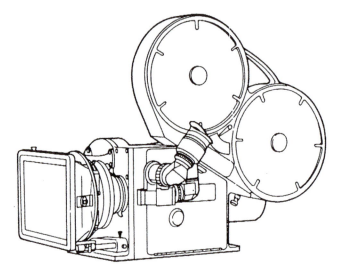

Figure 7.88   Photo-Sonics 35-4E/ER camera. (Courtesy of
Photo-Sonics Inc.)

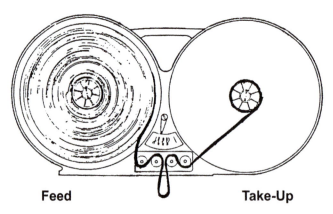

Figure 7.89   Photo-Sonics 35-4E/ER magazine. (Courtesy
of Photo-Sonics Inc.)

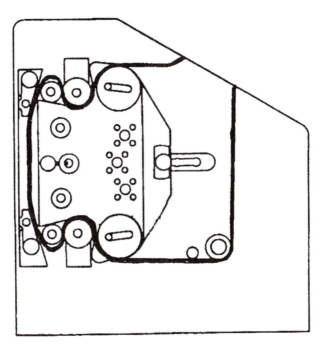

Figure 7.90   Photo-Sonics 35-4E/ER camera threading.
(Courtesy of Photo-Sonics Inc.)

PHOTO-SONICS 35-4ML

Format: 35 mm High Speed
Magazine sizes: 200′ and 400′ Displacement
Forward speeds: 10–200 fps

For camera and magazine illustrations and threading diagrams, see Figures 7.91 and 7.92.

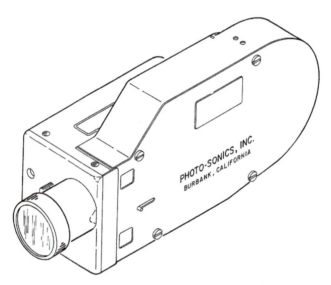

Figure 7.91 Photo-Sonics 35-4ML camera with 400′ magazine. (Courtesy of Photo-Sonics Inc.)

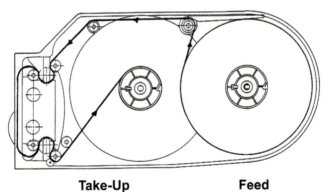

Take-Up   **Feed**

Figure 7.92 Photo-Sonics 35-4ML 400′ magazine. (Courtesy of Photo-Sonics Inc.)

8

Before, During, and After the Job

Now that you have read the first seven chapters and, it is hoped, have a basic understanding of how to do the job of a First and Second Assistant Cameraman, I'd like to mention some of the things you should do before you get the job, how to act when you have the job, and finally what to do when it's all over. Some of what is discussed here includes preparing a résumé, questions to ask during the interview, proper set etiquette, how to behave while on the job, freelance work and taxes, staying in contact with crew people after the job, and more.

Some people are not cut out for this type of work because of the uncertainty of when and where the next job will be, but if you are good at what you do and have established a good reputation in the industry, with a lot of professional contacts, you should have no problem finding work on a regular basis.

First I want to discuss the differences and similarities between union and non-union work. Most likely when you start out you will work on non-union productions, but there may come a time after gaining more experience when you decide that you would like to join the union or you may be on a non-union production that switches to union during the course of production.

The following information is based on my knowledge and experience from working on both non-union and union productions and also from being a member of International Cinematographers Guild Local 600.

UNION OR NON-UNION

Many people ask me what the primary difference is between a union production and a non-union production. There can be many answers

379

to this question, but my very simple answer is as follows. In general, on a non-union production you may work long hours, with overtime, meal penalties, and short turnarounds, and may not be adequately compensated for it. On a union production you may still work long hours with overtime and meal penalties, but due to union regulations, you must be compensated for all of these things. Please don't misunderstand me here because many of my jobs have been on non-union productions, and I was treated fairly in every way. But union productions have minimum wage requirements, overtime, meal penalty, and turnaround rules that must be adhered to. Union productions have a specific requirement as to the crew positions that must be filled within the camera department as well.

The most typical jobs that a beginning filmmaker encounters are independent non-union productions. Many of these are low-budget productions and are often first-time productions by a company or individual. But many non-union productions may be done by established individuals or companies that have simply not signed the agreement with the various production unions. These can include independent feature films, television pilots, commercials, music videos, educational and industrial films, and more.

A non-union production doesn't mean that it is not a reputable production, just that they are not required to abide by the union rules and regulations with regard to the crew. Many non-union productions that I have worked on included union actors, and, as such, the production company was required to follow all SAG (Screen Actors Guild) or AFTRA (American Federation of Television and Radio Artists) rules and regulations. Even though they may not be a union production with regard to the crew, they still must abide by basic state and federal guidelines regarding employment and fair treatment of their workers.

One of the biggest problems I have encountered on some non-union productions is their failure to provide a meal or a meal break six hours after the call time. Having worked in Los Angeles for so many years, I know that the working conditions for the motion picture industry clearly state that a minimum 30-minute meal break must be given six hours after the crew call. There have been a few times when I or another member of the crew needed to remind the Producer or Production Manager about this regulation. In most cases, though, the non-union productions abide by this guideline.

One of the key differences between union and non-union work is the pay scale. Often on a non-union production you will be asked to work for a flat rate per day. What this means is that no matter how many hours you work in a day, your rate of pay is a set amount. If you work 8, 10, 12, or more hours, you are still paid the same rate of pay. I try to avoid these types of jobs whenever possible. A production that

pays a flat rate will often not be as efficient as one that pays a specific rate with overtime. When speaking with a Producer or Production Manager about my daily rate for a non-union production, I usually quote a rate based on a 10-hr day, with overtime to be paid after 10 hours, usually time and a half up to a specific number of hours and then double time after that. I am almost always willing to negotiate if the producer cannot meet my rate. A number of factors will affect my decision to take a job at less than my usual rate of pay. One of these is the people I will be working with. If the DP is someone I have worked with in the past and enjoy working with, I will often accept the job at less than my rate, knowing that in the future the DP will do his or her best to get me on higher paying shows. Giving up a little bit now will most likely lead to gains later on. The Producer often negotiates, but I almost never accept a flat-rate deal, and whatever deal I do accept, I get it in writing on a deal memo or contract for the production. It is important to get this information in writing so that you have something to refer to later on in case there is ever a question or problem.

When you first start working, you must determine your daily pay rate. In most cases when you are contacted about your availability for a job, you are asked about your daily rate. You need to be able to quote an accurate amount based on the position, type of job, and length of production. When I started working in this industry, I worked for anything from $50 to $200 a day as a Second Assistant Cameraman or Loader, depending on how much experience I had at the time, the type of production, and finally what the company was willing to pay. When I started working as a First Assistant Cameraman, my daily rate went up because I had much more experience and felt comfortable quoting a higher rate. Each person's situation is going to be a bit different. If you are serious about working in this industry, I strongly urge you to be willing to negotiate your rate. Don't be so firm that you constantly lose work. The decision is ultimately yours, but if you show your flexibility and willingness to work for a little less than your normal rate, you will not only get more work, but you will establish a good reputation with many production companies. If and when you join the union, your pay rate will be determined by your classification and the current rate for that classification as established by the union.

IATSE and Local 600

The International Alliance of Theatrical Stage Employees, Moving Picture Technicians, Artists and Allied Crafts of the United States, Its Territories and Canada (IATSE) represents over 110,000 workers in the

motion picture industry. Directors of Photography, Camera Operators, Assistants, Technicians, Still Photographers, Film Loaders, Digital Imaging Technicians, Video Controllers, Camera Utility, and Digital Utility are some of the job classifications covered by the International Cinematographers Guild Local 600, which is only one of the many union locals in the United States and Canada.

When I first joined the union, there were three separate camera locals in the United States: Local 644 on the East Coast, Local 666 in the Midwest, and Local 659 on the West Coast. My original membership was in Local 659 on the West Coast. In 1996 all three were merged into one and became International Cinematographers Guild Local 600. Even though there is now one national local, there are still three distinct regions of Local 600: the Eastern Region, Central Region, and Western Region. The region you live in will determine the procedures and rules for joining.

Joining the Union

How do you actually go about joining the International Cinematographers Guild? It is not that complicated, but it does involve a little bit of work, and you may need to gather some documentation as proof of your non-union work. If you are interested in joining the union, you should work on non-union productions and build up your résumé. In some cases you may need a specific number of paid days or hours worked in a particular classification before applying for membership. Whether or not you ever join the union is a matter of personal preference. I know a lot of people who have had successful careers without joining the union and a lot of people who have had successful careers because they joined the union. Your decision depends on a number of factors. If you know some other camera people in the union and know that you will be able to get union jobs, then it may be a benefit to you to join. This is especially true if you are working in one of the larger film markets, such as New York or Los Angeles. If you are located in an area outside of these large markets, it may not be to your advantage to join the union, both from a practical and a financial standpoint. A union job is one in which the Producer or production company has signed a signatory agreement with the union agreeing to abide by its rules and regulations. Virtually all of the major studio productions, productions done by the major production companies, or major television network productions are union jobs. When in doubt, just ask if a job is a union job when inquiring about the availability of work. Also keep in mind that the union doesn't get you jobs. They have an availability list that you can put

your name on, but getting the job is up to you. Once you have been hired on a union job, the union will make sure that you are treated fairly and are paid a proper wage for the work that you do.

There are a number of ways that you can become a member of the International Cinematographers Guild Local 600. Depending on which region you live in, the membership requirements are a bit different. I will give you some basic information on how I joined, but if you would like more specific information on any of the requirements for membership for any position, I suggest that you contact a membership representative at the Local 600 office in the region in which you reside. You can find their contact information by going to the Links page of the companion web site of this book at www.cameraassistant-manual.com. As stated previously, there are a number of ways to join. You may be required to prove that you have a specific number of paid, non-union days in the classification for which you are applying. You may be asked to take a written and/or hands-on test to demonstrate your knowledge of certain cameras and the camera department responsibilities, or you may simply be asked to submit a résumé of your previous non-union work as evidence of your experience. It all depends on the region in which you reside, the classification you are applying for, and where you apply for membership.

When I first joined, I was living and working in Los Angeles, so my membership was governed by the Western Region. To work in the 13 states that encompass the Western Region, you must be placed on what is called the Industry Experience Roster, which is maintained by an organization called the Contract Services Administration Trust Fund. Being placed on the roster doesn't automatically mean you are a member of the union, and being a member of the union doesn't mean you are on the roster. The two are separate, and you must apply to both. You can be a member of Local 600 without being on the Industry Experience Roster.

For the Western Region, the way that I was placed on the Industry Experience Roster is as follows: If you have 100 days of paid work, either union or non-union, within three years of the date of your application, in the classification that you are applying for, you may submit an application to the union for that classification. The 100 days must be within a three-year period immediately preceding the date of application. I joined as a First Assistant Cameraman because I had accumulated the required 100 days of paid non-union work in the three-year period preceding my application. I submitted all of the required paperwork, including letters from Producers, Cinematographers, and/or Production Managers to verify that I had done the job of 1st AC on the various productions. I also provided copies of crew lists, call sheets, and paycheck receipts as proof of

my work. All of this documentation was submitted along with the Contract Services application form and an I-9 form as proof of my eligibility to work in the United States. When all of your paperwork has been received, processed, and verified, if you meet all of the requirements, you will then be placed on the Industry Experience Roster. Once on the roster you may then apply to Local 600 for membership. You will be asked to put a down payment on your initiation fee and to attend a new member orientation meeting. In addition to being placed on the Industry Experience Roster, you must also pass certain safety tests if you will be working on any union productions within the Western Region. These tests are also administered by the Contract Services Administration Trust Fund. Your specific classification will determine which safety tests you must take.

There are other methods to join the Western Region as well as the Eastern and Central Regions. The requirements may be different for Directors of Photography and Camera Operators than they are for Camera Assistants, and these requirements for membership may change periodically, so I strongly recommend that you check the Local 600 office in the region where you reside to find out the requirements for applying for membership. No matter what region you join, there are fees for joining as well as quarterly dues that you must pay. At the time of publication of this edition of the book the current initiation fees range from approximately $3,500 to $12,000 depending on the classification you are applying for. Currently, the initiation fee for an Assistant Cameraman is approximately $6,000. These are the fees just to become a member. You must also pay quarterly dues and other fees. The quarterly dues are assessed whether you are working or not, so you should be sure that you will be able to get union work before spending a great deal of money to join. Quarterly dues range from approximately $150 to $350, depending on your classification. Please be aware that the initiation fees and quarterly dues are subject to change at any time, usually yearly. In addition to quarterly dues, you must also pay a small percentage of your gross earnings when employed on a union production.

When you make the decision to join, you must then decide which classification you will apply for. If all of your non-union work is as a 1st AC, then that is the classification you should apply for. You cannot apply for a union classification for which you have little or no experience. If your work is split between 1st AC and 2nd AC, you may need to decide which would be more beneficial to you. In some regions you may choose to join simply as a Camera Assistant, but in other regions you may need to specify whether it is First Assistant or Second Assistant. When you are a member, you can rerate to a new

classification if you have the appropriate experience in that classification and pay the new initiation fees and dues.

When you are a member of International Cinematographers
Guild Local 600, you should be confident that you will be paid a fair
wage and be treated fairly on all union jobs that you take. Keep in
mind that the guild has different rates based on where you live and
work and on the type of production. In addition, there are different
rates for studio work versus location work. For example, a 1st AC may
be paid approximately $40 per hour for work on one hour episodic
television productions and approximately $42 per hour for work on
a feature film. A 1st AC who works with a specialized piece of equipment, such as Panavision cameras, is paid at the Technician rate of
$46 to $50 per hour instead of the 1st AC rate because special training and experience are required. When working in SD or HD video,
there are specific rates for each classification as well. They range from
approximately $30 to $58 per hour, depending on your classification.
The rates for DP, Camera Operator, and Camera Assistant are the same
as for filmed productions. The common practice is to pay 1½ times
the hourly rate after 8 hours worked, up to 12 hours, and two times
the hourly rate after 12 hours worked. These amounts are subject to
change at any time, and if you are a member of the union, you will
receive yearly updates of any rate changes. The current rates are available only to union members on the union's web site. In addition to
minimum wage rates, the union also requires a minimum turnaround
time between shifts. This is the time between wrap on one day and
call time for the next day's shooting. The typical turnaround time for
a Technician, Camera Assistant, and Loader is 9 hours, and for the
Camera Operator and DP it is 11 hours. The good news here is that on
virtually all union productions you will most likely be working with
union actors and they must be given a 12-hour turnaround, which
means that you will usually get a 12-hour turnaround. The union also
requires that you be paid a meal penalty if the meal break is not given
within six hours from the call time or from the end of the previous
meal break. The only time the meal penalty is not assessed is when
you are in the middle of shooting a shot for a scene and wish to finish
the shot before breaking for the meal. It is quite common for the First
Assistant Director to announce to the crew that they would like to finish the current shot before breaking, and in most cases the crew will
agree. When the shot is finished, you may not move on to a new shot
or scene until after the crew has been given a meal break. The meal
penalty starts at approximately $7.50 for the first half hour or fraction
of a half hour and increases for each subsequent half hour period that
you don't get the meal break.

The standard meal period is not less than half an hour nor more than one hour if the production company provides the meal, and the time starts when the last person goes through the meal line and gets their food. If the production company does not provide a meal, the standard meal break is one hour.

No matter what decision you make about whether or not to join the union, I am sure that you will have a successful and rewarding career in the camera department. Good luck and happy shooting.

BEFORE THE JOB

Keep in mind that the film industry is unlike any other business or industry. Before starting in this business, many people have no idea what they are up against. First, this is not a nine-to-five typical job. Most days you will work a minimum of 12 hours. Working more than 12 hours a day is not uncommon in this business, so don't make dinner plans for a particular evening because you probably won't be there on time. Some days will start at 6:00 p.m. and end at 6:00 a.m. I have had many of these and it's just something you get used to when working in this business. When working these hours I always found it funny that they would call a lunch break at midnight.

Most, if not all, of your jobs will come from word of mouth and recommendations from other camera people and people you have worked with. In most cases you will not work for a single company or studio. The film industry is made up of freelance workers in many different job categories. As stated earlier, being freelance is great for some people, but others find it to be unsuitable and get out of the business quickly. As a freelance camera person, you will always be working to find that next job. You must be aware of what productions are coming up and be especially familiar with the latest cameras and equipment. When looking for work, it is equally important who you know as well as what you know. Many of my jobs have come from recommendations from other DPs or Camera Assistants with whom I have worked.

When starting out it may be to your advantage to work at a camera rental company. You will get to know many of the cameras and accessories that a Camera Assistant uses, plus you will have the opportunity to meet DPs and Camera Assistants who come into the rental company. The downside to working at a camera rental company is that it takes you out of the job market for production work.

When you start looking for production jobs, you may need to accept jobs for little or no pay just to prove that you are a hard worker and know what you are doing. Don't be afraid to start out as a Camera Trainee or Camera PA, carrying cases and doing other jobs within the

camera department. Show that you are willing to work hard, and you will most likely be hired for pay on a future production. Two or three of my first feature film jobs as a 2nd AC were for little or no pay. I did them to gain experience and have something to put on the résumé.

When you are not working, try to learn as much as possible. Cameras and related equipment change rapidly, so it is important that you are knowledgeable about the most current pieces of equipment that you will be working with. Attend seminars that are often offered by camera rental companies. If you are a member of the union, you will have the opportunity to attend many different seminars and workshops about the latest equipment. Obtain camera instruction books or manuals and other camera-related books. Many camera manufacturer web sites offer their manuals for downloading. Many of these manuals are available on the companion web site for this book. The more you can learn when first starting out, the better chances you will have of getting work.

The Résumé and Business Cards

One of the first things you should do is prepare a résumé. At the beginning of your career you will have minimal experience. If you have recently graduated from film school, you will have some experience on student productions. I recommend that your beginning résumé should list any production experience that you may have. This includes Production Assistant, Craft Service, Grip, Electrician, and any other jobs you may have done. At the top of the résumé, just above the listing of your production experience, you should state that your goal is to work in the camera department so that anyone reading it will know that you do have a specific goal, but they will also see that you have worked on production sets so you know what goes on. When you have acquired more camera-related experience, then you should remove the jobs that are not related to the camera department and also remove the statement about your goal. You don't want to look like a jack-of-all-trades and master of none. It will soon be quite clear from your list of production credits that you are applying for a position within the camera department.

Your résumé should include your basic contact information: name, address, and telephone numbers. If you have a cell phone, or fax machine, be sure to include the numbers. If you don't already have a cell phone, and I don't know why anyone in this day would not have one, get one as soon as possible so you don't miss out on any job calls. Also include an email address or addresses. If you have a web site, include that address as well. As a freelance Camera Assistant,

prospective employers need to be able to get in touch with you. The difference between getting a job or not may be as simple as whether or not your contact information is accurate and the person calling can actually get in touch with you. In many cases if you are not available or don't respond to a phone message in a timely manner, it means that the job will be offered to another filmmaker.

Next, your résumé should list your production credits. There are so many different ways to list your credits. I have looked at so many résumés from Camera Assistants and no two have been formatted alike. The main thing is to keep it clean, simple, and easy to read. Don't use fancy fonts or colors that make it difficult to read. These things don't matter. One of the most common ways to list your credits is to start with the most recent job at the top and continue down the page with your other production credits to the oldest at the end. This is commonly referred to as reverse chronological order. One exception to this is if you have any production credits from well-known, recognizable productions. Those credits should be listed first because as the DP or Production Manager looks at your résumé, these titles will jump out at them and indicate that you are qualified for the job.

Another way to format your résumé is to categorize the credits according to the type of production or according to your position. In other words, you may list all your television credits, then features, music videos, commercials, etc. Or you may list all your First Assistant work and then Second Assistant, Loader, etc. The format that you use for the résumé is up to your personal preference, and if you are not sure I recommend asking friends and colleagues in the business if you can look at their résumé. Most résumés that I have seen contain similar basic information. This includes the title of the production; type of production (feature film, television show, commercial, and so forth); whether the job performed was that of a 1st AC, 2nd AC, or Loader; the name of the DP; and sometimes the name of the Director, Producer, or production company.

If you are applying for a job in the camera department (and if you are reading this book I hope you are), many Production Managers or DPs who you interview with will most often ask, "What DPs have you worked with?" In preparing my résumé, I have included the names of all DPs who I have worked with on the many productions that I have worked on during my career. For a brief time I worked as both a 2nd AC and 1st AC, so my résumé listed all of my production credits for those positions. In recent years I have worked as both a Camera Operator or 1st AC, so my résumé now lists all of my production credits for these positions as well as my past experience as a 2nd AC. My current résumé lists my credits in subcategories based on the job that I performed as well as the type of production: television,

feature film, commercial, music video, and other credits. You will be constantly updating your résumé and one thing you should not do is to list a production on the résumé that you have not worked on yet. Some people will book themselves on a job and immediately update their résumé with the production information. Then for one reason or another, the production gets canceled and you forget to remove the production from the résumé. Then sometime in the future when somebody is looking at your résumé they see this listing and may know that you didn't work on the show. It's best not to list anything until you have actually worked on it for at least one day. Then it is legitimate work and you won't have any problems in the future.

Following your list of credits, I recommend listing any special skills and especially equipment knowledge that relates to your experience. It is very helpful for anyone reading your résumé to know if you have experience with the particular camera that will be used on the production you are applying for. You may also list any industry-related organizations or unions that you belong to. Next you may list your education, including the name of the school, years attended, and degree earned. And finally at the end of the résumé you should include the following statement: "References available upon request." It is common practice to not list reference information unless it is asked for. When giving names of references, be sure that you have their permission. See Figures 8.1 and 8.2 for examples of two different résumé templates that you may use. There are many different styles for film résumés and these are only two examples.

My current résumé may be viewed on the companion web site for this book at www.cameraassistantmanual.com or at my personal web site at www.davidelkins.com.

The most important thing to remember about your résumé is don't lie. If you didn't work on a production, don't list it. If you have never used a particular camera, don't list it. If you don't have certain special skills, don't list them. And as stated earlier, especially important is don't list a production until you have actually worked on it for at least one day. Only list things that have actually been shot and you have actually worked on. This may sound like common sense but I know of people who "pad" their résumé by listing credits and experience that they don't have in order to make themselves look good. If you do this, it will be discovered sooner than later and will only cause you more problems than it is worth. It will affect whether or not you get hired on future jobs.

Now that your résumé is done, you need to get that first job. Send it out to as many production companies and Cinematographers as possible. Talk to friends in the industry to get leads on jobs. This business is all about networking so the more people in your network

Name
Address
City, State, Zip

Home Phone   Cell Phone
Email   Web Site

EXPERIENCE

FEATURES
Title, Your Position, Name of DP, Name of Director
Title, Your Position, Name of DP, Name of Director
Title, Your Position, Name of DP, Name of Director

TELEVISION
Title, Your Position, Name of DP, Name of Director
Title, Your Position, Name of DP, Name of Director
Title, Your Position, Name of DP, Name of Director

COMMERCIALS
Title of Spot or Product Name, Your Position, Name of DP, Name of Director
Title of Spot or Product Name, Your Position, Name of DP, Name of Director
Title of Spot or Product Name, Your Position, Name of DP, Name of Director

MUSIC VIDEOS
Artist Name – Song Title, Your Position, Name of DP, Name of Director
Artist Name – Song Title, Your Position, Name of DP, Name of Director
Artist Name – Song Title, Your Position, Name of DP, Name of Director

OTHER
Title, Type of Production (Short, Documentary, Industrial, Educational), Your Position, Name of DP, Name of Director
Title, Type of Production (Short, Documentary, Industrial, Educational), Your Position, Name of DP, Name of Director
Title, Type of Production (Short, Documentary, Industrial, Educational), Your Position, Name of DP, Name of Director

CAMERAS AND SPECIAL EQUIPMENT KNOWLEDGE
Aaton Penelope, Arriflex Arricam, Panavision Platinum, Arriflex Alexa, RED One, RED Scarlet, Canon 5D DSLR, Panasonic Varicam, Etc.

SPECIAL SKILLS
Steadicam, Underwater, Aerial, Etc.

UNION OR OTHER ORGANIZATION AFFILIATIONS
Member of the International Cinematographers Guild IATSE Local 600

EDUCATION
Name of College or University – Degree Received – Name of Major – Year of Graduation

References available upon request

Figure 8.1   One example of a résumé template.

the better your chances of getting work. There are many web sites as well as film industry-related trade papers or magazines that list current jobs. Two of the most common publications are *Daily Variety* and *The Hollywood Reporter*. These publications are available on most newsstands, by subscription, and also online. Each week they

Name
Address
City, State, Zip

Home Phone
Email

Cell Phone
Web Site

EXPERIENCE

FIRST ASSISTANT CAMERAMAN - *Television*
Title, Name of DP, Name of Director
Title, Name of DP, Name of Director

FIRST ASSISTANT CAMERAMAN – *Feature Films*
Title, Name of DP, Name of Director, Name of Producer
Title, Name of DP, Name of Director, Name of Producer

FIRST ASSISTANT CAMERAMAN – *Commercials*
Title of Spot or Product Name, Name of DP, Name of Director
Title of Spot or Product Name, Name of DP, Name of Director

FIRST ASSISTANT CAMERAMAN – *Music Videos*
Artist Name – Song Title, Name of DP, Name of Director
Artist Name – Song Title, Name of DP, Name of Director

SECOND ASSISTANT CAMERAMAN – *Television*
Title, Name of DP, Name of Director
Title, Name of DP, Name of Director

SECOND ASSISTANT CAMERAMAN – *Feature Films*
Title, Name of DP, Name of Director
Title, Name of DP, Name of Director

SECOND ASSISTANT CAMERAMAN – *Commercials*
Title of Spot or Product Name, Name of DP, Name of Director
Title of Spot or Product Name, Name of DP, Name of Director

SECOND ASSISTANT CAMERAMAN – *Music Videos*
Artist Name – Song Title, Name of DP, Name of Director
Artist Name – Song Title, Name of DP, Name of Director

CAMERAS AND SPECIAL EQUIPMENT KNOWLEDGE
Aaton Penelope, Arriflex Arricam, Panavision Platinum, Arriflex Alexa, RED One, RED Scarlet, Canon 5D DSLR, Panasonic Varicam, Etc.

SPECIAL SKILLS
Steadicam, Underwater, Aerial, Etc.

UNION OR OTHER ORGANIZATION AFFILIATIONS
Member of the International Cinematographers Guild IATSE Local 600

EDUCATION
Name of College or University – Degree Received – Name of Major – Year of Graduation

References available upon request

Figure 8.2   Another example of a résumé template.

list current productions along with productions in the preproduction or planning stages. Keep in mind that many of these listings may be for union productions, and unless you have extensive union experience and know somebody on the show, you will most likely not receive a reply to your inquiry. In addition to the publications

already mentioned, there are many other industry magazines and publications as well as many excellent web sites that contain job information. There are also many excellent film-related web sites where you can post your résumé for others to see. As I stated previously, if you have friends or colleagues in the film industry, you may also ask them for any job leads. Don't be afraid to ask people you have worked with if they know of any future jobs. Also, don't be afraid to tell other crew people about jobs you know of. When mailing or emailing your résumé, you should always include a brief cover letter that introduces yourself and explains why you are writing to the company. Show you are seriously interested in the position and your résumé will get read. Otherwise it may just end up in the circular file under somebody's desk, or the trash folder on somebody's computer. Mail your letter to as many productions as interest you. If you are able to obtain a telephone number for the production company, wait about a week and then call them. Ask if your résumé was received, and ask if you can come in for a personal interview. Show that you are seriously interested in the job. The old saying that the squeaky wheel gets the grease does apply in the film business. Telephoning and showing that you are truly interested may be the difference between your getting the job and someone else getting it.

In addition to your résumé you should have professional business cards printed. It is quite common to share business cards with other crew members on the last day of a production. Someone is more likely to remember you and to save your contact information if they have a business card rather than a Post-It note or a ripped off corner of the call sheet with your number written on it. Your business card should look professional but doesn't need to be over the top. Keep it simple and be sure to include all of your contact information. As with your résumé, don't use fancy fonts that are difficult to read. Your web site may only have your email address, but your business card should contain all of your contact information, including phone numbers, email, and web address. You can go to a commercial printing company to get your business cards printed, but there are also many web sites that offer professional looking and inexpensive business cards. I have used a site called www.vistaprint.com and have been very happy with their prices and service. They offer a number of templates to choose from or you can design your own.

Email and Web Sites

As I stated earlier, you should have an email address and it should be a professional email address and not one with the silly name you

made up in high school for your Hotmail or Yahoo account. You want people to take you seriously. If you don't have one, get one. Some people set up a special email account for film jobs only, so they don't get lost in the inbox of your personal account that family and friends may use. This is something you may want to consider as well. I also recommend setting up your own personal web site. Today we live in an age of technology and you will often be asked for your email address and even your web site address. The web site is a great place to showcase your work, post your résumé, and provide a quick way for prospective employers to find out as much as possible about you and your career. For your web site, try to have your own hosted domain such as I have at www.davidelkins.com. This will give you more credibility than something like www.davidelkins.webhost.com. There are many hosting companies out there that have very reasonable pricing for hosting a web site. And if you have your own domain you will usually be able to set up multiple email accounts and you can set up a professional email address as I have with david@davidelkins.com. I use a web hosting company called GoDaddy which has a number of options for hosting and very reasonable prices. And once you are working, the costs for setting up and maintaining your web site can be claimed as business expenses on your taxes. More on taxes later in this chapter.

In addition to having a web site you should get your name listed in various online directories devoted to the film industry. Two very good online resources are LA411 and NY411, which list production companies, rental companies for equipment, and crew listings, just to name a few. Most states also have film commissions that publish online production directories for the state. Some larger states even have regional film commissions with separate online directories. While these listings don't guarantee that you will get a job, they do provide a wider range of resources for people to find you and potentially contact you for work.

The Job Interview

Now that you have prepared your résumé and sent it out, you should get ready to go on that first job interview. In many cases the DP, Production Manager, or both will conduct the interview. Dress professionally, arrive a little early for the interview, and be prepared. Have additional copies of your résumé with you in case anyone asks for one. Take your business cards with you so that you can give them out with your résumé.

An important part of the interview is asking the right questions. There are many things that you need to know about the job before

starting, and you have the right to ask these questions. The following are some key questions that you should ask when interviewing for a job on any production. They are listed in no specific order.

- What format is the film being shot in?—16 mm, 35 mm, HD, or SD?
- What camera system will be used?—If you haven't worked in the format or with the equipment being used, you may need to get some quick training before starting the job.
- Is it a union or non-union crew?—You should know this up front because if you are not a member of the union, you cannot work on union jobs. There are exceptions to this and you should check before accepting a job and then finding out you cannot do it.
- What is the rate for the position I am applying for?—Be prepared to quote your daily rate and also be willing to negotiate.
- Is the daily rate based on 10 hours, 12 hours, or more?—If it is based on anything more than 12 hours then you should worry. Do the math and you may find out that you're not getting paid a fair wage.
- Is this a flat rate or is there overtime pay after a specific number of hours?—The last thing you want to do is to work an extra-long work day and then find out when you get paid that there was no overtime.
- How often will I be paid or how soon after the completion of production will I be paid?—You may be used to getting paid weekly or bi-weekly, but on some freelance, independent contractor jobs you must invoice the company and then wait for payment, which could take 30 days or longer.
- Does this rate include prep and wrap days?—Some productions try to get you to do the prep and/or wrap days for half your daily rate. But don't be afraid to negotiate for a full day's rate. Even if the prep will only take half a day, you are being taken out of the workforce for that day and cannot accept any jobs, for which you may have been paid your full rate. It can't hurt to ask, and if they are willing to negotiate then that's better for you. But in any case, I would almost never turn down a job because I am only being paid a half-day rate to prep. In my opinion some money is better than no money.
- Do you pay a box or kit rental?—As a professional you have a great deal of money invested in your tools and equipment. It cannot hurt to ask the production to pay a kit fee. If they are willing to do so, then it's a bit more for you, and a great way to get back some of the money you have invested. But if they won't or cannot pay a box or kit rental, the last thing you should do is leave your tools at home. You'll need them to do the job no matter what.

- Would you be willing to rent any equipment from me?—If you own any special equipment such as filters or batteries, ask if you can rent them. It's a little more income for you and may save the production some cost on the equipment from the rental house. As with other items here, be willing to negotiate.
- Is the shooting local or on a distant location?—If you are working away from home for an extended period you may need to make arrangements for your mail and other personal things. You will also need to take certain personal items with you on location that you wouldn't normally take on a local job. More on this later in the book.
- If it is a distant location, do you pay travel expenses, per diem, and lodging?—Like I said with the kit rental, it can't hurt to also ask if the production will pay some or all of your travel expenses for work on distant locations. If you are driving a few hours from your home to work, then it's only reasonable to be reimbursed for gas. If they tell you that they won't or cannot pay for travel I would recommend pushing for it and trying to negotiate. Fuel costs and wear and tear on your vehicle should be something you are compensated for when working for a production. There are no standard set rates for per diem, which is money paid for the basic, daily expenses like food, laundry, etc., that you may incur when working on a distant location. I recommend that you do the math before interviewing for the job so you know exactly how much these costs are and you can negotiate properly.
- Are meals provided?—As I stated earlier in the section on unions, this is the biggest problem I have encountered. You should get a meal after six hours and also have the opportunity to grab some snacks in between. It helps keep your energy level up and helps you to do a better job. Make sure this is covered in the deal memo.
- How many weeks of shooting will there be?—This is useful to know so that you can plan on any future work or other events.
- Is the workweek five or six days?—Never work a seven day week.
- How many hours per day do you anticipate shooting?—Twelve is normal; anything over 12 is usually too much.
- What are the scheduled start and end dates of the shooting schedule?—This is important to know because you may have another job lined up as soon as this one finishes. If the current job goes over schedule you may lose the other job. If you have to leave early because the current job goes over, you need to know if it is your responsibility to find a replacement. It helps to know ahead of time what the production company's plan is if things go over schedule.

- Are any other crew positions still available?—Recommend other crew members who you have worked with in the past.
- If the production is canceled before starting will I be paid anything?—This is rare but it cannot hurt to ask the question anyway. It is especially important if you have turned down other work in order to accept this job. It's not fair to you if you have committed to a production and then for one reason or another it is canceled at the last minute. Only once in my entire career have I been paid a cancellation fee for a show.
- May I receive a copy of the footage for use on my professional reel?—Most Camera Assistants don't have a reel, but this question is important to ask if you are the Camera Operator or Director of Photography. It's not always easy to get this, even if the deal memo states that you will receive it. As a Camera Operator I have often had to rent the DVD or video so that I could copy shots for my professional reel.

These are some of the typical questions that you should ask during the interview. You may come up with others as you work more.

The Deal Memo

When you have completed the basic part of the job interview, you will often be asked to sign a deal memo. This is a contract between you and the production that outlines the terms and conditions of your employment as well as the pay scale, overtime rate, if meals are included, equipment rentals, etc. It is viewed as legal protection for the production company as well as for you, the employee. If you talk to anyone in the film industry I am sure they will have a story about not being paid or having to wait weeks and months to be paid by a production company, even though they had a signed deal memo. Be sure to obtain a copy of all paperwork that you sign so that if there are any problems or questions later you can refer to it.

Without a signed deal memo you may find yourself in a heated argument with the Producer or Production Manager about being paid for some of the most basic things. Don't assume you'll get overtime pay; get it in writing on the deal memo. Producers are all about the bottom line and saving money, and they'll do almost anything to avoid paying their crew for even the most basic work. I have a personal story as an example of this that follows in the section During the Job.

It is important to ask how many hours your rate is based on. This will affect your overtime rate if and when you work any overtime hours. Be sure to ask this upfront during your interview. The After the Job section later in this chapter discusses daily rates and invoicing for

services in more detail. Even if you are working on a free production, which you will often do when you first start out, you should still have a signed deal memo. Although you may be working for "free" and not being paid for the job of Camera Assistant, you may still be receiving compensation for travel, per diem or other expenses. Be sure to completely read the deal memo before signing it so that you are sure that there are no hidden clauses or restrictions. You need to be sure that you will be treated as a professional by the production company and their representatives. An example of a basic, general Camera Department Deal Memo can be found in Appendix C (Figure C.22), and also on the companion web site for the book at www.cameraassistantmanual.com.

If you have any special camera-related equipment that may be used on the production, ask if the company will rent it from you instead of from the camera rental company. Many Camera Assistants own camera batteries, filters, or other camera equipment. Give the production company a fair price to make it worth renting from you. One thing you should remember when owning and renting your equipment is that you may be taking business away from a rental house that you will be dealing with regularly in the course of your career. Don't jeopardize your reputation with a rental company just to make a few extra dollars.

Sometimes you may have to work for little or no money to prove yourself, as I did when first starting out. Don't be discouraged by rejection because you will send out hundreds of résumés and may get only one or two replies. Be persistent, and eventually you will get that first big break. If you want that first job badly enough and are willing to work to get it, the job will come and you will be on your way to a successful career.

DURING THE JOB

As with most jobs in the film industry, a Camera Assistant is a freelance worker. This means that you will not be employed by one company but will go from job to job working a few days, weeks, or months at a time before you need to find that next production job. In some cases, although you are considered a freelance worker, you will be treated as an employee because state and federal taxes will be taken out of your pay. In the cases in which you are considered an independent contractor, taxes are not taken out of your pay but you will still be held responsible for paying those taxes at the end of the year. Later in this chapter I'll discuss taxes and what you need to know when working as an employee or independent contractor.

Once you have been hired for the job, you should follow some basic guidelines while on the set. There is a proper set etiquette that should be followed by all crew members on any production. How you conduct yourself is just as important as, and in some cases more important than, knowing how to do the job properly. You are a professional and should act accordingly. Another Camera Assistant once told me the following: Be serious when necessary, friendly at all times, and quiet most of the time. If you do this you will be much happier, have more jobs than you can handle, and have a very successful career.

Some people in the film industry let it go to their head and often develop an ego. Don't let this happen to you. Just because you are part of a film crew doesn't mean you are better than anybody else. And, just because you have the basic knowledge to do the job doesn't mean that you know everything. I learn something new on every job I do. Be willing to learn something new. It will make you much happier. Don't forget to thank other crew members for their efforts and help. And, most important, if you make a mistake, admit it. Never try to blame your errors on someone else. A friend shared a story with me that illustrates this point. A Camera Assistant on a show took the magazines home with him one night to make sure that they were all loaded for the next day's shooting. The next day the crew arrived at the designated meeting area and boarded the crew van to travel to the location. After about 10 or 15 minutes into the trip, the Camera Assistant realized that he had left the magazines at home. For the remainder of the trip he tried to think of a way out of his predicament but did and said nothing. When they arrived at the location he made some telephone calls but couldn't get anybody. Just as he was about to inform the DP of his error, it started to rain and the shoot was canceled for the day. Fortunately for him nobody ever found out about his error. But if it hadn't started raining, he would have been forced to admit his mistake. I think that it would have been best to admit the mistake as soon as it was discovered and take the consequences. We are only human, and we sometimes make mistakes. Trying to cover them up only creates more problems.

The first time you step onto a professional film set you may feel like a stranger in a foreign land. Learn the names of other crew members as quickly as possible. Also learn the names of the cast. Write them down on a notepad if necessary or keep a copy of the call sheet handy so that you can refer to it. If you have any questions, don't hesitate to ask. Don't attempt to do something that you may not be familiar with. It is important to stay within your own department and give help only if it is asked for, especially on union productions. This may sound selfish, but there are good reasons for doing this. On union shoots there are specific guidelines regarding each department and the

job responsibilities within that department. I was on a union show as 1st AC, and during a setup for a new scene, the DP asked me to move the camera dolly a few inches. I unlocked the dolly, moved it, and as I was locking it in place, the Key Grip was right in my face and said, "If you touch that dolly again I'll report you to the union." The DP began to explain that he had asked me to move the dolly, and the Key Grip proceeded to yell at him as well, saying that there was a specific crew member to do that job and nobody else. Although I had worked with that Key Grip many times in the past, I learned a valuable lesson that day: When working on a union production, don't touch a piece of equipment that is not part of your department unless specifically asked to do so by someone in that department.

Many of your jobs will come from recommendations from other crew members, especially from people within your own department. Work hard, do a good job, and always be willing to give a little extra in the performance of your job. Whenever possible, make your superior look good. By doing this you will have more job offers than you know what to do with. Whenever a question or problem arises, it is best to follow the chain of command. Start within your department. If you are the 2nd AC, then go to the 1st AC with your question or problem. If he or she can't help, then you should both go to the DP. Going over someone's head will only make you look bad and could risk your possible employment on future productions.

Each day you will be given a call sheet with a call time, which is the time that you should be on the set ready to work, not the time that you are to arrive at work. I recommend arriving at work at least 30 minutes before the call time. Showing up a little early shows your professionalism and desire to do a good job. If you will be traveling to an area that you are not familiar with, be sure to look at any maps and call sheets the night before so that you have an approximate idea where you are going and what time you should leave home so that you get there on time. You should have local maps available in case you need to find your way to a particular location. I recommend getting a GPS unit for your car, which will help you when traveling to unfamiliar locations. These units are very inexpensive and portable.

When traveling to a distant location for a job, be sure that you take certain personal items with you. You should have an extra change of clothes and various personal hygiene items on the camera truck in case of emergency. You may be away from home for an extended period, so be prepared. Even if not on a distant location you should have a change of clothes and other items with you because you never know when you may need them. See Appendix D for a complete listing of personal items that you I recommend you should have with you on a production.

As a freelance filmmaker it is important to be able to prove that you have experience. You may want to get listed in an industry directory or on a crew web site, and without proof of your work, they won't accept your listing. You should save the call sheets from every production you work on. It is a very important document that is distributed to the crew at the end of each shooting day and it provides key information for the next day of shooting. As stated earlier in this chapter, if you decide to join the union you will need to provide proof of your experience. The call sheet is one of the best ways to do this. In my home office I have a box that contains the call sheets from almost every show that I have done in the course of my career. With today's technology you may receive the call sheet in a digital format in your email. I recommend creating a folder on your computer so that you may store all of these digital call sheets for future reference. You can print any of them out at any time when needed. And if you receive paper call sheets, and have a scanner connected to your computer, you can scan the call sheets to save on your computer so you don't have a lot of paper cluttering up your home.

You'll discover very quickly that when working on a film set there is a lot of what I often refer to as "hurry up and wait." There may be a lot of downtime depending on the nature of the shoot. When the camera crew is working during the shot, the Grips and Electricians and others may be waiting around. When the Grips and Electricians are setting up the lighting plan, the camera crew may be waiting around. There are a number of things that you can do to keep busy during the downtime so that your day goes by faster. This is especially important if the Producer walks by and sees you just sitting around. He/she may think you are lazy and not realize you simply have nothing to do at this particular moment. If they walk by and you are busy, it looks better for you. Depending on whether you are the First or Second Assistant or the Loader, there are a number of tasks you can be doing in order to keep busy when not actually working for the shot.

Clean and organize the equipment on the camera carts, clean the cases, check that batteries are fully charged and, if not, plug them in to charge them. As the 2nd AC or Loader, check that all magazines are loaded and all paperwork is completed. This will give you less to do at the end of the day so you may leave earlier. Check and inventory the raw stock and expendables and let the production office know if you need anything. You don't want to run out of film or an important expendable item at a critical moment during production. As a First Assistant, practice guessing distances so you can improve your focus pulling. If you have a Camera Trainee or Production Assistant who is interested in learning more, help them and answer any questions they have. Show them how to do certain parts of the job. These are just a

few of the things that you can do so that you keep busy in between setups and shots. I would rather be busy than just sitting around and I hope you would as well.

When you are actively working and not just doing busy work, the job can be very stressful at times, no matter what position you are in. How you handle that pressure will be a sign of whether or not you are a true professional. Always be prepared for the job, have the right attitude, and be flexible whenever possible. Many times the shot that was planned changes on the spot and you need to go with the flow. Getting uptight and angry will not help you do the shot, and if you are the 1st AC, will most often cause you to blow the focus during the shot. Being prepared also means having the right tools and equipment to do the job. If you are properly prepared, your confidence level will increase which will then reduce your stress level. Stay relaxed and concentrate on the task at hand, the focus of the upcoming shot, etc. Think back to the last time you had a similar type of focus pull and how you handled it. It will make it a little easier this time. There are a lot of distractions on set, before and even during a shot. Don't let these things distract you from performing your job. Concentrate on the task at hand and basically ignore everything and everyone else around you. Keep in mind the statement that I often use when speaking with students in classes and workshops that I have taught, "It's only a movie." When you look at the bigger picture, it's not that important. If you screw up you may lose the job but at the end of the day you can go home, think about it, and the next day start looking for that next film job. Making mistakes is human and knowing how to handle them and deal with the day-to-day pressures of your job is what makes you a professional.

Being safety conscious is important on any film set. No shot is so important that you should jeopardize an actor or crew person's safety. As stated earlier, my favorite saying when speaking with beginners and students is, "It's only a movie." It's not so important that you need to jeopardize somebody's safety, especially your own. If you have a concern, it should be brought up immediately. I have refused to do certain shots because I felt that my personal safety was in jeopardy. In most cases you will be respected for your professionalism and willingness to speak up. Professionalism is an important aspect of the job in many different ways.

You are a professional and should act accordingly. You should also be treated as a professional. If you feel that you are being treated unfairly, you should mention it immediately. A situation that I was in a few years ago illustrates this point. This follows up the discussion in the previous section about deal memos. I was hired on a production as the 2nd AC. During the interview I was told that an overtime rate would be paid on hours worked past 12 hours per day and signed

a deal memo accordingly. We were using two cameras, and as the 2nd AC, the job sometimes required me to continue working 45 minutes to an hour or more after most of the crew had wrapped and gone home for the day. I had to prepare the film to be sent to the lab, complete all paperwork, and get the equipment ready for the next day's shooting. At the start of the second week of filming, the Production Manager came to me and told me that he couldn't pay me for the overtime hours that I had put on my time card. I reminded him of the agreement regarding overtime pay, and he told me that overtime was based on when the official wrap time was called for the entire crew. I explained that my job required me to work longer each day to complete the extra duties. He said he was sorry but that he could only pay overtime based on the crew wrap time. I looked at him and said, very sternly but in a calm voice, "Fine, when you call wrap tonight, I am going home. You can unload the film and complete all of the paperwork." At this point I walked back onto the set. A short time later the Producer called me into his office. I explained that we had agreed on an overtime deal during the job interview, and if he wasn't going to honor his agreement then I would leave then, and he could find someone else to do the job. I also explained that I was not trying to pad my hours and I only indicated the time that I had actually worked. He then told me to put any overtime hours on the time card and promised to honor his original agreement. By standing up for what was right, I showed my professionalism. I did not let the Production Manager or Producer force me into a situation that was unfair. From that day until the end of production, the Producer showed greater respect for me because of my willingness to stand up for what I felt was right.

Another part of being professional is having the right tools and equipment for the job. Many of the tools in your ditty bag may not be used regularly, but having that one special item when it is needed may be the difference between you and someone else being hired for the next job. Some of the items in my toolkit have only been used once or twice, but because I had them it made the job easier. Be sure to have at least the basic tools and accessories to fulfill your job responsibilities. Appendix D lists many of the fundamental tools and accessories that you should have in you ditty bag or toolkit.

Wrap time is the time that filming ends and the crew packs up to go home for the day. When the Assistant Director calls wrap, you should put everything away and leave as quickly as possible. Especially as the 2nd AC, if you have kept up on the magazines and paperwork throughout the day, you should have minimal work to do at the wrap. As the 1st AC puts away the camera and other equipment, the 2nd AC will unload all magazines and prepare the film for delivery to the lab. Remember, the faster you wrap, the sooner you get home.

On-Set Etiquette

As part of a film crew, there will be many times when you are filming on location, in offices, business establishments, private homes, and so on. Whenever you are on a location you should respect these people's homes, businesses, and property. Being part of a film crew doesn't give you the right to act as you please. The proper attitude and behavior apply as much to location work as they do when you are working on a stage or in a studio. No matter how bad the day is going, having a positive attitude is key. How you act on the job today will affect your chances of getting jobs in the future. When filming in any situation, whether it is on location or in a studio, there are certain commonsense guidelines that you should be aware of. Avoid any type of sexual, racial, political, or religious comments that could offend others. Avoid the use of profanity as much as possible. Don't wear any clothing that contains slogans, sayings, or images that may offend others. The use of drugs or alcohol before, during, or after work is not recommended. Avoid negative comments or opinions about other crew members, production companies, rental companies, or equipment. The production community is very small, and any bad things you may say now will come back to haunt you sooner or later. Any of the abovementioned behaviors only shows a nonprofessional attitude. Here are some important rules to be aware of on any film set:

- Always make the DP and your immediate superior look good.
- Stay in your own department, and let other crew members do their jobs. Be aware of everything going on in your department.
- Come to work early. Showing up late is a sure way to get fired and not get called for future work.
- Be enthusiastic and work hard. Go that extra mile. Work efficiently and effectively. If you take your time and move slowly throughout the day, you'll get a reputation for being lazy. Nobody will hire you. Work quickly but never run on set.
- Respect and treat the equipment as if it were your own. If you don't handle the equipment properly, lose or damage items, it shows that you simply don't care.
- Learn the names of coworkers and actors. Respect and support all the people that you work with.
- Keep your eyes and ears open at all times.
- Don't be afraid to ask questions.
- Don't be afraid to admit if you don't know how to do something or how to use a particular piece of equipment. It's better to admit this than to do something wrong that could injure somebody or cause damage to equipment.

- Don't have an ego.
- Admit your mistakes. It is the sign of a professional.
- Don't do or say things that may offend others.
- Don't complain in front of other crew members or actors. If you have a problem, bring it to your superior and do it off set away from others.

AFTER THE JOB

Invoicing and Time Cards

Being truthful on your time card is just as important as being truthful on your résumé. During the job interview you should have worked out the deal for overtime and other time-related issues. As the earlier story illustrates, the 2nd AC often needs to stay later than many other crew members. Be sure that the Production Manager or Producer understands that upfront so that there are no questions later on when you put the additional time on your time card. By filling in your time card accurately and truthfully, you will also show your professionalism and will get more jobs. On most productions you will fill out a time card at the end of each week of filming, or at the end of production if the production was less than a full week. If you have worked as an independent contractor, you often will submit an invoice to the production company for your equipment and/or services. I cannot stress enough the importance of being truthful on your time card or invoice. The example I mentioned previously illustrates this. You don't want to be known as the person who pads their time card or invoice, because if you do, you won't be hired for future jobs. See Figure 8.3 for an example of a typical film industry crew time card.

When invoicing, be sure to submit your invoice promptly. How long should you wait before receiving payment? I usually try to find this out during my interview or when hired for the job. Most companies pay on a 30-day basis, which means that you won't be paid until 30 days after they receive your invoice. So the sooner you submit the invoice, the sooner you get paid. If you haven't received any payment after 30 days from the end of production, you should call the production office to inquire. My invoice contains the following statement: *Payment is due 30 days from date of invoice. Payment not received is subject to interest charge of 1½% per month.* If I haven't received payment in the proper amount of time, I submit a new invoice with the interest charge added. This usually gets the attention of the production company, and they submit payment very quickly. A sample

CREW TIME CARD

PICTURE	PROD #	GUAR. HOURS	RATE	WEEK ENDING
NAME	SOCIAL SECURITY #	JOB CLASSIFICATION/OCC CODE	ACCOUNT #
		LOCATION	

WORK STATE	CITY	ACCT. CODE	DATE	LOC	DAY	CALL	OUT	IN	OUT	IN	WRAP	RE-RATE	OCC. CODE	TOTAL HOURS	1X	1.5X	2X	MEAL PNLTY	ACCT.	RATE	TYPE	HRS	TOTAL
					SUN																		
					MON																		
					TUE																		
					WED																		
					THU																		
					FRI																		
					SAT																		

TOTAL HOURS

COMMENTS

TOTAL AMOUNT

ACCT. #	MEALS-ALLOW. 861	MEALS-TAX 860	PER DIEM ADV. D18	ACCT. #	LODGING-ALLOW 861	LODGING-TAX 860	PER DIEM ADV D18	ACCT. #	MEAL MONEY-TAX 867
ACCT. #	BOX RENTAL 853	ACCT. #	CAR ALLOW. 856	ACCT. #	MILEAGE-ALLOW. 852	MILEAGE-TAX 858	MILEAGE ADV. D20	ACCT. #	2ND CAMERA 680
			PER DIEM BASED ON		CN DIEM – ALLOW.	CN DIEM – TAX			SALARY ADVANCE D21
ACCT. #	HAZARD 653	ACCT. #	_____ DAYS @ _____ US $ PER DAY	ACCT. #		ACCT. #		ACCT. #	

Employee Signature   Approved

Figure 8.3   Film industry time card.

invoice for freelance work can be found in Appendix C (Figure C.21) and also on the companion web site for the book.

If you have signed a deal memo, check it because the terms of payment may be specified there. Often in this business you will be paid based on a daily rate. Be sure to find out exactly what your rate will be if you haven't quoted a specific rate. Don't forget to ask about how many hours the rate applies to. Is it based on a 10-hr workday, 12-hr workday, or longer? Sometimes you will be asked to work for your rate based on a 14-hr day or even longer. I recommend staying away from these jobs. They are probably low paying, and when you calculate it out you are often making less than minimum wage. As stated in Chapter 4, on union productions and many non-union productions it is common to break down the hour into tenths of an hour. Each six minute block of time equals 0.1 of an hour. This makes it much easier to calculate the total time worked because you will most often finish at odd times and not exactly on the hour. It is also quite common to write the time in military time on your time card. For example, if you finish work at 10:25 p.m., this would be rounded to the nearest tenth of an hour and written as 22.5 on the time card. Table 8.1 lists the times for tenths of an hour conversion.

Table 8.1 Tenths of an Hour Conversion

1–6 minutes = 0.1 hour
7–12 minutes = 0.2 hour
13–18 minutes = 0.3 hour
19–24 minutes = 0.4 hour
25–30 minutes = 0.5 hour
31–36 minutes = 0.6 hour
37–42 minutes = 0.7 hour
43–48 minutes = 0.8 hour
49–54 minutes = 0.9 hour
55–60 minutes = 1.0 hour

Whether you invoice for your services or fill out a time card, you should know what your base hourly rate is along with overtime rates. Tables 8.2, 8.3, and 8.4 show typical daily rates and break them down into hourly rates. Table 8.2 shows the typical daily rates and breaks them down into straight hourly rates based on 8 hours, 10 hours, and 12 hours. In other words, the 8-hr day hourly rate is simply the daily

Table 8.2   Payroll Conversion Table for 8-, 10-, and 12-Hour Base Rate

Daily Rate	Straight Hourly Rate Based on 8 Hours (Daily Rate divided by 8)	1.5×8-Hour Rate	2×8-Hour Rate	Straight Hourly Rate Based on 10 Hours (Daily Rate divided by 10)	1.5×10-Hour Rate	2×10-Hour Rate	Straight Hourly Rate Based on 12 Hours (Daily Rate divided by 12)	1.5×12-Hour Rate	2×12-Hour Rate
$ 50.00	6.25	9.38	12.50	5.00	7.50	10.00	4.17	6.26	8.34
$ 75.00	9.38	14.07	18.76	7.50	11.25	15.00	6.25	9.38	12.50
$ 100.00	12.50	18.75	25.00	10.00	15.00	20.00	8.33	12.50	16.66
$ 125.00	15.63	23.45	31.26	12.50	18.75	25.00	10.42	15.63	20.84
$ 150.00	18.75	28.13	37.50	15.00	22.50	30.00	12.50	18.75	25.00
$ 175.00	21.88	32.82	43.76	17.50	26.25	35.00	14.58	21.87	29.16
$ 200.00	25.00	37.50	50.00	20.00	30.00	40.00	16.67	25.01	33.34
$ 225.00	28.13	42.20	56.26	22.50	33.75	45.00	18.75	28.13	37.50
$ 250.00	31.25	46.88	62.50	25.00	37.50	50.00	20.83	31.25	41.66
$ 275.00	34.38	51.57	68.76	27.50	41.25	55.00	22.92	34.38	45.84
$ 300.00	37.50	56.25	75.00	30.00	45.00	60.00	25.00	37.50	50.00
$ 325.00	40.63	60.95	81.26	32.50	48.75	65.00	27.08	40.62	54.16
$ 350.00	43.75	65.63	87.50	35.00	52.50	70.00	29.17	43.76	58.34
$ 375.00	46.88	70.32	93.76	37.50	56.25	75.00	31.25	46.88	62.50
$ 400.00	50.00	75.00	100.00	40.00	60.00	80.00	33.33	50.00	66.66
$ 425.00	53.13	79.70	106.26	42.50	63.75	85.00	35.42	53.13	70.84
$ 450.00	56.25	84.38	112.50	45.00	67.50	90.00	37.50	56.25	75.00
$ 475.00	59.38	89.07	118.76	47.50	71.25	95.00	39.58	59.37	79.16
$ 500.00	62.50	93.75	125.00	50.00	75.00	100.00	41.67	62.51	83.34

Table 8.3 Payroll Conversion Table—10-Hour Day Rate Converted to 8-Hour Day

Daily Rate for 10-Hour Day	8-Hour Day, Hourly Rate (10-Hour Rate divided by 11)	1.5×8-Hour Rate	2×8-Hour Rate
$ 50.00	4.55	6.83	9.10
$ 75.00	6.82	10.23	13.64
$ 100.00	9.09	13.64	18.18
$ 125.00	11.36	17.04	22.72
$ 150.00	13.64	20.46	27.28
$ 175.00	15.91	23.87	31.82
$ 200.00	18.18	27.27	36.36
$ 225.00	20.45	30.68	40.90
$ 250.00	22.73	34.10	45.46
$ 275.00	25.00	37.50	50.00
$ 300.00	27.27	40.91	54.54
$ 325.00	29.55	44.33	59.10
$ 350.00	31.82	47.73	63.64
$ 375.00	34.09	51.14	68.18
$ 400.00	36.36	54.54	72.72
$ 425.00	38.64	57.96	77.28
$ 450.00	40.91	61.37	81.82
$ 475.00	43.18	64.77	86.36
$ 500.00	45.45	68.18	90.90

rate divided by 8, the 10-hr day hourly rate is the daily rate divided by 10, and so on. Table 8.3 shows the daily rate based on a 10-hr day, with the rate converted to an hourly rate based on 8 hours. Overtime is then paid at the rate of 1½ times your hourly rate after 8 hours. For example, if you are being paid a daily rate of $300, then your hourly rate based on an 8-hr day would be $27.27, and your overtime rate would be $40.91. Then, for a 10-hr day, it calculates as follows: $(8 \times 27.27) + (2 \times 40.91) = \$299.98$, which is approximately $300 or your daily rate. Table 8.4 shows the daily rate based on a 12-hr day with the rate converted to an hourly rate based on 8 hours. Overtime is then paid at the rate of 1½ times your hourly rate after 8 hours. For

Table 8.4 Payroll Conversion Table—12-Hour Day Rate Converted to 8-Hour Day

Daily Rate for 12-Hour Day	8-Hour Day, Hourly Rate (12-Hour Rate divided by 14)	1.5 × 8-Hour Rate	2 × 8-Hour Rate
$ 50.00	3.57	5.36	7.14
$ 75.00	5.36	8.04	10.72
$ 100.00	7.14	10.71	14.28
$ 125.00	8.93	13.40	17.86
$ 150.00	10.71	16.07	21.42
$ 175.00	12.50	18.75	25.00
$ 200.00	14.29	21.44	28.58
$ 225.00	16.07	24.11	32.14
$ 250.00	17.86	26.79	35.72
$ 275.00	19.64	29.46	39.28
$ 300.00	21.43	32.15	42.86
$ 325.00	23.21	34.82	46.42
$ 350.00	25.00	37.50	50.00
$ 375.00	26.79	40.19	53.58
$ 400.00	28.57	42.86	57.14
$ 425.00	30.36	45.54	60.72
$ 450.00	32.14	48.21	64.28
$ 475.00	33.93	50.90	67.86
$ 500.00	35.71	53.57	71.42

example, if you are being paid a daily rate of $300, then your hourly rate based on an 8-hr day would be $21.43, and your overtime rate would be $32.15. Then, for a 12-hr day, it calculates as follows: $(8 \times 21.43) + (4 \times 32.15) = \$300.04$, which is approximately $300 or your daily rate.

The Next Job

After finishing each production job you need to start thinking about what you will do next. But first be sure that everything is cleaned up

from the previous production, all equipment is wrapped and returned, and remaining film stock and expendables are returned to the production company. You also need to be sure that your final time card, time sheet, or independent contractor invoice is completed and submitted to the production company for final payment. When everything is finished with the most recent production, you must decide if you will be taking some time off or if you will immediately start looking for that next job. If you plan on looking for the next job you will most likely be contacting other camera persons with whom you have worked in the past. As stated earlier in this book, the film industry is all about networking. It's important to keep your list of professional contacts up to date so that you can contact them in hopes of getting that next job. Start making calls and sending emails so that you can get started on that next project. But don't forget to take some time off in between, in order to recharge and refresh.

Networking

What you do after a job may be just as important as what you do during the job. Remember that the film industry relies heavily on word of mouth and networking. Stay in touch with the appropriate people after a job so that you won't have to worry about where the next job is coming from. Many of your jobs will come from the recommendations of other crew people who you have worked with. By staying in touch, you will keep your name fresh in their minds, and when the next job comes up, they may call you. It is especially important to stay in touch with the camera crew members who you have worked with. Call them periodically to let them know that you are available for any future projects. Often a Camera Assistant may get a job call, but because of a conflict with another job, he or she will have to turn it down. If you stay in touch with other camera crew people, you may be recommended for a job that another Camera Assistant turned down. Many of my jobs came this way. Also, if you must turn down a job because of a conflicting job, be sure to recommend a fellow Camera Assistant for the position.

And remember, whenever you are forced to turn down a job, be sure to tell the production company that it is because of a conflict with another job. A production company will be more inclined to call you again if they know that you work steadily. Steady work is usually an indication that you are good at what you do.

Here are some things to remember so that you will always get contacted for future work. Always return phone calls and emails in a timely manner. You may be busy at the moment the call comes in, but as soon as you are able return the call. Check your email daily and

reply to important messages immediately, especially if it is about a future job. Don't be inflexible when it comes to your day rate. When asked about my rate I often ask what amount they have in the budget. If the Producer or Production Manager doesn't give me this information then I quote my rate and follow it with, "but I am willing to negotiate." This lets them know what my normal rate is and that I value my work. Always be willing to negotiate, and if they won't pay a fair wage then you have the option of saying no and not taking the job.

After a job, call or email the DP to thank him or her for having you as part of the crew. Let the DP know that you would like to work with him or her again, and ask if you may call from time to time to keep in touch. You may also want to call the production company and express your interest in working with them again. Sometimes the first person to be hired for a job is the most recent person with whom they have spoken. Let's hope that person is you.

Good luck, don't get discouraged, and I wish you all the best for a long and rewarding career in the camera department.

The Freelance Filmmaker and Taxes

Some of the following information applies to things you should do before, during, and after the job but I have chosen to place it in a separate category rather than split it up into three categories. Before I continue I want to make it very clear that I am not a tax professional and the information that I am providing is based on my experience and information that my tax preparers have given me through the years. Tax laws change every year so always check with your accountant or tax preparer for the most current and up-to-date tax information.

When working as an employee you typically receive a W-2 form at the end of the year which shows your gross income as well as any state and federal taxes withheld from your income. If you don't claim the proper number of deductions, you may still owe some taxes at the end of the year but it usually won't be as much as when working as an independent contractor.

When working as an independent contractor you typically receive a 1099 form at the end of the year which shows your gross income. There are no taxes taken out of your pay, but this doesn't mean that you don't owe the taxes. You will still be responsible for them at the end of the year when you pay your income tax. It's a good idea to save a percentage of your independent contractor income so that when tax time comes you are not stuck with a large tax bill.

There are some expenses that you have as an independent contractor that may be claimed as deductions on your income taxes each

year. The most important thing for you to do is to keep accurate and detailed records of all of these so that you have proof in case of an audit. I recommend keeping separate records of all income and expenses when working as an employee and as an independent contractor. Some of your expenses as an employee may be deductible and if you have separate records it will be easier to deal with at the end of the year when it's time to complete your taxes. Save pay stubs for all jobs and keep receipts for all purchases related to your jobs.

See Figures 8.4 and 8.5 for examples of worksheets that you may use in order to keep track of your income and expenses. These worksheets are a combination of a worksheet that I have used through the years and a worksheet that my colleague Leon Sanginiti uses. I would like to especially thank Leon for his help in preparing this section of the book. The worksheets can also be found on the companion web site for the book.

Using the worksheets as a guide, the following are some basic guidelines to help you, but, as I stated earlier, always check with a professional tax preparer who is familiar with the film industry.

Many of the tools, equipment, supplies, and expendables that you purchase for your job can be deducted on your taxes. For example, if you are an Camera Assistant and purchase a Magliner cart to transport your equipment on set, you can claim the cost of the cart. Any expendables you buy, such as camera tape, lens fluid, markers, etc., are deductible.

Certain office and computer-related expenses such as pens, paper, Post-It notes, printer paper, blank CDs or DVDs, computer software, hardware, and other office supplies may be deducted if they are used specifically for your work as a Camera Assistant, etc. You may be using the supplies during production to take notes, make copies, print out camera reports, equipment lists, and other things for the production.

Most of us today have a cell phone. Since many of the jobs you get will come from others with whom you have worked, it is critical that they be able to contact you. The costs of your cell phone that are directly related to work calls may be deducted. If you use the same phone for personal use you will need to keep very accurate records as to the percentage of use that relates to your business. Also if you have a separate phone line in your home and/or a separate fax number in order to receive equipment lists or other documents, those costs are also deductible.

Earlier in this chapter I mentioned that you should have a business card and also a web site to promote yourself. The design and printing costs for the business cards as well as the costs to design and host your web site can be claimed on your taxes. If you are a

Income Worksheet

		Tax Year	Page
Name			SS #
Address			
City		State	Zip
Home Phone	Cell Phone		
Email			

W-2 Wages

Production/Employer/Payroll Co.	Production Title	Wages	Federal Tax	SS Tax	Medicare	State Tax	Local

1099 Wages

Production Co.	Payroll Co.	Production Title	1099 Gross Wages

Figure 8.4 Income worksheet.

Expense Worksheet	Tax Year		Page
Name		SS #	
Address			
City	State	Zip	
Home Phone	Cell Phone		
Email			

CATEGORY	AMOUNT
Work Tools, Equipment & Supplies	
Hand tools	
Work clothing	
Camera related equipment	
Lighting related equipment	
Grip related equipment	
Expendables	
Miscellaneous	
Other	
Office Expense	
Pens, Pencils, Paper, Pads, Post-it Notes, General Office Supplies & Stationery	
Printer ink, Toner, Copy Paper	
Data CDs, Flash Drives, Hard Drives, CD Storage	
Stamps, Labels, Envelopes	
Shipping Supplies, Tape, Storage Boxes,	
Postage & Shipping	
Stamps	
Shipping	
Other Office Expense	
Store Memberships	
Backup Data Service	
Computer Expense	
Hardware	
Software	
Tax Software	
Miscellaneous Computer Supplies	
Communication Expense	
Cell Phone	
Separate Business Phone Line	
Separate Business Fax Line	
Internet Service	
Web Site Domain	

Figure 8.5   Expense worksheet.

Expense Worksheet	Tax Year	Page
Name	**SS #**	
CATEGORY		**AMOUNT**
Advertising		
Business Cards		
Web Site Hosting		
Professional Videos, CDs and DVDs		
Local Film Guide Fees		
Print Advertising		
Miscellaneous Expenses		
Union Dues		
Accounting Fees		
Legal Fees		
Memberships in Professional Organizations		
Education &Training Fees		
Trade Publication Subscriptions		
Business Credit Card Finance Charges		
Licenses		
Job Search Fees		
Movie Tickets		
Video Rentals		
Video Purchases		
Business Travel		
Air, train or bus fare		
Hotel & motel expenses		
Rental vehicle		
Taxi & other transportation costs		
Gas, oil & other auto expense while traveling		
Computer rental while traveling		
Internet access while traveling		
Phone calls while traveling		
Tips other than for meals		
Dry cleaning		
Costs of shipping baggage, supplies & equipment necessary for business		
Costs of storing baggage, supplies & equipment during business travel		
Meals & Entertainment – 50% deductible		
Meals while traveling for business		
Admission & registration for trade shows, conventions, conferences		
Tickets, food, drinks for entertaining business associates		
Hosting a business dinner at your home		
Hosting a business dinner at a restaurant or private club		
Meals for potential customers		

Figure 8.5 (*continued*)

Expense Worksheet		Tax Year		Page	
Name			SS #		
CATEGORY					**AMOUNT**
Vehicle Information					
Vehicle Make, Model & Year					
Odometer Reading		Start of Year		End of Year	
Total Business Mileage					
Vehicle Expenses					
Gasoline					
Oil					
Tires					
Repairs and Maintenance					
Vehicle Insurance					
License/Registration Fees					
State Smog Inspection Fees					
State Inspection Fees					
Garage Rent					
Other Vehicle Expenses					
Towing Charges					
Auto Club Dues					
Washing, waxing, detailing					
Accessories (Steering wheel covers, seat covers, cup holders, etc.)					
Small parts (Bulbs, wipers, etc.)					
Car & truck repair tools					
Tools for fixing flat tires					
Vehicle Lease Payments					
Vehicle Interest if Financed					
Vehicle Property Taxes					
Business Parking Fees					
Business Tolls					
Business Local Transportation					
Home Office Expenses – Direct					
Maintenance & Repairs (painting, etc)					
Furnishings					
Phone & Internet (If on separate lines)					
Home Office Expenses – Indirect (Percentage of home devoted to business)					
Home mortgage or Rent					
Mortgage Interest					
Homeowner's/Renters Insurance					
Home Utilities					
Home maintenance and repairs					
Depreciation					

Figure 8.5   (*continued*)

member of the union or a professional organization, the union dues and membership fees are business expenses that are deductible. Any specialty magazines or trade publications that are directly related to your business may be claimed. For example, I subscribe to *American Cinematographer* and am able to claim the subscription fees on my income taxes.

Many of us attend various workshops, seminars, and industry expos in order to stay up to date on the most current equipment and technology. Any costs related to those events, such as registration fees, may be claimed on your taxes. If you travel for any of these events, be sure to keep records of all of your travel expenses. Rental cars, hotel costs, meals, and more may also be claimed as deductions on your yearly taxes.

When working as an independent contractor there are many vehicle expenses that you can also claim. You should keep detailed records of your mileage to and from film jobs. Use a small notebook or purchase a vehicle expense record book at a local office supply store. Your mileage to and from the job can be claimed, when working as an independent contractor. Keep records of gas and oil, maintenance fees, supplies, registration costs, lease payments, interest, etc., so you can claim them at tax time.

As a filmmaker you may also claim the costs of any movies you attend, and videos you rent or purchase. My tax accountant in Los Angeles once explained it to me that as a Camera Operator it was important for me to view other works so that I can better do my job. At the time he listed it as Professional Viewings on my taxes.

One additional tax-related item that I hesitate to go into detail about is a home office. Many of us may have a separate room in our home where we store our film-related equipment and conduct business. If you have a separate phone line and computer in this room and *only* conduct film-related business on this phone and computer, you may be able to claim the space as a "home office" on your taxes. There are a few rules regarding the use of a home office and one of these is that it must be used exclusively for your business purposes and no personal business. Also no personal items may be kept in the room in order for it to be claimed as a home office.

As freelance filmmakers our actual work is done outside of the home, but we still devote time in a home office to billing for our services, making and receiving work-related phone calls, updating our reels and résumés, faxing, emailing, etc. When claiming a home office deduction you need to calculate the percentage of your home that is devoted to the business use by dividing the square footage of the home office space by the total square footage of your home. You should also keep separate records of the expenses dealing with

the space. There are essentially two types of expenses and can be deducted, "direct" expenses and "indirect" expenses. Direct expenses are those that directly relate to the office space itself, like painting, furniture, phone and internet bills, maintenance, etc. Indirect expenses are those that relate to your overall home expenses, such as home utilities, mortgage payments, interest, insurance, etc. The indirect expenses are calculated based on the percentage of your home that is used for the home office. Claiming a home office can be very tricky so I strongly recommend that you consult a tax preparer who is familiar with our industry.

As you can see from the previous paragraphs along with the details included on the worksheets, there are many expenses that you can claim on your taxes. I'll remind you again because it is very important. Because the tax laws change each year it is very important that you always check with your tax professional before claiming any expenses on your taxes. I urge you to use a tax professional who has experience with and is familiar with the film industry.

If you choose to do your own taxes each year using one of the commercially available tax preparation software packages, be sure to read and follow the current tax regulations. All of the previous information is based on what I have been told over the years by the professional tax accountants that have assisted in the preparation of my yearly tax returns. Again, I am not a tax professional and I don't claim to be, so *always* check with a professional tax preparer.

Appendix A

Film Stock

Currently there is only one manufacturer of professional motion picture film stock: Eastman Kodak. Kodak offers a wide variety of film stocks for both 16 mm and 35 mm professional cinematography. It also has film for Super 8 mm use and you should check the Kodak web site for more information on these stocks. The 16 mm and 35 mm film stocks may be available in color and black and white, in negative and reversal. Emulsions are available in slow-, medium-, and high-speed exposure index (EI) ratings. Some of the film stocks are balanced for shooting in tungsten light (3200° K), and some are balanced for shooting in daylight (5600° K). Table A.1 contains a listing of the current film stocks available from Eastman Kodak at publication time.

Rolls of film come in various lengths because of the different camera and magazine sizes in use today. Motion picture film is available on plastic cores or daylight spools, sometimes referred to as camera spools. See Figures 4.5 and 4.6 in Chapter 4 for illustrations of plastic cores and daylight spools. Table A.2 lists the standard packaging sizes for motion picture film. When choosing a film stock, check with the manufacturer or distributor to be sure that it is available in the size and type that will suit your filmmaking needs. Not all films are available in all roll sizes. Also be sure that the sizes of the rolls you order correspond to the camera and/or the size of the camera magazines that you will be using. If you plan to use daylight spools, be sure that the camera has the ability to accept internal loads or that you are able to load daylight spools into magazines. And remember that film is available in double perf and single perf formats so be sure that you know which you are ordering.

I do not recommend using daylight spools in a magazine, although you can do it. When using a daylight spool in a magazine, the flanges of the spool will often rub against the cover of the magazine, causing unnecessary noise. If you will be using the Aaton A-Minima 16 mm camera, be aware that it only takes 200-ft daylight spools that are specially designed for the camera by Eastman Kodak

Table A.1   Professional Motion Picture Film Stock

Film Stock		Format	Color Balance	EI Tungsten	EI Daylight
EASTMAN KODAK COLOR NEGATIVE					
7201	Vision 2 50D	16 mm	Daylight	12 w/80A	50
7203	Vision 3 50D	16 mm	Daylight	12 w/80A	50
7207	Vision 3 250D	16 mm	Daylight	64 w/80A	250
7213	Vision 3 200T	16 mm	Tungsten	200	125 w/85
7219	Vision 3	16 mm	Tungsten	500	320 w/85
7230	500T	16 mm	Tungsten	500	320 w/85
5201	Vision 2 50D	35 mm	Daylight	12 w/80A	50
5203	Vision 3 50D	35 mm	Daylight	12 w/80A	50
5207	Vision 3 250D	35 mm	Daylight	64 w/80A	250
5213	Vision 3 200T	35 mm	Tungsten	200	125 w/85
5219	Vision 3	35 mm	Tungsten	500	320 w/85
5230	500T	35 mm	Tungsten	500	320 w/85
EASTMAN KODAK COLOR REVERSAL					
7285	Ektachrome	16 mm	Daylight	25 w/80A	100
5285	Ektachrome	35 mm	Daylight	25 w/80A	100
EASTMAN KODAK BLACK & WHITE NEGATIVE					
7222	Double-X	16 mm	B & W	200	250
5222	Double-X	35 mm	B & W	200	250
EASTMAN KODAK BLACK & WHITE REVERSAL					
7266	Tri-X	16 mm	B & W	160	200

Table A.2   Film Stock Packaging Sizes

16mm	35mm
100ft Daylight Spool	100ft Daylight Spool
200ft Daylight Spool	200ft Plastic Core
400ft Daylight Spool	400ft Plastic Core
400ft Plastic Core	1000ft Plastic Core
800ft Plastic Core	

Company. See the Eastman Kodak web site for specific films that are available for the Aaton A-Minima.

When filming on distant locations, it may be necessary to ship the film to the lab for processing. You will often have many cans of film from each day's shooting that must be carefully packed into boxes for shipping. Chapter 4 gives specific instructions on how to properly pack and ship your film from a distant location. To help you better prepare your film cans for shipping, Table A.3 gives the individual weight of a full can of film for all sizes that are currently available in both 16mm and 35mm.

Table A.3   Individual Film Can Weights

16mm		35mm	
100ft Daylight Spool	6.5 oz.	100ft Daylight Spool	13 oz.
200ft Daylight Spool	9.6 oz.	200ft Core	1lb 3 oz.
400ft Daylight Spool	1lb 11 oz.	400ft Core	2lb 7 oz.
400ft Core	1lb 10 oz.	1000ft Core	5lb 13 oz.
800ft Core	2lb 7 oz.		

Appendix B

Equipment, Software, and Apps

As an Assistant Cameraman you should have a working knowledge of all of the equipment that you will use on a daily basis. This section contains basic listings of the various cameras, accessories, filters, heads, tripods, and more that you should be familiar with. These lists are by no means complete and only include the most commonly used equipment that you may be working with. Equipment is being added, updated, and even discontinued on a regular basis, so it is not possible or practical to try to list every piece of equipment that you may or may not be working with. In addition to the equipment lists I have included information on some of the software that is available to the Cinematographer along with some of the most popular apps that are currently available for the iPhone, iPod Touch and iPad, and other smart phones or electronic devices.

There are a few different ways to become familiar with a new piece of equipment. One is to learn at an industry-related seminar that may be offered by a vendor, one of the union locals, or some other organization. Another is to contact a rental house and ask if they would show you the item at their convenience. And finally you can be hired on a film and obtain on-the-job training and experience with a particular piece of equipment. Whenever a new piece of equipment is introduced into the industry, you should make every effort to learn about it as quickly as possible. You never know if that next job call may be using the new item, and, if you are familiar with it, your chances of landing the job are much greater. The more you know the more jobs you may get.

Often when a new piece of equipment is introduced, the manufacturer may offer a seminar or workshop to industry professionals so that they can get introduced to the new item and become familiar with it. The International Cinematographers Guild and Society of Camera Operators as well as many camera rental companies periodically

conduct seminars and workshops to introduce filmmakers to specific pieces of equipment. Many manufacturers offer an instruction or operations manual for specific equipment. The manual may be free or may be available for purchase. In any case, I recommend having manuals for any equipment that you will be working with. I have an extensive library of film books along with camera and equipment manuals that I refer to on a regular basis. You cannot be expected to know everything about a specific piece of equipment, and if you have the manual, you may be able to troubleshoot any problems without having to contact the rental house. Many camera manuals are available for download at the manufacturer web site or the companion web site for this book. Please go to www.cameraassistantmanual.com in order to access many of these manuals.

When working with a piece of equipment for the first time it is a good idea to check it out with the rental house so that you are familiar with how it works. Most rental houses are willing to help and show you any piece of equipment that you are not familiar with. But don't just walk into a rental house and expect them to drop everything to show you a particular piece of equipment. Call them ahead of time. Ask them when it would be convenient for you to come in so that they can show it to you. This is especially important if the equipment is being rented from that rental house. If you establish a good relationship with them, they will be more willing to help you out in the future.

CAMERAS

The following is a list of the most commonly used 16 mm, 35 mm, 65 mm, digital and video cameras in use today. Many of the cameras listed in previous editions of this book are not listed here because they are not used much anymore or have been discontinued by the manufacturer. Remember that equipment is changing every day and by the time you read this, one or more of these pieces of equipment may no longer be available for rental or may not even exist. If you are not familiar with a specific camera or other piece of equipment, ask the rental house personnel to show it to you and explain how it works. Chapter 7 contains simple illustrations and threading diagrams of most of the film cameras and their magazines listed here. Keep in mind that the illustrations in Chapter 7 are not meant to teach you how to thread cameras or magazines. They are intended only as a guide for you to refer to in case you have forgotten how to thread a particular camera or magazine.

16 mm Cameras

Aaton A-Minima
Aaton Xterà
Aaton XTR-Plus
Aaton XTR-Prod
Arriflex 16 SR1
Arriflex 16 SR2 (regular and high speed)
Arriflex 16 SR3 and SR3 Advanced (regular and high speed)
Arriflex 416
Arriflex 416 Plus (regular and high speed)
Ikonoscope A-Cam
Panavision Panaflex 16
Photo-Sonics Actionmaster 500 (high speed)
Photo-Sonics 1VN (high speed)

35 mm Cameras

Aaton 35-III
Aaton Penelope
Arriflex 235
Arriflex 35 BL3 and BL4
Arriflex 35-3
Arriflex 435
Arriflex 435 Advanced
Arriflex 535A and 535B
Arriflex Arricam Lite
Arriflex Arricam Studio
Bell & Howell Eyemo
Moviecam Compact
Moviecam Super America
Moviecam SL
Panavision Panaflex Golden
Panavision Panaflex Golden G-II
Panavision Panaflex Lightweight II
Panavision Panaflex Millennium
Panavision Panaflex Millennium XL2
Panavision Panaflex Panastar I and II (high speed)
Panavision Panaflex Platinum
Photo-Sonics 4B/4C (high speed)
Photo-Sonics 4E/ER (high speed)
Photo-Sonics 4ML (high speed)

65 mm Cameras

Arriflex 765
Panavision Panaflex 65 Studio Camera
Panavision 65 Handheld Camera
Panavision 65 High Speed Camera

Digital and Video Cameras

Arriflex Alexa
Arriflex D-21
Canon 5D DSLR
Canon 7D DSLR
Canon XL2
Canon GL2
Canon XL H1
Canon XL-H1A
Panasonic AG-AF100
Panasonic AG-HVX200
Panasonic AG-DVX100
Panasonic AG-HPX170
Panasonic AJ-HPX2000
Panasonic AJ-HPX3000
Panasonic AJ-HDC27H
Panasonic AJ-HPX2700
Panasonic AJ-HPX3700
Panasonic AJ-HDX900
Panasonic AG-HPX500
Panavision Genesis
Phantom 65 Gold
Phantom Flex
RED Epic
RED MX-1
RED One
RED Scarlet
Sony F23 HD
Sony F35 HD
Sony F65 HD
Sony PMW-EX1
Sony PMW-EX3
Sony HDW-F900
Sony PDW-510

Sony SRW-9000
Sony PMW-F3
Thomson Viper HD
Weisscam HS-2

CAMERA LENSES AND ACCESSORIES

In addition to becoming familiar with the cameras you will be working with, you should also have a thorough understanding of the basic
accessories that are used with virtually all professional motion picture
cameras. The camera is only one part of the entire package. The more
you know about the lenses and basic accessories, as well as the many
advanced accessories, the more jobs you will have.

Lenses and Lens Accessories

Rather than list each individual lens, I am listing only some of the
specialty lenses along with lens accessories that you should become
familiar with. Refer to the Film Camera Equipment Checklist in
Appendix C (Figure C.1) for a more complete listing of lenses and lens
accessories currently in use.

1.4X Extender
2X Extender
Arriflex Alura Zooms
Arriflex Master Primes
Arriflex Compact Primes
Arriflex Lightweight Zoom
Arriflex Ultra 16 Lenses
Arriflex Ultra Primes
Arriflex Variable Primes
Arriflex Shift and Tilt Lenses
Aspheron Attachment for 9.5 mm and 12 mm Zeiss Lenses
Century Precision Optics Periscope
Innovision Probe
Low Angle Prism
Mesmerizer
Mutar Attachment for Zeiss 10 mm–100 mm Zoom Lens
Panavision Lightweight Zooms
Panavision Frazier Lens System
Revolution Lens System

Shift and Tilt Bellows Lens System
Snorkle Lens

Camera Accessories

Arriflex Arricam Speed Control Box
Arriflex Arricam Timing Shift Box
Arriflex 35-3 Hand Held Door
Arriflex 35-3 Video Door
Arriflex 435 Single Frame Shutter
Arriflex External Sync Unit (ESU-1)
Arriflex External Display (EXD-1)
Arriflex Hand Crank (HC-1)
Arriflex Iris Control Unit (ICU)
Arriflex Integrated Video System (IVS)
Arriflex Lens Control System (LCS)
Arriflex Lens Data Archive (LDA)
Arriflex Remote Control Unit (RCU-1)
Arriflex Remote Switch (RS-4)
Arriflex Steadicam Magazines (Arricam, 35-3, 435, and 535)
Arriflex Shoulder Magazines (Arricam, 35-3 and 435)
Arriflex Wireless Focus Unit (WFU-3)
Arriflex Wireless Remote Control (WRC-2)
Arriflex Wireless Zoom Unit (WZU-3)
Arriflex Wireless Compact Unit (WCU-3)
Auxiliary Carry Handle
Camera Barney
Camera Hand Grip
Capping Shutter
CE Crystal Speed Control
Clamp-on Matte Box or Lens Shade
cmotion Lens Control System
Coaxial Video Cable
Director's Viewfinder
Eyebrow
Eyepiece Extension
Eyepiece Heater
Eyepiece Leveler
Film/Video Synchronizer
Focus Whip
Follow Focus
Hard Mattes

HMI Speed Control
Image Shaker
Intervalometer
Iris Rods
Junction Box
Lens Light
Lens Shade
Magazine Barney
Matte Box
Medium Iris Rods
Microforce Handle for Sachtler
Microforce Motor
Microforce Zoom Control
Obie Light
Panavision Digital Remote Switch
Panavision Focus, T-Stop, Zoom, Speed, Aperture Controller (FTZSAC)
Panavision LAC
Panavision Panaflasher
Panavision Remote Digital Control (RDC)
Panavision Zoom Control
Panavision Zoom Holder
Precision Speed Control
Preston F I + Z
Rain Cover
Rain Deflector
Remote Switch
Rubber Donuts
Sliding Balance Plate
Speed Crank
Utility Base Plate
Video Monitors
Video Tap
Zoom Bridge Support

On-Board Video Monitors

More and more assistants are using on-board video monitors, especially in this day of digital productions. The on-board monitor is often needed to help the assistant judge the focus of a shot or simply to know what the camera is framing for critical focus racks, etc. There are many different types and sizes of monitors available and it is up to the assistant which one they may want to use. On-board video

monitors are a common part of the Camera Assistant's toolkit or ditty bag, but they may also be rented with the camera gear.

Astro 3004
Astro 3014
ikan D7w
ikan D7
ikan D5w
ikan D5
ikan VX7i
ikan VH8
ikan MR7
ikan VK7
ikan VK5
ikan VX9e
ikan VL7
ikan V8000T
ikan V8000W
ikan VG7
Manhattan 071A2
Manhattan HD089B2
Manhattan HD089C2
Manhattan HD5
Marshall V-LCD50
Marshall V-LCD651STX
Marshall V-LCD70XHB
Marshall V-LCD70XP
Panasonic BT-LH910GJ
Small HD DP4
Small HD DP6
Transvideo Cinemonitor IIIa
Transvideo Rainbow Xtreme
Transvideo Rainbow II
Transvideo Starlite Color
TV Logic LQM-071W
TV Logic LVM-074W
TV Logic LVM-084W
TV Logic LVM-091W
TV Logic VFM-056W

Specialized Camera Accessories

There are so many specialized accessories available to the camera department that it would be nearly impossible to describe all of them

here. I have chosen to give a brief description of some of the most common camera accessories, including some that I have used and am familiar with. Remember, if there is any piece of equipment that you are not familiar with, you should check with the rental house when renting and prepping the camera package.

Arriflex Remote Control Unit (RCU-1)

The Arriflex Remote Control Unit or RCU is a handheld controller that allows you to operate the camera from a remote head, with the RCU displaying all camera information. The RCU allows you to perform speed changes and should be used along with the Iris Control Unit so that you may also compensate the f-stop. You may dial in a speed change by hand during the shot or you may preprogram a speed ramp to occur over a period of time. The display of the RCU is similar to the display on the camera. The RCU works with most of the current generation of Arriflex cameras, including the 16 SR3, 416, 535, 535B, 435 and 235.

Arriflex External Display (EXD-1)

The Arriflex External Display is a small, handheld remote device that enables the assistant to view all of the information that is shown in the on-camera display. The EXD-1 works with all models of the 16SR3, 416, 235, 435, and 535. It shows camera speed, shutter angle, and contains the Mode, Sel, Set, Run and Phase buttons that are also found on the side of the camera.

Arriflex Wireless Remote Control (WRC-2)

The Arriflex Wireless Remote Control Unit or WRC-2 works with all of the current generation of Arriflex cameras, including the Arricam, 435 Xtreme, 435 Advanced, 435ES, 235, 535B, SR3 and 416. It has all of the functions found in the RCU-1 and WRC-1 along with many new features. The WRC-2's range of functions adapts to the camera it is being used with and you are not restricted by the use of cables to connect the unit to the camera. The WRC-2 allows you to perform speed changes, shutter angle changes, and t-stop changes, all from a small handheld unit.

Arriflex Iris Control Unit (ICU-1)

Any speed changes that you may do with the RCU will require you to also compensate your t-stop accordingly. This is accomplished by using the Arriflex Iris Control Unit or ICU. Whenever using the RCU, you should also use the ICU. The motor unit of the ICU attaches to the

iris rods of the camera and then engages the gears of the aperture ring. After careful calibration, the ICU works along with the RCU so that whenever a speed change is performed, the proper aperture exposure change is done along with it. The ICU works with many of the current generation as well as some of the older Arriflex cameras, including the 16 SR2, 16 SR3, 35-3, 535, 535B, 435, 435ES, and 765.

Arriflex Wireless Compact Unit 3 (WCU-3)

Similar to the Wireless Remote Control, the Wireless Compact Unit WCU-3 allows the user to remotely control camera on/off, focus, and aperture. It contains an adjustable hand grip, backlit buttons, and may be used either wirelessly or with an optional cable. The WCU-3 works with most of the current generation of Arriflex cameras, including the Arricam Studio, Arricam Lite, 435, 416 Plus, and 416 Plus HS.

cmotion

The cmotion system is a lightweight, ergonomic, modular lens control system that allows you to control focus, t-stop, and zoom on a variety of film and digital camera systems. Depending on the configuration, it can control up to four separate motors, giving the assistant control over all lens functions. If working in 3D you can slave the motors together, giving you control of up to eight motors.

Combined with the cdisplay II, the assistant can now see exactly what is happening on the compact 4.3-in. touch screen display, which displays all pertinent lens data. More and more Camera Assistants are choosing the cmotion lens control system over one manufactured by either Arriflex or Panavision.

Panavision Focus, T-stop, Zoom, Speed, Aperture Controller—FTZSAC

The Panavision FTZSAC system is a specially designed modular unit that gives you control over the three lens variables: focus, t-stop, and zoom. By using this device along with the Smart Shutter accessory, you can now control five different camera variables. The FTZSAC system can be used on any Panavision Panaflex camera system, including the high-speed Panastar cameras and the 16 mm Panaflex 16.

Panavision Remote Digital Control (RDC)

The Panavision RDC is a specially designed control for use by the Camera Assistant. It can be used as a wireless control or it may be hardwired to the camera. The RDC can be used with most of the

Panavision film cameras and controls the focus, t-stop, camera speed, shutter angle, and speed ramps. It contains an LCD screen that displays much of the camera information and can also display a video image.

CAMERA FILTERS

A wide variety of filters are available for motion picture cameras. Each filter has its own specific effect and is chosen based on the Cinematographer's preference. They may be used to adjust the color balance or to give a certain look to the image such as softening the image or adding a fog-like effect. Filters are available in many different sizes, as well as varying densities, with the lower numbers being lighter density and the higher numbers being heavier density. The most common camera filters for motion picture photography are manufactured by Tiffen, Harrison & Harrison, Mitchell, Schneider Optics, Formatt Filters, Ltd., Wilson Film Services, and Fries Engineering. The following are the various sizes that most of the filters are available in and also the most commonly used filters for motion picture photography. The numbers following some of the filters indicate their available densities. The smaller numbers indicate a very light effect and the larger numbers indicate a heavier effect. For example, a Diffusion ⅛ would have a lesser effect on the image than a Diffusion 2.

Filter Sizes

40.5 mm round
48 mm round
Series 9—3½ in. round
4½ in. round
138 mm—5½ in. round
3 in. × 3 in. square
4 in. × 4 in. square
4 in. × 5.65 in. Panavision
5.65 in. × 5.65 in. square.
5 in. × 6 in.
6.6 in. × 6.6 in. square

Filters

85, 85N3, 85N6, 85N9, 85B, 85C, 85 Pola
85B, 85BN3, 85BN6, 85BN9, 85B Pola

ND3, ND6, ND9, ND12

80A, 80B, 80C

81A, 81B, 81C, 81EF

82, 82A, 82B, 82C

812 Warming

Absorptive ND3, Absorptive ND6, Absorptive ND9

Black Diffusion/FX—½, 1, 2, 3, 4, 5

Black Dot Texture Screens—1, 2, 3, 4, 5

Black Frost—⅛, ¼, ½, 1, 2

Black Net—1, 2, 3, 4, 5

Black Pro Mist—⅛, ¼, ½, 1, 2, 3, 4, 5

Black Soft Net—1, 2, 3, 4, 5

Black Supafrost—00, 00+, 0, 0+, 1, 1+

Bronze Glimmerglass—1, 2, 3, 4, 5

Classic Soft—⅛, ¼, ½, 1, 2

Clear (Optical Flat)

Color Compensating—Blue, Cyan, Green, Magenta, Red, Yellow

Color Grads—Cool Blue, Red, Green, Blue, Cyan, Yellow, Magenta, Pink, Sunset, Sepia, Chocolate, Tobacco, Cranberry, Plum, Tangerine, Straw, Grape, Skyfire, Twilight, Tropic Blue, Amber, Gold, Paradise Blue, Sapphire Blue, Storm Blue

Cool Day for Night

Coral—⅛, ¼, ½, 1, 2, 3, 4, 5, 6, 7, 8

Coral Grad—⅛, ¼, ½, 1, 2, 3, 4, 5

Day for Night

Diffusion—½, 1, 1½, 2, 2½, 3

Digital Diffusion/FX—¼, ½, 1, 2, 3, 4, 5

Digital HT

Digital HV

Diopters—+½, +1, +1½, +2, +3

Double Fog—⅛, ¼, ½, 1, 2, 3, 4, 5

Enhancer

Fluorescent Light Correction—FLD (daylight), FLB (tungsten)

Fog—⅛, ¼, ½, 1, 2, 3, 4, 5

Glimmerglass—1, 2, 3, 4, 5

Gold Diffusion/FX—½, 1, 2, 3, 4, 5

Haze 1, Haze 2

IR—T1/2, T1, IRND, Hot Mirror, Hot Mirror IR, Hot Mirror IRND, 80C Hot Mirror, 80D Hot Mirror

LLD

Low Contrast—⅛, ¼, ½, 1, 2, 3, 4, 5

Low Light Ultra Contrast—1, 2, 3, 4

Mitchell Diffusion—A, B, C, D, E

Monochrome Day for Night

Neutral Blended Ratio Attenuator—1, 1½, 2, 2½, 3
ND3 Grad, ND6 Grad, ND9 Grad, ND12 Grad (Hard Edge and Soft
   Edge)
Nude/FX—1, 2, 3, 4, 5, 6
Polarizing—Linear, Circular
Sky 1A
Smoque—1, 2, 3, 4
Soft Centric—¼, ⅓, ½, 1, 2
Soft Contrast—1, 2, 3, 4, 5
Soft FX—1, 2, 3, 4, 5
Softnet—Black, White, Red, Skintone—1, 2, 3, 4, 5
Solid Color—Red, Green, Blue, Cyan, Yellow, Magenta, Grape,
   Plum, Sepia, Chocolate, Tobacco, Tangerine, Cranberry, Tropic
   Blue, Straw, Antique Suede, Gold, Cool Blue, Storm Blue
Split Diopters—+½, +1, +1½, +2, +3
Star—4 pt., 6 pt., 8 pt. (available in 1 mm, 2 mm, 3 mm, or 4 mm
   grid pattern)
Supafrost—00, 00+, 0, 0+, 1, 1+
Tru Pol
Ultra Contrast—⅛, ¼, ½, 1, 2, 3, 4, 5
Ultra Pol
UV
UV Haze
UV 410
Warm Black Frost—⅛, ¼, ½, 1, 2
Warm Black Pro Mist—⅛, ¼, ½, 1, 2
Warm Classic Soft—⅛, ¼, ½, 1, 2
Warm Pro Mist—⅛, ¼, ½ , 1, 2
Warm Soft FX—½, 1, 2, 3, 4, 5
Warm White Frost—⅛, ¼, ½, 1, 2
White Frost—⅛, ¼, ½, 1, 2
White Net—1, 2, 3, 4, 5
White Pro Mist—⅛, ¼, ½, 1, 2, 3, 4, 5

Filters for Black-and-White Cinematography

#8 Yellow
#11 Green
#12 Yellow
#15 Deep Yellow
#16 Orange
#21 Orange

#23A Light Red
#25 Red
#29 Dark Red
#47 Blue
#47B Dark Blue
#58 Green

HEADS AND TRIPODS

In addition to having a working knowledge of the cameras, accessories, and filters in use today, a Camera Assistant should know the various heads and tripods on which the cameras may be mounted. The following are the most commonly used heads and tripods.

Fluid Heads

Cartoni C-20
Cartoni C-40
Cartoni C-60
Cartoni C-20 Dutch Head
Cartoni C-40 Dutch Head
Cartoni Lambda
Cartoni Master
Cartoni Omega
Cartoni Sigma
O'Connor 120EX
O'Connor 120EXe
O'Connor 1030D
O'Connor 1030DS
O'Connor 2065
O'Connor 2575
O'Connor 100 and 100C
O'Connor 50 D
O'Connor 50-200
Ronford Baker Fluid 7 MK III
Ronford Baker Fluid 7 MK IV
Ronford Baker Fluid 7 MK IV 3-Axis
Ronford Baker Fluid 2015
Ronford Baker Fluid 2003
Ronford Baker Fluid 2004
Sachtler Cine 7 + 7

Sachtler Studio 9 + 9
Sachtler Cine 30 HD
Sachtler Cine 75 HD
Sachtler Video 25 Plus
Sachtler Video 60 Plus Studio
Sachtler Video 75 Plus
Sachtler Video 90
Sachtler Dutch Head
Tango Swing Head
Vinten Pro 10
Vinten Vision 3AS
Vinten Vision 5AS
Vinten Vision 8AS
Vinten Vision 10AS
Vinten Vision 100
Vinten Vision 250
Weaver-Steadman 2-Axis
Weaver-Steadman 3-Axis
Weaver-Steadman Multi-Axis

Gear Heads

Arriflex Arrihead
Cinema Products Mini-Worrall
Cinema Products Worrall
GearNex
Mitchell Lightweight
NCE/Ultrascope MK III
Panavision Panahead
Panavision Super Panahead
Technovision Technohead MK III

Tripods

Bazooka
Gimble Tripod
O'Connor Wooden Tripod with Mitchell Flat Top Casting—standard and baby
O'Connor Wooden Tripod with Ball Top Casting—standard and baby

Panavision Panapod with Mitchell Flat Top Casting—standard and baby

Ronford Aluminum Tripod with Mitchell Flat Top Casting—standard and baby

Ronford Aluminum Tripod with Ball Top Casting—standard and baby

Sachtler Aluminum Tripod with Ball Top Casting—standard and baby

Ti Stix Titanium Tripod with Mitchell Flat Top Casting—standard and baby

Ti Stix Titanium Tripod with Ball Top Casting—standard and baby

Miscellaneous Heads, Camera Mounts, or Mounting Platforms

Camera Slider
Cardellini Head Lock
Cinesaddle
Dutch Head
Gyro Stabilizer
Hi-Hat
Low-Hat
Power Pod
Rocker Plate
Skate Cam
Steadybag
Tilt Plate
vBag

SOFTWARE AND APPS

Software

There are a number of software applications available for budgeting, scheduling, editing, and postproduction work. Not much is out there for Cinematographers or Camera Assistants. One software application that is very useful for the camera department, especially the Cinematographer, is from Tiffen, one of the premier manufacturers of camera filters for film and digital cameras. The Tiffen DFX Software is a very useful tool when trying to decide what filters to use for your

project. With the software installed on your laptop or desktop you are able to simulate the look of many of the most popular Tiffen filters, specialized lenses, lighting and photographic effects as well as many lab processes. Using your digital still camera you can take location photos, test photos of sets, makeup effects, wardrobe and more, import them into your computer, and using the Tiffen DFX software you can overlay any number of filters over the image to see the effect. This can be extremely helpful in preproduction when determining the equipment package and what filters you may want to order, and also during production when you are not sure which filter to use for a particular shot. It can be extremely helpful when discussing the shot with a Director because it allows you to show the Director how the shot will look with various filters. The software can be purchased directly from the Tiffen filter web site at www.tiffen.com; click on DFX Sofware on the left side of the screen.

Apps

These days many of us have some type of smart phone or other electronic device, and there are many cinematography-related apps available for these devices. Because of ever changing technology I will mention only a few of them here, because by the time you read this, as with equipment, some may no longer exist. Most of the apps listed below are for the iPhone, iPod Touch, or iPad. While there may be cinematography apps available for other devices, in my research I have been unable to locate very many of them. I have indicated those that are available for multiple devices. For a more complete discussion and listing of cinematography-specific applications for your iPhone, iPod Touch, or iPad, please check the companion web site for the book at www.cameraassistantmanual.com, which will be updated on a regular basis.

AJA DataCalc (iPhone, iPod Touch, and iPad)

The AJA DataCalc computes storage requirements for professional audio and video media. The application works with many of the most popular video formats, including Apple ProRes, DVCProHD, HDV, XDCAM, DV, CineForm, REDCODE, Avid DNxHD.

Artemis Director's Viewfinder (iPhone, iPod Touch, iPad, and Android)

Artemis is a digital director's viewfinder for the iPhone and the new iPod Touch with built-in camera. It works in the same way that a

traditional director's viewfinder works but with more features. You can select a camera along with a specific aspect ratio and lenses, and the app allows you to compose shots with the same field of view as you will be shooting with. You can also save the images, which is ideal for location scouting.

Crew Time Card

By entering all the specific information regarding the job, including rate of pay, guaranteed hours, etc., you can generate an industry standard time card which calculates your wages, meal penalties, overtime pay, and more. We all must complete time cards when working in this business and the Crew Time Card app saves you time by doing all the calculations for you. This is a great application for anybody working in the film and television industry.

FilmCalc (iPhone, iPod Touch, and iPad)

The Film Calculator is a useful app for Directors of Photography, Camera Assistants, Still Photographers, and more. It allows you to calculate the following: depth of field, focal length to lens angle, lens angle to focal length, diopter needed for macro shot, time to film length, shooting time to screen time, and HMI flicker free speeds, just to name a few. Film Calculator is also available for Windows and Mac OS desktop and laptop computers.

Helios Sun Position Calculator (iPhone, iPod Touch, and iPad)

This is a sun position calculator that will graphically represent the position of the sun, on any given day, in any given place. It was designed as an aid to Cinematographers working in natural light, and who need to plan their filming around the constantly changing character of sunlight.

Kodak Cinema Tools (iPhone, iPod Touch, iPad, and Android)

This app contains a depth-of-field calculator, film calculator, film term glossary, and contact tool. The depth-of-field calculator is designed to be used with any film format, along with an f-stop range from f/1.4 to f/22. The film calculator allows you to determine the running time for any length of film in any format. You have the option of entering the film length in either feet or meters. The glossary provides access to an extensive listing of filmmaking terminology. The contact tool allows you to contact any Kodak film rep with a simple

tap of a button. You can also browse the Kodak directory of world-wide offices as well as locate film labs near your specific location. And if you are not sure what all that information is on a Kodak film can label, it contains a feature called "How to Read a Film Can Label," along with a breakdown of the different colors of tape used to seal Kodak film cans.

Panascout (iPhone, iPod Touch, and iPad)

With the first photography app from Panavision, you can shoot like the pros. Panavision is the premier designer, manufacturer, and supplier of motion picture camera equipment in the world. With the Panascout you can simulate the Cinematographer's viewpoint from a professional cinema camera. You can frame photos in four professional aspect ratios, including 2.40:1, 1.85:1, 1.78:1, and 1.33:1. With the hot button you can access the Panavision web site, allowing the user to find the nearest Panavision facility, check out the gear at the Panastore, and find any technical documentation in the Reference Library.

pCAM Film+Digital Calculator (iPhone, iPod Touch, and iPad)

In my opinion pCAM is the most extensive and best app designed for Cinematographers and the camera department. It can be used by Directors of Photography, Camera Operators, Camera Assistants, Gaffers, Key Grips, Script Supervisors, and more. With this app you are able to calculate the following: depth of field, hyperfocal distances, splits/aperture finder, field of view (picture sizes), field of view preview (with images to size shots), angle of view, focal length (lens) matching, exposure, running time to length, shooting to screen time, HMI flicker free speeds, color correction, diopter selection, macro, time lapse, underwater distance, scene illumination, light coverage, mired shift, and conversion calculator. It also contains a Siemens Star for checking lens focus and an insert slate. See Chapter 5 for various screen shot images from the pCAM application. The developer of the app is a working Camera Assistant who understands that calculations must be done quickly and simply on the run. At the present time it works on the iPhone, iPod Touch, and iPad. Go to the companion web site for the book at www.cameraassistantmanual.com for a link to the PDF version of the complete pCAM User Guide.

SL Director's Viewfinder (Android)

The SL Director's Viewfinder works in the same way that a traditional director's viewfinder works but with more features. It is designed

for Directors and Cinematographers, and is helpful when blocking and planning shots or when scouting locations. It allows you to see what your shot will look like using the specific format and lens focal lengths that you will be shooting with.

Sun Surveyor Lite (Android)

Like the Helios Sun Position Calculator for the iPhone, iPod and iPad, the Sun Surveyor allows you to predict the position of the sun, on any given day, in any given place.

Toland ASC Digital Assistant (iPhone, iPod Touch, and iPad)

Named after legendary ASC Cinematographer Gregg Toland, this app allows you to calculate your depth of field, field of view, shutter angle and speed change calculations, and specific camera information. It also includes a log feature for the assistant to keep track of specific information for each shot.

As previously mentioned, the above is only a small sampling of some of the best apps currently available for a Cinematographer. For a more complete discussion and listing of cinematography-specific applications for your iPhone, iPod Touch or iPad, please check the companion web site at www.cameraassistantmanual.com, which I intend to keep updated on a regular basis.

Appendix C

Camera Department Checklists, Production Forms, and Labels

As a Camera Assistant, you will assist the cinematographer in preparing equipment lists, complete camera reports and inventory forms, keep shooting logs, and complete many other types of paperwork, forms, and labels in the day-to-day performance of your job. Included in this section are a variety of checklists, forms, and labels that you may use during the course of your work as a Camera Assistant. Using these checklists, forms, and labels will make your job go much smoother each day and also help you and the camera department be much more organized.

All of these forms and labels are available for download on the companion web site for this book at www.cameraassistantmanual. com. They are available as Microsoft Word document template forms and also as PDF forms. The PDF forms may be opened and filled out using the Adobe Reader free software. You may print the filled out PDF forms, but to fill out and save a completed PDF form, you must have the full version of Adobe Acrobat software.

FORMS AND CHECKLISTS

The equipment checklists are provided to help you in the ordering and preparation of camera equipment and expendables. By using them, you will be sure that you have all equipment and supplies needed for your shoot. In most cases it is the Director of Photography that determines the basic equipment package for the specific production. But many Cinematographers may not be up to date on all of the special accessories and items used by a Camera Assistant. It is quite common for the DP to ask the Camera Assistant to help prepare the list of camera equipment, filters, etc.

FILM CAMERA EQUIPMENT CHECKLIST

Production Title

CAMERAS

Camera	
Aaton 35	
Aaton A-Minima	
Aaton Penelope	
Aaton XTR Plus	
Aaton XTR Prod	
Arriflex Arricam Studio	
Arriflex Arricam Lite	
Arriflex 235	
Arriflex 435	
Arriflex 535	
Arriflex 35 BL3	
Arriflex 35 BL4	
Arriflex 35-3	
Arriflex 2C	
Arriflex 416 Plus	
Arriflex 416 Plus High Speed	
Arriflex 16 SR3	HS
Arriflex 16 SR2	HS
Bell & Howell Eyemo	
Leonetti Ultracam	
Moviecam Super America	
Moviecam Compact	
Moviecam SL	
Panavision Millennium XL	
Panavision Millennium	
Panavision Panaflex Platinum	
Panavision Panaflex Gold II	
Panavision Panaflex Gold	
Panavision Panaflex–X	
Panavision Panastar I	
Panavision Panastar II	
Panavision Panaflex–16	
Panavision XL-2	
Photo Sonics 4ER	
Photo Sonics 4C	
Photo Sonics 4 ML	
Photo Sonics Actionmaster 500	
Photo Sonics 1VN	
Photo Sonics NAC	

GROUND GLASS

1.33	2.35/2.40
1.33/1.78	TV
1.33/1.85/2.40	TV/1.85
1.66	Super TV
1.78	Super 16
1.85	Super 35
1.85/Academy	
1.33/1.78/S35	

MAGAZINES

200	800
250	1000
400	1200
500	
Reverse	High Speed
Arricam Shoulder	
Arricam Steadicam	
Arri 35-3 Shoulder	
Arri 35-3 Steadicam	
Arri 535 Steadicam	
Arri 435 Shoulder	
Arri 435 Steadicam	

VIDEO ASSIST

Arri 35-3 Video Door	
B & W Video Tap	
Color Video Tap	
Wireless Transmitter	
Transvideo Monitor	
Arriflex IVS	
Panavision MAV	
Panavision PAV2	
Panavision XLV	
4" Monitor	Watchman
5" Monitor	Video 8
6" Monitor	VHS Deck
6.5" Monitor	DVD Deck
8.4" Monitor	DV Deck
9" Monitor	
10" Monitor	
12" Monitor	25' Coaxial
15" Monitor	50' Coaxial
17" Monitor	
19" Monitor	
26" Monitor	
Adapters, Connectors	

HANDHELD

Left-Hand Grip
Right-Hand Grip
Shoulder Pad
Shoulder Brace
Follow Focus
Clamp-on Matte Box
Arri 35-3 Handheld Door
Lens Shade
Handheld Microforce Handle

PRIME LENSES

3.5 mm	30 mm
4 mm	32 mm
5.9 mm	35 mm
6 mm	40 mm
8 mm	50 mm
9.5 mm	55 mm
9.8 mm	60 mm
10 mm	65 mm
12 mm	75 mm
14 mm	85 mm
14.5 mm	100 mm
16 mm	125 mm
17 mm	135 mm
17.5 mm	150 mm
18 mm	180 mm
20 mm	210 mm
21 mm	
24 mm	
25 mm	
27 mm	
28 mm	
29 mm	

ZOOM LENSES

7 – 56	18 – 100
7 – 63	18.5 – 55.5
7 – 81	20 – 60
8 – 64	20 – 100
9 – 50	20 – 120
9.5 – 57	20 – 125
10.4 – 52	23 – 460
10 – 30	24 – 275
10 – 100	24 – 290
10 – 150	25 – 80
10.5 – 210	25 – 250
11 – 110	25 – 625
11 – 165	27 – 68
11.5 – 138	28 – 70
12 – 120	35 – 140
12 – 240	40 – 200
14 – 70	48 – 550
14.5 – 50	50 – 500
16 – 44	85 – 200
17 – 35	135 – 420
17 – 75	150 – 450
17 – 102	150 – 600
17.5 – 34	190 – 595
17.5 – 75	270 – 840
18-90	

CEC   © DEE

Figure C.1   Film camera equipment checklist.

FILM CAMERA EQUIPMENT CHECKLIST – Page 2

Production Title

TELEPHOTO LENSES		ARRIFLEX LENSES		PANAVISION LENSES	
200 mm	800 mm	**MASTER PRIMES**		**G-SERIES ANAMORPHIC LENSES**	
300 mm	1000 mm	12 mm	35 mm	35 mm	60 mm
400 mm	1200 mm	14 mm	40 mm	40 mm	75 mm
500 mm	2000 mm	16 mm	50 mm	50 mm	100 mm
600 mm		18 mm	65 mm	**ANAMORPHIC ZOOM**	
		21 mm	75 mm	**AWZ2** 40 – 80	
		25 mm	100 mm	**ATZ** 70 -200	
MACRO LENSES		27 mm	135 mm	**PRIMO PRIMES**	
16 mm	75 mm	32 mm	150 mm	24 mm	85 mm
24 mm	90 mm	**ULTRA 16 LENSES**		30 mm	125 mm
32 mm	100 mm	6 mm	18 mm	65 mm	
40 mm	140 mm	8 mm	25 mm	**PRIMO SLZ ZOOM 3:1**	
50 mm	200 mm	9.5 mm	35 mm	135 – 420	
60 mm	280 mm	12 mm	50 mm	**PRIMO SLZ ZOOM 4:1**	
		14 mm		17.5 – 75	
SLANT FOCUS LENSES		**COMPACT PRIMES**		**PRIMO SLZ ZOOM 11:1**	
24 mm	63 mm	18 mm	35 mm	24 – 275	
34 mm	90 mm	21 mm	50 mm	**PRIMO MACRO ZOOM**	
45 mm		25 mm	85 mm	14.5 - 50	
		28 mm		**COMPACT ZOOM**	
SHIFT & TILT LENSES				**PCZ** 19 – 90	
14 mm	60 mm	**ULTRA PRIMES**		**LIGHTWEIGHT ZOOMS**	
18 mm	80 mm	8R	32 mm	17.5 – 34	
20 mm	90 mm	10 mm	40 mm	27 – 68	
24 mm	110 mm	12 mm	50 mm	85 – 200	
28 mm	120 mm	14 mm	65 mm		
35 mm	135 mm	16 mm	85 mm		
45 mm	150 mm	20 mm	100 mm		
50 mm		24 mm	135 mm	**LENS ACCESSORIES**	
		28 mm	180 mm	1.4X Extender	
EYEMO LENSES		**VARIABLE PRIMES**		2X Extender	
14 mm	24 mm	**VP1** 16 – 30		Aspheron for 9.5 & 12	
15 mm	35 mm	**VP2** 29 – 60		Century Periscope	
17 mm	50 mm	**VP3** 55 – 105		cmotion lens control system	
18 mm				Innovision Probe	
20 mm		**LIGHTWEIGHT ZOOM**		Low-Angle Prism	
		LWZ 15.5 – 45		Mesmerizer	
				Microforce Motor	
OPTICAL ACCESSORIES		**ALURA STUDIO ZOOMS**		Microforce Zoom Control	
Long Eyepiece Extension		18-80		Microforce Extension Cable	
Medium Eyepiece Extension		45-250		Mutar for 10-100	
Eyepiece Leveler				Panavision/Frazier Lens System	
Super Wide Eyepiece		**MASTER MACRO**		Panavision Zoom Control	
		Master Macro 100		Panavision Zoom Holder	
				PL to Bayonet Mount	
		ARRIFLEX MASTER DIOPTERS		Revolution Lens System	
		+ 0.5		Snorkel	
		+ 1.0		Squishy Lens	
		+ 2.0		Zoom Power Cables	

CEC   © DEE

Figure C.1   (*continued*)

FILM CAMERA EQUIPMENT CHECKLIST – Page 3

Production Title

ARRIFLEX ACCESSORIES	PANAVISION ACCESSORIES	MISCELLANEOUS ACCESSORIES
Arricam Speed Control Box	Digital Remote Switch	Short Iris Rods
Arricam Timing Shift Box	Filter Frame Gel Punch	Medium Iris Rods
BP-3 Bridgeplate	Flange Focal Depth Set	Long Iris Rods
BP-5 Bridgeplate	FTZSAC	Lens Bridge Support
BP-8 Bridgeplate	LAC	Bridge Plate
BP-9 Bridgeplate	Modular Combo Matte Box	Sliding Balance Plate
CLM-2 - Controlled Lens Motor	Modular Follow Focus	Studio Follow Focus
Controlled Focus Motor	Modular Follow Focus Remote	Mini Follow Focus
Director's Viewfinder	On-Board Battery Brackets	Follow Focus Right Hand Knob
ESU – External Sync Unit	On-Board Video Monitor	Focus Gears
EXD-1 External Display	Panaclear Auxiliary Handle	Focus Whip – 6", 12"
FF-3 2-Speed Studio Follow Focus	Panafinder Director's Finder	Speed Crank
FF-4 Studio Follow Focus	Panaflasher	4 x 4 Studio Matte Box
FF-5 Studio Follow Focus	Panatape II	4 x 5 Studio Matte Box
HC-1 Hand Crank	Panatate 360-Degree Mount	4 x 5.65 Studio Matte Box
HD-IVS	Panavision Universal Autobase	5 x 6 Studio Matte Box
ICU—Iris Control Unit	Panavision/Century Swing Shift	6.6 x 6.6 Studio Matte Box
IVS—Integrated Video System	Phaseable Synchronizer System	9 x 9 Studio Matte Box
LCC—Laptop Camera Controller	Preston Focus, Iris, Zoom Control	4 x 4 Filter Trays
LCS—Lens Control System	Remote Focus & T–Stop	4 x 5.65 Filter Trays
LDA - Lens Data Archive	Smart Lens System	6.6 x 6.6 Filter Trays
Lens Data Box	Smart Shutter Control II	6.6 x 6.6 Step Down to 4 x 5.65
LFF-1 – Lightweight Follow Focus	Telescoping Eyepiece Extension	4 x 4 Clamp–on Matte Box
LS-9 Lens Support		4 x 5.65 Clamp–on Matte Box
LS-10 Lens Support	***ARRIFLEX MATTE BOXES***	Matte Box Adapter Rings
MBP-1 Mini Base Plate	MB-14 Production Matte Box	Matte Box Bellows
MBP-2 Mini Base Plate 2	MB-16 Production Matte Box	Rubber Donuts
MFF-1 Mini Follow Focus	MB-19 Production Matte Box	Lens Shade
MFF-2 Mini Follow Focus	MB-20 I Compact Matte Box	4 1/2" Clamp-on Shade
On-Board Video Monitor	MB-20 II Compact Matte Box	138mm Clamp-on Shade
QR-HD1 Quick Release Baseplate	MB-20 Compact Matte Box Super Wide	Hard Mattes
RCU—Remote Control Unit	MB-28 Compact Matte Box	Extra Filter Retaining Rings
RPC —Ramp Preview Controller	MB-29 Compact Matte Box	Eyebrow
RS-4 – Remote Switch	LMB-3 Lightweight Matte Box	French Flag
Single-Frame Shutter for 435	LMB-4A Lightweight Matte Box	Utility Base Plate
TSB – 435 Time Shift Box	LMB-5 Lightweight Matte Box	Auto Base
ULB-3 Universal Lightweight Bracket	LMB-15 Lightweight Matte Box	Auxiliary Carry Handle
UMC-3 - Universal Motor Control	MMB-1 Mini Matte Box	Camera Barney
WBU-4 – Wireless Battery Unit	MMB-2 Mini Matte Box	Magazine Barney
WFU-3 – Wireless Focus Unit		Rain Cover/Weather Protector
WHA – Wired Hand grip Attachment		Rain Deflector
Wireless LCS		Director's Finder
WMU-3 – Wireless Main Unit		Microforce Handle
WRC-1—Wireless Remote Control		Oppenheimer Handle
WRC-2—Wireless Remote Control		
WRS – Wireless Remote System		
WZU-3 – Wireless Zoom Unit		Filters—See Filters Checklist
ZMU-3 Zoom Main Unit		
WZE-3 Wireless Zoom Extension		

CEC   © DEE

Figure C.1 (*continued*)

FILM CAMERA EQUIPMENT CHECKLIST – Page 4

Production Title

ELECTRONIC ACCESSORIES	SUPPORT	HEADS
Camera Shaker	Standard Tripod	*GEAR HEADS*
Capping Shutter	Baby Tripod	Arrihead
CE Crystal Speed Control	Bazooka	Arrihead 2
Cine Tape Measure	Spreader	Arrihead Reduction Gears
Eyepiece Heater	High Hat	Panahead
Eyepiece Heater Cable	Low Hat	Super Panahead
Film/Video Synchronizer	Rocker Plate	Mitchell Gear Head
HMI Speed Control	Tilt Plate	Mini Worral
Image Shaker	Camera Slider	Worral Gear Head
Intervalometer	Cardelini Head Lock	*FLUID HEADS*
Junction Box	Steadybag	Cardelini Spider Mount
Lens Light	Cine Saddle – Large	Cartoni C 20 S
Moviecam Sync Box	Cine Saddle – Small	Cartoni C 40 S
Obie Light	Rolling Spreader	Cartoni Dutch
Precision Speed Control	vBag Small	Cartoni Lambda H 520
Preston FI + Z	vBag Medium	Cartoni Lambda 3-Axis
Remote Follow Focus	vBag Large	Cartoni Omega
Remote Switch	Ball to Mitchell Adapter	Cartoni Sigma
Wireless Follow Focus		O'Connor 1030
		O'Connor 2060
		O'Connor 2575
		O'Connor 100
	MISCELLANEOUS	O'Connor 50-200
	Daylight Spools & Boxes	O'Connor Ultimatte
	400' Film Cans	O'Connor 50-200
	800' Film Cans	Ronford Fluid 7
		Ronford 30
BATTERIES & CABLES		Ronford Fluid 2015
12-Volt Block	1200' Film Cans	Ronford Fluid 2003
24-Volt Block		Ronford Fluid 2004
12/24 Blocks	400' Black Bags	Sachtler Studio 7 + 7
12-Volt Belt	800' Black Bags	Sachtler Studio 9 + 9
24-Volt Belt	1000' / 1200' Black Bags	Sachtler Studio 65
12/24 Belt		Sachtler Studio 80 II
Chargers	2" Film Cores	Sachtler 7502 Cine 75 HD
12-Volt On–Board	3" Film Cores	Sachtler Horizon
24-Volt On–Board		Sachtler Studio 80
On–Board Chargers	Camera Reports	Sachtler Video 90
Arriflex SR2 On–Board Adapter	Inventory Forms	Sachtler Dutch
Arriflex SR3 On–Board Adapter	Film Can Labels	Tango Swing Head
Panavision On-Board Battery Bracket		Vinten
Power Cables	Changing Bag	Weaver Steadman 2-Axis
Power Cable Extension	Changing Tent	Weaver Steadman 3-Axis
Junction Box	Slate	Weaver Steadman Multi-Axis
	Expendables — See Checklist	
	Miscellaneous Forms & Labels	

CEC   © DEE

Figure C.1   (*continued*)

FILTERS CHECKLIST

Production Title

	40.5	48	4 ½	138	4 X 4	4 X 5.65	6.6 X 6.6		40.5	48	4 ½	138	4 X 4	4 X 5.65	6.6 X 6.6
TIFFEN															
COLOR CONVERSION FILTERS								*PROTECTION/UV FILTERS*							
85, 85N3, 85N6, 85N9								Clear							
85B, 85BN3, 85BN6, 85BN9								Haze 1							
85C								Haze 2							
80A,80B,80C,80D								Haze 2A							
LLD								Sky 1A							
85/Polarizer								UV							
85B/Polarizer								UV 17							
NEUTRAL DENSITY FILTERS								UV Haze							
ND3, ND6, ND9								Warm UV							
ND1.2								*IR FILTERS*							
LIGHT BALANCING FILTERS								T1							
81A								T 1/2							
81B								IRND							
81C								Hot Mirror							
81D								Hot Mirror IR							
81EF								Hot Mirror IRND							
82								Hot Mirror 80C							
82A								Hot Mirror 80D							
82B								*EFFECTS FILTERS*							
82C								Center Spot							
Fluorescent FLB								Close-Up +1, +2, +4							
Fluorescent FLD								Cool Day for Night							
WARMING / ENHANCING FILTERS								Digital Diff. FX ¼, ½, 1, 2, 3, 4, 5							
812 Warming								Diopter +½, +1, +1 ½, +2, +3, +4							
Enhancer								Double Fog 1/8, ¼, ½, 1, 2, 3, 4, 5							
CONTRAST FILTERS								Fog 1/8, ¼, ½, 1, 2, 3, 4, 5							
Low Con 1/8, ¼, ½, 1, 2, 3, 4, 5								HDTV / FX 1, 2, 3, 4, 5, 6							
Soft Con 1, 2, 3, 4, 5								Monochrome Day for Night							
Ultra Con 1/8, ¼. ½, 1, 2, 3, 4, 5								Nude FX 1, 2, 3, 4, 5, 6							
								Sepia 1, 2, 3							
POLARIZING FILTERS								Smoque 1, 2, 3, 4							
Polarizer								Soft F/X ¼, 1, 2, 3, 4, 5							
Circular Polarizer								Split Diopter +½, +1, +2, +3							
Linear Polarizer								Star 1, 2, 3, 4 ☐4pt. ☐6pt. ☐8pt.							
Warm Polarizer								Warm Center Spot							
Ultra Pol								Wrm Soft F/X ½, 1, 2, 3, 4, 5							
FCL															© DEE

Figure C.2 Filters checklist.

FILTERS CHECKLIST – Page 2

Production Title

TIFFEN
DIFFUSION FILTERS

	40.5	48	4 ½	138	4 X 4	4 X 5.65	6.6 X 6.6		40.5	48	4 ½	138	4 X 4	4 X 5.65	6.6 X 6.6
Black Diffusion/FX ½, 1, 2, 3, 4, 5								Warm Black Pro-Mist 1/8, ¼. ½, 1, 2, 3, 4, 5							
Black Net 1, 2, 3, 4, 5								Warm Pro-Mist 1/8, ¼. ½, 1, 2, 3, 4, 5							
Black Pro-Mist 1/8, ¼. ½, 1, 2, 3, 4, 5								White Net 1, 2, 3, 4, 5							
Black Soft Net 1, 2, 3, 4								White Soft Net 1, 2, 3, 4							
Bronze Glimmerglass 1, 2, 3, 4, 5															
Diffusion 1/8, ¼. ½, 1, 2, 3															
Glimmerglass 1, 2, 3, 4, 5															
Gold Diffusion/FX ½, 1, 2, 3, 4, 5															
Pro-Mist 1/8, ¼. ½, 1, 2, 3, 4, 5															
Red Soft Net 1, 2, 3, 4															
Skintone Soft Net 1, 2, 3, 4															

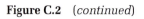

COLOR FILTERS | COLOR GRAD FILTERS

	40.5	48	4 ½	138	4 X 4	4 X 5.65	6.6 X 6.6		40.5	48	4 ½	138	4 X 4	4 X 5.65	6.6 X 6.6
Antique Suede 1, 2, 3								Blue 1, 2, 3, 4, 5							
Blue 1, 2, 3, 4, 5								Chocolate 1, 2, 3							
Chocolate 1, 2, 3								Cool Blue 1, 2, 3, 4, 5							
Cool Blue 1, 2, 3, 4, 5								Coral 1/8, ¼. ½, 1, 2, 3							
Coral 1/8, ¼. ½, 1, 2, 3, 4, 5								Cranberry 1, 2, 3							
Cranberry 1, 2, 3								Cyan 1, 2, 3, 4, 5							
Cyan 1, 2, 3, 4, 5								Grape 1, 2, 3							
Grape 1, 2, 3								Green 1, 2, 3, 4, 5							
Green 1, 2, 3, 4, 5								Magenta 1, 2, 3, 4, 5							
Magenta 1, 2, 3, 4, 5								ND3, ND6, ND9 Hard Edge							
Pink 1, 2, 3, 4, 5								ND3, ND6, ND9 Soft Edge							
Plum 1, 2, 3								Pink 1, 2, 3, 4, 5							
Red 1, 2, 3, 4, 5								Plum 1, 2, 3							
Straw 1, 2, 3								Red 1, 2, 3, 4, 5							
Tangerine 1, 2, 3								Skyfire 1, 2, 3							
Tobacco 1, 2, 3								Straw 1, 2, 3							
Tropic Blue 1, 2, 3								Sunset 1, 2, 3							
Yellow 1, 2, 3, 4, 5								Tangerine 1, 2, 3							
								Tobacco 1, 2, 3							
								Tropic Blue 1, 2, 3							
								Twilight 1, 2, 3							
								Yellow 1, 2, 3, 4, 5							

FCL   © DEE

Figure C.2   (*continued*)

FILTERS CHECKLIST – Page 3

Production Title	

SCHNEIDER

	40.5	48	4 ½	138	4 X 4	4 X 5.65	6.6 X 6.6
COLOR CONVERSION FILTERS							
85, 85N3, 85N6, 85N9, 85N12							
NEUTRAL DENSITY FILTERS							
ND3, ND6, ND9, ND12							
Absorptive ND3, ND6, ND9							
Reflective ND3, ND6, ND9							
POLARIZING FILTERS							
Linear True Pol							
Circular True Pol							
85/True Pol Linear							
85/True Pol Circular							
81EF/True Pol							
WARMING / ENHANCING FILTERS							
81 EF							
81-One Warming							
81-Two Warming							
Coral 1/8, ¼, ½, 1, 2							
Enhancer							
CONTRAST FILTERS							
DigiCon 1/8, ¼, ½, 1, 2							
Low Con 2000 1/8, ¼, ½, 1, 2							
SOLID COLOR							
Antique Suede 1, 2, 3							
Chocolate 1, 2, 3,							
Gold 1, 2, 3							
Golden Sepia 1, 2, 3							
Green 10CC							
Magenta 10CC							
Magenta 20CC							
Magenta 30CC							
Maui Brown 1, 2, 3							
Sahara Gold							
Sapphire Blue 1, 2, 3							
Storm Blue 1, 2, 3							
Tobacco 1, 2, 3							

	40.5	48	4 ½	138	4 X 4	4 X 5.65	6.6 X 6.6
DIFFUSION FILTERS							
Classic Soft 1/8, ¼, ½, 1, 2							
Classic Black Soft 1/8, ¼, ½, 1, 2							
Dbl. Classic Bl.Soft 1/8, ¼, ½, 1, 2							
HD Classic Soft 1/8, ¼, ½, 1, 2							
Hollywood Bl.Magic 1/8, ¼, ½, 1, 2							
Warm Classic Soft 1/8, ¼, ½, 1, 2							
Black Frost 1/8, ¼, ½, 1, 2							
Warm Black Frost 1/8, ¼, ½, 1, 2							
White Frost 1/8, ¼, ½, 1, 2							
Warm White Frost 1/8, ¼, ½, 1, 2							
PROTECTION/UV FILTERS							
Clear							
UV 410							
IRND							
EFFECTS FILTERS							
Achromat Diopter +1, +2, +3							
Day for Night							
Diopter +½, +1, +2, +3, +4							
Split Diopter +½, +1, +2, +3							
Soft Centric 1/4, 1/3, ½, 1, 2							
COLOR GRADS							
Amber 1, 2, 3							
Antique Suede 1, 2, 3							
Chocolate 1, 2, 3,							
Classic Sunset							
Coral 1/2, 1, 2, 3							
Gold 1, 2, 3							
Golden Sepia 1, 2, 3							
Magenta 1, 2, 3							
ND3, ND6, ND9, ND12							
ND3, ND6, ND9, ND12 Attenuators							
Paradise Blue 1, 2, 3							
Sapphire Blue 1, 2, 3							
Storm Blue 1, 2, 3							
Tobacco 1, 2, 3							

FCL © DEE

Figure C.2 (*continued*)

FILTERS CHECKLIST – Page 4

Production Title

HARRISON & HARRISON FILTERS

	40.5	48	4 ½	138	4 X 4	4 X 5.65	6.6 X 6.6
85, 85N3, 85N6, 85N9							
Black Dot Texture 1, 2, 3, 4, 5							
Blue 1, 2, 3, 4, 5							
Coral 1/8, ¼. ½, 1, 2, 3							
Cyan 1, 2, 3, 4, 5							
Day for Night							
Diffusion ¼, 1, 2, 3, 4, 5							
Double Fog ¼, ½, 1, 2, 3, 4, 5							
Fog ¼. ½, 1, 2, 3, 4, 5							
Green 1, 2, 3, 4, 5							
Low Con ¼. ½, 1, 2, 3, 4, 5							
Magenta 1, 2, 3, 4, 5							
ND3, ND6, ND9							
Neu. Blend. Ratio Att. 1, 1½, 2, 2½, 3							
Polarizer							
Red 1, 2, 3, 4, 5							
Scenic Fog 1, 2, 3, 4, 5							
Yellow 1, 2, 3, 4, 5							

HARRISON & HARRISON GRADS

	40.5	48	4 ½	138	4 X 4	4 X 5.65	6.6 X 6.6
Blue 1, 2, 3, 4, 5							
Cyan 1, 2, 3, 4, 5							
Green 1, 2, 3, 4, 5							
Magenta 1, 2, 3, 4, 5							
ND3, ND6, ND9 Grads							
Red 1, 2, 3, 4, 5							
Yellow 1, 2, 3, 4, 5							

FILTERS FOR BLACK & WHITE

	40.5	48	4 ½	138	4 X 4	4 X 5.65	6.6 X 6.6
#6 Yellow							
#8 Yellow							
#9 Yellow							
#11 Green							
#12 Yellow							
#13 Green							
#15 Deep Yellow							
#16 Orange							
#21 Orange							
#23A Light Red							
#25 Red							
#25A Red							
#29 Dark Red							
#47 Blue							
#47B Dark Blue							
#56 Light Blue							
#58 Green							
#61 Dark Green							

OTHER FILTERS

	40.5	48	4 ½	138	4 X 4	4 X 5.65	6.6 X 6.6
Mitchell A, B, C, D, E							
Pancro ND3, ND6, ND9, ND12							
Pancro ND3, ND6, ND9, ND12 Grads							
Pancro ND Center Spot							
Pancro Optical Flat							

FCL   © DEE

Figure C.2 *(continued)*

Figure C.1 is a Film Camera Equipment Checklist, and Figure C.2 is a Filters Checklist. These checklists will help when you are working with the DP to prepare the listing of camera equipment that will be needed for the shoot. Figure C.3 is the Expendables Inventory and Checklist, which will ensure that you have all the expendables needed to complete the job. You may use this form to place your initial order for expendables as well as to keep track of your expendables inventory during the course of the production.

Figure C.4 is a Film Camera Prep Checklist that will be helpful during the preproduction camera prep that is performed at the camera rental house. This list will help you to be sure that you have all the necessary equipment and that it functions properly. It is very important to leave the rental house, after completing the camera prep, knowing that you have everything and that it all works properly.

Figure C.5 is a Non-prep Disclaimer for use by the assistant or DIT in charge of prepping the camera equipment. Unfortunately there are some producers today who don't see the need to perform a complete camera prep, or they don't want to pay the assistant to do one and rely on the rental house to send the equipment out complete. Fortunately this has only happened to me once or twice in my career. In some cases, when the equipment arrives or when the AC arrives on set for the first day of filming, the equipment package is not complete, batteries are not charged, or items are not compatible. Since the 1st AC is the one usually responsible for all camera equipment on set, it is imperative for him/her to perform a complete prep and to be properly compensated for the job of performing the prep. The Non-prep Disclaimer is to be used if the production company does not allow the assistant to perform the prep. Hopefully it will protect the assistant in the event that they don't do the prep and there is something wrong with the equipment.

Figures C.6, C.7, and C.8 are equipment forms that you may need in the day-to-day performance of your job. Figure C.6 is the Equipment Received Log that allows you to keep a record of all equipment received during the course of the production. You will soon learn that on many occasions you will need additional equipment as shooting progresses. It may be a case of an additional camera for one or more days of shooting or a special lens for a particular shot and you can use this form to keep track of the new equipment received.

Figure C.7, the Returned Equipment Log, allows you to keep a record of all equipment returned to the rental house during the course of the production. Often when you have additional equipment such as a second camera, special lens or other equipment, it may only be needed for one or two days of shooting. When you are finished with the additional equipment, you should return it to the rental house so that the production company does not incur any additional rental fees. When you return the equipment, list each piece on the equipment returned log.

EXPENDABLES INVENTORY & CHECKLIST

Production Title

1" CAMERA TAPE – CLOTH	1" PAPER TAPE
White	White
Black	Black
Red	Red
Yellow	Yellow
Blue	Green
Grey	Orange
Green	Light Blue
Teal	Fluorescent Pink
Burgundy	Fluorescent Green
Dark Blue	Fluorescent Orange
Fluorescent Pink	Fluorescent Yellow
Fluorescent Green	
Fluorescent Orange	½" PAPER TAPE
Fluorescent Yellow	White
	Black
¾" CAMERA TAPE – CLOTH	Red
White	Yellow
Black	Blue
Red	Green
Yellow	Orange
Grey	Fluorescent Orange
Dark Blue	Fluorescent Pink
	Yellow Measure Tape
½" CAMERA TAPE – CLOTH	
White	2" PAPER TAPE
Black	White
Red	Black
Neon Blue	Red
Brown	Yellow
Yellow	Blue
Grey	Green
Teal	Orange
2" GAFFER TAPE – CLOTH	MISCELLANEOUS TAPE
White	"Warning Exposed Film" – 1" Tape
Black	"Do Not X-Ray" – 1" Tape
Gray	Magazine & Film Can – 2" White Cloth Tape
Red	Magazine & Film Can – 2" Yellow Cloth Tape
Yellow	Magazine & Film Can – 2" Blue Cloth Tape
Bright Blue	Magazine & Film Can – 2" Red Cloth Tape
Dark Blue	Transfer Tape (Snot Tape)
Green	
Brown	CHART TAPE
Fluorescent Orange	1/8" Chart Tape ☐ White ☐ Yellow ☐ Black
Fluorescent Yellow	3/16" Chart Tape ☐ White ☐ Yellow ☐ Black
Fluorescent Pink	1/4" Chart Tape ☐ White ☐ Yellow ☐ Black
Fluorescent Green	

ECL   © DEE

Figure C.3   Expendables inventory and checklist.

EXPENDABLES INVENTORY & CHECKLIST – Page 2	
Production Title	

MARKERS – PERMANENT	GREASE PENCILS, CHINA MARKERS, CHALK
Fine-Point Sharpies – Black	Stabilo Grease Pencil – White
Fine-Point Sharpies – Red	Stabilo Grease Pencil – Red
Fine-Point Sharpies – Blue	Stabilo Grease Pencil – Yellow
Fine-Point Sharpies – Silver	Stabilo Grease Pencil – Black
Extra Fine-Point Sharpies – Black	Stabilo Grease Pencil – Blue
Extra Fine-Point Sharpies – Red	Stabilo Grease Pencil – Green
Extra Fine-Point Sharpies – Blue	Stabilo Grease Pencil – Orange
Double Tip Sharpies – Black	Stabilo Grease Pencil – Brown
Double Tip Sharpies – Red	
Double Tip Sharpies – Blue	Dixon Peel-Off China Markers - White
Retractable Sharpie – Black	Dixon Peel-Off China Markers - Yellow
Retractable Sharpie – Red	Dixon Peel-Off China Markers - Red
Retractable Sharpie – Blue	Dixon Peel-Off China Markers - Black
Super Sharpie – Black	Dixon Peel-Off China Markers - Green
Super Sharpie – Red	Dixon Peel-Off China Markers - Blue
Super Sharpie – Blue	Dixon Peel-Off China Markers - Orange
Mini Sharpie – Black	
Mini Sharpie – Red	School Chalk – White
Mini Sharpie – Blue	School Chalk – Colors
Marks-A-Lot Permanent Marker - Black	Chalk Holder
Marks-A-Lot Permanent Marker - Red	Railroad Chalk - White
Marks-A-Lot Permanent Marker - Blue	Railroad Chalk - Blue
Marks-A-Lot Permanent Marker - Green	Railroad Chalk - Red
	Railroad Chalk - Yellow
MARKERS - ERASABLE	Railroad Chalk - Green
Staedtler Marking Pen – Black	Railroad Chalk Holder
Staedtler Marking Pen – Red	Lumber Crayon - White
Staedtler Marking Pen – Blue	Lumber Crayon - Blue
Staedtler Marking Pen – Green	Lumber Crayon - Red
	Lumber Crayon - Green
Vis–A–Vis Felt Marker – Black	Lumber Crayon - Yellow
Vis–A–Vis Felt Marker – Red	Lumber Crayon – Fluorescent Pink
Vis–A–Vis Felt Marker – Blue	Lumber Crayon Holder
Vis–A–Vis Felt Marker – Green	
Kleen Slate Erasable Slate Marker – Black	**OFFICE SUPPLIES**
Kleen Slate Erasable Slate Marker – Red	Medium Point Ballpoint Pens – Black
Kleen Slate Erasable Slate Marker – Blue	Medium Point Ballpoint Pens – Blue
Kleen Slate Erasable Slate Markers – 4-pack	Fine Point Ballpoint Pens – Black
Expo 2 Erasable Slate Marker – Black	Fine Point Ballpoint Pens – Blue
Expo 2 Erasable Slate Marker – Red	Highlighter – Yellow
Expo 2 Erasable Slate Marker – Blue	Highlighter – Pink
Marks-A-Lot Erasable Slate Marker - Black	Highlighter – Blue
Marks-A-Lot Erasable Slate Marker - Red	Highlighter - Green
Marks-A-Lot Erasable Slate Marker - Blue	Lined Legal Pad – 8 1/2" x 11"
Eraser for Dry Erase Marker	Memo Pad ☐ 3" x 5" or ☐ 5 ½" x 8 ½"
	Post-It Pads
	Scissors

ECL   © DEE

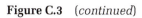

Figure C.3   (*continued*)

EXPENDABLES INVENTORY & CHECKLIST – Page 3

Production Title

STICK-ON LETTERS	GRAY CARDS, COLOR CHARTS, SLATES
1/2" Stick-on Letters & Numbers – Black	Kodak Gray Card Plus
1/2" Stick-on Letters & Numbers – Red	Gray Card
1/2" Stick-on Letters & Numbers – Blue	Macbeth Color Checker
	Framing Chart
3/4" Stick-on Letters & Numbers – Black	Focus Chart
3/4" Stick-on Letters & Numbers – Red	Insert Slate
3/4" Stick-on Letters & Numbers – Blue	Sync Slate
	WRATTEN GELS
1" Stick-on Letters & Numbers – Black	Kodak Wratten Gel – 85
1" Stick-on Letters & Numbers – Red	Kodak Wratten Gel – 85 N3
1" Stick-on Letters & Numbers – Blue	Kodak Wratten Gel – 85 N6
	Kodak Wratten Gel – 85 N9
P-TOUCH LABEL TAPE	Kodak Wratten Gel – 81EF
½" Black on White	Kodak Wratten Gel – 80 A
½" Black on Clear	Kodak Wratten Gel – 82 B
½" Black on Yellow	Kodak Wratten Gel – 85 B
½" Red on White	Kodak Wratten Gel – ND 3
	Kodak Wratten Gel – ND 6
¾" Black on White	Kodak Wratten Gel – ND 9
¾" Black on Clear	
¾" Black on Yellow	**CABLE TIES, RIP-TIES, VELCRO**
¾" Blue on White	Plastic Cable Ties ☐ 3 ½" ☐ 5 ½" ☐ 7 ½"
	Plastic Cable Ties ☐ 11" ☐ 14"
1" Black on White	Rip Tie Velcro Cable Wrap ☐ 6" ☐ 9"
1" Black on Clear	Rip Tie Velcro Cable Wrap ☐ 14"
1" Red on White	Bongo Tie Cable Ties
	Velcro ☐ 1" ☐ 2" ☐ 4"
LENS/FILTER CLEANING SUPPLIES	
Rosco Lens Tissue	**BATTERIES**
Rosco Lens Fluid	AAA Alkaline
Pancro Lens Fluid	AA Alkaline
Ultra Clarity Lens Cleaner	C Alkaline
Mikros Cloth Regular	D Alkaline
Mikros Cloth Jumbo	9–Volt Alkaline
Kimwipes Small	PX-28L
Kimwipes Large	DL-123
CANNED AIR	CR-2
Dust-Off	**MISCELLANEOUS**
Dust-Off Nozzle	Camera Log Book
Dust-Off Plus	Orangewood Sticks
Dust-Off Plus Nozzle	Camera Wedges
Dust-Off Jr.	Powder Puffs for Slate
	6" Cotton Swabs
EYEPIECE COVERS	Foam-Tip Swabs
Chamois Eyepiece Covers – Large Round	Mag Lite Replacement Bulbs
Chamois Eyepiece Covers – Small Round	Small Visqueen Equipment Covers
Chamois Eyepiece Covers – HD Round	Large Visqueen Equipment Covers
Chamois Eyepiece Covers – Small Oval	Small Plastic Storage Bags
	Medium Plastic Storage Bags

ECL   © DEE

Figure C.3   *(continued)*

EXPENDABLES INVENTORY & CHECKLIST – Page 4

Production Title

CLEANING SUPPLIES, LUBRICANTS	*FORMS*
Paper Towels	Box Rental
Box of Rags	Camera Equipment Checklist
409 Spray Cleaner	Camera Prep Checklist
Simple Green Spray Cleaner	Camera Department Contact List
Denatured Alcohol	Camera Department Log Sheet
Goo Gone	Camera Department Time Sheet
Goof Off	Daily Film Inventory
Lighter Fluid	Damaged Equipment Log
WD-40	Deal Memo
Silicone Spray	Digital Camera Reports
Pledge Furniture Polish	Equipment Received Log
CRC-656 Lubricant	Expendables Inventory & Checklist
Sanford Expo Towelettes	Film Camera Reports
Sanford Expo 2 Slate Cleaner	Filter Checklist
Medium Plastic Trash Bags	Film Developing Purchase Order
Large Plastic Trash Bags	Film Stock Request
	Job Information Form
	Non-prep Disclaimer
ALTOIDS MINTS	Personal Time Sheet and Invoice
Peppermint	Raw Stock Inventory
Cinnamon	Returned Equipment Log
Wintergreen	Short End Inventory
Spearmint	
	I-9 Employment Eligibility
	LABELS
CANS, BAGS, CORES	Develop Normal
100' Daylight Spools & Boxes	Do Not X-Ray
200' Daylight Spools & Boxes	Film Can
400' Daylight Spools & Cans	One Light Workprint
	Prep for Video Transfer
200' Film Cans	Recan
400' Film Cans	Short End
800' Film Cans	
1000' Film Cans	
1200' Film Cans	
	OTHER
200' Black Bags	
400' Black Bags	
800' Black Bags	
1000' Black Bags	
1200' Black Bags	
Film Cores ☐ 2" ☐ 3"	

ECL   © DEE

Figure C.3   (*continued*)

FILM CAMERA PREP CHECKLIST	
Production Title	
Camera Rental Company	
SPREADER	
☐	Runners slide smoothly and lock in all positions.
☐	Tripod points fit into spreader receptacles.
☐	
TRIPODS – BABY & STANDARD	
☐	Legs slide smoothly and lock in all positions.
☐	Top casting accommodates the head base (flat or bowl).
☐	Wooden legs are free from cracks and splinters.
☐	
HIGH HAT OR LOW HAT	
☐	Mounted on smooth flat piece of wood or other suitable material.
☐	Top casting accommodates the head base (flat or bowl).
☐	
FLUID HEAD	
☐	Base fits top casting of tripod and locks securely (Mitchell flat base or bowl shape).
☐	Camera lock down screw fits into camera body, adapter plate or sliding base plate.
☐	Pan and tilt movement is smooth at all tension settings.
☐	Tension adjustments for pan or tilt engage and do not slip.
☐	Pan and tilt locks securely at all settings.
☐	Eyepiece leveler attaches to head securely.
☐	Head contains a mounting bracket for the front box.
☐	
DUTCH HEAD	
☐	Easily mounted to main fluid head.
☐	Tilt movement is smooth at all tension settings.
☐	Tension adjustments for tilt engage securely and do not slip.
☐	Tilt locks securely at all settings.
☐	
GEAR HEAD	
☐	Base fits tripod top casting and locks securely. (All gear heads should have a Mitchell flat base).
☐	Camera lock down screw fits into camera body, adapter plate or sliding base plate.
☐	Pan and tilt movement is smooth at all speed settings. Pan and tilt locks securely at all settings.
☐	Gears shift smoothly.
☐	Tilt plate operates smoothly and locks securely in all positions. (Only on gear heads with built in tilt plate.)
☐	Eyepiece leveler attaches to head securely.
☐	Head contains a mounting bracket for the front box.
☐	
SLIDING BASE PLATE	
☐	Mounts securely onto head and adapter plate mounts securely onto camera.
☐	Slides smoothly and locks in all positions.
☐	
CPC	© DEE

Figure C.4   Film camera prep checklist.

	FILM CAMERA PREP CHECKLIST – Page 2
	Production Title
	Camera Rental Company
	CAMERA BODY
☐	Fits securely on head or adapter plate.
☐	Interior and exterior is clean and free of dirt and dust. Interior is free of emulsion buildup and film chips.
☐	Aperture plate, pressure plate and gate areas are clean and free of any burrs.
☐	Pressure plate is easily removable.
☐	Lens port opening is clean.
☐	Mirror is clean and free from scratches. (Do not clean mirror yourself)
☐	Magazine port opening is clean.
☐	On certain cameras, especially Panavision, electrical contacts in the magazine port opening are clean.
☐	Footage counter and tachometer function properly.
☐	On-off switch functions properly.
☐	The movement of the shutter, pull-down claw, and registration pin is synchronized.
☐	The mirror shutter stops in the viewing position when the camera is switched off.
☐	Pitch control functions properly to quiet camera.
☐	The variable speed switch functions properly.
☐	Ground glass is clean and is marked for the correct aspect ratio.
☐	Variable shutter operates smoothly through its entire range of openings.
☐	Doors close tightly and latches lock securely to protect from light leaks.
☐	Contrast viewing filter on eyepiece functions properly.
☐	Behind-the-lens filter slot is clear and free of any obstruction.
☐	Illuminated ground glass markings function properly and are adjustable in intensity. (If ground glass is removed, be sure to reinsert it properly.)
☐	Rain covers are available and fit properly for all lens and magazine configurations.
☐	
☐	
	VIEWFINDER
☐	Long and short eyepieces mount properly and focus easily to the eye.
☐	Eyepiece heater and magazine heater functions properly.
☐	Eyepiece magnifier functions properly.
☐	Diopter adjustment functions properly.
☐	Contrast viewing filters work correctly.
☐	
☐	
	FOCUS EYEPIECE
☐	Set eyepiece diopter for your vision.
☐	With lens removed, point camera at a bright light source.
☐	While looking through eyepiece, turn the diopter adjustment ring until the crosshairs or grains of the ground glass are sharp.
☐	If possible, lock the adjustment ring and mark it so that it can be returned to your setting if it should get moved.
☐	
☐	
☐	
CPC	© DEE

Figure C.4   (*continued*)

FILM CAMERA PREP CHECKLIST – Page 3

Production Title
Camera Rental Company

MAGAZINES

- ☐ Fit securely on camera body.
- ☐ Doors fit properly and lock securely
- ☐ Interior is clean and free of dirt, dust and film chips.
- ☐ Footage counter functions properly.
- ☐ Have different size magazines for various shooting situations.
- ☐ Magazine torque motor functions to properly to take-up film.
- ☐ Magazine heater (if available) functions properly.
- ☐ Electrical contacts on magazine are clean and function properly.
- ☐

CAMERA AND MAGAZINE BARNEYS

- ☐ Obtain proper size barneys for cameras and magazines.
- ☐ Check heated barneys to be sure that they function properly.
- ☐

SCRATCH TEST MAGAZINES

- ☐ Check all magazines on all cameras.
- ☐ Load a dummy load (approximately 20-30 feet) into each magazine.
- ☐ Place magazine on camera and thread film in camera.
- ☐ Run approximately 10-20 feet of film through the magazine.
- ☐ Remove film from take-up side and examine under bright light for any scratches. Check emulsion side and base side for scratches.
- ☐ When using high speed or variable speed cameras check magazines at various speeds.
- ☐
- ☐

LENSES

- ☐ Contains the proper mount for the camera being used.
- ☐ Lens seats properly in camera body.
- ☐ Mirror shutter does not strike rear element of lens when spinning.
- ☐ Front and rear glass elements are clean and free from scratches.
- ☐ Front element coating is not scratched or worn away.
- ☐ Iris (t-stop) diaphragm operates smoothly.
- ☐ Focus gear threads properly.
- ☐ Focus distance marks are accurate.
- ☐ On zoom lenses the zoom motor operates smoothly.
- ☐ Zoom lens tracks properly. (See below)
- ☐ Lens shade mounts securely to each lens.
- ☐ Zoom lens holds focus throughout the zoom range.
- ☐ Matte box bellows fits securely around all lenses.
- ☐ Obtain various size rubber donuts to insure a tight seal with matte box.
- ☐ Support rods are proper size for the lens being used.
- ☐
- ☐

CPC   © DEE

Figure C.4 (*continued*)

FILM CAMERA PREP CHECKLIST – Page 4

Production Title

Camera Rental Company

ZOOM LENS – TRACKING

☐	Place zoom lens on camera body.
☐	Look through lens and line up the cross hair of the ground glass on a point in your prep area.
☐	Lock the head so that the camera cannot pan or tilt.
☐	Look through lens and slowly zoom lens all the way in to telephoto and all the way out to wide angle.
☐	Look to see that the cross hair does not shift too noticeably from the original point. A small amount of shifting is acceptable.
☐	If there is too much shifting (up/down or left/right) have the lens checked before taking it.
☐	
☐	

POWER ZOOM CONTROL & MOTOR

☐	Check that zoom motor is mounted securely to lens.
☐	Connect zoom control and motor and check that they function properly.
☐	Check all power cables to be sure that they are in working order.
☐	
☐	

ALL LENSES – CHECK FOCUS

☐	Mount lens to camera.
☐	Set aperture (t-stop) to its widest setting.
☐	Using your tape measure, place a focus chart at a specific distance as marked on lens.
☐	Look through viewfinder and focus chart to your eye.
☐	Check that measured distance matches the eye focused distance.
☐	Check each lens at various distances including closest focusing point and infinity.
☐	When checking a zoom lens, set it to its most telephoto focal length for checking focus.
☐	
☐	
☐	

MATTE BOX

☐	Mounts properly and securely to iris rods, camera body or lens.
☐	Operates smoothly with each lens.
☐	Does not vignette with wide angle lenses.
☐	Contains the proper adapter rings and rubber donut or bellows for each lens.
☐	Filter trays are the correct size and slide in and out smoothly.
☐	Rotating filter rings operate smoothly and lock securely in position.
☐	Geared filter trays operate smoothly.
☐	Swing away matte box operates smoothly.
☐	Eyebrow or shade mounts securely and can be adjusted easily.
☐	Hard mattes mount securely and are the correct size for each lens.
☐	
☐	
☐	
☐	

CPC   © DEE

Figure C.4   *(continued)*

FILM CAMERA PREP CHECKLIST – Page 5

Production Title

Camera Rental Company

FOLLOW-FOCUS MECHANISM

- ☐ Check that follow-focus mounts securely to iris rods or camera body.
- ☐ Engage follow focus gear to lens gear.
- ☐ Check that it operates smoothly with each lens.
- ☐ Have correct focusing gears for zooms and primes.
- ☐
- ☐

FOLLOW-FOCUS ACCESSORIES

- ☐ Check all accessories to be sure that they fit and operate smoothly – focus whip, speed crank, right hand extension, marking disks, etc.
- ☐
- ☐

FILTERS

- ☐ All filters are correct size for matte box and lens shades being used.
- ☐ All filters are clean and free from scratches.
- ☐ Rotating polarizer operates smoothly.
- ☐ Filter set contains an optical flat.
- ☐ When using more than one camera, have enough filters for all cameras.
- ☐ Check graduated filters for hard or soft edge.
- ☐
- ☐

OBIE LIGHT OR EYE LIGHT

- ☐ Mounts securely to camera and operates correctly at each setting.
- ☐ Spare bulb is included with light.

LENS LIGHT (ASSISTANT'S LIGHT)

- ☐ Mounts securely to camera and is easily adjustable.
- ☐ Spare bulb and power cable is provided.
- ☐
- ☐

PRECISION SPEED CONTROL

- ☐ Mounts easily to camera and operates correctly for both high speed and slow motion.
- ☐ Spare power cable is provided.
- ☐
- ☐

HMI SPEED CONTROL

- ☐ Mounts easily to camera and operates correctly for both high speed and slow motion.
- ☐ Spare power cable is provided.
- ☐
- ☐
- ☐
- ☐

CPC   © DEE

Figure C.4   (*continued*)

FILM CAMERA PREP CHECKLIST – Page 6

Production Title

Camera Rental Company

SYNC BOX

☐ Connect sync box and test to be sure that you can sync to computer screen or video monitor if necessary.

☐ Camera must have an adjustable shutter in order to properly use the sync box.

☐

☐

VIDEO TAP & MONITOR

☐ Connect video tap and monitor to be sure that you have proper image on screen.

☐ Obtain extra cables and connectors.

☐ Be sure that monitor can be powered from AC as well as battery power.

☐ Check On-Board Video Monitor if one is being used. Be sure that it mounts securely to the camera.

☐

☐

HANDHELD ACCESS ORIES

☐ Obtain proper accessories and magazines if shooting any handheld shots – left and right hand grips, shoulder pad, light weight matte box, mini follow focus, on board or belt batteries, small magazines.

☐ Mount all accessories and check for proper fit and comfort of operator.

☐ Check hand grip with on/off switch to be sure that it functions properly.

☐

☐

REMOTE START SWITCH

☐ Connect to camera and be sure that it functions properly.

☐ Obtain extension cable for switch if necessary.

☐

☐

BATTERIES & CABLES

☐ Have enough batteries for all cameras and accessories.

☐ Check all cables for any frayed or loose wires.

☐ Check that there are no loose pins in the plugs or connectors.

☐ Check that all cables connect properly to camera body and batteries.

☐ Obtain extra batteries if shooting in cold weather or when doing high speed work.

☐ Obtain proper charges for all batteries being used.

☐ Obtain extra power cables – each camera should have at least two power cables.

ADDITIONAL ITEMS

☐

☐

☐

☐

☐

☐

☐

CPC   © DEE

Figure C.4 (*continued*)

NON-PREP DISCLAIMER		
TO PRODUCTION OFFICE: Please print this form, sign at bottom, and return signed copy by FAX, E-mail or printed hard copy to verify that you have read, understand and agree to the below conditions.		
Date:		
Prod. Title:	Prod. #:	
Prod. Company:		
Address:		
City:	State:	Zip:
Phone:	Fax:	
Email:		
Start Date:	End Date:	
Name:		
Address:		
City:	State:	Zip:
Phone:	Fax:	
Cell Phone:	Email:	
Position: ☐ 1st AC	☐ 2nd AC	☐ DIT

It is my strong recommendation that I or somebody that I recommend have the opportunity to perform a complete prep of the camera rental equipment at the rental house. If a complete and adequate prep is not carried out, I will not assume any responsibility for failure of equipment to operate and perform correctly. If equipment is ordered by the production company without a prep being performed, and does not arrive on set in working order, or if batteries are not adequately charged for camera operation, and pieces of equipment are missing or lack compatibility I will not be held responsible.

Employee Printed Name | Position

Employee Signature | Date

Approved and Accepted:

Prod. Co. Rep. Printed Name | Signature | Date

NPD | © DEE

Figure C.5 Non-prep disclaimer.

EQUIPMENT RECEIVED LOG Page # ____ of ____

Production Title

DATE RECEIVED	DESCRIPTION (ITEM NAME & SERIAL NUMBER)	RENTAL COMPANY NAME	NOTES

ERL

Figure C.6 Equipment received log.

DATE RETURNED	DESCRIPTION (ITEM NAME & SERIAL NUMBER)	RENTAL COMPANY NAME	NOTES

RETURNED EQUIPMENT LOG

Production Title

Page # __ of __

REL

© DEE

Figure C.7 Returned equipment log.

Figure C.8 is a Missing or Damaged Equipment Log that allows you to keep a record of all equipment that may be lost or damaged during the course of the production. Let's hope you don't need to use this form, but in case you do, it is available for your use.

Figures C.9 through C.23 are additional forms that I have created for use by the camera department. Most of these are based on industry standard forms that I have used, and they have been created using the best information from these forms and then modifying or adding to them. I have specially created other forms that I have used successfully for many years. These include a Film Camera Report, Digital Camera Report, two versions of a Daily Film Inventory Form, a camera department log sheet, a weekly time sheet, an invoice that can be used when providing services as an independent contractor, an example of a simple deal memo, and an equipment rental agreement, just to name a few. The first form is a Job Information Form, which can be seen in Figure C.9. I found that whenever I received a telephone call regarding work, I usually scribbled down the information on a piece of scrap paper. I created this form so that when a job call comes in, I can fill in all of the pertinent information regarding the job, and it also helps me to remember to ask the right questions regarding the job.

Chapter 3 contains three different types of industry standard camera reports. Figure C.10 shows a generic Film Camera Report that could be used any time you are shooting film, no matter what laboratory you are working with. It contains all of the pertinent information, as well as a space to write in the name of the lab that will be processing the film. While most labs provide copies of their camera reports, there may be instances when you don't have time to get them or you simply run out of the lab reports. This custom camera report will serve the purpose until you can obtain additional reports from the lab. The companion web site for the book contains a full-page version of the Film Camera Report along with a smaller version with two camera reports on a single 8½×11in. sheet of paper. You may want to print these out and have them printed on three-part or four-part carbonless paper for use on your individual productions.

Figure C.11 shows a Film Developing Purchase Order. Many labs and production companies require the use of a purchase order when submitting rolls of film for developing. If the lab or production company doesn't have its own purchase order form, you may use this one when submitting film. Unlike a standard purchase order form, this form is specifically designed for use when submitting film for processing.

Figure C.12 is a Digital Camera Report designed specifically for shooting digital productions. It contains spaces to record the information that is specific to shooting with a digital camera along with some of the same information that is recorded on a Film Camera Report. As

MISSING OR DAMAGED EQUIPMENT LOG

Page # ___ of ___

Production Title

DATE MISSING OR DAMAGED	DESCRIPTION (ITEM NAME & SERIAL NUMBER)	RENTAL COMPANY NAME	NOTES

DEL

© DEE

Figure C.8   Missing or damaged equipment log.

JOB INFORMATION							

Date:

Prod. Title:		Prod. #:

Format	☐ Film	☐ 16 mm	☐ 35 mm	☐ Digital	☐ SD	☐ HD

Prod. Company:

Address:

City:	State:	Zip:

Phone:	Fax:	E-mail:

Contact Person:	Title:

Shooting Date(s):

Position:	☐ DP	☐ Operator	☐ 1st AC	☐ 2nd AC	☐ Loader	☐ D.I.T.
	☐ Other					

☐ Union	☐ Non-union Rate:		☐ Daily – 8 Hours	☐ Daily – 10 Hours
☐ Daily – 12 Hours	☐ Weekly Other			
☐ Invoice	☐ Time Card	Box or Kit Rental ☐ Y ☐ N	Amount:	

Additional Information:

☐ Local	☐ Distant	Travel Dates (If applicable)

Per Diem

Director of Photography:

Phone:	Fax:	E-mail:

Camera Rental Company:

Address:

City:	State:	Zip:

Phone:	Fax:	E-mail:

Contact Person:	Title:

Camera (See Equipment Checklist)

Prep Date(s)

Laboratory:

Address:

City:	State:	Zip:

Phone:	Fax:	E-mail:

Contact Person:	Title:

Additional Information:

JIF   © DEE

Figure C.9   Job information form.

FILM CAMERA REPORT

Laboratory:						Page # of
Prod. Co.:						
Prod. Title:						
Director:			D.P.:			
1st AC:		2nd AC:			Loader:	
Date:		Prod. #:			Camera:	
Mag #:		Roll #:			Footage:	
Film Type:			Emulsion #:			

SCENE	TAKE	DIAL	FEET	LENS	T-STOP	REMARKS

☐ 16mm	☐ Super 16mm	☐ 35mm	☐ Color	☐ B & W	Good	
☐ Process Normal	☐ One Light Print		☐ Best Light Print		No Good	
☐ Prep for Video	☐ Time to Gray Card		☐ Timed Workprint		Waste	
☐ Special Developing	☐ Time to These Lights ____ — ____ — ____				Short End	
☐ Other					Total	

COMMENTS	

FCR   © DEE

Figure C.10   Film camera report.

CAMERA DEPARTMENT **FILM DEVELOPING PURCHASE ORDER**	**PURCHASE ORDER #**

Laboratory:	Date:

Address:

City:	State:	Zip:

Phone:	Fax:

Prod. Title:	Prod. No.

Prod. Co.

Contact Name:

Address:

City:	State:	Zip:

Phone:	Fax:

Film Type and Format   ☐ 16mm ☐ Super 16mm ☐ 35mm ☐ 65mm ☐ Color ☐ B & W

Number of 400-ft Rolls/Cans:	Footage:	Roll Numbers:
Number of 1000-ft Rolls/Cans:	Footage:	
Number of Other Rolls/Cans:	Footage:	
Total Number of Rolls/Cans :	Total Footage:	

☐ Process Normal   ☐ One Light Print   ☐ Best Light Print
☐ Prep for Video Transfer   ☐ Time to Gray Scale   ☐ Timed Work Print
☐ Special Processing   ☐ Time to These Lights ____ — ____ — ____
☐ Push   ☐ Pull   ☐ 1 Stop   ☐ 2 Stops
☐ Print All   ☐ Print Circle Takes Only
☐ Other

TRANSFER TO	☐ MINI DV	☐ DVC-PRO	☐ DV-CAM	☐ HD CAM
	☐ BETA	☐ DIGI BETA	☐ HARD DRIVE	
	☐ OTHER			

Special Instructions:

☐ Vault Original   ☐ Return Original with Order
☐ Other

_____	_____
Signature	Date

DPO	© DEE

Figure C.11   Film developing purchase order.

DIGITAL CAMERA REPORT		Date:		Page # of	

Prod. Co.:   Prod. #:

Prod. Title:

Director: D.P.:

1st AC: 2nd AC:

D.I.T./Data

Camera: Roll #:   Mag #:   Project FPS:

Codec: ISO/EI: White Bal: Shutter Angle:

Recording Media: ☐ Hard Drive   ☐ RED SS Drive   ☐ S x S   ☐ P-2

☐ SD Card   ☐ Compact Flash   ☐ Other

SCENE	TAKE	CLIP/FILE	LENS	F-STOP	REMARKS

Total # Clips: Total GB:

COMMENTS:

DCR   © DEE

Figure C.12   Digital camera report.

with the Film Camera Report, the companion web site for this book also contains a full-page version of the Digital Camera Report along with a smaller version that contains two camera reports on a single 8½ × 11 in. sheet of paper. These may also be printed out on three-part or four-part carbonless paper for use on your individual productions.

The Daily Film Inventory forms shown in Figures C.13 and C.14 are used to keep a daily record of film stock used for each roll shot during the day. I have included two different versions so that you can choose the one that is better suited to your production. There are many styles of the film inventory form that I have seen over the years, so you may come across one that is different from these two. These two are variations of what I have used most often during my career, but you should use whatever one works best for you, or make up your own. As with the Film and Digital Camera Reports, the companion web site for this book also contains a full-page version of the Daily Film Inventory forms along with a smaller version that contains two forms on a single 8½ × 11 in. sheet of paper. These may also be printed out on three-part or four-part carbonless paper for use on your individual productions.

Figure C.15, the Short End Inventory Form, was designed to allow me to better keep track of short ends created and used during the course of a production. Figure C.16 allows you to keep track of all raw stock on hand for every size roll of film, including short ends. I realize that the Daily Film Inventory and Short End Inventory forms each indicate how much raw stock is on hand, but they are not specific enough. The Raw Stock Inventory Form breaks down available stock more precisely into each size roll. The Production Manager or even the Director of Photography often wants a precise count of how much film and what size rolls are available for each film stock. Figure C.17, the Camera Department Film Log Sheet, may be used by the camera department to keep track of specific information for each shot or only for particular shots when shooting film. This form contains much more information than is included on the camera report and is useful if it becomes necessary to reshoot a scene after principal photography is completed. It can also be helpful when shooting coverage or reverse angles of a scene later in the day or even later in the production schedule. Having all of the information regarding lens focal length, distance to subject, filters, etc. will make it easier to match a shot later on in production. As indicated in Chapter 4, there is a small pocket-size book called *The Camera Log* that many Camera Assistants use on set. This form contains much of the same information that is in that book. Figure C.18, the Camera Department Digital Log Sheet, is similar to the film log sheet except that it is used when shooting in the digital format.

DAILY FILM INVENTORY						Page #		of	

Prod. Co.:					Day #:		Date:	
Prod. Title:						Prod. #:		
Laboratory:								

Film Type:

LOADED	ROLL #	GOOD	NG	WASTE	TOTAL	SE	FILM ON HAND	
							Previous	
							Today (+)	
							Today (-)	
							Total	
							400' Rolls	
							1000' Rolls	
							Short Ends	
							Other	
	TOTALS	GOOD	NG	WASTE	TOTAL	Comments:		
	Today							
	Previous (+)							
	Total to Date							

Film Type:

LOADED	ROLL #	GOOD	NG	WASTE	TOTAL	SE	FILM ON HAND	
							Previous	
							Today (+)	
							Today (-)	
							Total	
							400' Rolls	
							1000' Rolls	
							Short Ends	
							Other	
	TOTALS	GOOD	NG	WASTE	TOTAL	Comments:		
	Today							
	Previous (+)							
	Total to Date							

TOTAL FILM USE	GOOD	NG	WASTE	TOTAL	TOTAL FILM ON HAND	
Today					Previous	
Previous (+)					Today (+)	
Total to Date					Today (-)	
					Total	

DFI-1   © DEE

Figure C.13 Daily film inventory form #1.

DAILY FILM INVENTORY						Page #		of	
Prod. Co.:					Day #:		Date:		
Prod. Title:							Prod. #:		
Laboratory:									
FILM TYPE	ROLL #	LOADED	GOOD	NO GOOD	WASTE		TOTAL		SE
TOTALS		LOADED	GOOD	NO GOOD	WASTE		TOTAL		SE
	Today								
	Previous (+)								
	Total to Date								
Film on Hand	Film Type								TOTALS
Previous Balance									
(+) Received Today									
(–) Used Today									
Total To Date									

DFI-2 © DEE

Figure C.14   Daily film inventory form #2.

SHORT END INVENTORY			Page #		of	
Prod. Co.:						
Prod. Title:				Prod. #:		
SHORT ENDS CREATED DURING PRODUCTION						
DATE CREATED	FILM STOCK	SHORT END AMOUNT	DATE USED	AMOUNT USED	AMOUNT REMAINING	
SEI					© DEE	

Figure C.15   Short end inventory form.

SHORT END INVENTORY				Page #		of	
Prod. Co.:							
Prod. Title:					Prod. #:		
SHORT ENDS OBTAINED FROM OTHER SOURCE(S)							
DATE ON CAN	FILM STOCK	AMOUNT INDICATED ON CAN	DATE USED	AMOUNT USED	AMOUNT REMAINING	ACTUAL AMOUNT OF SHORT END	
SEI						© DEE	

Figure C.15 *(continued)*

RAW STOCK INVENTORY						Page #		of	

Prod. Co.:				Day #:		Date:	
Prod. Title:					Prod. #:		

Film Stock

	100'	200'	400'	800'	1000'	1200'	SHORT ENDS
Previous							
Today (+)							
Today (-)							
To Date							

Total on Hand to Date

Film Stock

	100'	200'	400'	800'	1000'	1200'	SHORT ENDS
Previous							
Today (+)							
Today (-)							
To Date							

Total on Hand to Date

Film Stock

	100'	200'	400'	800'	1000'	1200'	SHORT ENDS
Previous							
Today (+)							
Today (-)							
To Date							

Total on Hand to Date

Film Stock

	100'	200'	400'	800'	1000'	1200'	SHORT ENDS
Previous							
Today (+)							
Today (-)							
To Date							

Total on Hand to Date

Film Stock

	100'	200'	400'	800'	1000'	1200'	SHORT ENDS
Previous							
Today (+)							
Today (-)							
To Date							

Total on Hand to Date

RSI   © DEE

Figure C.16   Raw stock inventory form.

SCENE	ROLL	LENS	STOP	FPS	FOCUS	FILTER	LENS HEIGHT	REMARKS / SCENE DESCRIPTION
								SCENE DESCRIPTION

CAMERA DEPARTMENT LOG SHEET - FILM

Page #   of

Prod. Company   Day #   Date

Prod. Title   Prod. #

CLS-F   © DEE

Figure C.17 Camera department film log sheet.

SCENE	ROLL	CLIP/FILE	LENS	STOP	FPS	FOCUS	FILTER	LENS HEIGHT	REMARKS/SCENE DESCRIPTION

CAMERA DEPARTMENT LOG SHEET - DIGITAL

Page # ___ of ___

Prod. Company ___ Day # ___ Date ___

Prod. Title ___ Prod. # ___

CLS-D

© DEE

Figure C.18 Camera department digital log sheet.

Figure C.19, the Film Stock Request Form is used to request additional film stock from the production office during the course of production. This form makes it easier to request the correct roll sizes and type of film for the production.

As mentioned in Chapter 4, the 2nd AC, and sometimes the Loader, is often responsible for keeping track of hours worked by each member of the camera department. Figure C.20 is a weekly time sheet that allows the 2nd AC or Loader to write in the hours for all key members of the department along with any day players who may come on the production. Figure C.21 is a combination individual time sheet and invoice. It can be used to keep track of hours worked and also may be submitted at the conclusion of production for payment when working as an independent contractor. Because of the nature of the film business, you will often be asked to work as an independent contractor. This means that you will most likely not fill out a time card or time sheet, but rather submit an invoice for your services. Figure C.21 can serve as your time sheet and invoice when working as an independent contractor. Quite often you will be asked to sign a deal memo before the production. The deal memo is a contract between you and the production company. It will detail the terms of your employment for the duration of the production and is to be signed by you and a representative of the production company. Most production companies have their own form of deal memo, but if not you may use the generic deal memo shown in Figure C.22. As a freelance Camera Assistant you may also have some equipment that you will rent to the production company during the course of the production. Figure C.23 is an example of an equipment rental agreement that can be used between you and the production company. So that you can keep in touch with the members of your camera crew, Figure C.24 is a Camera Department Contact List so that you can enter the name, address, phone numbers, email address, etc., of all members of the camera department.

LABELS

As indicated in Chapter 3, when preparing film for delivery to the lab, each film can must be labeled. To ensure that all of the proper information is included on the film can, Figure C.25 is a film can label that you can use when sending film to the lab for developing. If you would like to print these from the companion web site for this book, I recommend using one of the following Avery brand labels that are available at any office supply store: #5164, #5264, or #8164. You may also use any generic 3.33×4 in. label similar to the Avery labels.

FILM STOCK REQUEST

Date:	Prod. #:
Prod. Title:	
Requested By:	
D.P.:	
Position: ☐ 1st AC ☐ 2nd AC ☐ Loader ☐ Camera PA ☐ Other	

16mm

Quantity	Film Type	Daylight Spool	Core Load
		☐ 100' ☐ 200' ☐ 400'	☐ 400' ☐ 800' ☐ 1200'
		☐ 100' ☐ 200' ☐ 400'	☐ 400' ☐ 800' ☐ 1200'
		☐ 100' ☐ 200' ☐ 400'	☐ 400' ☐ 800' ☐ 1200'
		☐ 100' ☐ 200' ☐ 400'	☐ 400' ☐ 800' ☐ 1200'
		☐ 100' ☐ 200' ☐ 400'	☐ 400' ☐ 800' ☐ 1200'
		☐ 100' ☐ 200' ☐ 400'	☐ 400' ☐ 800' ☐ 1200'
		☐ 100' ☐ 200' ☐ 400'	☐ 400' ☐ 800' ☐ 1200'
		☐ 100' ☐ 200' ☐ 400'	☐ 400' ☐ 800' ☐ 1200'
		☐ 100' ☐ 200' ☐ 400'	☐ 400' ☐ 800' ☐ 1200'

NOTE: 16 mm, 200-foot Daylight Spools are only available for the Aaton A-Minima Camera

35mm

Quantity	Film Type	Daylight Spool	Core Load
		☐ 100'	☐ 200' ☐ 400' ☐ 1000'
		☐ 100'	☐ 200' ☐ 400' ☐ 1000'
		☐ 100'	☐ 200' ☐ 400' ☐ 1000'
		☐ 100'	☐ 200' ☐ 400' ☐ 1000'
		☐ 100'	☐ 200' ☐ 400' ☐ 1000'
		☐ 100'	☐ 200' ☐ 400' ☐ 1000'
		☐ 100'	☐ 200' ☐ 400' ☐ 1000'
		☐ 100'	☐ 200' ☐ 400' ☐ 1000'
		☐ 100'	☐ 200' ☐ 400' ☐ 1000'
		☐ 100'	☐ 200' ☐ 400' ☐ 1000'

Notes:	
Date Needed:	

Signature	Date

FSR   © DEE

Figure C.19   Film stock request form.

| CAMERA DEPARTMENT WEEKLY TIME SHEET | | | | | | | Page # | | of | |

Prod. Company:

Prod. Title: Prod. #:

Week Ending:

D.P.		Name						SS #			
DAY	DATE	CALL	1ST MEAL		2ND MEAL		WRAP	1x	1.5x	2x	TOTAL
			OUT	IN	OUT	IN					
Sunday											
Monday											
Tuesday											
Wednesday											
Thursday											
Friday											
Saturday											
							TOTAL HOURS				

Camera Operator		Name						SS #			
DAY	DATE	CALL	1ST MEAL		2ND MEAL		WRAP	1x	1.5x	2x	TOTAL
			OUT	IN	OUT	IN					
Sunday											
Monday											
Tuesday											
Wednesday											
Thursday											
Friday											
Saturday											
							TOTAL HOURS				

1st AC		Name						SS #			
DAY	DATE	CALL	1ST MEAL		2ND MEAL		WRAP	1x	1.5x	2x	TOTAL
			OUT	IN	OUT	IN					
Sunday											
Monday											
Tuesday											
Wednesday											
Thursday											
Friday											
Saturday											
							TOTAL HOURS				

2nd AC		Name						SS #			
DAY	DATE	CALL	1ST MEAL		2ND MEAL		WRAP	1x	1.5x	2x	TOTAL
			OUT	IN	OUT	IN					
Sunday											
Monday											
Tuesday											
Wednesday											
Thursday											
Friday											
Saturday											
							TOTAL HOURS				

CTS   © DEE

Figure C.20 Camera department weekly time sheet.

| CAMERA DEPARTMENT WEEKLY TIME SHEET | | | | | | | | Page # | | | of | |

| Prod. Company: |
| Prod. Title: Prod. #: |
| Week Ending: |

Position				Name					SS #			
DAY	DATE	CALL	1ST MEAL		2ND MEAL		WRAP	1x	1.5x	2x	TOTAL
			OUT	IN	OUT	IN					
Sunday											
Monday											
Tuesday											
Wednesday											
Thursday											
Friday											
Saturday											
						TOTAL HOURS					

Position				Name					SS #			
DAY	DATE	CALL	1ST MEAL		2ND MEAL		WRAP	1x	1.5x	2x	TOTAL
			OUT	IN	OUT	IN					
Sunday											
Monday											
Tuesday											
Wednesday											
Thursday											
Friday											
Saturday											
						TOTAL HOURS					

Position				Name					SS #			
DAY	DATE	CALL	1ST MEAL		2ND MEAL		WRAP	1x	1.5x	2x	TOTAL
			OUT	IN	OUT	IN					
Sunday											
Monday											
Tuesday											
Wednesday											
Thursday											
Friday											
Saturday											
						TOTAL HOURS					

Position				Name					SS #			
DAY	DATE	CALL	1ST MEAL		2ND MEAL		WRAP	1x	1.5x	2x	TOTAL
			OUT	IN	OUT	IN					
Sunday											
Monday											
Tuesday											
Wednesday											
Thursday											
Friday											
Saturday											
						TOTAL HOURS					

CTS   © DEE

Figure C.20   (*continued*)

CAMERA CREW TIME SHEET AND INVOICE

Name: Date:

Address:

City: State: Zip:

Home Phone: SS# or Fed. ID #

Cell Phone: Email:

Prod. Title: Prod. #:

Prod. Co.:

Address:

City: State: Zip:

Phone: Fax:

For Services Rendered As   ☐ DP   ☐ Operator   ☐ 1st AC   ☐ 2nd AC
☐ Loader   ☐ DIT   ☐ Other

RATE: ☐ Weekly   ☐ Hourly   ☐ Daily   Hours

OVERTIME: ☐ Yes   ☐ No   RATE: ☐ 1 ½ X   ☐ 2 X   After   Hours

For Week Ending:

DAY	DATE	CALL	1ST MEAL		2ND MEAL		WRAP	1x	1.5x	2x	TOTAL
			OUT	IN	OUT	IN					
Sunday											
Monday											
Tuesday											
Wednesday											
Thursday											
Friday											
Saturday											
							TOTAL HOURS				

ADDITIONAL CHARGES OR SERVICES

TOTAL AMOUNT DUE

PAYMENT IS DUE 30 DAYS FROM DATE OF INVOICE
PAYMENT NOT RECEIVED IS SUBJECT TO INTEREST CHARGE OF 1 ½% PER MONTH

Signature   Date

Production Office Approval (Print Name)   Date

Production Office Approval (Signature)   Date

Paid by Check #   Date

PTS   © DEE

Figure C.21   Personal time sheet and invoice.

CAMERA DEPARTMENT DEAL MEMO

Date:	

Prod. Title: Prod. #:

Prod. Company:

Address:

City: State: Zip:

Phone: Fax: E-mail:

Start Date: End Date:

Name:

Address:

City: State: Zip:

Phone: Cell Phone:

Email:

SS# or Fed. ID #:

Position: ☐ DP   ☐ Camera Operator   ☐ 1st AC   ☐ 2nd AC   ☐ Loader

☐ Other:

Union/Guild:

Shoot Rate: ☐ Weekly   ☐ Hourly   ☐ Daily   Hours

Prep Rate: ☐ Weekly   ☐ Hourly   ☐ Daily   Hours

Overtime Rate: After   Hours   ☐ **SEE TERMS ON PAGE 2**

BOX / EQUIPMENT RENTAL   PER ☐ DAY   ☐ WEEK

(SEE EQUIPMENT RENTAL AGREEMENT)

Travel Accommodations:

Expenses/Per Diem:

Other:

Employer of Record:

Address:

City: State: Zip:

Phone:

SCREEN CREDIT WILL BE AWARDED AT PRODUCER'S DISCRETION.
IF AWARDED SCREEN CREDIT, INDICATE HOW YOU WOULD LIKE YOUR NAME TO READ

CDM   © DEE

Figure C.22   Camera department deal memo.

CAMERA DEPARTMENT DEAL MEMO – Page 2

TERMS AND CONDITIONS

1. If an hourly rate is stated, Employee will be paid straight time for the first eight hours worked and _____ times the straight time rate after eight hours worked and _____ times after twelve hours worked. Deals are for ANY _____ consecutive days out of seven, including weekends.

2. Weekend and holiday work must be authorized, in advance, by the Production Manager.

3. Any sixth day worked will be paid at _____ times the straight time rate for the first _____ hours worked and double time thereafter.   Any seventh day worked is paid at _____ times the straight time rate for the first _____ hours worked and double time thereafter.

4. Holidays not worked are not paid. Holidays worked are paid at _____ times straight time only for hours actually worked.

5. Payment for services is due 30 days after date of invoice or 30 days from the last date worked.

6. Petty cash expenses not accompanied by original receipts will not be reimbursed.

7. Timecards must reflect hours worked and must be turned in on time. Timecards turned in late will result in late payment.

8. Employee acknowledges that personal property rented to the Production Company as part of the Box/Equipment Rental must be insured by the Employee.

9. Box/Equipment Rentals will be prorated for any partial week worked.

10. Production Company reserves the right to suspend work without compensation, if a force majeure or labor dispute occurs.

11. Director of Photographer and Camera Operator will be provided a reel of the product on a master format when made available to the Producer.

Additional Terms:

Approved and Accepted:

Prod. Co. Rep. Printed Name	Signature	Date
Employee Printed Name	Signature	Date

CDM   © DEE

Figure C.22 *(continued)*

BOX / EQUIPMENT RENTAL AGREEMENT

Name:	Date:
Address:	
City:	State: Zip:
Phone:	SS# or Fed. ID#:

Prod. Title:	Prod. No.
Prod. Co.	
Address:	
City:	State: Zip:
Phone:	

The above named production company agrees to rent the equipment listed below from employee beginning on _____ and ending on _____ . The rental rate shall be _____ per ☐ day ☐ week. Company agrees to take full responsibility for the safety of equipment and agrees to replace or repair any equipment lost or damaged while being rented by the company. Total value for equipment listed below and/or on additional sheet(s) is $ _____

Any extensions beyond the above listed dates will be charged at the daily rate for rental of equipment unless other arrangements have previously been made. Employee acknowledges that personal property rented to the Production Company as part of this Box/Equipment Rental Agreement must be insured by the Employee.

☐ Invoice will be submitted weekly	☐ Charges will be listed on weekly time card

EQUIPMENT INVENTORY (Attach additional pages if necessary)

ITEM	SERIAL #	VALUE

- Box and equipment rentals are subject to 1099 reporting.
- *The Production Company is not responsible for any claims of loss or damage to box/equipment rental items that are not listed on the inventory.*

Approved and Accepted:

_____	_____	_____
Prod. Co. Rep. Printed Name	Signature	Date
_____	_____	_____
Employee Printed Name	Signature	Date

BER   © DEE

Figure C.23   Box/equipment rental agreement.

BOX / EQUIPMENT RENTAL AGREEMENT		Page #	of	
Name:		Date:		
Prod. Title:		Prod. No.		

EQUIPMENT INVENTORY		
ITEM	SERIAL #	VALUE

Approved and Accepted:

Prod. Co. Rep. Printed Name	Signature	Date

Employee Printed Name	Signature	Date

BER   © DEE

Figure C.23 (*continued*)

CAMERA DEPARTMENT CONTACT LIST		Page #		of	

Prod. Company:			
Prod. Title:		Prod. #:	

DP

Name:	Home Phone:
Address:	Cell Phone:
City:	State: Zip:
Email:	Other:

Camera Operator

Name:	Home Phone:
Address:	Cell Phone:
City:	State: Zip:
Email:	Other:

1st AC

Name:	Home Phone:
Address:	Cell Phone:
City:	State: Zip:
Email:	Other:

2nd AC

Name:	Home Phone:
Address:	Cell Phone:
City:	State: Zip:
Email:	Other:

Loader

Name:	Home Phone:
Address:	Cell Phone:
City:	State: Zip:
Email:	Other:

Position

Name:	Home Phone:
Address:	Cell Phone:
City:	State: Zip:
Email:	Other:

Position

Name:	Home Phone:
Address:	Cell Phone:
City:	State: Zip:
Email:	Other:

CCL	© DEE

Figure C.24   Camera department contact list.

CAMERA DEPARTMENT CONTACT LIST – page 2	Page #		of	

Prod. Company:		
Prod. Title:	Prod. #:	

Position		
Name:	Home Phone:	
Address:	Cell Phone:	
City:	State:	Zip:
Email:	Other:	

Position		
Name:	Home Phone:	
Address:	Cell Phone:	
City:	State:	Zip:
Email:	Other:	

Position		
Name:	Home Phone:	
Address:	Cell Phone:	
City:	State:	Zip:
Email:	Other:	

Position		
Name:	Home Phone:	
Address:	Cell Phone:	
City:	State:	Zip:
Email:	Other:	

Position		
Name:	Home Phone:	
Address:	Cell Phone:	
City:	State:	Zip:
Email:	Other:	

Position		
Name:	Home Phone:	
Address:	Cell Phone:	
City:	State:	Zip:
Email:	Other:	

Position		
Name:	Home Phone:	
Address:	Cell Phone:	
City:	State:	Zip:
Email:	Other:	

CCL	© DEE

Figure C.24 (*continued*)

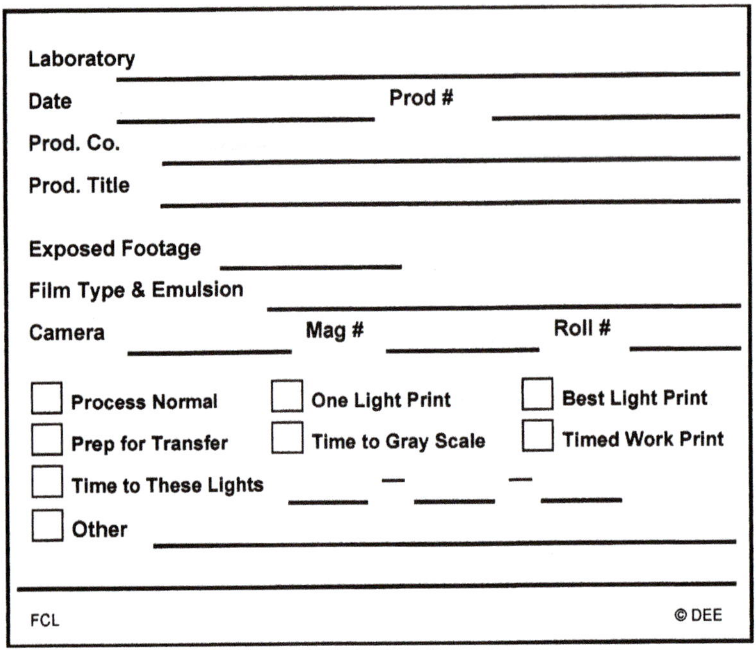

Laboratory		
Date	Prod #	
Prod. Co.		
Prod. Title		
Exposed Footage		
Film Type & Emulsion		
Camera	Mag #	Roll #

☐ Process Normal   ☐ One Light Print   ☐ Best Light Print

☐ Prep for Transfer   ☐ Time to Gray Scale   ☐ Timed Work Print

☐ Time to These Lights   —   —

☐ Other

FCL   © DEE

Figure C.25 Film can developing label.

At the end of the shooting day or at the end of production, you may have film left over that has not yet been shot. There may be short ends or even full rolls that were loaded into a magazine but not used. These rolls must be unloaded from the magazines, placed in a black bag and film can, sealed, and labeled so that they can either be sold or used on a future production. Figures C.26 and C.27 are short end and recan labels that you may use for labeling these cans of unexposed film stock. If you would like to print these from the companion web site for this book, I recommend using one of the following Avery brand labels that are available at any office supply store: #5163, #5263, or #8163. You may also use any generic 2×4 in. label similar to the Avery labels.

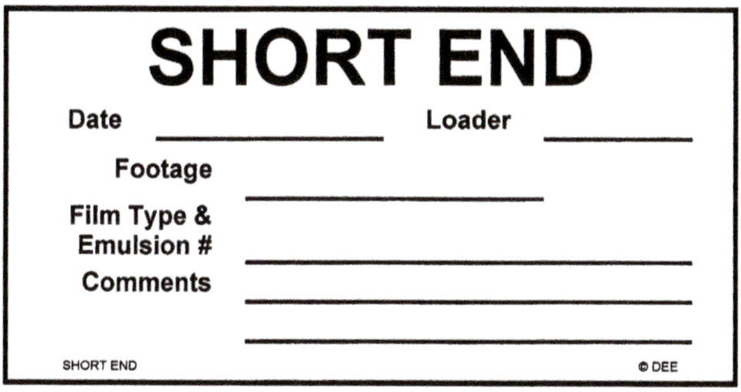

SHORT END

Date ____________ Loader ________

Footage ________________

Film Type &
Emulsion # ________________________

Comments ________________________

____

SHORT END © DEE

Figure C.26 Short end label.

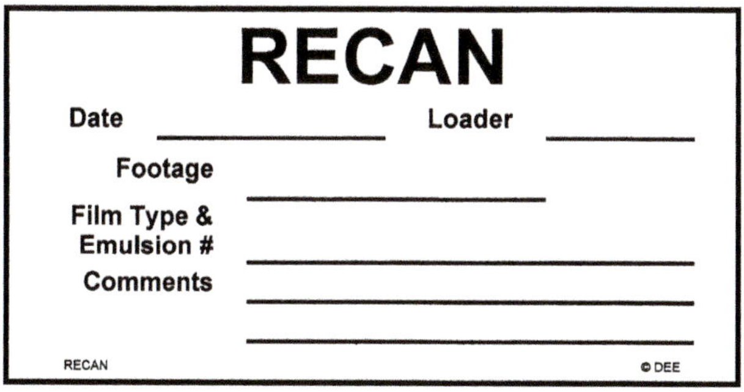

RECAN

Date ____________ Loader ________

Footage ________________

Film Type &
Emulsion # ________________________

Comments ________________________

____

RECAN © DEE

Figure C.27 Recan label.

If you plan to ship the film from a distant location, it is important to label the shipping carton properly so that the film does not get exposed to harmful X-rays. Figure C.28 is a label that you should place on all sides of the carton when shipping film. If you would like to print these from the companion web site for this book, I recommend using one of the following Avery brand labels that are available at any office supply store: #5163, #5263, or #8163. You may also use any generic 2×4 in. label similar to the Avery labels.

Figure C.28   X-ray warning label.

Appendix D

Tools, Accessories, and Expendables

Many professions require that you have your own tools and equipment to do the job. This is the case with a professional Assistant Cameraman. Without the basic tools, accessories, and expendables, you will not be able to perform your job properly and may not be hired for future jobs. Some of the tools are basic everyday tools that you will need to mount the camera onto a particular platform or to perform minor repairs on the camera. Others are specialized pieces of equipment or tools that are unique to the film industry. Many assistants also have certain specialty items in their ditty bag based on personal preference.

Your toolkit or ditty bag should also include many of the items on the Camera Expendables Inventory and Checklist (Figure C.3). As you work more and more, your ditty bag or kit will go through many changes as you improve upon it and make it as complete as possible to suit your individual needs. No two assistants' toolkits or ditty bags are alike. It is all based on personal preference, the types of jobs that you are accepting, and the specific tools that each individual needs to perform their job. If you are only working on digital productions you may want to have specific items that you would never need on film shoots. I have tried to include some digital tools and items that you may need in the following lists.

Because you will invest a lot of money in the various tools and accessories needed to do your job, I recommend having a protective case or cases to keep them in. Most assistants have one or more cases or bags that contain all of the tools, accessories, and supplies needed to do the job. The type of bag or case you choose is up to you. The important thing to remember is that this is your career, and you will use these tools and supplies for a long time. Keep them safe, protected, and organized in a case or bag so that they are always available when needed and you can carry them with you without too much difficulty. Some use soft-side bags with various size compartments, while others choose to keep their equipment in hard-side cases for

more protection. The type of bag or case you use should be based on what works best for you. In addition to having bags or cases for your tools and equipment, I recommend that you have some type of rolling four-wheel cart or dolly to assist in moving all of the camera equipment from place to place in the course of a shooting day. Two of the most popular carts among Camera Assistants today are the Yaeger & Sons Cart and the Backstage TR-04 Cart. In addition to these, many assistants have also used the Magliner Gemini Jr. and Gemini Sr. There are also a few companies that have modified or made their own version of these carts. Filmtools sells the Magliner carts as well as versions called the Liberator Jr. and Liberator Sr. These are excellent carts as well, and both the Magliner and Liberator carts can be customized with a wide range of accessories to suit your individual needs. I have used the Magliner Gemini Jr. cart for many years and am very happy with it. Many Camera Assistants add extra shelves and other accessories to these carts for them to be used most efficiently for transporting equipment while on stage or location, and in many cases an assistant may have two or more carts that they take from job to job. In addition to the Magliner or Liberator carts, many Camera Assistants use a rolling utility cart manufactured by Rubbermaid. See Figure D.1 for an illustration of the Backstage TR-04 Cart. See Figures D.2 and D.3 for illustrations of the Magliner cart andFigure D.4 for an illustration of

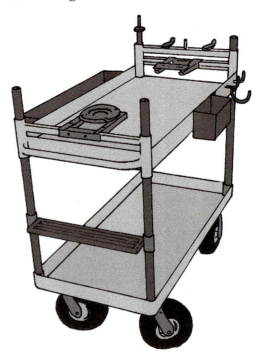

Figure D.1   Backstage TR-04 camera cart.

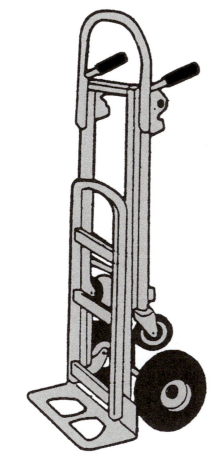

Figure D.2   Magliner cart folded for storage and transporting.

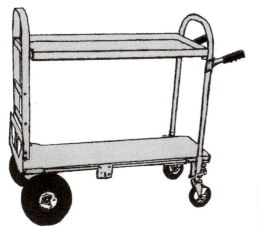

Figure D.3   Magliner cart with top and bottom shelves, set up for use.

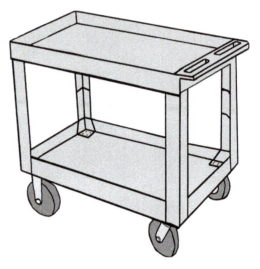

Figure D.4 Rubbermaid-style
utility cart.

the Rubbermaid cart. Choose the type and style of cart based on your particular needs. These carts can be very expensive depending on the accessories you add, but if you take care of them they will last for many, many years.

No matter where you are filming, it is important to protect the camera equipment and keep it organized. When filming in homes or buildings, you may be able to use a spare room for storage of the camera equipment. If not, you must have a protective area where you can keep the equipment close at hand. When filming on exterior locations this is especially important. In recent years I have seen many assistants, myself included, provide their own pop-up tent for use as shelter by the camera department. These are available at many department stores and specialty outdoor equipment or sporting goods stores, and are excellent for providing a shaded area not only for the camera equipment but also for the camera crew when they are not actively working on the shot. The most common size is 10×10 ft, which can be set up by two people in just a few minutes. When moving to a new location, the tent can be taken down and folded up just as quickly. When folded up it takes very little space on the camera truck. A small investment in one of these tents will go a long way in helping you to get future jobs. When you're not working, they are also great to take camping, on a picnic, or on a trip to the beach. And like the carts, many assistants may have more than one of these tents for use on production. See Figure D.5 for an illustration of the tent used by many Camera Assistants.

The following list contains some of the basic tools and accessories along with a list of expendables that you should have in your

ditty bag or AC kit. I have included a brief description of what each item is used for and there are additional descriptions or definitions included in the Glossary at the end of the book. I have tried to group them according to general tools and specialized film tools, but there may be some items that would fit into both categories and are only listed in one. Please keep in mind that this is by no means a complete list of all the items that you should have.

AC TOOLS AND ACCESSORIES

- Magliner, Liberator, Rubbermaid, Yaeger, Backstage, or other type of equipment cart or carts—for ease in transporting equipment (see Figures D.1 through D.4)
- Pop-up tent—to protect equipment and crew from sun when working outside (see Figure D.5)

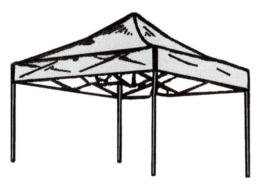

Figure D.5   Pop-up tent.

- Assorted medium and large canvas tote bags—for carrying a variety of camera accessories (e.g. LL Bean Boat Bag) (see Figure D.6)

Figure D.6   Canvas tote bag.

- Ditty bag or tool case—for assistant's tools and accessories (see Figure D.7)

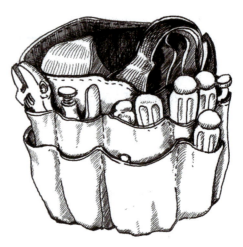

Figure D.7 Camera Assistant ditty bag.

- Small portable video monitor—for critical focus or to see the framing of the shot (see Figure D.8)
- Laptop computer—to be used for record keeping and/or storage of digital media

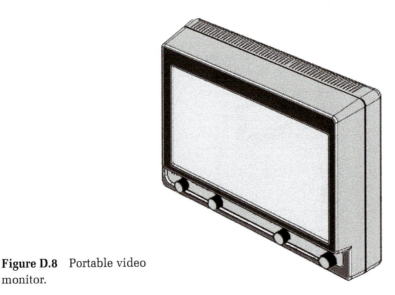

Figure D.8 Portable video monitor.

- PDA, smart phone or similar device—for keeping a record of contacts as well as useful apps for the day-to-day performance of the job
- Portable GPS—so you don't get lost on the way to the locations
- Rangefinder (Hilti PD-40)—to be used for critical focus
- AC pouch and belt—to keep basic tools handy and nearby
- Set of jeweler's screwdrivers—to be used for making repairs/adjustments to camera equipment
- 4-in-1 screwdriver—to be used for making repairs/adjustments to camera equipment
- Slotted screwdrivers (⅛ in., ³⁄₁₆ in., ¼ in., ⁵⁄₁₆ in.)—to be used for making repairs/adjustments to camera equipment
- Phillips screwdrivers (#1, #2)—to be used for making repairs/adjustments to camera equipment
- T-handle stubby screwdriver—to be used for making repairs/adjustments to camera equipment
- Magnetic screwdriver—to be used for making repairs/adjustments to camera equipment
- Allen wrenches (hex key wrenches)—metric and American—to be used for making repairs/adjustments to camera equipment (see Figure D.9)

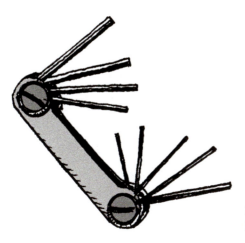

Figure D.9 Allen wrench (hex key).

- Adjustable wrench—to be used for making repairs/adjustments to camera equipment
- Large and small vise grips—to be used for making repairs/adjustments to camera equipment
- Regular and needle-nose pliers—to be used for making repairs/adjustments to camera equipment (see Figure D.10)

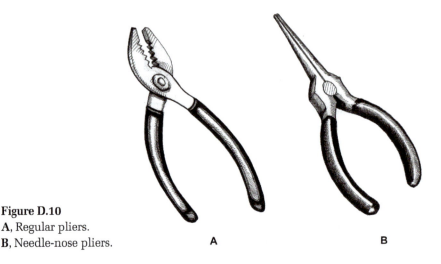

Figure D.10
A, Regular pliers.
B, Needle-nose pliers.

A   B

- Leatherman, Gerber, or similar multipurpose tool—to be used for making repairs/adjustments to camera equipment (see Figure D.11)

Figure D.11
Multipurpose tool.

- Swiss Army knife or similar pocket knife—to be used for making repairs/adjustments to camera equipment (see Figure D.12)
- Razor knife and spare blades—for cutting gels, tape, or other items
- Wire cutters—for cutting wire or cables if necessary
- Scissors—for trimming tape or anything that needs cutting
- Tweezers—for removing small film chips from inside the camera (be sure not to use metal tweezers on any metal part of the camera)
- Small C-clamps—to attach or secure camera equipment or other items to a specific point

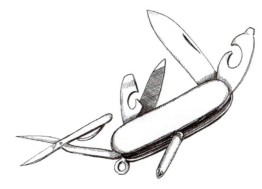

Figure D.12   Swiss Army-style pocket knife.

- Dental mirror—for checking sync of shutter when adjusting shutter angle for certain shots or for checking interior of camera body for loose film chips
- Clamp-on jar opener—can be used as a simple zoom control or follow focus if you don't have those accessories, and can also be used to remove tight screw-on filters (see Figure D.13)

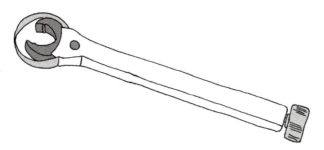

Figure D.13   Jar opener that may be used for following focus or zooming.

- Small and large flashlights—to be used when filming in dark locations and also for checking the gate on the camera (Mini Maglite, Maglite, Surefire) (see Figure D.14)
- Lighted magnifier—for checking the gate on the camera (see Figure D.15)
- Tape measures: metal (25 ft) and cloth or fiberglass (50 ft)—to measure distances for focus (see Figure D.16)
- Bubble level and small pocket level—to check that camera equipment is level before shooting (see Figure D.17)

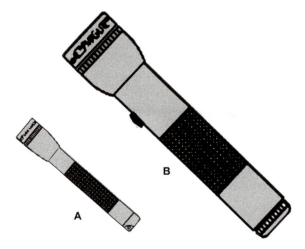

Figure D.14   **A**, Small Maglite flashlight.
B, Large Maglite flashlight.

Figure D.15
Lighted magnifier.

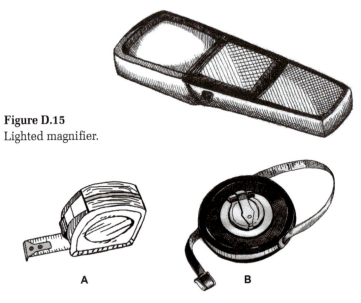

Figure D.16   **A**, Metal tape measure. **B**, Cloth tape measure.

Figure D.17   **A**, Bubble level. **B**, Pocket level.

- ⅜–16 bolts, short and long—for attaching camera to non-standard mounting platform
- ¼–20 bolts, short and long—for attaching camera to non-standard mounting platform
- 1-in. and 2-in. brush—for keeping exterior of camera clean (see Figure D.18)

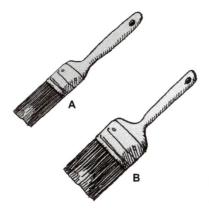

Figure D.18
A, 1-in. brush. **B**, 2-in. brush.

- 3-to-2 electrical adapters, cube taps, power strips, and extension cords—for charging batteries and powering any electrical device (see Figure D.19)
- Soldering iron—for making repairs to power cables
- Voltmeter—to check the voltage of batteries

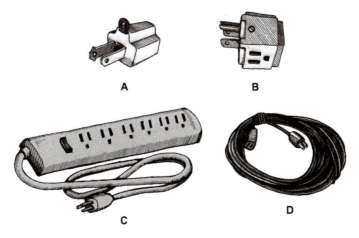

Figure D.19   A, 3-to-2 adapter. **B**, Cube tap. **C**, Power strip.
D, Extension cord.

Specialized Film Industry Tools

- Large and small sync slate—to be used to identify each shot at the beginning of the shot (see Figure 4.40 for an illustration of a sync slate)
- Insert slate—to be used to identify each shot at the beginning of the shot (see Figure 4.42 for an illustration of an insert slate)
- Large clapper sticks—for slating multiple camera shots
- Changing bag or changing tent—for loading/unloading of film when a darkroom is not available (see Figure 4.33 for illustrations of the changing bag and changing tent)
- French flag with arm—for keeping stray light from striking the front of the lens or filters in the matte box (see Figure 5.29 for an illustration of a French flag)
- 6-in. focus whip—to be attached to the follow-focus mechanism in order to give you more control when pulling focus (see Figure 5.6 for an illustration of a focus whip)
- Laser pointer—can be used as a simple tool for judging the distance to an actor for moving dolly shots
- Lens brush—to clean dust/dirt off the glass elements of the lens
- Magazine brush—to clean the interior of the magazines before loading (should have stiff bristles)
- Cardellini, mini cardellini or similar type clamps with ⅝-in. baby pin—for attaching on-board monitors, on-board lights, or other objects to camera or other device
- ⅜–16 to ¼–20 reducer—to be used when mounting accessories to camera or other device and the mounting hole is a different size
- Anton Bauer PowerTap Multi—for mounting additional electronic accessories to a camera with only one output
- Personal earpiece for walkie talkies—for communicating with other members of the camera crew that may have walkie talkies
- Extra Ronford Baker Quick Release Plate—great item to have when using multiple heads/cameras so you don't need to switch plates from one camera to another
- Ultralight, Noga arm, or similar arm/bracket for on-board monitor—for mounting on-board monitor to camera or other device
- Terrycloth wrist bands—to be used in place of foam or chamois eyepiece covers (they are washable so they can be used over and over)
- Color chart and gray scale or gray card—to be shot at beginning of roll for reference in postproduction
- Framing chart—to be shot at beginning of roll for reference in postproduction

- Camera oil (Mitchell, Panavision, Arriflex)—to keep the camera movement or mechanism lubricated
- Camera silicone lubricant—to keep the pull down claw lubricated
- Depth-of-field charts or calculator—for checking depth of field on critical shots (see Figures 5.34 and 5.35 for illustrations of depth-of-field calculators)
- Rubber T-marks, shot bag T-marks or shot bag sausage marks—for marking actors outside
- Golf tees—for marking actors outside
- Space blanket—for covering and protecting the camera
- Camera covers—for covering and protecting the camera
- Engraved filter tags—for labeling the matte box to indicate what filters are currently in place (see Figure 5.42 for an illustration of filter tags)
- Blower bulb syringe—for blowing dust and dirt off lens elements and filters (see Figure D.20)

Figure D.20
Blower bulb syringe.

- Small spring clamps (grip clamps)—for securing space blanket or camera covers (see Figure D.21)

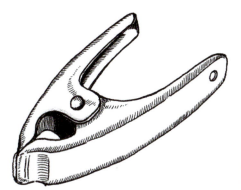

Figure D.21
Spring clamp (grip clamp).

- Ground glass puller—for removing ground glass from certain Arriflex cameras (Hirschmann Forceps) (see Figure D.22)

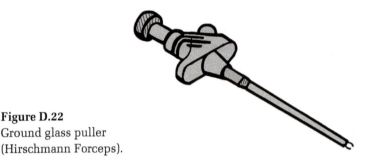

Figure D.22
Ground glass puller
(Hirschmann Forceps).

- Eye and hearing protection—to protect your eyes from objects or substances being projected toward the camera and to protect your ears from gunshots, explosions or other loud sounds on the set (see Figure D.23)

Figure D.23 **A**, Eye protection. **B**, Hearing protection.

A

B

- Assorted video connectors and cables—for connecting the video tap on the camera to the video monitor (see Figure D.24)
- Empty filter pouches (various sizes)—for storage of filters or other delicate objects
- Lens wrap—for protecting lenses when they are being transported out of their cases
- Camera fuses—for replacement in the camera if existing fuse blows during shooting
- Oil dropper or syringe—for applying oil or silicone lubricant
- Duvetyne (black cloth)—for covering matte box or lens to protect it from stray light
- Convex mirror—can be used to check for lens flares
- Extra camera power cables—for use when existing power cable becomes damaged

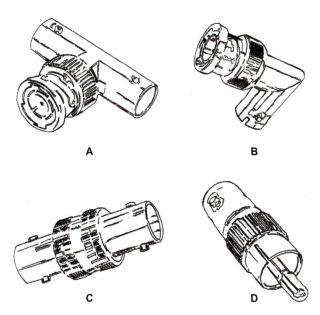

A   B

C   D

Figure D.24   **A**, BNC T-connector. **B**, BNC Right-angle
adapter. **C**, BNC barrel connector. **D**, BNC-to-RCA
adapter.

- 10-ft BNC video cable—to be used as jumper from dolly to video
  cable attached to monitor
- Sound blankets (furniture blankets)—to protect floors when placing equipment cases in homes or businesses, or for covering and
  protecting equipment on location
- Folding stool or small chair—for assistant to have a place to sit
  when resting between shots
- Work gloves—to protect hands when carrying equipment
- Fingerless gloves—to protect hands when carrying camera or
  other equipment (fingerless allows the assistant to be able to fol-
  low focus or thread camera without removing the gloves)
- Front box—to be mounted on the gear or fluid head for storage
  of key tools and accessories used regularly by the First Assistant
  Cameraman (see Figure D.25)
- *American Cinematographer Manual* (*ASC Manual*) —to be used
  as a reference (see Figure D.26)
- *Professional Cameraman's Handbook*—to be used as a reference
- *The Camera Assistant's Manual*—to be used as a reference (see
  Figure D.27)
- Various camera instruction manuals—to be used as a reference

Figure D.25 Front box used by many 1st ACs.

Figure D.26 ASC Manual.

Figure D.27 The Camera Assistant's Manual.

Arriflex Special Tools

Some companies, such as Arriflex, sell special tools or toolkits that are needed when working with their camera equipment. If you know or think you may be working with Arriflex cameras on a regular basis, you may want to pick up these tools for your ditty bag. These are some of the tools you will need when making any minor repairs or adjustments on the Arriflex 16 SR2, 16 SR3, 416, 235, 435, 535, or Arricam cameras. Some tools may also be used on the newer Arriflex digital cameras such as the Alexa and D-21 along with the older-style Arriflex film cameras.

- Arricam Combi Tool
- 235 Shutter Angle Tool
- 416 Shutter Angle Tool
- 1.3 mm hex driver
- 1.5 mm hex driver

- 2 mm hex driver
- 3 mm hex driver
- 5 mm hex driver
- Small Phillips screwdriver
- Large Phillips screwdriver
- Slotted screwdriver
- Special bushing tool

With today's technology, many productions are being shot using digital cameras instead of film cameras. Some of these cameras allow you to upgrade the firmware by downloading it to an SD card and then uploading it to the camera. As an assistant working with this new technology you may want to have a couple of extra SD cards along with a card reader in your kit. The typical size currently needed for these downloads is 4GB but you may also want to have one or two 8GB cards or larger just in case. I have a very nice memory card reader that accepts all SD cards and cost under $15.00. Figure D.28 shows an SD card.

Digital Supplies

- Memory/media cards—for downloading firmware updates and storing look files for certain digital cameras (see Figure D.28)

Figure D.28
SD memory card.

- Memory card reader—for downloading firmware updates and storing look files for certain digital cameras
- Hard drive—for backing up footage (500 GB or 1 TB)
- Battery backup—to power laptop and hard drives in case of power failure
- HDMI to SDI adapters—for connecting digital camera to monitors or other devices
- Digital cables and adapters—for connecting digital camera to monitors or other devices

EXPENDABLES

- 1-in. camera tape—black, white, red, yellow, blue, gray, green, teal, burgundy, purple, dark blue, fluorescent pink, fluorescent green, fluorescent orange, fluorescent yellow—for labeling magazines, camera cases, or other taping needs (see Figure D.29)

A   B

Figure D.29
A, Camera tape.
B, Exposed film tape.

- 2-in. gaffer tape—black, gray, white, yellow, red, green, brown, bright blue, dark blue, fluorescent orange, fluorescent yellow, fluorescent pink, fluorescent green—for securing items to camera equipment or other taping needs
- ½-in. or 1-in. paper tape—black, red, green, yellow, white, orange, light blue, dark blue, purple, fluorescent orange, fluorescent pink, fluorescent green, fluorescent yellow—for marking actors
- 2-in. photo black paper tape—for taping holes in darkroom or other taping needs
- 1-in. electrical tape—red, blue, green, yellow, white—in humid conditions it can be used in place of cloth tape when labeling magazines and cases
- 2-in. gorilla tape—extra strong tape for securing items
- 2-in. magazine tape—red, blue, yellow, white—special tape for labeling magazines with specific spaces for certain information
- ⅛-in., ³⁄₁₆-in., or ¼-in. chart tape—white or yellow—for making focus marks on the lens
- Transfer tape (snot tape)—for securing nets to the back or front of lenses
- Lens tissue and lens cleaner—for cleaning lenses and filters (see Figure D.30)
- Pancro lens cleaner—for cleaning lenses and filters
- Sensor cleaning kit for digital camera sensors—for cleaning the sensor on digital camera
- Compressed air with nozzle (Dust-Off) (see Figure D.31)
- Cotton swabs (Q-Tips) or foam-tip swabs
- Kimwipes—large and small for cleaning filters
- Silicone spray, WD-40 or CRC 656 lubricant—for lubricating any moving parts that are sticking like tripod legs (*do not use on interior of any camera*)

Figure D.30   **A**, Lens tissue. **B**, Lens cleaner.

Figure D.31
Compressed air (Dust-Off).

- Orangewood sticks—for cleaning the gate area of a film camera
- Eyepiece covers—soft covers for covering the eyecup so that it is comfortable for the camera operator
- Rip-tie hook and loop cable ties—for securing camera and video cables
- Assorted size plastic cable ties—4-in., 6-in., 8-in., 11-in., 14-in.—for securing camera and video cables
- Bongo ties—for securing camera and video cables
- Ratchet straps, bungee cords—for securing camera and other equipment

- Rope or sash cord—for securing camera and other equipment
- Velcro—for attaching and securing small items to camera or other equipment
- Erasable felt-tip markers (Vis-A-Vis or Staedtler)—black, red, green, blue—for marking the white focus disk on follow-focus mechanisms
- Erasable slate marker—for writing information on the slate
- Kleenslate erasers—for writing information on the slate
- Makeup powder puffs—for erasing information on the slate
- Permanent felt-tip markers, fine point, extra fine point, and wide tip (Sharpies)—red, black, blue, silver—for making labels with 1-in. camera tape
- Ballpoint pens—for completing camera reports, time cards, and other paperwork
- Three-ring binder—for organized storage of all camera department paperwork
- Clipboard—can be used with camera reports as a hard writing surface
- Pads of paper—for making notes or any other writing that may need to be done
- Grease pencils (Stabilo)—white, yellow, red—to be used for marking lens for focus or zoom lens moves
- Chalk—white and colors—for marking actors or camera positions on pavement or sidewalks

Figure D.32 Camera wedges.

- Camera wedges—for leveling the camera on uneven surfaces (see Figure D.32)
- Stick-on letters—black, red, blue, green—for labeling the slate
- Handheld electronic label maker—for labeling the slate
- Electronic labeler tape—white, red, blue, green, yellow—for labeling the slate

- Lighter fluid or Goo Gone—for cleaning sticky residue from slate or other equipment
- Kodak Wratten gels (85, 85N3, 85N6, 85N9, ND3, ND6, ND9, 80A)—for use as behind-the-lens filters
- Spare batteries (AAA, AA, C, D, 9-volt)—for powering light meters, flashlights, magnifiers, and other devices
- Spare Mini Maglite bulbs—for use in case flashlight bulb burns out
- Small plastic storage bags—for storage of small parts and equipment
- Trash bags—for trash and also for covering camera and equipment in wet or rainy situations
- Spray cleaner, rags, and paper towels—for cleaning equipment during shooting and especially at wrap

MISCELLANEOUS ITEMS

- Spare cores and daylight spools—for threading film in the magazines (see Figures 4.5 and 4.6 for illustrations of cores and daylight spools)

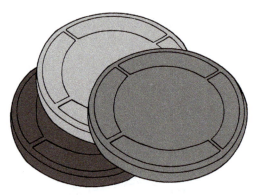

Figure D.33   Film cans.

- Extra film cans and black bags (400 ft and 1000 ft)—for canning exposed film, short ends and recans (see Figure D.33)
- Camera reports and film inventory forms—for keeping a record of shots (see Figure D.34)
- Camera log—for keeping a record of shot information (see Figure 4.12 for illustrations of pages from a camera log)
- Camera rental catalogs—for checking availability and/or pricing of additional equipment

Figure D.34   Camera reports and inventory forms.

As mentioned in the opening paragraph, along with the preceding items, you should have some type of case or cases, either hard side or soft side, to store and transport all of these items. Your tools and accessories are important for the performance of your job, so it is a very good idea to protect them and keep them in good condition when they are not being used. The type of case you use is a matter of personal preference. When I first started I used a couple of soft-side tool bags. As I acquired more tools, I slowly moved into hard-side cases to provide better protection for my equipment. Now I use some hard-side cases, some soft-side cases, and an assortment of soft-side canvas tote bags. I also have a Magliner cart, a Liberator Jr. cart and two Rubbermaid utility carts. This list is subject to change depending on the individual needs of each assistant. You may find a particular item that helps you to perform the job better. The basic items in the ditty bag or toolkit are essentially standard throughout the industry. Additional specialty items are based on individual needs and what is required for you to do your job completely. No two AC ditty bags or kits are identical.

As noted previously, many Camera Assistants have a belt pouch that they wear on their belt to keep specific items available at all times. These are items that are needed regularly during shooting and may include the following: permanent felt-tip markers, ball-point pens, grease pencil, lens tissue, lens cleaner, slate marker with powder puff or other eraser attached, small flashlight, magnifier with light, and depth-of-field calculator. Many Camera Assistants also make a small loop of rope on which to keep a roll of black and white camera tape with them in case they need to make marks or labels of any kind.

PERSONAL BAG

As stated in Chapters 3 and 4, I recommend having a personal bag with extra clothing, towels, and toiletry items with you as well. You may need an extra shirt, shoes, or coat, and it's best to be prepared. Having an extra sweatshirt, thermal underwear, and cold weather boots can make the difference between being comfortable and enjoying the job or being miserable because you are cold, wet, and uncomfortable. I have heard many Camera Assistants recommend a coat that unzips from both the top and the bottom. This makes it easy to access any tool belt you may be wearing and still have the upper part of your body covered.

The following list includes many of the items that I keep in my personal bag. You may modify this list to suit your individual needs. You don't need to keep everything listed in the bag. Set it up based on the location where you are filming and the season. Obviously you won't need the winter parka in the middle of the summer. I have chosen not to include any explanation as to why you would need each item because I believe that for the most part it is self-explanatory.

- Pants, shirt, sweatshirt, underwear (regular and thermal), socks (regular and thermal)
- Winter parka or jacket (cold-weather filming)
- Wool or cotton knit cap (cold-weather filming)
- Wide-brimmed hat (filming in sun or heat)
- Snow boots (cold-weather filming)
- Down vest (cold-weather filming)
- Sneakers and/or work shoes/boots
- Rain gear—jacket and pants
- Towels and face cloths
- Disposable moist towelettes
- Small blanket
- First aid kit, aspirin, ibuprofen, prescription medication
- Toothbrush, toothpaste, razors, shave cream, deodorant
- Comb, brush, mirror, soap, shampoo
- Insect repellent, skin cream
- Sunglasses and sunscreen
- Travel radio/alarm clock

As you gain more experience as a Camera Assistant, you will probably find other tools and accessories that you will keep in your ditty bag or AKS case. An AKS case is any case that contains a wide variety of tools, equipment, and supplies. Its literal translation is "All Kinds of Stuff" or "All Kinds of S**t." Please remember that this list

is meant only as a guide for people starting out who want to acquire the basics for doing the job.

Finally, because you will have a great deal of money invested in your tools and equipment, I strongly urge you to obtain an insurance policy to cover your tools and equipment in the event that they get lost, stolen, or damaged. Many homeowner's or renter's policies do not cover specialized tools for your profession, so you may have to obtain a separate insurance policy. You may have to contact a company that deals specifically with insurance for the motion picture industry. Check with your insurance agent regarding this. Paying a few dollars per month for insurance coverage will be worth it in the long run. Imagine if your tools were lost or stolen. How would you be able to properly perform your job without the basic tools of your profession?

Appendix E

Tables and Formulas

Included in this section are many tables and formulas that a Camera Assistant may refer to for a variety of information. The tables include footage tables, hyperfocal distances, f-stop compensation for changes in frames per second (fps), f-stop compensation for various filters used, footage to time conversions, time to footage conversions, and many more. The formulas include feet per minute, exposure time, hyperfocal distance, depth of field, feet to meters, meters to feet, screen time to running time, and more. Please keep in mind that the terms *f-stop* and *t-stop* are used interchangeably in this material.

For those of you using an iPhone, iPod Touch, or iPad, much of this information is available to you in the application called pCAM Film+Digital Calculator. In my opinion the pCAM Film+Digital Calculator is the best and most complete application currently available for use by the camera department. Some of the features include a depth-of-field calculator, the ability to view a sample image in the field of view screen, exposure compensation, running time to film length, HMI flicker free speeds, just to name a few. The application was developed by Assistant Cameraman David Eubank and you may find more information on his web site at www.davideubank.com. I have used this application successfully for many years, first with the Palm OS operating system and now on the iPhone, and strongly recommend it to anyone working as a Camera Assistant in the film industry. See Chapter 5 for screen shots from the pCAM Film+Digital Calculator application.

Another excellent application is the Toland ASC Digital Assistant, which is also available for the iPhone, iPod Touch, and iPad. It allows you to calculate your depth of field, exposure changes, running time and footage use, angle of view, and also to keep a log that can be accessed later. See Chapter 5 for screen shots from the Toland ASC Digital Assistant.

TABLES

The following are selected tables that you may refer to in the day-to-day course of filming. They are all available on the companion web site for this book, which can be found at www.cameraassistantmanual.com.

Film Speed (Exposure Index–DIN) Comparisons

The film speed is most often expressed as an EI (Exposure Index) number and is indicated on each can of film. The term *ASA* when referring to film speed is not used as often, but some people may still use this term. EI and ASA numbers are most often the same. The German numbering system uses a system called DIN numbers to indicate the film speed. Table E.1 shows the comparison between EI/ASA numbers and DIN numbers.

Standard Feet per Minute and Frames per Foot at 24 and 25 Frames per Second

The standard film speed in the United States is 24 frames per second and in Britain, Europe, and Australia it is 25 frames per second. These speeds give the illusion of normal motion when projected. Many calculations are based on the standard information for each film format at these fps. Table E.2 lists the standard frames per foot and feet per minute when shooting at 24, 25, or 30 fps. Table E.3 lists the standard frames per meter and meters per minute when shooting at 24, 25, or 30 fps.

Intermediate F-stop/T-stop Values

When the Director of Photography (DP) measures the light, the f-stop/t-stop reading that he or she gets will not always be exactly on one of the values mentioned in Chapter 1. The value of the light measurement often falls between two f-stop/t-stop numbers. Table E.4 gives the intermediate values between each successive pair of f-stop/t-stop numbers. For example, the value that is halfway between f/4 and f/5.6 is f/4.8.

F-stop/T-stop Compensation When Using Filters

During the course of shooting, the DP may ask that various filters be placed on the camera to achieve a specific effect or to correct for the color temperature. Quite often, placing a filter in front of the lens reduces the amount of light that reaches the film. Remember that if a filter requires an exposure compensation, the amount of compensation refers to how much you should open up the lens aperture. Table E.5 lists the f-stop/t-stop compensation for various filters that you may use. This table is by no means complete and only lists some of

Table E.1   Comparison of EI/ASA and DIN Numbers

EI/ASA	DIN
12	12
16	13
20	14
25	15
32	16
40	17
50	18
64	19
80	20
100	21
125	22
160	23
200	24
250	25
320	26
400	27
500	28
640	29
800	30

Table E.2   Frames per Foot and Feet per Minute for 24, 25, and 30 Frames per Second

Film Format	Frames per Foot	Feet per Minute at 24 fps	Feet per Minute at 25 fps	Feet per Minute at 30 fps
Super 8	72	20	20.83	25
16 mm	40	36	37.5	45
35 mm, 2-perf format	32	45	46.88	56.25
35 mm, 3-perf format	21.33	67.5	70.31	84.38
35 mm, 4-perf format	16	90	93.75	112.5
65 mm, 5-perf format	12.8	112.5	117.19	140.62

Table E.3   Frames per Meter and Meters per Minute for 24, 25, and 30 Frames per Second

Film Format	Frames Per Meter	Meters Per Minute at 24 fps	Meters Per Minute at 25 fps	Meters Per Minute at 30 fps
Super 8	236.21	6.1	6.35	7.625
16 mm	131.23	10.97	11.43	13.72
35 mm, 2-perf format	105	13.72	14.29	17.15
35 mm, 3-perf format	70	20.57	21.43	25.72
35 mm, 4-perf format	52.5	27.43	28.57	34.29
65 mm, 5-perf format	42	34.29	35.72	42.86

Table E.4   Intermediate F-Stop/T-Stop Values for ¼, ⅓, ½, ⅔, and ¾ Stops

Full Stop	¼ Stop	⅓ Stop	½ Stop	⅔ Stop	¾ Stop	Full Stop
1	1.09	1.12	1.18	1.26	1.30	1.4
1.4	1.54	1.59	1.68	1.78	1.83	2
2	2.18	2.24	2.38	2.52	2.59	2.8
2.8	3.08	3.17	3.36	3.56	3.67	4
4	4.36	4.49	4.76	5.04	5.19	5.6
5.6	6.17	6.35	6.73	7.13	7.34	8
8	8.72	8.98	9.51	10.08	10.37	11
11	12.34	12.70	13.45	14.25	14.67	16
16	17.45	17.96	19.03	20.16	20.75	22
22	24.68	25.40	26.91	28.51	29.34	32
32	34.90	35.92	38.05	40.32	41.50	45

the most commonly used filters. For example, when using an 85 filter, you must open up your exposure ⅔ of a stop from the exposure without the filter. If you are not sure about the exposure compensation of a particular filter, you can check with the company where you rented the camera equipment. A quick way to determine the exposure compensation for a particular filter is to take a light reading with your incident meter in the light you are shooting under. Then hold the

Table E.5   F-Stop/T-Stop Compensation for Various Filters

Filter	F-Stop/T-Stop Compensation (Open Aperture)	Filter	F-Stop/T-Stop Compensation (Open Aperture)
85	$^2/_3$	80A	2
85 N3	$1^2/_3$	80B	$1^2/_3$
85 N6	$2^2/_3$	80C	1
85 N9	$3^2/_3$	81A, 81B, 81C	$^1/_3$
LLD	0	81EF	$^2/_3$
ND 3	1	812	$^1/_3$
ND 6	2	82A	$^1/_3$
ND 9	3	82B	$^1/_3$
Polarizer	2	85B	$^2/_3$
Optical Flat	0	85C	$^1/_3$
Enhancer	1	Diopter	0
FLB	1	UV	0
FLD	1	Sky 1-A	0
Fog, Double Fog	0	Haze 1	0
Contrast (Low, Soft, Ultra)	0	Haze 2	0
Black Dot	1	Warm UV	$^1/_3$
Pro Mist	0	Soft Net	$^1/_3 - ^2/_3$
Warm Pro Mist	$^1/_3$	Coral, Sepia	Based on Density
Soft F/X	0		

filter over the photosphere of the light meter and take another reading. Compare the difference, and you will have determined your exposure compensation for that filter.

F-stop/T-stop Compensation When Using Filters for Black-and-White Film

When shooting black-and-white film, the DP may use certain filters to change the way that specific colors appear. On black-and-white film,

Table E.6   F-Stop Compensation when Using Filters for Black and White

Filter	F-Stop/T-Stop Compensation (Open Aperture)	
	Daylight	Tungsten
#8 YELLOW	1	$2/3$
#11 GREEN	2	$1 2/3$
#12 YELLOW	1	$2/3$
#15 DEEP YELLOW	$1 2/3$	1
#16 ORANGE	$1 2/3$	$1 2/3$
#21 ORANGE	$2 1/3$	2
#23A LIGHT RED	$2 2/3$	$1 2/3$
#25 RED	3	$2 2/3$
#29 DARK RED	$4 1/3$	2
#47 DARK BLUE	$2 1/3$	3
#47B DARK BLUE	3	4
#58 DARK GREEN	3	3

all colors are reproduced as a specific shade of gray. By using a filter, the DP can alter or change how light or dark the shade of gray is for a particular color. Table E.6 lists the f-stop compensation for the most common filters used in black-and-white photography. For example, when using a #12 yellow filter, you must open up your f-stop 1 stop when shooting in daylight and ⅔ of a stop when shooting in tungsten light.

F-stop/T-stop Compensation for Changes in Frames per Second

When you change the speed that the film travels through the camera (i.e. the fps), you are changing how long each frame is exposed to light. If you run the camera at a higher speed, each frame is exposed to light for less time, and if you run the camera at a slower speed, each frame is exposed to light for a longer time. Table E.7 lists the f-stop/t-stop compensation for various changes in frames per second. For example, if you change the camera speed to 60 fps, you must open your f-stop 1⅓ stops.

Table E.7   F-Stop/T-Stop Compensation for Changes in Frames per Second

Frames Per Second	F-Stop/T-Stop Compensation	Frames Per Second	F-Stop/T-Stop Compensation
5	Close 2¼	36–39	Open ⅔
6	Close 2	40–44	Open ¾
7	Close 1¾	45–52	Open 1
8	Close 1⅔	53–58	Open 1¼
9	Close 1⅓	59–64	Open 1⅓
10–11	Close 1¼	65–71	Open 1½
12–13	Close 1	72–78	Open 1⅔
14	Close ¾	79–88	Open 1¾
15–16	Close ⅔	89–104	Open 2
17	Close ½	105–117	Open 2¼
18–19	Close ⅓	118–128	Open 2⅓
20–22	Close ¼	129–143	Open 2½
23–26	0	144–156	Open 2⅔
27–29	Open ¼	157–176	Open 2¾
30–32	Open ⅓	177–209	Open 3
33–35	Open ½		

F-stop/T-stop Compensation for Changes in Shutter Angle

Similar to changing camera speed, if you change the shutter angle, you affect how much light strikes the film. Increasing the shutter angle allows more light to reach the film, and decreasing the shutter angle allows less light to reach the film. Table E.8 lists the f-stop/t-stop compensation for various changes in shutter angle. For example, when you change the shutter angle to 90 degrees, you must open the f-stop 1 stop.

Hyperfocal Distances

Hyperfocal distance is a special case of depth of field. It is sometimes defined as the closest point in front of the lens that will be in

Table E.8 F-Stop/T-Stop Compensation for Changes in Shutter Angle

Shutter Angle	F-Stop/T-Stop Compensation
197–200	Close ¼
166–196	Full Exposure
148–165	Open ¼
135–147	Open ⅓
121–134	Open ½
111–120	Open ⅔
99–110	Open ¾
83–98	Open 1
74–82	Open 1 ¼
68–73	Open 1⅓
61–67	Open 1½
56–60	Open 1⅔
50–55	Open 1¾
42–49	Open 2
37–41	Open 2¼
34–36	Open 2⅓
31–33	Open 2½
28–30	Open 2⅔
25–27	Open 2¾
22.5–24	Open 3

acceptable focus when the lens is focused to infinity. In other words, it is the closest focus distance at which objects at infinity and close to the lens are in focus. It is this focus point that gives the maximum depth of field for a given shooting situation. At certain times during filming, you may need to know the hyperfocal distance for a particular shot. Tables E.9 and E.10 list the hyperfocal distances for various focal length lenses for both 16 mm and 35 mm formats. All amounts are rounded to the nearest inch. For example, from Table E.10, when shooting in 35 mm with a 29 mm lens and an f-stop of 5.6, the hyperfocal distance is 19 ft 5 in. You may also determine the hyperfocal distance for a given situation if you are using the pCAM Film+Digital Calculator application discussed in Chapter 5.

Table E.9 16 mm Hyperfocal Distances—Circle of Confusion = .0006"

Focal Length	F-Stop								
	1	1.4	2	2.8	4	5.6	8	11	16
5.9	7' 6"	5' 4"	3' 9"	2' 8"	1' 11"	1' 4"	11"	8"	6"
8	13' 10"	9" 9"	6' 11"	4' 11"	3' 6"	2' 6"	1' 9"	1' 3"	11"
9.5	19' 6"	13' 9"	9' 9"	6' 11"	4' 11"	3' 6"	2' 6"	1' 9"	1' 3"
10	21' 7"	15' 3"	10' 10"	7' 8"	5' 5"	3' 10"	2' 9"	1' 11"	1' 5"
12	31'	22'	15' 6"	11'	7' 9"	5' 6"	3' 11"	2' 9"	2'
14	42' 3"	29' 11"	21' 2"	15'	10' 7"	7' 6"	5' 4"	3' 9"	2' 7"
16	55' 2"	39'	27' 7"	19' 8"	13' 10"	9' 10"	6' 11"	4' 11"	3' 6"
17	62' 3"	44' 1"	31' 2"	22' 1"	15' 7"	11' 1"	7' 10"	5' 8"	3' 11"
18	69' 10"	49' 5"	34' 11"	24' 9"	17' 6"	12' 5"	8' 9"	6' 3"	4' 5"
20	86' 2"	60' 11"	43' 1"	30' 6"	21' 7"	15' 3"	10' 10"	7' 8"	5' 5"
21	95'	67' 2"	47' 6"	33' 8"	23' 10"	16' 10"	11' 11"	8' 6"	6'
24	124' 1"	87' 9"	62' 1"	43' 11"	31' 1"	22'	15' 7"	11'	7' 10"
25	134' 8"	95' 3"	67' 4"	47' 8"	33' 9"	23' 10"	16' 11"	12'	8' 6"
27	157'	111' 1"	78' 7"	55' 7"	39' 4"	27' 10"	19' 8"	14'	9' 11"
28	168' 10"	119' 5"	84' 6"	59' 9"	42' 3"	29' 11"	21' 2"	15'	10' 8"
29	181' 2"	128' 1"	90' 7"	64' 1"	45' 4"	32' 1"	22' 9"	16' 1"	11' 5"
32	220' 7"	156'	110' 4"	78' 1"	55' 3"	39' 1"	27' 8"	19' 7"	13' 11"
35	263' 10"	186' 7"	132'	93' 4"	66' 1"	46' 9"	33' 1"	23' 5"	16' 7"
40	344' 7"	243' 8"	172' 4"	121' 11"	86' 3"	61'	43' 2"	30' 7"	21' 8"
50	538' 4"	380' 9"	269' 3"	190' 5"	134' 9"	95' 4"	67' 5"	47' 9"	33' 10"
60	775' 2"	548' 2"	387' 8"	274' 2"	193' 11"	137' 2"	97' 1"	68' 8"	48' 8"
65	909' 9"	643' 4"	455'	321' 9"	227' 7"	161'	113' 11"	80' 7"	57' 1"
75	1211' 2"	856' 6"	605' 9"	428' 5"	303'	214' 4"	151' 7"	107' 3"	75' 11"
85	1555' 8"	1100' 1"	778'	550' 2"	389' 2"	275' 3"	194' 8"	137' 9"	97' 6"
100	2153' 1"	1522' 7"	1076' 9"	761' 5"	538' 6"	380' 11"	269' 5"	190' 7"	134' 11"
120	3100' 5"	2192' 5"	1550' 5"	1096' 5"	775' 5"	548' 5"	387' 11"	274' 5"	194' 2"
135	3923' 11"	2774' 9"	1962' 2"	1387' 7"	981' 4"	694'	490' 10"	347' 3"	245' 8"
150	4844' 3"	3425' 7"	2422' 4"	1713'	1211' 5"	856' 9"	606'	428' 7"	303' 3"
180	6975' 7"	4932' 8"	3488' 1"	2466' 8"	1744' 4"	1233' 7"	872' 6"	617' 1"	436' 6"

Table E.10   35 mm Hyperfocal Distances—Circle of Confusion = .001"

Focal Length	F-Stop								
	1	**1.4**	**2**	**2.8**	**4**	**5.6**	**8**	**11**	**16**
5.9	4' 6"	3' 2"	2' 3"	1' 7"	1' 2"	10"	7"	5"	4"
8	8' 4"	5' 10"	4' 2"	2' 11"	2' 1"	1' 6"	1' 1"	9"	7"
9.5	11' 8"	8' 3"	5' 10"	4' 2"	2' 11"	2' 1"	1' 6"	1' 1"	9"
10	12' 11"	9' 2"	6' 6"	4' 7"	3' 3"	2' 4"	1' 8"	1' 2"	10"
12	18' 8"	13' 2"	9' 4"	6' 7"	4' 8"	3' 4"	2' 4"	1' 8"	1' 2"
14	25' 4"	17' 11"	12' 8"	9'	6' 5"	4' 6"	3' 3"	2' 3"	1' 8"
16	33' 1"	23' 5"	16' 7"	11' 9"	8' 4"	5' 11"	4' 2"	3'	2' 1"
17	37' 5"	26' 5"	18' 9"	13' 3"	9' 5"	6' 8"	4' 9"	3' 4"	2' 5"
18	41' 11"	29' 8"	21'	14' 10"	10' 6"	7' 5"	5' 3"	3' 9"	2' 8"
20	51' 9"	36' 7"	25' 11"	18' 4"	13'	9' 2"	6' 6"	4' 8"	3' 4"
21	57'	40' 4"	28' 7"	20' 2"	14' 4"	10' 2"	7' 2"	5' 1"	3' 8"
24	74' 6"	52' 8"	37' 3"	26' 5"	18' 8"	13' 3"	9' 5"	6' 8"	4' 9"
25	80' 10"	57' 2"	40' 5"	28' 7"	20' 3"	14' 4"	10' 2"	7' 3"	5' 2"
27	94' 3"	66' 8"	47' 2"	33' 5"	23' 8"	16' 9"	11' 10"	8' 5"	6'
28	101' 4"	71' 8"	50' 9"	35' 11"	25' 5"	18'	12' 9"	9' 1"	6' 5"
29	108' 9"	76' 11"	54' 5"	38' 6"	27' 3"	19' 4"	13' 8"	9' 8"	6' 11"
32	132' 4"	93' 8"	66' 3"	46' 10"	33' 2"	23' 6"	16' 8"	11' 10"	8' 4"
35	158' 4"	112'	79' 3"	56' 1"	39' 8"	28' 1"	19' 11"	14' 1"	10'
40	206' 10"	146' 3"	103' 6"	73' 2"	51' 10"	36' 8"	26'	18' 5"	13' 1"
50	323' 1"	228' 6"	161' 7"	114' 4"	80' 11"	57' 3"	40' 6"	28' 8"	20' 4"
60	465' 2"	329'	232' 8"	164' 7"	116' 5"	82' 5"	58' 4"	41' 4"	29' 3"
65	545' 11"	386' 1"	273' 1"	193' 2"	136' 8"	96' 8"	68' 5"	48' 5"	34' 1"
75	726' 10"	514'	363' 6"	257' 2"	181' 11"	128' 8"	91' 1"	64' 6"	45' 8"
85	933' 6"	660' 2"	466' 11"	330' 3"	233' 7"	165' 3"	116' 11"	82' 9"	58' 7"
100	1292'	913' 8"	646' 2"	457'	323' 3"	228' 8"	161' 9"	114' 6"	81' 1"
125	2018' 8"	1427' 6"	1009' 6"	714'	505'	357' 2"	252' 8"	178' 10"	126' 7"
135	2354' 6"	1665'	1177' 6"	832' 9"	589'	416' 7"	294' 8"	208' 6"	147' 7"
150	2906' 9"	2055' 6"	1453' 7"	1028'	726' 1"	514' 3"	363' 9"	257' 4"	182' 2"
180	4185' 7"	2959' 10"	2093' 1"	1480' 3"	1046' 10"	740' 5"	523' 9"	370' 6"	262' 2"

Feet per Second, Feet per Minute, Meters per Second, and Meters per Minute

In the United States, at 24 fps, 16 mm film travels through the camera at the rate of 36 feet per minute, 35 mm 3-perf format film travels through the camera at the rate of 67.5 feet per minute, and 35 mm 4-perf format film travels through the camera at the rate of 90 feet per minute. In Britain, Europe and Australia, at 25 fps, 16 mm film travels through the camera at the rate of 11.43 meters per minute, 35 mm 3-perf format film travels through the camera at the rate of 21.43 meters per minute, and 35 mm 4-perf format film travels through the camera at the rate of 28.57 meters per minute. Because you will not always be filming at sync speed, Tables E.11 and E.12 list feet per second, feet per minute, meters per second, and meters per minute for various frames per second for each format. For example, in the United States, when shooting 16 mm film at 18 fps, the film travels through the camera at the rate of 27 ft per minute.

Table E.11   Feet per Second and Feet per Minute

FPS	16 mm		35 mm 2-perf		35 mm 3-perf		35mm 4-perf	
	Feet per Second	Feet per Minute	Feet per Second	Feet per Minute	Feet per Second	Feet per Minute	Feet per Second	Feet per Minute
6	.15	9	.188	11.25	.28	16.9	.375	22.5
12	.3	18	.375	22.5	.56	33.8	.75	45
18	.45	27	.5625	33.75	.85	50.7	1.125	67.5
24	.6	36	.75	45	1.13	67.5	1.5	90
25	.625	37.5	.7812	46.875	1.17	70.31	1.5625	93.75
30	.75	45	.9375	56.25	1.41	84.5	1.875	112.5
36	.9	54	1.125	67.5	1.69	101.4	2.25	135
48	1.2	72	1.5	90	2.25	135.2	3	180
60	1.5	90	1.875	112.5	2.82	169	3.75	225
72	1.8	108	2.25	135	3.38	202.8	4.5	270
96	2.4	144	3	180	4.5	270.4	6	360
120	3	180	3.75	225	5.63	338	7.5	450

Table E.12   Meters per Second and Meters per Minute

FPS	16 mm		35 mm 2-perf		35 mm 3-perf		35 mm 4-perf	
	Meters per Second	Meters per Minute	Meters per Second	Meters per Minute	Meters per Second	Meters per Minute	Meters per Second	Meters per Minute
6	.046	2.74	.057	3.42	.086	5.14	.115	6.875
12	.092	5.49	.114	6.86	.172	10.29	.229	13.71
18	.137	8.23	.172	10.29	.257	15.43	.343	20.57
24	.183	10.97	.229	13.72	.343	20.57	.457	27.43
25	.191	11.43	.238	14.29	.357	21.43	.476	28.57
30	.229	13.72	.286	17.15	.429	25.72	.572	34.29
36	.274	16.46	.343	20.57	.514	30.86	.686	41.14
48	.366	21.95	.457	27.43	.686	41.14	.914	54.86
60	.457	27.43	.572	34.29	.857	51.43	1.14	68.57
72	.549	32.92	.686	41.14	1.03	61.71	1.37	82.29
96	.732	43.89	.914	54.86	1.37	82.29	.83	109.71
120	.915	54.87	1.14	68.57	1.71	102.86	2.29	137.14

Running Time to Film Length and Film Length to Running Time

You will often need to determine if you have enough film to complete a certain shot. Tables E.13 to E.16 list the approximate running times for full rolls of film at various frames per second. All amounts are rounded to the nearest minute and second. For example, from Table E.15 you can determine that when shooting 35 mm 3-perf format and using a 400-ft roll at a speed of 36 fps, the roll will last approximately 3 minutes and 56 seconds.

Tables E.17 to E.20 show the amount of film used for different times at various frames per second. All lengths are rounded to the nearest foot and inch. For example, from Table E.20, you can determine that when shooting the 35 mm 4-perf format at 24 fps, a shot that lasts 14 seconds is approximately 21 ft in length. Tables E.21 to E.24 show the amount of time for different film lengths at various frames per second. All amounts are rounded to the nearest minute and second. For example, from Table E.21 you can determine that when shooting 16 mm at 48 fps, 60 ft of film will last approximately 50 seconds.

Table E.13 Running Times for 16 mm Format

FPS	16 mm Running Time				
	100 feet	**200 feet**	**400 feet**	**800 feet**	**1200 feet**
6	11 min. 7 sec.	22 min. 13 sec.	44 min. 26 sec.	1 hr 28 min. 53 sec.	2 hr 13 min. 20 sec.
12	5 min. 33 sec.	11 min. 7 sec.	22 min. 13 sec.	44 min. 26 sec.	1 hr 6 min. 40 sec.
18	3 min. 42 sec.	7 min. 24 sec.	14 min. 49 sec.	29 min. 38 sec.	44 min. 26 sec.
24	2 min. 46 sec.	5 min. 33 sec.	11 min. 7 sec.	22 min. 13 sec.	33 min. 20 sec.
25	2 min. 40 sec.	5 min. 20 sec.	10 mi 40 sec.	21 mi 2 sec.	32 min.
30	2 min. 13 sec.	4 min. 26 sec.	8 min. 53 sec.	17 min. 46 sec.	26 min. 40 sec.
36	1 min. 51 sec.	3 min. 42 sec.	7 min. 25 sec.	14 min. 49 sec.	22 min. 13 sec.
48	1 min. 23 sec.	2 min. 46 sec.	5 min. 33 sec.	11 min. 7 sec.	16 min. 40 sec.
60	1 min. 7 sec.	2 min. 13 sec.	4 min. 26 sec.	8 min. 53 sec.	13 min. 20 sec.
72	55 sec.	1 min. 51 sec.	3 min. 42 sec.	7 min. 25 sec.	11 min. 7 sec.
96	41 sec.	1 min. 23 sec.	2 min. 46 sec.	5 min. 33 sec.	8 min. 20 sec.
120	33 sec.	1 min. 7 sec.	2 min. 13 sec.	4 min. 26 sec.	6 min. 40 sec.

Table E.14   Running Times for 35 mm 2-Perf Format

FPS	35 mm 2-Perf Running Time				
	100 feet	200 feet	400 feet	1000 feet	2000 feet
6	8 min. 53 sec.	17 min. 46 sec.	35 min. 33 sec.	1 hr 28 min. 53 sec.	2 hr 7 min. 46 sec.
12	4 min. 26 sec.	8 min. 53 sec.	17 min. 46 sec.	44 min. 26 sec.	1 hr 28 min. 53 sec.
18	2 min. 57 sec.	5 min. 55 sec.	11 min. 51 sec.	29 min. 37 sec.	59 min. 15 sec.
24	2 min. 13 sec.	4 min. 26 sec.	8 min. 53 sec.	22 min. 13 sec.	44 min. 26 sec.
25	2 min. 8 sec.	4 min. 16 sec.	8 min. 32 sec.	21 min. 20 sec.	42 min. 40 sec.
30	1 min. 46 sec.	3 min. 33 sec.	7 min. 6 sec.	17 min. 46 sec.	35 min. 33 sec.
36	1 min. 28 sec.	2 min. 57 sec.	5 min. 55 sec.	14 min. 48 sec.	29 min. 37 sec.
48	1 min. 6 sec.	2 min. 13 sec.	4 min. 26 sec.	11 min. 6 sec.	22 min. 13 sec.
60	53 sec.	1 min. 46 sec.	3 min. 33 sec.	8 min. 53 sec.	17 min. 46 sec.
72	44 sec.	1 min. 28 sec.	2 min. 57 sec.	7 min. 24 sec.	14 min. 48 sec.
96	33 sec.	1 min. 6 sec.	2 min. 13 sec.	5 min. 33 sec.	11 min. 6 sec.
120	26 sec.	53 sec.	1 min. 46 sec.	4 min. 26 sec.	8 min. 53 sec.

Table E.15   Running Times for 35 mm 3-Perf Format

FPS	35mm 3-Perf Running Time				
	100 feet	**200 feet**	**400 feet**	**1000 feet**	**2000 feet**
6	5 min. 55 sec.	11 min. 51 sec.	23 min. 42 sec.	59 min. 15 sec.	1 hr 58 min. 30 sec.
12	2 min. 57 sec.	5 min. 55 sec.	11 min. 51 sec.	29 min. 37 sec.	59 min. 15 sec.
18	1 min. 58 sec.	3 min. 57 sec.	7 min. 54 sec.	19 min. 45 sec.	39 min. 30 sec.
24	1 min. 28 sec.	2 min. 57 sec.	5 min. 55 sec.	14 min. 48 sec.	29 min. 37 sec.
25	1 min. 25 sec.	2 min. 50 sec.	5 min. 41 sec.	14 min. 13 sec.	28 min. 26 sec.
30	1 min. 11 sec.	2 min. 22 sec.	4 min. 44 sec.	11 min. 51 sec.	23 min. 42 sec.
36	59 sec.	1 min. 58 sec.	3 min. 57 sec.	9 min. 52 sec.	19 min. 45 sec.
48	44 sec.	1 min. 28 sec.	2 min. 57 sec.	7 min. 24 sec.	14 min. 48 sec.
60	35 sec.	1 min. 11 sec.	2 min. 22 sec.	5 min. 55 sec.	11 min. 51 sec.
72	29 sec.	59 sec.	1 min. 58 sec.	4 min. 56 sec.	9 min. 52 sec.
96	22 sec.	44 sec.	1 min. 28 sec.	3 min. 42 sec.	7 min. 24 sec.
120	17 sec.	35 sec.	1 min. 11 sec.	2 min. 57 sec.	5 min. 55 sec.

Table E.16 Running Times for 35 mm 4-Perf Format

FPS	35 mm 4-Perf Running Time				
	100 feet	**200 feet**	**400 feet**	**1000 feet**	**2000 feet**
6	4 min. 26 sec.	8 min. 53 sec.	17 min. 46 sec.	44 min. 26 sec.	1 hr 28 min. 53 sec.
12	2 min. 13 sec.	4 min. 26 sec.	8 min. 53 sec.	22 min. 13 sec.	44 min. 26 sec.
18	1 min. 28 sec.	2 min. 57 sec.	5 min. 55 sec.	14 min. 48 sec.	29 min. 37 sec.
24	1 min. 6 sec.	2 min. 13 sec.	4 min. 26 sec.	11 min. 6 sec.	22 min. 13 sec.
25	1 min. 4 sec.	2 min. 8 sec.	4 min. 16 sec.	10 min. 40 sec.	21 min. 20 sec.
30	53 sec.	1 min. 46 sec.	3 min. 33 sec.	8 min. 53 sec.	17 min. 46 sec.
36	44 sec.	1 min. 28 sec.	2 min. 57 sec.	7 min. 24 sec.	14 min. 48 sec.
48	33 sec.	1 min. 6 sec.	2 min. 13 sec.	5 min. 33 sec.	11 min. 6 sec.
60	26 sec.	53 sec.	1 min. 46 sec.	4 min. 26 sec.	8 min. 53 sec.
72	22 sec.	44 sec.	1 min. 28 sec.	3 min. 42 sec.	7 min. 24 sec.
96	16 sec.	33 sec.	1 min. 6 sec.	2 min. 46 sec.	5 min. 33 sec.
120	13 sec.	26 sec.	53 sec.	2 min. 13 sec.	4 min. 26 sec.

Table E.17   Running Time to Film Length—16 mm

SEC.	Frames Per Second											
	6	12	18	24	25	30	36	48	60	72	96	120
1	2"	4"	6"	7"	8"	9"	11"	1'2"	1'6"	1' 10"	2' 5"	3'
2	4"	7"	11"	1' 2"	1' 3"	1' 6"	1' 10"	2' 5"	3'	3' 7"	4' 10"	6'
3	6"	11"	1' 5"	1' 10"	1' 11"	2' 3"	2' 8"	3' 7"	4' 6"	5' 5"	7' 2"	9'
4	7"	1' 2"	1' 10"	2' 5"	2' 6"	3'	3' 7"	4' 10"	6'	7' 2"	9' 7"	12'
5	9"	1' 6"	2' 3"	3'	3' 2"	3' 9"	4' 6"	6'	7' 6"	9'	12'	15'
6	11"	1' 10"	2' 8"	3' 7"	3' 9"	4' 6"	5' 5"	7' 2"	9'	10' 10"	14' 5"	18'
7	1' 1"	2' 1"	3' 2"	4' 2"	4' 5"	5' 3"	6' 4"	8' 5"	10' 6"	12' 7"	16' 10"	21'
8	1' 2"	2' 5"	3' 7"	4' 10"	5'	6'	7' 2"	9' 7"	12'	14' 5"	19' 2"	24'
9	1' 4"	2' 8"	4' 1"	5' 5"	5' 8"	6' 9"	8' 1"	10' 10"	13' 6"	16' 2"	21' 7"	27'
10	1' 6"	3'	4' 6"	6'	6' 3"	7' 6"	9'	12'	15'	18'	24'	30'
11	1' 8"	3' 4"	5'	6' 7"	6' 11"	8' 3"	9' 11"	13' 2"	16' 6"	19' 10"	26' 5"	33'
12	1' 10"	3' 7"	5' 5"	7' 2"	7' 6"	9'	10' 10"	14' 5"	18'	21' 7"	28' 10"	36'
13	2'	3' 11"	5' 10"	7' 10"	8' 2"	9' 9"	11' 8"	15' 7"	19' 6"	23' 4"	31' 2"	39'
14	2' 1"	4' 2"	6' 4"	8' 5"	8' 9"	10' 6"	12' 7"	16' 10"	21'	25' 2"	33' 7"	42'
15	2' 3"	4' 6"	6' 9"	9'	9' 5"	11' 3"	13' 6"	18'	22' 6"	27'	35'	45'
16	2' 5"	4' 10"	7' 2"	9' 7"	10'	12'	14' 5"	19' 2"	24'	28' 10"	38' 5"	48'
17	2' 7"	5' 1"	7' 8"	10' 2"	10' 8"	12' 9"	15' 4"	20' 5"	25' 6"	30' 7"	40' 10"	51'
18	2' 8"	5' 5"	8' 1"	10' 10"	11' 3"	13' 6"	16' 2"	21' 6"	27'	32' 5"	43' 2"	54'
19	2' 11"	5' 8"	8' 7"	11' 5"	11' 11"	14' 3"	17' 1"	22' 10"	28' 6"	34' 2'	45' 7"	57'
20	3'	6'	9'	12'	12' 6"	15'	18'	24'	30'	36'	48'	60'
21	3' 2"	6' 4"	9' 6"	12' 7"	13' 2"	15' 9"	18' 11"	25' 2"	31' 6"	37' 8"	50' 5"	63'
22	3' 4"	6' 4"	9' 6"	12' 7"	13' 9"	15' 9"	18' 11"	25' 2"	31' 6"	37' 10"	50' 5"	63'
23	3' 6"	6' 11"	10' 4"	13' 10"	14' 5"	17' 3"	20' 8"	27' 7"	34' 6"	41' 5"	55' 2"	69'
24	3' 7"	7' 2"	10' 10"	14' 5"	15'	18'	21' 7"	28' 10"	36'	43' 2"	57' 7"	72'
25	3' 9"	7' 6"	11' 3"	15'	15' 8"	18' 9"	22' 6"	30'	37' 6"	45'	60'	75'
26	3' 11"	7' 10"	11' 8"	15' 7"	16' 3"	19' 6"	23' 5"	31' 2"	39'	46' 7"	62' 4"	78'
27	4' 1"	8' 1"	12' 2"	16' 2"	16' 11"	20' 3"	24' 4"	32' 5"	40' 6"	48' 7"	64' 10"	81'
28	4' 2"	8' 5"	12' 7"	16' 10"	17' 6"	21'	25' 2"	33' 7"	42'	50' 5"	67'2"	84'
29	4' 4"	8' 8"	13' 1"	17' 5"	17' 2"	21' 9"	26' 1"	34' 10"	43' 6"	52' 2"	69' 7"	87'
30	4' 6"	9'	13' 6"	18'	18' 9"	22' 6"	27'	36'	45'	54'	72'	90'
31	4' 8"	9' 4"	13' 11"	18' 7"	19' 5"	23' 3"	27' 11"	37' 2"	46' 6"	55' 10"	74' 5"	93'
32	4' 10"	9' 7"	14' 5"	19' 2"	20'	24'	28' 10"	38' 5"	48'	57' 7"	76' 10"	96'
33	4' 11"	9' 11"	14' 11"	19' 10"	20' 8"	24' 9"	29' 8"	39' 7"	49' 6"	59' 5"	79' 2"	99'
34	5' 1"	10' 2"	15' 4"	20' 5"	21' 3"	25' 6"	30' 7"	40' 10"	51'	61' 2"	81' 7"	102'

(Continued)

Table E.17 (Continued)

SEC.	Frames Per Second											
	6	12	18	24	25	30	36	48	60	72	96	120
35	5' 3"	10' 6"	15' 9"	21'	21' 11"	26' 3"	31' 6"	42'	52' 6"	63'	84'	105'
36	5' 5"	10' 10"	16' 2"	21' 7"	22' 6"	27'	32' 5"	43' 2"	54'	64' 10"	86' 5"	108'
37	5' 7"	11' 1"	16' 7"	22' 2"	23' 2"	27' 9"	33' 4"	44' 5"	55' 6"	66' 7"	88' 10"	111'
38	5' 8"	11' 5"	17' 1"	22' 10"	23' 9"	28' 6"	34' 2"	45' 7"	57'	68' 5"	91' 2"	114'
39	5' 11"	11' 8"	17' 7"	23' 5"	24' 5"	29' 3"	35' 1"	46' 10"	58' 6"	70' 2"	93' 7"	117'
40	6'	12'	18'	24'	25'	30'	36'	48'	60'	72'	96'	120'
41	6' 2"	12' 4"	18' 6"	24' 7"	25' 8"	30' 9"	36' 11"	49' 2"	61' 6"	73' 10"	98' 5"	123'
42	6' 4"	12' 7"	18' 11"	25' 2"	26' 3"	31' 6"	37' 10"	50' 5"	63'	75' 6"	100' 10"	126'
43	6' 6"	12' 11"	19' 4"	25' 10"	26' 11"	32' 3"	38' 8"	51' 7"	64' 6"	77' 5"	103' 2"	129'
44	6' 7"	13' 2"	19' 10"	26' 5"	27' 6"	33'	39' 7"	52' 10"	66'	79' 2"	105' 7"	132'
45	6' 9"	13' 6"	20' 3"	27'	28' 2"	33' 9"	40' 6"	54'	67' 6"	81'	108'	135'
46	6' 11"	13' 10"	20' 8"	27' 7"	28' 9"	34' 6"	41' 5"	55' 2"	69'	82' 10"	110' 5"	138'
47	7' 1"	14' 1"	21' 2"	28' 2"	29' 5"	35' 3"	42' 4"	56' 5"	70' 6"	84' 7"	112' 10"	141'
48	7' 2"	14' 5"	21' 7"	28' 10"	30'	36'	43' 2"	57' 6"	72'	86' 5"	115' 2"	144'
49	7' 4"	14' 8"	22' 1"	29' 5"	30' 8"	36' 9"	44' 1"	58' 10"	73' 6"	88' 2"	117' 7"	147'
50	7' 6"	15'	22' 6"	30'	31' 3"	37' 6"	45'	60'	75'	90'	120'	150'
51	7' 8"	15' 4"	22' 11"	30' 7"	31' 11"	38' 3"	45' 11"	61' 2"	76' 6"	91' 10"	122' 5"	153'
52	7' 10"	15' 7"	23' 5"	31' 2"	32' 6"	39'	46' 10"	62' 5"	78'	93' 7"	124' 10"	156'
53	7' 11"	15' 11"	23' 11"	31' 10"	33' 2"	39' 9"	47' 8"	63' 7"	79' 6"	95' 5"	127' 2"	159'
54	8' 1"	16' 2"	24' 4"	32' 5"	33' 9"	40' 6"	48' 7"	64' 10"	81'	97' 2"	129' 7"	162'
55	8' 3"	16' 6"	24' 9"	33'	34' 5"	41' 3"	49' 6"	66'	82' 6"	99'	132'	165'
56	8' 5"	16' 10"	25' 2"	33' 7"	35'	42'	50' 5"	67' 2"	84'	100' 10"	134' 5"	168'
57	8' 7"	17' 1"	25' 8"	34' 2"	35' 8"	42' 9"	51' 4"	68' 5"	85' 6"	102' 7"	136' 10"	171'
58	8' 8"	17' 5"	26' 1"	34' 10"	36' 3"	43' 6"	52' 2"	69' 7"	87'	104' 5"	139' 2"	174'
59	8' 11"	17' 8"	26' 7"	35' 5"	36' 11"	44' 3"	53' 1"	70' 10"	88' 6"	106' 2"	141' 7"	177'
60	9'	18'	27'	36'	37' 6"	45'	54'	72'	90'	108'	144'	180'

Table E.18   Running Time to Film Length—35 mm 2-Perf

SEC.	Frames Per Second											
	6	12	18	24	25	30	36	48	60	72	96	120
1	2"	5"	7"	9"	9"	11"	1' 2"	1' 6"	1' 11"	2' 3"	3'	3' 9"
2	5"	9"	1' 2"	1' 6"	1' 7"	1' 10"	2' 3"	3'	3' 9"	4' 6"	6'	7' 6"
3	7"	1' 2"	1' 8"	2' 3"	2' 4"	2' 10"	3' 5"	4' 6"	5' 7"	6' 9"	9'	11' 3"
4	9"	1' 6"	2' 3"	3'	3' 2"	3' 9"	4' 6"	6'	7' 6"	6'	12'	15'
5	11"	1' 10"	2' 10"	3' 9"	3' 11"	4' 8"	5' 7"	7' 6"	9' 4"	11' 3"	15'	18' 9"
6	1' 2"	2' 3"	3' 4"	4' 6"	4' 8"	5' 7"	6' 9"	9'	11' 3"	13' 6"	18'	22' 6"
7	1' 4"	2' 7"	3' 11"	5' 3"	5' 6"	6' 7"	7' 10"	10' 6"	13' 2"	15' 9"	21'	26' 3"
8	1' 6"	3'	4' 6"	6'	6' 3"	7' 6"	9'	12'	15'	18'	24'	30'
9	1' 8"	3' 4"	5' 1"	6' 9"	7'	8' 5"	10' 2"	13' 6"	16' 10"	20' 3"	27'	33' 9"
10	1' 10"	3' 9"	5' 7"	7' 6"	7' 10"	9' 4"	11' 3"	15'	18' 9"	22' 6"	30'	37' 6"
11	2' 1"	4' 2"	6' 2"	8' 3"	8' 7"	10' 4"	12' 4"	16' 6"	20' 7"	24' 9"	33'	41' 3"
12	2' 3"	4' 6"	6' 9"	9'	9' 4"	11' 3"	13' 6"	18'	22' 6"	27'	36'	45'
13	2' 5"	4' 10"	7' 4"	9' 9"	10' 2"	12' 2"	14' 7"	19' 6"	24' 4"	29' 3"	39'	48' 9"
14	2' 7"	5' 3"	7' 10"	10' 6"	10' 11"	13' 2"	15' 9"	21'	26' 3"	31' 6"	42'	52' 6"
15	2' 10"	5' 7"	8' 5"	11' 3"	11' 9"	14' 1"	16' 11"	22' 6"	28' 2"	33' 9"	45'	56' 3"
16	3'	6'	9'	12'	12' 6"	15'	18'	24'	30'	36'	48'	60'
17	3' 2"	6' 4"	9' 7"	12' 9"	13' 3"	15' 11"	19' 2"	25' 6"	31' 10"	38' 3"	51'	63' 9"
18	3' 4"	6' 9"	10' 2"	13' 6"	14' 1"	16' 10"	20' 3"	27'	33' 9"	40' 6"	54'	67' 6"
19	3' 7"	7' 2"	10' 8"	14' 3"	14' 10"	17' 10"	21' 4"	28' 6"	35' 7"	42' 9"	57'	71' 3"
20	3' 9"	7' 6"	11' 3"	15'	15' 7"	18' 9"	22' 6"	30'	37' 6"	45'	60'	75'
21	3' 11"	7' 10"	11' 10"	15' 9"	16' 5"	19' 8"	23' 7"	31' 6"	39' 4"	47' 3"	63'	78' 9"
22	4' 2"	8' 3"	12' 4"	16' 6"	17' 2"	20' 7"	24' 9"	33'	41' 3"	49' 6"	66'	82' 6"
23	4' 4"	8' 7"	12' 11"	17' 3"	18'	21' 7"	25' 10"	34' 6"	43' 2"	51' 9"	69'	86' 3"
24	4' 6"	9'	13' 6"	18'	18' 9"	22' 6"	27'	36'	45'	54'	72'	90'
25	4' 8"	9' 4"	14' 1"	18' 9"	19' 6"	23' 5"	28' 2"	37' 6"	46' 10"	56' 3"	75'	93' 9"
26	4' 10"	9' 9"	14' 7"	19' 6"	20' 4"	24' 4"	29' 3"	39'	48' 9"	58' 6"	78'	97' 6"
27	5' 1"	10' 2"	15' 2"	20' 3"	21' 1"	25' 4"	30' 4"	40' 6"	50' 7"	60' 9"	81'	101' 3"
28	5' 3"	10' 6"	15' 9"	21'	21' 10"	26' 3"	31' 6"	42'	52' 6"	63'	84'	105'
29	5' 5"	10' 10"	16' 4"	21' 9"	22' 8"	27' 2"	32' 7"	43' 6"	54' 4"	65' 3"	87'	108' 9"
30	5' 7"	11' 3"	16' 10"	22' 6"	23' 5"	28' 2"	33' 9"	45'	56' 3"	67' 6"	90'	112' 6"
31	5' 10"	11' 7"	17' 5"	23' 3"	24' 3"	29' 1"	34' 10"	46' 6"	58' 2"	69' 9"	93'	116' 3"
32	6'	12'	18'	24'	25'	30'	36'	48'	60'	72'	96'	120'
33	6' 2"	12' 4"	18' 7"	24' 9"	25' 9"	30' 11"	37' 2"	49' 6"	61' 10"	74' 3"	99'	123' 9"

(Continued)

Table E.18   (Continued)

SEC.	Frames Per Second											
	6	12	18	24	25	30	36	48	60	72	96	120
34	6' 4"	12' 9"	19' 2"	25' 6"	26' 7"	31' 10"	38' 3"	51'	63' 9"	76' 6"	102'	127' 6"
35	6' 7"	13' 2"	19' 8"	26' 3"	27' 4"	32' 10"	39' 4"	52' 9"	65' 7"	78' 9"	105'	131' 3"
36	6' 9"	13' 6"	20' 3"	27'	28' 2"	33' 9"	40' 6"	54'	67' 6"	81'	108'	135'
37	6' 11"	13' 10"	20' 10"	27' 9"	28' 11"	34' 8"	41' 7"	55' 6"	69' 4"	83' 3"	111'	138' 9"
38	7' 2"	14' 3"	21' 4"	28' 6"	29' 8"	35' 7"	42' 9"	57'	71' 3"	85' 6"	114'	142' 6"
39	7' 4"	14' 7"	21' 11"	29' 3"	30' 5"	36' 7"	43' 10"	58' 6"	73' 2"	87' 9"	117'	146' 3"
40	7' 6"	15'	22' 6"	30'	31' 3"	37' 6"	45'	60'	75'	90'	120'	150'
41	7' 8"	15' 4"	23' 1"	30' 9"	32'	38' 5"	46' 2"	61' 6"	76' 10"	92' 3"	123'	153' 9"
42	7' 10"	15' 9"	23' 7"	31' 6"	32' 10"	39' 4"	47' 3"	63'	78' 9"	94' 6"	126'	157' 6"
43	8' 1"	16' 2"	24' 2"	32' 3"	33' 7"	40' 4"	48' 4"	64' 6"	80' 7"	96' 9"	129'	161' 3"
44	8' 3"	16' 6"	24' 9"	33'	34' 4"	41' 3"	49' 6"	66'	82' 6"	99'	132'	165'
45	8' 5"	16' 10"	25' 4"	33' 9"	35' 2"	42' 2"	50' 7"	67' 6"	84' 4"	101' 3"	135'	168' 9"
46	8' 7"	17' 3"	25' 10"	34' 6"	35' 11"	43' 2"	51' 9"	69'	86' 3"	103' 6"	138'	172' 6"
47	8' 10"	17' 7"	26' 5"	35' 3"	36' 8"	44' 1"	52' 10"	70' 6"	88' 2"	105' 9"	141'	176' 3"
48	9'	18'	27'	36'	37' 6"	45'	54'	72'	90'	108'	144'	180'
49	9' 2"	18' 4"	27' 7"	36' 9"	38' 3"	45' 11"	55' 2"	73' 6"	91' 10"	110' 3"	147'	183' 9"
50	9' 4"	18' 9"	28' 2"	37' 6"	39' 1"	46' 10"	56' 3"	75'	93' 9"	112' 6"	150'	187' 6"
51	9' 7"	19' 2"	28' 8"	38' 3"	39' 10"	47' 10"	57' 4"	76' 6"	95' 7"	114' 9"	153'	191' 3"
52	9' 9"	19' 6"	29' 3"	39'	40' 7"	48' 9"	58' 6"	78'	97' 6"	117'	156'	195'
53	9' 11"	19' 10"	29' 10"	39' 9"	41' 5"	49' 8"	59' 7"	79' 6"	99' 4"	119' 3"	159'	198' 9"
54	10' 2"	20' 3"	30' 4"	40' 6"	42' 2"	50' 7"	60' 9"	81'	101' 3"	121' 6"	162'	202' 6"
55	10' 4"	20' 7"	30' 11"	41' 3"	43'	51' 7"	61' 10"	82' 6"	103' 2"	123' 9"	165'	206' 3"
56	10' 6"	21'	31'	42'	43' 9"	52' 6"	63'	84'	105'	126'	168'	210'
57	10' 8"	21' 4"	32' 1"	42' 9"	44' 6"	53' 5"	64' 2"	85' 6"	106' 10"	128' 3"	171'	213' 9"
58	10' 10"	21' 9"	32' 7"	43' 6"	45' 4"	54' 4"	65' 3"	87'	108' 9"	130' 6"	174'	217' 6"
59	11' 1"	22' 2"	33' 2"	44' 3"	46' 1"	55' 4"	66' 4"	88' 6"	110' 7"	132' 9"	177'	221' 3"
60	11' 3"	22' 6"	33' 9"	45'	46' 10"	56' 3"	67' 6"	90'	112' 6"	135'	180'	225'

Table E.19 Running Time to Film Length—35 mm 3-Perf

SEC.	Frames Per Second											
	6	12	18	24	25	30	36	48	60	72	96	120
1	3"	7"	10"	1' 2"	1' 2"	1' 5"	1' 8"	2' 3"	2' 10"	3' 5"	4' 6"	5' 7"
2	7"	1' 2"	1' 8"	2' 3"	2' 4"	2' 10"	3' 5"	4' 6"	5' 7"	6' 9"	9'	11' 3"
3	10"	1' 8"	2' 7"	3' 5"	3' 6"	4' 3"	5' 1"	6' 9"	8' 6"	10' 2"	13' 6"	16' 11"
4	1' 1"	2' 2"	3' 5"	4' 6"	4' 8"	5' 7"	6' 9"	9'	11' 3"	13' 6"	18'	22' 6"
5	1' 5"	2' 10"	4' 4"	5' 7"	5' 10"	7' 1"	8' 6"	11' 3"	14' 1"	16' 11"	22' 6"	28' 2"
6	1' 8"	3' 5"	5' 1"	6' 10"	7'	8' 6"	10' 2"	13' 6"	16' 11"	20' 3"	27'	33' 10"
7	2'	3' 11"	6'	7' 11"	8' 2"	9' 11"	11' 10"	15' 9"	19' 9"	23' 8"	31' 6"	39' 5"
8	2' 2"	4' 6"	6' 10"	9'	9' 5"	11' 3"	13' 6"	18'	22' 7"	27' 1"	36'	45' 1"
9	2' 6"	5'	7' 8"	10' 1"	10' 7"	12' 8"	15' 3"	20' 3"	25' 5"	30' 5"	40' 6"	50' 8"
10	2' 10"	5' 7"	8' 6"	11' 4"	11' 9"	14' 1"	16' 11"	22' 6"	28' 2"	33' 10"	45'	56' 4"
11	3' 1"	6' 2"	9' 5"	12' 5"	12' 11"	15' 6"	18' 7"	24' 9"	31' 1"	37' 2"	49' 6"	61' 11"
12	3' 5"	6' 8"	10' 2"	13' 6"	14' 1"	16' 11"	20' 3"	27'	33' 10"	40' 7"	54'	67' 7"
13	3' 7"	7' 4"	11' 1"	14' 7"	15' 3"	18' 4"	21' 11"	29' 3"	36' 7"	43' 11"	58' 6"	73' 2"
14	3' 11"	7' 10"	11' 11"	15' 10"	16' 5"	19' 9"	23' 7"	31' 6"	39' 6"	47' 4"	63'	78' 10"
15	4' 2"	8' 5"	12' 10"	16' 11"	17' 7"	21' 2"	25' 4"	33' 9"	42' 4"	50' 8"	67' 6"	84' 6"
16	4' 6"	9'	13' 7"	18'	18' 9"	22' 6"	27' 1"	36'	45' 2"	54' 1"	72'	90' 1"
17	4' 10"	9' 6"	14' 6"	19' 1"	19' 11"	23' 11"	28' 9"	38' 3"	47' 11"	57' 6"	76' 6"	95' 8"
18	5'	10' 1"	15' 4"	20' 4"	21' 1"	25' 4"	30' 5"	40' 6"	50' 9"	60' 10"	81'	101' 4"
19	5' 4"	10' 7"	16' 2"	21' 5"	22' 3"	26' 9"	32' 11"	42' 9"	53' 7"	64' 2"	85' 6"	106' 11"
20	5' 7"	11' 2"	17'	22' 5"	23' 5"	28' 2"	33' 10"	45'	56' 5"	67' 7"	90'	112' 7"
21	5' 11"	11' 10"	17' 11"	23' 7"	24' 7"	29' 7"	35' 6"	47' 3"	59' 2"	71'	94' 6"	118' 3"
22	6' 2"	12' 4"	18' 8"	24' 10"	25' 9"	31' 1"	37' 2"	49' 6"	62' 1"	74' 4"	99'	123' 11"
23	6' 5"	12' 11"	19' 7"	25' 11"	26' 11"	32' 5"	38' 11"	51' 9"	64' 11"	77' 9"	103' 6"	129' 6"
24	6' 8"	13' 5"	20' 5"	27'	28' 2"	33' 10"	40' 7"	54'	67' 7"	81' 2"	108'	135' 2"
25	7'	14'	21' 4"	28' 1"	29' 4"	35' 3"	42' 3"	56' 3"	70' 6"	84' 6"	112' 6"	140' 9"
26	7' 4"	14' 7"	22' 1"	29' 4"	30' 6"	36' 8"	43' 11"	58' 6"	73' 4"	87' 11"	117'	146' 5"
27	7' 7"	15' 1"	23'	30' 5"	31' 8"	38' 1"	45' 7"	60' 9"	76' 2"	91' 3"	121' 6"	152'
28	7' 10"	15' 8"	23' 10"	31' 6"	32' 10"	39' 6"	47' 4"	63'	78' 11"	94' 7"	130' 6"	163' 3"
29	8' 1"	16' 2"	24' 8"	32' 7"	34'	40' 11"	49'	65' 3"	81' 9"	98'	130' 6"	163' 3"
30	8' 5"	16' 10"	26' 6"	33' 9"	35' 2"	42' 4"	50' 8"	67' 6"	84' 7"	101' 5"	135'	168' 11"
31	8' 8"	17' 5"	26' 5"	34' 11"	36' 4"	43' 8"	52' 5"	69' 9"	87' 5"	104' 10"	139' 6"	174' 6"
32	9'	17' 11"	27' 2"	36'	37' 6"	45' 1"	54' 1"	72'	90' 3"	108' 2"	144'	180' 2"
33	9' 2"	18' 6"	28' 1"	37' 1"	38' 8"	46' 6"	55' 8"	74' 3"	93' 1"	111' 6"	148' 6"	185' 10"
34	9' 6"	19'	28' 11"	38' 4"	39' 10"	47' 11"	57' 6"	76' 6"	95' 11"	114' 11"	153'	191' 5"
35	9' 10"	19' 7"	29' 10"	39' 5"	41'	49' 4"	59' 2"	78' 9"	98' 8"	118' 4"	157' 6"	197' 1"

(Continued)

Table E.19   (Continued)

SEC.	Frames Per Second											
	6	12	18	24	25	30	36	48	60	72	96	120
36	10' 1"	20' 2"	30' 7"	40' 6"	42' 3"	50' 9"	60' 9"	81'	101' 6"	121' 7"	162'	202' 7"
37	10' 5"	20' 8"	31' 6"	41' 7"	43' 4"	52' 2"	62' 6"	83' 3"	104' 4"	125' 1"	166' 6"	208' 4"
38	10' 7"	21' 4"	32' 4"	42' 10"	44' 6"	53' 7"	64' 3"	85' 6"	107' 2"	128' 6"	171'	213' 11"
39	10' 11"	21' 11"	33' 2"	43' 11"	45' 8"	55'	65' 11"	87' 9"	110'	131' 10"	175' 6"	219' 7"
40	11' 2"	22' 5"	34'	45'	46' 11"	56' 5"	67' 7"	90'	112' 10"	135' 2"	180'	225' 2"
41	11' 6"	23'	34' 11"	46' 1"	48' 1"	57' 10"	69' 4"	92' 3"	115' 7"	138' 7"	184' 6"	230' 10"
42	11' 10"	23' 6"	35' 8"	47' 4"	49' 3"	59' 3"	71'	94' 6"	118' 6"	142'	189'	236' 6"
43	12'	24' 1"	36' 7"	48' 5"	50' 5"	60' 7"	72' 7"	96' 9"	121' 3"	145' 4"	193' 6"	242' 1"
44	12' 4"	24' 7"	37' 5"	49' 6"	51' 7"	62'	74' 4"	99'	124' 1"	148' 8"	198'	247' 9"
45	12' 7"	25' 2"	38' 4"	50' 7"	52' 9"	63' 6"	76' 1"	101' 3"	126' 11"	152' 1"	202' 6"	253' 4"
46	12' 11"	25' 10"	39' 1"	51' 10"	53' 11"	64' 11"	77' 9"	103' 6"	129' 9"	155' 6"	207'	259'
47	13' 2"	26' 4"	40'	52' 11"	55' 1"	66' 3"	79' 5"	105' 9"	132' 6"	158' 11"	211' 6"	264' 7"
48	13' 5"	26' 11"	40' 10"	54'	56' 3"	67' 8"	81' 2"	108'	135' 4"	162' 3"	216'	270' 3"
49	13' 8"	27' 5"	41' 8"	55' 1"	57' 5"	69' 1"	82' 10"	110' 3"	138' 2"	165' 7"	220' 6"	275' 11"
50	14'	28'	42' 6"	56' 4"	58' 11"	70' 6"	84' 6"	112' 6"	141'	169'	225'	281' 6"
51	14' 4"	28' 7"	43' 5"	57' 5"	60' 1"	71' 11"	86' 2"	114' 9"	143' 10"	172' 5"	229' 6"	287' 2"
52	14' 7"	29' 1"	44' 2"	58' 6"	61' 3"	73' 4"	87' 11"	117'	146' 7"	175' 9"	234'	292' 9"
53	14' 10"	29' 8"	45' 1"	59' 7"	62' 6"	74' 9"	89' 7"	119' 3"	149' 6"	179' 2"	238' 6"	298' 5"
54	15' 1"	30' 2"	45' 11"	60' 10"	63' 8"	76' 2"	91' 3"	121' 6"	152' 3"	182' 6"	243'	304'
55	15' 5"	30' 10"	46' 10"	61' 11"	64' 10"	77' 6"	93'	123' 9"	155' 1"	185' 11"	247' 6"	309' 8"
56	15' 8"	31' 5"	47' 7"	63'	66'	79'	94' 7"	126'	158'	189' 3"	252'	315' 3"
57	16'	31' 11"	48' 6"	64' 1"	67' 2"	80' 4"	96' 4"	128' 3"	160' 9"	192' 8"	256' 6"	320' 11"
58	16' 2"	32' 6"	49' 4"	65' 4"	68' 4"	81' 9"	98'	130' 6"	163' 7"	196'	261'	326' 6"
59	16' 6"	33'	50' 2"	66' 5"	69' 6"	83' 2"	99' 8"	132' 9"	166' 5"	199' 5"	265' 6"	332' 2"
60	16' 10"	33' 7"	51'	67' 6"	70' 4"	84' 7"	101' 5"	135'	169' 2"	202' 10"	270'	337' 10"

Table E.20   Running Time to Film length—35 mm 4-Perf

SEC.	Frames Per Second											
	6	12	18	24	25	30	36	48	60	72	96	120
1	5"	9"	1' 2"	1' 6"	1' 7"	1' 11"	2' 3"	3'	3' 9"	4' 6"	6'	7' 6"
2	9"	1' 6"	2' 3"	3'	3' 2"	3' 9"	4' 6"	6'	7' 6"	9'	12'	15'
3	1' 2"	2' 3"	3' 5"	4' 6"	4' 8"	5' 8"	6' 9"	9'	11' 3"	13' 6"	18'	22' 6"
4	1' 6"	3'	4' 6"	6'	6' 3"	7' 6"	9'	12'	15'	18'	24'	30'
5	1' 11"	3' 9"	5' 8"	7' 6"	7' 10"	9' 5"	11' 3"	15'	18' 9"	22' 6"	30'	37' 6"
6	2' 3"	4' 6"	6' 9"	9'	9' 5"	11' 3"	13' 6"	18'	22' 6"	27'	36'	45'
7	2' 8"	5' 3"	7' 11"	10' 6"	10' 11"	13' 2"	15' 9"	21'	26' 3"	31' 6"	42'	52' 6"
8	3'	6'	9'	12'	12' 6"	15'	18'	24'	30'	36'	48'	60'
9	3' 5"	6' 9"	10' 2"	13' 6"	14' 1"	16' 11"	20' 3"	27'	33' 9"	40' 6"	54'	67' 6"
10	3' 9"	7' 6"	11' 3"	15'	15' 8"	18' 9"	22' 6"	30'	37' 6"	45'	60'	75'
11	4' 2"	8' 3"	12' 5"	16' 6"	17' 2"	20' 7"	24' 9"	33'	41' 3"	49' 6"	66'	82' 6"
12	4' 6"	9'	13' 6"	18'	18" 9"	22' 6"	27'	36'	45'	54'	72'	90'
13	4' 11"	9' 9"	14' 7"	19' 6"	20' 4"	24' 5"	29' 3"	39'	48' 9"	58' 6"	78'	97' 6"
14	5' 3"	10' 6"	15' 9"	21'	21' 11"	26' 3"	31' 6"	42'	52' 6"	63'	84'	105'
15	5' 8"	11' 3"	16' 11"	22' 6"	23' 5"	28' 2"	33' 9"	45'	56' 3"	67' 6"	90'	112' 6"
16	6'	12'	18'	24'	25'	30'	36'	48'	60'	72'	96'	120'
17	6' 5"	12' 9"	19' 2"	25' 6"	26' 7"	31' 11"	38' 3"	51'	63' 9"	76' 6"	102'	127' 6"
18	6' 9"	13' 6"	20' 3"	27'	28' 2"	33' 9"	40' 6"	54'	67' 6"	81'	108'	135'
19	7' 2"	14' 3"	21' 5"	28' 6"	29' 8"	35' 7"	42' 9"	57'	71' 3"	85' 6"	114'	142' 6"
20	7' 6"	15'	22' 6"	30'	31' 3"	37' 6"	45'	60'	75'	90'	120'	150'
21	7' 11"	15' 9"	23' 7"	31' 6"	32' 10"	39' 5"	47' 3"	63'	78' 9"	94' 6"	126'	157' 6"
22	8' 3"	16' 6"	24' 9"	33'	34' 5"	41' 3"	49' 6"	66'	82' 6"	99'	132'	165'
23	8' 8"	17' 3"	25' 11"	34' 6"	35' 11"	43' 2"	51' 9"	69'	86' 3"	103'6"	138'	172' 6"
24	9'	18'	27'	36'	37' 6"	45'	54'	72'	90'	108'	144'	180'
25	9' 5"	18' 9"	28' 2"	37' 6"	39' 1"	46' 11"	56' 3"	75'	93' 9"	112' 6"	150'	187' 6"
26	9' 9"	19' 6"	29' 3"	39'	40' 8"	48' 9"	58' 6"	78'	97' 6"	117'	156'	195'
27	10' 2"	20' 3"	30' 5"	40' 6"	42' 2"	50' 7"	60' 9"	81'	101' 4"	121' 6"	162'	202' 6"
28	10'6"	21'	31' 6"	42'	43' 9"	52' 6"	63'	84'	105'	126'	168'	210'
29	10' 11"	21' 9"	32' 7"	43' 6"	45' 4"	54' 5"	65' 3"	87'	108' 10"	130' 6"	174'	217' 6"
30	11' 3"	22' 6"	33' 9"	45'	46' 11"	56' 3"	67' 6"	90'	11' 6"	135'	180'	225'
31	11' 8"	23' 3"	34' 11"	46' 6"	48' 5"	58' 2"	69' 9"	93'	116' 4"	139' 6"	186'	232' 6"
32	12'	24'	36'	48'	50'	60'	72'	96'	120'	144'	192'	240'
33	12' 5"	24' 9"	37' 2"	49' 6"	51' 7"	61' 11"	74' 3"	99'	123' 10"	148' 6"	198'	247' 6"
34	12' 9"	25' 6"	38' 3"	51'	53' 2"	63' 9"	76' 6"	102'	127' 5"	153'	204'	255'
35	13' 2"	26' 3"	39' 5"	52' 6"	54' 8"	65' 8"	78' 9"	105'	131' 4"	157' 6"	210'	262' 6"

(Continued)

Table E.20 (Continued)

SEC.	Frames Per Second											
	6	**12**	**18**	**24**	**25**	**30**	**36**	**48**	**60**	**72**	**96**	**120**
36	13' 6"	27'	40' 6"	54'	56' 3"	67' 6"	81'	108'	135'	162'	216'	270'
37	13' 11"	27' 9"	41' 8"	55' 6"	57' 10"	69' 5"	83' 3"	111'	138' 10"	166'6"	222'	277' 6"
38	14' 3"	28' 6"	42' 9"	57'	59' 5"	71' 3"	85' 6"	114'	142' 6"	171'	228'	285'
39	14' 8"	29' 3"	43' 11"	58' 6"	60' 11"	73' 2"	87' 9"	117'	146'4"	175'6"	234'	292' 6"
40	15'	30'	45'	60'	62' 6"	75'	90'	120'	150'	180'	240'	300'
41	15' 5"	30' 9"	46'2"	61' 6"	64' 1"	76' 11"	92' 3"	123'	153' 10"	184' 6"	246'	307' 6"
42	15' 9"	31' 6"	47' 3"	63'	65' 8"	78' 9"	94' 6"	126'	157. 6"	189'	252'	315'
43	16' 2"	32' 3"	48' 5"	64' 6"	67' 2"	80' 8"	96' 9"	129'	161' 4"	193' 6"	258'	322' 6"
44	16' 6"	33'	49' 6"	66'	68' 9"	82' 6"	99'	132'	165'	198'	264'	330'
45	16' 11"	33' 9"	50' 8"	67' 6"	70' 4"	84' 5"	101' 4"	135'	168' 10"	202' 6"	270'	337' 6"
46	17' 3"	34' 6"	51' 9"	69'	71' 11"	86' 3"	103' 6"	138'	172' 6"	207'	276'	345'
47	17' 8"	35' 3"	52' 11"	70' 6"	73' 5"	88' 2"	105' 10"	141'	176' 4"	211' 6"	282'	352' 5"
48	18'	36'	54'	72'	75'	90'	108'	144'	180'	216'	288'	360'
49	18' 5"	36' 9"	55' 2"	73' 6"	76' 7"	91' 11"	110' 4"	147'	183' 10"	225'	300'	375'
50	18' 9"	37' 6"	56' 3"	75'	78' 2"	93' 9"	112' 6"	150'	187' 6"	225'	300'	375'
51	19' 2"	38' 3"	57' 5"	76' 6"	79' 8"	95' 8"	114' 10"	153'	191' 4"	229' 6"	306'	382' 6"
52	19' 6"	39'	58' 6"	78'	81' 3"	97' 6"	117'	156'	195'	234'	312'	390'
53	19' 11"	39' 9"	59' 8"	79' 6"	82' 10"	99' 5"	119' 4"	159'	198' 10"	238' 6"	318'	397' 6"
54	20' 3"	40' 6"	60' 9"	81'	84' 5"	101' 4"	121' 6"	162'	202' 6"	243'	324'	405'
55	20' 8"	41' 3"	61' 11"	82'6"	85' 11"	103' 1"	123' 10"	165'	206' 3"	247' 6"	330'	412' 6"
56	21'	42'	63'	84'	87'6"	105'	126'	168'	210'	252'	336'	420'
57	21' 5"	42' 9"	64' 2"	85' 6"	89' 1"	106' 11"	128' 4"	171'	213' 10"	256' 6"	342'	427' 6"
58	21' 9"	43' 6"	65' 3"	87'	90' 7"	108' 10"	130' 6"	174'	217' 6"	261'	348'	435'
59	22' 2"	44' 3"	66' 5"	88'6"	92' 2"	110' 7"	132' 10"	177'	221' 4"	265' 6"	354'	442' 6"
60	22' 6"	45'	67' 6"	90'	93'9"	112' 6"	135'	180'	225'	270'	360'	450'

Table E.21   Film Length to Running Time—16 mm

FEET	Frames Per Second											
	6	12	18	24	25	30	36	48	60	72	96	120
1	7 sec.	3 sec.	2 sec.	2 sec.	1 sec.	1 sec.	1 sec.	1 sec.	.7 sec.	.6 sec.	.4 sec.	.3 sec.
2	13 sec.	7 sec.	4 sec.	3 sec.	3 sec.	3 sec.	2 sec.	2 sec.	1 sec.	1 sec.	1 sec.	.7 sec.
3	20 sec.	10 sec.	7 sec.	5 sec.	5 sec.	4 sec.	3 sec.	3 sec.	2 sec.	2 sec.	1 sec.	1 sec.
4	27 sec.	13 sec.	9 sec.	7 sec.	6 sec.	5 sec.	4 sec.	3 sec.	3 sec.	2 sec.	2 sec.	1 sec.
5	33 sec.	17 sec.	11 sec.	8 sec.	8 sec.	7 sec.	6 sec.	4 sec.	3 sec.	3 sec.	2 sec.	2 sec.
6	40 sec.	20 sec.	13 sec.	10 sec.	9 sec.	8 sec.	7 sec.	5 sec.	4 sec.	3 sec.	3 sec.	2 sec.
7	47 sec.	23 sec.	16 sec.	12 sec.	11 sec.	9 sec.	8 sec.	6 sec.	5 sec.	4 sec.	3 sec.	2 sec.
8	53 sec.	27 sec.	18 sec.	13 sec.	12 sec.	11 sec.	9 sec.	7 sec.	5 sec.	4 sec.	3 sec.	3 sec.
9	1 min.	30 sec.	20 sec.	15 sec.	14 sec.	12 sec.	10 sec.	7 sec.	6 sec.	5 sec.	4 sec.	3 sec.
10	1 min. 7 sec.	33 sec.	22 sec.	17 sec.	16 sec.	13 sec.	11 sec.	8 sec.	7 sec.	6 sec.	4 sec.	3 sec.
20	2 min. 13 sec.	1 min. 7 sec.	44 sec.	33 sec.	32 sec.	27 sec.	22 sec.	17 sec.	13 sec.	11 sec.	8 sec.	7 sec.
30	3 min. 20 sec.	1 min. 40 sec.	1 min. 7 sec.	50 sec.	48 sec.	40 sec.	33 sec.	25 sec.	20 sec.	17 sec.	13 sec.	10 sec.
40	4 min. 26 sec.	2 min. 13 sec.	1 min. 29 sec.	1 min. 7 sec.	1 min. 4 sec.	53 sec.	44 sec.	33 sec.	27 sec.	22 sec.	17 sec.	13 sec.
50	5 min. 33 sec.	2 min. 47 sec.	1 min. 51 sec.	1 min. 23 sec.	1 min. 20 sec.	1 min. 6 sec.	56 sec.	42 sec.	34 sec.	28 sec.	21 sec.	17 sec.
60	6 min. 40 sec.	3 min. 20 sec.	2 min. 13 sec.	1 min. 40 sec.	1 min. 36 sec.	1 min. 20 sec.	1 min. 7 sec.	50 sec.	40 sec.	33 sec.	25 sec.	20 sec.
70	7 min. 47 sec.	3 min. 53 sec.	2 min. 35 sec.	1 min. 57 sec.	1 min. 52 sec.	1 min. 33 sec.	1 min. 18 sec.	58 sec.	47 sec.	39 sec.	29 sec.	23 sec.
80	8 min. 54 sec.	4 min. 26 sec.	2 min. 58 sec.	2 min. 14 sec.	2 min. 8 sec.	1 min. 46 sec.	1 min. 29 sec.	1 min. 6 sec.	54 sec.	44 sec.	33 sec.	26 sec.
90	10 min.	5 min.	3 min. 20 sec.	2 min. 30 sec.	2 min. 24 sec.	2 min.	1 min. 40 sec.	1 min. 15 sec.	1 min.	50 sec.	38 sec.	30 sec.
100	11 min. 7 sec.	5 min. 33 sec.	3 min. 42 sec.	2 min. 47 sec.	2 min. 40 sec.	2 min. 13 sec.	1 min. 51 sec.	1 min. 23 sec.	1 min. 7 sec.	55 sec.	41 sec.	33 sec.
200	22 min. 14 sec.	11 min. 6 sec.	7 min. 24 sec.	5 min. 34 sec.	5 min. 20 sec.	4 min. 26 sec.	3 min. 42 sec.	2 min. 46 sec.	2 min. 13 sec.	1 min. 51 sec.	1 min. 23 sec.	1 min. 7 sec.
400	44 min. 28 sec.	22 min. 12 sec.	14 min. 48 sec.	11 min. 7 sec.	10 min. 40 sec.	8 min. 53 sec.	7 min. 25 sec.	5 min. 33 sec.	4 min. 26 sec.	3 min. 42 sec.	2 min. 46 sec.	2 min. 13 sec.
800	88 min. 53 sec.	44 min. 26 sec.	29 min. 38 sec.	22 min. 13 sec.	21 min. 20 sec.	17 min. 46 sec.	14 min. 49 sec.	11 min. 7 sec.	8 min. 53 sec.	7 min. 25 sec.	5 min. 33 sec.	4 min. 26 sec.
1200	133 min. 24 sec.	66 min. 36 sec.	44 min. 24 sec.	33 min. 20 sec.	32 min.	26 min. 40 sec.	22 min. 13 sec.	16 min. 40 sec.	13 min. 20 sec.	11 min. 7 sec.	8 min. 20 sec.	6 min. 40 sec.

Table E.22 Film Length To Running Time—35 mm 2-Perf

FEET	Frames Per Second											
	6	12	18	24	25	30	36	48	60	72	96	120
1	5 sec.	3 sec.	2 sec.	1 sec.	1 sec.	1 sec.	.8 sec.	.6 sec.	.5 sec.	.4 sec.	.4 sec.	.2 sec.
2	10 sec.	6 sec.	4 sec.	2 sec.	2 sec.	2 sec.	2 sec.	1 sec.	1 sec.	.8 sec.	.6 sec.	.6 sec.
3	16 sec.	8 sec.	6 sec.	4 sec.	4 sec.	4 sec.	2 sec.	2 sec.	2 sec.	1 sec.	1 sec.	.8 sec.
4	21 sec.	10 sec.	8 sec.	6 sec.	6 sec.	4 sec.	4 sec.	2 sec.	2 sec.	2 sec.	1 sec.	1 sec.
5	26 sec.	13 sec.	9 sec.	7 sec.	6 sec.	5 sec.	4 sec.	3 sec.	3 sec.	2 sec.	2 sec.	.7 sec.
6	32 sec.	16 sec.	10 sec.	8 sec.	7 sec.	6 sec.	5 sec.	4 sec.	3 sec.	3 sec.	2 sec.	2 sec.
7	37 sec.	18 sec.	12 sec.	9.3 sec.	9 sec.	7 sec.	6 sec.	5 sec.	4 sec.	3 sec.	2 sec.	2 sec.
8	42 sec.	21 sec.	14 sec.	11 sec.	10 sec.	9 sec.	7 sec.	5 sec.	4 sec.	4 sec.	3 sec.	2 sec.
9	48 sec.	24 sec.	16 sec.	12 sec.	12 sec.	10 sec.	8 sec.	6 sec.	5 sec.	4 sec.	3 sec.	2 sec.
10	53 sec.	27 sec.	18 sec.	13 sec.	13 sec.	11 sec.	9 sec.	7 sec.	5 sec.	4 sec.	3 sec.	3 sec.
20	1 min. 47 sec.	53 sec.	36 sec.	27 sec.	26 sec.	21 sec.	18 sec.	13 sec.	11 sec.	9 sec.	7 sec.	5 sec.
30	2 min. 40 sec.	1 min. 20 sec.	53 sec.	40 sec.	38 sec.	32 sec.	27 sec.	20 sec.	16 sec.	13 sec.	10 sec.	8 sec.
40	3 min. 33 sec.	1 min. 47 sec.	1 min. 11 sec.	53 sec.	51 sec.	43 sec.	36 sec.	27 sec.	21 sec.	18 sec.	13 sec.	11 sec.
50	4 min. 26 sec.	2 min. 13 sec.	1 min. 29 sec.	1 min. 7 sec.	1 min. 4 sec.	53 sec.	44 sec.	33 sec.	27 sec.	22 sec.	17 sec.	13 sec.
60	5 min. 20 sec.	2 min. 40 sec.	1 min. 47 sec.	1 min. 20 sec.	1 min. 17 sec.	1 min. 4 sec.	53 sec.	40 sec.	32 sec.	27 sec.	20 sec.	16 sec.
70	6 min. 13 sec.	3 min. 7 sec.	2 min. 4 sec.	1 min. 33 sec.	1 min. 30 sec.	1 min. 15 sec.	1 min. 2 sec.	47 sec.	37 sec.	31 sec.	23 sec.	19 sec.
80	7 min. 6 sec.	3 min. 33 sec.	2 min. 22 sec.	1 min. 47 sec.	1 min. 42 sec.	1 min. 25 sec.	1 min. 11 sec.	53 sec.	43 sec.	36 sec.	27 sec.	21 sec.
90	8 min.	4 min.	2 min. 40 sec.	2 min.	1 min. 55 sec.	1 min. 36 sec.	1 min. 20 sec.	1 min.	48 sec.	40 sec.	30 sec.	24 sec.
100	8 min. 53 sec.	4 min. 26 sec.	2 min. 58 sec.	2 min. 13 sec.	2 min. 8 sec.	1 min. 47 sec.	1 min. 29 sec.	1 min. 7 sec.	53 sec.	44 sec.	33 sec.	27 sec.
200	17 min. 46 sec.	8 min. 53 sec.	5 min. 56 sec.	4 min. 27 sec.	4 min. 16 sec.	3 min. 33 sec.	2 min. 58 sec.	2 min. 13 sec.	1 min. 47 sec.	1 min. 29 sec.	1 min. 7 sec.	53 sec.
400	35 min. 33 sec.	17 min. 46 sec.	11 min. 51 sec.	8 min. 53 sec.	8 min. 32 sec.	7 min. 7 sec.	5 min. 56 sec.	4 min. 26 sec.	3 min. 33 sec.	2 min. 58 sec.	2 min. 13 sec.	1 min. 46 sec.
1000	1 hour 28 min. 53 sec.	44 min. 27 sec.	29 min. 38 sec.	22 min. 13 sec.	21 min. 20 sec.	17 min. 47 sec.	14 min. 49 sec.	11 min. 7 sec.	8 min. 53 sec.	7 min. 24 sec.	5 min. 33 sec.	4 min. 27 sec.
2000	2 hours 57 min. 46 sec.	1 hours 28 min. 53 sec.	59 min. 16 sec.	44 min. 27 sec.	42 min. 40 sec.	35 min. 33 sec.	29 min. 38 sec.	22 min. 13 sec.	17 min. 47 sec.	14 min. 49 sec.	11 min. 7 sec.	8 min. 53 sec.

Table E.23   Film Length to Running Time—35 mm 3-Perf

FEET	Frames Per Second											
	6	**12**	**18**	**24**	**25**	**30**	**36**	**48**	**60**	**72**	**96**	**120**
1	4 sec.	2 sec.	1 sec.	.9 sec.	.8 sec.	.7 sec.	.6 sec.	.4 sec.	.4 sec.	.3 sec.	.2 sec.	.2 sec.
2	7 sec.	4 sec.	2 sec.	2 sec.	1 sec.	1 sec.	1 sec.	.9 sec.	.7 sec.	.6 sec.	.4 sec.	.4 sec.
3	11 sec.	5 sec.	4 sec.	4 sec.	2 sec.	2 sec.	2 sec.	1 sec.	1 sec.	.9 sec.	.7 sec.	.5 sec.
4	14 sec.	7 sec.	5 sec.	4 sec.	3 sec.	3 sec.	2 sec.	2 sec.	1 sec.	1 sec.	.9 sec.	.7 sec.
5	18 sec.	9 sec.	6 sec.	4 sec.	4 sec.	4 sec.	3 sec.	2 sec.	2 sec.	1 sec.	1 sec.	.9 sec.
6	21 sec.	11 sec.	7 sec.	5 sec.	5 sec.	4 sec.	4 sec.	3 sec.	2 sec.	2 sec.	1 sec.	1 sec.
7	25 sec.	12 sec.	8 sec.	6 sec.	5 sec.	5 sec.	4 sec.	3 sec.	3 sec.	2 sec.	2 sec.	1 sec.
8	28 sec.	14 sec.	9 sec.	7 sec.	6 sec.	6 sec.	5 sec.	4 sec.	3 sec.	2 sec.	2 sec.	1 sec.
9	32 sec.	16 sec.	11 sec.	8 sec.	7 sec.	6 sec.	5 sec.	4 sec.	3 sec.	2 sec.	2 sec.	2 sec.
10	36 sec.	18 sec.	12 sec.	9 sec.	8 sec.	7 sec.	6 sec.	4 sec.	4 sec.	3 sec.	2 sec.	2 sec.
20	1 min. 11 sec.	36 sec.	24 sec.	18 sec.	17 sec.	14 sec.	12 sec.	9 sec.	7 sec.	6 sec.	4 sec.	4 sec.
30	1 min. 47 sec.	53 sec.	35 sec.	26 sec.	26 sec.	21 sec.	18 sec.	13 sec.	11 sec.	9 sec.	7 sec.	5 sec.
40	2 min. 22 sec.	1 min. 11 sec.	47 sec.	35 sec.	34 sec.	28 sec.	24 sec.	18 sec.	14 sec.	12 sec.	9 sec.	7 sec.
50	2 min. 57 sec.	1 min. 29 sec.	59 sec.	44 sec.	42 sec.	36 sec.	30 sec.	22 sec.	18 sec.	15 sec.	11 sec.	9 sec.
60	3 min. 33 sec.	1 min. 47 sec.	1 min. 11 sec.	53 sec.	51 sec.	43 sec.	35 sec.	26 sec.	22 sec.	18 sec.	13 sec.	11 sec.
70	4 min. 12 sec.	2 min. 5 sec.	1 min. 23 sec.	1 min. 2 sec.	59 sec.	50 sec.	41 sec.	31 sec.	25 sec.	21 sec.	15 sec.	13 sec.
80	4 min. 44 sec.	2 min. 22 sec.	1 min. 34 sec.	1 min. 10 sec.	1 min. 8 sec.	57 sec.	47 sec.	35 sec.	29 sec.	24 sec.	18 sec.	14 sec.
90	5 min. 20 sec.	2 min. 40 sec.	1 min. 46 sec.	1 min. 19 sec.	1 min. 16 sec.	1 min. 4 sec.	53 sec.	40 sec.	32 sec.	27 sec.	20 sec.	16 sec.
100	5 min. 55 sec.	2 min. 58 sec.	1 min. 58 sec.	1 min. 29 sec.	1 min. 25 sec.	1 min. 11 sec.	59 sec.	44 sec.	35 sec.	30 sec.	22 sec.	18 sec.
200	11 min. 50 sec.	5 min. 55 sec.	3 min. 56 sec.	2 min. 58 sec.	2 min. 50 sec.	2 min. 22 sec.	1 min. 58 sec.	1 min. 29 sec.	1 min. 11 sec.	59 sec.	44 sec.	35 sec.
400	23 min. 40 sec.	11 min. 50 sec.	7 min. 53 sec.	5 min. 56 sec.	5 min. 41 sec.	4 min. 44 sec.	3 min. 56 sec.	2 min. 58 sec.	2 min. 22 sec.	1 min. 58 sec.	1 min. 29 sec.	1 min. 11 sec.
1000	59 min. 10 sec.	29 min. 35 sec.	19 min. 43 sec.	14 min. 49 sec.	14 min. 13 sec.	11 min. 50 sec.	9 min. 52 sec.	7 min. 24 sec.	5 min. 55 sec.	4 min. 56 sec.	3 min. 42 sec.	2 min. 58 sec.
2000	118 min. 18 sec.	59 min. 10 sec.	39 min. 27 sec.	29 min. 38 sec.	28 min. 26 sec.	23 min. 40 sec.	19 min. 43 sec.	14 min. 47 sec.	11 min. 50 sec.	9 min. 52 sec.	7 min. 24 sec.	5 min. 55 sec.

Table E.24   Film Length To Running Time—35 mm 4-Perf

FEET	Frames Per Second											
	6	12	18	24	25	30	36	48	60	72	96	120
1	3 sec.	1 sec.	.9 sec.	.7 sec.	.6 sec.	.5 sec.	.4 sec.	.3 sec.	.3 sec.	.2 sec.	.2 sec.	.1 sec.
2	5 sec.	3 sec.	2 sec.	1 sec.	1 sec.	1 sec.	.9 sec.	.7 sec.	.5 sec.	.4 sec.	.3 sec.	.3 sec.
3	8 sec.	4 sec.	3 sec.	2 sec.	2 sec.	2 sec.	1 sec.	1 sec.	.8 sec.	.7 sec.	.5 sec.	.4 sec.
4	11 sec.	5 sec.	4 sec.	3 sec.	3 sec.	2 sec.	2 sec.	1 sec.	1 sec.	.9 sec.	.7 sec.	.5 sec.
5	13 sec.	7 sec.	4 sec.	3 sec.	3 sec.	3 sec.	2 sec.	2 sec.	1 sec.	1 sec.	.9 sec.	.7 sec.
6	16 sec.	8 sec.	5 sec.	4 sec.	3 sec.	3 sec.	3 sec.	2 sec.	2 sec.	1 sec.	1 sec.	.8 sec.
7	19 sec.	9 sec.	6 sec.	5 sec.	5 sec.	4 sec.	3 sec.	2 sec.	2 sec.	2 sec.	1 sec.	.9 sec.
8	21 sec.	11 sec.	7 sec.	5 sec.	5 sec.	4 sec.	4 sec.	3 sec.	2 sec.	2 sec.	1 sec.	1 sec.
9	24 sec.	12 sec.	8 sec.	6 sec.	5 sec.	5 sec.	4 sec.	3 sec.	2 sec.	2 sec.	2 sec.	1 sec.
10	27 sec.	13 sec.	9 sec.	7 sec.	6 sec.	5 sec.	4 sec.	3 sec.	3 sec.	2 sec.	2 sec.	1 sec.
20	53 sec.	27 sec.	18 sec.	13 sec.	12 sec.	11 sec.	9 sec.	7 sec.	5 sec.	4 sec.	3 sec.	3 sec.
30	1 min. 20 sec.	40 sec.	26 sec.	20 sec.	19 sec.	16 sec.	13 sec.	10 sec.	8 sec.	7 sec.	5 sec.	4 sec.
40	1 min. 47 sec.	53 sec.	35 sec.	27 sec.	25 sec.	21 sec.	18 sec.	13 sec.	11 sec.	9 sec.	7 sec.	5 sec.
50	2 min. 14 sec.	1 min. 6 sec.	44 sec.	34 sec.	32 sec.	27 sec.	22 sec.	17 sec.	14 sec.	11 sec.	9 sec.	7 sec.
60	2 min. 40 sec.	1 min. 20 sec.	53 sec.	40 sec.	38 sec.	32 sec.	26 sec.	20 sec.	16 sec.	13 sec.	10 sec.	8 sec.
70	3 min. 7 sec.	1 min. 33 sec.	1 min. 2 sec.	47 sec.	44 sec.	37 sec.	31 sec.	23 sec.	19 sec.	15 sec.	12 sec.	9 sec.
80	3 min. 34 sec.	1 min. 46 sec.	1 min. 10 sec.	54 sec.	51 sec.	42 sec.	35 sec.	26 sec.	22 sec.	18 sec.	14 sec.	10 sec.
90	4 min.	2 min.	1 min. 19 sec.	1 min.	57 sec.	48 sec.	40 sec.	30 sec.	24 sec.	20 sec.	15 sec.	12 sec.
100	4 min. 26 sec.	2 min. 13 sec.	1 min. 29 sec.	1 min. 7 sec.	1 min. 4 sec.	53 sec.	44 sec.	33 sec.	26 sec.	22 sec.	16 sec.	13 sec.
200	8 min. 53 sec.	4 min. 26 sec.	2 min. 58 sec.	2 min. 13 sec.	2 min. 8 sec.	1 min. 46 sec.	1 min. 29 sec.	1 min. 7 sec.	53 sec.	44 sec.	33 sec.	26 sec.
400	17 min. 47 sec.	8 min. 53 sec.	5 min. 56 sec.	4 min. 26 sec.	4 min. 16 sec.	3 min. 33 sec.	2 min. 58 sec.	2 min. 13 sec.	1 min. 46 sec.	1 min. 29 sec.	1 min. 7 sec.	53 sec.
1000	44 min. 26 sec.	22 min. 13 sec.	14 min. 49 sec.	11 min. 7 sec.	10 min. 40 sec.	8 min. 53 sec.	7 min. 24 sec.	5 min. 33 sec.	4 min. 26 sec.	3 min. 42 sec.	2 min. 46 sec.	2 min. 13 sec.
2000	88 min. 53 sec.	44 min. 26 sec.	29 min. 37 sec.	22 min. 13 sec.	21 min. 20 sec.	17 min. 46 sec.	14 min. 48 sec.	11 min. 7 sec.	8 min. 53 sec.	7 min. 24 sec.	5 min. 33 sec.	4 min. 26 sec.

Table E.25   Meters to Feet Conversion Table

Meters	Feet/Inches
.1 meter	3.9 inches
.2 meter	7.9 inches
.3 meter	11.8 inches
.4 meter	15.7 inches
.5 meter	19.7 inches
.6 meter	23.6 inches
.7 meter	27.6 inches
.8 meter	31.5 inches
.9 meter	35.4 inches
1 meter	3 feet 3.4 inches
2 meters	6 feet 6.7 inches
3 meters	9 feet 10.1 inches
4 meters	13 feet 1.5 inches
5 meters	16 feet 4.8 inches
6 meters	3.9 inches
7 meters	7.9 inches
8 meters	26 feet 3 inches
9 meters	29 feet 6.3 inches
10 meters	32 feet 9.7 inches

Feet to Meters and Meters to Feet

Because you may not always be shooting in the United States and using feet and inches as your means of measurement, you may need to convert feet and inches to meters or vice versa. Tables E.25 and E.26 are conversion tables for converting feet and inches to meters or meters to feet and inches.

FORMULAS

You may often not be able to find specific information needed to calculate depth of field, exposure time, feet per minute, etc. The following formulas may be useful to calculate these and some other values. Remember when using formulas that contain mixed values for

Table E.26   Feet to Meters Conversion Table

Feet	Meters
1 foot	.30 meter
2 feet	.61 meter
3 feet	.91 meter
4 feet	1.22 meters
5 feet	1.52 meters
6 feet	1.83 meters
7 feet	2.13 meters
8 feet	2.44 meters
9 feet	2.74 meters
10 feet	3.05 meters
15 feet	4.57 meters
20 feet	6.10 meters
30 feet	9.14 meters
40 feet	12.19 meters
50 feet	15.24 meters

measurements (millimeters versus inches), you will need to convert so that all values are in the same format.

Depth of Field—Near

Note: This formula is for basic depth-of-field calculations for simple lenses.

$$\text{depth of field} = \frac{\text{hyperfocal distance} \times \text{focus distance}}{\text{hyperfocal distance} + \text{focus distance}}$$

Depth of Field—Far

Note: This formula is for basic depth-of-field calculations for simple lenses.

$$\text{depth of field} = \frac{\text{hyperfocal distance} \times \text{focus distance}}{\text{hyperfocal distance} - \text{focus distance}}$$

Hyperfocal Distance

$$\text{Hyperfocal distance} = \frac{\text{focal length}^2}{\text{circle of confusion} \times \text{f-stop}}$$

Electrical

$$\text{amps} = \frac{\text{watts}}{\text{volts}}$$

Or

$$\text{watts} = \text{volts} \times \text{amps}$$

Exposure Time/Shutter Speed

$$\text{exposure time} = \frac{\text{shutter angle}}{360 \times \text{frames per second}}$$

F-stop

$$\text{f-stop} = \frac{\text{focal length of lens}}{\text{diameter of lens opening}}$$

Feet per Minute for 16 mm

$$\text{feet per minute (16mm)} = \frac{\text{frames per second} \times 60}{40}$$

Feet per Minute for 35 mm 2-Perf Format

$$\text{feet per minute (35mm, 2-perf format)} = \frac{\text{frames per second} \times 60}{32}$$

Feet per Minute for 35 mm 3-Perf Format

$$\text{feet per minute (35mm, 3-perf format)} = \frac{\text{frames per second} \times 60}{21.33}$$

Feet per Minute for 35 mm 4-Perf Format

$$\text{feet per minute (35mm, 4-perf format)} = \frac{\text{frames per second} \times 60}{16}$$

Meters per Minute for 16 mm

$$\text{meters per minute (16mm)} = \frac{\text{frames per second} \times 60}{131.23}$$

Meters per Minute for 35 mm 2-Perf Format

$$\text{meters per minute (35mm, 2-perf format)} = \frac{\text{frames per second} \times 60}{105}$$

Meters per Minute for 35 mm 3-Perf Format

$$\text{meters per minute (35mm, 3-perf format)} = \frac{\text{frames per second} \times 60}{70}$$

Meters per Minute for 35 mm 4-Perf Format

$$\text{meters per minute (35mm, 4-perf format)} = \frac{\text{frames per second} \times 60}{52.5}$$

Screen Time

$$\text{Screen time} = \frac{\text{camera running time (seconds)} \times \text{frames per second}}{24}$$

Feet and Inches to Meters

$$\text{meters} = \frac{(\text{feet} \times 12) + \text{inches}}{39.37}$$

Meters to Feet and Inches

$$\text{Feet} = \text{meters} \times 3.2808$$

Mm to Inches

1mm	$= .03938$ inches
25mm	$= .9845$ inch ≈ 1 inch
50mm	$= 1.969$ inches ≈ 2 inches
75mm	$= 2.9535$ inches ≈ 3 inches
100mm	$= 3.938$ inches ≈ 4 inches

Recommended Reading

Alton, John, 1995. Painting with Light. University of California Press, Berkeley and Los Angeles, CA.

Anderson, Jack, 2011. Shooting Movies Without Shooting Yourself in the Foot. Focal Press, Boston, MA.

Arijon, Daniel, 1991. Grammar of the Film Language. Silman-James Press, Los Angeles, CA.

Ballinger, Alex, 2004. New Cinematographers. Collins Design, New York.

Barclay, Steven, 2000. The Motion Picture Image: From Film to Digital. Focal Press, Boston, MA.

Bergery, Benjamin, 2002. Reflections: Twenty-One Cinematographers at Work. ASC Press, Hollywood, CA.

Bernstein, Steven, 1988. The Technique of Film Production, 2nd ed. Focal Press, Boston, MA.

Billups, Scott, 2008. Digital Moviemaking 3.0. Michael Wiese Productions, Los Angeles, CA.

Block, Bruce, 2008. The Visual Story, Creating the Visual Structure of Film, TV and Digital Media, 2nd ed. Focal Press, Boston, MA.

Bloedow, Jerry, 1991. Filmmaking Foundations. Focal Press, Boston, MA.

Bognar, Desi K., 1999. International Dictionary of Broadcasting and Film, 2nd ed. Focal Press, Boston, MA.

Box, Harry C., 2003. Set Lighting Technician's Handbook, 3rd ed. Focal Press, Boston, MA.

Braverman, Barry, 2009. Video Shooter. Focal Press, Boston, MA.

Brown, Blain, 1994. The Filmmaker's Pocket Reference. Focal Press, Boston, MA.

Brown, Blain, 2007. Motion Picture and Video Lighting, 2nd ed. Focal Press, Boston, MA.

Brown, Blain, 2011. Cinematography Theory and Practice, 2nd ed. Focal Press, Boston, MA.

Browne, Steven E., 1992. Film-Video Terms and Concepts. Focal Press, Boston, MA.

Burum, Stephen (Ed.), 2006. American Cinematographer Manual (9th ed.). ASC Press, Hollywood, CA.

Cardiff, Jack, 1996. Magic Hour. Faber & Faber, London.

Carlson, Verne, Carlson, Sylvia, 1991. Professional Lighting Handbook, 2nd ed. Focal Press, Boston, MA.

Carlson, Verne, Carlson, Sylvia, 1994. Professional Cameraman's Handbook, 4th ed. Focal Press, Boston, MA.

Case, Dominic, 2001. Film Technology in Post Production. Focal Press, Boston, MA.

Cheshire, David, 1979. The Book of Movie Photography. Alfred A. Knopf, New York.

Clarke, Charles, 1989. Highlights and Shadows. The Scarecrow Press, Lanham, MD.

Clarke, Charles, 1994. Charles Clarke's Professional Cinematography. ASC Press, Hollywood, CA.

Coe, Brian, 1982. The History of Movie Photography. Zoetrope, New York.

Courter, Philip R., 1982. The Filmmakers Craft: 16 mm Cinematography. Van Nostrand Reinhold, New York.

Cunningham, Megan, 2005. The Art of the Documentary. New Riders, Berkeley, CA.

Daley, Ken, 1980. Basic Film Technique. Focal Press, Boston, MA.

Dancyger, Ken, 1993. The Technique of Film and Video Editing. Focal Press, Boston, MA.

Dancyger, Ken, 1999. The World of Film and Video Production: Aesthetics and Practices. Wadsworth Publishing, Belmont, CA.

De Leeuw, Ben, 1997. Digital Cinematography. Academic Press/Morgan Kaufmann, San Diego, CA.

Dmytryk, Edward, 1988. Cinema: Concept & Practice. Focal Press, Boston, MA.

Kodak Co, Eastman, 1983. The Book of Film Care. Eastman Kodak Co., Rochester, NY.

Kodak Co, Eastman, 1983. Kodak Motion Picture Film. Eastman Kodak Co., Rochester, NY.

Kodak Co, Eastman, 1990. Handbook of Kodak Photographic Filters. Eastman Kodak Co., Rochester, NY.

Kodak Co, Eastman, 1992. Eastman Professional Motion Picture Films. Eastman Kodak Co., Rochester, NY.

Kodak Co, Eastman, 1996. Exploring the Color Image. Eastman Kodak Co., Rochester, NY.

Kodak Co, Eastman, 2010. Cinematographer's Field Guide, 14th ed. Eastman Kodak Co., Rochester, NY.

Ettedgui, Peter, 1999. Cinematography—Screencraft Series. Focal Press, Boston, MA.

Fauer, Jon, 1996. Arriflex 16SR3—The Book. Arriflex, Blauvelt, NY.

Fauer, Jon, 1999. Arriflex 16SR Book, 3rd ed. Focal Press, Boston, MA.

Fauer, Jon, 1999. Arriflex 35 Book, 3rd ed. Focal Press, Boston, MA.

Fauer, Jon, 1999. Arriflex 435 Book, 3rd ed. Arriflex, Blauvelt, NY.

Fauer, Jon, 2001. DVCAM, A Practical Guide to the Professional System. Focal Press, Boston, MA.

Fauer, Jon, 2001. Shooting Digital Video: DVCAM, MiniDV and DVC Pro. Focal Press, Boston, MA.

Fauer, Jon, 2002. Arricam Book. ASC Press, Hollywood, CA.

Ferncase, Richard K., 1992. Basic Lighting Worktext for Film and Video. Focal Press, Boston, MA.

Ferncase, Richard K., 1994. Film and Video Lighting Terms and Concepts. Focal Press, Boston, MA.

Ferrara, Serena, 2000. Steadicam: Techniques and Aesthetics. Focal Press, Boston, MA.

Fielding, Raymond, 1967. A Technological History of Motion Pictures and Television. University of California Press, Berkeley, CA.

Fielding, Raymond, 1985. The Technique of Special Effects Cinematography. Focal Press, Boston, MA.

Frost, Jacqueline B., 2009. Cinematography for Directors. Michael Wiese Productions, Los Angeles, CA.

Galer, Mark, Child, John, 2003. Photographic Lighting: Essentials, 2nd ed. Focal Press, Boston, MA.

Garvey, Helen, 1985. Before You Shoot. Shire Press, Santa Cruz, CA.

Gloman, Chuck B., Letourneau, Tom, 2002. Placing Shadows: Lighting Techniques for Video Production. Focal Press, Boston, MA.

Grierson, Tim, Goodridge, Mike, 2011. FilmCraft: Cinematography. Focal Press, Boston, MA.

Gross, Lynne S., Ward, Larry W., 2004. Digital Moviemaking, 5th ed. Wadsworth Publishing, Belmont, CA.

Grotticelli, Michael, 2001. American Cinematographer Video Manual, 3rd ed. ASC Press, Hollywood, CA.

Happe, L.Bernard, 1971. Basic Motion Picture Technology. Focal Press, Boston, MA.

Harrison, H.K., 1981. Mystery of Filters II. Harrison and Harrison, Porterville, CA.

Hart, Douglas C., 1995. The Camera Assistant: A Complete Professional Handbook. Focal Press, Boston, MA.

Hershey, Fritz Lynn, 1996. Optics and Focus for Camera Assistants. Focal Press, Boston, MA.

Hines, William, 1997. In: Los Angeles, CA (Ed.), Operating Cinematography for Film and Video. Ed-Venture Films/Books, Los Angeles, CA.

Hines, William, 1999. In: Los Angeles, CA (Ed.), Job Descriptions for Film, Video and CGI. Ed-Venture Films/Books, Los Angeles, CA.

Hirschfeld, Gerald, A.S.C, 2005. Image Control: Motion Picture and Video Camera Filters and Lab Techniques. ASC Press, Hollywood, CA.

Hurbis-Cherrier, Mick, 2011. Voice and Vision: A Creative Approach to Narrative Film and DV Production, 2nd ed. Focal Press, Boston, MA.

Jackman, John, 2010. Lighting for Digital Video and Television, 3rd ed. Focal Press, Boston, MA.

James, Jack, 2005. Digital *Intermediates for Film and Video.* Focal Press, Boston, MA.

Kennel, Glenn, 2006. Color and Mastering for Digital Cinema. Focal Press, Boston, MA.

Kindem, Gorham, 1987. The Moving Image: Production Principles and Practice. Scott, Foresman, Glenview, IL.

Krasilovsky, Alexis, 1997. Women Behind the Camera. Praeger Publishing, Westport, CT.

Lancaster, Kurt, 2010. DSLR Cinema. Focal Press, Boston, MA.

Lazslo, Andrew, 1999. Every Frame a Rembrandt: Art and Practice of Cinematography. Focal Press, Boston, MA.

Lazslo, Andrew, 2004. It's a Wrap. ASC Press, Hollywood, CA.

Lowell, Ross, 1992. Matters of Light & Depth. Broad Street Books, Philadelphia, PA.

Lyver, Des, Swainson, Graham, 1999. Basics of Video Lighting, 2nd ed. Focal Press, Boston, MA.

Lyver, Des, Swainson, Graham, 1999. Basics of Video Production, 2nd ed. Focal Press, Boston, MA.

Macdonald, Scott, 1988. A Critical Cinema. University of California Press, Berkeley, CA.

Malkiewicz, Kris, Mullen M., David, 2005. Cinematography, 3rd ed. Fireside, New York.

Malkiewicz, Kris, Rogers, Robert E., 1986. Film Lighting. Fireside, New York.

Maltin, Leonard, 1978. The Art of the Cinematographer: A Survey and Interview with Five Masters. Dover, New York.

Mamer, Bruce, 2008. Film Production Technique: Creating the Accomplished Image, 5th ed. Wadsworth Publishing, Belmont, CA.

Mascelli, Joseph V., 1998. The Five C's of Cinematography. Silman-James Press, Los Angeles, CA.

Mercado, Gustavo, 2010. The Filmmaker's Eye—Learning (and Breaking) the Rules of Cinematic Composition. Focal Press, Boston, MA.

Miller, Pat P., 1999. Script Supervising and Film Continuity, 3rd ed. Focal Press, Boston, MA.

Millerson, Gerald, 1991. Lighting for Video, 3rd ed. Focal Press, Boston, MA.

Millerson, Gerald, 1994. Video Camera Techniques. Focal Press, Boston, MA.

Millerson, Gerald, 1999. Lighting for Television and Film, 3rd ed. Focal Press, Boston, MA.

Mitchell, Mitch, 2004. Visual Effects for Film and Television. Focal Press, Boston, MA.

Ohanian, Thomas A., Phillips, Michael E., 1996. Digital Filmmaking: The Changing Art and Craft of Making Motion Pictures. Focal Press, Boston, MA.

Penney, Edmund F., 1991. The Facts on File Dictionary of Film and Broadcast Terms. Facts on File, New York.

Perisic, Zoran, 1999. Visual Effects Cinematography. Focal Press, Boston, MA.

Petrie, Duncan, 1996. The British Cinematographer. British Film Institute, London, England.

Pincus, Edward, Ascher, Steven, 1984. The Filmmaker's Handbook. New American Library, New York.

Rahmel, Dan, 2004. Nuts and Bolts Filmmaking. Focal Press, Boston, MA.

Ratcliff, John, 1999. Timecode: A User's Guide. Focal Press, Boston, MA.

Ray, Sidney F., 1992. The Photographic Lens, 2nd ed. Focal Press, Boston, MA.

Ray, Sidney F., 2003. Applied Photographic Optics, 3rd ed. Focal Press, Boston, MA.

Rickitt, Richard, 2007. Special Effects: The History and Technique. Billboard Books, New York.

Roberts, Kenneth H., Sharples Jr., Win, 1971. A Primer for Filmmaking: A Complete Guide to 16 and 35mm Film Production. Bobbs-Merrill, New York.

Rogers, Pauline B., 1998. Contemporary Cinematographers on Their Art. Focal Press, Boston, MA.

Rogers, Pauline B., 1999. Art of Visual Effects—Interviews on the Tools of the Trade. Focal Press, Boston, MA.

Rogers, Pauline B., 1999. More Contemporary Cinematographers on Their Art. Focal Press, Boston, MA.

Samuelson, David W., 1979. Motion Picture Camera Data. Focal Press, Boston, MA.

Samuelson, David W., 1984. Motion Picture Camera Techniques. Focal Press, Boston, MA.

Samuelson, David W., 1987. Motion Picture Camera and Lighting Equipment. Focal Press, Boston, MA.

Samuelson, David W., 1996. Panaflex Users' Manual, 2nd ed. Focal Press, Boston, MA.

Samuelson, David W., 1998. Hands-On Manual for Cinematographers, 2nd ed. Focal Press, Boston, MA.

Sawicki, Mark, 2007. Filming the Fantastic: A Guide to Visual Effects Cinematography. Focal Press, Boston, MA.

Schaefer, Dennis, Salvato, Larry, 1985. Masters of Light: Conversations with Contemporary Cinematographers. University of California Press, Berkeley, CA.

Schroeppel, Tom, 1982. The Bare Bones Camera Course for Film and Video, 2nd rev. ed. Tom Schroeppel, Tampa, FL.

Schroeppel, Tom, 1998. Video Goals: Getting Results with Pictures and Sound. Tom Schroeppel, Tampa, FL.

Singleton, Ralph S, Conrad, James A., 2000. Filmmaker's Dictionary, 2nd ed. Lone Eagle Publishing Co, Beverly Hills, CA.

Souto, Mario Raimondo, 1969. The Technique of the Motion Picture Camera. Focal Press, Boston, MA.

Stone, Judy, 1997. Eye on the World: Conversations with International Filmmakers. Silman-James Press, Los Angeles, CA.

Swartz, Charles S., 2004. Understanding Digital Cinema. Focal Press, Boston, MA.

Taub, Eric, 1987. Gaffers, Grips and Best Boys. St. Martin's Press, New York.

Thompson, Roy, 1998. Grammar of the Shot. Focal Press, Boston, MA.

Underdahl, Douglas, 1993. The 16 mm Camera Book. Media Logic, New York.

Uva, Michael G., 2009. The Grip Book, 4th ed. Focal Press, Boston, MA.

Uva, Michael G., Uva, Sabrina, 2001. Uva's Basic Grip Book. Focal Press, Boston, MA.

Uva, Michael G., Uva, Sabrina, 2001. Uva's Guide to Cranes, Dollies and Remote Heads. Focal Press, Boston, MA.

Van Hurkman, Alexis, 2010. Color Correction Handbook: Professional Techniques for Video and Cinema. Peachpit Press, Berkeley, CA.

Van Sikill, Jennifer, 2005. Cinematic Storytelling. Michael Wiese Productions, Los Angeles, CA.

Viera, Dave, Viera, Maria, 2004. Lighting for Film and Digital Cinematography, 2nd ed. Wadsworth Publishing, Belmont, CA.

Ward, Peter, 2000. Digital Video Camerawork. Focal Press, Boston, MA.

Ward, Peter, 2001. Studio and Outside Broadcast Camerawork. Focal Press, Boston, MA.

Ward, Peter, 2002. Picture Composition, 2nd ed. Focal Press, Boston, MA.

Watkinson, John, 2008. The Art of Digital Video. Focal Press, Boston, MA.

Wheeler, Leslie J., 1953. Principles of Cinematography. Fountain Press, Indianola, IN.

Wheeler, Paul, 2001. Digital Cinematography. Focal Press, Boston, MA.

Wheeler, Paul, 2005. Practical Cinematography, 2nd ed. Focal Press, Boston, MA.

Wheeler, Paul, 2007. High Definition Cinematography, 2nd ed. Focal Press, Boston, MA.

Wilson, Anton, 1994. Anton Wilson's Cinema Workshop, 4th ed. ASC Press, Hollywood, CA.

Zone, Ray (Ed.), 2001. Writer of Light: The Cinematography of Vittorio Storaro. ASC Press, Hollywood, CA

Zone, Ray, 2002. New Wave King: The Cinematography of Laszlo Kovacs, ASC. ASC Press, Hollywood, CA.

Glossary

Aaton: Trade name of a brand of professional motion picture camera.

Abby Singer Shot: The next-to-the-last shot of the day. The term is named for Abby Singer. According to Mr. Singer, the term was started during the mid-1950s while he was an Assistant Director at Universal Studios. To keep ahead of things, he would inform the crew that they would shoot the current shot plus one more shot before moving to a different area of the studio. Through the years other Assistant Directors began referring to the next-to-the-last shot of the day as the Abby Singer Shot.

AC: Abbreviation for Assistant Cameraman.

Academy Aperture: An image with an aspect ratio of 1.33:1. It is the standard image size of a 4-perf frame of 35 mm motion picture film. It may also be referred to as 1.37:1.

Acetate Base: A film base that is much more durable than the older nitrate film base, which was highly flammable. Film that is coated onto an acetate base is sometimes referred to as safety film.

AKS: A slang term used to refer to an assortment of equipment, tools, and accessories. Its literal translation is "All Kinds of Stuff" or "All Kinds of S**t."

American Cinematographer Manual: See *ASC Manual*.

American Society of Cinematographers (ASC): An honorary organization of Cinematographers. It is not a labor guild or union. To become a member you must be invited to join by the current membership.

Anamorphic Lens: A film lens that allows you to film widescreen format when using standard 35 mm film. It produces an image that is compressed to fit the film frame. The developed print of the film is projected through an anamorphic projector lens, which un-squeezes the image and makes it appear normal on the screen.

Angle of View: The angle covered by the camera lens. It may also be called field of view.

Anti-Halation Backing: The dark coating on the back of the unexposed film stock that prevents light from passing through the film, causing a flare or fogging of the film image.

Aperture (Camera): The opening in the aperture plate that determines the precise area of exposure of the frame of film.

Aperture (Lens): The opening in the lens, formed by an adjustable iris, through which light passes to expose the film. The size of this opening is expressed as an f-stop number.

Aperture Plate: A metal plate within the camera that contains the camera aperture opening. Light passes through this opening before striking the film, creating the image.

Arriflex: Trade name for a brand of professional motion picture cameras.

ASA: An older term that was used to refer to the speed of the film or the sensitivity of the film to light. See Exposure Index.

ASC: Abbreviation for American Society of Cinematographers.

ASC Manual: A technical manual published by the American Society of Cinematographers. It contains useful information used by the camera crew, including information on cameras, lighting, filters, depth of field, exposure compensation, film speed tables, etc.

Aspect Ratio: The relationship between the width of the image and its height.

Aspheron: A 16 mm lens attachment designed for the 9.5 mm and the 12 mm Zeiss prime lenses. It is used to increase the angle of view of these wide-angle lenses.

Assistant Cameraman (AC): A member of the camera crew whose job responsibilities include maintaining and setting up the camera, changing lenses, loading film, measuring focus distances, focusing and zooming during the shot, clapping the slate, placing tape marks for actors, keeping camera reports and other paperwork, etc. The camera department usually consists of the First Assistant Cameraman (1st AC) and the Second Assistant Cameraman (2nd AC). See First Assistant Cameraman and Second Assistant Cameraman.

ATSC: An abbreviation for Advanced Television Systems Committee, which developed the standards for digital television transmission.

B & W: Abbreviation for black and white.

Baby Legs, Baby Tripod, Babies: A short tripod used for low-angle shots or any shots where the standard size tripod is not appropriate. In Britain a slang term for the Baby Legs/Tripod is Shorts.

Barney: A flexible, padded, and insulated cover used to reduce noise coming from the camera or magazine. It is available in a heated version that is used to keep the camera and magazine warm in extremely cold shooting situations.

Barrel Connector: A metal connector that allows two BNC video cables to be interconnected to make a longer cable.

Base: The smooth, transparent surface on which the film emulsion is attached. In the earlier days of filmmaking, a nitrate base was used, which was highly flammable. Today a safer acetate-type base is used for all film stocks.

Batteries: Rechargeable power supply used to power the camera. The most common are block batteries, but they are also available as belt and on-board batteries.

Battery Cables: Power cables that are used to connect the camera or any other accessory to the battery and that supply the power from the battery to the camera or accessory being used.

Battery Charger: Electrical device used to keep the batteries fully charged when they are not being used.

Belt Battery: A belt containing the cells of the battery that may be worn by the Operator or the Camera Assistant when doing handheld shots. It may also be used when a block battery is impractical.

Black and White (B & W):   Any film shot without using color film, or a film shot using color film with the color removed during postproduction to give a black-and-white image.

Black Bag: A small plastic or paper bag that contains the raw film stock when it is packaged inside the film can. Exposed film is also placed in the black bag and in the can before being sealed and sent to the lab for processing. Some Camera Assistants also refer to the film changing bag as the black bag.

Black Dot Texture Screen: A diffusion filter that looks like a clear piece of glass containing small black dots in a random pattern.

Block Battery: A large camera battery that is enclosed in a hard-side case that contains the cells of the battery and often a built-in charger.

Breathing: The characteristic of some lenses that gives the illusion of zooming when you are adjusting the focus of the lens.

Buckle Switch: A switch within the camera that acts as a safety shut-off device in the event of a film jam or rollout within the camera. Also called buckle trip switch.

Camera: The basic piece of equipment used to photograph images. Most cameras consist of a lens that projects the image onto the film stock, a shutter to regulate the light striking the film, a viewfinder that enables the Camera Operator to view the image during filming, some type of mechanism to transport the film through the camera, a motor that drives the transport mechanism, and a lightproof container, called a magazine, that holds the film before and after exposure.

Camera Angle: The position of the camera in relation to the subject being filmed.

Camera, Handheld: A camera that has been set up so that the Camera Operator may hold it on his or her shoulder during filming. It may be used to film moving shots or point-of-view shots of an actor walking or moving through the scene.

Camera Jam: A malfunction that occurs when the film backs up in the camera and becomes piled up in the camera movement.

Camera Left: The area to the left side of the camera as seen from the Camera Operator's point of view. As the actor faces the camera, camera left is to the actor's right.

Camera Mount: Any type of device that the camera is mounted on for support. It may be mounted on a head and placed on a dolly, tripod, high hat, camera car, etc.

Camera Oil: A special type of oil used for lubricating the movement in the camera. The camera rental house or camera manufacturer usually supplies it.

Camera Operator: The member of the camera crew who looks through and operates the camera during filming. He or she maintains the composition of the shot by making smooth pan and tilt moves as instructed by the Director and Director of Photography.

Camera Package: Umbrella term used for the camera, lenses, magazines, batteries, head, tripod, and all other camera equipment needed for shooting.

Camera Rental House: A company that specializes in the rental and maintenance of motion picture camera equipment.

Camera Report: A form that is filled in with the pertinent information for each roll of film shot.

Camera Right: The area to the right side of the camera as seen from the Camera Operator's point of view. As the actor faces the camera, camera right is to the actor's left.

Camera Speed: The rate at which the film is transported through the camera during filming. It is expressed in frames per second, abbreviated fps. In the United States normal sync camera speed is 24 fps.

Camera Tape (1-in.): Cloth tape, usually 1-inch wide, which is used for making labels on cases, film cans, magazines, and any other labels that may be required. It is also used for wrapping cans of exposed film and unexposed film and short ends.

Camera Truck: A large enclosed truck used to transport and store all camera equipment when filming on location. It is usually set up with a workbench, shelves for storage of equipment, and a darkroom for loading and unloading film.

Camera Wedge: A small wooden wedge that may be used to help level the camera when it is placed on uneven surfaces.

Cameraman: See Director of Photography.

Cartoni: Trade name of a brand of professional fluid camera head.

Chamois: Cloth used for cleaning the camera and magazines.

Changing Bag: A lightproof, heavyweight cloth bag used to load and unload film when a darkroom is not available. It consists of two bags sewn together, one inside the other. The top of each bag contains a zipper that gives access to the inside of the bag, and two sleeves that contain elastic cuffs, on the opposite side of the bag from the zippers.

The magazine is placed inside the inner bag and both zippers are then closed. With the zippers closed and the Camera Assistant's arms placed inside the sleeves, it forms a light-tight compartment for loading and unloading the film stock.

Changing Tent: Very similar in design to a changing bag except that it forms a dome-shaped tent over the working surface. It is constructed of two layers, similar to the construction of the changing bag, and contains a double-zippered opening, with one sleeve on each side of the opening.

Cinematographer: See Director of Photography.

Cinematography: The art and craft of recording images on motion picture film.

Clap Sticks: Wooden sticks attached to the slate, which are clapped together at the beginning of a sync sound take. See Slate.

Clapper Board: See Slate.

Clapper/Loader: A member of the camera crew who is responsible for clapping the slate for the shot, loading and unloading the film in the magazines, and other duties. This term is used primarily in Britain, Europe, and Australia. In the United States, this crew member is the Second Assistant Cameraman (2nd AC).

Closing Down the Lens: Turning the diaphragm adjustment ring on the lens to a higher f-stop number, which results in a smaller diaphragm opening. Also referred to as stopping down the lens.

Coaxial Cable: See Video Cables.

Coaxial Magazine: A magazine that contains two side-by-side compartments, separated by a common dividing wall. One compartment is for the feed side and the other for the take-up side. Coaxial refers to the fact that these two distinct compartments share the same axis of rotation.

Codec: A combination of the terms compressor–decompressor or coder–decoder. The term is generally used to refer to the compression rate used for recording the digital image. Some of the common codecs currently used are JPEG, MPEG 2, MPEG4. Some examples of how the codec is indicated on the camera and written on the camera are indicated as follows: Pro Res 422, Pro Res 422 HQ, and Pro Res 4444.

Collapsible Core: A permanent core in the take-up side of the film magazine onto which the film is wound after it has been exposed.

Color Chart: A card or chart that contains strips of colors corresponding to the primary and complementary colors. It is photographed at the beginning of a roll and is used by the lab to assist in developing and processing the film.

Color Grad Filter: A filter that is half color and half clear. Used when a specific color effect is desired.

Color Temperature: A measurement scale in degrees Kelvin that indicates the specific color of a light source.

Combination Filter: Two different filter types that are combined into one filter, for example an 85 combined with a neutral density (85ND3, 85ND6, 85ND9) or an 85 combined with a polarizer (85Pola).

Combination Meter: A light meter that contains both an incident meter and a spot meter in one device.

"Common Marker" or "Common Slate": What the Second Assistant Cameraman calls out when slating a shot for two or more cameras by using only one slate. When using only one slate, all cameras point toward the slate at the start of the shot.

Compressed Air: Canned air used for blowing out the magazine and camera body. Also used to clean dust from lenses and filters. In the United States a common brand is Dust-Off. In Britain a common brand is Kenair. It is often simply referred to as Air.

Conversion Filter: A filter used to convert one color temperature to another. The two most common conversion filters are the 85 and the 80A. See 85 Filter and 80A Filter.

Coral Filter: Filter that is used to warm up the overall scene and to enhance skin tones. It is also used to make slight adjustments in Kelvin temperature for different times of day.

Core: Plastic disks around which the raw stock film is wound. They are usually 2 or 3 inches in diameter.

Cotton Swabs: Long wooden sticks with a small piece of cotton wrapped around one end, which can be used to remove excess oil when oiling the camera.

Crosshairs: A cross shape that is located on the ground glass/viewing screen of the camera's viewing system. The cross is positioned in the exact center of the film frame to assist the Camera Operator in framing the shot.

Crystal Motor: The most common type of camera motor for motion picture cameras. A built-in crystal allows the motor to run at precise speeds, especially when filming with sound, without the use of a cable running from the camera to the sound recorder.

CTB: A blue-colored gel that is placed on tungsten lights to convert the color temperature to the color temperature of daylight. It stands for Color Temperature Blue and is available in varying densities ranging from 1/8 CTB to Full CTB.

CTO: An orange-colored gel that is used to convert the color temperature of daylight to the color temperature of tungsten light. It stands for Color Temperature Orange and is available in varying densities ranging from 1/8 CTO to Full CTO.

Dailies: The developed and printed scenes from the previous day's filming, which are viewed by the key production personnel each day. These may also be in video format instead of a film print. Also called Rushes.

Daily Film Inventory: A form filled in with information relating to how much film is shot each day. It lists all film stocks and roll numbers used for the day, with a breakdown of good and no-good takes, waste footage, and any short ends made.

Darkroom: A small, lightproof room, usually 4 × 4 feet in size, on a stage or in a camera truck, which is used for the loading and unloading of film.

Day Player: A crew member who is hired for one or more days, usually when additional cameras are being used or to fill in for another member of the film crew.

Daylight: A light source with a color temperature of approximately 5600° Kelvin.

Daylight Spool: A spool usually made of metal or plastic that has opaque edges onto which the raw stock is tightly wound. It allows the film to be loaded into the camera in daylight or subdued light. Also referred to as a camera spool.

Depth of Field: The range of distance within which all objects will be in acceptable sharp focus. It is an area in front of and behind the principal point of focus that will also be in acceptable focus.

Diaphragm: The adjustable metal blades within the lens that control the size of the opening through which the light enters the lens. It may also be called an iris. The size of the opening is expressed by an f-stop number.

Diffusion Filter: A filter that is used to slightly decrease the sharpness of the image. It is good for smoothing out facial blemishes or wrinkles. It can also be used for dreamlike effects. When used, this filter may give the appearance that the image is out of focus.

Digital Imaging Technician (DIT):   A person who provides on-set operation, troubleshooting, and maintenance of digital cameras, waveform monitors, monitors, digital recorders, and other related equipment. The Digital Imaging Technician is responsible for all image manipulation and color correction, in-camera recording, and troubleshooting and assisting in fulfilling the requirements and vision of the Cinematographer in film-style digital production.

DIN: An abbreviation meaning Deutsche Industrie Norm. It is the German system for rating the film stock's sensitivity to light or film speed.

Diopter: A filter that allows you to focus on something much closer than the lens would normally allow.

Director of Photography (DP):   The person in charge of lighting the set and photographing a film. The DP oversees all aspects of the camera department and the camera crew as well as the grip and lighting crews on a production during filming. He or she may also be called the Cinematographer or Lighting Cameraman.

Displacement Magazine: A magazine that usually contains the feed and take-up sides in the same compartment of the magazine. In most displacement magazines, as the magazine sits on the camera, the feed side is toward the front, and the take-up side is toward the rear.

DIT: Abbreviation for Digital Imaging Technician.

Ditty Bag: A tool bag that usually contains many compartments of different sizes, which is used by the Camera Assistant to hold tools and supplies needed for filming. Some of the items kept in the ditty bag include basic hand tools, the slate, tape measure, pens, markers, and camera tape. May also be called a set bag and in Britain it may be referred to as a standby bag.

Dolly: A four-wheeled platform on which a camera is mounted for moving shots. It may also have a boom arm, which allows the camera to be raised or lowered for a shot.

Donut: A circular piece of rubber of various sizes, approximately ¼ or ½ in. thick with a circle cut out of the center. It is placed around the front of the lens and is used to seal the opening between the lens and the matte box to prevent light from entering the matte box from behind the lens and reflecting off the filters and into the lens.

Double Fog: See Fog Filter.

Double Perf: Film stock that contains perforations on both sides of the film frame.

Downloading: The act of unloading the film from the camera and magazine.

DP: Abbreviation for Director of Photography.

Dummy Load: A short roll of raw stock film that is too small to be used for shooting. It may be used to test the magazines for scratches during the camera prep or to practice loading and threading magazines and cameras. In Britain it may be referred to as Gash Stock.

Dutch Angle: Framing a shot with the camera tilted either left or right so that the image will appear diagonally within the frame.

Dutch Head: A special type of head that allows you to shoot Dutch angle shots.

Eastman Kodak: Trade name of a brand of professional motion picture film stock. Sometimes shortened and referred to as Kodak.

EI: Abbreviation for Exposure Index.

80A Filter: Conversion filter used to convert daylight-balanced film for filming with tungsten light sources. When using this filter, you must adjust your exposure by two stops. The 80A filter is blue in color.

85 Filter: Conversion filter used to convert tungsten-balanced film for filming under daylight conditions. When using this filter, you must adjust your exposure by ⅔ stop. The 85 filter is orange in color.

Emulsion: The part of the film stock that is sensitive to light. The emulsion is where the photographic image is recorded.

End Slate: See Tail Slate.

Enhancing Filter: A filter used to improve the color saturation of red-, orange-, and rust brown-colored objects in the scene while having little effect on other colors.

Expendables: Items such as tape, pens, markers, batteries, etc. that are used up or expended by the camera department during the course of a production. In Britain they may be referred to as stores or consumables.

Exposed Film: Any film that has been run through the camera and contains a photographed image.

Exposure: The f-stop or t-stop that has been set on the lens for a particular shot. It can also be used to refer to the act of subjecting the film to light. The degree of exposure is determined by how much light strikes the film and for how long the light is allowed to strike the film.

Exposure Index (EI):   A numeric value assigned to a film stock that is a measurement of the film's speed or sensitivity to light.

Exposure Meter: A measuring device used to determine the amount or intensity of light that is illuminating a scene. The two main types of exposure meters are incident and reflected. The reflected meter may also be called a spot meter. See Incident Meter; Light Meter; and Spot Meter.

Exposure Time: The amount of time that each frame of film is exposed to light. For normal motion picture photography, the standard exposure time is expressed as 1/50 of a second with a film speed of 24 frames per second.

EXT: Abbreviation for an exterior scene in the script.

Eyebrow: A small flag that mounts directly to the matte box and is used to block any light from hitting the lens. It may also be called a sunshade or French flag. In Britain it may also be referred to as a top chopper. The side flags used on the matte box may be referred to as side chops.

Eyepiece: The attachment on the camera that allows the Camera Operator to view the scene as it is being filmed. The eyepiece often contains an adjustable diopter to compensate for the differences in each person's vision and an eyecup for comfort and to protect the operator's eye.

Eyepiece Covers: Small round covers that are usually made of foam or chamois material, and placed on the eyepiece so that it is more comfortable for the Camera Operator. In Britain they may be referred to as teddy bears, or TBAs.

Eyepiece Extension: A long version of the camera eyepiece that is used when a short eyepiece is not convenient or comfortable for the Camera Operator. It is used most often when the camera is mounted to a gear head or fluid head.

Eyepiece Heater: A heater element used to keep the eyepiece warm when shooting in cold-weather situations. It prevents the eyepiece from fogging. It may also be called an eyepiece warmer.

Eyepiece Leveler: An adjustable rod that is used to keep the eyepiece level while the camera is tilting. The eyepiece leveler allows the eyepiece to remain at a comfortable position for the Camera Operator when doing extreme tilt moves with the fluid or gear head.

Feed Side: The side of the magazine or camera that contains the fresh, unexposed film.

Field of View: The angle covered by the camera lens. It may also be called angle of view.

Film Can: A metal or plastic container that holds the fresh raw stock. It is used along with the black bag to wrap any exposed film or short ends that are created during shooting.

Film Plane: The point located behind the lens where the film is held in place during exposure. It is the plane where the rays of light that enter the lens come together in sharp focus.

Film Speed: The rating assigned to the film based on its sensitivity to light. The film speed may be expressed as an EI, ASA, DIN, or ISO number.

Film-to-Video Synchronizer: A device used when filming a video monitor or computer screen image with a film camera. Because the standard frame rate of video is different from that of film, the synchronizer must be used between the camera and the video source.

Filter: A piece of optically correct glass placed in front of a lens to cause a change in the image. Gel-type filters are used on lights to create specific lighting effects. Some cameras also have the ability to accept a behind-the-lens gel filter.

Filter Trays: Sliding trays that are used to hold a filter in the matte box.

First Assistant Cameraman (1st AC), First Camera Assistant: A member of the camera crew whose duties include overseeing all aspects of the camera department, setting up and maintaining the camera, changing lenses and filters, loading film into the camera, keeping the camera in working order, and maintaining focus during shooting. The 1st AC works closely with the Director of Photography and the Camera Operator and coordinates any additional camera crew members who are needed during the course of production. In Britain, Europe, and Australia, this position is referred to as the Focus Puller.

Fish Eye Lens: A wide-angle lens that distorts the image to great effect.

Flare: A bright spot or flash of light in the photographic image that may be caused by lights shining directly into the lens or by reflections from shiny surfaces.

FLB Filter: Filter used when shooting under fluorescent lights with indoor type B films.

FLD Filter: Filter used when filming under fluorescent lights with daylight-type film.

Fluid Head: A mounting platform for the camera that allows the Camera Operator to do smooth pan and tilt moves during shooting. Its internal elements contain a highly viscous fluid that controls the amount of tension on the pan and tilt components of the head.

Foam-Tip Swab: A long wooden or plastic stick with a small piece of foam on one end. It may be used to remove any excess oil when oiling the camera. See Cotton Swabs.

Focal Length: The distance between the optical center of the lens and the film plane when the lens is focused at infinity. Lenses are always referred to by their focal length, which is usually expressed in millimeters, such as 25 mm, 32 mm, 50 mm, 75 mm, etc.

Focal Plane: The specific point behind the lens where the image is focused onto the film stock. As the film travels through the camera, it is held between the pressure plate and the aperture plate in the film gate. Also referred to as the film plane.

Focal Plane Shutter: A rotating shutter located at the focal plane that alternately blocks light from striking the film and then allows the light to strike the film. It works along with the mirror shutter of the camera.

Focus: The point in the scene that appears sharp and clear when viewed through the camera eyepiece. It may also refer to the act of adjusting the lens to produce a sharp image.

Focus Chart: A special chart that is used when testing photographic lenses. It is used to help determine if the lens focus is accurate.

Focus Extension: An accessory for the follow-focus mechanism that attaches to the right side of the follow focus so you can pull focus from either side of the camera. A flexible focus accessory, called a focus whip, may be attached to either side of the follow-focus mechanism.

Focus Puller: A member of the camera crew who is responsible for maintaining focus during a shot. This term is used primarily in Britain, Europe, and Australia. In the United States, the Focus Puller is the First Assistant Cameraman (1st AC).

Focus Whip: An extension that allows the Assistant to step back from the camera and still be able to follow focus for a shot. It is a flexible extension that may be 6, 12 or 18 inches long. Also referred to as a whip.

Fog Filter (Double Fog):   Filter that simulates the effect of natural fog. A fog filter causes any light in the shot to have a flare.

Follow Focus, Following Focus: The act of turning the focus barrel of the lens during the shot so that the actors stay in focus as they move through the scene. It may also be referred to as pulling focus.

Follow-Focus Mechanism: A geared attachment that mounts to the camera and engages the gears on the lens. It enables the 1st AC to follow focus or pull focus during the shot.

Footage Counter: A digital or dial type of gauge on the camera that indicates how many feet of film have been run through the camera.

Format: A term most often used to indicate the film gauge you are shooting, such as 16 mm, 35 mm, or 65 mm.

Four-Inch Lens (4-in. Lens): A slang term used in the early days of filmmaking to indicate a 100 mm lens.

FPS: Abbreviation for Frames per Second.

Frame: An individual photographic image. A motion picture is made up of thousands of individual frames.

Frame Rate: The speed that the film runs through the camera. It is expressed in terms of frames per second (fps).

Frames per Second (FPS): The standard measurement for film speed as it runs through the camera or projector. In the United States, 24 fps is the standard film speed; in Britain, Europe, and Australia, 25 fps is the standard film speed.

French Flag: A small flag that is mounted onto the camera and used to help keep any lights from causing a flare in the lens. It consists of a flexible arm onto which the flag is attached and positioned so that the flag prevents light from striking the lens.

Friction Head: An early type of mounting platform for the camera that allows the Camera Operator to perform smooth pan and tilt moves when composing the scene. Its internal elements create friction by rubbing against each other, creating the tension for the pan and tilt portions of the head. Friction heads are not used very much today, but they were used quite often in the earlier days of filmmaking.

Front Box: A wooden storage box that attaches to the front of the camera head and is used to hold a variety of tools and accessories. It is used by the 1st AC for storing the tape measure, mini flashlight, depth-of-field charts, pens, markers, compressed air, lens cleaner, gum, mints, etc. It may also be used to hold the DP's meters.

F-Stop: The setting on the lens that indicates the size of the aperture. It is an indication of the amount of light entering the lens and does not take into account any light loss due to absorption. The standard series of f-stop numbers is 1, 1.4, 2, 2.8, 4, 5.6, 8, 11, 16, 22, 32, etc. In theory these numbers go infinitely in both directions.

Fuji: Trade name for a brand of professional motion picture film stock.

Full Aperture: The entire area of the film frame that extends out to the perforations on the film. When looking through the eyepiece, it extends beyond the frame lines inscribed on the ground glass.

Gaffer: The chief lighting technician and head of the lighting/electrical crew on a film set. The Gaffer works closely with the Director of Photography to light the set according to the DP's instructions.

Gaffer Tape (2 in.):   Cloth tape, usually 2 in. wide, that is used for any taping job that requires tape wider than the 1-in. camera tape.

Gate: The part of the camera where the film is held while it is being exposed. Quite often when referring to the gate, we include the aperture plate, pressure plate, pull down claw, and registration pin.

Gear Head: A mounting platform for the camera that allows the Camera Operator to do smooth pan and tilt moves during shooting. It is operated by turning two control wheels that are connected to gears in the head. One control wheel, which is mounted on the left side of the head, is used for panning the camera. The other control wheel is mounted at the back of the head and is used for making any tilt moves.

Gel: Heat resistant cellophane material placed in front of a light source. It may be used to change the intensity of the light or to change the color of the light.

Good (G):   Any takes on the camera report that the Director chooses as his or her preference for each scene. The take number and footage amount are circled on the camera report, and it is these takes that are to be printed or transferred by the lab. The Editor will choose among the good takes when editing the film together.

Graduated Filter, Grad Filter: A partial filter in which half is clear and the other half contains the filter.

Grand: British slang term that refers to a 1000 foot roll of film.

Grayscale, Gray Card: The grayscale is a standard series of tonal shades ranging from white to gray to black. The gray card is a solid color gray. Both may be photographed at the beginning of each film roll and are used by the lab when processing the film to ensure the correct tonal values in the film.

Grease Pencils: Erasable pencils used for making focus marks directly on the lens or focus-marking disk.

Grip: Film crew member responsible for laying dolly track, setting C-stands and flags, moving large set pieces, and much more. A jack-of-all-trades on the set. A film set will have many different Grips on set, including the Key Grip, Dolly Grip, and Best Boy Grip.

Ground Glass: A small piece of optical material, onto which a portion of the light from the lens is focused, to allow the Camera Operator to see the image that the lens is seeing. It is inscribed with lines that indicate the aspect ratio being used for filming and to assist the Operator in composing the shot.

Guild Kelly Calculator: Trade name for a brand of depth-of-field calculator used by many 1st ACs. There are currently three types in use today: 16 mm, 35 mm, and HD Kelly Calculators.

Hair: A very fine piece of emulsion that appears in the gate and can look like an actual hair. It may be caused by the emulsion being scraped off of the film as it travels through the gate. If it is not

removed from the gate, it will appear as a large rope on the screen when the film is projected.

Handheld: Any shot that is done by the Camera Operator physically holding the camera on his or her shoulder while filming. It is often used for point-of-view shots of an actor walking or moving through the scene. See Camera, Handheld.

Handheld Accessories: Any item needed to make handheld shots easier. These items may include left- and right-hand grips, shoulder pad, smaller clamp-on-style matte box, and smaller film magazines.

Hard Mattes: Covers for the matte box that have a square or rectangular opening cut out of the center and placed in front of the matte box to block any unwanted light from striking the lens.

Harrison & Harrison: Trade name of a brand of motion picture camera filter.

HD: Abbreviation for high-definition video.

Head: A platform for mounting the camera that allows the Camera Operator to make smooth pan and tilt moves during the shot. The two most commonly used heads are fluid heads and gear heads.

Head Slate: A slate that is photographed at the beginning of a shot.

High Angle: A shot that is done with the camera placed high above the action and pointed down toward the subject or action.

High Definition (HD):   A video format that captures images at a much higher quality than VHS, Beta, or any other previous video format. HD is said to have an image quality as good as 35 mm motion picture film.

High Hat (Hi Hat):   A very low camera mount used when filming low-angle shots.

High Speed: Any filmed shot that is done at a speed greater than normal sync speed.

HMI Lights (Hydrargyrum Medium Arc Iodide):   Lighting devices that produce a color temperature that is equivalent to the color temperature of natural daylight. They are often used when filming daylight interior scenes to help supplement the existing daylight coming through the windows.

HMI Speed Control: A camera speed control used when filming with HMI lights.

Hyperfocal Distance: A special case of depth of field that may be defined as the closest point in front of the lens that will be in acceptable focus when the lens is focused to infinity. In other words, it is the closest focus distance at which objects at infinity and close to the lens are both in focus. It is the focus point that gives you the maximum depth of field for a given shooting situation.

IATSE: An abbreviation for the primary motion picture union that oversees all craft unions and guilds in the film industry. The full name is International Alliance of Theatrical Stage Employees, Moving

Picture Technicians, Artists and Allied Crafts of the United States, Its Territories and Canada.

ICG: Abbreviation for International Cinematographers Guild.

Inching Knob: A small knob that may be located either inside or outside the camera body that allows you to slowly advance or inch the film through the movement.

Incident Light: The light from all sources that falls on the subject being filmed.

Incident Meter: A light meter used to measure the amount of incident light that is falling on the subject.

Insert Slate: A small scene slate used to identify any MOS or insert shots being filmed. The typical insert slate does not contain clapper sticks.

INT: Abbreviation for an interior scene in the script.

Intermittent Movement: The starting and stopping movement of the film transport mechanism as it advances the film through the camera.

International Cinematographers Guild: The union that represents Directors of Photography, Camera Operators, Assistants, Visual Effect Supervisors, Still Photographers and Publicists. In order to become a member you must demonstrate professional experience in one of the above categories.

Iris: An adjustable diaphragm that is used to control the amount of light that is transmitted through the lens. The iris of the lens consists of overlapping leaves that form a circular opening to vary the amount of light coming through the lens.

Iris Rods: Metal rods of varying lengths that are used to support the matte box, follow focus, or other accessory on the camera.

ISO: Abbreviation for International Standards Organization. It is a rating of the film stock's sensitivity to light and is sometimes used in place of ASA or EI.

Keepers: A small arm or lever that engages the sprocket roller ensuring that the film perforations are aligned with the roller. If the film perforations are not locked and aligned to the roller, the film will not travel smoothly through the camera.

Kelvin: The temperature scale used for measuring the color temperature of a light source.

Kimwipe: Soft tissue-like material similar to lens tissue that is used for cleaning filters or any other small cleaning job. Kimwipes should not be used to clean lenses.

Kodak: Trade name for a brand of professional motion picture film stock. Also known by its full name, Eastman Kodak.

Lab or Laboratory: The facility where the film is sent to be processed, developed, and printed or transferred to video or some digital format.

Latitude: The ability of the film emulsion to be underexposed or overexposed and still produce an acceptable image.

Left-Hand Grip: An attachment for the camera used when shooting handheld shots that is placed on the left side of the camera and allows the Camera Operator to hold the camera steady in a comfortable position for shooting.

Legs: A slang term used to refer to the tripod for the camera. Baby legs refer to the smaller tripod, and standard legs refer to the larger tripod.

Lens: An optical device through which light rays pass to form a focused image on the film. Lenses are usually referred to by their focal length, and the two types are prime lenses and zoom lenses. See Prime Lens and Zoom Lens.

Lens Cleaner: Special liquid that is used along with lens tissue to clean lenses and filters.

Lens Extender: An attachment that is placed between the lens and the camera that increases the focal length of the lens being used. The most common lens extenders are the 1.4X, which increases the focal length by 1.4 times the actual focal length, and the 2X, which doubles the focal length.

Lens Light: A small light, mounted to a flexible arm that is attached to the camera and that allows the 1st AC to see the lens focus and zoom markings when filming on a dark set. It is sometimes called an Assistant's Light, Little Light, or Niner Light.

Lens Shade: A rubber or metal device that either screws on or is clamped onto the front of the lens. It may be used to hold round filters and to keep any stray light from striking the front element of the lens. It may also be called a sunshade.

Lens Speed: The lens speed refers to the widest f-stop to which the lens opens up. The smaller the f-number, the faster the lens.

Lens Tissue: Special tissues used to clean lenses and filters along with lens cleaner.

L-Handle: See Speed Crank.

Light Meter: A measuring device that is used to measure the amount of light illuminating the scene. See Combination Meter; Exposure Meter; Incident Meter; Reflected Meter; and Spot Meter.

LLD Filter: A filter used when filming with tungsten-balanced film in low-light daylight situations. It is usually used in early morning or late afternoon and requires no exposure compensation.

Loader: The member of the camera crew who is responsible for loading and unloading the film into the magazines. A loader is usually used on larger productions when two or more cameras are being used.

Lock Off: Any shot that is done with the pan and tilt mechanisms of the camera head locked so that the camera is not moved during filming.

Long Lens: Term used to refer to a telephoto lens or a lens that has a focal length that is longer than that of a normal lens.

Loop: A slack length of film between the sprocket wheels and camera or projector gate. It is designed to absorb the tension caused by intermittent movement, thus avoiding the tearing of film as it travels through the camera. If the loop is not set correctly, the film may become jammed in the camera or magazine, and the camera may not run properly.

Low Angle: A shot that is done with the camera placed below the action and pointed up toward the subject or action.

Low-Contrast Filter: A filter that lowers the contrast by causing light to spread from highlight areas to shadow areas. Also referred to as lo-con filter.

Low Hat: A very low camera mount used when filming low-angle shots. It is similar to the high hat, but it enables you to get the camera lower.

Mag: Abbreviation for magazine.

Magazine: A removable, lightproof chamber that contains the film before and after exposure. See Coaxial Magazine and Displacement Magazine.

Magliner: The trade name of a four-wheel folding hand truck used by many Camera Assistants to expedite the moving of the many equipment cases on a film set. The two most common types of Magliner carts are the Gemini Jr. and the Gemini Sr.

Maglite Bulbs: Replacement bulbs for the small flashlight usually used by most Camera Assistants.

Marks: Small pieces of colored tape, chalk marks, or any other item placed on the ground and used to identify various positions. They are used to indicate where the actor is to stand for the shot, where the dolly starts and stops its move, or as a reference for focus used by the First Assistant Cameraman. The most common actor mark is the T-Mark. In Britain a mark placed at the side of an actor's foot is referred to as a Sidey.

Matte Box: An accessory that mounts to the front of the camera to shield the lens against unwanted light and also used to hold any filters.

Mini Maglite: Small pocket-type flashlight used by most crew people.

Mirrored Shutter: A shutter that incorporates a mirror into its design so that the image may be reflected to the viewfinder when the shutter is closed to the film. When the shutter is open, the light goes to the film so that the film may be exposed.

Mitchell: A trade name of one of the earlier models of motion picture cameras. It is also the name of a type of diffusion filter used in front of the camera lens. See Mitchell Diffusion.

Mitchell Diffusion: The trade name of a brand of motion picture camera diffusion filters. See Diffusion Filter.

Mitchell Flat Base: A type of top casting of the high hat, low hat, tripod, or dolly onto which the head is mounted.

Monitor: A television or video screen used by the Director during filming to check the framing of the shot and the quality of the performance. It is used in conjunction with a video camera that is incorporated into the film camera viewing system.

MOS: Any shot that is done without recording synchronous sound. It is an abbreviation for minus optical sound.

Multicamera: The use of two or more cameras simultaneously to shoot a scene from more than one angle.

Mutar: A 16 mm lens attachment that is designed for use on a Zeiss 10–100 mm zoom lens. It is used to increase the angle of view of the lens.

ND: Abbreviation for neutral density filter.

Negative Film Stock: Film that, when processed, produces a negative image of the scene. In other words, it is a film stock that renders all lights, darks, and colors as their opposite on the developed original. A positive print must be made of this negative for viewing purposes.

Neutral Density Filter (ND): A filter used to reduce the amount of light that strikes the film. Neutral density filters are gray and come in varying densities.

Nitrate Base Film: A highly flammable film stock used in the early days of filmmaking. It was made up of cellulose nitrate that was capable of self-igniting under certain circumstances. It is no longer used for the manufacture of motion picture film.

No Good (NG): Any take that is not printed or circled on the camera report. On the daily film inventory report form it refers to the total amount of footage for all takes on the camera report that are not to be printed or transferred by the lab.

Normal Lens: A lens that essentially gives an approximate image size as that seen by the human eye if viewed from the position of the camera.

NTSC: An abbreviation for National Television System Committee. It is the analog television system used in most of North America as well as some other countries.

Obie Light: A light that is mounted on the camera directly over the matte box. Its common use is to highlight the actor's eyes.

O'Connor: Trade name for a brand of professional motion picture fluid head.

1.85 (One–Eight–Five): The standard aspect ratio for most of today's theatrical motion pictures. It may also be written as 1.85:1, which means that the picture area is 1.85 times as wide as it is high.

One-Inch Lens (1-in. Lens):   A slang term used in the early days of filmmaking to indicate a 25 mm lens.

One-Light Print: A print made from the negative with no color correction. It is made by using one printer light setting for all shots within the roll of film.

1/3–2/3 Rule: The rule that states that one-third of the depth of field is in front of the focus point and two-thirds is behind the focus point.

Opening Up the Lens: Turning the diaphragm adjustment ring on the lens to a smaller f-stop number, which results in a larger diaphragm opening. Opening up allows more light to strike the film.

Operator: See Camera Operator.

Optical Flat: A clear piece of optically corrected glass that is placed in front of the lens to protect the lens. It is also used to help reduce the sound coming from the camera. Most of the sound from a camera comes out from the lens port opening, so an optical flat in front of the lens helps to cut down this sound, making the Sound Mixer's job easier.

Orangewood Sticks: Wooden sticks that are used to remove emulsion buildup in the gate or aperture plate. The aperture plate or gate should only be cleaned with these sticks.

Overcrank: Running the camera at a speed that is higher than normal sync speed. This causes the action to appear in slow motion when it is projected at sync speed of 24 frames per second. The term originated in the early days of filmmaking when all cameras were cranked by hand.

Overexpose: Allowing too much light to strike the film as it is being exposed. This results in the photographic image having a washed-out look or being much lighter than normal.

Pan or Panning: The horizontal or left and right movement of the camera.

Panavision: Trade name of a brand of professional motion picture camera.

Paper Tape (⅛ in. or ¼ in.):   Tape that is most often used to make focus marks on the lens. It is wrapped around the barrel of the lens so that you may mark it for following or pulling focus.

Paper Tape (½ in. or 1 in.):   Tape that may be used for making actor's marks, labeling equipment, or any other taping job during production.

Paper Tape (2 in.):   Tape that is used for many of the same types of things as gaffer tape. Used for hanging items on painted walls because the glue is not as strong as that on gaffer tape, so it will not remove paint when taken down. It may also be used to seal any cracks or holes in the darkroom.

Perforations, Perfs: Equally spaced holes that are punched into the edges of the film along the entire length of the roll. These holes are engaged by the teeth of the sprockets in the film magazines and

camera movements, allowing the film to accurately travel through the camera before and after exposure.

Persistence of Vision: The phenomenon that allows the human eye to retain an image for a brief moment after it has been viewed. This allows the illusion of movement when a series of still pictures are projected on a screen at a specified rate of speed. At normal sync speed of 24 frames per second, a series of still frames projected on the screen appear to be moving continuously to the human eye.

Pitch: The distance between the top edge of one perforation to the top edge of the next perforation. This distance is measured along the length of the film.

Polarizing Filter: A filter that is used to reduce glare and reflections from reflective, nonmetallic surfaces. It is also used to enhance or darken a blue sky or water.

Powder Puffs: Soft makeup-type pads that are used to erase information that is written on an acrylic slate with erasable slate markers.

Precision Speed Control: An external speed control attachment that allows you to vary the speed of the camera.

Prep: The time during preproduction when the equipment is checked to ensure that it is in working order.

Pressure Plate: A flat, smoothly polished piece of metal that puts pressure on the film, keeping it flat against the aperture plate and steady as it travels through the gate.

Primary Colors: For the purposes of cinematography, the three primary colors of light are red, blue, and green. When equal amounts of these three colors of light are combined, they form what is known as white light. All colors of light are made up of varying combinations of these primary colors. The corresponding complementary colors are cyan, yellow, and magenta, respectively.

Prime Lens: A lens of a single, fixed focal length. Examples of prime lenses are 25 mm, 35 mm, 50 mm, 75 mm, 100 mm, etc.

Print All: The instructions given to the lab that tell them to print all of the takes on a given roll of exposed film.

Print Circle Takes Only: The instructions given to the lab that tell them to print only the takes that have been circled on the camera report for a specific roll of film.

Production Company: The name of the company that is producing the film. It may be a small independent company or a major Hollywood studio.

Production Number: A specific number assigned to a film production or television episode as assigned by the production company. By having a specific production number for each project, a production company can keep track of the various expenses and things needed for each project.

Production Title: The working title of the film as assigned by the production company.

Professional Cameraman's Handbook: An indispensable manual used by both Camera Assistants and Directors of Photography. It contains illustrations and descriptions of the many different cameras and related pieces of equipment in use today.

Pro-Mist Filter: A diffusion filter that is used to soften harsh lines in an actor's face.

Pull Down Claw: These are the small hooks or pins, located in the camera movement, that engage the perforations of the film and pull the film into position between the aperture plate and pressure plate so that it may be exposed.

Pulling Focus: See Following Focus.

Quick Release Plate: A detachable plate that is used to secure the camera to the tripod head. It allows for quick and easy removal and attachment of the camera.

Rain Cover: A waterproof cover used to protect the camera and magazine in extreme weather conditions, including snow and rain. It contains openings for the lens and viewfinder.

Raw Stock: Fresh unexposed and unprocessed film stock.

Reflected Light: Any light that is bouncing off or being reflected by an object.

Reflected Meter: A light meter used to measure the amount of reflected light that is bouncing off or reflected by an object.

Reflex Camera: Any camera that allows viewing through the lens during filming. The camera contains a mirrored shutter that directs the image to the viewfinder for the Camera Operator to see the shot.

Reflex Viewing System: A viewing system that allows the Camera Operator to view the image as it is being filmed.

Registration: The accurate positioning of the film in the film gate as it is running through the camera. Any variation causes a jump or blur in the photographic image. During the camera prep, the registration may be checked by filming a registration chart and then viewing the results.

Registration Chart: A chart containing a series of crossed lines that is used during the camera prep to check the registration of the camera. By shooting a double-exposed image of the chart and then viewing the results, you can tell if the registration of the camera is accurate.

Registration Pins: Part of the camera movement that consists of a small pin that holds the film securely in the gate while it is being exposed. Some cameras contain a single registration pin, while many professional cameras contain two registration pins. These cameras are often referred to as dual-pin registered cameras.

Remote Switch: An external attachment that allows the camera to be switched on and off from a distance.

Reversal: Film that, when processed, produces a positive image of the scene. It may also be called positive film, and it may be viewed directly.

Right-Hand Grip: A camera accessory item used when filming hand-held shots. As the name implies, it attaches to the right-hand side of the camera and is used to hold the camera steady during shooting. It usually contains an on/off switch for the Camera Operator to start and stop the camera.

Rocker Plate: A very low-angle camera mount that allows the Camera Operator to make smooth pans and tilts without using a fluid head or gear head.

Roll Number: The number assigned to a roll of film when it is placed on the camera. Each time a new roll of film is placed on the camera, the next higher number is assigned to that roll.

Ronford Baker: Trade name of a brand of professional motion picture fluid head and tripod.

Rubber Donut: See Donut.

Rushes: See Dailies.

Sachtler: Trade name of a brand of professional motion picture camera fluid head and tripod.

Samuelson Mark II Calculator: Trade name of a brand of depth-of-field calculator used by most 1st ACs.

Scene: The basic unit of a script with action occurring in a single setting.

Scene Number: The number assigned to a scene based on its place in the script. A scene is a section of the film as it takes place in a particular location or time in the story. Normally each time the location or the time changes, a new scene number is assigned to the action.

Script Supervisor: The person on the film crew who keeps track of the action for each scene. He or she keeps detailed notes for each shot regarding actor movement, placement of props, dialogue spoken, etc. The Script Supervisor tells the 2nd ACs what the scene and take number are for each shot.

SE: An abbreviation for short end.

Second Assistant Cameraman (2nd AC), Second Camera Assistant: The member of the camera crew whose duties include assisting the First Assistant Cameraman (1st AC), clapping the slate for the shot, keeping camera reports, placing marks for actors, and loading and unloading film into the magazines. The 2nd AC reports directly to the 1st AC during production. In Britain, Europe, and Australia, this position is referred to as the Clapper/Loader.

Second Camera: An additional camera used for filming shots or scenes at the same time as the primary or main camera.

"Second Marker," "Second Slate," or "Second Sticks": What the 2nd AC calls out when slating a shot a second time. The first slate may have been missed by the Camera Operator or Sound Mixer.

Setup: The basic component of a film's production, referring to each camera position or angle.

Short End (SE): A roll of unexposed raw stock that is less than a full size roll but larger than a waste roll or dummy load.

Short Eyepiece: A smaller version of the camera eyepiece that is used especially when filming handheld shots. It may also be used on the camera in certain filming situations where the long eyepiece is too uncomfortable or in an awkward position.

Shoulder Pad: A small pad that attaches to the underside of the camera when doing handheld shots to make it more comfortable for placing the camera on the Camera Operator's shoulder. If a shoulder pad is not available, you may use a rolled-up sweatshirt, jacket, towel, or anything else that can be used as padding.

Shutter: The mechanical device in a camera that rotates during filming to alternately block light from the film and then allow it to strike the film.

Shutter Angle: A measurement in degrees of the open part of the camera shutter that allows light to strike the film.

Silicone: A type of lubricant that is available in a spray or liquid form. The spray is used to lubricate various components, including the sliding base plate or tripod legs if they begin to stick. The liquid type is usually used to lubricate the pull down claws of certain cameras. When using silicone on the camera pull down claw, you should only use the type recommended for the particular camera you are using, and it should be provided by the camera rental company.

16 mm: A film gauge, introduced in 1923, that was used mainly for nontheatrical or amateur productions. It is most commonly used today for music videos, commercials, and many television series.

65 mm/70 mm: Film gauge that is most often used for release prints of theatrical films. It is very rarely used for actual productions. Arriflex and Panavision are two companies that have manufactured 65 mm cameras for filming.

Slate: A board marked with the pertinent identifying information for each scene photographed. It should contain the film's title, Director's name, Cameraman's name, date, camera roll number, scene number, and take number. The two main types of slates are sync and insert. See Insert Slate and Sync Slate.

Slate Markers: Erasable markers that are used to mark information on acrylic slates. It is usually some type of dry erase marker.

Sliding Base Plate: An attachment used for mounting the camera to the head. It is usually a two-part plate, with the bottom piece (base

plate) mounted to the tripod head and the top piece (bridge plate) mounted to the camera.

SOC: Abbreviation for the Society of Camera Operators.

Society of Camera Operators: An honorary organization composed of several hundred men and women who make their living operating film and/or video cameras.

Soft-Contrast Filter: A filter that lowers the contrast by darkening the highlight areas.

Soft Focus: Indicates a shot or scene that appears to be out of focus to the viewer's eye.

Space Blanket: A large cover used to protect the camera and equipment from the sun and weather. It is usually a bright silver color on one side and may be red, green, blue, or another color on the opposite side.

Speed (Camera):   The rate at which the film travels through the camera. Standard sync speed in the United States is 24 frames per second, and in Britain, Europe, and Australia it is 25 frames per second.

Speed (Film):   An indication of the film's sensitivity to light. The film speed may be referred to as EI, ISO, ASA, or DIN number.

Speed (Lens):   The f-stop or t-stop setting of the lens at its widest opening. The smaller this number, the faster the lens. Fast lenses are used many times for filming in extreme low-light situations.

Speed Crank: An L-shaped handle that attaches to the follow-focus mechanism. It is used when the 1st AC or Focus Puller has a very long focus change to do during a shot. In Britain it may also be referred to as a right-angle crank, focus crank, toffee hammer, Jimmy bar, or a Tommy bar.

Split Diopter: A filter that may be used to maintain focus on two objects, one in the foreground and one in the background. The split diopter is round, and only half of it contains the diopter. The remaining half of the filter is clear.

Split Focus: The technique of setting the focus so that a foreground object and a background object are both in focus for a shot or scene. It is usually best to check with the DP to see if he or she wants you to try to do a split focus for a shot.

Spot Meter: An exposure meter that takes a light reading by measuring the light that is reflected by an object.

Spreader: A metal or rubber device that has three arms and opens up to form a horizontal Y-shape to support the legs of the tripod. It prevents the legs of the tripod from slipping out from under the camera. It may also be called a spider or a triangle.

Sprocket Holes: Equally spaced holes punched into the edges of film stock so that it may be advanced through the camera or projector. See Perforations.

Sprockets: Small teeth or gears inside the camera or projector that advances the film by engaging in the perforations of the film.

Stabilo Grease Pencil: The brand name of an erasable marker used by many 1st ACs. It is available in many colors and may be used to make focus marks on lenses or on the white focus-marking disk of the follow-focus mechanism.

Standard Legs, Standards: A slang term to indicate the tripod on which the camera and head are mounted. Most standard tripods can be adjusted in height from approximately 4 ft to 6 or 7 ft. In Britain the slang term for the standard legs/tripod is talls.

Star Filter: A filter placed in front of the lens to give highlights to any lights that appear in the scene. The star filter produces lines coming from bright lights in the scene, depending on the texture of the star filter.

Stick-on Letters (1/2 in. or 3/4 in.):   Plastic or vinyl adhesive-backed letters and numbers that are used to label the slate with information related to the production.

Sticks: Slang term used to refer to the tripod. Also slang for the sync slate or clap sticks.

Stop: An abbreviation meaning the f-stop or t-stop.

Stop Pull: The technique of changing the f-stop or t-stop setting of the lens during a shot.

Stopping Down the Lens: See Closing Down the Lens.

Sunshade: A small flag or hood that attaches directly to the matte box or the lens to help prevent any light from striking the lens or the filter. It may also be called an eyebrow, French flag, or lens shade. See Eyebrow; French Flag; and Lens Shade.

Supa Frost Filter: Trade name of a brand of motion picture camera diffusion filter.

Sync: Abbreviation for synchronization or synchronized. It is usually used to indicate a film or scene that is shot with sound being recorded simultaneously.

Sync Slate: Slate used for identifying all shots done with sound. It contains two hinged pieces of wood that are clapped together at the beginning of each sound take.

Sync Speed: The speed that gives motion pictures the appearance of normal motion to the viewer. In the United States, sync speed is 24 frames per second, and in Britain, Europe, and Australia it is 25 frames per second.

Tachometer: A dial or meter located on the camera that shows the speed while the camera is running.

Tail Slate: A slate that is photographed at the end of a shot. When doing a tail slate, the slate is held upside down. Often called an end board in Britain.

Take, Take Number: The number assigned to a scene each time it is photographed. It refers to a single, uninterrupted shot filmed by the camera. Each time a scene or portion of a scene is shot, it is given a new take number.

Take-up Side: The side of the magazine or camera that contains the exposed film.

Tape Measure: A device used by the 1st AC to measure the distance from the film plane of the camera to the subject. The typical tape measure is 50 ft long and is made of cloth or fiberglass material.

Telephoto Lens: A lens of long focal length that allows you to photograph close shots of faraway objects. It has a small angle of view.

35 mm: The standard film gauge, introduced in 1889, that is used for most professional theatrical and television productions. It is used primarily for larger productions because of its excellent image quality.

Three-Inch Lens (3-in. Lens): A slang term used in the early days of filmmaking to indicate a 75 mm lens.

Tiffen: Trade name of a brand of motion picture camera filter.

Tilt: The vertical or up and down movement of the camera.

Tilt Plate: An accessory that is attached between the camera and the head and is used when doing extreme tilt angles with the camera. It allows the Camera Operator to tilt the camera at a much steeper angle than is possible with the standard gear head or fluid head. Many gear heads contain a built-in tilt plate for these types of shots.

Total (T): A section on the camera report and also on the film inventory form that indicates the combined total of all Good, No Good, and Waste footage.

Tracking (Lens): The ability of a zoom lens to stay centered on a particular point throughout the range of its zoom.

Triangle: See Spreader.

Tripod: A three-legged camera support that can be adjusted in height. When choosing a tripod, be sure that its top-casting piece is the same as the head that will be used for filming. For example, a tripod with a flat base will not accept a head with a bowl base without some type of adapter piece. In Britain the standard tripod may be referred to as talls and the baby tripod may be referred to as shorts. See Baby Legs and Standard Legs.

T-Stop: A number that is similar to the f-stop, but is much more precise. It indicates the exact amount of light that is transmitted through the lens.

Tungsten: Any light source with a color temperature of approximately 3200° Kelvin.

Two-Inch Lens (2-in. Lens): A slang term used in the early days of filmmaking to indicate a 50 mm lens.

Undercrank: To operate the camera at any speed that is slower than the normal sync-sound speed of 24 or 25 frames per second. As with

the term overcrank, it originated in the early days of filmmaking when all cameras were cranked by hand.

Underexpose: Exposing the film to less light than you would for a normal exposure. By allowing too little light to expose the shot, you end up with a very dark image.

Variable Shutter: A camera shutter that allows you to change the angle for specific filming situations. It allows you to make longer or shorter exposures while the speed of the camera remains constant. It may be used to make fades and dissolves within the camera. It may also be used by the DP to control the exposure and change the depth of field of a shot without changing the exposure setting on the lens. On some cameras that contain variable shutters, you can adjust the shutter angle while the camera is running.

Variable-Speed Camera Motor: A motor that allows you to change the speed of the camera for certain types of shots. It enables you to film at very slow speeds or very fast speeds, depending on the effect that you want.

Video Assist: A system that incorporates a video camera into the film camera viewing system. The image that strikes the mirror shutter of the camera is split so that part of it goes to the viewfinder and part goes to the video camera. The image from the video camera is then sent to a video monitor for the Director to view.

Video Cables: Any cables needed to connect the video tap to the video monitor or recorder.

Video Monitor: A television monitor that is used along with the video tap to allow the Director to view the shot during filming. See Video Assist.

Video Tap: A video camera that is incorporated into the film camera viewing system during shooting. It allows the Director to view the shot on the video monitor as it is being filmed. See Video Assist.

Viewfinder: The attachment on the camera that allows the Camera Operator to view the action. Today's modern film cameras all contain a reflex viewfinder system. This allows the Camera Operator to line up the shot and view it exactly as it will appear on film. The image coming through the lens is reflected onto a mirror shutter and is focused onto a viewing screen or ground glass, which is seen through the viewfinder by the Camera Operator. See Eyepiece.

Vignetting: A term used to indicate that a portion of the matte box or lens shade is visible or blocking the frame when viewing through the lens. It usually occurs on a very wide-angle lens.

Vinten: Trade name of a brand of professional fluid camera head.

Vitesse: Trade name of a brand of professional motion picture gear head.

Waste (W):   The amount of footage remaining on a roll that is left over after the Good and No Good footage have been totaled. It is too

small to be called a short end and may be used as a dummy load. It is written in a section of the camera report and also on the film inventory report form.

Weaver Steadman: A trade name of a brand of professional motion picture fluid head.

Whip: A slang term used for a type of follow-focus extension. It usually consists of a small round knob attached to a long flexible cable, which then connects to the follow-focus mechanism on the camera. It may also be called a focus whip.

Wide-Angle Lens: A lens that has a very short focal length or a focal length less than that of a normal lens. It may exaggerate perspective and covers a large angle of view.

Wrap: The period at the end of a day's shooting or at the completion of the film or production, when all of the equipment is packed away. At the conclusion of a production, the wrap usually consists of cleaning and packing the equipment and returning it to the rental house.

Wratten Filter: An optically correct gel filter that is used on a camera lens in place of or in addition to a glass filter. In many cases the gel filter is placed behind the lens in a special gel filter holder.

Zeiss: Trade name of a brand of professional motion picture camera lens.

Zoom: An effect that is achieved by turning the barrel of the zoom lens, to change the focal length of the lens, so that the object in the frame appears to get larger or smaller in the frame.

Zoom In: The act of changing the focal length of the lens so that the angle of view decreases and the focal length of the lens increases. By doing this, the subject becomes larger in the frame. Zooming in decreases depth of field.

Zoom Lens: A lens that has varying focal lengths. It allows you to change the focal length by turning an adjustment ring on the barrel of the lens. An object can be held in focus while the angle of view and size of the object are changed during the shot.

Zoom Motor: An electric motor that attaches to the zoom lens to allow you to do a smooth zoom move during a shot. It may be built into the lens, or it may be an additional item that you must attach to the lens.

Zoom Out: The act of changing the focal length of the lens so that the angle of view increases and the focal length of the lens decreases. By doing this, the subject becomes smaller in the frame. Zooming out increases depth of field.

Index